Red Dot Design
Yearbook 2016/2017

Edited by Peter Zec

reddot award
product design

About this book

"Working" presents the current best products relating to the workplace. All of the products in this book are of outstanding design quality and have been successful in one of the world's largest and most renowned design competitions, the Red Dot Design Award. This book documents the results of the current competition in the field of "Working", also presenting its most important players – the design team of the year, the designers of the best products and the jury members.

Über dieses Buch

„Working" stellt die aktuell besten Produkte rund um das Themengebiet „Arbeitsplatz" vor. Alle Produkte in diesem Buch sind von herausragender gestalterischer Qualität, ausgezeichnet in einem der größten und renommiertesten Designwettbewerbe der Welt, dem Red Dot Design Award. Dieses Buch dokumentiert die Ergebnisse des aktuellen Wettbewerbs im Bereich „Working" und stellt zudem seine wichtigsten Akteure vor – das Designteam des Jahres, die Designer der besten Produkte und die Jurymitglieder.

Contents
Inhalt

Professor Dr Peter Zec
Preface of the editor
Vorwort des Herausgebers

Dear Readers,

Last year we celebrated the 60th anniversary of the Red Dot Design Award. This year marks another anniversary – albeit a considerably smaller and more personal one: 25 years ago, I joined the Design Zentrum and took over management of the competition. I still remember well how informal everything was at the time – a small team, a manageable design community, and a competition that was predominantly national in terms of reach. And yet the potential was huge, because at the beginning of the 1990s more and more companies discovered as part of the increasing globalisation of the markets that design can make the decisive difference. In the 25 exciting years that followed, the competition grew and became more international. I am delighted and honoured to have been part of it.

Just how big and popular the Red Dot Award: Product Design has since become is reflected impressively in this Red Dot Design Yearbook 2016/2017, which for the first time is being published in four volumes: "Living", "Doing", "Working" and "Enjoying". When you leaf through the pages of this book, you will see lots of well-known brands from all over the world. All of them entered their best products in the Red Dot Award: Product Design for scrutiny by the jury of 41 design experts. Personally, I still find it fascinating even after 25 years to watch the jury members as they examine the products, try them out and ultimately rate them. On the following pages, we will introduce you to the products that won over this year's jury with their high design quality.

I wish you an inspiring read.

Sincerely, Peter Zec

Liebe Leserin, lieber Leser,

im vergangenen Jahr haben wir das 60-jährige Bestehen des Red Dot Design Awards gefeiert. In diesem Jahr gibt es wieder ein Jubiläum – wenn auch ein deutlich kleineres und persönlicheres: Vor 25 Jahren kam ich zum Design Zentrum und übernahm die Leitung des Wettbewerbs. Ich kann mich noch gut erinnern, wie familiär damals alles war – ein kleines Team, eine überschaubare Designgemeinschaft, ein eher nationaler Wettbewerb. Und doch war das Potenzial riesig, denn Anfang der 1990er Jahre entdeckten im Zuge der zunehmenden Globalisierung der Märkte immer mehr Unternehmen, dass Design den Unterschied machen kann. Es folgten 25 spannende Jahre des Wachstums und der Internationalisierung des Wettbewerbs. Es ist mir eine Freude und eine Ehre, dass ich dabei sein durfte.

Wie groß und beliebt der Red Dot Award: Product Design heute ist, belegt das vorliegende Red Dot Design Yearbook 2016/2017 eindrucksvoll, das erstmals in vier Bänden erscheint: „Living", „Doing", „Working" und „Enjoying". Beim Durchblättern der Bücher werden Ihnen viele bekannte Marken aus aller Welt begegnen. Sie alle sind mit ihren besten Produkten beim Red Dot Award: Product Design angetreten, um sich dem Urteil unserer Jury aus 41 Designexperten zu stellen. Für mich selbst ist es auch nach 25 Jahren immer noch faszinierend, den Jurymitgliedern dabei über die Schulter zu schauen, wie sie die Produkte in Augenschein nehmen, ausprobieren und schließlich bewerten. Auf den folgenden Seiten zeigen wir Ihnen die Produkte, die in diesem Jahr mit ihrer hohen Designqualität überzeugen konnten.

Ich wünsche Ihnen eine inspirierende Lektüre.

Ihr Peter Zec

The title "Red Dot: Design Team of the Year" is bestowed on a design team that has garnered attention through its outstanding overall design achievements. This year, the title goes to the Blackmagic Industrial Design Team led by Simon Kidd. This award is the only one of its kind in the world and is extremely highly regarded even outside of the design scene.

Mit der Auszeichnung „Red Dot: Design Team of the Year" wird ein Designteam geehrt, das durch seine herausragende gestalterische Gesamtleistung auf sich aufmerksam gemacht hat. In diesem Jahr geht sie an das Blackmagic Industrial Design Team led by Simon Kidd. Diese Würdigung ist einzigartig auf der Welt und genießt über die Designszene hinaus höchstes Ansehen.

In recognition of its feat, the Red Dot: Design Team of the Year receives the "Radius" trophy. This sculpture was designed and crafted by the Weinstadt-Schnaidt based designer, Simon Peter Eiber.

Als Anerkennung erhält das Red Dot: Design Team of the Year den Wanderpokal „Radius". Die Skulptur wurde entworfen und angefertigt von dem Designer Simon Peter Eiber aus Weinstadt-Schnaidt.

2016	Blackmagic Industrial Design Team led by Simon Kidd
2015	Robert Sachon & Bosch Home Appliances Design Team
2014	Veryday
2013	Lenovo Design & User Experience Team
2012	Michael Mauer & Style Porsche
2011	The Grohe Design Team led by Paul Flowers
2010	Stephan Niehaus & Hilti Design Team
2009	Susan Perkins & Tupperware World Wide Design Team
2008	Michael Laude & Bose Design Team
2007	Chris Bangle & Design Team BMW Group
2006	LG Corporate Design Center
2005	Adidas Design Team
2004	Pininfarina Design Team
2003	Nokia Design Team
2002	Apple Industrial Design Team
2001	Festo Design Team
2000	Sony Design Team
1999	Audi Design Team
1998	Philips Design Team
1997	Michele De Lucchi Design Team
1996	Bill Moggridge & Ideo Design Team
1995	Herbert Schultes & Siemens Design Team
1994	Bruno Sacco & Mercedes-Benz Design Team
1993	Hartmut Esslinger & Frogdesign
1992	Alexander Neumeister & Neumeister Design
1991	Reiner Moll & Partner & Moll Design
1990	Slany Design Team
1989	Braun Design Team
1988	Leybold AG Design Team

Red Dot: Design Team of the Year 2016
Blackmagic Industrial Design Team led by Simon Kidd
Reshaping an Industry by Rethinking its Products

Blackmagic Design is dedicated to making highest quality video affordable to everyone – an approach that has had a lasting impact on the industry in the past 15 years. The products combine a user focus and innovative technology with a design and a pricing structure that make them relevant not just for professionals but also for consumers. In recent years, the Blackmagic Industrial Design Team under the leadership of Simon Kidd has recorded notable successes in the Red Dot Award: Product Design. This year, the design team from Blackmagic Design is being awarded the "Red Dot: Design Team of the Year" title of honour for its consistently strong and ground-breaking design achievements.

Blackmagic Design hat den Anspruch, höchste Videoqualität für jedermann erschwinglich zu machen – ein Ansatz, der die Branche in den vergangenen 15 Jahren nachhaltig verändert hat. Die Produkte verbinden Nutzerorientierung und innovative Technik mit einem Design und einer Preisgestaltung, die sie nicht nur für Profis, sondern auch für Konsumenten interessant machen. Beim Red Dot Award: Product Design erzielte das Blackmagic Industrial Design Team unter der Leitung von Simon Kidd in den letzten Jahren große Erfolge. In diesem Jahr wird das Designteam von Blackmagic Design für seine kontinuierlich hohen und wegweisenden Gestaltungsleistungen mit dem Ehrentitel „Red Dot: Design Team of the Year" ausgezeichnet.

Revolutionary: The extremely compact Blackmagic Cinema Camera makes digital film recordings in cinema quality affordable for everyone.
Revolutionär: Die extrem kompakt gestaltete Blackmagic Cinema Camera macht digitale Filmaufnahmen in Kinoqualität für alle erschwinglich.

"The discontented man finds no easy chair," said Benjamin Franklin. And discontented, if not extremely dissatisfied, was Grant Petty – though the chair in his post-production work space was the least of his problems. Instead he was at odds with the technical equipment, which he found ugly, impractical and unreliable. History has shown that mounting dissatisfaction can move people to achieve major accomplishments. In the case of Grant Petty and Blackmagic Design, the accomplishment was to revolutionise not only his own professional life but the entire film industry.

Film and video production was his passion, and post-production his métier. But right from the start of his career, in television, he was very much bothered by what he considered to be an inefficient and dysfunctional technology. The longer he worked there, the more frustrated he became with products that made his life difficult and that stymied creativity. "Often we would have to work all night, because there was a job that had to go out in the morning, and the equipment we were using just kept failing us! We were working with broadcast products that were unreliable, difficult to use and often very badly designed. You can't imagine how angry that makes you, especially when these things cost hundreds of thousands of dollars, if not a million!"

His frustration with his industry's status quo grew so big that he decided to look for alternatives and solutions himself. His workplace: a kitchen table in Melbourne, Australia. His goal: giving film enthusiasts, both laymen and professionals, tools that foster creativity and that are affordable. His start-up capital: 2,000 dollars.

„Der unzufriedene Mensch findet keinen bequemen Stuhl", sagte Benjamin Franklin. Und unzufrieden war Grant Petty. Höchst unzufrieden sogar. Dabei war der Stuhl in seinem Postproduktions-Arbeitsraum noch sein geringstes Problem. Wesentlich unbequemer waren die technischen Geräte: unschön, unpraktisch, unzuverlässig. Nun zeigt die Geschichte, dass die wachsende Unzufriedenheit eines Einzelnen oder einer Gruppe mächtige Folgen haben kann. Und gravierende Folgen hatte sie auch im Falle von Grant Petty und Blackmagic Design – nicht nur für sein Berufsleben, sondern für die gesamte Filmindustrie.

Die Film- und Videoproduktion war seine große Leidenschaft; seine Arbeit als Postproduktions-Techniker das, was er schon immer tun wollte. Doch schon als er beim Fernsehen anfing, fiel ihm auf, wie schlecht die Technik funktionierte. Je länger er dort arbeitete, desto frustrierter wurde er angesichts der Produkte, die ihm das Leben schwer machten und kreative Ideen regelmäßig ausbremsten. „Wir mussten oft die Nächte durcharbeiten, weil die Beiträge morgens gesendet werden sollten, aber die Technik uns im Stich ließ. Wir arbeiteten mit Produkten, die unzuverlässig und kompliziert zu bedienen waren. Man kann sich kaum vorstellen, wie wütend einen das macht – vor allem, wenn die Sachen auch noch Hunderttausende Dollars oder eine Million kosten."

Seine Unzufriedenheit mit dem Status quo der Branche wurde so groß, dass er beschloss, selbst nach Alternativen und Lösungen zu suchen. Sein Arbeitsplatz: ein Küchentisch in Melbourne, Australien. Sein Ziel: filmbegeisterten Laien wie Profis professionelles, durchdachtes Werkzeug an die Hand zu geben, das die Kreativität fördert und zudem erschwinglich ist. Sein Startkapital: 2.000 Dollar.

Action hero: The Blackmagic Pocket Cinema Camera is designed to film high-quality videos in difficult surroundings, and is used regularly for Hollywood motion pictures – including for example "Mad Max: Fury Road".
Act onheld: Die Blackmagic Pocket Cinema Camera ist für das Filmen von qualitativ hochwertigen Videos in schwierigen Umgebungen konzipiert und kommt regelmäßig bei Hollywood-Drehs zum Einsatz – unter anderem bereits in „Mad Max: Fury Road".

The first project: the digitisation of the television industry

In 2002, Grant Petty, founder and CEO of Blackmagic Design, launched his first industry-changing product: the DeckLink video capture card. Until then, uncompressed video material could only be processed on computers specifically built for that purpose, and which were extremely expensive. Petty: "I remember asking a manufacturer's sales director why they built the systems this way and he actually said to me that 'these guys can afford it,' which I was shocked to be told. The fundamental problem was that myself and my friends could not afford it at all." That's when Petty decided he could take no more and began developing the capture card. As a first ever, the card allowed users to upload high-resolution material onto each computer and to edit it with any video software.

Today, almost fifteen years later, Blackmagic Design is one of the world's leading manufacturers of creative video technology. There's hardly a film, hardly a television production that does not use products developed by Petty. Blackmagic Design has thus fundamentally changed the industry with regard to software and hardware solutions alike.

A corporate culture subscribed to trial and error

The corporate culture of Blackmagic is built on solving problems just as much as on unleashing creativity. The innovation process starts with identifying a weakness of a given program or technical device. However, rather than just solving the problem, the team reconceptualises the product from scratch. In that process, the product is completely disassembled and analysed and the configuration of all parts is put into question.

Das erste Projekt: die Computerisierung der TV-Industrie

2002 brachte Grant Petty, der Initiator und CEO von Blackmagic Design, sein erstes Produkt auf den Markt, das die Branche verändern sollte: die Video-Capture-Karte DeckLink. Bis dahin konnte unkomprimiertes Videomaterial nur auf speziell dafür gebauten Computern bearbeitet werden, die extrem teuer waren. Petty: „Einmal fragte ich den Verkaufsleiter eines Herstellers dieser Million-Dollar-Geräte nach der Preisgestaltung. Er antwortete einfach: ‚Diese Leute können sich das leisten.' Ich war wirklich schockiert, denn meine Freunde und ich konnten es uns eben nicht leisten." Petty beschloss, das nicht länger hinzunehmen, und entwickelte die Capture-Karte. Angeschlossen an einen Computer, ermöglichte die Karte es erstmals, hochauflösendes Material auf jeden Computer zu laden und mit jeder Video-Software zu editieren.

Heute, kaum fünfzehn Jahre später, ist Blackmagic Design einer der weltweit führenden Hersteller kreativer Videotechnologie. Kaum ein Film, kaum eine Fernsehproduktion, bei denen Pettys Produkte nicht zum Einsatz kommen. Blackmagic Design hat die Branche nachhaltig verändert, mit Software- und Hardware-Lösungen gleichermaßen.

Die Unternehmenskultur: Experimentieren geht über Studieren

Dies gelang durch eine problemorientierte und kreative Herangehensweise, die das Herzstück der Firmenkultur bildet. Der Innovationsprozess startet mit der Identifizierung einer Schwachstelle von Programmen oder technischen Geräten. Statt jedoch nur das konkrete Problem zu lösen, besteht der nächste Schritt darin, das jeweilige Produkt von Grund auf neu zu denken.

"We love video as a creative medium and that's why we strive to make it available and easily usable to as many people as possible."
„Wir lieben Video als kreatives Medium, und deswegen möchten wir jedem Menschen die Möglichkeit eröffnen, optimal mit diesem Medium zu arbeiten."

Grant Petty – CEO Blackmagic Design

But above all, the process involves plenty of experimenting. Indeed, Petty calls it a "new culture of experimentation" that embraces trials, and as part of that, errors. After all, we can only learn from mistakes. He continues: "I think that really shows the difference in how we approach these things, and how other companies do it. The way I see it, it is this creative culture that sets us apart. The business world usually won't make a decision unless they can predict the outcomes. That sort of culture kills creativity."

Design beginnings: Blackmagic Design and Simon Kidd

Petty's next major undertaking was to remove video technology from the computer so that high-quality videos could be recorded or played back with an external device. Fortunately, new interfaces such as USB 3.0 and Thunderbolt had been marketed that were able to deliver the required speed and high data throughput. This second endeavour culminated in the product UltraStudio Pro, a standalone device that had to be well designed.

At the same time, in 2006, Blackmagic set up its own industrial design team. From the beginning, Simon Kidd was on board. An Australian national, Kidd had been active for many years in establishing industrial design as a strategic tool in the original equipment manufacturers sector in China to deliver products to the US market under iconic brands such as Black & Decker, Colgate-Palmolive and Schick Energizer. Prior to that, he worked as a designer in the United Kingdom, designing products for companies such as Roche, British Telecom and Marconi.

Es wird auseinandergenommen, analysiert, jede einzelne Komponente infrage gestellt. Vor allem aber wird viel experimentiert. Petty nennt es eine „neue Kultur des Experimentierens", bei der auch missglückte Ansätze willkommen sind. Aus Fehlern kann man schließlich lernen. „Ich denke, das ist es, was unsere Herangehensweise von der anderer Unternehmen unterscheidet. In meinen Augen ist diese Innovationskultur unsere größte Stärke. In der Geschäftswelt werden normalerweise keine Entscheidungen getroffen, wenn das Ergebnis nicht vorhersehbar ist. Eine solche Firmenkultur erstickt jedoch jegliche Kreativität schon im Keim", so Petty.

Die Designanfänge: Blackmagic Design und Simon Kidd

Pettys nächstes Großprojekt bestand darin, die Videotechnologie aus dem Computer auszulagern, um mit einem externen Gerät qualitativ hochwertiges Videomaterial aufzeichnen oder wiedergeben zu können. Neue Schnittstellen wie USB 3.0 und Thunderbolt lieferten mit ihrer Schnelligkeit und dem hohen Datendurchsatz die notwendigen technischen Voraussetzungen. Erstmals plante Blackmagic Design mit UltraStudio Pro also ein eigenständiges Gerät, das gut gestaltet sein musste.

Zu diesem Zeitpunkt, 2006, bekam das Unternehmen sein eigenes Industrial Design Team. Von Anfang an dabei: Simon Kidd. Der Australier hatte zuvor einige Jahre lang in China OEMs dabei unterstützt, Industriedesign als strategisches Werkzeug bei der Herstellung von Produkten zu etablieren, die unter Markennamen wie Black & Decker, Colgate-Palmolive und Schick Energizer auf den Markt kommen sollten. Zuvor gestaltete er in Großbritannien Produkte für Unternehmen wie Roche, British Telecom und Marconi.

Future-proof: Blackmagic Design wants its customers to be able to use HD and Ultra HD technology – for the same price and in the same product.
The Blackmagic Studio Camera in Ultra HD marked the first step in this direction.
Bereit für die Zukunft: Kunden von Blackmagic Design sollen HD- und Ultra-HD-Technologie nutzen können – zum gleichen Preis und im selben Produkt.
Die Ultra-HD-fähige Blackmagic Studio Camera war der erste Schritt in diese Richtung.

Together with Petty, Kidd built the design department. Kidd says: "It was a fantastic opportunity, namely because by building the design capability 'from scratch' we were able to handpick a world class team of designers who are specifically tailored to products we make. Not only were we able to recruit from scratch, but we also had the freedom to develop systems, process and design philosophies that were specifically built to suit to this new and evolving business." He summarises his design philosophy as follows: "Our key philosophy is to integrate design into the complete product development process. Rather than superficially wrapping styling around a product, we leverage it in every part of the creation process helping to deliver a more wholly considered final product."

One of the first products designed under Simon Kidd's direction was UltraStudio Pro. When it finally came on the market, the film and video industry first thought it was a product for home use – that's how unaccustomed they were to user-friendly design. "It was a completely unique design language for the video industry. For Blackmagic Design, the new challenge was to educate an entire market into understanding that rack-mounted broadcast equipment could also be elegant and still be the highest broadcast quality," says Kidd. Thus, UltraStudio Pro was a first step in that direction.

UltraStudio Pro already had the hallmark features for which Blackmagic Design products are known for today, namely, state-of-the-art functionality, ergonomics and user interface design for professional filmmakers. Yet, in addition Simon Kidd and his team succeeded in giving the products a lightness and elegance hitherto known only from consumer electronics – thereby breaking with conventions and practices that had been long established in the TV and film industry.

Gemeinsam mit Petty baute Kidd die Designabteilung auf. „Es war eine fantastische Chance", so Kidd. „Da wir bei null anfingen, konnten wir uns die richtigen Leute für unsere Produkte heraussuchen: Designer, die ein großes technisches Verständnis mitbringen. Außerdem konnten wir Systeme, Prozesse und eine Designphilosophie entwickeln, die perfekt auf unsere Aufgaben zugeschnitten waren." Diese Designphilosophie definiert er folgendermaßen: „Unsere Philosophie ist es, die Gestaltung in den kompletten Produktentwicklungsprozess zu integrieren. Statt ein Produkt nur ansprechend zu verpacken, folgen wir einem ganzheitlichen Ansatz: Wir setzen Design während des gesamten Prozesses gezielt ein, damit am Ende ein perfekt durchdachtes und gestaltetes Produkt steht."

Eines der ersten unter Simon Kidds Leitung gestalteten Produkte sollte also das UltraStudio Pro werden. Als es schließlich auf den Markt kam, hielt die bis dahin nicht unbedingt designverwöhnte Branche es zunächst für ein Produkt für den privaten Gebrauch – so ungewohnt war die Gestaltung. „Das Design war einzigartig in der Videoindustrie. Die Herausforderung bestand jetzt darin, einem ganzen Markt beizubringen, dass auch Rack-montierte Geräte elegant und gleichzeitig hochprofessionell sein können", so Kidd. Aber der Anfang war gemacht.

Im UltraStudio Pro war bereits all das angelegt, was die Produkte von Blackmagic Design bis heute prägt: Die Produkte sind vor allem Arbeitsmittel für Profis, das heißt, Funktionalität, Ergonomie und Benutzerschnittstellen-Gestaltung spielen die Hauptrolle. Dennoch gelingt es Simon Kidd und seinem Team, den Produkten eine Eleganz und Leichtigkeit mitzugeben, wie man sie eigentlich eher aus der Unterhaltungselektronik kennt – ein Bruch mit den bis dahin bekannten Gestaltungsmustern der TV- und Filmindustrie.

Miniaturised design: The Blackmagic Micro Cinema Camera is an extremely small professional quality digital film camera that's perfect for use on quadcopters, as a crash cam, or hidden on set for reality TV.
Miniaturdesign: Die Blackmagic Micro Cinema Camera ist eine extrem kleine professionelle Digitalfilmkamera, perfekt für den Einsatz auf Quadrokoptern, als Crash Cam oder als versteckte Kamera am Set für Reality-TV-Shows.

Further, thanks to the company's rigorous efforts to achieve the best possible price-performance ratio, which was pushed in particular by Petty, the resulting products were interesting not only for professionals but also for consumers.

The design process: attention to detail

With this approach, Blackmagic Design fundamentally changed an industry that was traditionally conservative in the space of a decade. Since then, the company has become known for its unconventional product solutions that combine sophisticated technology with a mature and evolved design. To achieve this, designers and engineers collaborate closely early in the design phase. Everything is about detail, about capturing the essence of the product in its entirety, and about understanding how it is used.

"Design quality is the unseen attention to detail that makes a product feel intuitive. It is the thinking that the designer does, so that the user doesn't have to," says Kidd. Pragmatic considerations thus play an equally important role: The product design is generally streamlined to the bare essentials, the goal being to simplify the usability as well as the construction and manufacturing processes for purposes of both reliability and cost-effectiveness.

"When you pick up one of our products, I believe you can see the commitment our team has made to creating the very best product possible," says Kidd. Quite clearly, not only Kidd believes that but the design world as well: In the Red Dot Design Award, Blackmagic submitted 18 products

Im Zusammenspiel mit dem Preis-Leistungs-Verhältnis, das Petty so am Herzen liegt, entstehen so Produkte, die eben nicht nur für Profis, sondern auch für Konsumenten interessant sind.

Der Designprozess: Aufmerksamkeit für das Detail

In den folgenden zehn Jahren sollte Blackmagic Design mit diesem Ansatz eine traditionell eher konservative Branche grundlegend verändern. Es wurde bekannt für seine unkonventionellen Produktlösungen, die anspruchsvolle Technik mit einer formvollendeten Ausarbeitung verbinden. Dafür arbeiten Designteam und Ingenieure schon in der Konzeptphase eng zusammen. Alles dreht sich um die Details, darum, das Produkt komplett zu durchdringen, zu verstehen, wie es genutzt wird.

„Designqualität ist die unsichtbare Aufmerksamkeit für das Detail, damit ein Produkt intuitiv verständlich ist. Es sind die Gedanken, die sich ein Designer macht, damit Anwender nicht mehr darüber nachdenken müssen", erklärt Kidd. Pragmatische Erwägungen spielen eine ebenso große Rolle: Die Produktgestaltungen werden auf das absolut Wesentliche rationalisiert. Ziel ist es, die Bedienbarkeit, Konstruktion und Herstellung zu vereinfachen, um sowohl Zuverlässigkeit als auch Wirtschaftlichkeit zu erreichen.

„Wenn man eines unserer Produkte in die Hand nimmt, kann man vielleicht erahnen, welchen Einsatz das Team gezeigt hat, damit am Ende das bestmögliche Produkt steht", so Kidd. Der Erfolg scheint ihm recht zu geben: Beim Red Dot Design Award reichte Blackmagic in den vergangenen fünf Jahren 18 Produkte ein.

over the past five years. Of those, 13 were awarded a Red Dot and five even received the highest award of the competition, the Red Dot: Best of the Best. And as if that wasn't enough, now Simon Kidd and the Blackmagic Industrial Design Team were named Red Dot: Design Team of the Year 2016 for their pioneering and standard-setting design performance.

The acid test: Blackmagic Design buys DaVinci

However, the year 2009 was to show whether Petty and Kidd's approach to the development and design of their own products would be applicable to other products. In that year, Blackmagic Design was given the opportunity to purchase and improve on the colour correction system DaVinci, which had been the status quo in Hollywood for decades. From the beginning, Petty was sceptical as to whether the product could be saved, saying: "I remember when we purchased DaVinci, that the product was so poorly constructed that Simon put his sunglasses in the gaps between the panels. These were really basic things, but back then they just didn't care. That particular product, with that gap in the panels, was selling back then at 350,000 dollars."

Finally, his desire for challenges won the upper hand. He took over the entire company, and gave the design team the task of giving DaVinci a complete overhaul. "The design team was tasked with completely reinventing DaVinci as a mass producible product. It was from the ground up. What Blackmagic Design did to DaVinci was to apply the rules of mass production to every part of the product." The result was nothing less than a reinvention of DaVinci. From the user interface to the colour correction control panel down to the system design, everything was overhauled. The sale price was 30,000 dollars. Petty was satisfied. His philosophy had proved viable, and his team powerful. Hollywood now makes ample use of the new DaVinci system because of its reliability, speed and performance. Among other things, it was used to produce Oscar-winning films such as "The Theory of Everything", "The Grand Budapest Hotel" and "Avatar".

To allow as many people as possible to benefit from the product, Petty made a stripped back version of the software available for free to video makers.

The reinvention of the movie camera: Blackmagic Design becomes camera producer

Once Blackmagic Design had acquired DaVinci, it realised that many DaVinci users were unhappy with the poor colour correction results – primarily because much of the original content was coming from video cameras. Video cameras can produce beautiful images, given their integrated colour correction, but when compared to 'digital film cameras' they are unable to capture the full spectrum of light. This meant that many users were unable to exploit key functionality of the DaVinci software which requires the full spectrum of light for optimum results.

Das Ergebnis: Dreizehnmal wurden die Arbeiten mit einem Red Dot prämiert, fünfmal sogar mit der höchsten Auszeichnung des Wettbewerbs, dem Red Dot: Best of the Best. Jetzt wurden Simon Kidd und das Blackmagic Industrial Design Team für ihre wegweisenden Gestaltungsleistungen zum Red Dot: Design Team of the Year 2016 gekürt.

Die Feuerprobe: Blackmagic Design kauft DaVinci

2009 sollte sich jedoch erst einmal zeigen, ob Pettys und Kidds Herangehensweise an die Entwicklung und Gestaltung eigener Produkte auch auf fremde Produkte anwendbar wäre: Blackmagic Design bekam die Chance, das in Hollywood seit Jahrzehnten etablierte Farbkorrektursystem „DaVinci" zu übernehmen. Anfangs war Petty skeptisch, ob sich das Produkt überhaupt retten ließe: „Als wir DaVinci kauften, konnte Simon seine Sonnenbrille in die Spalten zwischen den einzelnen Komponenten legen, so schlecht war die Konstruktion. Jedes Gerät war ein Einzelstück und hatte eine andere Software-Version aufgespielt, da es kein Update-System gab. Trotzdem wurde es für 350.000 Dollar verkauft."

Letztlich gewann jedoch seine Lust auf Herausforderungen die Oberhand. Er übernahm das Unternehmen. Und das Designteam die Aufgabe, DaVinci komplett zu überarbeiten. „Wir mussten DaVinci völlig neu gestalten, um ein serientaugliches Produkt zu bekommen; jedes Teil musste daraufhin überprüft werden." Das Ergebnis war nicht weniger als eine Neuerfindung DaVincis – von der Benutzeroberfläche über die Farbkorrektur-Schalttafel bis hin zum Systemdesign wurde alles neu gedacht. Der Verkaufspreis: 30.000 Dollar. Petty war zufrieden. Seine Philosophie hatte sich als tragfähig, sein Team als schlagkräftig erwiesen. Und auch Hollywood nutzt das neue DaVinci-System wegen seiner Zuverlässigkeit, Schnelligkeit und Leistungsstärke viel und gerne – unter anderem für Oscar-prämierte Filme wie „Die Entdeckung der Unendlichkeit", „Grand Hotel Budapest" und „Avatar".

Damit wieder möglichst viele Menschen von dem Produkt profitieren, stellt Petty die Software kreativen Videomachern in einer abgespeckten Version kostenlos zur Verfügung.

Die Neuerfindung der Filmkamera: Blackmagic Design wird Kameraproduzent

Durch die Übernahme DaVincis wurde Blackmagic Design für ein weiteres Problem sensibilisiert. DaVinci-Nutzer, die mit Videokameras arbeiteten, bemängelten die schlechten Farbkorrektur-Resultate. Die Erklärung dafür ist recht einfach: Im Gegensatz zu Digitalkameras produzieren Videokameras durch eine integrierte Farbkorrektur schöne Bilder, ohne dabei jedoch das volle Lichtspektrum einzufangen. DaVinci benötigt aber möglichst die gesamte Bandbreite, damit alle Möglichkeiten ausgeschöpft werden können.

The dilemma is that video cameras were affordable but weren't delivering the required quality; and that digital film cameras, for their part, were delivering quality but were unaffordable for most consumers, with a price tag of around 50,000 dollars.

Petty, embracing this as the next major challenge for his firm, then began thinking strategically about the camera market. He wanted to develop an affordable digital movie camera that would also be compatible with the accessories of digital SLR cameras which many potential customers already had at home.

In keeping with the company's corporate philosophy, the team then engaged in a detailed examination and thorough experimentation with the configuration of parts. Simon Kidd explained the design process as follows: "Designing a camera is a complex process and it takes a significant amount of refinement, prototyping and testing to put together a really great product. You need to understand the exact requirements of the user and design quite precisely around these. Ergonomics and balance need to be spot on, controls – buttons, dials and keys – need to be in exactly the right position and the user interface needs to be a seamless part of the design."

The questioning of established, conventional design principles resulted in a product with an innovative design language – the Blackmagic Cinema Camera. The camera is extremely compact while nevertheless offering feature film quality. Its rather minimalist camera geometry renders it compatible with a wide range of accessories, which is important especially for professionals. Finally, a simple touchscreen menu allows for an intuitive operation.

Grant Petty had every reason to be satisfied. In 2012, he brought the camera on the market at a price of 3,000 dollars. Therewith he not only broke into a new market but also revolutionised a good part of the film and television industry by making filming in 'cinema quality' affordable for all.

This was followed soon after with the launch of yet another camera: the Blackmagic Pocket Cinema Camera. The best proof of the quality of the Blackmagic cameras is perhaps that they are now regularly in use in Hollywood, for example in the movie "Mad Max: Fury Road". Camera assistant Michelle Pizanis said: "We made Tom Hardy wear a body harness with the Blackmagic camera rigged to it for a chase in a tunnel. The camera was ideal in this situation, and everyone was happy with the footage."

Fast-forward into the future: Ultra HD-enabled products

The subsequent big challenge for Blackmagic Design was closely linked to the developments in the computer industry. Monitors are continually getting larger, both with regard to screen size and resolution, meaning that images shot in HD quality will eventually lag behind. Petty then subjected his entire product range to an elaborate examination with regard to this challenge.

Das Dilemma: Videokameras waren bezahlbar, lieferten aber nicht die nötige Qualität; digitale Filmkameras lieferten diese Qualität, waren aber mit einem Preis um die 50.000 Dollar für den normalen Nutzer unbezahlbar.

Dieses Problem wurde zum Ausgangspunkt für den nächsten Meilenstein in der Geschichte des Unternehmens: Petty fing an, sich Gedanken über den Kameramarkt zu machen. Er wollte eine bezahlbare digitale Filmkamera entwickeln, die zudem mit dem Zubehör digitaler Spiegelreflexkameras kompatibel sein würde, das viele potenzielle Kunden bereits zu Hause hatten.

Wieder wurde jedes Detail neu durchdacht, es wurde experimentiert, bis kein Bauteil auf dem anderen blieb. Simon Kidd über den Gestaltungsprozess: „Eine Kamera zu gestalten ist ein überaus komplexer Prozess, der viele Modellbau- und Testphasen erfordert. Es geht darum, die genauen Anforderungen des Nutzers zu verstehen und gestalterisch umzusetzen. Deswegen spielt auch die Mensch-Maschine-Schnittstelle eine besondere Rolle – alles muss exakt positioniert und intuitiv bedienbar sein und sich gleichzeitig nahtlos in die Gehäusegestaltung einfügen."

Das grundsätzliche Hinterfragen bis dahin üblicher Gestaltungsmaximen mündete in einem Produkt mit einer innovativen Formensprache – der Blackmagic Cinema Camera. Die Kamera ist extrem kompakt gestaltet. Gleichzeitig ermöglicht sie Aufnahmen in Kinofilmqualität. Die schlichte Kamerageometrie erlaubt das Anbringen von Zubehör, was insbesondere für Profis wichtig ist. Ein übersichtliches Touchscreen-Menü ermöglicht eine intuitive Bedienung.

Grant Petty hatte allen Grund, zufrieden zu sein. Er brachte die Kamera 2012 zu einem Preis von 3.000 Dollar auf den Markt. Damit hatte er nicht nur einen neuen Markt betreten, sondern auch einen weiteren Bereich der Film- und Fernsehbranche erfolgreich revolutioniert, indem er Filmaufnahmen in Kinoqualität für alle erschwinglich machte.

Es folgte die Blackmagic Pocket Cinema Camera. Wie gut die Kameras tatsächlich sind, zeigt sich vielleicht am besten daran, dass sie mittlerweile regelmäßig bei Hollywood-Drehs zum Einsatz kommen – unter anderem in dem Film „Mad Max: Fury Road". Kameraassistentin Michelle Pizanis: „Für eine Verfolgungsjagd durch einen Tunnel schnallten wir Tom Hardy eine mit der Blackmagic-Kamera ausgestattete Körperweste um. Die Kamera erwies sich als ideal und alle Beteiligten waren mit dem Filmmaterial zufrieden."

Der Schritt in die Zukunft: Ultra-HD-fähige Produkte

Die nächste große Herausforderung für Blackmagic Design war eng mit den Entwicklungen in der Computerindustrie verknüpft. Die Bildschirme werden immer größer und hochauflösender, sodass Aufnahmen, die in HD-Qualität gedreht sind, künftig hinter den Möglichkeiten zurückbleiben würden. Mit diesem potenziellen Problem im Hinterkopf unterzog Petty seine gesamte Produktpalette einer eingehenden Überprüfung. Er kam zu dem Schluss, dass jedes einzelne Produkt überarbeitet und Ultra-HD-fähig gemacht werden müsse.

Completely rethinking cameras: At 2.5 kg, the extremely light Super 35 digital film camera Blackmagic URSA Mini achieves the perfect balance of weight distribution and size through its design.
Kameras völlig neu denken: Die mit 2,5 kg extrem leichte Super-35-Digitalfilmkamera Blackmagic URSA Mini optimiert durch ihre Gestaltung das Verhältnis von Gewichtsverteilung und Größe.

17

Perfect minimalism: Blackmagic Cintel is a futuristic film scanner with an impressive minimalist look.
Its predecessor was too big to fit through a door.
Minimalismus in Perfektion: Der Blackmagic Cintel ist ein futuristischer Filmscanner mit einer beeindruckend minimalistischen Ästhetik.
Sein Vorgänger passte durch keine Tür.

He concluded that each and every product had to be redesigned and made Ultra HD-capable. The goal was to allow customers to use HD and Ultra HD technology for the same price. Although a mammoth task, it also bore the opportunity to revamp existing products and to create new ones. This examination led fairly quickly to the development of three products, each characterised by a pioneering design: the live broadcast digital film camera Blackmagic Studio Camera, the film scanner Blackmagic Cintel and the digital film camera Blackmagic URSA Mini.

The art of miniaturisation

As much as these products differ, all three have in common that they are extremely compact. This is particularly evident in the case of the Cintel scanner. Blackmagic Design had bought the scanner manufacturer Cintel in 2013 with the aim to make the digitisation of 35mm motion picture film faster, easier and cheaper. Because even though 35mm film has fallen out of fashion, it does provide a top quality Ultra HD resolution, and indeed has been doing so for over a hundred years now.

"The original Cintel didn't fit through any door," says Kidd. So the first step was to remove all unnecessary and outdated components from the device and to focus on the essentials in the new design. "We redesigned the scanner with a 'space frame'. This gave us the rigidity that we needed to reduce the overall size and weight." What emerged was a futuristic film scanner with an impressive minimalist aesthetic. Indeed, the Cintel scanner is so compact that it can even be hung on the wall.

"I think this example is a good illustration of how we approach things. We want to make a difference and create products that are technically mature and affordable. And we want to blow our customers' minds. We love video as a creative medium and that's why we strive to make it available and easily usable to as many people as possible," says Petty.

If Petty was a newcomer to the field of post-production today, he would probably be much more satisfied with the equipment being used now than with what was the standard at the beginning of his career. He has achieved a lot by making the technology of a largely self-contained, elitist industry available to a broad audience. In addition, he has improved the technology by reconceptualising, redesigning and revamping products from the ground up. However, we can only imagine that a person with an inquisitive and keen mind as his would hardly sit contentedly back in his chair and would instead work to continually bring the state of the art to yet another level.

Für den gleichen Preis sollten seine Kunden in Zukunft HD- und Ultra-HD-Technologie nutzen können. Eine Mammutaufgabe, die allerdings auch die Chance barg, vorhandene Produkte neu zu gestalten und neue zu kreieren. Im Zuge dieses Prozesses entstanden in rascher Folge drei Produkte, die sich wiederum durch eine wegweisende Gestaltung auszeichnen: die digitale Live-Broadcast-Filmkamera „Blackmagic Studio Camera", der Filmscanner „Blackmagic Cintel" und die digitale Filmkamera „Blackmagic URSA Mini".

Die Kunst der Miniaturisierung

So sehr sie sich auch sonst unterscheiden, ist allen drei Produkten gemein, dass sie extrem kompakt gestaltet sind. Besonders deutlich wird dies am Beispiel des Cintel. Blackmagic Design hatte den Filmscanner-Hersteller Cintel 2013 gekauft, mit dem Ziel, die Digitalisierung von 35-mm-Bewegtbildmaterial schneller, einfacher und kostengünstiger zu gestalten. Denn obwohl der 35-mm-Film aus der Mode gekommen ist, liefert er eine Auflösung in bester Ultra-HD-Qualität – und das bereits seit über hundert Jahren.

„Der ursprüngliche Cintel passte durch keine Tür", so Kidd. Also bestand der erste Schritt darin, alle unnötigen und veralteten Komponenten aus dem Gerät herauszunehmen und sich bei der Neukonstruktion auf das Wesentliche zu konzentrieren. „Wir haben den Scanner mit einem ‚Space Frame', einem hochfesten Strukturrahmen, neu gestaltet. Dadurch bekam er die nötige Steifigkeit, die wir brauchten, um die Gesamtgröße und das Gewicht deutlich reduzieren zu können", so Kidd. Auf dieser Basis ist ein futuristischer Filmscanner mit einer beeindruckend minimalistischen Ästhetik entstanden, der dank seiner kompakten Ausmaße sogar an die Wand gehängt werden kann.

„Ich denke, dieses Beispiel verdeutlicht ganz gut, wie wir an Dinge herangehen. Wir möchten wirklich etwas bewegen; Produkte machen, die technisch ausgereift und bezahlbar sind. Und die unsere Kunden zum Staunen bringen. Wir lieben Video als kreatives Medium, und deswegen möchten wir jedem Menschen die Möglichkeit eröffnen, optimal mit diesem Medium zu arbeiten", resümiert Petty.

Würde Petty heute wieder in der Postproduktion arbeiten, könnte er wohl um einiges zufriedener mit seinem Arbeitsgerät sein als zu Beginn seiner Laufbahn. Er hat bereits vieles erreicht, indem er die Technik einer weitgehend in sich geschlossenen, elitären Branche einer breiten Masse zugänglich gemacht hat. Und er hat vieles verbessert, indem er Produkte neu gedacht, neu entwickelt und neu gestaltet hat. Aber wer mit einem solch wachen Blick auf seine Branche schaut, wird wohl nie restlos zufrieden sein können.

Red Dot: Design Team of the Year 2016
Interview: Simon Kidd
Director of Industrial Design
Blackmagic Design

Simon Kidd has built and led the Blackmagic Industrial Design Team since its inception ten years ago. Red Dot talked to him about his work at Blackmagic Design.

What does Blackmagic Design stand for?

Blackmagic Design is dedicated to making the highest quality video affordable to everyone. Design plays an integral role in achieving this, it's part of our DNA.

Can you sum up Blackmagic Design's design philosophy in just a few words?

Our key philosophy is to integrate design into the complete product development process. Rather than superficially wrapping styling around a product, we leverage it in every part of the creation process helping to deliver a more wholly considered final product.

You have been Director of Industrial Design at Blackmagic Design since the inception of the design department. How would you describe your role as head of the design team?

I lead a large team of dedicated and passionate designers and engineers. So first and foremost, my role is about empowering them to deliver their best work. Essentially this involves setting out the design philosophies, systems and processes to provide the guidance and structure for them to work within. However, I am still a hands-on designer. I believe it is the sum of the details that makes a product great and for this reason I am involved in every project that comes through the studio.

The role has a particularly broad scope – industrial design, design engineering, and the mass production of all mechanical parts. Bringing all three functions together was a deliberate decision for a number of key reasons; firstly, it ensures that the essence of the concept is not lost during the design-engineering phase – designers and engineers work closely together to ensure that the concepts are maintained, and even improved on, during the engineering stages.

Simon Kidd hat das Blackmagic Industrial Design Team vor zehn Jahren aufgebaut und leitet es seitdem. Red Dot hat mit ihm über seine Arbeit bei Blackmagic Design gesprochen.

Wofür steht Blackmagic Design?

Das Ziel von Blackmagic Design ist es, erstklassige Videoaufnahmen für alle erschwinglich zu machen. Das Design spielt dabei eine zentrale Rolle, es ist Teil unserer DNA.

Kurz und knapp – was ist die Designphilosophie von Blackmagic Design?

Unser Kerngedanke ist die Integration von Design in den Gesamtprozess der Produktentwicklung. Wir wollen Design nicht oberflächlich um das Produkt legen, sondern in alle Teile des Entstehungsprozesses einbinden, um damit zu einem besser durchdachten Endprodukt beizutragen.

Seit der Gründung der Designabteilung sind Sie als Leiter des Industriedesigns bei Blackmagic Design dabei. Wie sieht Ihre Rolle als Leiter des Designteams aus?

Ich leite ein Team von engagierten und leidenschaftlichen Designern und Ingenieuren. In meiner Rolle geht es also hauptsächlich darum, ihnen zu ermöglichen, ihr Bestes zu geben. Das heißt vor allem, Designphilosophien, Systeme und Prozesse zu etablieren, an denen sie sich bei der Arbeit orientieren können und die ihre Arbeit strukturieren. Ich bin aber selbst auch noch aktiv in den Gestaltungsprozess eingebunden. Ich denke, es ist die Summe der Details, die ein Produkt zu einem tollen Produkt werden lässt. Deswegen bin ich in jedes Projekt involviert, das unser Designbüro durchläuft.

Meine Rolle ist also sehr weit gefasst – Industriedesign, Konstruktionstechnik sowie die Serienproduktion aller mechanischen Teile fallen in meinen Bereich. Es war eine bewusste Entscheidung, alle drei Aspekte zusammenzuführen.

Secondly, we can control very closely the manufactured outcomes ensuring the details from the initial concept follow through into the final product – subtleties of form, tolerancing of parts and quality of finishes. And finally, we can feed key learnings from the engineering and manufacturing stages back into the front end of the product development cycle. We think of this as a 'closed loop' and it enables us to continue to learn all the time and consistently improve what we do.

Could you please describe the design process at Blackmagic Design?

Very collaborative. We have a tight-knit team that has worked together for a long time. We bounce ideas off each other to quickly solve problems and come up with the best solution. The process is fluid and we move fast. We've developed some key pieces of intellectual property around the process of industrial design; this has enabled us to drive product development cycles with far greater speed and efficiency than many other brands in the space. Being first to market with new technologies, in well designed high quality products, has been rewarded with loyal customers who really appreciate what we do.

What sort of designers make a good fit for your team?

We like to bring 'T' shaped people into our team. That is, they are rooted firmly with a core strength, such as industrial design, but also show a deep empathy toward other related functions such as engineering, manufacturing and even quality control. This makes them incredible designers because they understand at a very early stage in the design process the impact that every decision has on the final product.

Die Gründe hierfür sind vielfältig: Erstens wird dadurch gewährleistet, dass die Grundidee bei der Konstruktion nicht verloren geht. Die Designer und Ingenieure arbeiten eng zusammen, um sicherzustellen, dass die Konzepte im Laufe der Konstruktionsphasen erhalten bleiben und sogar verbessert werden. Zweitens können wir die Produktionsergebnisse so sehr genau kontrollieren und eine durchgängige Umsetzung der Details von der ursprünglichen Idee bis zum Endprodukt sicherstellen. Es geht dabei um Feinheiten der Formgebung, Teiletoleranzen und die Qualität der Verarbeitung. Zu guter Letzt können wir wichtige Erkenntnisse aus den Konstruktions- und Produktionsphasen direkt in den frühen Produktentwicklungszyklus einarbeiten. Wir betrachten dieses Verfahren als einen geschlossenen Kreislauf, der es uns erlaubt, permanent zu lernen und unsere Arbeit ständig zu verbessern.

Wie sieht der Designprozess bei Blackmagic Design aus?

Sehr kollaborativ. Wir haben ein gut eingespieltes, eng aufeinander abgestimmtes Team, das seit vielen Jahren zusammenarbeitet. Wir tauschen uns aus, um Probleme schnell zu lösen und die beste Lösung zu finden. Dieser Prozess ist fließend und bringt uns rasch vorwärts. Wir haben einige Kernstücke im Bereich geistigen Eigentums während dieses Industriedesign-Prozesses entwickelt. Mit dieser Herangehensweise können wir Produktentwicklungszyklen viel schneller und effizienter vorantreiben als viele andere Marken in diesem Bereich. Es gelingt uns immer wieder, als Erster mit neuen Technologien sowie durchdachten und hochwertigen Produkten auf den Markt zu kommen. Dafür werden wir mit treuen Kunden belohnt, die das, was wir machen, wirklich schätzen.

> "Design quality is the unseen attention to detail that makes a product feel intuitive."
>
> „Designqualität ist die unsichtbare Aufmerksamkeit für das Detail, damit ein Produkt intuitiv verständlich ist."

Simon Kidd – Director of Industrial Design

Similarly, we like to blur the lines between industrial designers and product engineers, we like teams to work fluidly and develop a respect for all disciplines that are required to bring a product to market.

How important are aesthetics in a technology-driven field as cinematography?

They're critical. First and foremost aesthetics are driven out of the product's functionality – enhancing the human-machine interface, improving clarity of controls and reflecting the ergonomics: these are critical elements of any camera. Secondly, they drive an emotive appeal that forms the bond between the product and user, often projecting the aspirations that the user may have. And finally, they're an integral part of communicating key messages about the Blackmagic Design brand.

Often our aesthetics are driven from key functional aspects of a product, for example the CNC machined chassis of our original Cinema Camera not only acts as the backbone of the camera but also functions as a heat sink. This large thermal mass of aluminium cools the delicate image sensor and helps maintain beautiful image quality. Customers love hearing this story; they often have no idea that such an elegant visual element performs such a critical engineering function.

We also like to promote engineering aspects of the products, like the top vent pattern on URSA Mini, or the transverse fins on the Micro Cinema Camera. These reflect the highly complex nature of the internal workings and create a dynamic visual element that is driven by core functionality.

Welche Art von Designern passt gut in Ihr Team?

In unserem Team haben wir gerne „generalisierende Spezialisten". Das heißt, sie sind Fachleute in einem Bereich wie beispielsweise dem Industriedesign, können aber auch grundlegende Kenntnisse in anderen verwandten Bereichen wie dem Ingenieurwesen, der Produktion oder sogar der Qualitätskontrolle vorweisen. Das macht sie zu unglaublich guten Designern, da sie bereits in einer sehr frühen Phase des Designprozesses in der Lage sind, die Auswirkung jeder Entscheidung auf das Endprodukt nachvollziehen zu können. Ebenso verwischen wir gerne die Trennlinien zwischen Industriedesignern und Produktingenieuren. Die Teams sind flexibel, die Übergänge fließend, sodass alle Beteiligten Respekt für all diejenigen Disziplinen entwickeln, die erforderlich sind, um ein Produkt auf den Markt zu bringen.

Wie wichtig ist die Ästhetik bei einem technologieorientierten Bereich wie der Kinematografie?

Sie ist entscheidend. Die Ästhetik ist überwiegend von der Funktion des Produktes geprägt – eine optimierte Mensch-Maschine-Schnittstelle, übersichtlichere Bedienelemente und eine perfekte Ergonomie sind allesamt kritische Bestandteile jeder Kamera. Daneben hat die Ästhetik einen emotionalen Wert, der den Verbraucher an das Produkt bindet und es ihm erlaubt, seine Erwartungen auf das Produkt zu projizieren. Letztlich bildet die Ästhetik einen wesentlichen Bestandteil bei der Vermittlung der Kernbotschaften der Marke Blackmagic Design.

Too often products try to 'cover up', wrapping superfluous layers around technology. We prefer to celebrate it.

And how do you maintain a consistent design language?

We make a wide range of products for many different segments of the video production industry. They're designed for quite different functions, users and environments. But rather than trying to create a singular visual language, we prefer to unite the products through their inherent qualities. We design the products to reflect the Blackmagic Design brand through physical aspects such as materials, finishes, internal structures, and key touch points such as latches, buttons and connections.

We don't believe that our products need to look the same, but they do need to exude the same qualities. Across more than 100 product lines, used in a wide range of environments, this is tricky to achieve. It requires a great deal of discipline, adhering to a robust design process and staying true to the brand.

Would you say that the design of your products is a materialisation of a technological quality?

Absolutely. Not only do we use the aesthetic elements of the products to communicate a message, we want the physical elements of the camera, their detailing and their tolerancing, to reflect the precision and accuracy of the internal engineering. It is a key way that we communicate to our customers – that the products are of a high quality, even though they are an affordable price.

Unsere Ästhetik leitet sich oft aus den wichtigen funktionalen Aspekten eines Produktes ab. Zum Beispiel stellt das CNC-bearbeitete Gehäuse unserer innovativen Cinema Camera nicht nur das Rückgrat der Kamera dar, sondern dient auch als Kühlkörper. Diese große thermische Masse aus Aluminium kühlt den empfindlichen Bildsensor und hilft dabei, eine hohe Bildqualität zu erhalten. Unsere Kunden sind von dieser Geschichte begeistert, denn sie wissen oft nicht, dass ein solch optisch ansprechendes Element auch eine entscheidende konstruktive Funktion erfüllt.

Zudem betonen wir gerne konstruktionsbedingte Produktmerkmale wie zum Beispiel die obere Öffnung des URSA Mini oder die Querlamelle bei der Micro Cinema Camera. Diese spiegeln die hohe Komplexität des Innenlebens wider und bilden ein dynamisches optisches Element, das aus der zentralen Funktion resultiert. Allzu oft wird bei Produkten versucht, sie „einzuhüllen", um damit die Technologie unnötig zu verpacken. Wir zelebrieren lieber die Technologie.

Wie gelingt es Ihnen, eine konsequente Designsprache beizubehalten?

Wir bieten eine breite Palette an Produkten für viele verschiedene Bereiche der Videoproduktion. Sie werden für ganz unterschiedliche Funktionen, Benutzer und Umgebungen entworfen. Unser Fokus liegt weniger auf einer einheitlichen Designsprache als vielmehr darauf, die Produkte durch ihre inneren Eigenschaften zu vereinen. Wir entwerfen die Produkte so, dass sie die Marke Blackmagic Design durch technische Aspekte wie Material, Verarbeitung, interne Strukturen sowie wichtige Berührungspunkte wie zum Beispiel Riegel, Knöpfe und Verbindungen widerspiegeln.

What role does the aspect of user-centred design play in your design work?

We make products for a highly technical professional industry, so understandably our customers have very high demands. Not only do our products need to be well designed, of great quality and be very reliable, they need to specifically cater for the user's workflow. To achieve this, we spend a great deal of time studying the way they work and the environments they operate in.

Our high end digital camera URSA is a good example of this. After an exhaustive study of 'on set' film crews we identified three key 'work zones' around the camera – the camera operator, the focus assistant and the audio engineer. We set about creating a camera that specifically catered for needs of each of these users providing the specific controls that each required. The result is a product that has superior ergonomics, a much more organised workflow and controls laid out in a considered and logical way.

... and how important is sustainability in your process?

We tend to take a more long-term approach to sustainability. Further than using recyclable materials, we develop products that include technologies that will increase their lifespan.

In the case of our digital film camera URSA, this approach comes in the form of an upgradable image sensor. We found that image sensor technology was moving so fast that cameras were becoming obsolete within a few years of their release – despite the fact that the body of the camera was still cutting edge. So we found a way to make the image sensor 'user-upgradable' and implemented this technology in URSA. Not only did this create a hugely sustainable product but it also delighted our customers who now had a camera that would last for many years to come.

How do you enjoy working with your customers?

There is a privilege in creating for a creative industry – they appreciate the effort. Prior to Blackmagic the industry was dominated by bland utilitarian design that was forced on users in overly expensive and complicated products.

Our end users are highly creative, and highly technically skilled people. There are similarities with industrial designers. We want them to enjoy using their products and appreciate the thought we've put in – much the same as we do.

Has your work changed your way of seeing movies?

When you design the tools that are used to make movies, you get a real understanding of the effort and hard work that goes into creating a motion picture, it's a collaboration of a large creative and technical team working under intense pressure toward a common goal. Interestingly it's like designing a product.

Wir denken nicht, dass unsere Produkte alle gleich aussehen müssen – aber sie müssen alle die gleichen Eigenschaften vorweisen. Bei hundert verschiedenen Produktlinien, die in einer Vielzahl unterschiedlicher Umgebungen verwendet werden, kann das eine Herausforderung sein. Es erfordert ein großes Maß an Disziplin, die Einhaltung eines soliden Gestaltungsprozesses sowie Markentreue.

Würden Sie sagen, dass das Design Ihrer Produkte die Manifestation ihrer technologischen Qualität ist?

Absolut. Wir verwenden die ästhetischen Merkmale der Produkte dazu, eine Botschaft zu vermitteln. Darüber hinaus müssen die physischen Bestandteile der Kamera, ihre Details sowie ihre Toleranzen die Präzision und Genauigkeit des Innenlebens widerspiegeln. Das ist eine zentrale Botschaft an unsere Kunden – nämlich, dass die Produkte hochwertig und trotzdem erschwinglich sind.

Welche Rolle spielt die benutzerorientierte Gestaltung bei Ihrer Designarbeit?

Da wir Produkte für eine hoch technische und professionelle Branche herstellen, haben unsere Kunden natürlich sehr hohe Anforderungen. Unsere Produkte brauchen nicht nur ein gutes Design, hohe Qualität und eine hohe Zuverlässigkeit, sie müssen auch zum individuellen User-Workflow passen. Das erreichen wir dadurch, dass wir viel Zeit damit verbringen, die Funktionsweise der Produkte und die Umgebung, in der sie eingesetzt werden, zu verstehen.

Unsere High-End-Digitalkamera URSA ist ein gutes Beispiel dafür. Nach einer eingehenden Beobachtung von Filmcrews bei der Arbeit haben wir drei „Hauptarbeitsbereiche" im Umgang mit der Kamera identifiziert: Kameramann/-frau, Kameraassistent/-in und Tontechniker/-in. Dann haben wir mit der Konstruktion einer Kamera angefangen, welche der speziellen Bedürfnissen dieser drei Benutzergruppen gerecht wird und die jeweiligen spezifischen Kontrollen aufweist. Das Ergebnis ist ein Produkt mit einer überlegenen Ergonomie, einem viel besser organisierten Workflow sowie einer Benutzerschnittstelle, die durchdacht und logisch aufgebaut ist.

... und wie wichtig ist der Aspekt der Nachhaltigkeit?

Wir gehen das Thema Nachhaltigkeit eher langfristig an. Über den Einsatz wiederverwendbarer Materialien hinaus entwickeln wir vor allem Produkte, deren Lebensdauer sich durch die integrierte Technik erhöht.

Im Falle unserer digitalen Filmkamera URSA ist dieser Ansatz etwa in Form eines aufrüstbaren Bildsensors umgesetzt. Wir haben gemerkt, dass die Bildsensortechnologie sich so schnell weiterentwickelte, dass Kameras nach wenigen Jahren bereits veraltet waren, obwohl der Kamerakörper immer noch den Stand der Technik darstellte. Deshalb haben wir eine Lösung gefunden, den Bildsensor aufrüstbar zu gestalten. Diese Technologie haben wir in die URSA implementiert. Das hat zum einen ein enorm nachhaltiges Produkt geschaffen und zum anderen unsere Kunden gefreut, die nun eine Kamera haben, die sie lange begleiten wird.

People just see the outcome, but when you have an understanding of the process that was required to get there, you have a greater appreciation of the end result. So it's very hard not to 'appreciate' a lot of the films you watch.

Our Cinema Cameras were used on "Mad Max: Fury Road", in some incredibly tough to shoot scenes. Not only was this a testament to the camera's rugged design, but it showcased the ways creative people can utilise the benefits of our cameras – they're affordable, functional and miniaturised. Using multiple Blackmagic Cinema Cameras in tight spaces allowed them to create many of the unique action scenes in that movie – it's real 'edge of the seat' stuff. Watching that film and appreciating the creative ways people have used our product is extremely satisfying.

Do you have a role model in design?

I admire Apple. Not just for their design, but for their consideration of the entire engineering and manufacturing process and the effect it has on front end design decisions. They have set new benchmarks for the quality and tolerancing of mass produced products.

What does it mean to you to be the
Red Dot: Design Team of the Year?

It's an incredible honour for our team and the entire Blackmagic Design business. To be recognised among the top design-led businesses in the world truly endorses our commitment to making the highest quality video affordable to everyone through really well designed, high-quality and innovative products. We're a young company with an evolving design legacy and we consider this to be validation of the work that we've done to date … and inspiration for the team to go forward.

Wie ist die Zusammenarbeit mit Ihren Kunden?

Es ist ein Privileg, für eine kreative Branche zu gestalten – die Kunden schätzen unsere Arbeit. Vor Blackmagic war die Branche von einem rein zweckmäßigen Design dominiert, die Produkte überteuert und kompliziert.

Unsere Endnutzer sind sehr kreativ und technisch versiert. Es gibt Ähnlichkeiten mit Industriedesignern. Wir möchten, dass sie ihre Produkte gerne verwenden und unseren Aufwand schätzen – genau so, wie wir das tun.

Hat Ihre Arbeit etwas daran geändert, wie Sie jetzt Filme sehen?

Wenn man die Werkzeuge gestaltet, die beim Drehen von Filmen verwendet werden, entwickelt man ein tiefes Verständnis für den Aufwand und die harte Arbeit, die dahintersteckt. Ein Film ist das Resultat aus der Zusammenarbeit eines großen kreativen und technischen Teams, das unter großem Druck auf ein gemeinsames Ziel hinarbeitet. Interessanterweise ist es ähnlich, wenn man ein Produkt entwirft. Die meisten Leute sehen nur das Ergebnis – wenn man aber den Prozess dahinter versteht, schätzt man das Endergebnis umso mehr. Es ist also schwierig, die gesehenen Filme nicht zu schätzen.

Unsere Cinema Cameras wurden beim Dreh von „Mad Max: Fury Road" eingesetzt, und einige Szenen waren unheimlich herausfordernd. Das spricht nicht nur für das robuste Kameradesign, sondern zeigt auf, wie Kreative die Vorteile unserer Kameras ausnutzen können – sie sind bezahlbar, funktionell und sehr klein gehalten. Durch die Verwendung von mehreren Blackmagic Cinema Cameras bei beengten Platzverhältnissen gelang es den Filmemachern, viele der großartigen Action-Szenen in diesem Film zu verwirklichen. Es ist eine wirklich spannende Sache, sich diesen Film anzusehen und zu erleben, wie kreativ unser Produkt verwendet wurde.

Haben Sie ein Designvorbild?

Ich bewundere Apple. Nicht nur wegen des Designs, sondern weil Apple den gesamten Konstruktions- und Produktionsprozess berücksichtigt und sich dies bereits früh auf grundlegende Designentscheidungen auswirkt. Apple hat neue Maßstäbe für die Qualität und Produktionstoleranzen von Serienprodukten gesetzt.

Was bedeutet es für Sie, zum Red Dot: Design Team of the Year gekürt zu werden?

Es ist eine unglaubliche Ehre für unser Team bei Blackmagic Design und für das ganze Unternehmen. Die Auszeichnung als eines der besten designgeführten Unternehmen der Welt bestätigt unser Ziel, durch durchdachte, hochwertige und innovative Produkte erstklassige Videoaufnahmen für alle erschwinglich zu machen. Wir sind ein junges Unternehmen mit stetig wachsender Designerfahrung, und wir sehen diesen Titel als Bestätigung unserer bisherigen Arbeit und als Inspiration für die Zukunft.

Red Dot: Design Team of the Year 2016: the entire Blackmagic Industrial Design Team
with CEO Grant Petty and Design Director Simon Kidd
Red Dot: Design Team of the Year 2016: das gesamte Blackmagic Industrial Design Team
mit CEO Grant Petty und Design Director Simon Kidd

Red Dot: Best of the Best
The best designers of their category
Die besten Designer ihrer Kategorie

The designers of the Red Dot: Best of the Best
Only a few products in the Red Dot Design Award receive the "Red Dot: Best of the Best" accolade. In each category, the jury can assign this award to products of outstanding design quality and innovative achievement. Exploring new paths, these products are all exemplary in their design and oriented towards the future.

The following chapter introduces the people who have received one of these prestigious awards. It features the best designers and design teams of the year 2016 together with their products, revealing in interviews and statements what drives these designers and what design means to them.

Die Designer der Red Dot: Best of the Best
Nur sehr wenige Produkte im Red Dot Design Award erhalten die Auszeichnung „Red Dot: Best of the Best". Die Jury kann mit dieser Auszeichnung in jeder Kategorie Design von außerordentlicher Qualität und Innovationsleistung besonders hervorheben. In jeder Hinsicht vorbildlich gestaltet, beschreiten diese Produkte neue Wege und sind zukunftsweisend.

Das folgende Kapitel stellt die Menschen vor, die diese besondere Auszeichnung erhalten haben. Es zeigt die besten Designer und Designteams des Jahres 2016 zusammen mit ihren Produkten. In Interviews und Statements wird deutlich, was diese Designer bewegt und was ihnen Design bedeutet.

Humanscale Design Studio

"Effortless functionality and honest design."

„Mühelose Funktionalität und ehrliches Design."

What was your goal when you designed your award-winning product?
To design a minimal sit-to-stand workstation that is easily adaptable to different office environments.

How do you define design quality?
A well-designed product's function should be intuitive. The design must be distilled only to what's essential.

Where will your industry be in ten years; what trends and developments do you expect to see?
The modern office environment will continue to evolve in order to accommodate an increasingly mobile workforce. Workplace design is being inspired by residential design as the line between home and office blurs.

Welches Ziel verfolgten Sie bei der Gestaltung Ihres ausgezeichneten Produkts?
Einen minimalistischen Sitz-/Steh-Arbeitsplatz zu gestalten, der sich verschiedenen Bürolandschaften leicht anpasst.

Wie definieren Sie Designqualität?
Die Funktion eines gut gestalteten Produkts sollte intuitiv erfahrbar sein. Die Gestaltung muss auf das Wesentliche reduziert sein.

Wo wird Ihre Branche in zehn Jahren stehen, mit welchen Trends und Entwicklungen rechnen Sie?
Die moderne Bürolandschaft wird sich weiter entwickeln, um immer mobileren Arbeitskräften entgegenzukommen. Da die Grenzen zwischen Heim und Arbeit verschwimmen, wird die Arbeitsplatzgestaltung zunehmend auch vom Wohndesign beeinflusst.

reddot award 2016
best of the best

Manufacturer
Humanscale, New York, USA

QuickStand Lite™
Monitor Arm

See page 58
Siehe Seite 58

Jia-Sheng Wong, Chun-Fu Lin, Yao-Hsing Tsai
TPV design

"To passionately explore demands with stunning and creative solutions."
„Es gilt, mit verblüffenden und kreativen Lösungen leidenschaftlich Bedürfnisse zu erkunden."

What inspires you?
The environment and the people living in it.

How do you define design quality?
A good design should be intuitive, durable, detailed, with well-controlled cost; a good design should offer a desirable user experience.

Where will your industry be in ten years; what trends and developments do you expect to see?
The future display will not be a boring box linked with conventional interface devices. The future display will be more immersive, interactive and beautiful with elements such as virtual reality, eye-tracking and mind control.

Was inspiriert Sie?
Die Umwelt und die Menschen, die in ihr leben.

Wie definieren Sie Designqualität?
Gutes Design sollte intuitiv, langlebig und detailliert sein, mit gut kontrollierten Kosten. Gutes Design sollte auch ein begehrenswertes Benutzererlebnis bieten.

Wo wird Ihre Branche in zehn Jahren stehen, mit welchen Trends und Entwicklungen rechnen Sie?
Das Display der Zukunft wird keine langweilige Box sein, die mit konventionellen Schnittstellengeräten verbunden ist. Das Display der Zukunft wird immersiver, interaktiver und einfach schöner sein, mit Komponenten wie virtueller Realität, Blickerfassung und Gedankensteuerung.

reddot award 2016
best of the best

Manufacturer
Top Victory Investments Ltd,
New Taipei City, Taiwan

GAMA
POS System

See page 82
Siehe Seite 82

34

Beat Fahrni
ugomo ag

"Everybody said: it's impossible. Then someone came along who didn't know that and just did it."

„Alle sagten: Das geht nicht. Dann kam einer, der wusste das nicht, und hat's einfach gemacht."

Why did you become a designer?
The term design stands for forming, designing and creating. To think of something and to follow up on it, to be part of the process, part of the creation right up to the point where a product comes into being – that is what fascinates and drives me.

What are the challenges in your everyday work?
The challenge is daily to grapple with things, to ask critical questions about what is considered as given, and always to strive for the best possible solution. For we encounter a lot of scepticism in our everyday life, that something may not be correct or won't work properly. Tenacity is vital, as is a belief in something, and a well-functioning team that grows even closer together when things go wrong and continually keeps on going forward.

Warum sind Sie Designer geworden?
Der Begriff Design steht für Formen, Gestalten, Kreieren. Einen Gedanken zu denken und weiterzuverfolgen, den Prozess mitzuerleben, mitzugestalten bis zur Entstehung eines Produkts – das fasziniert und treibt mich an.

Welche Herausforderungen begegnen Ihnen in Ihrem Arbeitsalltag?
Die Herausforderung besteht darin, sich täglich mit allem auseinanderzusetzen, das Gegebene kritisch zu hinterfragen und immer bestrebt zu sein, die bestmöglichen Lösungen zu finden. Denn in unserem Arbeitsalltag begegnen wir viel Skepsis, dass etwas nicht richtig sein oder nicht vernünftig funktionieren könnte. Da braucht es Beharrlichkeit, den Glauben an die Sache und ein gut eingespieltes Team, das bei Rückschlägen noch näher zusammenrückt und immer wieder weitermacht.

reddot award 2016
best of the best

Manufacturer
ugomo ag, Thun, Switzerland

uTerminal
Time Recording Terminal
Zeiterfassungsterminal

See page 92
Siehe Seite 92

LOOP

"Our challenge was to be completely disruptive in a highly conservative sector,
and have this disruptive change accepted naturally."

„Unsere Herausforderung war es, in einer konservativen Branche vollkommen
revolutionär zu sein und zu erreichen, dass diese Veränderung wie selbstverständlich angenommen wird."

What inspires you?
Given that we were creating a workstation with a completely new relationship
between man and machine, we focused
our efforts on finding alternatives to
the obvious solutions for direct interaction such as tablet interfaces. We looked
for inspiration from new interaction
solutions that were appropriate for the
scale, user context and focus of the
application.

**What are the challenges in your
everyday work?**
Our challenge is to help our clients to
understand how their users operate, and
how to find out the key points to offer
them added value.

Was inspiriert Sie?
Da wir einen Arbeitsplatz schaffen wollten,
der Mensch und Maschine in eine gänzlich neue Beziehung zueinander bringt,
haben wir unsere Bemühungen darauf ausgerichtet, Alternativen zu den offensicht-
lichen Lösungen für direkte Interaktion
wie beispielsweise Tablet-Schnittstellen
zu finden. Wir haben Inspiration in neuen
interaktiven Lösungen gesucht, die für
den Umfang, den Benutzerkontext und
die Zielrichtung des Anwendungsgebiets
passend waren.

**Welche Herausforderungen begegnen
Ihnen in Ihrem Arbeitsalltag?**
Unsere Herausforderung besteht darin,
unseren Kunden verstehen zu helfen,
wie ihre Nutzer arbeiten und wie sie die
wesentlichen Aspekte in Erfahrung bringen, um diesen einen Mehrwert bieten
zu können.

reddot award 2016
best of the best

Manufacturer
Indra, Torrejón de Ardoz (Madrid), Spain

CWP V3 / Evolution
Air Traffic Controller Working Position
Fluglotsen-Arbeitsplatz

See page 94
Siehe Seite 94

François Lessard, Nicolas Lebrun
Creaform Inc (Ametek Inc)

"Fail early, succeed faster. If you're not failing,
you're not going to innovate."

„Früh scheitern, schneller erfolgreich sein.
Wer nicht scheitert, schafft keine Neuerungen."

How do you define design quality?
Design quality is a very important aspect. It means that the whole product is unanimous to all contributors. It means the design is accepted and well understood.

What are the challenges in your everyday work?
We have to fight against paradigms. We always try to reconsider everything. Push the limits. Try to be resilient.

What does winning the Red Dot: Best of the Best mean to you?
It really means a lot to us. The exclusivity and fame it brings make it almost unattainable, but when you are passionate about designing, it becomes a great accomplishment after all. At the end of the day, we guess it means we got the job done.

Wie definieren Sie Designqualität?
Designqualität ist ein sehr wichtiger Aspekt und bedeutet, dass das gesamte Produkt für alle Beteiligten ausnahmslos positiv erfahren und seine Gestaltung akzeptiert und gut verstanden wird.

Welche Herausforderungen begegnen Ihnen in Ihrem Arbeitsalltag?
Wir müssen gegen Paradigmen ankämpfen und versuchen, ständig alles zu überdenken, die Möglichkeiten auszureizen und widerstandsfähig zu bleiben.

Was bedeutet die Auszeichnung mit dem Red Dot: Best of the Best für Sie?
Sie bedeutet uns sehr viel. Der Ruhm und die Exklusivität, die sie mit sich bringt, sind kaum zu erreichen. Aber wenn man mit Leidenschaft gestaltet, bringt sie eine große Erfüllung mit sich. Am Ende des Tages heißt das wohl, dass wir unsere Aufgabe gut gemacht haben.

reddot award 2016
best of the best

Manufacturer
Creaform Inc (Ametek Inc),
Lévis, Québec, Canada

MetraSCAN 3D / HandyPROBE / C-Track
Portable 3D Measurement System
Tragbares 3D-Messsystem

See page 120
Siehe Seite 120

CleanSpace Design Team

"Rigorous simplicity – in both design and operation."
"Rigorose Einfachheit – sowohl in der Gestaltung als auch in der Handhabung."

What inspires you?
We are inspired by raising the industry benchmark for industrial personal respiratory protection. To create a mask for workers who are at risk of airborne hazards and can work safer.

Where will your industry be in ten years; what trends and developments do you expect to see?
Our industry hasn't seen revolutionary innovation for over 20 years. The CleanSpace respirator design is a watershed event. This new design will trigger established companies to reinvest in their design projects.

What does winning the Red Dot: Best of the Best mean to you?
Winning the most respected design award in the world is for us like winning an Oscar. It is a feeling of honour and pride.

Was inspiriert Sie?
Wir wurden inspiriert von der Anhebung des Branchenstandards für individuellen Atemschutz in der Industrie, um für durch Schadstoffe in der Luft gefährdete Arbeiter eine Maske zu entwerfen, mit der sie sicherer arbeiten können.

Wo wird Ihre Branche in zehn Jahren stehen, mit welchen Trends und Entwicklungen rechnen Sie?
Unsere Branche hat seit mehr als 20 Jahren keine revolutionäre Innovation mehr erlebt. Die Gestaltung der CleanSpace-Atemschutzmaske stellt einen Wendepunkt dar. Dieses neue Design wird für etablierte Unternehmen der Auslöser sein, wieder in ihre Designprojekte zu investieren.

Was bedeutet die Auszeichnung mit dem Red Dot: Best of the Best für Sie?
Der Gewinn dieses weltweit angesehensten Designpreises ist für uns, als hätten wir den Oscar gewonnen. Wir fühlen uns sehr geehrt und sind stolz.

reddot award 2016
best of the best

Manufacturer
PAFtec Australia Pty Ltd, Sydney, Australia

CleanSpace Ultra
Respirator
Atemschutzmaske

See page 154
Siehe Seite 154

Tribecraft

"As an interdisciplinary team, we jointly discover, develop and design clever solutions and promising products for selected customers."
„Gemeinsam entdecken, entwickeln und gestalten wir als interdisziplinäres Team clevere Lösungen und zukunftsträchtige Produkte für ausgewählte Auftraggeber."

What was your goal when you designed your award-winning product?
To convey something radically new in a self-evident, confident way that was at the same time unobtrusive in interior design.

What are the challenges in your everyday work?
To be of one mind about the aim, but to have the freedom to choose the right route, independently of others.

How do you define design quality?
By comparing it to a good script: never go for easy laughs and therefore make the result strong, coherent and believable.

What do you see as being the biggest challenges in your industry at present?
To design products and systems in such a way that they will become or remain trustworthy over a long period of time – in an environment in which personal data has become a form of currency.

Welches Ziel verfolgten Sie bei der Gestaltung Ihres ausgezeichneten Produkts?
Radikal Neues selbstverständlich, selbstbewusst, aber innenarchitektonisch zurückhaltend zu vermitteln.

Welche Herausforderungen begegnen Ihnen in Ihrem Arbeitsalltag?
Sich über das Ziel einig zu werden und sich die Freiheit herauszunehmen, den dazu passenden Weg unabhängig zu wählen.

Wie definieren Sie Designqualität?
Durch die Analogie mit einem guten Drehbuch: niemals die billigen, einfachen Lacher abholen, sondern das Werk stark, stimmig und glaubwürdig machen.

Worin sehen Sie aktuell die größten Herausforderungen in Ihrer Branche?
Produkte und Systeme so zu gestalten, dass sie belastbar vertrauenswürdig werden oder auf lange Sicht bleiben – in einem Umfeld, in dem persönliche Daten zur Währung geworden sind.

reddot award 2016
best of the best

Manufacturer
Zehnder Group International AG,
Gränichen, Switzerland

Zehnder Zmart
Radiator
Heizkörper

See page 164
Siehe Seite 164

Jesse Laivo – Link Design and Development Oy
Mikko Toivonen – Chiller Oy
Ville Hirvonen – Link Design and Development Oy

"Break out of the ordinary and follow your gut."
„Man muss den üblichen Rahmen sprengen und seinem Bauchgefühl folgen."

What was your goal when you designed your award-winning product?
To create a product that would be approachable and intuitive to use. We aimed to indicate functions in a way that makes the product understandable at one glimpse. The design embodies beauty of simplicity in the user interface.

How do you define design quality?
Quality comes from the benefit that a product provides for the user. It means purposeful design that brings a product to life.

What are the challenges in your everyday work?
Finding real issues behind a design problem and coming up with a purpose-driven solution. At the same time, it is the force that prompts our curiosity, creativity and dedication.

Welches Ziel verfolgten Sie bei der Gestaltung Ihres ausgezeichneten Produkts?
Ein Produkt zu gestalten, das zugänglich und in der Handhabung intuitiv sein würde. Wir haben versucht, Funktionen so zu zeigen, dass sie auf einen Blick verständlich sind. Die Gestaltung der Benutzeroberfläche verkörpert die Ästhetik der Einfachheit.

Wie definieren Sie Designqualität?
Qualität ergibt sich aus dem Nutzen, den ein Produkt seinem Anwender bietet, und bedeutet, dass eine zielgerichtete Gestaltung ein Produkt mit Leben erfüllt.

Welche Herausforderungen begegnen Ihnen in Ihrem Arbeitsalltag?
Die wirkliche Thematik hinter einem Gestaltungsproblem zu identifizieren und dann eine zielgerechte Lösung zu entwickeln. Das ist gleichzeitig auch die Kraft, die unsere Neugier, Kreativität und Hingabe antreibt.

reddot award 2016
best of the best

Manufacturer
Chiller Oy, Tuusula, Finland

Vari Pro
Thermostat

See page 168
Siehe Seite 168

Andreas Haug, Harald Lutz, Bernd Eigenstetter, Tom Schönherr
Phoenix Design GmbH + Co. KG

"Design with logic, morals and magic."
„Design mit Logik, Moral und Magie."

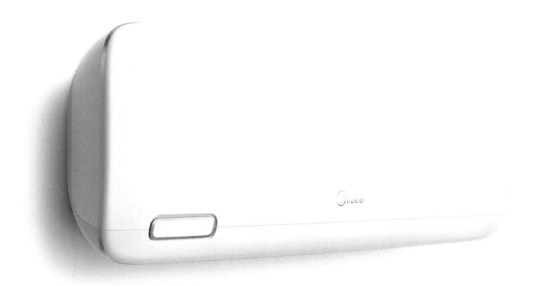

reddot award 2016
best of the best

Manufacturer
Midea Air-Conditioning Equipment Co., Ltd., Foshan, China

Hybrid Air Conditioner
Hybrid-Klimaanlage

See page 172
Siehe Seite 172

Philips Design

"Everything we do is based on people and their needs. That has always been our starting point."

„Alles, was wir tun, basiert auf Menschen und ihren Bedürfnissen. Das ist immer unser Ausgangspunkt."

What inspires you?
People, how they work, provide or receive care and the challenges they face experiencing today's medical solutions.

What do you see as being the biggest challenges in your industry at present?
Healthcare design is still in the pioneer ng stage. We are now at a point where we see a shift towards design-led innovation alongside clinical science and engineering.

Where will your industry be in ten years; what trends and developments do you expect to see?
The world's population is rising, people are getting older and the need for health-care is increasing. At the same, the digitalisation of healthcare solutions and services continues.

Was inspiriert Sie?
Menschen, wie sie arbeiten, Pflegeleistungen ausführen oder in Anspruch nehmen, und die Herausforderungen, vor die sie die heutigen medizinischen Lösungen stellen.

Worin sehen Sie aktuell die größten Herausforderungen in Ihrer Branche?
Design im Gesundheitswesen steckt immer noch in der Anfangsphase. Wir sind jetzt an einem Punkt angelangt, an dem wir nicht nur Entwicklungen in der klinischen Forschung und Technik sehen, sondern auch durch Design bestimmte Innovationen.

Wo wird Ihre Branche in zehn Jahren stehen, mit welchen Trends und Entwicklungen rechnen Sie?
Die Weltbevölkerung wächst, die Menschen werden älter und der Bedarf an Gesundheitsversorgung nimmt zu. Gleichzeitig schreitet die Digitalisierung von medizinischen Lösungen und Dienstleistungen weiter fort.

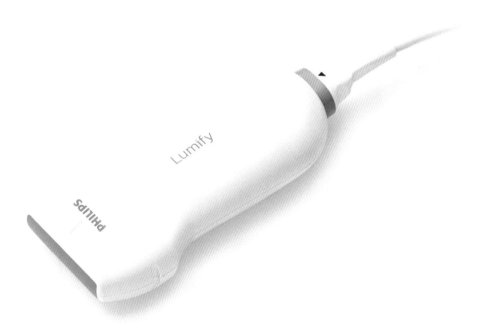

reddot award 2016
best of the best

Manufacturer
Royal Philips, Eindhoven, Netherlands

Lumify
Ultrasound System
Ultraschallsystem

See page 194
Siehe Seite 194

Held+Team

"Specialists in medical design."

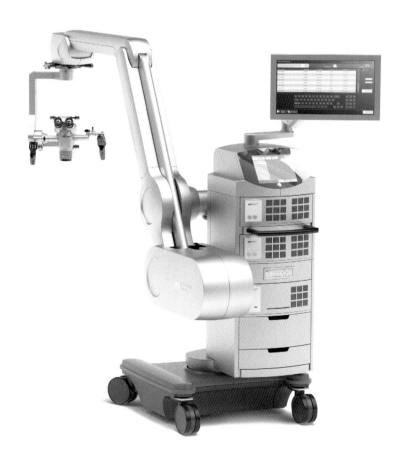

What inspires you?
Calm.

Why did you become a designer?
At the time, the wide variety of tasks
appealed to me.

What are the challenges in your
everyday work?
The ever stricter regulations are a major
challenge for a designer who focuses
solely on medical and laboratory technologies.

How do you define design quality?
When dealing with medical technology,
usability has always been of the highest
priority for me. If one manages, in addition, to give a product an appearance
that fulfils the manufacturer's brand
values, then I believe the result to be a
success.

Was inspiriert Sie?
Ruhe.

Warum sind Sie Designer geworden?
Die Vielfältigkeit der möglichen Aufgaben
hat mich damals sehr gereizt.

Welche Herausforderungen begegnen
Ihnen in Ihrem Arbeitsalltag?
Als Designer, der sich nur mit Medizin- und
Labortechnik beschäftigt, sind die immer
strikteren regulatorischen Vorgaben eine
der großen Herausforderungen.

Wie definieren Sie Designqualität?
In der Medizintechnik kam Usability für
mich schon immer an erster Stelle. Wenn
es gelingt, dem Produkt darüber hinaus
eine Erscheinung mitzugeben, die den
Markenwerten des Herstellers gerecht wird,
empfinde ich das Ergebnis als gelungen.

reddot award 2016
best of the best

Manufacturer
Haag-Streit Surgical GmbH,
Wedel, Germany

FS 5-33
Floor Stand for Operating Microscopes
Stativ für Operationsmikroskope

See page 208
Siehe Seite 208

Paul Doczy, Mark Menendez
Dell Experience Design Group

"Keep it simple, purposeful and intuitive: validate with confident, iconic design."
„Halte es einfach, zweckmäßig und intuitiv: Beweise das mit einem selbstbewussten, ikonischen Design."

What was your goal when you designed your award-winning product?
We knew we needed to make a bold statement with the introduction of Dell's first Edge Gateway. The quality must be undeniably industry-leading. We wanted a design language that further communicates a high level of quality and reliability through a bold visual statement and robust material selection.

What inspires you?
We draw inspiration from the occasional everyday products that take design to a higher standard than is expected of them. Just because a product is highly functional in its application does not mean its design cannot have a high level of refinement and elegance.

Welches Ziel verfolgten Sie bei der Gestaltung Ihres ausgezeichneten Produkts?
Uns war klar, dass die Einführung des ersten Edge Gateway von Dell einen starken Auftritt haben und die Qualität unbestreitbar marktführend sein musste. Wir wollten außerdem eine Formensprache erzielen, die durch eine kühne optische Erscheinung und eine stringente Auswahl der Materialien ein hohes Maß an Wertigkeit und Zuverlässigkeit vermittelt.

Was inspiriert Sie?
Uns inspirieren alltägliche Gelegenheitsprodukte, die Design auf ein höheres Niveau heben, als man von ihnen erwarten würde. Nur weil ein Produkt äußerst funktional in seiner Anwendung ist, heißt das noch lange nicht, dass seine Gestaltung nicht auch ein hohes Maß an Feinheit und Eleganz besitzen kann.

reddot award 2016
best of the best

Manufacturer
Dell Inc., Round Rock, Texas, USA

Dell Edge Gateway 5000 Series
Internet Gateway

See page 258
Siehe Seite 258

Javier A. Cesar
HP Inc.

"A product is the utmost brand expression, with immense power to drive customer loyalty."

„Ein Produkt ist der höchste Ausdruck einer Marke und hat die immense Macht, die Kundenbindung zu stärken."

What inspires you?
I get inspired mainly by two things: technology as an enabler of new product architectures and the way people interact with things.

How do you define design quality?
Authentic design quality is the result of how well a product embodies an innovative concept, relevant functionalities and a great user experience into a unique and iconic industrial design. Of course, the whole wrapped up in a flawless implementation, otherwise it all loses meaning.

What do you see as being the biggest challenges in your industry at present?
It's about making the whole customer's workflow a streamlined, even enjoyable process; printing is just one part within a larger picture of productivity needs.

Was inspiriert Sie?
Mich inspirieren vornehmlich zwei Dinge: die Technik als Wegbereiter für neue Produktarchitekturen und das Zusammenspiel zwischen Menschen und Dingen.

Wie definieren Sie Designqualität?
Echte Designqualität hängt davon ab, wie gut ein Produkt ein innovatives Konzept, relevante Funktionalitäten und eine großartige Nutzererfahrung in ein einzigartiges und ikonisches Industriedesign verwandelt. Selbstverständlich muss das Ganze tadellos umgesetzt werden, sonst verliert es seinen Sinn.

Worin sehen Sie aktuell die größten Herausforderungen in Ihrer Branche?
Es geht darum, den gesamten Workflow des Kunden in einen optimierten, ja sogar angenehmen Prozess zu verwandeln. Drucken ist dabei nur ein Teil innerhalb des größeren Rahmens der Produktivitätsanforderungen.

reddot award 2016
best of the best

Manufacturer
HP Inc.,
Sant Cugat del Vallès (Barcelona), Spain

HP PageWide XL
Large-Format Printer
Großformatdrucker

See page 328
Siehe Seite 328

Offices
Büro

QuickStand Lite™
Monitor Arm

Manufacturer
Humanscale, New York, USA

In-house design
Humanscale Design Studio

Web
www.humanscale.com

reddot award 2016
best of the best

Contemporary flexibility

In today's working world, the most diverse scenarios of individual work and teamwork coexist equally. The QuickStand Lite monitor arm suits this diversity with a sophisticated concept. Its design impresses with an elegant form language that blends well into any office environment. On the basis of a well thought-through functionality, it is especially suitable for use in hot-desking spaces, where several users share one workplace. This monitor arm supports a variety of hardware components, while an intelligent, built-in cable management system keeps work surfaces clear and uncluttered. An innovation in design is the counterbalance mechanism, since it allows users to transition from sitting to standing positions with ease. The monitor arm features an adjustable keyboard platform, which, just like the monitor arm, provides exceptional stability while typing. Additional ergonomic comfort for the ideal sit/stand workplace is offered through the tool's 20" height range and 5.5" vertical range, allowing easy adjustments to the different body heights of users. The QuickStand Lite monitor arm can hold single or dual monitors of up to 25 pounds. It fascinates every day with its innovative functionality – turning static office desks into active workspaces.

Zeitgemäße Flexibilität

In der aktuellen Arbeitswelt existieren die verschiedensten Szenarien von Einzel- und Teamarbeit ebenbürtig nebeneinander. Der Monitorarm QuickStand Lite wird dieser Vielfalt mit einem ausgereiften Konzept gerecht. Seine Gestaltung beeindruckt mit einer eleganten Formensprache, dank der er sich gut in jede Büroumgebung einfügt. Auf der Basis einer durchdachten Funktionalität ist er insbesondere für den Einsatz in Hot-Desking-Bereichen geeignet, in denen sich mehrere Mitarbeiter einen Arbeitsplatz teilen. Dieser Monitorarm passt zu einer Vielzahl von Hardware-Komponenten, ein kluges, integriertes Kabelmanagement sorgt außerdem für Ordnung am Arbeitsplatz. Eine gestalterische Innovation ist der Mechanismus zum Gewichtsausgleich, da er dem Nutzer ein müheloses Wechseln zwischen Sitzen und Stehen ermöglicht. Der Monitorarm verfügt über eine einstellbare Tastaturablage, die sich, ebenso wie die Monitorarmstütze, auch bei der Eingabe von Texten als ausgesprochen stabil erweist. Zusätzlichen ergonomischen Komfort für den idealen Sitz-/Steh-Arbeitsplatz bietet ein Höheneinstellbereich von 51 cm und ein seitlicher Einstellbereich von 14 cm, um sich den unterschiedlichen Körpergrößen der Nutzer problemlos anpassen zu können. Der Monitorarm QuickStand Lite eignet sich zudem für Einzel- oder Doppelmonitore mit einem Gewicht bis 11,3 kg. Er begeistert täglich durch seine innovative Funktionalität – der statische Büroschreibtisch wird so in einen aktiven Arbeitsbereich verwandelt.

Statement by the jury

The QuickStand Lite monitor arm combines minimalistic elegance with sophisticated and conclusive functionality, allowing it to perfectly adjust to changing work situations. The innovative counterbalance mechanism ensures high flexibility. A well-balanced design language as well as high-grade materials visualise a high standard of quality.

Begründung der Jury

Minimalistische Eleganz verbindet sich beim Monitorarm QuickStand Lite mit einer ausgeklügelten und schlüssigen Funktionalität. Sie erlaubt es, sich den wechselnden Arbeitssituationen perfekt anzupassen. Die Innovation des integrierten Gewichtsausgleichs sorgt für eine hohe Flexibilität. Eine ausgewogene Formensprache sowie hochwertige Materialien visualisieren den hohen Qualitätsanspruch.

Designer portrait
See page 30
Siehe Seite 30

Play&Work
Office Furniture System
Büromöbelsystem

Manufacturer
Nowy Styl Group, Krosno, Poland
Design
WertelOberfell GbR (Gernot Oberfell, Ian Wertel),
Munich, Germany
Web
www.nowystylgroup.com
www.werteloberfell.com

The objective of the Play&Work office furniture system is to promote its users' productivity and well-being. Thanks to the wide range of configuration options, it supports communication and provides enough space for teamwork as well as for individual work. The system consists of different desks, also in combination with cabinets and panels, available in metal and upholstered, and comes with a wide range of colourful accessories made of metal, wood or wool. The system combines these elements into functional and ergonomic office furniture, which allows for extensions and upgrades according to individual requirements.

Statement by the jury
The particularity of this office furniture system is that it allows for versatile configurations, supporting different working styles and office routines.

Ziel des Büromöbelsystems Play&Work ist es, die Produktivität und das Wohlbefinden seiner Nutzer zu fördern. Dank der zahlreichen Konfigurationsoptionen unterstützt es die Kommunikation und bietet genügend Platz für Teamwork, aber auch für individuelles Arbeiten. Das System besteht aus verschiedenen Schreibtischen, auch in Verbindung mit Schränken und Trennwänden, die aus Metall sowie gepolstert erhältlich sind, und in einer großen Auswahl an farbenfrohem Zubehör aus Metall, Holz und Wolle. Das System verbindet diese Elemente zu funktionalen und ergonomischen Büromöbeln, die sich nach Wunsch erweitern und ausbauen lassen.

Begründung der Jury
Die Besonderheit dieses Büromöbelsystems ist, dass es sich vielseitig konfigurieren lässt und so die unterschiedlichen Arbeitsweisen im Büroalltag unterstützt.

SW
Office System
Bürosystem

Manufacturer
Okamura Corporation, Yokohama, Japan
In-house design
Takayuki Yamamoto
Web
www.okamura.jp

The SW with fast electric height adjustment creates a refreshing work environment, since it is suitable as both a traditional desk and conference table. The curved edge reduces pressure on the forearms. When the desktop height is lowered to 72 cm, it automatically stops and then slowly settles to the set height. An optional coloured wall grants privacy and prevents objects from falling off the desk, while a cable that runs through the rear of the desktop into a cable tray prevents, for example, cables tearing. The eco-friendly motor consumes only 0.1 watt in standby mode and has been designed for a long life span of 30,000 height adjustments.

Der SW mit schneller elektrischer Höheneinstellung schafft ein erfrischendes Arbeitsumfeld, da er sich sowohl als herkömmlicher Schreibtisch wie auch als Konferenztisch eignet. Die abgerundete Kante reduziert den Druck auf die Unterarme. Wenn die Tischplatte auf auf 72 cm eingestellt wird, hält sie automatisch einmal an und rastet dann auf der eingestellten Höhe ein. Eine optionale farbige Wand gewährt Sichtschutz und Halt für Gegenstände, und ein auf der Rückseite in einer Kabelrinne verlaufendes Kabel verhindert z. B. Kabelrisse. Der umweltfreundliche Motor verbraucht im Bereitschaftszustand 0,1 Watt und wurde für eine Beanspruchung von 30.000 Höheneinstellungen entworfen.

Statement by the jury
The SW office system scores with its sophisticated construction, which places particular importance on ergonomics as well as convenient operation.

Begründung der Jury
Das Bürosystem SW punktet mit seiner durchdachten Konstruktion, die besonderen Wert auf Ergonomie wie auf eine praktische Handhabung legt.

moll T7
Desk
Schreibtisch

Manufacturer
moll Funktionsmöbel GmbH, Gruibingen, Germany
In-house design
Hans Looser, Martin Moll
Design
pearl creative (Tim Storti. Christian Rummel),
Ludwigsburg, Germany
Web
www.moll-funktion.com
www.pearlcreative.com

The moll T7 desk can be integrated into any room. It features a safe electrically motorised height adjustment that is lockable and requires two-handed operation, thus covering the entire range of users and applications – from the seated child to standing adults. The high-capacity drawer with push-to-open function offers enough room for diverse utensils and documents. An optional cable duct with power management provides storage for power adapters and keeps the workplace neat and clean. The inlay of the table top is colour-coded and strongly contributes to its distinctive look. It is available in six different colours, including two solid wood versions.

Der Schreibtisch moll T7 lässt sich in jeden Raum integrieren. Eine sichere elektromotorische Höhenverstellung erfolgt über eine abschließbare Zweihand-Bedienung und deckt die gesamte Bandbreite – vom sitzenden Kind bis zum stehenden Erwachsenen – ab. In seiner Großraumschublade mit Push-to-Open-Funktion findet sich genug Raum für verschiedenste Utensilien und Unterlagen. Eine optionale Kabelführung mit Power-Management schafft Stauraum für Netzteile und hält den Arbeitsplatz aufgeräumt. Das Inlay der Tischplatte ist farblich abgesetzt und prägt das Aussehen stark mit. Sechs unterschiedliche Farben, darunter zwei Massivholzausführungen, stehen hierbei zur Wahl.

Statement by the jury
Suitable for all relevant heights, this desk offers individual applications and also in terms of colours a spectrum for every taste.

Begründung der Jury
Für alle relevanten Einstellhöhen geeignet, bietet dieser Schreibtisch individuelle Einsatzmöglichkeiten und auch farblich ein Spektrum für jeden Geschmack.

ANTEO® ALU
Office Chair
Bürostuhl

Manufacturer
KÖHL GmbH Sitzmöbel, Rödermark, Germany
In-house design
Web
www.koehl.com

Anteo Alu combines aesthetics with ergonomic comfort. The high backrest lends the chair a distinctive silhouette, which is additionally emphasised by the aluminium frame construction. Manufactured from high-quality materials and cover fabrics such as leather, Tube, Network or SlimLine, the office chair offers a variety of design options to adapt to individual seating requirements. To expand its ergonomic functionality, it can be equipped with the Köhl Air-Seat. This allows multidimensional micro-movements, better providing the intervertebral discs with nutrients and stimulating the low-laying back muscles.

Statement by the jury
The design of the Anteo Alu is characterised by classic, elegant forms, satisfying ergonomic demands.

Anteo Alu verbindet Ästhetik mit ergonomischem Sitzkomfort. Die hohe Rückenlehne schafft eine markante Silhouette, die durch die Alu-Rahmenkonstruktion zusätzlich hervorgehoben wird. Hergestellt aus hochwertigen Materialien und Bezugsstoffen wie Leder, Tube, Network oder SlimLine, weist der Bürostuhl eine Vielzahl an Variationsmöglichkeiten auf, die sich an individuelle Sitzbedürfnisse anpassen lassen. Um die ergonomische Funktionalität zu erweitern, ist die Ausstattung mit dem Köhl Air-Seat möglich. Dies erlaubt mehrdimensionale Bewegungen im Sitzen, sodass die Bandscheiben besser mit Nährstoffen versorgt werden und die tiefer liegende Rückenmuskulatur stimuliert wird.

Begründung der Jury
Die Gestaltung des Anteo Alu zeichnet sich durch eine klassische, elegante Formgebung aus, die gleichzeitig ergonomischen Ansprüchen genügt.

Monico
Office Chair
Bürostuhl

Manufacturer
F.-Martin Steifensand Büromöbel GmbH,
Freystadt-Rettelloh, Germany
Design
Justus Kolberg, Hamburg, Germany
Web
www.original-steifensand.de

The Monico office chair range was designed as a flexible modular system, combining a clear form language and sophisticated functions for individual sitting. The heart of the system is the backrest with its Y-shaped brace and curved form. It has a technical appeal, yet with its curves and smooth transitions, is also highly aesthetic. All other components such as the sitting mechanisms, armrests, seats and star bases can be combined individually depending on personal comfort requirements.

Statement by the jury
The combination of a simple aesthetic design and high functionality makes this office chair series elegant and practical.

Die Bürostuhlfamilie Monico wurde als flexibler Baukasten konzipiert und verbindet eine klare Formensprache mit ausgereifter Funktion für individuelles Sitzen. Herzstück ist die Rückenlehne mit Y-förmiger Spange und gebogener Lehne. Sie mutet technisch an, wirkt durch Rundungen und fließende Übergänge aber ebenso ästhetisch. Die weiteren Komponenten wie Sitzmechaniken, Armlehnen, Sitze oder Fußkreuze lassen sich beliebig nach den jeweiligen Komfortansprüchen kombinieren.

Begründung der Jury
Die Kombination aus schlichter ästhetischer Formgebung und hoher Funktionalität macht diese Bürostuhlfamilie elegant und praktikabel.

Coza
Office Chair
Bürostuhl

Manufacturer
Boss Design, Dudley, Great Britain
In-house design
Design
Design Ballendat, Braunau, Austria
Web
www.boss-design.co.uk
www.ballendat.com

The dynamically designed Coza supports a flexible work environment. It fulfils the increasing demands on ergonomic conference chairs and offers high comfort without the need for manual adjustment. Its visual impact is based on a single line – an organic ribbon that sweeps from under the seat and over the arm and backrests. The result is a slim, sophisticated form adapting to the human body.

Statement by the jury
The Coza office chair fascinates with a self-contained design. With its dynamically curved arm and backrests it is a real eye-catcher.

Der dynamisch gestaltete Coza unterstützt ein flexibles Arbeitsumfeld. Er wird den steigenden Anforderungen an ergonomische Konferenzstühle gerecht und bietet hohen Komfort, ohne dass manuelle Verstellmöglichkeiten nötig sind. Seine visuelle Wirkung beruht auf einer einzigen Linie – einer organischen Schleife, die unterhalb des Sitzes beginnt und über die Armlehnen und die Rückenlehne gezogen ist. Ergebnis ist eine schlanke, raffinierte Form, die sich dem menschlichen Körper anpasst.

Begründung der Jury
Der Bürostuhl Coza begeistert durch seine eigenständige Gestaltung. Mit seinen dynamisch geschwungenen Arm- und Rückenlehnen ist er ein echter Blickfang.

ray
Cantilever Chair
Freischwinger

Manufacturer
Brunner GmbH, Rheinau, Germany
Design
Jehs+Laub GbR, Stuttgart, Germany
Web
www.brunner-group.com
www.jehs-laub.com

ray is a chair that appears to be cast from one mould. Its flowing forms seamlessly blend into one another and the delicate curved back is invisibly mounted to the steel frame and shell. Even the cover fabrics are fastened to the shell in such a way that neither seams nor zippers are visible. The die-cast aluminium armrests are available in a chrome, polished aluminium or powder coating finish. The flexible skeleton is coated with moulded foam and is very robust.

Statement by the jury
The ray cantilever chair fascinates with its slim design that conveys elegance and dynamics. As well as functionality the chair's materials promise robustness.

ray ist ein Stuhl wie aus einem Guss. Seine fließenden Formen gehen nahtlos ineinander über und die filigran geschwungenen Lehnen sind unsichtbar an das Stahlgestell und die Schale montiert. Auch die Sitzbezüge sind so an der Schale befestigt, dass weder Nähte noch Reißverschlüsse zu sehen sind. Die Armlehnen aus Aluminium-Druckguss sind verchromt, poliert oder in farbiger Pulverbeschichtung erhältlich. Das bewegliche Skelett ist mit Formschaum ummantelt und sehr robust.

Begründung der Jury
Der Freischwinger ray begeistert mit seiner schlanken Gestaltung, die Eleganz und Dynamik vermittelt. Gleichzeitig funktional, sprechen seine Materialien für eine hohe Lebensdauer.

SITAGTEAM
Chair Family
Stuhlfamilie

Manufacturer
SITAG AG, Sennwald, Switzerland
Design
2DO-DESIGN, Stuttgart, Germany
Web
www.sitag.ch
www.2do-design.de

The cantilever of the Sitagteam office chair family meets a high standard in ergonomics and functionality. With its well-balanced, clear lines it shows a factual formal appearance, which makes it suitable for all areas of offices as well as for use in the home office. Finely tuned details and various colour options complement the sophisticated concept of this chair, which will always appear reserved, but not unspectacular.

Statement by the jury
The design of this cantilever chair convinces with elegance and simplicity. It is versatile in use and furthermore enables comfortable sitting.

Der Freischwinger der Sitagteam-Bürostuhlfamilie erfüllt einen hohen Anspruch an Ergonomie und Funktionalität. Mit seinen ausgewogenen, klaren Linien zeigt er ein formal-sachliches Erscheinungsbild und ist so in allen Bereichen des Büros oder auch im Homeoffice einsetzbar. Fein abgestimmte Materialien und verschiedene wählbare Farben ergänzen das ausgereifte Konzept eines Stuhls, der stets zurückhaltend, jedoch nicht unspektakulär erscheint.

Begründung der Jury
Die Gestaltung dieses Freischwingers überzeugt durch Eleganz und Schlichtheit. Er lässt sich flexibel einsetzen und ermöglicht darüber hinaus komfortables Sitzen.

Tabulator
Chair
Stuhl

Manufacturer
Ooland GmbH, Hamburg Germany
Design
Favaretto & Partners, Padua, Italy
Web
www.ooland.de
www.favarettoandpartners.com

The formal characteristic of this chair is the back part of the chair body. This detail is not only highly aesthetically pleasing, it is also of structural importance, as it reinforces the junction between seat and backrest, which is the most critical point when considering the stability of a chair. Its clean lines and the well-balanced combination of materials make it stand out from alternative products.

Statement by the jury
The Tabulator chair catches the eye with the distinctive design of its back part, which is not only an interesting formal feature, but also gives structure and stability.

Die formale Besonderheit dieses Stuhls ist das Rückenteil des Stuhlkörpers. Dieses Detail strahlt eine hohe Ästhetik aus und ist zudem von struktureller Bedeutung. Verstärkt es doch die Verbindung von Sitz und Rückenlehne, was der kritische Punkt im Hinblick auf die Stabilität eines Stuhls ist. Mit seinen klaren Linien und der ausgewogenen Materialkombination hebt er sich deshalb von alternativen Produkten ab.

Begründung der Jury
Der Stuhl Tabulator gefällt aufgrund der markanten Gestaltung seines Rückenteils, das nicht nur formal interessant ist, sondern ihm auch Struktur und Stabilität gibt.

Nico Less
Chair
Stuhl

Manufacturer
Donar d.o.o., Ljubljana, Slovenia
Design
Primož Jeza Studio, Ljubljana, Slovenia
Web
www.donar.si
www.primozjeza.com

With its highly simple design, the Nico Less chair is a tribute to the industrial designer Niko Kralj. At the same time, it is an expression of responsibility for the environment and is made of recycled materials: 60 per cent of recycled PP bottles and 40 per cent of non-woven textile. Two elements are linked with straps and can be combined in various lengths or stored in vertical stacks. Flexible and ergonomically adjusting to the body, the Nico Less is designed as a comfortable piece of seating furniture.

Statement by the jury
Nico Less stands out with its minimalist and unobtrusive design. The chair is furthermore produced of entirely sustainable materials.

Der sehr schlicht gestaltete Stuhl Nico Less ist eine Hommage an den Industriedesigner Niko Kralj. Zugleich ist er Ausdruck von Verantwortung der Umwelt gegenüber und aus recyceltem Material hergestellt: zu 60 Prozent aus PP-Flaschen und zu 40 Prozent aus ungewebten Textilien. Zwei Elemente sind mit den Trägern verbunden und können in verschiedenen Längen miteinander kombiniert oder in vertikalen Stapeln gestapelt werden. Flexibel und ergonomisch an den Körper angepasst, ist so ein bequemes Sitzmöbel entstanden.

Begründung der Jury
Nico Less fällt durch seine minimalistische und zurückhaltende Gestaltung auf. Der Stuhl wird außerdem aus vollständig nachhaltigen Materialien produziert.

Use Me
Table System
Tischsystem

Manufacturer
SitLand SpA, Nanto, Italy
Design
Scagnellato – Bertolini – Ferrarese, Padua, Italy
Web
www.sitland.com

Use Me is a multi-purpose table system with a minimalist design, which is available with or without castors or sliders as well as in different colours and finishes. Suitable for a wide variety of applications, the version with pad system offers discreet storage options, which are automatically activated when inclining the table top, permitting the use and placement of tablets, smartphones or books on the desktop. The table top tilts up to 30 degrees to support an ergonomically correct sitting position by preventing the typical forward-leaning posture.

Use Me ist ein minimalistisch gestaltetes Mehrzweck-Tischsystem und wahlweise mit Rollen oder Gleitern sowie in unterschiedlichen Farben und Oberflächen erhältlich. Geeignet für vielfältige Anwendungen bietet die Version mit Pad-System dezente Ablagemöglichkeiten, die sich beim Abwinkeln der Tischplatte automatisch aktivieren, um die optimale Position für Tablets, Smartphones oder Bücher zu schaffen. Die um 30 Grad neigbare Tischplatte fördert gleichzeitig die korrekte ergonomische Position des Nutzers, indem sie seine sonst übliche nach vorne gebeugte Haltung unterbindet.

Statement by the jury
Available in a variety of configurations, the Use Me table system skilfully combines ergonomics, easy operation and a simple design.

Begründung der Jury
Dem in verschiedenen Ausführungen erhältlichen Tischsystem Use Me gelingt es, Ergonomie, Handhabbarkeit und eine schlichte Gestaltung gekonnt miteinander zu verbinden.

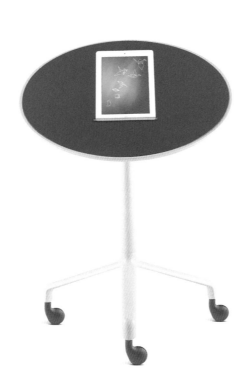

repiroue
Chair
Stuhl

Manufacturer
Okamura Corporation, Yokohama, Japan
In-house design
Naho Ono
Web
www.okamura.jp

The compact repiroue chair is suitable for a multitude of purposes. The sophisticated combination of sitting and standing allows for quick and playfully easy posture changes. The forward tilt of the seat provides a natural half-standing position and so reduces strain on the lumbar spine. By distributing the body's weight to the soles of the feet and the seat, it reduces leg tiredness compared to standing. The omnidirectional tilting pillar provides an ergonomic seating angle regardless of a person's physique. The ring lever under the seat makes height adjustment possible from any position to suit all people regardless of their stature.

Der kompakte Stuhl repiroue eignet sich für verschiedenste Verwendungszwecke. Die raffinierte Kombination aus Sitzen und Stehen lässt sich spielend von einer in die andere Position bringen. Die Vorwärtsneigung der Sitzfläche ermöglicht eine halb stehende Haltung und verringert so die Belastung der Lendenwirbelsäule. Durch Verteilung des Körpergewichts auf die Fußsohlen und die Sitzfläche wird die Ermüdung der Beine im Vergleich zum Stehen reduziert. Die omnidirektionale Neigestütze bietet unabhängig vom Körperbau einen ergonomischen Sitzwinkel. Der Ringhebel unter dem Sitz ermöglicht aus jeder Position heraus eine von der Statur unabhängige Höheneinstellung.

Statement by the jury
The clear, simple design and the countless possibilities to adjust the repiroue chair to user requirements qualify it for the most different of locations.

Begründung der Jury
Das klare, schlichte Design und die zahlreichen Möglichkeiten, den Stuhl repiroue an Kundenwünsche anzupassen, qualifizieren ihn für unterschiedlichste Locations.

ADD
Modular Seating System
Modulares Sitzmöbelsystem

Manufacturer
Lapalma S.r.l., Cadoneghe, Italy
Design
Francesco Rota, Milan, Italy
Web
www.lapalma.it
www.francescorota.com

ADD is a versatile system of clearly designed, combinable seating furniture. It is flexible in use and thus not only meets the different needs in the contract market, for example in hotel rooms, lounge areas or offices, but is also suitable for residential premises. The modular system comprises straightforward seats and backs with removable upholstery, available in fabric, soft-leather or eco-leather. The frame in powder-coated aluminium comes in two different heights and it is equipped with elastic belts for more comfort.

Statement by the jury
The design of ADD convinces with an unobtrusive clarity. Thanks to its modularity, the system can be flexibly used in both public and private spaces.

ADD ist ein vielseitiges System aus klar gestalteten, kombinierbaren Sitzmöbeln. Sie lassen sich flexibel einsetzen und werden somit nicht nur verschiedensten Anforderungen im Objektbereich, etwa in einem Hotelzimmer, in Loungebereichen oder Büros, gerecht, sondern können auch in Wohnräumen genutzt werden. Das modulare System besteht aus geradlinigen Sitzmöbeln und Rückenlehnen, ist gepolstert und mit abziehbarem Bezug in Stoff, Softleder oder Kunstleder erhältlich. Sein Gestell aus pulverlackiertem Aluminium mit elastischen Riemen gibt es in zwei verschiedenen Höhen.

Begründung der Jury
Die Gestaltung von ADD überzeugt durch eine zurückhaltende Klarheit. Dank seiner Modularität lässt sich das System flexibel im öffentlichen wie privaten Raum einsetzen.

Orbit®
Cable Duct
Kabeldurchführung

Manufacturer
Q-LAB®, Prien, Germany
In-house design
Maximilian Rüttiger
Web
www.q-lab.de

The Orbit cable duct features a clear design and technical sophistication. A patented lever with magnet holder allows even thick cables to be easily fed through. The circular ring gap prevents plugs from accidentally slipping down. Thanks to its patented connection system providing connectability from the top and the bottom, it provides a modular construction kit for furniture electrification. In an aesthetically appealing way, cables can be fed from the ceiling into and through furniture. Fixed by a magnet holder, the lever is guaranteed not to loosen, even when installed headfirst. The metal surfaces in stainless steel, chrome or aluminium are manufactured by hand.

Statement by the jury
The innovation of the Orbit cable duct is its individual building kit system for cable ducting, which fulfils high demands in both design and technology.

Die Kabeldurchführung Orbit besitzt eine klare Linienführung und technische Ausgereiftheit. Ein patentierter Hebel mit Magnetschnapper ermöglicht das Hindurchführen auch dicker Kabelenden. Der umlaufende Ringspalt verhindert, dass Stecker ungewollt durchrutschen. Durch die patentierten Anschlussmöglichkeiten von oben und unten wird ein Baukasten zur Möbelelektrifizierung zur Verfügung gestellt. Kabel können ansprechend von der Decke in Möbel und durch Möbel hindurch geführt werden. Selbst beim Einbau kopfüber ist der unverlierbare Hebel durch einen Magnetschnapper fixiert. Die Metalloberflächen in Edelstahl, Chrom oder Aluminium werden in Handarbeit gefertigt.

Begründung der Jury
Die Innovation der Kabeldurchführung Orbit ist ihr individueller Systembaukasten zur Kabeldurchführung, der zugleich hohen Ansprüchen an Design und Technik genügt.

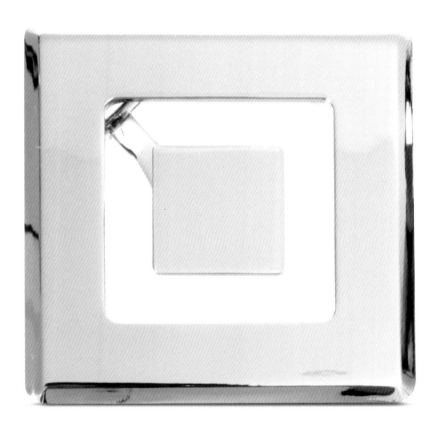 

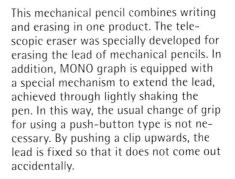

MONO graph
Mechanical Pencil
Druckbleistift

Manufacturer
Tombow Pencil Co., Ltd., Tokyo, Japan
In-house design
Kazuki Koda
Web
www.tombow.com

This mechanical pencil combines writing and erasing in one product. The telescopic eraser was specially developed for erasing the lead of mechanical pencils. In addition, MONO graph is equipped with a special mechanism to extend the lead, achieved through lightly shaking the pen. In this way, the usual change of grip for using a push-button type is not necessary. By pushing a clip upwards, the lead is fixed so that it does not come out accidentally.

Statement by the jury
With the MONO graph, writing and erasing skilfully go hand in hand. In addition, the pencil convinces with innovative mechanics which allow users to extend the lead by a simple shake.

Der Druckbleistift kombiniert Schreiben und Radieren in einem Produkt, wobei der herausdrehbare Radierer speziell für das Radieren von Druckbleistift-Minen entwickelt wurde. Außerdem ist der MONO graph mit einem speziellen Mechanismus zum Ausfahren der Mine ausgestattet. Sie wird durch leichtes Schütteln ausgefahren, wodurch das übliche Umgreifen zum Betätigen des Druckknopfes entfällt. Durch Hochdrücken des Clips wird die Mine fixiert, sodass sie nicht versehentlich herausfährt.

Begründung der Jury
Beim MONO graph gehen Schreiben und Radieren gekonnt Hand in Hand. Zudem überzeugt die innovative Mechanik, mit der sich die Mine durch einfaches Schütteln ausfahren lässt.

Hang-on
Ballpoint Pen
Kugelschreiber

Manufacturer
Wah Fook Holdings Ltd.,
ten Design Stationery, Hong Kong
In-house design
Shao Long Chen, Paul Lam, Jaman Lam
Web
www.ten-design-stationery.com
Honourable Mention

By a hook on the top of the ballpoint pen, the Hang-on can be flexibly attached to backpacks or shoulder bags. By pushing a button on the side of the pen, a special mechanism allows users to unlock the hook as well as refill the lead. With a slight push of this button, the refill is retracted and locked again. The beautiful and simple design is based on the observation of user behaviour.

Statement by the jury
The Hang-on ballpoint pen catches the eye with its clear and simple design and the inventive idea of replacing the traditional clip with an aesthetic hook.

An einem Haken am hinteren Ende des Kugelschreibers lässt sich der Hang-on flexibel an einen Rucksack oder eine Schultertasche anheften. Durch Drücken des seitlichen Knopfes kann man diesen Haken mithilfe eines speziellen Mechanismus öffnen sowie die Mine betätigen. Mit leichtem Druck auf diesen Knopf kann man die Mine einziehen und den Haken wieder schließen. Die schöne, schlichte Gestaltung geht auf die Beobachtung des Nutzerverhaltens zurück.

Begründung der Jury
Der Kugelschreiber Hang-on fällt durch seine klare und einfache Gestaltung ins Auge und die originelle Idee, den üblichen Clip durch einen formschönen Haken zu ersetzen.

MICRO CONSTRUCTION
Keyring with Ballpoint Pen
Schlüsselanhänger mit
Kugelschreiber

Manufacturer
TROIKA Germany GmbH,
Müschenbach, Germany
In-house design
Web
www.troika.org

The pens of the Troika Construction family were combined with the company's key holders to create this delicate ballpoint pen plus key holder. The compact product weighs 21 grams, is suitable for analogue as well as digital use as a stylus, and helps solve minor everyday problems through a ruler in centimetres and inches in addition to a flat- and Phillips-head screwdriver. The Micro Construction with its strong key holder ring is available in six elegant and trendy colours.

Statement by the jury
The Micro Construction is a real multi-talent: As a simply designed screwdriver, ruler, pen and key holder, it unites many functions into only one product.

Die Stifte der Troika-Construction-Familie wurden so mit den hauseigenen Schlüssel-anhängern verbunden, dass dieser filigrane Kugelschreiber plus Schlüsselanhänger entstand. Das kompakte Produkt wiegt 21 Gramm, lässt sich analog wie digital als Stylus verwenden und verhilft mit Zenti-meter- und Zoll-Lineal sowie Schlitz- und Kreuzschraubendreher außerdem, kleine Alltagsprobleme zu lösen. Den Micro Construction mit stabilem Ring als Schlüs-selanhänger gibt es in sechs edlen Trend-farben.

Begründung der Jury
Der Micro Construction ist ein echtes Multitalent: Als schlicht gestalteter Schrau-bendreher, Lineal, Stift oder Schlüsselan-hänger vereint er viele Funktionalitäten in einem Produkt.

EXPERT Dry
All-in-One Marker
Universalstift

Manufacturer
eagle kreativ, Nuremberg, Germany
Design
hillemanndesign, Kranzberg, Germany
Web
www.eaglekreativ.com
www.hillemanndesign.de

The Expert Dry is a professional-use pen for marking and tracing measured lines or drill holes. The refillable lead works on virtually all surfaces, the slim barrel reaches even difficult-to-access areas and is particularly suitable for marking drill holes. When the holder is attached to work clothes, the integrated sharpener allows for one-handed sharpening. The pen positively locks into the holder and is held securely.

Statement by the jury
The Expert Dry was carefully designed and, from form and materials to its functionality, blends very well into work environments.

Der Expert Dry ist ein Stift, mit dem sich Maßlinien oder Bohrungen im professio-nellen Einsatz markieren lassen. Die nach-füllbare Mine schreibt auf nahezu allen Untergründen; die Teleskopspitze erreicht auch schwer zugängliche Bereiche und eignet sich ausgesprochen gut für das An-zeichnen von Bohrpunkten. Ist der Köcher an der Arbeitskleidung befestigt, lässt sich mit dem im Clip integrierten Spitzer die Mine mit nur einer Hand anspitzen. Der Stift rastet formschlüssig in den Köcher ein und wird sicher gehalten.

Begründung der Jury
Der Expert Dry wurde mit Bedacht konzi-piert und fügt sich von der Formgebung über die Materialien bis hin zur Funktionali-tät sehr gut in sein Nutzungsumfeld ein.

Winsor & Newton Pigment Marker
Marker Pen
Malstift

Manufacturer
Colart, London, Great Britain
Design
Veryday (David Crafoord, Henrik Olsson),
Bromma, Sweden
Web
www.winsornewton.com
www.veryday.com

The innovative Pigment Marker pens are guaranteed to remain lightfast for over 100 years, so that artists can create lasting works of art. The objective of the design is to present professional marker users with an aesthetic and ergonomic tool which can be held comfortably even for long periods of time. Particular importance has been placed on elegant form, a comfortable grip and intuitive handling. The pens feature a chisel tip for broad strokes, a fine tip for delicate lines and detail work, and an ergonomic barrel design. Thanks to the use of Winsor & Newton's fine art pigment, the markers blend easily with minimal feathering or bleeding.

Die innovativen Pigmentmalstifte garantieren Lichtechtheit für mehr als 100 Jahre, sodass Künstler mithilfe der Marker Werke von Dauer schaffen können. Das Ziel der Gestaltung war es, professionellen Nutzern der Stifte ein ästhetisches sowie ergonomisches Utensil zu bieten, das auch über einen längeren Zeitraum bequem in der Hand liegt. Daher wurde besonderer Wert auf eine elegante Form, die angenehme Handhabbarkeit und einen intuitiven Umgang gelegt. Die Stifte verfügen über eine Keilspitze für breite Striche, eine Spitze für feine Linien und Detailarbeiten sowie eine ergonomische Kolbenkonstruktion. Dank der verwendeten Winsor & Newton-Kunstpigmente sind die Marker leicht mischbar bei nur minimalem Abfärben und Verlaufen.

Statement by the jury
This marker blends elegant design, simple handling and long-lasting pigment colour into a pen for highly demanding people.

Begründung der Jury
Bei diesem Marker verschmelzen elegante Formgebung, einfache Handhabung und die Langlebigkeit der Pigmentfarbe zu einem Malstift für Anspruchsvolle.

WINSOR & NEWTON PIGMENT MARKER™ CARMINE CARMIN CARMÍN

The Rock Book
Notebook
Notizbuch

Manufacturer
Taiwan Lung Meng Technology Co., Ltd.,
Tainan, Taiwan
In-house design
Ya Wen Kuo
Web
www.taiwanlm.com

The Rock Book notebook was designed from environmentally-friendly, water- and tear-resistant stone paper with the motto "purity". The unique quality of the cover as well as the dotted and ruled pages, which offer space for sketches, is achieved by the authentic colour of marble stone. The embossed line design on the cover represents the natural appearance of stone. The cover flap can be used as a bookmark and features a compartment for business cards.

Statement by the jury
The Rock Book fascinates with its elaborate embossing and the high quality of materials, making the notebook an elegant companion.

Das Notizbuch The Rock Book wurde aus umweltfreundlichem, wasser- und reißfestem Steinpapier unter dem Motto „Reinheit" gestaltet. Die besondere Qualität des Umschlags und der linierten wie gepunkteten Seiten für Skizzen wird durch die authentische Farbe von Marmorgestein erzielt. Das geprägte Liniendesign auf dem Einband repräsentiert die natürliche Anmutung von Stein. Die Einbandklappe kann als Lesezeichen verwendet werden und ist mit einer Tasche für Visitenkarten versehen.

Begründung der Jury
Das Notizbuch fasziniert durch seine aufwendigen Prägungen und die hohe Materialqualität. Sie machen The Rock Book zu einem edlen Begleiter.

nuuna by brandbook
Notebook Collection
Notizbuch-Kollektion

Manufacturer
brandbook, Frankfurt/Main, Germany
In-house design
Web
www.nuuna.com

Understanding notebooks as a storage for ideas, the nuuna collection was designed so that each notebook itself embodies an idea – visually, conceptually and haptically. They are made in Germany, consist of the finest Swedish paper, are thread-stitched, bound in innovative cover materials such as smooth bonded leather (recycled leather) and printed in a screen-printing process. Also the edges of the notebooks are integrated into the design concept, while materials in a metal or hologram look lend them a unique character.

Statement by the jury
The nuuna notebook collection fascinates with the diversity of cover materials as well as cover motifs, featuring an extremely high-quality manufacturing.

Weil Notizbücher als Ideenspeicher verstanden werden, wurde die nuuna-Kollektion so gestaltet, dass die einzelnen Bücher selbst eine Idee verkörpern – visuell, konzeptuell und haptisch. Sie sind made in Germany, bestehen aus schwedischem Feinstpapier, sind fadengeheftet, in innovative Covermaterialien wie Smooth Bonded Leather (recyceltes Lederfasermaterial) eingebunden und im Siebdruckverfahren bedruckt. Auch die Kanten des Buchblocks sind in das Designkonzept integriert, und Materialien in Metallic- oder Hologramm-Optik machen die Notizbücher besonders.

Begründung der Jury
Die Notizbuch-Kollektion nuuna begeistert durch die Vielfalt ihrer Covermaterialien sowie deren Motive. Dabei zeigt sie eine qualitativ überaus hochwertige Verarbeitung.

Qbook
Colourful Notebooks
Einfarbige Notizbücher

Manufacturer
Edica Sp. z o.o., Poznań, Poland
In-house design
Web
www.qbook.eu

The design objective of the Qbook notebooks was to be both unique in character and practical in use. Their cover is soft and flexible and can be rolled up and put into the pocket. Each Qbook is entirely coloured using one single colour, from the cover and edges to the endpaper, while the range is available in six colours and two sizes. It is FSC-certified and a useful companion for all people who want to write, draw or just scribble.

Statement by the jury
The single-coloured notebooks draw attention with their compact, reduced design, and thanks to their flexibility are particularly well suited for people on the go.

Das Gestaltungsziel der Notizbücher Qbook war, dass sie zugleich charaktervoll und praktisch sein sollten. Sie haben eine schlichte, rechteckige Form. Ihr Umschlag ist weich und flexibel, sie lassen sich einrollen und in die Tasche stecken. Qbook ist einfarbig durchgefärbt, vom Umschlag über die Kanten bis zum Versatzblatt, und in sechs Farben und zwei Formaten erhältlich. Es ist FSC-zertifiziert und ein nützlicher Begleiter für alle, die schreiben, zeichnen oder einfach nur kritzeln möchten.

Begründung der Jury
Die unifarbenen Notizbücher machen durch ihre handliche, reduzierte Gestaltung auf sich aufmerksam und eignen sich dank ihrer Flexibilität besonders gut für unterwegs.

DURAFRAME® POSTER SUN
Poster Frame
Poster-Rahmen

Manufacturer
DURABLE Hunke & Jochheim GmbH & Co. KG,
Iserlohn, Germany
In-house design
Klaus Jäger
Web
www.durable.de

Duraframe® Poster Sun is a user- and
design-oriented solution for the design
of shop windows. A self-cling plastic
film frame that can be fixed on show
windows allows the display and regular
update of information with an easy-to-
use magnetic fixture. The poster frame
comes in four sizes, can be removed
without leaving traces or marks and can
be repositioned multiple times. It is heat-
resistant up to 70 degrees Celsius, UV-
resistant and thus extremely resilient.

Statement by the jury
This poster frame looks good in any shop
window and especially stands out for
being easy to affix and remove without
leaving behind residuals.

Duraframe® Poster Sun ist eine anwen-
dungs- und designorientierte Lösung für
die Gestaltung eines Schaufensters. In dem
durch klebefreie Adhäsion haftenden Foli-
enrahmen lassen sich Informationen durch
die einfache magnetische Bedienbarkeit
stets aktuell präsentieren. Der Plakat-Rah-
men in vier Formaten kann rückstandslos
entfernt und immer wieder neu angebracht
werden. Er ist bis zu 70 Grad Celsius
hitzestabil, UV-beständig und somit hoch
belastbar.

Begründung der Jury
Dieser Poster-Rahmen macht sich gut in
jedem Schaufenster und sticht insbesondere
dadurch hervor, dass er sich leicht anbringen und ohne Rückstände wieder entfernen
lässt.

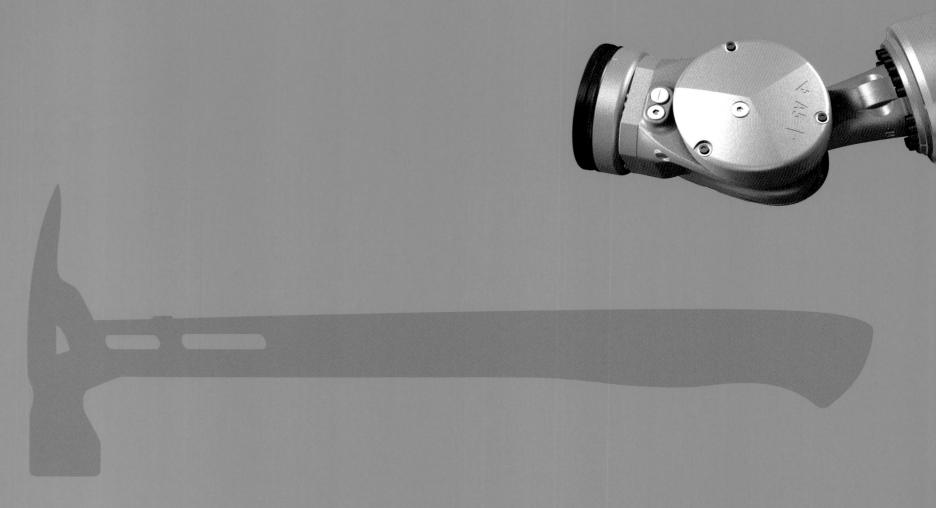

Industry and crafts
Industrie und Handwerk

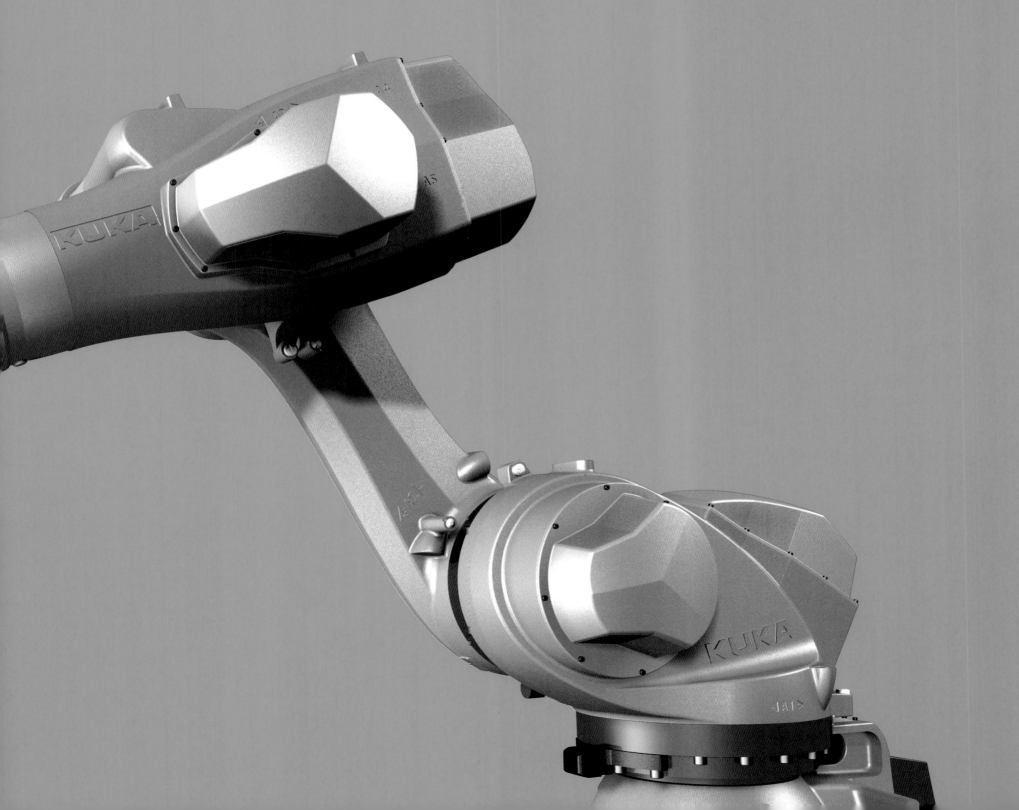

GAMA
POS System

Manufacturer
Top Victory Investments Ltd,
New Taipei City, Taiwan

In-house design
TPV design (Jia-Sheng Wong)

Web
www.tpvholdings.com

reddot award 2016
best of the best

The alphabet of good design

Interior design plays a crucial role in the retail industry. The entire shop appearance is an expression of the brand, inviting customers to feel relaxed. Following an integrated approach, the design of GAMA emerged as a novel POS system. At first glance, it impresses with flowing lines and a premium-quality appearance. The form was inspired by the ancient Greek letter "gamma", lending this system its visually enticing geometry. The integration of all components into one housing embodies an elegant solution. It consistently merges the functions of scanner, payment processing and printer into one clearly arranged device at the point of sale. Easy and intuitive to operate, the system delivers convenient access to users. As it comprises all functions needed in the retail business, it also provides comprehensive and competitive inventory management alongside the possibility to interactively display advertisements. GAMA thus delivers a high degree of innovative efficiency in the daily retail transaction processes. It enriches almost any interior with its geometric shape – redefining the relation between cashier, consumer and a POS system.

Das Alphabet guten Designs

Das Interieur spielt im Einzelhandel eine wichtige Rolle. Das gesamte Shop-Design ist Ausdruck der Marke und der Kunde soll sich rundum wohlfühlen. Mit einem integrativen Ansatz verwirklicht die Gestaltung von GAMA auf neue Art und Weise ein POS-System. Es beeindruckt auf den ersten Blick mit seinen fließenden Linien und der Anmutung von Wertigkeit. Die Form wurde inspiriert von dem griechischen Buchstaben „Gamma", was zu der faszinierenden Geometrie dieses Systems führte. Elegant gelöst wurde dabei die Integration aller Elemente in einem Gehäuse. Scanner, Bezahlmöglichkeit und Drucker sind schlüssig in die Form integriert und können damit einheitlich am Point of Sale bereitgestellt werden. Dem Nutzer bietet dieses System einen guten Zugang, er kann es leicht und intuitiv bedienen. Da es alle Funktionen für den Einzelhandel umfasst, erlaubt es auch ein wettbewerbsfähiges, vollständiges Bestandsmanagement und die Möglichkeit, interaktive Werbung darüber abzuwickeln. Auf diese Weise bietet GAMA ein hohes Maß an innovativer Effizienz während der täglichen Transaktionen. Mit seiner geometrischen Anmutung bereichert es das Ambiente – die Beziehung zwischen Bezahlvorgang, Konsument und POS-System wird neu definiert.

Statement by the jury

This space-saving solution fascinates with an elegant design idiom. The system satisfies high user demands and successfully balances form and function. It integrates all key elements at the point of sale, such as inventory management, advertisement, scanner, payment processing and printer, into one effective device. An overall sophisticated interpretation, the GAMA POS system sets new standards for the future of the retail sector.

Begründung der Jury

Diese platzsparende Lösung begeistert mit ihrer eleganten Formensprache. Das Design ist anspruchsvoll und schafft eine gelungene Balance zwischen Form und Funktion. Die wichtigsten Elemente am Point of Sale wie Bestandsmanagement, Werbung, Scannen, Bezahlvorgänge und Drucken werden in einem effektiven System integriert. Als rundum gelungene Interpretation ist das POS-System GAMA wegweisend für die Zukunft des Einzelhandels.

Designer portrait
See page 32
Siehe Seite 32

ULTIMO
POS Terminal

Manufacturer
Oxhoo, Lieusaint, France
In-house design
Web
www.oxhoo.com

The Ultimo POS terminal is equipped with an NFC-enabled reader and a camera, which are both mounted on the front in order to provide customers with direct access. In addition, a barcode reader can be attached to the frame of the swivelling and tiltable multitouch 15" screen. Concealed connectors give the terminal a tidy appearance. The aluminium housing is available in black or white. The screen can be mounted either to the middle or side of the base, or even attached to the wall.

Das POS-Terminal Ultimo ist mit einem NFC-fähigen Lesegerät und einer Kamera ausgestattet, die beide an der Front angebracht sind, um so einen direkten Zugriff vonseiten des Kunden zu ermöglichen. Zusätzlich kann an dem Rahmen des dreh- und kippbaren 15"-Multitouchscreens ein Barcodescanner installiert werden. Die versteckt liegenden Kabelanschlüsse sorgen für eine aufgeräumte Optik. Das Gehäuse aus Aluminium ist in Schwarz und Weiß erhältlich. Der Bildschirm kann entweder mittig oder seitlich an den Sockel montiert oder an der Wand befestigt werden.

Statement by the jury
This slim POS terminal houses many technical features. Its closed design highlights the independent nature of this product solution.

Begründung der Jury
In dem schlanken POS-Terminal stecken viele technische Features. Dabei unterstreicht die geschlossene Bauart, dass es sich um eine eigenständige Produktlösung handelt.

VariPOS 210
Mobile POS System

Manufacturer
Poindus Systems Corp., Taipei, Taiwan
In-house design
Frank Hu
Web
www.poindus.com

The VariPOS 210 is a mobile POS system on the basis of a 14" tablet. The ultralight aluminium housing fosters an elegant design, which blends into any commercial or gastronomic environment. A fast processor and a durable battery provide optimal performance with minimal use of energy. In addition, the system features a connector for an external power bank, in order to minimise the risk of data loss in the event of a power blackout.

Das VariPOS 210 ist ein mobiles Kassensystem auf Basis eines 14"-Tablets. Das ultraleichte Aluminiumgehäuse sorgt für ein elegantes Design, das sich in jede kaufmännische und gastronomische Umgebung einfügt. Ein schneller Prozessor und ein hochwertiger Akku sorgen für optimale Leistungsfähigkeit bei minimalem Energieverbrauch. Zudem verfügt das System über einen Anschluss für eine externe Powerbank, um das Risiko von Datenverlusten im Falle eines Stromausfalls zu verhindern.

Statement by the jury
The generous display and extremely narrow frame of this POS system combine to create a stylish and minimalist overall appearance.

Begründung der Jury
Das ausladende Display und der äußerst schmale Rahmen verbinden sich bei dem POS-System zu einem stilvoll-minimalistischen Gesamtbild.

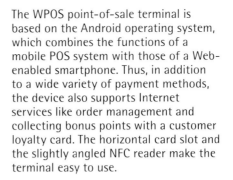

WPOS
Mobile POS Terminal

Manufacturer
Beijing Weipass Panorama Information
Technology Co., Ltd., Beijing, China
In-house design
Huiren La
Web
www.wangpos.com

The WPOS point-of-sale terminal is based on the Android operating system, which combines the functions of a mobile POS system with those of a Web-enabled smartphone. Thus, in addition to a wide variety of payment methods, the device also supports Internet services like order management and collecting bonus points with a customer loyalty card. The horizontal card slot and the slightly angled NFC reader make the terminal easy to use.

Statement by the jury
The multifunctionality of the WPOS is impressively demonstrated by the clearly offset black display and the colourful housing.

Das POS-Terminal WPOS basiert auf dem Android-Betriebssystem, welches die Funktionen eines mobilen Kassensystems mit denen eines internetfähigen Smartphones verbindet. Somit unterstützt das Gerät nicht nur eine Vielzahl unterschiedlicher Zahlungsarten, sondern auch webbasierte Dienste wie z. B. die Bestellung von Waren oder das Sammeln von Bonuspunkten mit einer Kundenkarte. Der horizontal verlaufende Kartenschlitz und das leicht angeschrägte NFC-Lesegerät sorgen für eine bequeme Handhabung.

Begründung der Jury
Die Multifunktionalität des WPOS wird eindrucksvoll durch das schwarze Display und das farbenfrohe Gehäuse demonstriert, die deutlich voneinander abgesetzt sind.

Chip&Pin SL31
Mobile Card Reader
Mobiler Kartenleser

Manufacturer
Shenzhen Popsecu Technology Co., Ltd.,
Shenzhen, China
Design
TGS Design Consultancy
(Weixue Liao, Hangdong Wang),
Shenzhen, China
Web
www.popsecu.cn
www.chinatgs.com

The Chip&Pin SL31 mobile card reader can be connected to a retailer's smartphone or tablet PC via Bluetooth or a USB cable. In order to make a payment, customers insert their debit or credit card into the lower slot of the card reader and enter their PIN code or signature on the 2.4" colour touchscreen. The touch-sensitive display enables the mobile card reader to be used in a way similar to a smartphone. The device is so small and flat that it fits into any trouser pocket.

Statement by the jury
The design of this mobile card reader is reduced to the essentials. The simple housing serves to frame the display and is aligned flush with it.

Der mobile Kartenleser Chip&Pin SL31 wird via Bluetooth oder USB-Kabel mit dem Smartphone oder Tablet-PC eines Händlers verbunden. Zum Bezahlen steckt der Kunde seine EC- oder Kreditkarte in den unteren Schlitz des Kartenlesers und gibt auf dem 2,4"-Farbtouchdisplay seinen PIN-Code oder seine Unterschrift ein. Der berührungsempfindliche Bildschirm ermöglicht eine Smartphone-ähnliche Bedienung. Das Gerät ist so klein und flach, dass es in eine Hosentasche passt.

Begründung der Jury
Das Design des Kartenlesers ist auf das Wesentliche reduziert. Das schlichte Gehäuse bildet einen Rahmen für das Display und schließt bündig mit diesem ab.

MC 500
Self-Service Scale
Selbstbedienungswaage

Manufacturer
Bizerba GmbH & Co. KG, Balingen, Germany
In-house design
Web
www.bizerba.com
Honourable Mention

The MC 500 self-service scale with
integrated pedestal can be placed in the
fruit and vegetable department immediately next to the goods being sold. The
large 15.6" touchscreen provides the
customer with a quick overview of the
product range in images and numbers.
The frameless display and a special coating simplify daily cleaning. The pedestal
can be opened on both sides, thus
providing storage space for label rolls,
cleaning agents and other items.

Statement by the jury
The self-contained form and softly
gleaming surfaces give rise to a
cohesive design, highlighting the scale's
originality.

Die Selbstbedienungswaage MC 500 mit
integrierter Standsäule kann in der Obst-
und Gemüseabteilung direkt neben der
Ware positioniert werden. Der große
15,6"-Touchscreen bietet dem Kunden mithilfe von Bildern und Nummern eine
schnelle Übersicht über das Warenangebot.
Das rahmenlose Display und eine spezielle
Beschichtung vereinfachen die tägliche
Reinigung. Die Standsäule kann von beiden
Seiten geöffnet werden und bietet Stauraum für Etikettenrollen, Reinigungsmittel
und andere Utensilien.

Begründung der Jury
Die geschlossene Form und die mattschim-
mernden Oberflächen stellen eine gestalterische Einheit her, welche die Eigenständigkeit der Waage unterstreicht.

HS-3510W
All-in-One POS Terminal

Manufacturer
Posiflex Technology Inc., New Taipei, Taiwan
In-house design
Web
www.posiflex.com

The HS-3510W all-in-one POS terminal is based on a fanless architecture featuring a 9.7" touchscreen, a detachable printer and an optional 2D barcode scanner. Furthermore, the terminal can be combined with additional peripheral devices such as a fingerprint sensor or a second customer display. Due to its small footprint, the system is suited for different counter styles and can be used in all areas with limited space.

Das All-in-one-POS-Terminal HS-3510W beruht auf einer lüfterlosen Konstruktion mit einem 9,7"-Touchscreen, einem abnehmbaren Drucker und einem optionalen 2D-Barcodescanner. Zusätzlich kann das Gerät mit weiteren Peripheriegeräten wie einem Fingerabdrucksensor oder einem zweiten Kundendisplay kombiniert werden. Durch seine kleine Standfläche ist das System für unterschiedliche Arten von Kassentresen geeignet und kann in allen Bereichen eingesetzt werden, in denen nur begrenzt Platz zur Verfügung steht.

Statement by the jury
This POS terminal provides excellent interface connectivity. Thanks to its unobtrusive design, it blends in well with any environment.

Begründung der Jury
Das POS-Terminal bietet eine ausgezeichnete Schnittstellenanbindung und fügt sich durch seine zurückhaltende Gestaltung harmonisch in jedes Umfeld ein.

CINEO C2020
ATM
Geldautomat

Manufacturer
Wincor Nixdorf International GmbH, Paderborn, Germany
In-house design
Frank Bleck, Gregor Pollmann
Web
www.wincor-nixdorf.com

The Cineo C2020 ATM allows users to withdraw cash with the help of a smartphone or an NFC card. The ATM's central control elements are its large touch display and its non-contact barcode and card reader. In order to guide the user through the transaction, entry and dispensing modules are specifically illuminated during the interaction. Identification is carried out either using a QR code, which is generated on a smartphone and then scanned via a barcode reader, or the PIN code of an NFC card, which is entered on the touchscreen.

Der Geldautomat Cineo C2020 ermöglicht das Abheben von Bargeld mit dem Smartphone oder einer NFC-Karte. Zentrale Bedienelemente des Geldautomaten sind der große Touchscreen und der kontaktlose Barcode- und Kartenleser. Um den Benutzer durch die Transaktion zu führen, werden die Eingabe- und Ausgabemodule während der Interaktion gezielt beleuchtet. Die Identifizierung erfolgt entweder über einen QR-Code, der auf dem Smartphone generiert und über einen Barcodeleser eingescannt wird, oder über den PIN-Code der NFC-Karte, der über den Touchscreen eingegeben wird.

Statement by the jury
With its minimalist design, the Cineo C2020 expresses a strong sense of integrity. This in turn conveys unrestricted security during the payment process.

Begründung der Jury
Der Cineo C2020 drückt in seiner reduzierten Gestaltung größtmögliche Seriosität aus. Damit vermittelt er dem Anwender uneingeschränkte Sicherheit beim Bezahlen.

MPAIO
Mobile POS Terminal

Manufacturer
SamilCTS Co., Ltd., Seongnam, South Korea
In-house design
Kyuyong Oh
Web
www.mpaio.com

The MPAIO mobile POS terminal supports customer needs in diverse ways and offers a variety of cashless payment options. Therefore, it can be used flexibly in very diverse business environments. The terminal may be connected to several different devices, such as barcode readers and magnetic card readers, via USB cable or Bluetooth. With its clear separation into an LCD display and a PIN pad, the user interface offers a high degree of clarity.

Das mobile POS-Terminal MPAIO unterstützt den Kundenservice in vielfältiger Weise und bietet diverse bargeldlose Zahlungsarten. Dadurch ist es in sehr unterschiedlichen Geschäftsumgebungen flexibel einsetzbar. Per USB-Kabel oder Bluetooth-Verbindung kann das Terminal mit verschiedenen Endgeräten wie beispielsweise einem Barcodescanner oder Magnetkartenleser verbunden werden. Die Benutzeroberfläche ist durch ihre klare Unterteilung in einen LCD-Bildschirm und ein PIN-Pad sehr übersichtlich.

Statement by the jury
The convenient size of this POS terminal is especially impressive. The design concept, which has been modelled after a mobile phone, enables intuitive operation.

Begründung der Jury
Das POS-Terminal besticht durch seine besonders handliche Größe. Das einem Mobiltelefon nachempfundene Gestaltungskonzept erlaubt eine intuitive Bedienung.

EVIS Manta
RFID Card Reader
RFID-Lesegerät

Manufacturer
EVIS AG, Volketswil, Switzerland
In-house design
Roland Frefel
Web
www.evis.ch

The Evis Manta is an RFID card reader which is connected to a POS cash register system in order to communicate with electronic data storage devices such as keys, cards and NFC-enabled smartphones. The ray-like pattern on the glass surface indicates the position of the RFID reader field. The two-line display which is backlit in a subtle blue, guides the customer safely through the sales process. The aluminium housing has a solid weight, which lends it positioning stability.

Statement by the jury
The minimalist design of the RFID card reader creates an exciting contrast with the device's black detailing and graphic surface.

Das Evis Manta ist ein RFID-Lesegerät, das an ein POS-Kassensystem angeschlossen wird, um mit elektronischen Datenträgern wie Schlüsseln, Karten oder NFC-fähigen Smartphones zu kommunizieren. Das strahlenförmige Muster auf der Glasoberfläche zeigt die Position des RFID-Lesefeldes an. Die dezente blaue Hintergrundbeleuchtung des zweizeiligen Displays führt den Kunden sicher durch den Verkaufsprozess. Das Gehäuse aus Aluminium verfügt über ein solides Gewicht, das stabil auf dem Untergrund aufliegt.

Begründung der Jury
Bei dem RFID-Lesegerät steht die minimalistische Formgebung in einem aufregenden Kontrast zu den schwarz abgesetzten Details und der grafischen Oberfläche.

IT 8250
Multifunctional Terminal
Multifunktionsterminal

Manufacturer
ISGUS GmbH, Villingen-Schwenningen, Germany
In-house design
Web
www.isgus.de

The IT 8250 multifunctional terminal with anti-glare 15" TFT display meets all requirements for time recording and plant data collection. The large buttons and function symbols enable easy and safe use of the touchscreen, even when wearing gloves. Information like orders, workflow and absence can thus be accessed directly at the workstation by staff. Thanks to its low housing depth, the terminal is also deployable in confined spaces.

Statement by the jury
This terminal convinces with its flat construction and seamless transitions. The functional look highlights its application in industrial environments.

Das Multifunktionsterminal IT 8250 mit entspiegeltem 15"-TFT-Display erfüllt alle Funktionen der Zeiterfassung und Betriebsdatenerfassung. Die großen Tasten und Funktionssymbole erlauben eine einfache und sichere Bedienung des Touchscreens auch mit Handschuhen. So können Aufträge, Arbeitsgänge, Fehlzeiten etc. vom Personal direkt am Arbeitsplatz eingesehen werden. Dank seiner geringen Gehäusetiefe ist das Terminal auch in beengten Raumverhältnissen einsetzbar.

Begründung der Jury
Das Terminal überzeugt durch eine flache Bauform und nahtlose Übergänge. Die sachliche Anmutung unterstreicht den Einsatz in einem industriellen Umfeld.

uTerminal
Time Recording Terminal
Zeiterfassungsterminal

Manufacturer
ugomo ag, Thun, Switzerland

In-house design
ugomo ag

Web
www.ugomo.com

reddot award 2016
best of the best

In the course of time

Since recording work time plays a central role in the organisation of companies, the classic time clock has accompanied generations of employees. Against this backdrop, the uTerminal embodies a contemporary and user-friendly solution for recording time. Featuring a robust unibody housing, this terminal can safely hold and protect an iPad on which the uTerminal app can be installed. Through a wireless network, the system can be easily integrated into any given infrastructure and seamlessly connected with any time management system. Directly interacting with the existing system, the app offers easy access to all aspects of recording time and thus embodies a quick, simple and cost-effective solution. Employees are accurately identified by QR codes via the iPad camera or by using an RFID Bluetooth reader with Legic or Mifare badges. The well thought-out design concept of uTerminal allows any number of terminals to be connected across the existing infrastructure. Thanks to the integrated communication capability, the uTerminal interacts immediately with the time recording software. Another important aspect is that the app can save all entries posted, even when used offline, and then transfer the values to the time recording software whenever the app is online again. The uTerminal thus embodies a highly sophisticated interpretation of contemporary time recording – a design that is perfectly adapted to modern work environments.

Im Wandel der Zeit

Da für die Organisation in Unternehmen die Zeiterfassung eine zentrale Rolle spielt, hat die klassische Stempeluhr Generationen von Arbeitnehmern begleitet. Das uTerminal stellt hier ein sehr zeitgemäßes und nutzerfreundliches System für die Zeiterfassung bereit. Gestaltet mit einem soliden Unibody-Gehäuse kann dieses Terminal ein iPad sicher aufnehmen, auf dem die uTerminal App installiert wird. Über ein drahtloses Netzwerk lässt es sich leicht in die bestehende Infrastruktur integrieren und nahtlos mit jedem Zeitmanagementsystem verbinden. Die mit diesem direkt interagierende App umfasst sämtliche Funktionen der Arbeitszeiterfassung und stellt damit eine schnelle, einfache und kostengünstige Lösung dar. Die Identifikation der Mitarbeiter erfolgt mit einem QR-Code über die iPad-Kamera oder mittels eines RFID-Bluetooth-Lesers mit Legic- oder Mifare-Badges. Das gut durchdachte Gestaltungskonzept von uTerminal erlaubt es, beliebig viele Terminals über die bestehende Infrastruktur anzuschließen. Dank der integrierten Kommunikation steht es sofort in Interaktion mit der angesteuerten Zeiterfassungssoftware. Ein wichtiger Aspekt ist auch, dass im Offline-Fall die gebuchten Einträge in der App sicher gespeichert und, sobald die App wieder online ist, übertragen werden. Das uTerminal ist damit eine überaus gelungene Interpretation zeitgemäßer Arbeitszeiterfassung – seine Gestaltung bildet auf perfekte Weise die moderne Arbeitswelt ab.

Statement by the jury

The uTerminal is an outstandingly designed product with a perfect internal arrangement. It integrates modern technologies in a meaningful and user-friendly manner. All individual elements merge exemplarily into an effective system for recording time. With its clear design idiom and open modularity approach, the uTerminal is ideally equipped and suited for further developments in the future.

Begründung der Jury

Das uTerminal ist ein ausgezeichnet gestaltetes Produkt, das in sich perfekt gegliedert ist. Aktuelle Technologien werden auf sinnvolle Weise und nutzerfreundlich integriert. Die einzelnen Elemente ergänzen sich beispielhaft zu einem effektiven System der Zeiterfassung. Mit seiner klaren Formensprache und offenen Modularität ist das uTerminal für die Entwicklungen der Zukunft bestens gerüstet.

Designer portrait
See page 34
Siehe Seite 34

CWP V3 / Evolution
Air Traffic Controller Working Position
Fluglotsen-Arbeitsplatz

Manufacturer
Indra, Torrejón de Ardoz
(Madrid), Spain

Design
LOOP, Sant Cugat del Vallès
(Barcelona), Spain

Web
www.indracompany.com
www.loop-cn.com

reddot award 2016
best of the best

Safe interaction

The constantly increasing complexity of air traffic in
international airspace calls for new systems and interfaces to control the airspace consistently for safety
reasons. The design of the CWP V3 / Evolution
responds to this need with a simple and, for air traffic
controllers, easy-to-understand concept. All functions
are consistently integrated into one elegant, clearly
arranged housing. The working position features an
intuitively operated interface that allows the controller to interact directly with the multi-touch screen,
or indirectly (traditional mode) in such a way that the
screen is vertical and the controller interacts through
a keyboard, a touch pad or a tablet computer. This
option ensures enhanced safety as the control unit
can thus be removed to continue controlling even in
the case of something unexpected happening in the
control room. This versatility also allows the controllers to more easily adapt to the shift towards gestural
interfaces. A key innovative aspect of this system is
that it offers the possibility of switching between different work modes and functional requirements
needed in a modern control room. All configuration
changes can be performed within five seconds elec-
tronically and silently. This working position for air
traffic controllers thus perfectly adapts to various
control room needs – it smartly conquers new paths
by responding to the increasing complexity in this
field with an elegant solution.

Sichere Interaktion

Mit der stetigen Zunahme der Flugbewegungen im internationalen Luftraum werden Überwachungssysteme
benötigt, die dieser Komplexität auf sinnvolle Weise
begegnen. Die Gestaltung von CWP V3 / Evolution erfüllt die damit einhergehenden Anforderungen mittels
eines einfachen und für den Fluglotsen leicht verständlichen Konzepts. Alle Funktionen sind sehr schlüssig in
einem klar und elegant anmutenden Gehäuse vereint.
Der Arbeitsplatz ist mit einem intuitiv bedienbaren Interface gestaltet, bei dem der Fluglotse direkt mit
einem Multi-Touch-Bildschirm interagiert oder indirekt
(Traditional Mode) mit vertikalem Bildschirm, indem die
Bedienung dann über eine Tastatur, ein Touchpad oder
einen Tablet-Computer erfolgt. Diese Option bietet viel
Sicherheit, da bei möglicherweise im Kontrollraum auf-
tretenden unerwarteten Situationen das Eingabeme-
dium portabel ist. Die hohe Variabilität erlaubt es dem
Nutzer auch, sich leichter dem Trend hin zu einer
Gestensteuerung anzupassen. Es ist daher ein zentraler
innovativer Aspekt dieses Systems, dass es die Möglichkeit bietet, zwischen den einzelnen Funktionsanfor-
derungen zu wechseln, die in einem modernen Kontrollraum benötigt werden. Die Anpassungen können
innerhalb von nur fünf Sekunden leise und komfortabel
stattfinden. Dieser Arbeitsplatz für Fluglotsen passt
sich damit perfekt den schwierigen Bedingungen an –
auf intelligente Weise gibt er Wege vor, den komplexen
Situationen im Kontrollraum stilvoll zu begegnen.

Statement by the jury
The CWP V3 / Evolution air traffic controller working
position fascinates with an innovative use of technology and materials. The design sensitively reflects and
responds to the complexity of requirements that people working in air traffic control face on a daily basis.
This sophisticated system impressively coordinates and
harmonises control room work processes. It offers a
high degree of comfort for the user and enhanced
safety in air traffic.

Begründung der Jury
Der Fluglotsen-Arbeitsplatz CWP V3 / Evolution begeistert mit einem innovativen Einsatz von Technologie
und Material. Die Gestaltung bildet auf sensitive Weise
die komplexen Anforderungen ab, mit denen die im
Bereich der Flugverkehrskontrolle Arbeitenden täglich
konfrontiert sind. Deren Tätigkeit wird durch dieses
ausgeklügelte System eindrucksvoll harmonisiert und
koordiniert. Es bietet dabei ein hohes Maß an Komfort
und mehr Sicherheit für den Luftverkehr.

Designer portrait
See page 36
Siehe Seite 36

TC70
Industrial Handheld Computer
Mobiler Industriecomputer

Manufacturer
Zebra Technologies, Holtsville, USA
In-house design
Web
www.zebra.com

The TC70 industrial handheld computer is not only dust- and waterproof, but also shock-protected thanks to its external metal housing which features rubberised surfaces. The touchscreen can be operated either by finger, even when wearing gloves, or by using a stylus for signatures. The expansion port allows accessories like card readers to be connected. Furthermore, the computer can also be used as a two-way radio thanks to its front-facing speaker and push-to-talk button.

Statement by the jury
Careful selection of materials and high-quality workmanship make the TC70 highly robust. Its modular structure accommodates a wide range of applications.

Der mobile Industriecomputer TC70 ist nicht nur staub- und wasserdicht, sondern aufgrund seines externen Metallgehäuses mit gummierten Oberflächen auch sturzfest. Der Touchscreen kann wahlweise per Finger, sogar mit Handschuhen, oder zur Unterschrifterfassung per Stift bedient werden. Ein Erweiterungssteckplatz ermöglicht z. B. den Anschluss eines Kartenlesegeräts. Zudem kann der Computer durch den nach vorne ausgerichteten Lautsprecher und den Push-to-talk-Button auch als Walkie-Talkie genutzt werden.

Begründung der Jury
Die sorgfältige Materialauswahl und hochwertige Verarbeitung machen den TC70 äußerst robust. Seine Modularität bietet vielseitige Einsatzmöglichkeiten.

TC8000
Mobile Industrial Computer
Mobiler Industriecomputer

Manufacturer
Zebra Technologies, Holtsville, USA
In-house design
Web
www.zebra.com

The TC8000 mobile industrial computer has been designed to increase productivity in warehouses and to reduce fatigue in workers. The slanted display makes it possible for users to read the data input during the scanning process, without having to bend the wrist. Thanks to its touch interface, the device weighs up to 33 per cent less than comparable models featuring a keypad. Furthermore, the novel touch technology also enables operation when wearing gloves, even in wet conditions.

Statement by the jury
The prominent design feature of the TC8000 is its pleasantly large size, which at the same time feels astonishingly light in the hand.

Der mobile Industriecomputer TC8000 ist darauf ausgelegt, die Produktivität im Warenlager zu steigern und ein ermüdungsfreies Arbeiten zu fördern. Das angeschrägte Display ermöglicht ein Ablesen der Eingabe bereits während des Scanvorgangs, ohne dafür das Handgelenk an- und abwinkeln zu müssen. Dank des Touch-Interfaces wiegt das Gerät bis zu 33 Prozent weniger als vergleichbare Modelle mit einer Tastatur. Zudem erlaubt die neuartige Touch-Technologie die Benutzung mit Handschuhen, sogar bei Nässe.

Begründung der Jury
Herausragendes Gestaltungsmerkmal des TC8000 ist, dass er ein angenehm großes Volumen mit sich bringt, dabei jedoch verblüffend leicht in der Hand liegt.

DS3600 Series
DS3600 Serie
Barcode Scanner

Manufacturer
Zebra Technologies, Holtsville, USA
In-house design
Web
www.zebra.com

The DS3600 series barcode scanner comes in two versions, corded and cordless. The ergonomically shaped pistol grip ensures a reliable hold. The housing is partly designed in neon green in order to make the scanner easy to find in poorly lit industrial buildings. The upper protective cap made from polycarbonate can be easily replaced if it gets damaged. The robust metal hook on the back attaches to forklifts and other vehicles.

Statement by the jury
With its robust design, which is characterised by sleek lines and distinct indentations, this barcode scanner blends excellently with any industrial environment.

Den Barcodescanner der Serie DS3600 gibt es in zwei Ausführungen, mit oder ohne Kabel. Der ergonomisch geformte Pistolengriff bietet einen sicheren Halt. Das Gehäuse ist teilweise in Neongrün gestaltet, damit der Scanner in schlecht beleuchteten Industriehallen schnell wiedergefunden werden kann. Die obere Schutzkappe aus Polycarbonat lässt sich bei Beschädigung einfach austauschen, der robuste Metallhaken auf der Rückseite dient zur Befestigung an Gabelstaplern oder anderen Fahrzeugen.

Begründung der Jury
Mit seinem robusten Design, das durch schnittige Linien und markante Vertiefungen geprägt ist, passt der Barcodescanner hervorragend in ein Industrieumfeld.

SIMATIC IPC547G
Industrial PC
Industrie-PC

Manufacturer
Siemens AG, Nuremberg, Germany
In-house design
Stephan Hühne
Design
at-design GbR (Jan Andersson),
Fürth, Germany
Web
www.siemens.com
www.atdesign.de

The Simatic IPC547G industrial PC in 19" format is particularly suitable for use as an industrial workstation and server for the parallel processing of large quantities of data. The housing fashioned entirely from metal ensures electromagnetic compatibility with other technical devices. The overpressure ventilation system results in low noise emissions and prevents dust from entering the housing. The respective status of temperature, fan and hard drive is shown on the LED display at the front.

Statement by the jury
This industrial PC is structured by vertical lines, engendering order and clarity. Thanks to the low depth of the housing, it is also extremely space-saving.

Der Industrie-PC Simatic IPC547G im 19"-Format eignet sich besonders als Industrie-Workstation und -Server für die parallele Verarbeitung großer Datenmengen. Das Ganzmetallgehäuse garantiert die elektromagnetische Verträglichkeit mit anderen technischen Geräten. Die Überdruckbelüftung sorgt für eine geringe Geräuschentwicklung und verhindert das Eindringen von Staub in das Gehäuse. Der Status von Temperatur, Lüfter und Festplatte wird über ein LED-Frontdisplay angezeigt.

Begründung der Jury
Der Industrie-PC ist durch vertikale Linien unterteilt, die Ordnung und Klarheit schaffen. Dank seiner geringen Gehäusetiefe ist er zudem äußerst platzsparend.

Industrial Box PC
Industrie-Box-PC

Manufacturer
Omron, 's-Hertogenbosch, Netherlands
Design
GBO, Helmond, Netherlands
Web
www.omron.com
www.gbo.eu

The design brief for developing this Industrial Box PC set out to prove to a sceptical market that PC technology works reliably in industrial environments. The solution is a monolithic rectangle shape with chamfered edges made of black cast aluminium. For future scalability, individual sections can be added or removed. The prominent cooling ribs, which convey a sense of power, dominate the front of the unit.

Statement by the jury
The Industrial Box PC conveys reliability and solidity – features that predestine it for use in the industrial field.

Die Aufgabe bei der Entwicklung dieses Industrie-Box-PCs bestand darin, einem skeptischen Markt zu beweisen, dass PC-Technologie in industriellen Umgebungen zuverlässig funktioniert. Die Lösung ist eine monolithische, rechteckige Form mit abgeschrägten Kanten aus schwarzem Aluminiumguss. Für die zukünftige Skalierbarkeit können einzelne Sektionen hinzugefügt oder entfernt werden. Die auffälligen Kühlrippen verleihen eine kraftvolle Anmutung und dominieren die Vorderseite des Geräts.

Begründung der Jury
Der Industrie-Box-PC vermittelt Zuverlässigkeit und Solidität – und damit Merkmale, die ihn für den Einsatz in der Industrie prädestinieren.

DuraForce XD
Professional Phablet
Profi-Phablet

Manufacturer
Kyocera Corporation, Kyoto, Japan
In-house design
Hidetoshi Hachiya
Web
www.kyoceramobile.com

The DuraForce XD combines the technical performance of a tablet with the convenient functionality of a smartphone. The 5.7" HD touchscreen is large enough to comfortably view data yet compact enough to be operated with one hand, even when wearing gloves. The housing is waterproof, shockproof and hazardous location safe, thus surviving extreme conditions in the construction, chemical and manufacturing industries.

Das DuraForce XD vereint die technische Leistungsfähigkeit eines Tablets mit der praktischen Funktionalität eines Smartphones. Der 5,7"-HD-Touchscreen ist groß genug, um Inhalte bequem ablesen zu können, aber gleichzeitig so kompakt, dass das Gerät mit nur einer Hand bedient werden kann, auch mit Handschuhen. Das Gehäuse ist wasserdicht, stoßfest und flammensicher, sodass es den extremen Anforderungen in der Bau-, Chemie- und Fertigungsbranche gerecht wird.

Statement by the jury
The DuraForce XD impresses with its robustness. Matt surfaces and distinct lines complete the tough look.

Begründung der Jury
Das DuraForce XD beeindruckt durch seine Widerstandsfähigkeit. Die matten Oberflächen und markanten Linien vervollständigen den robusten Look.

Black Marble
LED Display

Manufacturer
ROE Visual Co., Ltd., Shenzhen, China
In-house design
Chen Lu, Darhu Cai
Web
www.roevisual.com

The Black Marble LED display consists of tiles that are mounted onto the corresponding frame construction in different variations. The individual tiles can be quickly replaced using a magnet. The matt screen features an anti-glare coating, which does not even reflect bright spotlights, such as those used in TV studios and on concert stages. The LED spotlights enable both the presentation of video content and the staging of light shows.

Das LED-Display Black Marble besteht aus Kacheln, die in beliebigen Varianten in die zugehörige Rahmenkonstruktion montiert werden. Die einzelnen Kacheln lassen sich mithilfe eines Magneten schnell und einfach auswechseln. Der matte Bildschirm verfügt über eine Anti-Glare-Beschichtung, die auch grelles Scheinwerferlicht wie z.B. in Fernsehstudios oder auf Konzertbühnen nicht reflektiert. Die LED-Scheinwerfer ermöglichen sowohl die Darstellung von Videoinhalten als auch die Inszenierung von Lichtshows.

Statement by the jury
The modular structure of this LED display facilitates a high degree of flexibility and creativity, thus clearly accommodating the needs of the user.

Begründung der Jury
Der modulare Aufbau des LED-Displays ermöglicht ein hohes Maß an Flexibilität und Kreativität. Damit ist es ganz auf die Bedürfnisse des Nutzers abgestimmt.

Speedmaster XL 106
Sheetfed Offset Printing Press
Bogenoffset-Druckmaschine

Manufacturer
Heidelberger Druckmaschinen AG, Heidelberg, Germany
In-house design
Björn Wilke
Web
www.heidelberg.com

The Speedmaster XL 106 sheetfed offset printing press prints on paper and cardboard as well as foil and PVC. The modular concept enables machine configurations of up to 20 units connected in series. The precise geometric forms of the press clearly define the individual work areas. The portals are unobtrusive and at the same time clearly indicate the machine's input and output. The colour scheme has been reduced for maximum contrast, placing the design focus clearly on core and operating functions.

Die Bogenoffset-Druckmaschine Speedmaster XL 106 bedruckt neben Papier und Karton auch Folien und PVC. Das modulare Konzept ermöglicht Maschinenkonfigurationen mit bis zu 20 hintereinander geschalteten Werken. Die präzisen geometrischen Formen der Anlage sorgen für eine klare Gliederung der Arbeitsbereiche. Die Portale sind flächig zurückgenommen und zeigen zugleich deutlich den In- und Output der Maschine. Das Farbkonzept ist kontraststark reduziert, sodass der gestalterische Fokus eindeutig auf den Kern- und Bedienfunktionen liegt.

Statement by the jury
With its cubic form and pillar design, this printing press resembles an architectural structure, thus achieving a fascinating and unique spatial effect.

Begründung der Jury
Die Druckmaschine erscheint in ihrer kubischen Form samt Pfeilerkonstruktion wie ein architektonisches Gebäude und erzielt so eine faszinierende eigene Raumwirkung.

Speedmaster XL 162
Sheetfed Offset Printing Press
Bogenoffset-Druckmaschine

Manufacturer
Heidelberger Druckmaschinen AG, Heidelberg, Germany
In-house design
Heidelberg Industrial Design Team
Web
www.heidelberg.com

The Speedmaster XL 162 offers a wide range of large-format printing options for promotional and packaging materials. In addition, the machine is equipped with a coating unit, also enabling UV finishes. The curved surfaces of the printing units with their clean recesses facilitate optimum operation. The geometrically reduced slanting silver portal at the delivery provides safety for the user and directs the eye towards the finished print product. A fully automated printing plate exchanger enables the complete replacement of the printing plates in two minutes.

Die Speedmaster XL 162 bietet alle Möglichkeiten des Bedruckens von Werbe- und Verpackungsmaterialien in Großformat. Zudem ist die Maschine mit einem Lackierwerk ausgestattet, sodass auch UV-Veredelungen möglich sind. Die gewölbten Flächen der Druckwerke mit ihren klaren Einschnitten erlauben eine optimale Bedienung. Das geneigte silberne Portal am Ausleger ist geometrisch reduziert, gibt dem Bediener Sicherheit und leitet den Blick gezielt auf das fertige Druckprodukt. Ein vollautomatischer Plattenwechsler ermöglicht den kompletten Austausch der Druckplatten in zwei Minuten.

Statement by the jury
The design of this printing press captivates with its light/dark contrasts and slightly offset proportions, which create a fascinating impression of spatial depth.

Begründung der Jury
Das Design der Druckmaschine besticht durch Hell-Dunkel-Kontraste und leicht verschobene Proportionen, die einen reizvollen Eindruck von räumlicher Tiefe erzeugen.

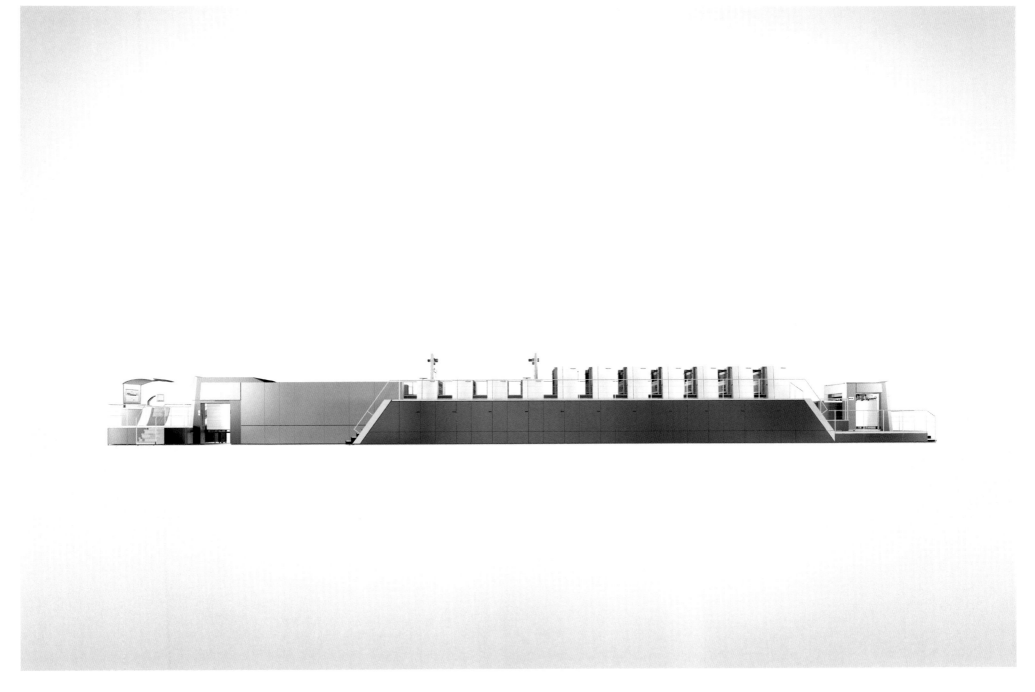

Omnifire 250
Digital Printing Press
Digital-Druckmaschine

Manufacturer
Heidelberger Druckmaschinen AG, Heidelberg, Germany
In-house design
Marc Bundschuh
Web
www.heidelberg.com

The Omnifire 250 combines advanced inkjet technology with highly precise robotics. This facilitates printing onto a wide range of 3D objects such as balls, drinking bottles or mobile phone sleeves. Thanks to its modular structure, the machine may be adjusted to the requirements of individual customers. The glass pane is framed by silver edges, directing the eye to the work area. The angular shape of the edges gives the machine a character of its own, while conveying the quality and precision of the innovative 4D printing process.

Die Omnifire 250 vereint fortschrittliche Inkjet-Technologie mit hochpräziser Robotik. So können verschiedenste 3D-Objekte wie Sportbälle, Trinkflaschen oder Mobiltelefon-Cover digital bedruckt werden. Aufgrund ihrer modularen Bauweise kann die Maschine an individuelle Kundenwünsche angepasst werden. Die Glasscheibe wird von silbernen Rändern eingefasst, wodurch der Blick auf den Arbeitsbereich gelenkt wird. Die kantige Form der Ränder verleiht der Maschine darüber hinaus einen eigenständigen Charakter und vermittelt gleichfalls die Qualität und Präzision des innovativen 4D-Druckverfahrens.

Statement by the jury
The clear geometric form of the printing press conveys its high technical standards. The protruding edges foster a sense of suspended lightness.

Begründung der Jury
Ihre klare Geometrie dokumentiert den hohen technischen Anspruch der Druckmaschine. Die überstehenden Kanten erzeugen eine schwebende Leichtigkeit.

FLUX Delta
3D Printer
3D-Drucker

Manufacturer
Flux Technology Corp., Taipei, Taiwan
In-house design
Web
www.flux3dp.com

The Flux Delta can be equipped with different modules, converting the 3D printer into, for example, a laser engraving device or a drawing pen. Each module is attached to the robotic arms using a magnetic bracket, so no tools are required for the installation. An integrated 3D scanner allows the user to scan any object into the printer. It can be controlled via a smartphone, tablet or any other Web-enabled device.

Statement by the jury
This 3D printer captivates with its modular expandability. The frame with its matt-black finish creates a sculptural silhouette.

Für den Flux Delta stehen verschiedene Module zur Verfügung, mit denen der 3D-Drucker beispielsweise in ein Lasergravur-Gerät oder einen Zeichenstift umgewandelt werden kann. Das jeweilige Modul wird über eine Magnethalterung an den Roboterarmen befestigt, für die Montage ist keinerlei Werkzeug notwendig. Ein integrierter 3D-Scanner ermöglicht es, jedes beliebige Objekt in den Drucker einzulesen. Die Steuerung erfolgt über ein Smartphone, Tablet oder anderes internetfähiges Gerät.

Begründung der Jury
Der 3D-Drucker begeistert durch seine modulare Erweiterbarkeit. Der Rahmen in einem matten, schwarzen Finish schafft eine skulptural anmutende Silhouette.

MetalFAB1
3D Metal Printer
3D-Metalldrucker

Manufacturer
Additive Industries, Eindhoven, Netherlands
Design
VanBerlo, Eindhoven, Netherlands
Web
www.additiveindustries.com
www.vanberlo.nl

The MetalFab1 3D metal printer is designed for the serial production of components for aerospace, automotive and medical applications as well as for other high-tech industries. The system consists of various standard modules that can be combined as needed. In the build chamber, up to four lasers can be used simultaneously. In parallel, up to four build chambers can handle a maximum of four different metal powders. Despite working almost autonomously, the process is made highly visible.

Statement by the jury
The MetalFab1 presents a highly coherent design with regard to form and materials. Thanks to its large, planar surfaces, the separate areas visually combine to form a whole.

Der 3D-Metalldrucker MetalFab1 wurde für die serielle Fertigung von Bauteilen für die Luftfahrt-, Automobil- und Medizinindustrie sowie für andere Hightech-Branchen entwickelt. Das System setzt sich aus verschiedenen Standardmodulen zusammen, die frei konfigurierbar sind. In der Baukammer sind bis zu vier Laser gleichzeitig im Einsatz. Parallel dazu können in bis zu vier Baukammern maximal vier unterschiedliche Metallpulver verarbeitet werden. Obwohl der Drucker nahezu selbständig arbeitet, sind die Arbeitsabläufe gut nachzuvollziehen.

Begründung der Jury
Die MetalFab1 präsentiert sich formal wie materiell äußerst stimmig. Dank der flächigen Bauart verbinden sich die separaten Bereiche zu einer visuellen Einheit.

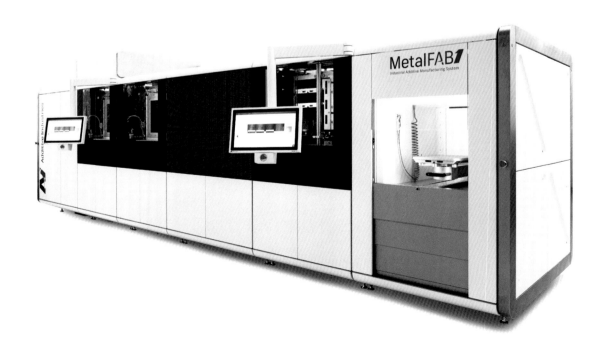

Cubicon Style
3D Printer
3D-Drucker

Manufacturer
HyVision System, Seongnam, South Korea
In-house design
Seom-Gyun Lee
Web
www.3dcubicon.com

The compact Cubicon Style 3D printer is self-contained on three sides in order to make it safe to use on a desk. The handleless glass door at the front can be opened and closed by exerting gentle pressure. As soon as the printing process starts, the object is illuminated from all four sides. The robust housing is characterised by its contrasting materials, combining matt-black anodised aluminium and glossy acrylic surfaces. The touch interface has pleasant tactile qualities.

Statement by the jury
This 3D printer convinces with its stylishly harmonised materials. The illuminated interior fosters an intense user experience.

Der kompakte 3D-Drucker Cubicon Style ist von drei Seiten geschlossen, um den Gebrauch auf einem Schreibtisch sicher zu machen. Die vordere grifflose Glastür lässt sich durch sanftes Drücken öffnen und schließen. Sobald der Druckvorgang beginnt, wird das Objekt von vier Seiten angeleuchtet. Das robuste Gehäuse zeichnet sich durch den Materialkontrast aus mattschwarz-eloxiertem Aluminium und glänzenden Acrylflächen aus. Die Touch-Oberfläche bietet eine angenehme Haptik.

Begründung der Jury
Der 3D-Drucker überzeugt durch seine stilvoll aufeinander abgestimmte Materialkomposition. Der beleuchtete Innenraum bietet ein intensives Nutzererlebnis.

ZD410
Thermal Printer
Thermodrucker

Manufacturer
Zebra Technologies, Lincolnshire, USA
In-house design
Web
www.zebra.com

The ZD410 thermal printer is very small and compact, making it particularly suited for printing labels and tags in work environments with little available desktop space, such as in laboratories or retail settings. The design concept is modelled on familiar characteristics from the consumer electronics sector, also enabling untrained personnel to operate the device as intuitively as possible. Geometric forms and colour coding help to make important operating elements quickly recognisable.

Der Thermodrucker ZD410 ist sehr klein und kompakt, sodass er insbesondere für das Drucken von Aufschriften und Etiketten in Arbeitsumgebungen geeignet ist, wo nur wenig Schreibtischfläche zur Verfügung steht, z. B. im Labor oder Einzelhandel. Das Gestaltungskonzept orientiert sich an bekannten Merkmalen der Verbraucherelektronik, damit auch ungeschultes Personal das Gerät möglichst intuitiv benutzen kann. Die geometrischen Formen und farblichen Kennzeichnungen helfen dabei, wichtige Bedienelemente schnell zu erkennen.

Statement by the jury
The tidy arrangement of the control elements and the calm, reduced colour scheme of this thermal printer facilitate clear understanding of its functions.

Begründung der Jury
Die übersichtliche Anordnung der Bedienelemente und die ruhige, reduzierte Farbgestaltung des Thermodruckers sorgen für ein klares Verständnis der Funktionen.

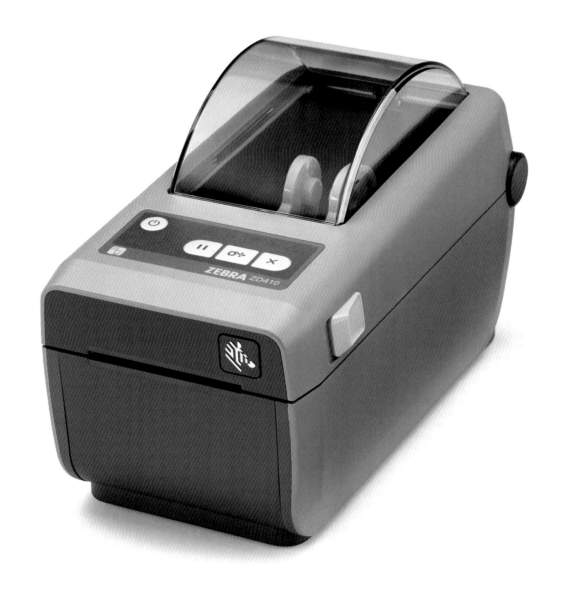

VarioInspect
LED Light Tunnel
LED-Lichttunnel

Manufacturer
Eisenmann Anlagenbau GmbH & Co. KG,
Böblingen, Germany
Design
Panik Ebner Design, Stuttgart, Germany
Web
www.eisenmann.com
www.panikebnerdesign.de

The VarioInspect LED light tunnel supports surface checks in the paint shop.
The LEDs are integrated into aluminium
profiles and create a uniform, smooth
reflection. The E-LED units enable finely
adjusted control, e.g. the light intensity
and temperature can be precisely regu-
lated, making it possible to detect even
the slightest blemishes in the paintwork
with ease. Running along a floor track is
a trolley that supplies materials, water,
power and compressed air for finishing
work. The number and spacing of portals
can be chosen as required.

Statement by the jury
The optimally aligned portal arches and
the flexibly adjustable brightness of the
VarioInspect lamps create excellent
lighting conditions and use of space.

Der LED-Lichttunnel VarioInspect unterstützt die Oberflächenkontrolle in der La-
ckiererei. Die Leuchten sind in Aluminiumprofilen gefasst und erzeugen ein
durchgehendes, ruhiges Reflexbild. Die
E-LED-Einheiten ermöglichen eine fein
angepasste Steuerung, z. B. lassen sich die
Lichtstärke und die Lichttemperatur sehr
genau regulieren, sodass auch kleinste
Unregelmäßigkeiten im Lack sichtbar werden. Der in einer Bodenschiene mitlaufende
Trolley stellt Material, Wasser, Strom und
Druckluft für Finish-Arbeiten bereit. Die
Anzahl und der Abstand der Portale sind
frei wählbar.

Begründung der Jury
Die optimal ausgerichteten Portalbögen
und die variabel anpassbaren Helligkeiten
der Leuchtmittel des VarioInspect schaffen
hervorragende Licht- und Raumverhält-
nisse.

EXCT
Linear Gantry
Linienportal

Manufacturer
Festo AG & Co. KG, Esslingen, Germany
In-house design
Web
www.festo.com

The EXCT linear gantry is more dynamic than conventional linear gantries and can be scaled to a wide range of strokes. It is mainly used in production processes with high cycle rates, such as in electronic manufacturing, medical technology and end line packaging. The portal achieves its high speed thanks to its fixed servomotors and revolving toothed belt. Due to these design features, less mass has to be set in motion, which results in a lower use of energy and fewer vibrations, thus also reducing wear and tear.

Das Linienportal EXCT bietet eine höhere Dynamik als konventionelle Linienportale und ist auf eine Vielzahl von Hüben skalierbar. Es kommt hauptsächlich bei Produktionsprozessen mit hohen Taktraten zum Einsatz, z. B. in der Elektronikfertigung, der Medizintechnik sowie im End Line Packaging. Die hohe Geschwindigkeit des Portals wird durch die feststehenden Servomotoren und einen umlaufenden Zahnriemen erreicht. Dadurch muss weniger Masse in Bewegung gesetzt werden, was zu einem niedrigeren Energieverbrauch führt, und es kommt zu weniger Erschütterungen, sodass der Verschleiß reduziert wird.

Statement by the jury
The appearance of this linear gantry is characterised by uncompromising clarity. The powerful design successfully highlights its performance.

Begründung der Jury
Das Aussehen des Linienportals ist von kompromissloser Klarheit geprägt. Die betont kraftvolle Formgebung unterstreicht gekonnt seine Leistungsfähigkeit.

VZQA
Pinch Valve
Quetschventil

Manufacturer
Festo AG & Co. KG, Esslingen, Germany
In-house design
Simone Mangcld
Web
www.festo.com

The VZQA pinch valve is used for controlling, filling and dosing liquid and gaseous media in the beverage, bio-pharmaceutical and chemical industries. It is based on a modular design principle involving just a few components, with which the suitable valve for any medium and environment can be configured. The integrated approach ensures a compact design and an unrestricted flow of the medium. With its reduced, slim construction, the valve incorporates into the piping system without taking up much space.

Das Quetschventil VZQA wird zum Steuern, Abfüllen und Dosieren von fließenden und gasförmigen Medien in der Getränke-, Biopharma- sowie Chemieindustrie verwendet. Es basiert auf einem modularen Baukastenprinzip, das aus wenigen Komponenten besteht. Daraus kann für jede Anwendung das passende Ventil hinsichtlich Medium und Umgebung konfiguriert werden. Der integrierte Antrieb sorgt für ein kompaktes Design und einen ungehinderten Durchfluss des Mediums. Mit seiner reduzierten, schlanken Bauform fügt es sich in die Rohrleitung ein, ohne viel Platz zu beanspruchen.

Statement by the jury
The pinch valve impresses with its tidy design and careful workmanship. It clearly conveys an air of robustness and premium quality.

Begründung der Jury
Das Quetschventil beeindruckt durch seine saubere Gestaltung und sorgfältige Verarbeitung. Es strahlt in hohem Maße Robustheit und Wertigkeit aus.

Die Achse
Linear Axis Module
Linearachsenmodul

Manufacturer
HIWIN GmbH, Offenburg, Germany
Design
Design Tech (Jürgen Schmid),
Ammerbuch, Germany
Web
www.hiwin.de
www.designtech.eu

The linear axis module called "Die Achse" is a flexible positioning tool for automation and machinery construction. It is based on a profiled rail guide and an aluminium profile with large grooves for secure mounting on the machine frame. The fact that the linear axis module is particularly suitable for applications with high speed is conveyed by the dynamic forms and smooth transitions between the end blocks and the profile; they appear as if cast in one piece. This impression is further enhanced by the consistent colour and surface design and by the continuous green line.

Statement by the jury
The self-contained form and clear geometry of the linear axis module convey high performance. Thanks to the choice of materials, it is robust and durable.

„Die Achse" ist ein flexibel einsetzbares Positionierungsmodul für die Automation und den Maschinenbau. Es basiert auf einer Profilschienenführung und einem Aluminiumprofil mit groß dimensionierten Nuten für eine stabile Befestigung am Maschinengestell. Dass die Achse speziell für Anwendungen mit hoher Geschwindigkeit geeignet ist, verdeutlichen die dynamische Form und die fließenden Übergänge zwischen den Endblöcken und dem Profil. Sie wirken wie aus einem Guss. Dieser Eindruck wird durch die konsequente Farb- und Oberflächengestaltung und die fortlaufende grüne Linie verstärkt.

Begründung der Jury
Die geschlossene Form und klare Geometrie des Linearachsenmoduls vermittelt eine hohe Leistungsfähigkeit. Dank der Materialwahl ist es robust und langlebig.

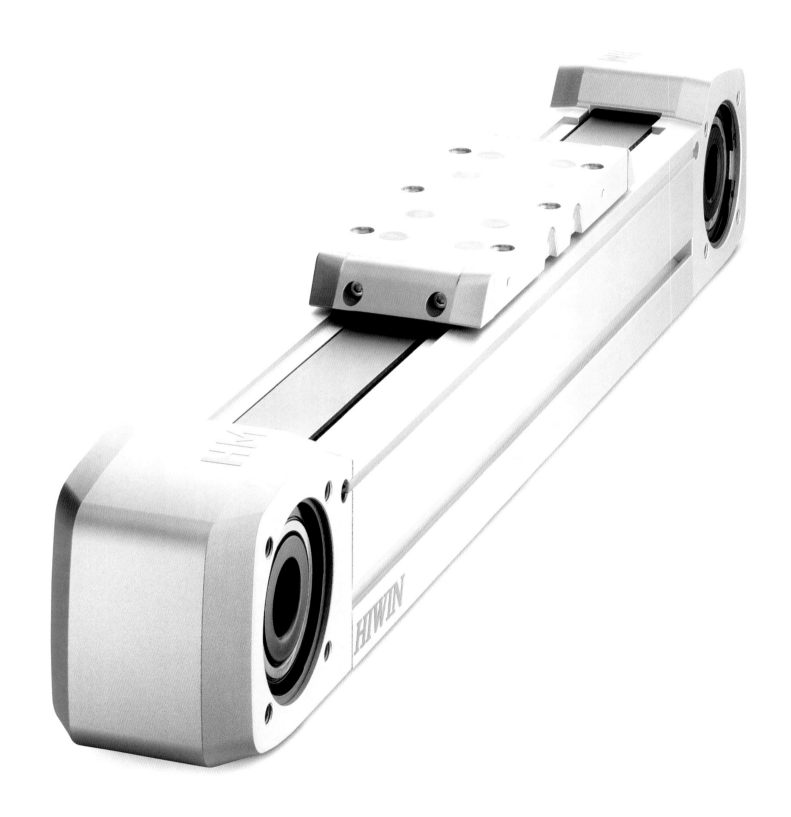

MELSEC iQ-R Series
MELSEC iQ-R-Baureihe
Programmable Logic Controllers
Modulares Steuerungssystem

Manufacturer
Mitsubishi Electric Corporation, Tokyo, Japan
In-house design
Takanori Miyake
Web
www.mitsubishielectric.co.jp

The MELSEC iQ-R Series has been developed specifically for automated machinery control carried out by less experienced staff. The housing is wider at the front in order to provide more space for the control and display unit. This makes printed characters easier to read, and the dot matrix LEDs can be expanded to form a larger display. The LEDs for the indication of errors are clearly positioned in a horizontal row at the top of the device. The controls and the wiring are situated behind a cover that opens vertically and swings completely out of the way.

Die Baureihe MELSEC iQ-R ist speziell auf die Steuerung von Maschinen durch weniger erfahrenes Personal ausgelegt. Das Gehäuse ist vorne breiter, um mehr Platz für die Bedien- und Anzeigeeinheit zu schaffen. So lassen sich Beschriftungen einfacher ablesen und die Punktmatrix-LEDs können zu einem größeren Display erweitert werden. Die für Fehlermeldungen zuständigen LEDs liegen gut sichtbar in einer waagerechten Reihe oben am Gerät. Die Steuerelemente und Verdrahtung befinden sich hinter einer sich senkrecht öffnenden Abdeckung, die vollständig aus dem Weg geklappt werden kann.

Statement by the jury
The straightforward layout of this control system makes a significant contribution to its safe use. The clean design enables quick access to all settings.

Begründung der Jury
Die Übersichtlichkeit des Steuerungssystems trägt in hohem Maße zur Sicherheit bei. Die saubere Gestaltung ermöglicht einen schnellen Zugriff auf alle Einstellungen.

AnkerBox
Mobile Charging Station
Mobile Ladestation

Manufacturer
Hunan Oceanwing E-commerce Co., Ltd., Changsha, China
In-house design
Lin Yen Ting, Bai Xue Feng, Zhang Chen Yu
Web
www.oceanwing.com
Honourable Mention

The AnkerBox is a publicly accessible charging station, which enables registered users to recharge their mobile devices on the go. An app indicates where the next charging station is located, for instance in a cafe or shop. Each station has either six or twelve rechargeable batteries, which can be taken out of the box and connected to an iOS or Android device. The different colours indicate which battery is suited to which device.

Die AnkerBox ist eine öffentlich zugängliche Ladestation, die registrierten Nutzern ermöglicht, ihre mobilen Endgeräte unterwegs aufzuladen. Eine App zeigt an, wo sich die nächstgelegene Ladestation befindet, z. B. in einem Café oder Geschäft. In jeder Station befinden sich entweder sechs oder zwölf Akkus, die aus der Box herausgenommen und an ein iOS- oder Android-Gerät angeschlossen werden können. Die unterschiedlichen Farben kommunizieren, welcher Akku sich für welches Gerät eignet.

Statement by the jury
The AnkerBox is based on an innovative idea: using it is as straightforward as its minimalist appearance.

Begründung der Jury
Hinter der AnkerBox steckt eine innovative Idee: Ihre Anwendung ist ebenso simpel wie ihr minimalistisches Erscheinungsbild

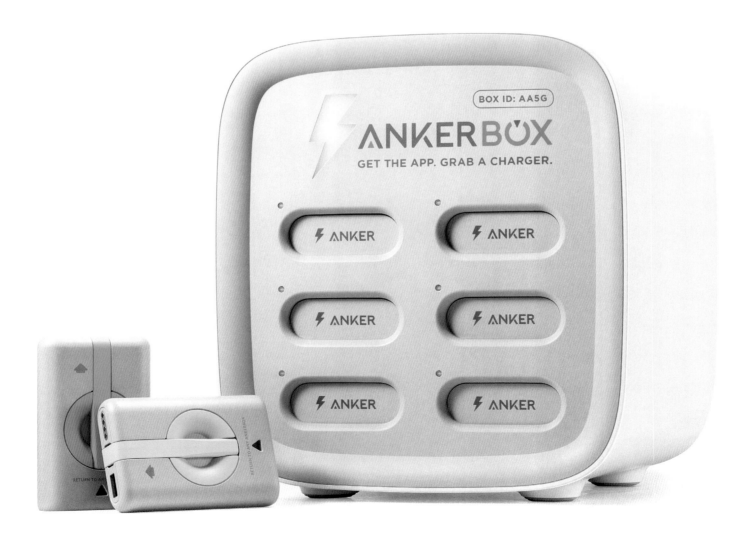

THEDRA
Water-Mixing Valve for Faucets
Mischkartusche

Manufacturer
SEDAL, Sant Andreu de la Barca, Spain
In-house design
Joan Porquer
Web
www.sedal.com

The Thedra water-mixing valve is a water- and energy-saving control unit for the operation of a single-lever water faucet. It is made of high-strength and high-density materials that withstand extreme loads. The ceramic set is packed with the so-called Sedalox ceramic material featuring Nano Shelter Technology that extends life twice as long. The redesign of the movable ceramic holder and the valve base results in a distinct noise-cancelling effect.

Die Mischkartusche Thedra ist eine wasser- und energiesparende Steuereinheit zur Bedienung eines Einhebel-Wasserhahns. Ihre hochfesten und hochdichten Materialien halten extremen Belastungen stand. Die Keramikteile bestehen aus sogenanntem Sedalox mit Nanoschutztechnologie, was die Lebensdauer um das Doppelte verlängert. Das Design der beweglichen Keramikhalterung und des Ventilfußes wurde überarbeitet, was für eine deutlich bessere Geräuschunterdrückung sorgt.

Statement by the jury
Thedra captivates with its well-conceived design and high-quality integration of robust materials, which ensure high performance and minimal wear and tear.

Begründung der Jury
Thedra besticht durch eine durchdachte Gestaltung und wertige Verarbeitung robuster Materialien, die für eine hohe Leistung und geringen Verschleiß sorgen.

SUN2000S
Photovoltaic Inverter
Photovoltaik-Wechselrichter

Manufacturer
Huawei Technologies Co., Ltd., Shenzhen, China
In-house design
Guan Yu
Design
designaffairs (Stefan Hillenmayer), Munich, Germany
Web
www.huawei.com
www.designaffairs.com

The SUN2000S photovoltaic inverter has a very lightweight aluminium housing with passive cooling. Indoor and outdoor assembly can be carried out in a time-efficient and user-friendly manner. Installation time is less than 15 minutes thanks to a convenient wall mount and an easily accessible cable connection area, as well as an app that completes the software setup in just two steps. The graphic interface displays the operating status in the form of an arc of light, which is inspired by a sunrise.

Der Photovoltaik-Wechselrichter SUN2000S hat ein sehr leichtes Aluminiumgehäuse mit passiver Kühlung. Die Innen- und Außenmontage kann zeitsparend und anwenderfreundlich durchgeführt werden. Aufgrund der praktischen Wandhalterung, dem gut zugänglichen Kabelanschlussbereich und einer App, welche die Inbetriebnahme in nur zwei Schritten abschließt, beträgt die Installationszeit weniger als 15 Minuten. Das grafische Interface zeigt den Betriebsstatus in Form eines Lichtbogens an, der von einem Sonnenaufgang inspiriert ist.

Statement by the jury
The aesthetics of the SUN2000S combines organic forms with a technical character, excellently reflecting its task of harnessing solar energy.

Begründung der Jury
Die Ästhetik des SUN2000S vereint organische Formen mit einem technischen Charakter. Dies spiegelt hervorragend seine Aufgabe wider, Solarenergie nutzbar zu machen.

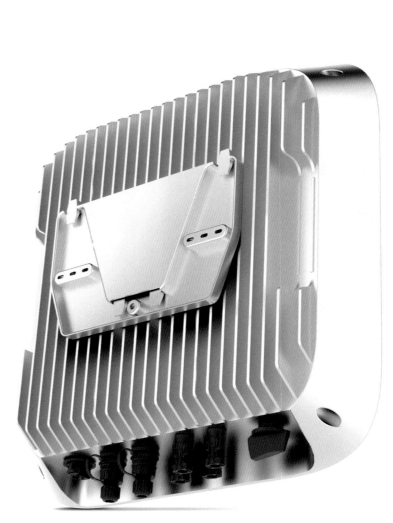

USB 3 uEye XC
Industrial Camera
Industriekamera

Manufacturer
IDS Imaging Development Systems GmbH,
Obersulm, Germany
Design
ipdd GmbH & Co. KG, Stuttgart, Germany
Web
www.ids-imaging.com
www.ipdd.com

The USB 3 uEye XC offers the comfort of a digital camera while simultaneously providing high-resolution images at increased speed. The look of the camera is modelled after its main field of application involving kiosk systems, access control, logistics and medical technology. Additional functions enable automated use. The magnesium housing with its compact dimensions is not only particularly space-saving, but also robust and lightweight.

Statement by the jury
This industrial camera captivates with its unconventional design, which gives rise to a multiform profile and demonstrates marked individuality.

Die USB 3 uEye XC verfügt über den Komfort einer Digitalkamera und liefert dabei selbständig mit hoher Geschwindigkeit hochauflösende Bilder. Das Aussehen der Kamera orientiert sich an ihren Haupteinsatzgebieten in Kiosksystemen, Zugangskontrollen, in der Logistik sowie Medizintechnik. Zusätzliche Funktionen ermöglichen den Automatikbetrieb. Das Gehäuse aus Magnesium ist mit seiner kompakten Abmessungen nicht nur besonders platzsparend, sondern auch robust und leicht.

Begründung der Jury
Die Industriekamera fasziniert durch ihre eigenwillige Geometrie, die ein vielförmiges Profil entstehen lässt und ausgesprochene Individualität beweist.

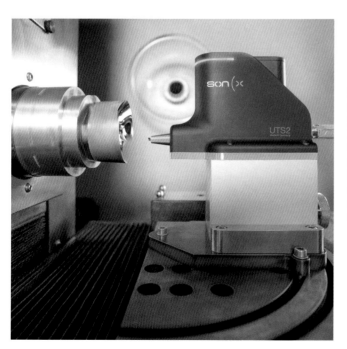

UTS2
Ultrasonic Tooling System
Ultraschall-Werkzeug-System

Manufacturer
son-x GmbH, Aachen, Germany
Design
Manuel Aydt, Pforzheim, Germany
crosscreative (Tom Nassal), Recklinghausen, Germany
Web
www.son-x.com
www.manuel-aydt.de
www.crosscreative.de

The UTS2 ultrasonic tooling system enables direct ultra-precision processing of hardened steel and glass. The housing has a clear geometric structure, which conveys the machine's high precision. The soft surface transitions direct the focus to the diamond tool tip. The blue status LED at the front and the illuminated ring around the on/off switch indicate that both mechanical and ultrasound processes are in progress.

Statement by the jury
Compact design and seamless surfaces give the UTS2 a valuable appearance, lending expression to the system's high quality.

Das Ultraschall-Werkzeug-System UTS2 ermöglicht die direkte Ultrapräzisionsbearbeitung von gehärtetem Stahl und Glas. Das Gehäuse ist geometrisch klar strukturiert, was die hohe Genauigkeit der Maschine widerspiegelt. Die weichen Flächenübergänge lenken den Fokus auf die Diamantwerkzeugspitze. Die blau leuchtende Status-LED im vorderen Bereich und der Leuchtring um den An-/Ausschalter zeigen visuell an, dass neben dem mechanischen auch ein Ultraschallprozess abläuft.

Begründung der Jury
Das UTS2 erlangt durch sein kompaktes Design und die nahtlose Beschaffenheit der Flächen eine wertige Optik, welche die hohe Qualität des Systems ausdrückt.

WLX
Modular Wide Belt Conveyor
Modularer Mattenkettenförderer

Manufacturer
FlexLink AB, Göteborg, Sweden
In-house design
Josef Snabb, Magnus Askerdal
Web
www.flexlink.com
Honourable Mention

The WLX modular wide belt conveyor in stainless steel is available as a module or a complete system. The conveyor is suited for the handling of pouches, liquid carton packaging or any packed food product. Focus areas of the design are cleanliness, operator safety and a low cost of ownership. The chain can easily be lifted by the operator, reducing heavy lifts and making the interior easy to clean. Small openings prevent pinch points, and there are no sharp edges. The conveyor design facilitates a constant cleaning result and short drying time, adding valuable production time.

Der modulare Mattenkettenförderer WLX aus Edelstahl ist als Komponente oder komplettes System erhältlich. Der Förderer eignet sich für das Handling von Beuteln, Kartons oder anderen verpackten Lebensmitteln. Bei der Entwicklung waren Reinigbarkeit, Bedienersicherheit und niedrige Betriebskosten wichtig. Die Kette lässt sich ohne Kraftaufwand anheben, sodass das innere einfach zu reinigen ist. Kleine Öffnungen verhindern Quetschungen. Es gibt keine spitzen Ecken und Kanten. Die Konstruktion ermöglicht einheitliche Reinigungsergebnisse und kurze Trocknungszeiten, was die Produktionszeit steigert.

Statement by the jury
The design of this wide belt conveyor was developed with a major focus on meeting high standards of hygiene and safety.

Begründung der Jury
Bei der Konstruktion des Mattenkettenförderers wurde sehr viel Wert darauf gelegt, hohe Ansprüche an die Hygiene und Sicherheit zu erfüllen.

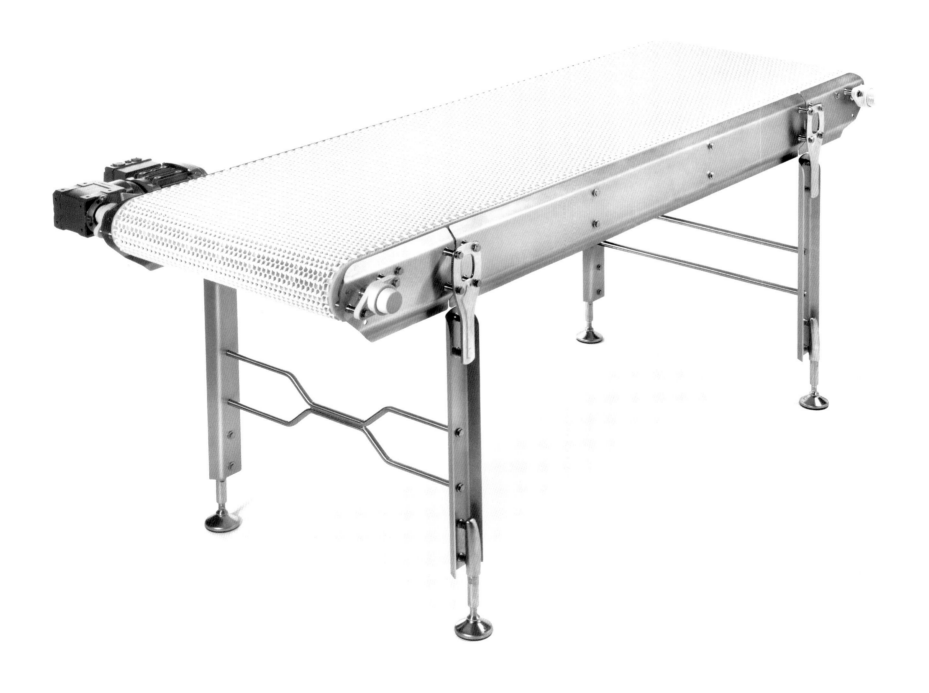

CR5000
Coin Recycler
Münzrecycler

Manufacturer
Crane Payment Innovations, CPI Manchester, Oldham, Great Britain
In-house design
Robert Blythin
Web
www.cranepi.com
Honourable Mention

The CR5000 coin recycler not only separates and validates coins of all common currencies but also actively filters debris. The number of components has been reduced to a minimum in order to increase the machine's reliability. In contrast to conventional models made of metal, this coin recycler is polymer-based, without compromising on robustness. The lit control panel at the front, with its easy-to-understand symbols, helps the user to identify possible error sources.

Der Münzrecycler CR5000 verarbeitet nicht nur Münzen aller gängigen Währungen, sondern befreit sie auch von Verschmutzungen. Die Anzahl der Bauteile wurde auf ein Minimum reduziert, um die Zuverlässigkeit der Maschine zu erhöhen. Im Gegensatz zu herkömmlichen Modellen aus Metall ist der Münzrecycler aus Polymer gefertigt, ohne dabei an Robustheit einzubüßen. Das beleuchtete Frontbedienelement mit seiner leicht verständlichen Symbolik hilft dem Anwender, mögliche Störungen schnell zu identifizieren.

Statement by the jury
The user interfaces of this coin recycler are distinctly marked using bright colours so as to facilitate safe and intuitive use.

Begründung der Jury
Die Benutzerschnittstellen des Münzrecyclers sind durch die leuchtenden Farben deutlich gekennzeichnet und ermöglichen so eine intuitive, sichere Bedienung.

SkyTender
Fully Automated
Beverage Trolley
Vollautomatischer
Getränketrolley

Manufacturer
SkyTender Solutions GmbH,
Herborn, Germany
In-house design
Web
www.skytendersolutions.com
Honourable Mention

The SkyTender beverage trolley is a fully automatic solution, which does not require an external electricity or water supply. At the touch of a button, the dispensing unit slides out of the trolley. At two dispensing points users can select hot, cold or carbonated beverages on the respective touchscreen. Waste resulting from empty cans or bottles is thereby eliminated. A specially developed filtration system guarantees consistent water quality. An integrated IT system facilitates the needs-oriented and predictive planning of the beverage inventory.

Statement by the jury
The SkyTender combines the functions of a beverage dispenser with the mobility of an airplane trolley in an innovative way.

Bei dem Getränketrolley SkyTender handelt es sich um eine vollautomatische Lösung, die ohne einen direkten Strom- oder Wasseranschluss auskommt. Die Zapfanlage fährt per Knopfdruck aus dem Wagen heraus. Die beiden Ausschankpunkte werden jeweils über einen Touchscreen bedient, es kann zwischen heißen, kalten und kohlensäurehaltigen Getränken gewählt werden. Abfall durch leere Dosen oder Flaschen wird so vermieden. Ein speziell entwickeltes Filtersystem garantiert eine konstante Wasserqualität. Das integrierte IT-System ermöglicht eine bedarfsgerechte und vorausschauende Planung des Getränkebestands.

Begründung der Jury
Auf innovative Weise verbindet der SkyTender die Funktionen eines Getränkeautomats mit der Mobilität eines Flugzeugtrolleys.

MetraSCAN 3D/HandyPROBE/C-Track
Portable 3D Measurement System
Tragbares 3D-Messsystem

Manufacturer
Creaform Inc (Ametek Inc),
Lévis, Québec, Canada

In-house design
François Lessard, Nicolas Lebrun

Web
www.creaform3d.com

reddot award 2016
best of the best

Form for precision

In many industrial areas, consistency and replication in the digital process chain are key to high added value. The portable 3D measurement system, consisting of the optical CMM scanner MetraSCAN 3D, the coordinate measuring machine (CMM) HandyPROBE as well as the C-Track tracker, was designed for engineers and their need for measurement accuracy and comprehensive flexibility. The result is a concept with perfectly matched and balanced components that are ready for operation even at unsteady conditions. The individual components are reliable and can interact with one another effectively. Optimised with FEA (Finite Element Analysis), its carbon structure is highly robust and provides a clear reduction in weight. In addition, they are marked by an ergonomic design and an intuitive approach towards handling. The C-Track optical tracker features high-performance dual-camera sensors. The device ensures high stability and is easy to transport thanks to an integrated handle. Another impressive innovation is the option to operate the HandyPROBE in two positions, allowing users to choose between a more stable "stylus pen style" and a more versatile "joystick style". This measurement system for professional engineering offers high user comfort and functionality – it aestheticises everyday work with its well-proportioned design idiom.

Form für die Präzision

In vielen Bereichen der Industrie ist die Durchgängigkeit der digitalen Prozesskette der Schlüssel für eine hohe Wertschöpfung. Das tragbare 3D-Messsystem, bestehend aus dem optischen CMM-Scanner MetraSCAN 3D, dem Koordinatenmessgerät (Coordinate Measuring Machine – CMM) HandyPROBE sowie dem Tracker C-Track, wurde für Ingenieure konzipiert, um genaue Messergebnisse und eine umfassende Flexibilität zu bieten. Das Ergebnis ist ein Konzept mit perfekt aufeinander abgestimmten Komponenten, die auch unter widrigen Bedingungen einsatzbereit sind. Die einzelnen Elemente arbeiten zuverlässig und können effektiv untereinander interagieren. Ihre durch FEA (Finite Element Analysis) optimierte Carbon-Struktur ist sehr robust und ermöglicht eine deutliche Verringerung des Gewichts. Sie zeichnen sich außerdem durch ihre ergonomische Gestaltung sowie die intuitive Art der Bedienung aus. Der optische Tracker C-Track verfügt über leistungsfähige Dual-Kamera-Sensoren. Er bietet eine hohe Stabilität und lässt sich mit einem schlüssig integrierten Griff leicht transportieren. Eine beeindruckende Innovation ist die Option, die Handy-PROBE in zwei Positionen zu bedienen, der Nutzer kann zwischen dem stabileren „Stylus Pen Style" und dem vielseitigeren „Joystick Style" wählen. Dieses Messsystem bietet für den beruflichen Alltag sehr viel Komfort und Funktionalität – mit seiner wohlproportionierten Formensprache ästhetisiert es den industriellen Bereich.

Statement by the jury

Thanks to this portable 3D measurement system, highly complex data can be collected with absolute accuracy. It fascinates with a lightweight structure, easy-to-use functionality, perfect ergonomics and an economical material usage. The system's components blend into a highly symbolic and emotionalising appearance. The device embodies an overall solution of high design quality with an exemplary character.

Begründung der Jury

Mittels dieses tragbaren 3D-Messsystems lassen sich hochkomplexe Daten mit absoluter Präzision erheben. Es begeistert mit seiner Leichtbaustruktur, einer gut handhabbaren Funktionalität, perfekter Ergonomie sowie sparsamem Materialeinsatz. Die Systemkomponenten vermitteln einen hohen symbolischen und emotionalen Gehalt. Es ist eine Gesamtlösung von hoher gestalterischer Qualität, die Vorbildcharakter besitzt

Designer portrait
See page 38
Siehe Seite 38

USTER TESTER 6
Yarn Evenness Tester
Garn-Prüfgerät

Manufacturer
Uster Technologies AG, Uster, Switzerland
Design
Industrial Designers, Chrétien & Apothéloz GmbH
(Christophe Apothéloz), Zürich, Switzerland
Web
www.uster.com
www.industrialdesigners.ch

The Uster Tester 6 is used in spinning mills to measure the evenness of yarn. Its main design characteristic is a curved structural form, lending the machine both visual elegance and practical value. The shape of the measuring unit is curved towards the front and provides an optimal guide path for the yarn, while the contoured base enables the operator to stand in an ideal position for accessing the touchscreen. The glossy and matt chrome finishes together with black components reflect the technical dimensions of the tester.

Der Uster Tester 6 wird in Spinnereien eingesetzt, um die Gleichmäßigkeit von Garnen zu prüfen. Das zentrale Gestaltungsmerkmal ist die gebogene Bauform, die dem Gerät sowohl optische Eleganz verleiht als auch von praktischem Nutzen ist. Die nach vorne gewölbte Front der Messeinheit gibt die optimale Führung des Garns vor, während der geschwungene Unterbau es dem Benutzer erlaubt, ideal zum Touchscreen zu stehen. Die Elemente aus glänzendem und mattem Chrom in Kombination mit Komponenten in Schwarz spiegeln die technische Dimension des Testinstruments wider.

Statement by the jury
Thanks to a successful combination of structural volumes and balanced proportions, this testing device has a visually open and light overall appearance.

Begründung der Jury
Dank eines gekonnten Zusammenspiels von Volumina und ausgewogener Proportionen wirkt das Prüfgerät insgesamt offen und optisch leicht.

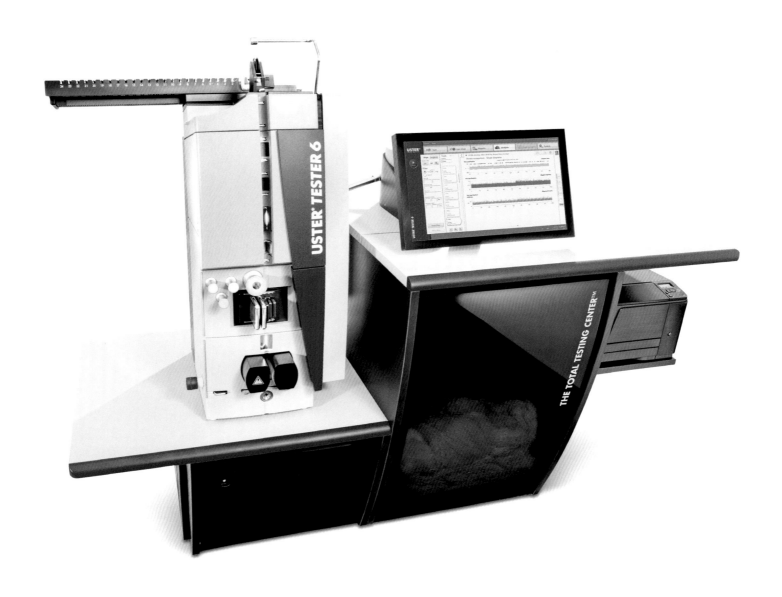

KONE DT6
Lift Performance Data Analysis Tool
Analysetool für Aufzuganlagen

Manufacturer
KONE Corporation, Hyvinkää, Finland
In-house design
Web
www.kone.com

Operators of lifts are required to employ the latest technology and to keep them functioning correctly. The Kone DT6 lift performance data analysis too with push-button operation enables lifts to be monitored remotely and collects standardised data on the ride quality for internal business analysis. The tool is directly connected to a lift and registers even the most minute vibrations and operation noises via three contact points. This enables the device to provide much more reliable measurements than a laptop or other peripheral devices.

Die Betreiber von Aufzuganlagen sind verpflichtet, diese auf dem aktuellen Stand der Technik und in ordnungsgemäßem Zustand zu halten. Das Analysetool Kone DT6 mit Drucktastenbedienung ermöglicht die Fernüberwachung von Aufzügen und sammelt standardisierte Daten über die Fahrqualität für die interne Geschäftsanalyse. Das Tool wird direkt an einen Aufzug gekoppelt und registriert über drei Kontaktpunkte kleinste Vibrationen und Fahrgeräusche. Dadurch bietet das System messtechnisch sehr viel zuverlässigere Informationen als ein Laptop oder andere Peripheriegeräte.

Statement by the jury
The Kone DT6 convinces with its smooth curved surfaces and flat form, which provide a stable support surface and allow it to assume any given position.

Begründung der Jury
Das Kone DT6 überzeugt durch seine rundlaufenden, glatten Oberflächen und die flache Form. Dadurch besitzt es eine stabile Auflagefläche und findet überall Platz.

Pegasus:Backpack
Mobile Mapping System
Mobiles Vermessungssystem

Manufacturer
Leica Geosystems AG,
Heerbrugg, Switzerland
Design
prodesign-Hetzenecker,
Fürstenfeldbruck, Germany
Web
www.leica-geosystems.com
www.prodesignnet.de

The Pegasus:Backpack was developed to
visually document work progress at
building sites. With a combination of
five cameras and two laser sensors,
which are all housed in the ultra-light-
weight, ergonomic and easy-to-carry
carbon-fibre chassis, a 3D view of indoor
and outdoor areas is created. Thanks to
robotic technology, lasers are used to
identify the position instead of GPS. A
durable ripstop nylon fabric protects the
high-tech instruments from water, sand
and dust. The batteries are hidden behind a zip fastener.

Statement by the jury
The Pegasus:Backpack presents a new
type of design in the mobile mapping
field. The sophisticated concept makes it
very convenient to carry.

Der Pegasus:Backpack wurde entwickelt,
um Arbeitsfortschritte auf Baustellen
bildlich zu dokumentieren. Mit einer Kom-
bination aus fünf Kameras und zwei
Lasersensoren, die alle in einem ultraleich-
ten und ergonomisch zu tragenden
Kohlefaser-Chassis untergebracht sind,
wird eine 3D-Ansicht von Innen- und
Außenbereichen erstellt. Durch Roboter-
technik wird die Position nicht mittels
GPS, sondern mit Lasern bestimmt.
Die Hightech-Instrumente sind durch ein
langlebiges Ripstop-Nylon-Gewebe vor
Wasser, Sand und Staub geschützt. Die
Batterien liegen versteckt hinter einem
Reißverschluss.

Begründung der Jury
Mit dem Pegasus:Backpack wurde eine
neue Art der Gestaltung für die Geo-
Datenerfassung entwickelt. Die durch-
dachte Konzeption bietet einen hohen
Tragekomfort.

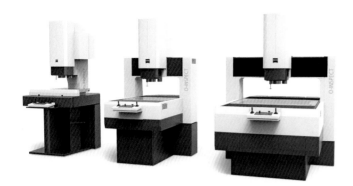

O-INSPECT
Multisensor Measuring Machines
Multisensor-Messgeräte

Manufacturer
Carl Zeiss Industrielle Messtechnik GmbH,
Oberkochen, Germany
Design
Henssler und Schultheiss Fullservice Product-
design GmbH, Schwäbisch Gmünd, Germany
Web
www.zeiss.de
www.henssler-schultheiss.de

The O-Inspect combines tactile scanning and optical measuring in one device. The different models were developed for various measuring volumes. The telecentric 12x zoom lens and the adaptive lighting system ensure an excellent reproduction quality of the workpieces requiring testing. Due to completely covered guideways and an integrated damping system, which compensates ground vibrations, the machines can be located directly at the production site.

Statement by the jury
Thanks to their almost architectural sense of lines, which is further highlighted by black-and-white contrasting, these measuring machines present an impressively clear design.

O-Inspect vereint taktiles Scannen und optisches Messen in einem Gerät. Die verschiedenen Modelle wurden für unterschiedliche Messvolumina konzipiert. Das telezentrische 12-fach Zoomobjektiv und das adaptive Beleuchtungssystem gewährleisten eine ausgezeichnete Abbildungsqualität der zu prüfenden Werkstücke. Dank der verkleideten Führungsbahnen und einer integrierten Dämpfung, die Bodenschwingungen ausgleicht, können die Geräte direkt in der Produktionsstätte stehen.

Begründung der Jury
Die Messgeräte sind durch die fast architektonische Linienführung, welche durch die Schwarz-Weiß-Kontraste noch betont wird, beeindruckend klar strukturiert.

ColorCube
Spectrophotometer
Spektralphotometer

Manufacturer
ColorLite GmbH, Katlenburg-Lindau,
Germany
In-house design
Web
www.colorlite.de

The ColorCube spectrophotometer compares a colour sample to a specific product's hue for the purpose of colour matching. Its unibody aluminium housing and high-performance LED light sources have high durability and ensure reliable measurement results. The device features user-friendly one-button operation and a visual pass/fail indicator. Using a glass plate lit either in green or red, it provides clear feedback on whether the measurements are within the tolerance range.

Statement by the jury
Its monolithic form gives the ColorCube an iconic character. The illuminated glass surface is a true eye-catcher.

Das Spektralphotometer ColorCube dient dazu, eine Farbprobe mit einem spezifischen Produktfarbton abzugleichen. Das Unibody-Gehäuse aus Aluminium und die Hochleistungs-LEDs haben eine lange Lebensdauer und sorgen für sichere Messergebnisse. Das Gerät verfügt über eine benutzerfreundliche Ein-Knopf-Bedienung und eine visuelle Pass-/Fail-Anzeige. Diese gibt durch die grün oder rot aufleuchtende Glasplatte eine klare Rückmeldung darüber, ob die Messwerte im Toleranzbereich liegen.

Begründung der Jury
Die monolithische Form verleiht dem ColorCube einen ikonischen Charakter. Die beleuchtete Glasoberfläche ist ein echter Hingucker.

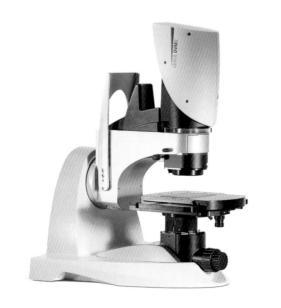

Leica DVM6
Digital Microscope
Digitalmikroskop

Manufacturer
Leica Microsystems AG,
Heerbrugg, Switzerland
In-house design
Design
Industrial Designers,
Chrétien & Apothéloz GmbH
(Christophe Apothéloz),
Zürich, Switzerland
Web
www.leica-microsystems.com
www.industrialdesigners.ch
Honourable Mention

With the Leica DVM6 digital microscope, objects the size of a grain of sand can be viewed using continuously variable magnification and displayed in a full-screen view. With the help of the rotation and tilting functions, the smallest details may be inspected from all sides and different angles. The microscope has been designed so that only one hand is sufficient to operate it. Its symmetrical form and compact dimensions allow for an easy grip for right-handers and left-handers alike.

Statement by the jury
The functional quality of this digital microscope is reflected in its form, characterised by elongated lines and dynamic curves.

Mit dem Digitalmikroskop Leica DVM6 lassen sich Objekte von der Größe eines Sandkorns stufenlos vergrößern und bildschirmfüllend darstellen. Mithilfe der Dreh- und Kippfunktionen können feinste Details von allen Seiten und aus verschiedenen Blickwinkeln betrachtet werden. Das Mikroskop ist so konzipiert, dass es mit nur einer Hand bedient werden kann. Durch die symmetrische Form und die kompakten Dimensionen fällt Rechts- und Linkshändern das Greifen gleichermaßen leicht.

Begründung der Jury
Der funktionale Charakter des Digitalmikroskops spiegelt sich in der Form wider, die durch gestreckte Linien und dynamische Schwünge geprägt ist.

Wiz Stick
Internet Security Dongle
Internetsicherheitsdongle

Manufacturer
kt, korea telecom, Seoul, South Korea
In-house design
Design
Designmu, Seoul, South Korea
Web
www.kt.com
www.designmu.com

You can also find this product in
Dieses Produkt finden Sie auch in
Working
Page 263
Seite 263

The Wiz Stick offers protection from hacker attacks and data theft. It is inserted into and removed from computers like a key and is therefore not restricted to a fixed workstation. In order to make it easy for users to carry the stick, it has been integrated into the company's identification card and can be worn comfortably around the neck hanging from a lanyard, where it is always within reach. In addition, it enables authentication via fingerprint scan, so that no passwords are required.

Statement by the jury
The Wiz Stick impresses with its state-of-the-art technology and high-quality design, which makes it look more like a fashionable accessory.

Der Wiz Stick schützt vor Hacker-Angriffen und Datendiebstahl. Er wird wie ein Schlüssel in den Computer ein- und ausgesteckt, sodass er nicht an einen festen Arbeitsplatz gebunden ist. Damit der Stick nicht separat mit sich geführt werden muss, ist er in den Firmenausweis integriert und wird bequem an einer Schlaufe um den Hals getragen, wo er immer griffbereit ist. Zudem ermöglicht er die Authentifizierung per Fingerabdruck-Scan, sodass Passwörter überflüssig werden.

Begründung der Jury
Der Wiz Stick beeindruckt mit fortschrittlicher Technologie und einem wertigen Design, das ihn mehr wie ein modisches Accessoire wirken lässt.

microScan3
Safety Laser Scanner
Sicherheitslaserscanner

Manufacturer
SICK AG, Waldkirch, Germany
In-house design
Design
2ND WEST GmbH, Rapperswil, Switzerland
Web
www.sick.com
www.2ndwest.ch

The microScan3 safety laser scanner features patented safeHDDM scan technology that converts a large scanning range into a compact structural design. Simultaneously, the new technology increases the device's reliability if there is dust or ambient light in the environment. The status indicators, the LEDs and the display are easily visible from many angles. Important diagnostic messages can be selected directly via keys while the machine is running and are shown in plain text on the display.

Statement by the jury
The functional areas and the operating panel of the microScan3 are clearly divided. The tidy design makes it intuitive to operate.

Der Sicherheitslaserscanner microScan3 verfügt über die patentierte safeHDDM-Scantechnologie, die eine große Schutzfeldreichweite in eine kompakte Bauform überführt. Gleichzeitig erhöht die neue Technologie die Zuverlässigkeit des Geräts bei Staub und Fremdlicht in der Umgebung. Die Statusanzeigen, LEDs und das Display sind aus vielen Blickwinkeln gut sichtbar. Wichtige Diagnosemeldungen können im laufenden Betrieb direkt über Tasten ausgewählt werden und erscheinen als Klartext auf dem Display.

Begründung der Jury
Die Funktionsbereiche und das Bedienfeld sind beim microScan3 klar unterteilt. Die übersichtliche Gestaltung ermöglicht eine intuitive Handhabung.

P-40
Endoscope
Endoskop

Manufacturer
Shenzhen Coantec Automation Technology Co., Ltd., Shenzhen, China
Design
Shenzhen Newplan Design Co., Ltd. (Shuai Liang, Jun Zhang), Shenzhen, China
Web
www.coantec.com
www.newplan.com.cn
Honourable Mention

The P-40 video endoscope has been developed for vehicle inspections in areas that are hard to access, such as the engine bay. The housing is characterised by its flat, lightweight shape and is waterproof. The connector socket framed in red links the camera probe to the joystick and can be removed from the housing, which makes it easy to replace the probes according to individual needs. The optimised angle between handle and joystick facilitates ergonomic handling.

Statement by the jury
This video endoscope captivates with its removable connector socket, which enables a quick replacement of the probes on site.

Das Videoendoskop P-40 dient zur Fahrzeuginspektion in schwer zugänglichen Bereichen wie dem Motorraum. Das Gehäuse zeichnet sich durch eine flache, leichte Bauweise aus und ist wasserdicht. Der rot eingefasste Anschlusssockel verbindet die Kamerasonde mit dem Joystick und kann aus dem Gehäuse herausgenommen werden. So lassen sich die Sonden je nach Anwendungssituation einfach und bequem austauschen. Der optimierte Winkel zwischen Griff und Joystick erlaubt eine ergonomische Handhabung.

Begründung der Jury
Das Videoendoskop besticht durch den herausnehmbaren Anschlusssockel, der einen schnellen Austausch der Sonden vor Ort ermöglicht.

AGV-31-MC500
Intelligent Transport Robot
Intelligenter Transportroboter

Manufacturer
Guangdong Jaten Robot & Automation Co., Ltd., Foshan, China
Design
Chinno Industrial Design Co., Ltd., Foshan, China
Web
www.jtrobots.com
www.chinno.cn

The AGV-31-MC500 intelligent transport robot moves independently through industrial buildings. It is equipped with warning lights, acoustic signals, infrared sensors and shock absorbers, which meet safety requirements. The design is inspired by the body position of a leopard that is ready to pounce. Due to the bevelled edges at the front, it is easier for the robot to reach underneath shelves. It is battery-powered and thus does not emit CO_2 or any other harmful substance. The robot's back footboard and maintenance doors ensure easy access.

Der intelligente Transportroboter AGV-31-MC500 bewegt sich selbständig durch die Werkhalle. Er ist mit Warnlichtern, akustischen Signalen, Infrarotsensoren und Stoßdämpfern ausgestattet, die für die notwendige Sicherheit sorgen. Bei der Gestaltung diente die Körperhaltung eines sprungbereiten Leoparden als Vorbild. Durch die vorderen abgeschrägten Kanten gelangt der Roboter leichter unter Regale. Er wird mit Batterien betrieben und stößt daher weder CO_2 noch andere Schadstoffe aus. Ein Trittbrett an der Rückseite und Wartungstüren gewährleisten eine gute Zugänglichkeit.

Statement by the jury
The front of the transport robot has face-like features, while the body displays an unobtrusive design, making it look both friendly and trustworthy.

Begründung der Jury
Die Front des Transportroboters trägt die Züge eines Gesichts, während der Korpus sehr zurückhaltend gestaltet ist. Dies wirkt sympathisch und vertrauenswürdig.

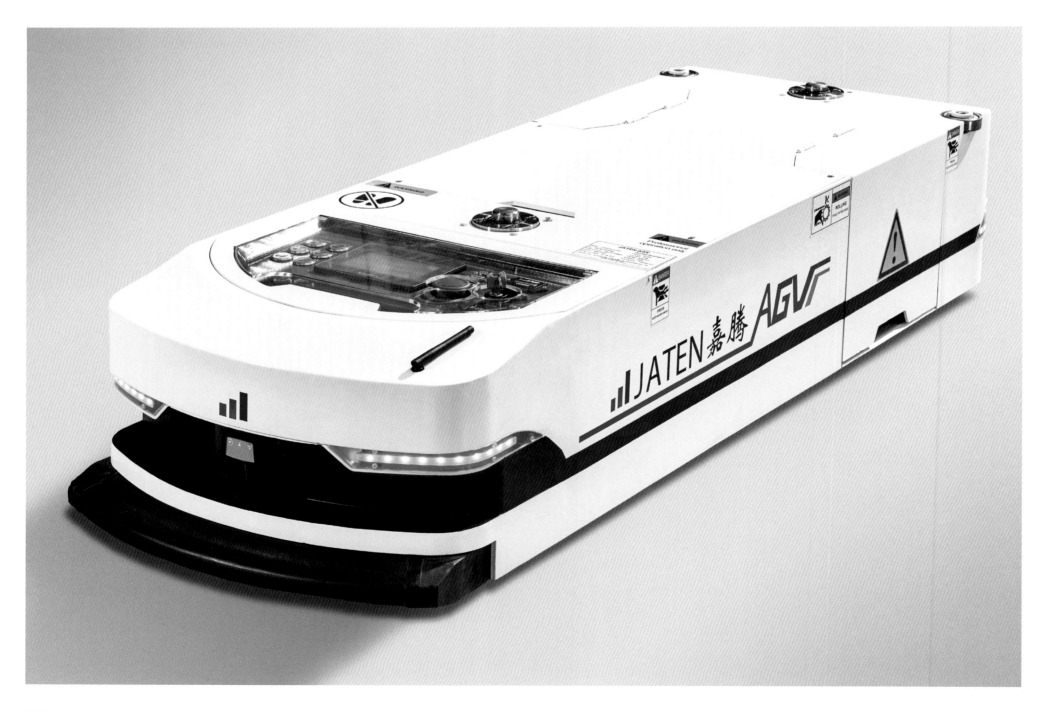

KR 120 nano F
Industrial Robot
Industrieroboter

Manufacturer
KUKA AG, Augsburg, Germany
In-house design
Achim Heinze, André Reekers, Dieter Schaab, Jorge Torres
Design
Sedmy Industriedesign, Augsburg, Germany
Web
www.kuka.com
www.relic.de

The KR 120 nano F industrial robot was optimised for the extreme conditions found in cleaning plants and washing cells. It is used in foundries and in the automotive industry. The mechanical parts of the robot are completely encapsulated and all electrical cables are installed inside the body. Its interior is pressurised with compressed air to prevent the infiltration of liquids. The coated surface is resistant to lye, acid, heat and corrosion. The design, with its expressive edges and metallic colour scheme, highlights the machine's toughness.

Der KR 120 nano F wurde für die extremen Bedingungen in Reinigungsanlagen und Waschzellen optimiert. Er wird in Gießereien und in der Motorenbaubranche eingesetzt. Der Roboter besitzt eine komplette Kapselung der Mechanik und einen durchgängig innenliegenden Kabelsatz. Sein Innenraum wird mit Druckluft beaufschlagt, um das Eindringen von Flüssigkeiten zu verhindern. Die beschichtete Oberfläche ist laugen-, säure-, hitze- und korrosionsbeständig. Das Design mit ausdruc<sstarken Kanten und einer metallischen Farbgebung unterstreicht die Resistenz der Maschine.

Statement by the jury
This powerful and agile robot has humanoid characteristics, which in addition to its technical dimensions lend it a unique emotional quality.

Begründung der Jury
Der kraftvolle und agile Roboter trägt humanoide Züge, die ihm neben seiner technischen Dimension auch eine besondere emotionale Qualität verleihen.

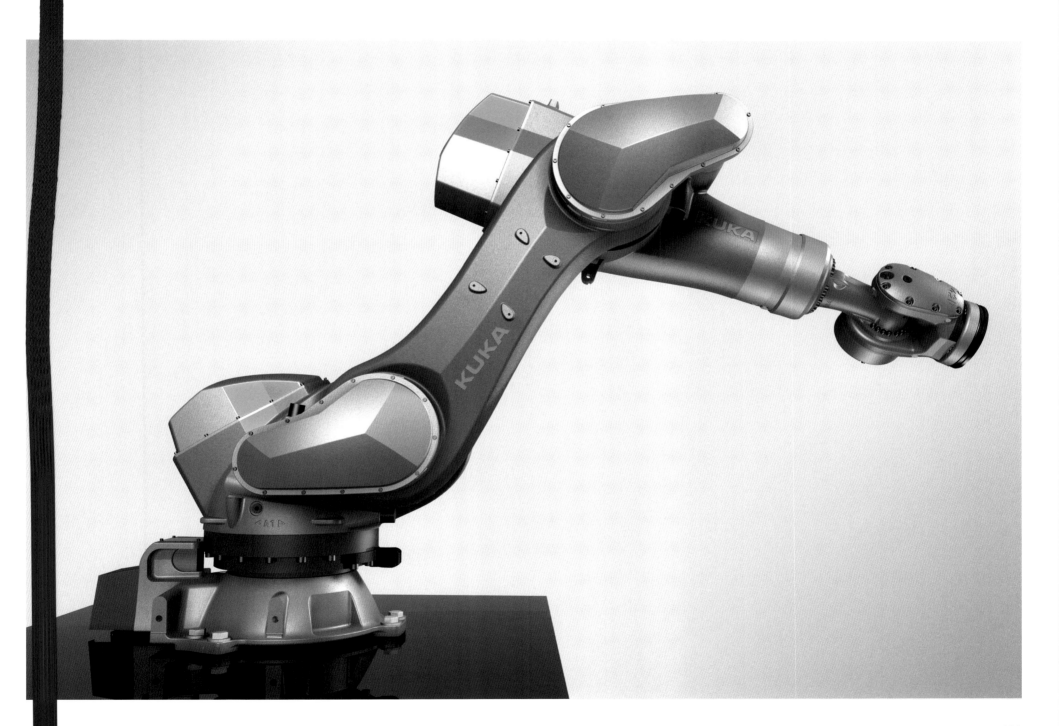

EXV-SF 16
High Lift Pallet Truck
Hochhubwagen

Manufacturer
STILL GmbH, Hamburg, Germany
Design
TEAMS Design (Ulrich Schweig), Esslingen,
Germany
Web
www.still.de
www.teamsdesign.com

The EXV-SF 16 high lift pallet truck
is no wider than a Euro-pallet, thus providing high manoeuvrability in confined
storage spaces. For a back-friendly,
shock- and vibration-free driving experience, the air-suspended stand-on
platform is adjustable to the driver's
weight. The lateral folding protection
arms are height-adjustable. The colour
display with its pictorial symbols promotes easy understanding, independent
of language.

Statement by the jury
The design of this high lift pallet truck
has been ergonomically thought out
down to the smallest detail. Its operation
is characterised by a strong self-explanatory quality.

Der Hochhubwagen EXV-SF 16 ist nicht
breiter als eine Europalette und dadurch
auch in engen Lagerräumen sehr wendig.
Für ein rückenschonendes, stoß- und
vibrationsfreies Fahrerlebnis sorgt die luft-
gedämpfte Standplattform, die an das
Gewicht des Fahrers angepasst werden
kann. Die ausklappbaren, seitlichen Schutz-
arme sind individuell in der Höhe verstellbar. Das Farbdisplay sorgt mit bildhaften
Symbolen für ein sprachunabhängiges
Verständnis.

Begründung der Jury
Die Gestaltung des Hochhubwagens ist bis
ins Detail ergonomisch durchdacht. Seine
Bedienung zeichnet sich durch ihre hohe
Selbsterklärungsqualität aus.

SKINNY POWER
Electric Stacker
Elektrostapler

Manufacturer
Ningbo Ruyi Joint Stock Co.,
Ltd., Ninghai, China
Design
ICO Creative Design Co.,
Ltd. (Yu Liao, Yin Bo Sun), Hefei, China
Web
www.xilin.com
www.ico-d.com

The Skinny Power electric stacker enables
the safe and fast stacking of pallets
with a minimum of power. It has a load-
carrying capacity of up to a ton. Due to
its reduced dimensions and particularly
small turning radius, the stacker is highly
manoeuvrable and can be used in narrow
aisles and in very confined spaces, such
as containers. The centrally located kill
switch ensures safe operation.

Statement by the jury
The electric pallet truck captivates with
its robust, round form and its extremely
short front chassis, which requires little
space.

Der Elektrostapler Skinny Power ermöglicht
das sichere und schnelle Einstapeln von
Paletten bei geringem Kraftaufwand. Seine
Tragkraft beträgt bis zu einer Tonne.
Aufgrund seiner geringen Dimensionen und
einem sehr kleinen Wenderadius ist der
Stapler besonders manövrierfähig und auch
in schmalen Gängen und auf engstem
Raum, z. B. in Containern, zu verwenden.
Der zentral gelegene Notausschalter garan-
tiert eine sichere Bedienung

Begründung der Jury
Der Elektrostapler punktet mit seiner robus-
ten runden Form und seiner extrem kurzen
Vorderbaulänge, wodurch er nur wenig
Platz in Anspruch nimmt.

AGV-37-ID2500
Intelligent Transport Robot
Intelligenter Transportroboter

Manufacturer
Guangdong Jaten
Robot & Automation Co., Ltd., Foshan, China
Design
Chinno Industrial Design Co.,
Ltd., Foshan, China
Web
www.jtrobots.com
www.chinno.cn
Honourable Mention

The AGV-37-ID2500 intelligent transport robot is equipped with an automated navigation system and does not require any equipment to be permanently installed on the ground in order to reliably transport materials from one place to another. The laser measuring system continuously identifies the vehicle's current position and scans the environment for obstacles. Since it is powered by batteries, the robot runs smoothly and cleanly. Its robust design with front-wheel drive makes it likewise suitable for use in rough work environments.

Statement by the jury
The mobility of this transport robot is successfully conveyed visually through its forward-leaning design.

Der intelligente Transportrobotor AGV-37-ID2500 ist mit einem Autonavigationssystem ausgestattet und benötigt keine fest am Boden installierten Vorrichtungen, um Material zielsicher von einem Ort zum anderen zu bringen. Das Lasermesssystem ermittelt permanent die aktuelle Fahrzeugposition und scannt die Umgebung auf Hindernisse ab. Durch den Batteriebetrieb läuft der Roboter ruhig und ist sauber im Gebrauch. Seine robuste Bauweise mit Vorderradantrieb ermöglicht den Einsatz auch in rauen Arbeitsumgebungen.

Begründung der Jury
Die Mobilität des Transportroboters drückt sich optisch überzeugend in seiner nach vorne geneigten Bauform aus.

Fingertip Controller
(7 Series Electric Forklifts)
Fingertip-Steuerung
(7er-Serie Elektrostapler)

Manufacturer
Doosan Corporation Industrial Vehicle,
Incheon, South Korea
In-house design
Doosan Infracore (Jin-Hup Yeu, Dong-Chearl
Lee, Hyun-Joong Kim, Eun-Sook Seo)
Web
www.doosan-iv.com
www.doosaninfracore.com
Honourable Mention

This fingertip controller makes the Doosan electric forklifts of the 7 series particularly effortless and efficient to use. The position control lever, which slides back, has an overlapping form. The user can lightly pull on the lever and carry out changes in position more easily than with existing models. Premium surface materials foster a luxurious tactile appeal and achieve, together with strong matt/glossy contrasting, a high emotional effect.

Statement by the jury
The fingertip controller provides a markedly large supporting surface, which enables users to work comfortably for extended periods of time.

Die Fingertip-Steuerung macht die Bedienung der Doosan Elektrostapler aus der 7er-Serie besonders mühelos und effizient. Der von vorne nach hinten verschiebbare Einstellhebel hat eine überlappende Form; der Benutzer kann den Hebel leicht ziehen und die Positionsänderungen bequemer vornehmen als bei bestehenden Modellen. Edle Oberflächenmaterialien sorgen für eine luxuriöse Haptik und erzielen gemeinsam mit den Matt-Glänzend-Kontrasten eine hohe emotionale Wirkung.

Begründung der Jury
Die Fingertip-Steuerung bietet eine ausgesprochen großzügige Auflagefläche, die ein komfortables Arbeiten über längere Zeiträume ermöglicht.

VP600
Commercial Vacuum Cleaner
Gewerbesauger

Manufacturer
Nilfisk Brøndby, Denmark
In-house design
Design
Attention, Copenhagen, Denmark
Web
www.nilfisk.com
www.attention-group.com

The VP600 commercial vacuum cleaner is
equipped with a high-performance
turbine. This ensures particularly quiet
operation so that the cleaning device
can also be used during office and business hours without distracting guests
or staff. The magnetic locking system enables easy opening of the filter chamber.
The device is available with either a standard or detachable power cord, as well as
with an automatically retractable cable.

Statement by the jury
This commercial vacuum cleaner
convinces with its pleasantly low sound
level. Its industrial character is underscored by the functional design.

Der Gewerbesauger VP600 ist mit einer
Hochleistungsturbine ausgestattet, die für
einen besonders geräuscharmen Betrieb
sorgt. Dadurch kann das Reinigungsgerät
auch während der Geschäfts- und
Betriebszeit benutzt werden, ohne Gäste
oder Mitarbeiter zu stören. Die Magnetver-
schlüsse gewährleisten ein einfaches Öff-
ner der Filterkammer. Das Gerät ist wahlweise mit einem Standard- oder abnehmbaren Netzkabel sowie mit einer automatischen Kabelaufwicklung erhältlich.

Begründung der Jury
Der Gewerbesauger überzeugt durch
seinen angenehm niedrigen Geräuschpegel.
Sein industrieller Charakter wird durch das
funktionale Design unterstrichen.

AQT 60-16
High Pressure Washer
Hochdruckreiniger

Manufacturer
Robert Bosch GmbH, Power Tools,
Leinfelden-Echterdingen, Germany
Design
Tatic Designstudio Srl (Aleks Tatic, Alessandro
Cereda, Silvina Iglesias), Milan, Italy
Web
www.bosch-pt.com
www.taticdesignstudio.com

The AQT 60-16 high pressure washer
features storage space for all accessories, including a gun and three lances, a
choice of nozzles, a cleaning agent container, a cable and a hose. The handle
can be extended to a height of 980 mm
or retracted completely into the body
for transport. The large footprint and the
additional footplate provide stability and
safety. The large wheels have been designed especially for uneven paths and
stairs and feature a self-cleaning tread
design.

Statement by the jury
The design of the AQT 60-16 is part cu-
larly geared towards high ease-of-use.
All accessories are visible at a glance and
easy to access.

Der Hochdruckreiniger AQT 60-16 verfügt
über Stauraum für das gesamte Zubehör
inklusive Pistole mit drei Lanzen, diverse
Düsen, Reinigungsmittelbehälter, Kabel und
Schlauch. Der Griff kann bis zu einer Höhe
von 980 mm ausgezogen oder für den
Transport komplett in den Korpus eingezo-
gen werden. Die große Standfläche und
eine extra Trittfläche bieten Stabilität und
Sicherheit. Die großen Räder wurden speziell für unebene Wege und Treppen entwickelt, das Profil der Reifen ist selbstreni-
gend.

Begründung der Jury
Die Gestaltung des AQT 60-16 ist in hohem
Maße auf den Bedienkomfort ausgelegt.
Das Zubehör ist auf einen Blick erfassbar
und schnell zugänglich.

OLED Exit Sign Luminaire
OLED-Rettungsschild

Manufacturer
RP-Technik GmbH, Rodgau, Germany
In-house design
Markus Weber
Web
www.notleuchte.de

The OLED exit sign luminaire is available in two renditions. As a wallmounted version, it blends in with the room's overall appearance. The electronics are concealed in the wall and only the thin pictograph pane is visible. The ceiling version is mounted on a pendant fitting and is available with labelling on either one or both sides. The electronics and power adapter are installed in the ceiling, so only the thin pane displaying the evenly illuminated pictograph remains visible.

Das OLED-Rettungsschild ist in zwei Varianten erhältlich. Als Wandeinbau integriert es sich in das Gesamtbild des Raumes. Die Elektronik verschwindet in der Wand, lediglich die dünne Piktogrammscheibe ist sichtbar. Als Deckenleuchte wird das Schild an einem Pendel montiert und ist sowohl einseitig als auch beidseitig beschriftet erhältlich. Elektronik und Stromversorgung werden in der Decke installiert, sichtbar bleibt nur die flache Scheibe mit der gleichmäßigen Ausleuchtung des Piktogramms.

Statement by the jury
Due to its flat design and concealed electronics, this high-quality sign appears to be hovering on the wall or in the room.

Begründung der Jury
Das hochwertig verarbeitete Schild wirkt aufgrund seiner flachen Bauform und der versteckten Elektronik so, als ob es frei an der Wand oder im Raum schwebt.

Scandic X
Telescopic Handle
Teleskopstiel

Manufacturer
VERMOP Salmon GmbH, Gilching, Germany
In-house design
Web
www.vermop.com

The Scandic X is characterised by an innovative connector system, which can fasten cleaning accessories at the push of a button. Instead of requiring a twisting movement, it can be adjusted to the optimal working height with just one click. The flexible ball at the handle enables users to keep their wrist steady while wiping, making it possible to avoid unnatural sequences of movement. Thanks to high-quality materials, the handle is durable and features high bending strength.

Statement by the jury
The Scandic X impresses with its connector system, which simplifies use considerably. The strong construction can withstand very high loads.

Der Scandic X zeichnet sich durch ein innovatives Adaptersystem aus, bei dem das Reinigungszubehör durch Drücken einer Taste fixiert wird. Ebenfalls mit nur einem Klick statt durch Drehen lässt sich die optimale Arbeitshöhe einstellen. Die bewegliche Kugel am Stiel sorgt für ein ruhiges Handgelenk beim Wischen, sodass ungünstige Bewegungsabläufe vermieden werden. Dank seiner hochwertigen Materialien besitzt der Stiel eine lange Lebensdauer und eine hohe Biegefestigkeit.

Begründung der Jury
Der Scandic X begeistert durch sein Adaptersystem, das die Handhabung stark vereinfacht. Die stabile Bauweise hält auch hohen Belastungen stand.

CHEP Quarter Pallet
CHEP Viertelpalette

Manufacturer
CHEP Deutschland GmbH, Cologne, Germany
In-house design
Karl Wesson, Sanjiv Takyar
Web
www.chep.com
Honourable Mention

This quarter pallet has been designed for the presentation of goods at the point of sale. The newly developed design includes the "Blue Click" system, with which cardboard boxes can be quickly and safely attached to the pallet. Thanks to their optimised feet, the pallets can be stacked with high stability while saving space. The ergonomic handle makes empty pallets easier to carry. Furthermore, the pallets' reduced weight saves transport costs, thus reducing CO_2 emissions.

Statement by the jury
The design of the quarter pallets incorporates ergonomic aspects and sustainability in equal measure.

Die Viertelpalette ist für die Präsentation von Waren am Verkaufsort konzipiert. Zum neu entwickelten Design gehört das „Blue Click"-System, mit dem Kartons schnell und sicher in der Palette befestigt werden können. Durch die optimierten Standfüße lassen sich die Paletten platzsparend und stabil ineinander stapeln, der ergonomische Handgriff erleichtert das Tragen leerer Paletten. Außerdem spart das reduzierte Gewicht der Paletten Transportkosten ein und verringert so die CO_2-Belastung.

Begründung der Jury
Bei der gestalterischen Weiterentwicklung der Viertelpalette wurden Aspekte der Ergonomie und Nachhaltigkeit gleichermaßen stark berücksichtigt.

BITOBOX EQ
Folding Box
Klappbox

Manufacturer
BITO-Lagertechnik, Bittmann GmbH, Meisenheim, Germany
In-house design
Andreas Mattes
Web
www.bito.com

The Bitobox EQ features an innovative seesaw mechanism to lock and unlock the sides, thus preventing fingers from being caught. Open grips with a rounded hand rest ensure that loads are evenly distributed onto the palms. Labels can be inserted into a pocket behind the transparent window which keeps them well protected and clean. Empty boxes can be folded, thereby reducing the box volume by 75 per cent.

Statement by the jury
Sophisticated ergonomic features and a robust design make this folding box easy and safe to use.

Die Bitobox EQ verfügt über einen innovativen Wippmechanismus zur Entriegelung der Seitenwände, der das Einklemmen der Finger verhindert. Die abgerundeten Griffe gewährleisten eine gleichmäßige Verteilung der Lasten auf die Handflächen. Etiketten werden in das Sichtfenster auf der Innenseite eingeschoben, wo sie gut geschützt sind und nicht verloren gehen können. Im leeren Zustand lässt sich die Box zusammenklappen, wodurch sich ihr Volumen um 75 Prozent verringert.

Begründung der Jury
Die durchdachte Ergonomie und robuste Gestaltung der Klappbox trägt in hohem Maße zu einem einfachen und sicheren Gebrauch bei.

DATRON neo
CNC Milling Machine
CNC-Fräsmaschine

Manufacturer
DATRON AG, Mühltal, Germany
In-house design
Frank Wesp
Web
www.datron.de

The Datron neo CNC milling machine uses a combination of camera and touch-screen. The software interface with its tile look guides the user through the milling process, similar to a smartphone. The camera function replaces the time-consuming task of entering values for the measurement of the workpiece. Ergonomic operation is achieved by loading the machine from the top and by offering a height- and angle-adjustable control terminal. The coherent design and innovative door concept focus on the milling area and provide an optimal view of the milling procedure inside the machining area.

Statement by the jury
The Datron neo consistently combines the functions and aesthetics of a smartphone, making it not only intuitive but also fun to use.

Die CNC-Fräsmaschine Datron neo verwendet eine Kombination aus Kamera und Touchscreen. Die Benutzeroberfläche in Kachel-Optik leitet den Anwender wie auf einem Smartphone durch den Fräsprozess. Die Kamerafunktion ersetzt die aufwendige Eingabe von Werten für das Vermessen des Werkstücks. Das Beladen der Maschine von oben sowie das höhen- und winkelverstellbare Bedienterminal ermöglichen ein ergonomisches Arbeiten. Das klare Design und das innovative Türkonzept fokussieren auf den Fräsbereich und bieten eine optimale Sicht auf den Fräsvorgang im Bearbeitungsraum.

Begründung der Jury
Datron neo stellt eine konsequente Verbindung aus Smartphone-Funktionen und -Ästhetik her. Dadurch ist die Bedienung nicht nur intuitiv, sondern macht auch Spaß.

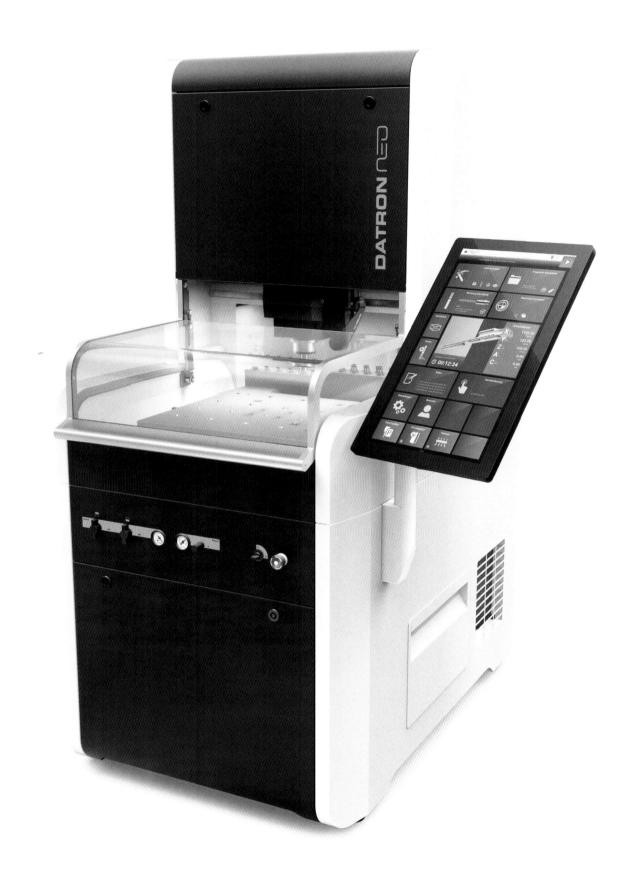

FXR
Milling and Boring Machine
Fräs- und Bohrmaschine

Manufacturer
SORALUCE & DANOBAT Group, Bergara, Spain
In-house design
Ibon Roman
Design
dhemen, Aia, Spain
Web
www.danobatgroup.com
www.dhemen.com

The FXR milling and boring machine is characterised by its modular structure and can be expanded with a range of optional accessories. The sound-protected operator cabin is equipped with a desk and a foldable chair, as well as a sound system, lighting and air conditioning. Furthermore, the cabin features a fully electric lifting system and a sliding door with a fold-out platform. While interaction areas are easily accessible, critical areas are well protected.

Statement by the jury
The sloping angles and narrow radii, which are further highlighted by the blue frames, give the FXR its highly distinctive silhouette.

Die Fräs- und Bohrmaschine FXR zeichnet sich durch eine modulare Bauweise aus und kann um eine Vielzahl optionaler Zubehörteile ergänzt werden. Die schallgeschützte Führerkabine ist mit einem Schreibtisch und einem klappbaren Stuhl ausgestattet sowie mit einer Musikanlage, einem Beleuchtungssystem und einer Klimaanlage. Zudem verfügt die Kabine über ein komplett elektrisches Hebesystem und über eine Schiebetür mit einer Plattform, die ausgeklappt werden kann. Während die Interaktionsbereiche leicht zugänglich sind, liegen kritische Bereiche gut geschützt.

Begründung der Jury
Die schrägen Winkel und engen Radien, die durch die blauen Rahmen noch mehr zur Geltung kommen, verleihen der FXR eine außergewöhnlich markante Silhouette.

ProfilCut Q Premium
Milling Tool
Fräswerkzeug

Manufacturer
Leitz GmbH & Co. KG, Riedau, Austria
Design
Phormolog OG, Kuchl, Austria
Web
www.leitz.org
www.phormolog.at

The ProfilCut Q Premium is a milling tool
for woodworking, which is used in the
manufacturing of windows, doors, furniture and flooring. The system achieves
a very high cutting speed of 120 metres
per second. The functional coating reduces friction, shock load and heat development during the milling process,
even under heavy loads. The ergonomic
design and the lightweight construction
of the tool body reduce noise significantly.

Statement by the jury
The high precision of this milling tool
is conveyed through its choice of top-
quality materials and meticulous workmanship, as well as its premium silver
design.

Der ProfilCut Q Premium ist ein Fräswerkzeug für die Holzbearbeitung, das bei der
Fertigung von Fenstern, Türen. Möbeln
und Böden zum Einsatz kommt. Das System erreicht eine sehr hohe Schnittge-
schwindigkeit von 120 Meterr pro Sekun-
de. Die Funktionsbeschichtung verringert
die Reibung, Stoßbelastung und Wärme-
entwicklung während des Fräsvorgangs,
auch unter starker Belastung. Das ergonomische Design und die Leichtbauweise des
Tragkörpers tragen zu einer erheblichen
Lärmreduzierung bei.

Begründung der Jury
Die hohe Präzision des Fräswerkzeugs
drückt sich in dem Einsatz von hochwertigen Materialien, einer sorgfältigen Verarbeitung sowie der edlen Silber-Optik aus

W-Dress
Grinding Wheel Dressing Machine
Schleifscheiben-Abrichtmaschine

Manufacturer
Strausak AG, Lohn-Ammannsegg, Switzerland
Design
Sard Innovation (Enrique Luis Sardi), Milan, Italy
Web
www.strausak-swiss.com
www.sardi-innovation.com

The W-Dress compact grinding wheel dressing machine is designed to carry out the shaping and sharpening of diamond and CBN grinding discs with a diameter of up to 250 mm. The easily accessible machining area provides access from three sides by simply lifting the hood. Even when closed, there is an unobstructed view of the machining area. The integrated vacuum cleaner ensures a tidy work environment.

Die kompakte Schleifscheiben-Abrichtmaschine W-Dress ist zum Formen und Schärfen von Diamant- und CBN-Schleifscheiben mit einem Durchmesser bis 250 mm geeignet. Der Arbeitsbereich ist leicht zugänglich, durch einfaches Anheben der Haube ist der Zugriff von drei Seiten möglich. Auch im geschlossenen Zustand besteht freie Sicht auf den Bearbeitungsinnenraum. Der integrierte Staubabsauger garantiert eine saubere Arbeitsumgebung.

Statement by the jury
This dressing machine features radiused edges and dynamic lines, which causes it to appear neither solid nor heavy despite its compact form.

Begründung der Jury
Die Abrichtmaschine ist mit abgerundeten Kanten und dynamischen Linien gestaltet. Dadurch wirkt sie in ihrer Kompaktheit weder schwer noch massiv.

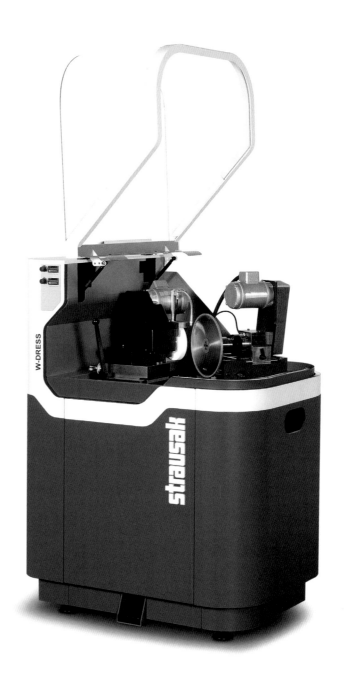

Planet V4
Double Disc Grinding Machine
Doppelseitenschleifmaschine

Manufacturer
Supfina Grieshaber GmbH & Co. KG,
Wolfach, Germany
Design
Design Tech, Ammerbuch, Germany
Web
www.supfina.com
www.designtech.eu

Due to its compact size, the Planet V4 double disc grinding machine requires only a small base area. The operating panel can be moved along the entire front of the machine. The dark, curved front with its large viewing area visually puts the machining space into the foreground. A vertical red line marks the boundary between the machine's front and rear. The light-coloured metal panels at the rear enable direct access to all the machine parts that require maintenance.

Statement by the jury
The grinding machine impresses with its smooth surfaces, radiused edges and clear layout, which combine to create a clean and modern design language.

Die Doppelseitenschleifmaschine Planet V4 beansprucht aufgrund ihrer kompakten Abmessungen nur eine geringe Grundfläche. Das Bedienpanel ist über die gesamte Front beweglich. Die dunkle, überspannte Front mit einem großen Sichtfeld rückt den Bearbeitungsinnenraum optisch in den Vordergrund. Eine vertikal verlaufende rote Linie markiert die Grenze zwischen dem vorderen und hinteren Maschinenbereich. Die hellen Blechpaneele im hinteren Bereich ermöglichen einen direkten Zugang zu den wartungsrelevanten Maschinenteilen.

Begründung der Jury
Die Schleifmaschine besticht durch ihre glatten Oberflächen, abgerundeten Kanten und klare Gliederung. Alles zusammen ergibt eine saubere und moderne Formensprache.

42 RB Range
42 RB Serie
Deburring Machine
Multirotationsbürstmaschine

Manufacturer
Timesavers International B.V.,
Goes, Netherlands
Design
Ko:work, Eindhoven, Netherlands
Web
www.timesaversint.com
www.kowork.nl

This deburring machine from the 42 RB Range is used for uniformly deburring and rounding edges of metal parts. The large access doors simplify maintenance and servicing. The machine features a broad front of windows and a clearly arranged control panel situated in one corner. This guarantees an open view of the machining area, enabling the work process to be continually monitored. A clearly visible LED bar indicates the current machine status.

Statement by the jury
This machine impresses with its clarity of design and self-contained form, which convey a sense of safety and reliability.

Die Multirotationsbürstmaschine der 42 RB Serie wird für das gleichmäßige Entgraten und Verrunden von Metallteilen eingesetzt. Die großen Zugangstüren vereinfachen die Reinigung und Wartung. Die Maschine besitzt eine breite Fensterfront und die übersichtliche Bedienkonsole befindet sich an einer Ecke. Dies gewährleistet eine freie Sicht auf den Maschinenraum und der Bearbeitungsprozess kann kontinuierlich überwacht werden. Eine gut sichtbare LED-Leiste zeigt den aktuellen Maschinenstatus an.

Begründung der Jury
Die Maschine besticht durch ihre gestalterische Klarheit und geschlossene Bauform, die ein Gefühl von Sicherheit und Zuverlässigkeit vermitteln.

S300
Metal Additive Manufacturing Machine
Additive Fertigungsanlage für Metallteile

Manufacturer
Xi'an Bright Laser Technologies Ltd.,
Xi'an, China
Design
Beijing Dongzhi Industrial Design Co., Ltd.
(Yue Jiao, Zonghui Zhang, Tao Li),
Beijing, China
Web
www.xa-blt.com
www.dzdesign.com.cn

The S300 metal additive manufacturing machine produces metal parts with high precision for applications in industries such as aviation and space travel. The method involves laser technology that manufactures components based on a virtual 3D model at a high processing speed. The machine is divided into three functional areas, which are at the same time connected by horizontal lines to form a coherent whole. The resulting geometric contours make the machine appear less bulky than it actually is.

Statement by the jury
The design of this manufacturing machine is characterised by remarkable simplicity and straight lines, highlighting its professional character.

Die additive Fertigungsanlage S300 stellt mit hoher Präzision Metallteile her, wie sie beispielsweise in der Luft- und Raumfahrt eingesetzt werden. Das Verfahren beruht auf einer Lasertechnologie, bei der die Bauteile basierend auf einem virtuellen 3D-Modell mit hoher Prozessgeschwindigkeit konstruiert werden. Die Anlage ist in drei Funktionsbereiche unterteilt, die durch horizontal verlaufende Linien dennoch als eine Einheit erscheinen. Die daraus entstehenden Geometrien lassen die Anlage weniger wuchtig wirken.

Begründung der Jury
Das Erscheinungsbild der Fertigungsanlage ist von beachtlicher Schlichtheit und Geradlinigkeit geprägt, was ihren professionellen Charakter unterstreicht.

BX 3
Cordless Direct Fastening Tool
Akku-Befestigungsgerät

Manufacturer
Hilti Corporation, Schaan, Liechtenstein
In-house design
Web
www.hilti.com

The BX 3 was developed for cordless use and enables the driving of nails into concrete, solid brick and steel. The housing encases the motor, tensioning belt and springs in an unusually asymmetrical, optimally balanced form. The dimensions and weight are reduced to a minimum, making the device easy to use. In addition, the power tool features an ergonomic, anti-slip and vibration-absorbing handle, as well as a support foot with a scaffolding hook. An LED lamp shows the current charge status of the battery.

Der BX 3 wurde für den kabellosen Betrieb entwickelt und ermöglicht das Setzen von Nägeln in Beton, Vollziegel und Stahl. Das Gehäuse umschließt Motor, Zugband und Spannfedern in einer ungewöhnlich asymmetrischen, optimal ausbalancierten Form. Die Abmessungen und das Gewicht sind auf ein Minimum reduziert, sodass das Werkzeug bequem zu handhaben ist. Darüber hinaus ist das Gerät mit einem ergonomischen, rutschfesten und vibrationsgedämpften Handgriff und einem Stützfuß mit Gerüsthaken ausgestattet. Eine LED-Lampe zeigt den aktuellen Ladezustand des Akkus an.

Statement by the jury
The housing of the cordless fastening tool conceals all technical innovations, allowing the design language to remain minimalist, functional and dynamic.

Begründung der Jury
Das Gehäuse des Akku-Befestigungsgeräts verbirgt alle technischen Installationen, sodass die Formensprache reduziert, funktional und dynamisch bleibt.

Folding Work Trestle
Klapp-Arbeitsbock

Manufacturer
Stanley Black & Decker, Rosh HaAjin, Israel
In-house design
Avi Faibish, Mickey Menirom
Web
www.stanleyblackanddecker.com

The folding metal work trestle has a high load capacity and is designed for a wide variety of sawing tasks. The extendable workpiece support makes it possible to process even long workpieces comfortably. After collapsing, the legs are secured by a latching mechanism, allowing the device to be transported safely and saving storage space. In addition, the integrated handle makes the work trestle easier to transport.

Statement by the jury
The sturdy construction of the folding work trestle reflects the high standards of functionality while giving it a minimalist look.

Der zusammenklappbare Arbeitsbock aus Metall besitzt eine hohe Tragkraft und ist für verschiedenartige Sägearbeiten konzipiert. Aufgrund der ausziehbaren Werkstückauflage ist es möglich, auch lange Werkstücke problemlos zu bearbeiten. Die Standbeine werden nach dem Zusammenklappen durch einen Verriegelungsmechanismus fixiert, sodass das Arbeitsgerät sicher transportiert und platzsparend gelagert werden kann. Darüber hinaus wird der Transport durch einen integrierten Tragegriff erleichtert.

Begründung der Jury
In der stabilen Konstruktion des Klapp-Arbeitsbocks spiegelt sich der hohe Anspruch an Funktionalität bei gleichzeitig formaler Einfachheit wider.

GWS 10,8-76 V-EC Professional
Cordless Angle Grinder
Akku-Winkelschleifer

Manufacturer
Robert Bosch GmbH, Power Tools, Leinfelden-Echterdingen, Germany
Design
TEAMS Design, Esslingen, Germany
Web
www.bosch-professional.com
www.teamsdesign.com

The GWS 10.8-76 V-EC Professional cordless angle grinder has been designed for mobile use. With a weight of only 900 grams, the device is very light and rests comfortably in the hand during use. The disc is attached vertically, which provides additional control when making cuts. Moreover, it is not necessary to additionally implement other tools, such as a handsaw. The brushless EC motor delivers high performance while enabling a compact design.

Statement by the jury
This angle grinder has a captivating ergonomic and lightweight design, which lends itself to versatile applications.

Der Akku-Winkelschleifer GWS 10,8-76 V-EC Professional ist für den mobilen Einsatz bestimmt. Mit einem Gewicht von nur 900 Gramm ist das Gerät sehr leicht und liegt bei der Arbeit gut in der Hand. Die Scheibe ist vertikal angebracht, wodurch Schneidarbeiten besonders kontrolliert ausgeführt werden können. Zudem ist es nicht notwendig, zusätzlich andere Werkzeuge wie beispielsweise eine Handsäge einzusetzen. Der bürstenlose EC-Motor liefert eine hohe Leistung und ermöglicht eine kompakte Bauweise.

Begründung der Jury
Der Winkelschleifer überzeugt durch seine ergonomische und leichte Bauform, wodurch er vielseitig eingesetzt werden kann.

WPB 36 LTX BL 230 Quick
Cordless Angle Grinder
Akku-Winkelschleifer

Manufacturer
Metabowerke GmbH, Nürtingen, Germany
In-house design
Web
www.metabo.com

The WPB 36 LTX BL 230 Quick cordless angle grinder with its 230-mm disc is able to provide the same performance as large corded devices. The dynamic shape and the rotatable U-shaped handle with soft-touch components give the grinder a lightweight and ergonomic design. The wide paddle switch provides safety and ease of use in a wide variety of working positions. The adjustment of the guard and the changing of discs can be carried out without additional tools.

Statement by the jury
A balanced distribution of weight enables excellent control over the angle grinder. The straight lines of the geometric design convey its high efficiency.

Der Akku-Winkelschleifer WPB 36 LTX BL 230 Quick mit einer 230-mm-Scheibe ist zu den gleichen Leistungen fähig wie eine große Netzmaschine. Die dynamische Formgebung und der drehbare Bügelhandgriff mit Softtouch-Komponenten verleihen dem Schleifer ein leichtes und ergonomisches Design. Der breite Paddle-Schalter bietet Sicherheit und Komfort in den unterschiedlichsten Anwendungspositionen. Um die Schutzhaube zu verstellen und die Scheibe auszuwechseln, ist kein zusätzliches Werkzeug notwendig.

Begründung der Jury
Die gleichmäßige Gewichtsverteilung ermöglicht eine ausgezeichnete Kontrolle über den Winkelschleifer. Die Geradlinigkeit seiner Geometrie drückt hohe Effizienz aus.

EY75A7 / EZ75A7
Impact Driver
Akku-Schlagschrauber

Manufacturer
Panasonic Corporation, Kadoma City,
Osaka Prefecture, Japan
In-house design
Design Center, Eco Solutions Company
(Kazuma Kubono)
Design
Design Group Italia (Edgardo Angelini),
Milan, Italy
Web
www.panasonic-powertools.eu
www.designgroupitalia.com

The EY75A7 / EZ75A7 impact driver with
a 117.8 mm short body and a newly
developed compact motor offers high
usability. An innovative self-drilling
screw mode limits the risk of stripping
the thread on fasteners or materials
during screwing-in by automatically
switching the rotation speed from high
to low speed. The ergonomic shape and
optimally balanced weight distribution
enable fatigue-free use. The dual voltage
specification with a 14.4-volt and
18-volt battery provides more flexibility.

Statement by the jury
This impact driver captivates with its
compact housing, which is visually highlighted by its monochrome colour
scheme.

Der Akku-Schlagschrauber EY75A7 / EZ75A7
mit einem 117,8 mm kleinen Gehäuse und
einem neu entwickelten Kompaktmotor
bietet eine hohe Benutzerfreundlichkeit.
Ein innovativer Auto-Schraub-Modus verhindert das Überdrehen der Schraube auf
Befestigungselementen und Materialien,
indem die Drehgeschwindigkeit beim Ein-
schrauben automatisch von hoch auf
niedrig wechselt. Die ergonomische Form
und die optimal austarierte Gewichtsverteilung ermöglichen ein ermüdungsfreies
Arbeiten. Die duale Spannungsversorgung
mit einem 18-Volt- und 14,4-Volt-Akku
sorgt für mehr Flexibilität.

Begründung der Jury
Der Akku-Schlagschrauber besticht durch
sein kompaktes Gehäuse, das durch die
monochrome Farbgebung optisch prägnant
hervorgehoben wird.

SF 8M / SF 10W
Cordless Drill Driver
Akku-Bohrschrauber

Manufacturer
Hilti Corporation, Schaan, Liechtenstein
In-house design
Web
www.hilti.com

The SF 8M cordless drill driver has been designed for metalworking, while the SF 10W has been especially developed for woodworking. Both driver drills are based on a 22-volt platform and feature a rugged metal chuck, making it suitable for extreme applications as well. Thanks to its powerful four-speed gear box, the torque can be precisely adjusted to the material thickness and drill-bit diameter. The rubberised grip ensures a low transfer of vibration to the hand. The LED lamp at the lower end of the grip optimally illuminates the working area.

Der Akku-Bohrschrauber SF 8M kommt bei der Metallbearbeitung zum Einsatz, während der SF 10W speziell für Holzarbeiten konzipiert ist. Beide Schrauber basieren auf einer 22-Volt-Plattform und verfügen über ein robustes Bohrfutter aus Metall, das auch extremen Anwendungsbedingungen standhält. Dank des leistungsstarken 4-Gang-Getriebes kann die Drehzahl präzise auf die Materialstärke und den Bohrdurchmesser abgestimmt werden. Der gummierte Handgriff sorgt für eine geringe Vibrationsbelastung der Hand. Die LED-Lampe am unteren Griffende leuchtet das Arbeitsfeld optimal aus.

Statement by the jury
The design of these cordless drills successfully combines an impressively compact shape with comprehensive technical features.

Begründung der Jury
Bei der Gestaltung der Akku-Bohrschrauber ist es gelungen, trotz umfangreicher technischer Ausstattung eine beeindruckend kompakte Bauform zu erreichen.

Bahco Fit Screwdriver
Bahco Fit Schraubendreher

Manufacturer
SNA Europe (Sweden) AB, Enköping, Sweden
In-house design
Jon Uranga Elorza, Olatz Arias Moreno
Web
www.bahco.com
Honourable Mention

The Bahco Fit screwdriver features a patented two-component handle, which is made of 75 per cent elastomer and ensures a pleasant grip. The vertical grooves provide maximum transfer of force and prevent the hand from slipping. A clearly visible identification mark on the grip enables users to quickly identify the right type of tip. The black tip of the shaft improves the user's accuracy when aligning it with the screw.

Statement by the jury
This screwdriver impresses with its structured surface that facilitates an optimal grip. Colour accents successfully highlight individual sections of the handle.

Der Bahco Fit Schraubendreher verfügt über einen patentierten 2-Komponenten-Griff, der zu 75 Prozent aus Elastomer besteht und für eine angenehme Haptik sorgt. Die vertikalen Einkerbungen gewährleisten eine maximale Kraftübertragung und verhindern, dass die Hand abrutscht. Eine deutlich sichtbare Kennzeichnung am Griff ermöglicht dem Anwender eine schnelle Auswahl des passenden Klingentyps. Die schwarz markierte Klingenspitze verbessert die Zielgenauigkeit beim Treffen der Schraube.

Begründung der Jury
Der Schraubendreher punktet durch seine strukturierte Oberfläche, die optimalen Halt gibt. Die Farbakzente heben einzelne Bereiche des Griffs gekonnt hervor.

GARANT 65 5550
Torque Wrench
Drehmomentschlüssel

Manufacturer
Hoffmann GmbH Qualitätswerkzeuge, Munich, Germany
Design
Böhler GmbH, Corporate Industrial Design, Fürth, Germany
Web
www.hoffmann-group.com
www.boehler-design.com

The Garant 65 5550 electronic torque wrench is used for the controlled tightening of screws and to carry out control measurements. During the tightening process, the torque is shown on the TFT colour display as a numerical value, as well as on a dial gauge. This minimises reading errors. After finishing the tightening process, the final torque value continues to be displayed as a shadow. An acoustic warning signal prevents users from tightening bolts over the maximum value.

Statement by the jury
Design elements were sparsely employed in the Garant 65 5550, ensuring that the user's attention is fully focused on the digital dial gauge.

Der elektronische Drehmomentschlüssel Garant 65 5550 wird für den kontrollierten Einzelanzug von Schrauben sowie für Kontrollmessungen verwendet. Während des Arbeitsvorgangs wird das Drehmoment auf dem TFT-Farbdisplay sowohl als numerischer Wert als auch auf einer Skalenmessuhr angezeigt. Dadurch werden Ablesefehler minimiert. Nach Beendigung des Anzugs wird der Endwert weiterhin als Schatten dargestellt. Ein akustisches Signal warnt vor dem Überschreiten des maximalen Anzugsmoments.

Begründung der Jury
Gestaltungselemente wurden beim Garant 65 5550 wohldosiert eingesetzt, sodass die Aufmerksamkeit voll und ganz auf der digitalen Skalenmessuhr liegt.

E-torc Q
Electronic Torque Wrench
Elektronischer Drehmomentschlüssel

Manufacturer
GEDORE TorqueTech GmbH & Co. KG, Solingen, Germany
In-house design
Stefan Czympiel
Web
www.gedore.com

The E-torc Q electronic torque wrench comprises three models for controlled clockwise and counterclockwise tightening in the range of 10 to 300 newton metres. The screwing operation is displayed on the large and clear 4.3" colour touch display. The analysis of the screwing operations therefore can be carried out directly on the wrench. The high-quality and rotatable aluminium housing, as well as the ergonomically shaped handle, enables safe and easy use in every measuring range.

Statement by the jury
The E-torc Q convinces with its clear design language, which is achieved through the tidy arrangement of all functional areas facing the user.

Der elektronische Drehmomentschlüssel E-torc Q umfasst drei Modelle für den kontrollierten Rechts- und Linksanzug im Bereich von 10 bis 300 Newtonmetern. Der Verschraubungsprozess wird über das große und übersichtliche 4,3"-Farbtouchdisplay visualisiert. So kann die Analyse der Schraubvorgänge direkt am Schlüssel durchgeführt werden. Das hochwertige und drehbare Aluminiumgehäuse sowie der ergonomisch gestaltete Griff ermöglichen eine einfache und sichere Handhabung über alle Messbereiche.

Begründung der Jury
Der E-torc Q überzeugt durch seine klare Formensprache, die durch eine saubere, dem Anwender zugewandte Anordnung der Funktionsbereiche erzielt wird.

790 ½
Roofing Hammer
Latthammer

Manufacturer
Joh. Hermann Picard GmbH & Co. KG,
Wuppertal, Germany
In-house design
Web
www.picard-hammer.de

The 790 ½ roofing hammer made from solid steel weighs only 800 grams and is therefore in the same weight class as tubular steel hammers, while being considerably more robust. The claw and the slim point are precisely wrought and inductively hardened. The weight-optimised head provides excellent balance and the strongest possible strike force. The carefully cut surface of the hammer blends smoothly into the grip, which is sheathed in core leather that absorbs moisture and releases it again once the work is done.

Statement by the jury
The simple design of the 790 ½ roofing hammer directs attention towards its leather grip. It has a particularly noble look thanks to its natural structure.

Der Latthammer 790 ½ aus Ganzstahl wiegt nur 800 Gramm und bewegt sich damit in derselben Gewichtsklasse wie Rohrstielhämmer, ist jedoch wesentlich robuster. Die Klaue und die schlanke Spitze sind präzise ausgearbeitet und induktiv gehärtet. Der gewichtsoptimierte Kopf sorgt für eine ausgewogene Balance und höchste Schlagkraft. Die sorgfältig geschliffene Oberfläche des Hammers geht nahtlos in den Griff über. Dieser ist mit Kernleder ummantelt, das Feuchtigkeit aufnimmt und nach getaner Arbeit wieder abgibt.

Begründung der Jury
Das schlichte Design des Latthammers 790 ½ lenkt die gesamte Aufmerksamkeit auf den Ledergriff. Dieser wirkt durch seine natürliche Struktur besonders edel.

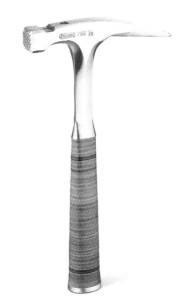

Fiskars Striking Tool Range
Fiskars Hammer-Sortiment

Manufacturer
Fiskars Finland Oy Ab, Helsinki, Finland
In-house design
Fiskars R&D Team
Web
www.fiskarsgroup.com

The Fiskars striking tool range is characterised by its vibration-reduction system, which absorbs the kinetic energy of the strike. This noticeably reduces the impact of the strike on the user. The ergonomically shaped grip and optimised balance point enable the user to feel the force and effect of the hammer, while at the same time having full control over the strike. The back claw makes it easier to pull nails out.

Statement by the jury
The differently structured areas of the hammer create an appealing formal tension. At the same time the hammer appears as if cast in one piece.

Das Hammer-Sortiment von Fiskars zeichnet sich durch ein Vibrationsreduktionssystem aus, das die kinetische Energie des Schlags auffängt. Dadurch werden die Auswirkungen des Schlags auf den Benutzer spürbar gemindert. Der ergonomisch geformte Griff und der optimierte Gleichgewichtspunkt ermöglichen es dem Benutzer, die Kraft und Wirkung des Hammers zu spüren und den Schlag gleichzeitig vollständig zu kontrollieren. Die hintere Klaue erleichtert das Herausziehen von Nägeln.

Begründung der Jury
Die unterschiedlich strukturierten Bereiche des Hammers schaffen eine ansprechende formale Grundspannung. Gleichzeitig wirkt er wie aus einem Guss.

Bostitch® BTHTHT550
Hammer Tacker
Hefthammer

Manufacturer
Stanley Black & Decker, New Britain, USA
In-house design
Jonathan Spence
Web
www.stanleyblackanddecker.com

The Bostitch BTHTHT550 hammer tacker is characterised by its angled form, which enables users to operate the tool without hitting their knuckles on the application surface. The anti-vibration handle with double shot construction helps reduce the recoil when driving in staples, helping to protect the hand and inhibiting early wear and tear. The anti-slip bumpers also help prevent the tool from sliding on sloped or angled surfaces.

Statement by the jury
The ergonomics of this hammer tacker have been thought out down to the smallest detail. The clearly structured surfaces convey its function as a reliable tool.

Der Hefthammer Bostitch BTHTHT550 zeichnet sich durch seine nach oben angewinkelte Form aus, die es dem Anwender ermöglicht, das Werkzeug zu verwenden, ohne sich den Knöchel an der Arbeitsfläche zu stoßen. Der Anti-Vibrations-Griff mit Doppelschussfunktion dämpft den Rückstoß beim Anbringen der Klammern, wodurch die Hand geschützt und das Werkzeug vor frühzeitigem Verschleiß bewahrt wird. Die Anti-Rutsch-Stoßfänger verhindern ein Abrutschen des Werkzeugs auf schrägen oder verwinkelten Flächen.

Begründung der Jury
Die Ergonomie des Hefthammers ist bis ins Detail durchdacht. Die klar strukturierten Oberflächen unterstreichen die Zuverlässigkeit des Werkzeugs.

Leica Lino L4P1
Multiline Laser
Multilinienlaser

Manufacturer
Leica Geosystems AG,
Heerbrugg, Switzerland
Design
Stan Maes Product Design (Stan Maes),
Dilsen-Stokkem, Belgium
Web
www.leica-geosystems.com
www.stanmaesproductdesign.com

The Leica Lino L4P1 multiline laser can read laser lines from a distance of up to 80 metres. The device is powered by lithium-ion batteries, which contributes to cost reduction and protection of the environment. The base, which can be rotated by 360 degrees, enables quick and precise alignment of the laser. The fine adjustment is carried out with the help of the adjustment screw. The device is protected against dust and spraying water, and the surrounding black shock absorber reduces the force of impact.

Statement by the jury
The shock absorber as central design element gives the Leica Lino L4P1 a distinct appearance. The battery compartment is discreetly located in the housing, thus saving space.

Mit dem Multilinienlaser Leica Lino L4P1 können die Laserlinien noch in einer Entfernung von 80 Metern erfasst werden. Das Gerät wird mit Lithium-Ionen-Akkus betrieben, was dazu beiträgt, Kosten zu sparen und die Umwelt zu schonen. Die um 360 Grad drehbare Basis ermöglicht ein schnelles und präzises Ausrichten des Lasers. Die Feineinstellung erfolgt durch Drehen der Justierschraube. Das Gerät ist staub- und spritzwassergeschützt, der umlaufende schwarze Stoßdämpfer fängt Stöße ab.

Begründung der Jury
Der Stoßdämpfer als zentrales Gestaltungsmerkmal verleiht dem Leica Lino L4P1 ein markantes Äußeres. Das Akkufach ist platzsparend und diskret in das Gehäuse verbaut.

Smart
Line Laser
Linienlaser

Manufacturer
SOLA-Messwerkzeuge GmbH, Götzis, Austria
In-house design
Martin Hinterauer
Design
mgdesign (Melih Gürleyik, Seyman Çay),
Istanbul, Turkey
Web
www.sola.at
www.mg-design.org

The Smart line laser is characterised by its high versatility in renovation and construction tasks. The housing forms a geometric line, which directs the focus to the opening for the laser diode, while at the same time providing a stable base. The device is switched on and off via a single rotary knob in order to make its operation as simple as possible. Its bright, self-levelling laser lines enable a large working area within a beam angle of 105 degrees.

Statement by the jury
The rounded shape of this line laser gives it an individual and highly recognisable look and also makes it convenient to use.

Der Linienlaser Smart zeichnet sich durch vielseitige Einsatzmöglichkeiten bei Renovierungs- und Bauarbeiten aus. Das Gehäuse bildet eine geometrische Linie, die den Blick auf die Öffnung für die Laserdiode lenkt und zugleich eine sichere Standfläche bietet. Das Gerät wird über einen einzelnen Drehschalter an- und ausgeschaltet, um die Bedienung möglichst einfach zu halten. Das helle, selbstnivellierende Laserkreuz erlaubt einen großen Arbeitsbereich innerhalb eines Abstrahlwinkels von 105 Grad.

Begründung der Jury
Die gerundete Form verleiht dem Linienlaser ein individuelles Aussehen mit hohem Wiedererkennungswert und ist noch dazu praktisch im Gebrauch.

Crossline
Line Laser
Linienlaser

Manufacturer
SOLA-Messwerkzeuge GmbH, Götzis, Austria
In-house design
Martin Hinterauer
Design
mgdesign (Melih Gürleyik, Seyman Çay),
Istanbul, Turkey
Web
www.sola.at
www.mg-design.org

Just a few hand movements are necessary for aligning the Crossline line laser, and for projecting a broad laser cross pattern onto walls and ceilings. The laser beam angle of 125 degrees creates a broad, highly visible panoramic line, which significantly simplifies alignment and installation tasks. The rotary knob on the side of the device controls the on/off function and the transport lock. The control panel for different user modes is located on top of the housing so as to enhance user-friendliness.

Statement by the jury
The dark borders of this line laser convey a robust and compact impression, while also cleverly highlighting the different functional areas.

Nur wenige Handgriffe sind notwendig, um den Linienlaser Crossline auszurichten und ein lotrechtes Laserkreuz an Wände und Decken zu projizieren. Der Laserabstrahlwinkel von 125 Grad erzeugt ein großflächiges, gut sichtbares Linienpanorama, das genaueste Ausrichtungs- und Montagearbeiten deutlich vereinfacht. Durch den seitlichen Drehregler wird das Gerät ein- und ausgeschaltet sowie die Transportsperre betätigt. Das Bedienfeld für unterschiedliche Anwendungsmodi ist benutzerfreundlich auf der Oberseite angebracht.

Begründung der Jury
Die dunklen Rahmungen des Linienlasers vermitteln den Eindruck von Robustheit und Kompaktheit. Zudem heben sie die Funktionsbereiche geschickt hervor.

Smart Wheel
Distance Measuring Device
Entfernungsmessgerät

Manufacturer
NWi, Budd Lake, USA
In-house design
David Xing, Shi Xin, Zeng Jinmin,
Zhou Chaojie, Yao Di
Web
www.nwismart.com
Honourable Mention

The Smart Wheel captures data points along a route walked by the users carrying the device. The collected information, including distances, pictures, notes and videos, is used to create digital and interactive maps. This helps construction projects to be planned with more simplicity and precision. The data are transferred in real time via Bluetooth to an app. Users can select any data points on the map and carry out additional calculations without having to go back on-site to remeasure.

Das Smart Wheel erfasst Datenpunkte entlang einer Wegstrecke, die der Anwender mit dem Gerät abgeht. Aus den gesammelten Informationen, wie Abstände, Bilder, Notizen und Videos, werden digitale und interaktive Karten erstellt, mit denen sich Bauprojekte einfacher und präziser planen lassen. Die Daten werden per Bluetooth und in Echtzeit an eine App übermittelt. Der Anwender kann alle Datenpunkte auf der Karte anwählen und zusätzliche Berechnungen durchführen, ohne noch einmal vor Ort nachmessen zu müssen.

Statement by the jury
The Smart Wheel triggers new design developments in the field of measuring technology. Its open architecture has a friendly and easily accessible look.

Begründung der Jury
Das Smart Wheel setzt neue gestalterische Impulse in der Messtechnik. Seine offene Architektur wirkt sympathisch und leicht zugänglich.

PD-C
Laser Range Meter
Laser-Distanzmessgerät

Manufacturer
Hilti Corporation, Schaan, Liechtenstein
In-house design
Design
Matuschek Design & Management, Aalen, Germany
HID Human Interface Design GmbH, Hamburg, Germany
Web
www.hilti.com
www.matuschekdesign.de
www.human-interface.de

The PD-C laser range meter gauges distance and calculates area and volume, in both indoor and outdoor environments. The high-resolution digital camera with zoom enables documentation of the construction process with the help of photos, while enabling the device to be accurately aimed at measuring points from a great distance. The meter is controlled via a touchscreen made from special-strength Gorilla Glass, which can also be operated while wearing gloves. The saved data may be transferred to other devices via Bluetooth or USB connectivity. The integrated lithium-ion battery maintains its charge for up to ten hours.

Das Laser-Distanzmessgerät PD-C berechnet Distanzen, Flächen und Volumina im Außen- und Innenbereich. Die hochauflösende Digitalkamera mit Zoom ermöglicht die Baudokumentation mithilfe von Fotos sowie das punktgenaue Anvisieren von Messpunkten auch auf größere Entfernungen. Das Gerät wird über einen Touchscreen aus hochfestem Gorilla-Glas gesteuert, der auch mit Handschuhen bedient werden kann. Die gespeicherten Daten lassen sich per Bluetooth- oder USB-Verbindung an andere Geräte übermitteln. Der integrierte Lithium-Ionen-Akku hält bis zu zehn Stunden.

Statement by the jury
Thanks to the exceptionally clear design of the PD-C, its functionality is easy to grasp and the meter is intuitive to use.

Begründung der Jury
Aufgrund der äußerst übersichtlichen Gestaltung des PD-C können die Funktionen schnell erfasst werden und das Messgerät lässt sich intuitiv bedienen.

optoNCDT 1320 / 1420
Laser Triangulation Sensors
Laser-Triangulationssensoren

Manufacturer
Micro-Epsilon Messtechnik GmbH & Co. KG, Ortenburg, Germany
Design
H-Design, Büro für Industrie- und Grafikdesign (Wolfgang Hartig), Langebrück, Germany
Micro-Epsilon Optronic GmbH (Christoph Grüber), Dresden, Germany
Web
www.micro-epsilon.com
www.h-design.de

The optoNCDT 1320 and optoNCDT 1420 laser triangulation sensors detect displacement, distance and position with high precision. Their very compact design with integrated controller and low weight makes the sensors also suited for applications in confined construction spaces and in conditions subject to high acceleration, such as on robotic arms. The model-specific colour coding of the cable entry and the communication with the Web interface enable intuitive use.

Die Laser-Triangulationssensoren optoNCDT 1320 und optoNCDT 1420 erfassen Weg, Abstand und Position mit hoher Präzision. Die sehr kompakte Bauform mit integriertem Controller und geringem Gewicht machen die Sensoren auch in beengten Bauräumen und für Anwendungen geeignet, bei denen hohe Beschleunigungen wirken, z. B. an Roboterarmen. Die modellspezifische Farbcodierung der Kabeldurchführung und die Kommunikation mit der Messtechnik über ein Webinterface ermöglichen eine intuitive Bedienung.

Statement by the jury
The design of the sensors has been specially developed for rough industrial conditions. The bevelled edge makes it easy to integrate them into the existing environment.

Begründung der Jury
Die Gestaltung der Sensoren ist ganz auf die rauen Bedingungen in der Industrie abgestimmt. Durch die abgeschrägte Kante sind sie einfach in die bestehende Umgebung zu integrieren

Zamo
Laser Measure
Laser-Entfernungsmesser

Manufacturer
Robert Bosch Elektrowerkzeuge GmbH,
Leinfelden-Echterdingen, Germany
Design
TEAMS Design,
Esslingen, Germany
Web
www.bosch-pt.com

The Zamo laser measure calculates distances using a convenient one-button control concept. The design of the second generation is modelled on the modern environment of consumer electronics in order to appeal to a larger target group. Nonetheless, the positioning of the company logo on the upward facing side of the tool creates a clear connection with the brand. All important measurement data are presented on the display and can thus be grasped at a glance.

Statement by the jury
With its curved front edge and slightly projecting, rounded outer edges, the Zamo has an eye-catching visual appearance. Its display is the main focus.

Der Laser-Entfernungsmesser Zamo misst Abstände und Strecken über eine komfortable 1-Knopf-Bedienung. Das Design der zweiten Gerätegeneration ist an das moderne Umfeld der Unterhaltungselektronik angelehnt, um eine breitere Zielgruppe anzusprechen. Die Platzierung des Unternehmenslogos auf der Oberseite des Werkzeugs stellt trotzdem eine klare Verbindung zur Marke her. Alle wichtigen Messinformationen werden über das Display dargestellt und sind so auf einen Blick schnell erfassbar.

Begründung der Jury
Durch die geschwungene Frontkante und die leicht überstehenden, abgerundeten Ränder erhält der Zamo eine aufmerksamkeitsstarke Optik. Das Display steht klar im Fokus.

GIS 1000 C Professional
Thermo Detector
Thermodetektor

Manufacturer
Robert Bosch Elektrowerkzeuge GmbH,
Leinfelden-Echterdingen, Germany
Design
TEAMS Design,
Esslingen, Germany
Web
www.bosch-pt.com

The GIS 1000 C Professional thermo detector features precise sensor technology for measuring the room temperature and relative humidity. Each detail, such as the camera, the two laser diodes and the LED, have been carefully designed. The curved lines of the soft-grip zones form a protective sleeve around the device. The keyboard and the colour display are integrated into the handle and can be controlled with a natural movement of the thumb.

Statement by the jury
Distinct surface structures lend a special visual and also tactile experience to the thermo detector.

Der Thermodetektor GIS 1000 C Professional ist mit präziser Sensortechnik zum Messen von Raumtemperatur und relativer Luftfeuchtigkeit ausgestattet. Jedes Detail, wie die Kamera, die zwei Laserdioden und die LED-Lampe, ist gestalterisch sorgfältig herausgearbeitet. Die geschwungenen Linien der Softgrip-Zonen bilden eine Schutzhülle um das Gerät. Die Tastatur und das Farbdisplay sind in den Handgriff integriert und lassen sich mit einer natürlichen Bewegung des Daumens steuern.

Begründung der Jury
Die ausgeprägten Oberflächenstrukturen machen den Thermodetektor nicht nur zu einem besonderen visuellen, sondern auch zu einem taktilen Erlebnis.

CleanSpace Ultra
Respirator
Atemschutzmaske

Manufacturer
PAFtec Australia Pty Ltd,
Sydney, Australia

In-house design
Alexander Virr

Web
www.cleanspacetechnology.com

reddot award 2016
best of the best

Form for safety

Respiratory masks are used in many industrial areas to protect workers from inhaling harmful dust and gases in the air. Respiratory contaminants are the leading cause of long-term occupational health issues. The CleanSpace Ultra was developed against the backdrop that respiratory protection design has hardly changed over the past 25 years. The aim was to combine the convenience of a negative pressure mask with the assured protection and comfort of a powered respirator. Weighing only 520 grams, this lightweight mask was developed by biomedical engineers who have miniaturised the core components to encase them in a compact ergonomic device. Thanks to this efficient design, the disadvantages of traditional respiratory masks, such as bulkiness and the obstruction of dangling hoses and belts, could be eliminated. Featuring an elegant design idiom, the CleanSpace Ultra delivers very good on-demand airflow thanks to the proprietary AirSensit system. The respiratory mask is intuitive to wear and durable at low total operating costs. It is thus especially suitable for high-volume deployment and high adoption by work teams in large industrial companies and in remote sites where close training and technical support cannot always be ensured. Balancing functionality with highly advanced ergonomics, the mask thus results in improved respiratory protection – its distinctively elegant appearance yields a high level of acceptance and long-term compliance among workers.

Form für die Sicherheit

Atemschutzmasken werden in vielen industriellen Bereichen genutzt, in denen gesundheitsschädliche Gase oder Stäube entstehen. Schadstoffe in der Luft sind der Hauptgrund für langwierige berufsbedingte Beeinträchtigungen. Die CleanSpace Ultra wurde vor dem Hintergrund entworfen, dass sich das Design von Atemschutzmasken in den vergangenen 25 Jahren kaum verändert hat. Das Ziel war es, die Zweckmäßigkeit einer Unterdruck-Maske mit dem Schutz und Komfort einer gebläseunterstützten Version zu kombinieren. Diese mit einem Gewicht von nur 520 Gramm sehr leichte Maske wurde von biomedizinischen Ingenieuren entwickelt, wobei die Kernkomponenten verkleinert und in ein kompaktes, ergonomisches Gehäuse eingebaut wurden. Durch diese effiziente Gestaltung konnten die Nachteile traditioneller Atemschutzmasken wie etwa umständlich anhängende Schläuche und Gürtel umgangen werden. Die CleanSpace Ultra weist eine elegante Formensprache auf und bietet aufgrund des proprietären AirSensit-Systems einen sehr guten Bedarfsluftstrom. Sie lässt sich intuitiv bedienen und ist langlebig bei geringen Gesamtbetriebskosten. Diese Atemschutzmaske eignet sich deshalb insbesondere für den Einsatz in großen industriellen Betrieben und an dezentralen Standorten, wo eine eingehende Schulung sowie technische Unterstützung nur bedingt sichergestellt werden können. Durch ihre Funktionalität im Einklang mit einer hochentwickelten Ergonomie trägt sie zu einem verbesserten Atemschutz bei – ihre einprägsame Eleganz führt zu hoher Regelkonformität und Akzeptanz bei den Anwendern.

Statement by the jury

Fundamentally questioning the form and function of a respiratory mask made the design of the CleanSpace Ultra emerge with an entirely new construction approach that combines many advantages. Its design idiom impressively embodies design of the 21st century. Equipped with the well thought-out AirSensit system, the mask delivers the highest degree of wearing comfort and ergonomics. This respiratory mask sets new standards for the safety of its users.

Begründung der Jury

Das grundlegende Hinterfragen der Form und Funktion einer Atemschutzmaske führte bei der Gestaltung der CleanSpace Ultra zu einer völlig neuen Konstruktion, die viele Vorteile in sich vereint. Ihre Formensprache verkörpert eindrucksvoll das Design des 21. Jahrhunderts. Die Ausstattung mit dem gut durchdachten AirSensit-System ermöglicht ein Höchstmaß an Tragekomfort und Ergonomie. Für die Sicherheit der Anwender setzt diese Atemschutzmaske neue Standards.

Designer portrait
See page 40
Siehe Seite 40

155

AIR+ Smart Mask
Respiratory Mask
Atemschutzmaske

Manufacturer
Innosparks Pte Ltd, Singapore
In-house design
Web
www.airplus-asia.com

The AIR+ Smart Mask combines a respiratory mask with a micro ventilator, which reduces heat, moisture and CO_2 that build up behind the mask. At the same time, the ventilator provides cool and fresh air, which is particularly noticeable when the mask is worn for long periods of time. The micro ventilator is reusable and disconnects from the mask for recharging. The mask is available in three different sizes and is thus suitable for children aged seven and above, as well as for adults. An integrated sizing gauge on the packaging helps in selecting the right size.

Die AIR+ Smart Mask kombiniert eine Atemschutzmaske mit einem Mikroventilator, der Hitze, Luftfeuchtigkeit und CO_2, die sich unter der Maske bilden, reduziert. Gleichzeitig sorgt der Ventilator für kühle, frische Luft. Dies macht sich besonders bei längerem Tragen der Maske positiv bemerkbar. Der Mikroventilator ist wiederverwendbar und wird zum Aufladen von der Maske abgenommen. Die Maske ist in drei verschiedenen Größen erhältlich und damit sowohl für Kinder ab sieben Jahren als auch für Erwachsene geeignet. Eine Schablone auf der Verpackung hilft bei der Wahl der passenden Größe.

Statement by the jury
With an innovative ventilator and a comfortable design that optimally adjusts to the face, this protective mask contributes to a higher quality of life.

Begründung der Jury
Die Schutzmaske trägt durch den innovativen Ventilator und ihr komfortables Design, das optimal dem Gesicht angepasst ist, zu mehr Lebensqualität bei.

Zenith
Safety Helmet
Schutzhelm

Manufacturer
KASK S.p.A., Chiuduno (Bergamo), Italy
In-house design
Web
www.kask.com

The Zenith safety helmet meets the highest safety standards while granting enhanced wearing comfort. With the help of its innovative quick-mount system, the Easy Click System, the helmet can be adapted to any head shape, ensuring a stable fit. The inner pad made from a high-tech 3D fabric prevents overheating by reliably wicking moisture away from the head. Its mounting mechanism for different types of face shields makes the helmet a versatile piece of equipment.

Statement by the jury
This safety helmet is characterised by an elegant design that looks both lightweight and robust at the same time. It can be easily and intuitively adjusted.

Der Schutzhelm Zenith erfüllt höchste Sicherheitsstandards und bietet ein komfortables Tragegefühl. Mithilfe eines innovativen Schnellbefestigungssystems, dem Easy Click System, lässt sich der Helm an jede Kopfform anpassen und garantiert stets einen stabilen Sitz. Das Innenpolster aus Hightech-3D-Gewebe schützt vor Überhitzung, indem es die Feuchtigkeit zuverlässig nach außen transportiert. Eine Vorrichtung zur Montage von verschiedenen Visieren macht den Helm vielseitig einsetzbar.

Begründung der Jury
Der Schutzhelm zeichnet sich durch ein formschönes Design aus, das zugleich leicht und robust wirkt. Er lässt sich schnell und intuitiv justieren.

Auto Darkening Welding Helmet
Schweißhelm mit Autoverdunklung

Manufacturer
OTOS, Seoul, South Korea
In-house design
Web
www.otos.co.kr

The Auto Darkening Welding Helmet automatically protects the wearer against sparks and splashes, as well as UV and infrared radiation. The anti-glare filter darkens once the electric arc is ignited; beforehand it is transparent. Thus the working environment remains visible at all times and the electrode can be precisely positioned before the welding begins. The filter cassette is 30 per cent larger than that of previous models, giving the user a broader field of vision and more freedom of movement.

Statement by the jury
The extended field of vision is an innovation that is fittingly highlighted by the helmet's large dimensions and dynamic lines.

Der Schweißhelm mit Autoverdunklung schützt automatisch gegen Funken, Spritzer, Ultraviolett- und Infrarotstrahlung. Der Blendschutzfilter verdunkelt sich erst, wenn der Lichtbogen gezündet wird, vorher ist er transparent. So bleibt die Arbeitsumgebung immer sichtbar und die Elektrode kann vor dem Schweißen präzise platziert werden. Die Filterkassette ist 30 Prozent größer als bei vorherigen Modellen, was dem Anwender ein größeres Sichtfeld und mehr Bewegungsfreiheit verleiht.

Begründung der Jury
Das erweiterte Sichtfeld stellt eine Innovation dar, die durch die großzügigen Dimensionen und dynamischen Linien des Helms passend in Szene gesetzt wird.

pheos c²
Safety Eyewear
Arbeitsschutzbrille

Manufacturer
UVEX Arbeitsschutz GmbH, Fürth, Germany
Design
Brandis Industrial Design (Michael Brandis, Nadine Sauerwein), Nuremberg, Germany
Web
www.uvex-safety.com
www.brandis-design.de

The lens of the pheos c² safety eyewear is finished with a special coating, which is scratch-resistant on the outside and anti-fog on the inside. This ensures unobstructed vision even under extreme conditions. Another innovative manufacturing method makes it possible to inject both the nose pad and the soft components directly into the single-piece lens. In combination with the flexible temples, this provides pleasant wearing comfort.

Statement by the jury
Thanks to high-quality workmanship, the safety eyewear optimally fits the face while providing excellent freedom of movement.

Die Scheibe der Arbeitsschutzbrille pheos c² verfügt über eine spezielle Beschichtung, die außen extrem kratzfest ist und von innen nicht beschlägt. Dies sorgt auch unter schwierigen Bedingungen für eine uneingeschränkte Sicht. In einem weiteren innovativen Beschichtungsverfahren werden das Nasenpad und die Weichkomponenten bei der Herstellung direkt in die Vollscheibe gespritzt. Dies sorgt in Verbindung mit den flexiblen Bügeln für einen angenehmen Tragekomfort.

Begründung der Jury
Die hochwertige Verarbeitung der Schutzbrille sorgt dafür, dass sie optimal mit dem Gesicht abschließt und hervorragende Bewegungsfreiheit bietet.

Granberg 5501
Work Gloves
Arbeitshandschuhe

Manufacturer
Granberg AS, Bjoa, Norway
In-house design
Virginijus Urbelis
Web
www.granberg.no

The Granberg 5501 work gloves meet the standards of the highest cut protection class. A flexible impact protection system on the back of the hand guards the user against crushing forces and other impacts, directing it away from the hand in the case of an accident. This is achieved thanks to protective grooves, which run traversely, lengthwise and diagonally across the back of the hand, as well as other impact-protection details in areas where stretching powers are the strongest. The nitrile coating on the palm of the gloves provides a strong grip on dry, wet and oily surfaces.

Die Arbeitshandschuhe Granberg 5501 haben die höchste Schnittschutzklasse. Ein flexibles Schlagschutzsystem auf dem Handrücken schützt gegen Quetschkräfte und andere Schläge und leitet diese im Falle eines Unfalls von der Hand ab. Dies wird durch die Protektor-Rillen erreicht, die quer, längs und diagonal über den Handrücken verlaufen, sowie durch getrennte Schlagschutzdetails in den Bereichen, wo die Dehnkräfte am stärksten wirken. Die Nitrilbeschichtung in der Handfläche sorgt für einen festen Griff auf trockenen, nassen und öligen Oberflächen.

Statement by the jury
The functional design of the work gloves unites the properties of protection and convenience. The light-grey lines and gaps highlight the impact protection.

Begründung der Jury
Das funktionale Design der Arbeitshandschuhe vereint die Eigenschaften Schutz und Komfort. Die hellgrauen Linien und Zwischenräume heben den Schlagschutz prägnant hervor.

Morakniv Craft
Craftsmen Knives
Handwerksmesser

Manufacturer
Morakniv AB, Mora, Sweden
Design
No Picnic AB (Petter Åstradsson),
Stockholm, Sweden
Web
www.morakniv.com
www.nopicnic.com

The craftsmen knives of the Morakniv Craft series are available in ten different variants and a range of steel qualities. A characteristic feature of the knives is the coil shape of the handle, which goes back to a centuries-old manufacturing technique from the city of Mora in Sweden. A rubber coating made of thermoplastic elastomer borders the handle in order to highlight the historical legacy. The protective sheath can be attached to a belt using a clip.

Statement by the jury
These high-quality knives combine traditional craftsmanship with modern design. The colours indicate the knives' respective purposes.

Die Handwerksmesser der Serie Morakniv Craft sind in zehn verschiedenen Ausführungen und Stahlqualitäten erhältlich. Charakteristisches Gestaltungsmerkmal der Messer ist die Spindelform des Griffs, die auf eine jahrhundertealte Fertigungstechnik der Stadt Mora in Schweden zurückgeht. Eine Gummierung aus thermoplastischem Elastomer umrahmt diesen Griff, um das historische Erbe hervorzuheben. Die Schutzhülle kann mit einem Clip am Gürtel befestigt werden.

Begründung der Jury
Bei den hochwertigen Messern wurde traditionelles Handwerk in ein modernes Design überführt. Die Farben machen den jeweiligen Zweck erfahrbar.

Leatherman Signal
Mulitool
Multifunktionswerkzeug

Manufacturer
Leatherman Tool Group, Inc., Portland, USA
In-house design
Kenny Lohr
Web
www.leatherman.de

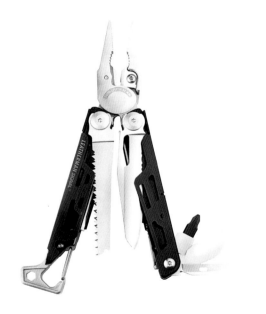

The Leatherman Signal combines classic tools like a saw, pliers, can opener and screwdriver with special tools like a whistle, blade grinder and fire starter, enabling users to help themselves in emergency situations even without modern technology. Furthermore, it is equipped with a hammer, wire cutters and file. With the help of the pocket clip or the snap hook, it can be attached to a trouser pocket or a backpack for quick access.

Statement by the jury
This multitool captivates with its cleverly conceived design concept, uniting 19 tools in the smallest of spaces.

Das Leatherman Signal kombiniert klassische Werkzeuge wie Säge, Zange, Dosenöffner und Schraubendreher mit speziellen Hilfsmitteln wie Signalpfeife, Klingenschleifer und Feuerstein, um sich in Notsituationen auch ohne moderne Technologien selbst helfen zu können. Darüber hinaus ist es mit einem Hammer, einem Drahtschneider und einer Feile ausgestattet. Mithilfe des Taschenclips oder Karabiners kann es für einen schnellen Zugriff an der Hosentasche oder am Rucksack befestigt werden.

Begründung der Jury
Das Multifunktionswerkzeug begeistert durch sein clever durchdachtes Gestaltungskonzept, das 19 Instrumente auf kleinstem Raum vereint.

Highbay | IL Up
LED Highbay
LED-Hallentiefstrahler

Manufacturer
HELLA KGaA Hueck & Co., HELLA Industries,
Lippstadt, Germany
Herbert Waldmann GmbH & Co. KG,
Villingen-Schwenningen, Germany
Design
HELLA KGaA Hueck & Co., HELLA Industries
(Christian Smarslik, Horst Feldkamp),
Lippstadt, Germany
Web
www.hella-industries.com
www.waldmann.com

The Highbay | IL Up, an LED highbay light, is divided into three components made from high-quality aluminium. Due to the physical separation of the heat sources and the addition of a thermal management system, which constantly monitors temperature, no cooling fins are required. At the same time, this results in a design without deep grooves, which makes the highbay easy to clean. For use in rough conditions, the LED modules can be protected with an additional protective plate made of glass.

Statement by the jury
This LED highbay appeals to the eye with its elegantly elongated form, which reinterprets the classical appearance of an industrial lamp.

Der LED-Hallentiefstrahler Highbay | IL Up ist in drei Bauteile aus hochwertigem Aluminium gegliedert. Durch die bauliche Trennung der Wärmequellen in Kombination mit einem Thermomanagement-System, das die Temperatur permanent überwacht, konnte auf den Einsatz von Kühlrippen verzichtet werden. Gleichzeitig entsteht dadurch eine Konstruktion ohne tiefe Rillen, sodass der Strahler einfach zu reinigen ist. In rauer Umgebung können die LED-Module durch eine zusätzliche Glasschutzscheibe geschützt werden.

Begründung der Jury
Der Hallentiefstrahler gefällt durch seine elegant gestreckte Form, die das klassische Erscheinungsbild einer Industrieleuchte neu interpretiert.

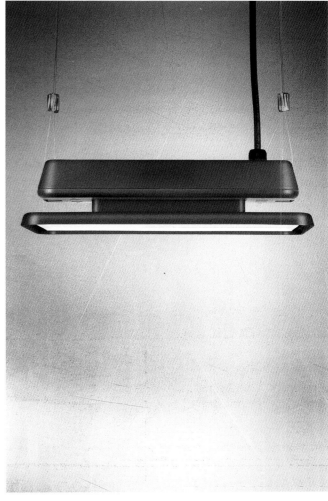

Series 976
Serie 976
LED Light
LED-Leuchte

Manufacturer
Franz Binder GmbH & Co. Elektrische
Bauelemente KG, Neckarsulm, Germany
In-house design
Web
www.binder-connector.de

The Series 976 LED light is protected against the infiltration of dust and water, which also makes it suitable for extreme industrial conditions. The high beam angle of 120 degrees enables optimal illumination. Due to its round design, the light is easy to install even in confined spaces. The M12 connector ensures a very high contact quality. The light is available in three different lengths.

Statement by the jury
This LED light is particularly slim and robust. It is very easy to hold along the metal edges, which finish flush with the body of the light.

Die LED-Maschinenleuchte der Serie 976 ist gegen das Eindringen von Staub und Wasser geschützt, sodass sie auch bei extremen industriellen Einsatzbedingungen standhält. Der hohe Abstrahlwinkel von 120 Grad ermöglicht eine optimale Ausleuchtung. Aufgrund ihrer runden Bauform ist die Leuchte auch bei beengten Platzverhältnissen einfach zu montieren. Der M12-Steckverbinder gewährleistet eine sehr gute Kontaktqualität. Die Leuchte ist in drei unterschiedlichen Längen erhältlich.

Begründung der Jury
Die LED-Leuchte ist ausgesprochen schlank und robust. Sie ist an den Metallrändern, die bündig mit dem Leuchtkörper abschließen, sehr gut zu halten.

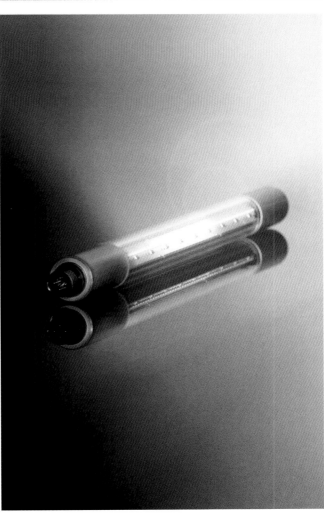

Heating and air conditioning technology
Heiz- und Klimatechnik

Zehnder Zmart
Radiator
Heizkörper

Manufacturer
Zehnder Group International AG,
Gränichen, Switzerland

Design
Tribecraft, Zürich, Switzerland

Web
www.zehnder-systems.com
www.tribecraft.ch

reddot award 2016
best of the best

New surfaces

As the final link in a complex chain of heat production for the home, radiators usually blend more or less effortlessly into a given interior. The aim in designing the Zehnder Zmart radiator was to create a new form for as many different spatial situations as possible. At the centre was the integration of the valve into the radiator in order to achieve a surface without visible interruption. The solution was to separate the "operational" and "actuational" functions of the thermostat and fully integrate the valve into the body of the radiator. This resulted in a seamless, enclosed cover extending over the front and sides of the radiator body. The hardly noticeable single opening is located at the air outlet on top. Since this opening is surrounded by a frame that merges seamlessly with the cover, the design was able to do entirely without a grille. The radiator is highly convenient to operate and can be mounted quickly and easily thanks to flexible connections. The user convenience is further enhanced by allowing the thermostat to be positioned on the left or right without the need to remove the radiator. Zehnder Zmart is much lighter than conventional radiators, features outstanding ecological heat-efficiency properties and is non-corrosive due to its polymer heating registers. The innovative design of this radiator turns it into a non-obtrusive interior element – emerging with clear surfaces that integrate seamlessly into almost any interior.

Neue Flächen

Ein Heizkörper ist der Endpunkt eines komplexen Systems der Wärmeerzeugung, der sich mehr oder weniger gut in das Interieur einfügt. Das Ziel der Gestaltung des Heizkörpers Zehnder Zmart war es, eine neue Form für möglichst viele Raumsituationen zu entwickeln. Im Mittelpunkt stand die Integration des sichtbaren Ventils, um so eine Fläche ohne optische Unterbrechung zu erhalten. Die Lösung liegt in der Trennung der Funktionen „Bedienung" und „Ventilantrieb" des Thermostats, um das Ventil ins Innere des Heizkörpers einzupassen. Es entsteht ein durchgängig geschlossenes Cover, welches sich über die Front und die Seitenpartien des Heizkörpers erstreckt. Die einzige, kaum sichtbare Öffnung befindet sich beim oben angeordneten Luftaustritt. Da die Öffnung von einem nahtlos in das Cover übergehenden Rahmen eingefasst ist, konnte auf ein Gitter verzichtet werden. Der Heizkörper lässt sich überaus komfortabel bedienen und ermöglicht dank flexibler Anschlüsse eine einfache und schnelle Montage. Den Komfort erhöht zusätzlich, dass der integrierte Thermostat variabel rechts oder links positioniert werden kann, ohne den Heizkörper zu demontieren. Zehnder Zmart ist deutlich leichter als herkömmliche Heizkörper, hat eine sehr gute Ökobilanz und die aus Kunststoff gefertigten Register sind korrosionsfrei. Die innovative Gestaltung dieses Heizkörpers macht ihn zu einem selbstverständlichen Raumelement – es entstehen klare Flächen, die sich nahtlos integrieren.

Statement by the jury

The design of the Zehnder Zmart radiator delivers a new spatial aesthetic. Since the valve was formally integrated, this radiator blends elegantly into almost any environment, allowing for new approaches in interior planning. It makes the otherwise often large, rectangular and usually massive radiator surfaces emerge with a well-proportioned appearance. The details are well thought-out, lending it a highly sophisticated appeal.

Begründung der Jury

Das Design des Heizkörpers Zehnder Zmart sorgt für eine neue Raumästhetik. Da das Ventil formal integriert wurde, fügt sich dieser Heizkörper elegant in die Umgebung ein und ermöglicht eine neue Art der Planung im Interieur. Auf beeindruckende Weise gelingt es der Gestaltung, einer großen rechteckigen, gewöhnlich massiven Fläche eine wohlproportionierte Formensprache zu verleihen. Die Gestaltung im Detail ist dabei ausgereift und durchdacht.

Designer portrait
See page 42
Siehe Seite 42

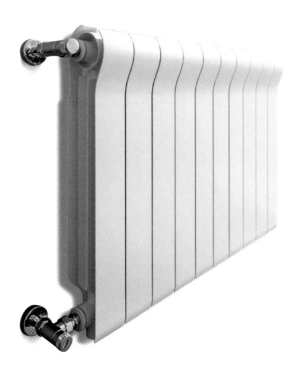

Ottimo
Radiator
Heizkörper

Manufacturer
Radiatori 2000 SpA, Ciserano (Bergamo), Italy
Design
Meneghello Paolelli Associati. Milan, Italy
Web
www.radiatori2000.it
www.meneghellopaolelli.com

The elegant, strikingly slim design of the Ottimo radiator has been made possible by use of die-cast aluminium. Through this innovative production process, thickness and weight of the metal elements could be minimised, resulting in a space-saving design while maintaining the same performance level. All products of the Ottimo series include a chrono-thermostat and can be combined with one another. The radiator is also available in an electric version.

Statement by the jury
The Ottimo radiator convinces with its slim design, and especially with its very filigree profile.

Die elegante, auffallend flache Gestaltung des Heizkörpers Ottimo wird durch die Verwendung von Druckguss-Aluminium ermöglicht. Durch diese innovative Produktionsweise konnten die Stärke und das Gewicht der Metallelemente minimiert werden; so nimmt der Heizkörper bei gleichbleibender Leistungsstärke deutlich weniger Raum ein. Alle Produkte der Ottimo-Serie haben eine Thermostat-Zeitschaltuhr und sind miteinander kombinierbar. Der Heizkörper ist auch in einer elektrischen Version erhältlich.

Begründung der Jury
Der Heizkörper Ottimo besticht mit einer flachen Bauweise und einer insbesondere im Profil sehr filigran wirkenden Gestaltung.

Regubox
Cabinet for the Building
Services Industry
Schrank für Haustechnik

Manufacturer
Oventrop GmbH & Co. KG, Olsberg, Germany
In-house design
Design
Design & Identität (Prof. Ulrich Hirsch), Brügge, Germany
Web
www.oventrop.de
www.designundidentitaet.de

The striking feature of the Regubox is its highly reduced, sophisticated design featuring a stainless-steel corpus with rounded corners and a frameless glass door. Behind the lockable glass door, technical components are concealed for surface heating systems or dwelling stations supplying individual residential units with heat and drinking water. The robust cabinet has a simple construction, is made of only a few components and is maintenance-free.

Statement by the jury
With its clear purist design and high-grade workmanship, the Regubox breaks with the conventional aesthetics of utility and engineering rooms.

Hervorstechendes Merkmal der Regubox ist ihre hochwertige, sehr reduzierte Gestaltung mit einem an den Ecken abgerundeten Edelstahlkorpus und einer rahmenlosen, abschließbaren Glastür. Dahinter verbergen sich technische Komponenten für Flächenheizungssysteme oder Wohnungsstationen, die einzelne Wohnungen mit Wärme und Trinkwasser versorgen. Der robuste Schrank ist einfach konstruiert, aus wenigen Teilen zusammengesetzt und wartungsfrei.

Begründung der Jury
Mit ihrer klaren, puristischen Gestaltung und hochwertigen Ausführung bricht die Regubox auf elegante Weise mit der gängigen Ästhetik von Technikräumen.

Buderus Logamax plus
GB192iT
Gas-Condensing Compact Heating System
Gas-Brennwert-Kompakt-
heizzentrale

Manufacturer
Bosch Thermotechnik GmbH, Buderus
Deutschland, Wetzlar, Germany
Design
designaffairs, Erlangen, Germany
Web
www.buderus.de
www.designaffairs.com

The outer appearance of this gas-con-
densing compact heating system is characterised by a robust yet elegant titanium glass surface with touchscreen.
The easily accessible interior shows a
bright and clear design. On a floor surface of 0.5 sqm, the energy-efficient
heating system offers an integrated hot
water tank. Thanks to its modular construction, it also allows for easy expandability with new technologies for hybrid
solutions.

Statement by the jury
With a high-grade and straightforward
interior and exterior design, the Logamax plus GB192iT communicates highest
efficiency and blends well into modern
living interiors.

Das äußere Erscheinungsbild dieser Gas-
Brennwert-Kompaktheizzentrale ist geprägt von einer robusten und dennoch
elegant wirkenden Titaniumglas-Ober-
fläche mit Touchscreen, während der gut
zugängliche Innenraum hell und übersichtlich gestaltet ist. Die energieeffiziente
Heizanlage bietet auf einer Grundfläche
von 0,5 qm einen integrierten Warmwas-
serspeicher und ist dank ihrer Modulbau-
weise auch um Hybridlösungen mit neuen
Technologien erweiterbar.

Begründung der Jury
Mit einer hochwertigen und aufgeräumten
Interieur- wie Exterieurgestaltung kom-
muniziert Logamax plus GB192iT höchste
Effizienz und fügt sich gut ins moderne
Wohnumfeld ein.

Vari Pro
Thermostat

Manufacturer
Chiller Oy, Tuusula, Finland

In-house design
Mikko Toivonen

Design
Link Design and Development Oy
(Jesse Laivo, Ville Hirvonen),
Espoo, Finland

Web
www.chiller.fi
www.linkdesign.fi

reddot award 2016
best of the best

Pure intelligence
Intelligent systems have made the organisation of home automation increasingly easy. They are oriented toward the needs and habits of users, optimised processes and are of paramount ecological relevance. The Vari Pro thermostat supports temperature regulation through intelligent technology customisable to the individual needs of users. The thermostat offers high convenience by indicating the current temperature, the desired temperature as well as the estimated time left to achieve that preset temperature. The status of all parameters can be intuitively checked at one glance. The device features an enticingly elegant LED circle that indicates the current operating mode. The interface design is supported by capacitive buttons giving users a mild feedback. The buttons make operating the device easier and help navigate the set-up menu. All components have been integrated into a slim housing of contemporary appearance. In order to simplify installation, the housing features only two frame parts, using a RJ9 connector to wire it up. The thermostat configures itself for convenience reasons with the help of a start-up wizard when powered up for the first time. The Vari Pro thermostat aestheticises everyday life – a design that emerged as a perfect form boasting intelligent technology.

Pure Intelligenz
Intelligente Systeme erleichtern zunehmend die häusliche Organisation. Sie orientieren sich an den Gewohnheiten der Bewohner, optimieren Abläufe und haben eine erhebliche ökologische Relevanz. Der Thermostat Vari Pro unterstützt die Temperatursteuerung mit einer den jeweiligen Bedürfnissen gut angepassten intelligenten Technologie. Er bietet dem Nutzer viel Komfort und zeigt die momentane, die gewünschte Temperatur sowie die verbleibende Zeit bis zum Erreichen der eingestellten Temperatur an. Intuitiv lässt sich dabei der Status aller Parameter auf einen Blick erfassen. Ein reizvolles gestalterisches Detail ist der elegante LED-Ring, der den aktuellen Betriebsmodus anzeigt. Ergänzt wird er durch kapazitive Tasten, die dem Nutzer ein dezentes Feedback geben. Sie erleichtern die Bedienung und werden ebenso zur Navigation im Set-up-Menü genutzt. Alle Komponenten sind in einem schlicht und modern anmutenden Gehäuse vereint. Um die Installation zu vereinfachen, besteht dieses nur aus zwei Rahmen, wobei zur Verkabelung ein RJ9-Stecker verwendet wird. Auf komfortable Weise konfiguriert sich der Thermostat selbst mithilfe eines Start-up-Wizards, wenn er zum ersten Mal in Betrieb genommen wird. Der Thermostat Vari Pro ästhetisiert den Alltag – die Gestaltung findet hier die perfekte Form für eine intelligente Technologie.

Statement by the jury
The Vari Pro thermostat conveys a simplicity that expresses masterly design skills. The design seamlessly merges all elements into a consistently intelligent system. Created with the needs of the user in mind, its innovative technology is integrated in a highly clever and coherent manner into one aesthetic form. The interface of this thermostat is intuitive to operate and offers a new outlook on convenience.

Begründung der Jury
Bei dem Thermostat Vari Pro überzeugt eine Einfachheit, die Ausdruck hohen gestalterischen Könnens ist. Alle Elemente fügen sich zu einem schlüssigen intelligenten System zusammen. Gestaltet mit dem Nutzer im Fokus, wird die innovative Technologie auf äußerst clevere Weise in eine ästhetische Form integriert. Das Interface dieses Thermostats lässt sich intuitiv bedienen und bietet eine neue Art von Komfort.

Designer portrait
See page 44
Siehe Seite 44

Element
Thermostat

Manufacturer
Vivint, Lehi, USA
In-house design
Vivint Innovation Center
Web
www.vivint.com

With the aid of smart home sensors throughout the house, the Element thermostat knows whether the residents are present or absent, regulating the temperature accordingly. The contact surface reacts promptly upon interaction yet remains plain white in standby mode. Thanks to its minimalist design approach, the thermostat blends harmoniously into different interior settings. The living room climate can be controlled remotely via smartphone and corresponding app.

Mithilfe von Smart-Home-Sensoren im ganzen Haus weiß der Thermostat Element, ob die Bewohner anwesend sind oder ob das Haus verlassen ist, und reguliert die Temperatur entsprechend. Im Ruhezustand ist die Oberfläche schlicht weiß, bei Interaktion reagiert sie jedoch prompt. Dank seines minimalistischen Gestaltungsansatzes fügt sich der Thermostat harmonisch in unterschiedliche Interieurs ein. Mittels Smartphone und entsprechender App kann das Wohnraumklima auch aus der Ferne reguliert werden.

Statement by the jury
The purist Element thermostat is user-friendly and makes saving energy simple and enjoyable.

Begründung der Jury
Puristisch und benutzerfreundlich präsentiert sich der Thermostat Element und macht das Energiesparen damit einfach und angenehm.

Evosense
Thermostatic Head
Thermostatkopf

Manufacturer
AB Markaryds Metallarmatur,
Markaryd, Sweden
In-house design
Design
Yellon AB (Örjan Nilsson), Jönköping, Sweden
Web
www.mma.se
www.yellon.se/design

The Evosense is a self-acting thermostat that regulates room temperature in an innovative way: it "feels" the room temperature and transfers this, according to the laws of physics, into motion by regulating a heating valve, which thus avoids overheating. The thermostat requires neither batteries nor other energy sources and therefore saves energy during its entire lifespan. By integrating high-grade materials and environmentally friendly processes, Evosense meets strict environmental classifications.

Statement by the jury
Contemporary, clear aesthetics attuned to modern radiators are combined in the Evosense with an intelligent concept of temperature control.

Evosense ist ein selbsttätiger Thermostat, der die Raumtemperatur auf innovative Weise reguliert: Er „fühlt" die Raumtemperatur und überträgt dies nach den Gesetzen der Physik in eine Bewegung, die ein Heizungsventil regelt. Damit schützt er vor Überheizung. Der Thermostat benötigt weder Batterien noch andere Energiequellen und spart so Energie. Durch den Einsatz hochwertiger Materialien und umweltschonender Prozesse erfüllt Evosense strenge Umweltklassifizierungen.

Begründung der Jury
Eine zeitgemäße, klare Ästhetik, die zu modernen Heizkörpern passt, verbindet sich bei Evosense mit einem intelligenten Konzept der Temperatursteuerung.

Junkers Control CT100
Intelligent Wi-Fi Room Controller
Intelligenter Wi-Fi-Raumregler

Manufacturer
Bosch Thermotechnik GmbH,
Wernau, Germany
In-house design
Tetiana Zavidalova, Erica Cusell
Design
VanBerlo, Eindhoven, Netherlands
Web
www.bosch-thermotechnology.com
www.vanberlo.nl

The Junkers Control CT100 enables the remote control of heating and hot water via smartphone or tablet. The appearance of the unit is characterised by a striking black high-tech glass surface that simultaneously serves as a touchscreen. In combination with a user-friendly app, the controller features well-conceived functions for saving energy, such as a presence function. Moreover, the self-learning app automatically adjusts the programmed functions to the user's actual behaviour.

Statement by the jury
This room controller takes a sophisticated approach to combining functionality and user-friendliness with an elegant appearance.

Junkers Control CT100 ermöglicht die Fernsteuerung von Heizung und Warmwasser per Smartphone oder Tablet. Das Erscheinungsbild des Geräts ist durch eine markante schwarze Hightech-Glasoberfläche geprägt, die zugleich als Touchscreen dient. Der Regler bietet in Verbindung mit einer nutzerfreundlichen App durchdachte Funktionen für das Energiesparen, wie z. B. eine Anwesenheitsfunktion. Zudem passt die selbstlernende App die programmierten Funktionen automatisch an das tatsächliche Verhalten der Nutzer an.

Begründung der Jury
Auf hohem Niveau verbindet dieser Raumregler Funktionalität und Benutzerfreundlichkeit mit einem eleganten Erscheinungsbild.

Danaus
Air Quality Sensor
Luftqualitätssensor

Manufacturer
Fangkuai Industrial Design Co., Ltd.,
Foshan, China
In-house design
Wei Tao Chen, Bo Yu Li
Web
www.sq-id.com

Danaus is an innovative air quality sensor for domestic use, which, thanks to its precise sensors, detects harmful emissions including fine dust, natural gas, formaldehyde, alcohol, soot, carbon monoxide, toluene and benzene. Additionally, it activates connected air-purifying mechanisms. The colour of the light ring indicates the currently measured air quality, with blue signaling that the quality is good. Thanks to its magnet mount, the unobtrusive aluminium unit can be flexibly used at various places around the house.

Statement by the jury
A purist design language in combination with high-quality materials lends the Danaus air quality sensor a timeless appearance.

Danaus ist ein innovativer Luftqualitätssensor für den Hausgebrauch, der dank seiner präzisen Sensoren gesundheitsschädliche Emissionen wie Feinstaub, Erdgas, Formaldehyd, Alkohol, Ruß, CO, Toluol, Benzol etc. aufspürt und gekoppelte Lüftungsmechanismen aktiviert. Die Farbe des Leuchtrings signalisiert die in diesem Moment gemessene Luftqualität, wobei Blau eine gute Qualität anzeigt. Mit seiner Magnetbefestigung kann der dezente Korpus aus Aluminium an wechselnden Orten im Haus flexibel eingesetzt werden.

Begründung der Jury
Eine puristische Formensprache in Verbindung mit hochwertigen Materialien verleiht dem Luftqualitätssensor Danaus eine zeitlose Anmutung.

Hybrid Air Conditioner
Hybrid-Klimaanlage

Manufacturer
Midea Air-Conditioning
Equipment Co., Ltd.,
Foshan, China

Design
Phoenix Design GmbH + Co. KG,
Stuttgart, Munich, Germany;
Shanghai, China

Web
www.midea.com
www.phoenixdesign.com

reddot award 2016
best of the best

Friendly climate

As autonomous systems, air conditioners in homes, offices and public spaces provide both heating and fresh air, creating a pleasant spatial atmosphere. The Hybrid Air Conditioner follows a new approach in terms of user-oriented form and function, making it not only easily accessible but also integrating users and their needs. The design features smooth and round lines of emotionalising appeal. The design idiom appeals to the senses and at the same time visualises the highly advanced technology. With the aim to promote wellbeing and health, this air conditioner not only supports the room climate but also improves air quality. In order to keep the room quality constant at all times, an integrated filter cleans both the prevalent room air and inflowing outside air. Another innovative design feature is the unit's innovative self-cleaning function, which, thanks to a UV light and integrated brushes, cleans and disinfects the filters on a regular basis. A light signal that is visible through the perforated plastic front indicates when the unit is in self-cleaning mode, thus addressing the need for safety and security of the people in the room. With its clear, unobtrusive design and natural appearance, the Hybrid Air Conditioner emerged as a friendly-looking and reliable partner within the user's personal private sphere.

Freundliches Klima

Als autonome Systeme sorgen Klimaanlagen vielerorts für die Belüftung oder Heizung von Räumen und gewährleisten ein angenehmes Raumklima. Die Hybrid-Klimaanlage geht neue Wege, ihre Form und Funktion sind dem Nutzer zugewandt, ermöglichen einen leichten Zugang und beziehen ihn ein. Die Gestaltung mit abgerundeten und weich anmutenden Linien emotionalisiert. Die Formensprache spricht die Sinne an und visualisiert zugleich die hochentwickelte Technologie. Mit der Zielsetzung, das Wohlbefinden und die Gesundheit zu fördern, unterstützt diese Klimaanlage das Raumklima und verbessert gleichzeitig die Luftqualität. Um dabei die Raumqualität ständig konstant zu halten, reinigt ein integrierter Filter die vorhandene Raum- wie auch die hereinströmende Außenluft. Ein wichtiger Aspekt ist zudem eine neuartige Selbstreinigungsfunktion, durch die die Filter mithilfe von UV-Licht und integrierten Bürsten regelmäßig gereinigt und desinfiziert werden. Über ein Lichtsignet wird dieser Reinigungsvorgang durch die perforierte Kunststofffront optisch sichtbar. Auf diese Weise wird das Sicherheitsbedürfnis der Menschen im Raum angesprochen. Mit ihrer klaren, zurückhaltenden Gestaltung und natürlichen Anmutung wird die Hybrid-Klimaanlage so zu einem freundlichen und verlässlichen Partner in der Privatsphäre.

Statement by the jury

The Hybrid Air Conditioner brings a fresh breeze into an otherwise rather tradition-defined area. It fascinates with its smooth and soft appearance that blends well into almost any interior. It impresses with technical details, among them an outstandingly innovative self-cleaning function. The organic and functional design of this air conditioner pushes the boundaries of traditional design in many respects.

Begründung der Jury

Mit der Hybrid-Klimaanlage weht ein frischer Wind in einem ansonsten eher traditionell geprägten Bereich. Sie begeistert mit ihrer weichen und sanften Anmutung, welche sich gut in nahezu jede Umgebung einfügt. Beeindruckend sind ihre technischen Qualitäten, wobei insbesondere die innovative Selbstreinigungsfunktion besticht. Die organische und funktionale Gestaltung dieser Klimaanlage ist wegweisend in vielerlei Hinsicht.

Designer portrait
See page 46
Siehe Seite 46

LG Residential 1-Way Cassette Air Conditioner
Klimaanlage

Manufacturer
LG Electronics Inc., Seoul, South Korea
In-house design
Yongduk Cha, Jinwon Kang, Sungmin Kim,
Hyunhee You, Inhyeuk Choi, Yuna Jo
Web
www.lg.com

The design of this one-way air conditioner is inspired by the sea. The intake grille design is reminiscent of the shape of slowly approaching waves, while the transparent section in the middle of the unit visualises waves sparkling in the sunlight. At the outlet, a large impeller wheel blows a cool breeze into the room. With its round, slim enclosure, the unit integrates discreetly into any ceiling environment. A display indicates operational status and air quality.

Statement by the jury
The design of this air-conditioning unit is inspired by ocean waves. This motif has been implemented consistently, yet also discreetly.

Die Gestaltung dieses 1-Wege-Klimageräts ist vom Meer inspiriert. Die Form des Einsauggitters erinnert an langsam heranrollende Wellen, der transparente Abschnitt in der Mitte des Geräts an Wellen, die im Sonnenlicht funkeln. Am Auslass sorgt ein großes Flügelrad dafür, dass die Klimaanlage eine kühle Brise in den Raum bläst. Mit seinem runden, schlanken Gehäuse integriert sich das Gerät dezent in die Deckenumgebung. Ein Display zeigt den Betriebsstatus und die Luftqualität an.

Begründung der Jury
Diese Klimaanlage ist in ihrer Formensprache von den Wellenbewegungen des Meeres inspiriert. Dieses Motiv wurde konsequent und zugleich dezent umgesetzt.

PZ Series Air-Conditioner
PZ-Serie Klimaanlage

Manufacturer
Midea Air-Conditioning Equipment Co., Ltd.,
Foshan, China
In-house design
Sanxin Li, Wei Pan
Web
www.midea.com
Honourable Mention

The air-conditioning systems of the PZ series are characterised by a combination of wood and metal, allowing them to harmoniously integrate into residential environments. The design of the air conditioners is slim and elegant. When the units are closed, they display a minimalist appearance, yet their open state renders a high-tech impression, reflecting their efficiency and functionality.

Statement by the jury
With a blend of wood and metal, this air-conditioner series has an appearance that is both welcoming and technical.

Die Klimaanlagen der PZ-Serie sind durch die Kombination von Holz und Metall gekennzeichnet, wodurch sie sich harmonisch in Wohnumgebungen integrieren lassen. Die Formgebung der Klimaanlagen ist schlank und elegant. In geschlossenem Zustand zeigen sie ein minimalistisches Erscheinungsbild, während sie geöffnet eine hochtechnologische Anmutung haben, die ihre Effizienz und Funktionalität widerspiegelt.

Begründung der Jury
Durch die Kombination von Holz und Metall wirkt diese Klimaanlagen-Serie wohnlich und technologisch zugleich.

Wukong i8 Intelligent Air Conditioner Partner
Thermostat for Air Conditioners
Thermostat für Klimaanlagen

Manufacturer
Shenzhen Galaxywind Network Systems Co., Ltd., Shenzhen, China
Design
Shenzhen White Design Co., Ltd.
(Zhang Xun, Huang Jin), Shenzhen, China
Web
www.galaxywind.com
www.whitedesign.com.cn
Honourable Mention

The Wukong i8 Intelligent Air Conditioner Partner is an innovative, intelligent thermostat that provides a safe and simple upgrade for traditional air-conditioning units. The energy-saving device is activated simply by connecting it to the air conditioner. Intelligent sensor technology, operated via remote control, monitors the unit. The thermostat can be integrated into business operating platforms and thus helps improve central energy management and reduce operating costs.

Wukong i8 Intelligent Air Conditioner Partner ist ein innovativer, intelligenter Thermostat, der traditionelle Klimaanlagen einfach und sicher aufrüstet. Um es in Betrieb zu nehmen, wird das energiesparende Gerät einfach an die Klimaanlage angeschlossen. Gesteuert wird es über eine intelligente Sensorik und per Fernbedienung. Der Thermostat lässt sich in Business-Betriebsplattformen integrieren und hilft so, das zentrale Energiemanagement zu verbessern und die Betriebskosten zu senken.

Statement by the jury
A high degree of user-friendliness characterises this purist thermostat for air-conditioning units.

Begründung der Jury
Eine hohe Benutzerfreundlichkeit kennzeichnet diesen puristisch gestalteten Thermostat für Klimaanlagen.

OA Air Conditioner
OA Klimaanlage

Manufacturer
Midea Air-Conditioning Equipment Co., Ltd., Foshan, China
In-house design
Sanxin Li, Jinpeng Shao
Web
www.midea.com

This wall-mounted circular air conditioner with its purist design provides both a comfortable room climate and, thanks to an integrated lighting function, also atmospheric illumination. The 360-degree circular air outlet optimises the air circulation area, resulting in a smooth and quiet operation of the unit. The light intensity adjusts automatically to the operating state and ambient brightness, thus creating a pleasant feeling of spaciousness.

Diese puristisch gestaltete, kreisförmige Wand-Klimaanlage sorgt nicht nur für ein angenehmes Raumklima, sondern dank integrierter Lichtfunktion auch für eine stimmungsvolle Beleuchtung. Die runde 360-Grad-Luftöffnung optimiert den Luftzirkulationsbereich, wodurch die Anlage ruhig und gleichmäßig arbeitet. Die Lichtstärke passt sich selbständig dem Betriebszustand und der Umgebungshelligkeit an. Dies schafft ein angenehmes Raumgefühl.

Statement by the jury
With its integrated light source and clear appearance, the OA Air Conditioner exudes a pleasant sense of calm.

Begründung der Jury
Mit ihrer eingebauten Lichtquelle und ihrem klaren Erscheinungsbild strahlt die OA Klimaanlage eine wohltuende Ruhe aus.

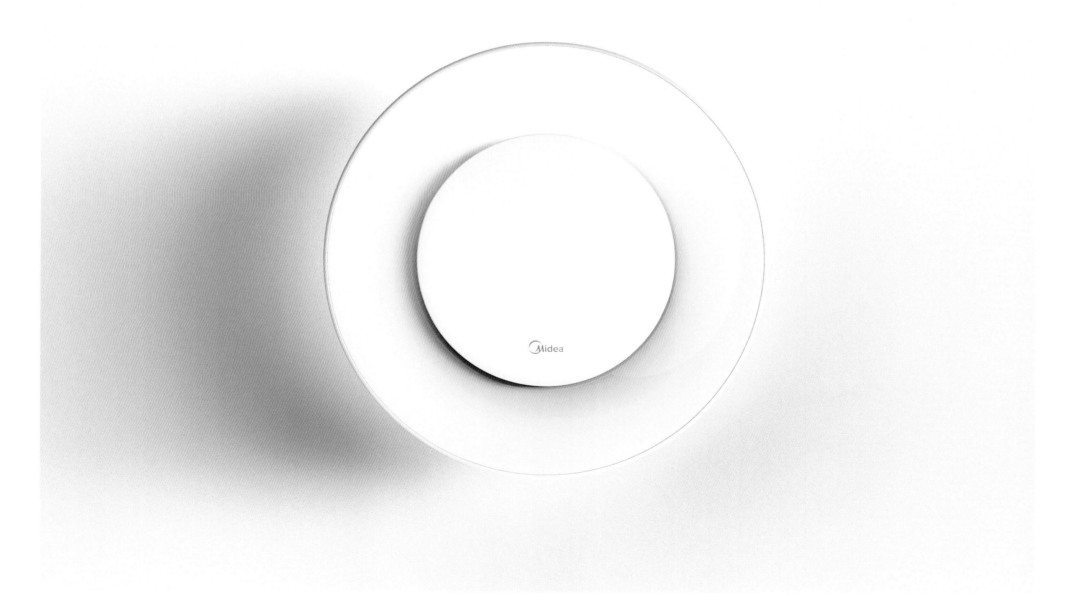

X360 Air Conditioner
X360 Klimaanlage

Manufacturer
Midea Air-Conditioning Equipment Co., Ltd., Foshan, China
In-house design
Bing Bai, Sanxin Li
Web
www.midea.com

The circular, extremely flat X360 air conditioner for wall mounting offers two different wind modes: rotating and 360 degrees. The central rotary wind damper and circular outlet opening are made of a premium aluminium-magnesium alloy. An integrated LED display communicates the selected programme.

Die kreisförmige, extrem flache Klimaanlage X360 für die Wandmontage bietet zwei verschiedene Wind-Einstellungen: rotierend und 360 Grad. Die zentrale Dreh-Windklappe und die ringförmige Austritts-öffnung sind aus einer hochwertigen Aluminium-Magnesium-Legierung gefertigt. Ein integriertes LED-Display kommuniziert das ausgewählte Programm.

Statement by the jury
With its balanced, minimalist design and elegant appearance, this air conditioner blends harmoniously into any given interior.

Begründung der Jury
Mit ihrer ausgewogenen, minimalistischen Formensprache und ihrer eleganten Anmutung fügt sich diese Klimaanlage in jedes Interieur ein.

Atmobot 3s
Air Purifier
Luftreiniger

Manufacturer
ECOVACS Robotics Co., Ltd., Suzhou, China
In-house design
Xiaowen Li, Xintong Yu
Web
www.ecovacs.com

The Atmobot 3s is a robotic air purifier
which is turned on by tapping the corpus
of the unit. Once activated, it establishes
a virtual map using a laser detection
system which subdivides the room into
sections for movement and purification
of air. With its intelligent sensors, the
robot detects particles and odours, while
also monitoring temperature and humidity. An indicator light on the top displays
the degree of air quality. The Atmobot 3s
can also be controlled by an app on a
mobile device.

Statement by the jury
The Atmobot 3s combines purist design
with intelligent functionality and impresses with a high degree of user-
friendliness.

Atmobot 3s ist ein Luftreinigungsroboter,
der mit einem Klopfen auf den Korpus ein-
geschaltet wird. Sobald er aktiviert ist,
erstellt er mithilfe eines Laser-Erkennungs-
systems eine virtuelle Karte, die den Raum
in Bewegungs- und Luftreinigungsab-
schnitte unterteilt. Dank intelligenter Sensoren erkennt der Roboter Partikel und
Gerüche und überwacht Temperatur sowie
Luftfeuchtigkeit. Eine Kontrollleuchte auf
der Oberseite zeigt die Luftqualität an.
Der Atmobot 3s lässt sich auch mobil per
App steuern.

Begründung der Jury
Der Atmobot 3s verbindet eine puristische
Gestaltung mit einer intelligenten Funktionsweise und punktet mit hoher Benutzerfreundlichkeit.

APD-1015B
Air Purifier & Dehumidifier
Luftwäscher & Luftentfeuchter

Manufacturer
Coway Co., Ltd., Seoul, South Korea
In-house design
Web
www.coway.com

This multifunctional device with integrated inverter filters and dehumidifies the air in indoor spaces in a particularly efficient and energy-saving way. The design focuses on user-friendliness, which is why the control unit was optically separated from the functional one: the generous user interface is situated on the inclined top of the device and is distinguished from the black air outlets by black-and-white contrasting. Energy-saving information can be easily obtained by the user on the circular display.

Statement by the jury
Thanks to a large, centred and slightly exposed control panel, this multifunctional device is easy to operate.

Dieses Multifunktionsgerät mit integriertem Wechselrichter filtert und entfeuchtet die Luft in Innenräumen besonders effizient und energiesparend. Der Gestaltungsfokus liegt auf der Benutzerfreundlichkeit, dafür wurde das Bedienteil optisch von der Funktionseinheit getrennt: Die großzügige Bedienoberfläche ist an der geneigten Oberseite des Geräts platziert und hebt sich durch den Schwarz-Weiß-Kontrast von den dunklen Luftauslässen ab. Über die kreisrunde Anzeige erhält der Nutzer Energiesparinformationen.

Begründung der Jury
Dank eines großen, zentrierten und leicht exponierten Bedienfeldes ist dieses multifunktionale Gerät einfach in der Handhabung.

HEMNES Air Purifier
HEMNES Luftreiniger

Manufacturer
Midea Air-Conditioning Equipment Co., Ltd., Foshan, China
In-house design
Sanxin Li, Lilong Zhou
Web
www.midea.com

The particular feature of this intelligent tabletop air purifier is its wood-textured surface, thanks to which the Hemnes can be perfectly integrated into residential environments. An innovative attribute is the drawer filter with a unique way of opening. The unit is monitored with a small remote control simultaneously serving as an air-testing device. As soon as it detects poor quality, the purifier starts automatically.

Statement by the jury
This air purifier pleases with its minimalist design. The wooden surface gives it the appearance of a piece of furniture so that it blends harmoniously into different living environments.

Das Besondere an diesem intelligenten Tisch-Luftreiniger ist seine Oberfläche in Holztextur. Dank dieser lässt sich Hemnes perfekt in Wohnumgebungen integrieren. Innovativ ist der Schubladenfilter mit seiner für einen Luftreiniger ungewöhnlichen Öffnungsweise. Gesteuert wird er mithilfe einer kleinen Fernbedienung, die gleichzeitig ein Luftprüfgerät ist. Sobald eine schlechte Luftqualität erfasst wird, startet es den Luftreiniger automatisch.

Begründung der Jury
Dieser Luftreiniger gefällt mit seiner minimalistischen Gestaltung. Die Holzoberfläche verleiht ihm die Anmutung eines Möbels, sodass er sich harmonisch in Wohnbereiche einfügt.

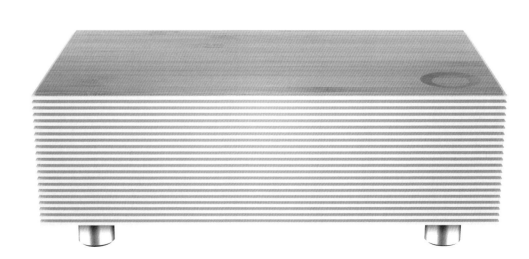

Super Air Cleaner
Super-Luftreiniger

Manufacturer
Tongyang Magic Inc., Seoul, South Korea
In-house design
Dongsu Kim, Dongwook Yoon, Jongsoo Kim
Web
www.magic.co.kr

The design of this air purifier was in-spired by a classic wood speaker shape. The 12,000 perforated holes on the front fulfil both an aesthetic and a functional purpose: by using the front absorption method, the overall size of the unit could be reduced, compared to similar devices, and the surface for cleaning widened by 25 per cent at the same time. The front colour LCD indicates air quality with colours and words (very good/good/poor/very poor).

Dieser Luftreiniger ist in seiner Gestaltung einem klassischen Holzlautsprecher nach-empfunden. Die 12.000 kleinen Perforie-rungen der Oberfläche erfüllen sowohl einen ästhetischen als auch einen funktio-nalen Zweck: Durch die Frontansaugme-thode konnte die Gesamtgröße des Geräts im Vergleich zu ähnlichen Produkten redu-ziert und die Fläche zur Reinigung der Luft gleichzeitig um 25 Prozent vergrößert wer-den. Das farbige LCD zeigt die Luftqualität mittels Farben und Worten (gut/normal/schlecht/sehr schlecht) an.

Statement by the jury
The design concept inspired by a wood speaker gives the Super Air Cleaner an independent appearance and ensures improved functionality.

Begründung der Jury
Das von einem Holzlautsprecher inspirierte Gestaltungskonzept verleiht dem Super Air Cleaner ein eigenständiges Erscheinungs-bild und sorgt zudem für eine bessere Funktionalität.

Dyson Pure Cool Link
Air Purifier
Luftreiniger

Manufacturer
Dyson Ltd, Malmesbury, Great Britain
In-house design
Web
www.dyson.com

The Dyson Pure Cool Link air purifier is connected to the Internet via Wi-Fi. With an intuitive smartphone app, the user can control the current air quality at home in real time and, as required, can also clean the air from anywhere. Through the efficient combination of a HEPA filter and an active carbon filter, the air purifier removes 99.95 per cent of all particles, down to a size of 0.1 microns. It filters pollen, mould spores, and fine dust from the air, but also odours, noxious fumes, allergens and bacteria.

Statement by the jury
An extremely efficient air purifying function is integrated into the already familiar, striking design of the Dyson air purifier.

Der Luftreiniger Dyson Pure Cool Link wird via Wi-Fi mit dem Internet verbunden. Per intuitiv bedienbarer Smartphone-App kann der Nutzer so auch von unterwegs die aktuelle Luftqualität daheim in Echtzeit kontrollieren und die Luft bei Bedarf reinigen. Durch die effiziente Kombination von HEPA- und Aktivkohlefilter entfernt der Luftreiniger 99,95 Prozent aller Partikel bis zu einer Größe von 0,1 Mikrometer. Er filtert Pollen, Schimmelsporen, Feinstaub, aber auch Gerüche, gesundheitsschädliche Ausdünstungen sowie Allergene und Bakterien aus der Luft.

Begründung der Jury
Eine äußerst effiziente Luftreinigungsfunktion wird hier harmonisch in die bereits vertraute markante Gestaltung des Dyson-Ventilators integriert.

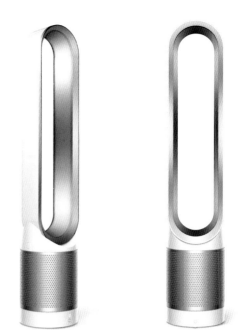

Sophia
Air Purifier
Luftreiniger

Manufacturer
WINIX Manufacturing Company, Seongnam. South Korea
In-house design
Chanwook Yeo, Seungho Kim
Web
www.winixcorp.com

The Sophia air purifier is characterised by a very slim design. It was developed with the growing number of single households in mind. With a depth of merely 200 mm, it consumes but little space. The intake vents are located at the front, left and right, thus guaranteeing optimum airflow and a high clean air delivery rate (CADR). A magnetic fastener at the front filter cover enables easy filter management and replacement.

Statement by the jury
The Sophia impresses with a slim, purist corpus and, simultaneously, high-performance figures.

Der Luftreiniger Sophia zeichnet sich durch eine sehr schlanke Bauweise aus. Er wurde insbesondere im Hinblick auf die wachsende Anzahl von Singlehaushalten entwickelt und nimmt mit einer Tiefe von 200 mm nur wenig Raum ein. Die Ansaugöffnungen befinden sich vorne, links und rechts und gewährleisten so einen optimalen Luftstrom und eine hohe Luftreinigungskapazität (CADR). Ein Magnetverschluss an der vorderen Filterabdeckung ermöglicht einen einfachen Filterwechsel.

Begründung der Jury
Sophia beeindruckt mit einem schlanken, puristisch gestalteten Korpus bei gleichzeitig hoher Leistung.

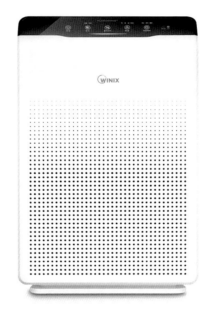

T1
Air Purifier
Luftreiniger

Manufacturer
Ningbo Taian New Material Technology Co.,
Ltd., Ningbo, China
In-house design
Jiangguo Huang, Chenjun Zhou
Web
www.ucheer.com

The compact T1 air purifier is based on
a purist and eco-friendly design concept.
Concealed behind the cubic, high-gloss
aluminium corpus is CH-CUT filter technology exclusively developed for the
purifier. Thanks to this technology, an
uninterrupted and highly efficient re-
moval of pollutants like formaldehyde
is possible without replacing the filter.
Both the functionality and the design
of the T1 are geared to durability,
making it an eco-friendly device that
efficiently and sustainably counteracts
air pollution in rooms.

Statement by the jury
The T1 convinces with a minimalist,
high-grade enclosure and innovative
functionality, giving the product a long
life cycle.

Dem kompakten Luftreiniger T1 liegt ein
puristisches und umweltfreundliches
Designkonzept zugrunde. Hinter dem
glänzenden kubischen Aluminiumkorpus
verbirgt sich eine eigens für den Luftreiniger entwickelte CH-CUT-Filtertechnologie.
Dank dieser Technologie ist eine ununter-
brochene und hochwirksame Auflösung
von Schadstoffen wie Formaldehyd auch
ohne Filterwechsel möglich. Sowohl Funktionsweise als auch Gestaltung des T1
sind auf Langlebigkeit ausgerichtet, was
ihn zu einem umweltfreundlichen Gerät
macht, das Luftverschmutzung in Räumen
effizient und dauerhaft entgegenwirkt.

Begründung der Jury
Der T1 überzeugt mit einem minimalistischen, hochwertigen Gehäuse und einer
innovativen Funktionsweise, die dem
Produkt Langlebigkeit verleihen.

U300
Humidifier
Luftbefeuchter

Manufacturer
BONECO AG, Widnau, Switzerland
In-house design
Manfred Fitsch
Web
www.boneco.com

The U300 humidifier combines air humidifying with simultaneous fragrancing. An ultrasonic system converts water into a microfine mist, which is released into the room through an outlet nozzle. Fragrance oils are diffused into the air from the removable fragrance container at the back of the unit. The flat dial integrated into the bottom of the unit allows continuous regulation, while its illuminated ring indicates the water status of the device.

Statement by the jury
This humidifier is distinguished by intuitive usage with pleasant results thanks to a consistent, sophisticated design concept.

Der Luftbefeuchter U300 befeuchtet die Raumluft und beduftet sie gleichzeitig. Mittels Ultraschallsystem wird das Wasser in mikrofeinen Nebel umgewandelt, der über eine Auslassdüse an die Umgebung abgegeben wird. Über den entnehmbaren Duftstoffbehälter auf der Rückseite des Geräts lassen sich Duftöle in die Raumluft einbringen. Der flächig im unteren Teil integrierte Drehknopf ermöglicht eine stufenlose Regelung, wobei sein Leuchtring den Status des Geräts anzeigt.

Begründung der Jury
Aufgrund eines stringent durchdachten Gestaltungskonzepts zeichnet sich dieser Luftbefeuchter durch eine intuitive Handhabung sowie eine angenehme Wirkung aus.

Tower
Turm
Air Purifier
Luftreiniger

Manufacturer
WINIX Manufacturing Company, Seongnam, South Korea
In-house design
Chanwook Yeo, Seungho Kim
Web
www.winixcorp.com

The visually striking feature of the Tower air purifier is its cylindrical shape, which distinguishes the unit, in terms of design, from traditional air purifiers. With this slim shape, the purifier requires less stand space and can also be used in small environments. The Tower is even available in a version featuring a Wi-Fi module, allowing the user to monitor air quality from a distance and to control the air purifier via smartphone or tablet.

Statement by the jury
The elegant and striking cylindrical design gives this air purifier a sculptural character. It also reduces the amount of space needed for the unit.

Visuell hervorstechendes Merkmal des Luftreinigers Turm ist seine zylindrische Form, mit der er sich gestalterisch von traditionellen Luftreinigern abhebt. Durch diese Formgebung benötigt er weniger Standfläche und kann auch in kleinen Räumen eingesetzt werden. Den Turm gibt es auch in einer Version mit Wi-Fi-Modul, die es dem Nutzer erlaubt, die Luftqualität aus der Ferne zu überprüfen und den Luftreiniger über Smartphone oder Tablet zu steuern.

Begründung der Jury
Seine elegante, markant zylindrische Formgebung verleiht diesem Luftreiniger einen skulpturalen Charakter. Zudem sorgt sie dafür, dass er wenig Platz in Anspruch nimmt.

Air Humidifier Series 5000
Air Humidifier
Luftbefeuchter

Manufacturer
Royal Philips, Eindhoven, Netherlands
In-house design
Philips Design
Web
www.philips.com

The units of the 5000 series are high-performance air humidifiers that purify air at the same time. The design allows for integration of innovative particle filtration technology, which ensures that the humidified air is clean and healthy. The corpus has a compact and classic-elegant design, and a user-friendly control system facilitates operation of the humidifiers.

Statement by the jury
The 5000 series air humidifiers convince with their high performance and compact design. The polished surface gives the units an elegant appearance.

Die Geräte der Serie 5000 sind leistungsstarke Luftbefeuchter, die die Luft gleichzeitig reinigen. Der Aufbau ermöglicht die Integration einer innovativen Partikelfiltrations-Technologie, durch die sichergestellt wird, dass die befeuchtete Luft auch sauber und gesund ist. Der Korpus ist kompakt und klassisch-elegant gestaltet, der Luftbefeuchter wird über ein benutzerfreundliches Kontrollsystem bedient.

Begründung der Jury
Die Luftbefeuchter der Serie 5000 punkten mit hoher Leistung bei kompakter Bauweise. Die glänzende Oberfläche verleiht den Geräten ein elegantes Erscheinungsbild.

LG Signature Hybrid Air Purifier
Luftreiniger

Manufacturer
LG Electronics Inc., Seoul, South Korea
In-house design
Sehwan Bae, Joosang Kim, Seungmin Yoo, Sungkyong Han, Yoojeong Han
Web
www.lg.com

The functionality of this air purifier is inspired by the natural phenomenon of rain washing pollutant particles from the air: the LG Signature Hybrid Air Purifier sucks in polluted air through the filter, washes it with clean water and emits fresh, clean air again. This process can be observed through a transparent section of the enclosure. The easily accessible water tank can be pulled out of the top for filling and cleaning.

Statement by the jury
This air purifier convinces with its eco-friendly functionality, highlighted and visualised by the transparent element.

Die Funktionsweise dieses Luftreinigers ist von dem natürlichen Phänomen inspiriert, dass der Regen Schmutzpartikel aus der Luft wäscht: Der LG Signature Hybrid Air Purifier saugt verschmutzte Luft durch den Filter ein, wäscht sie mit sauberem Wasser und bläst die frische, gereinigte Luft wieder aus. Dieser Vorgang lässt sich durch einen transparenten Bereich im Gehäuse beobachten. Der gut erreichbare Wassertank kann zum Befüllen und Reinigen nach oben herausgezogen werden.

Begründung der Jury
Dieser Luftreiniger überzeugt mit einer umweltfreundlichen Funktionsweise, die durch das transparente Element hervorgehoben und nachvollziehbar gemacht wird.

M3 Series Gas Heater
Gas Water Heater
Gas-Durchlauferhitzer

Manufacturer
Haier Group, Qingdao, China
Design
Haier Innovation Design Center
(Wang Haoxing, Song Lei, Hu Xiaodong, Wang Haili, Liu Li),
Qingdao, China
Web
www.haier.com

The gas water heaters of the M3 series are constructed in such a way that the hitherto exposed housing elements are now harmoniously integrated into the surface, resulting in a reduced design and easier cleaning of the unit. The pre-warm cycle or "zero cold water" function is indicated by a progress bar on the display. A carbon-monoxide alarm at the side of the housing guarantees secure operation.

Die Gas-Durchlauferhitzer der M3-Serie sind so konstruiert, dass Gehäuseelemente, die bislang freiliegend waren, jetzt harmonisch in die Oberfläche integriert sind. Dadurch ist die Gestaltung reduzierter und die Geräte sind leichter sauber zu halten. Der Vorwärm-Zyklus oder „Zero-Cold-Water"-Funktion wird über einen Fortschrittsbalken auf dem Display angezeigt. Ein Kohlenmonoxid-Alarm an der Seite des Gehäuses bietet Sicherheit.

Statement by the jury
With a solid design characterised by smooth surfaces, the heaters of the M3 series foster an appealing and reliable overall impression.

Begründung der Jury
Durch eine solide Gestaltung mit glatten Oberflächen hinterlassen die Geräte der M3-Serie einen ansprechenden und zuverlässigen Gesamteindruck.

ANNI ECO Water Heater
Heat Pump Water Heater
Warmwasser-Wärmepumpe

Manufacturer
Aini Electrical Appliance Manufacture Co., Ltd., Foshan, China
In-house design
Yong Liang Chen, Guang Biao Luo
Design
Fangkuai industrial design Co., Ltd. (Wei Tao Chen, Bo Yu Li, Hua Xiang Ou Yang), Hefei, China
Web
www.gdaini.com
www.sq-id.com

This heat pump water heater is an energy-saving and highly efficient central water heater. With regard to a comfortable and healthy user experience, the Anni Eco combines a hot water circulation system with a water purifier function. Thanks to its triangular shape, the unit can be installed in a space-saving way in corners when necessary. A smart controller system enables monitoring and controlling via a smartphone.

Diese Warmwasser-Wärmepumpe ist ein energiesparender und sehr effizienter zentraler Warmwasserbereiter. Im Hinblick auf ein komfortables und gesundes Benutzererlebnis kombiniert Anni Eco ein Warmwasser-Zirkulationssystem mit einer Wasserreinigungsfunktion. Mit seiner dreieckigen Grundform lässt sich das Gerät bei Bedarf platzsparend in einer Ecke installieren. Ein „Smart Controller System" erlaubt die Überwachung und Steuerung via Smartphone.

Statement by the jury
The Anni Eco Water Heater convinces with a high degree of functionality and also with a design enabling an optimised use of space.

Begründung der Jury
Der Anni Eco Water Heater überzeugt gleichermaßen mit hoher Funktionalität wie mit einer Gestaltung, die eine optimale Raumausnutzung zulässt.

EcoTouch Ai1 Air
Heat Pump
Wärmepumpe

Manufacturer
WATERKOTTE GmbH, Herne, Germany
Design
industrialpartners GmbH,
Frankfurt/Main, Germany
Web
www.waterkotte.de
www.industrialpartners-communication.de

The EcoTouch Ai1 Air, an air heat pump, consists of indoor and outdoor unit that harmonise with regard to their reduced and clear design. The outdoor unit made of corrosion-resistant aluminium is cost-efficient and, with its newly developed fan, also energy-efficient and silent. By means of inverter technology, the compressor performance is adjusted to the heat demand, optimising efficiency and reducing operating costs.

Statement by the jury
The EcoTouch Ai1 Air combines clear, unobtrusive design with the implementation of energy-efficient technology.

Die Luft-Wärmepumpe EcoTouch Ai1 Air setzt sich aus Innen- und Außeneinheit zusammen, die mit ihrer reduzierten, klaren Gestaltung harmonisch aufeinander abgestimmt sind. Die Außeneinheit mit einem Gehäuse aus korrosionsbeständigem Aluminium ist sparsam und dank Neuentwicklungen beim Ventilator energieeffizient und geräuscharm. Mittels Invertertechnik passt sich die Verdichterleistung dem Wärmebedarf an, dies optimiert die Wirkung und reduziert die Betriebskosten.

Begründung der Jury
Die EcoTouch Ai1 Air verbindet eine unaufdringliche, klare Gestaltung mit dem Einsatz energieeffizienter Technik.

EcoTouch Ai1 Geo
Heat Pump
Wärmepumpe

Manufacturer
WATERKOTTE GmbH, Herne, Germany
Design
industrialpartners GmbH,
Frankfurt/Main, Germany
Web
www.waterkotte.de
www.industrialpartners-communication.de

The EcoTouch A1 Geo geothermal heat pump uses ground or groundwater close to the surface as a heat source. The underlying design concept combines economy, energy efficiency and modern control technology with a discreet contemporary and, at the same time, elegant appearance. The heat pump is controlled directly on the device or via a touch-screen through an intuitive user interface or using a mobile terminal.

Statement by the jury
With its elegant-minimalist design, the EcoTouch Ai1 Geo blends harmoniously into any environment. Moreover, it convinces with its user-friendly control system.

Die Erdwärmepumpe EcoTouch A1 Geo nutzt als Wärmequelle das oberflächennahe Erdreich oder Grundwasser. Das ihr zugrundeliegende Gestaltungskonzept vereint Wirtschaftlichkeit, Energieeffizienz und moderne Steuerungstechnik mit einer zeitgemäß schlichten und zugleich eleganten Erscheinung. Die Wärmepumpe wird entweder direkt am Gerät über ein Touchdisplay mit intuitiv bedienbarer Benutzeroberfläche gesteuert oder über ein mobiles Endgerät.

Begründung der Jury
Mit ihrem elegant-minimalistischen Design fügt sich die EcoTouch Ai1 Geo in jede Umgebung ein. Zudem überzeugt sie mit einer benutzerfreundlichen Steuerung.

Basic Line Ai1 Geo
Heat Pump
Wärmepumpe

Manufacturer
WATERKOTTE GmbH, Herne, Germany
Design
industrialpartners GmbH,
Frankfurt/Main, Germany
Web
www.waterkotte.de

The Basic Line Ai1 Geo is a complete system offering all heating functions required. The geothermal heat pump derives its energy from the ground and provides heat in the winter, cooling in the summer and hot water all year round. The basic equipment includes a 170-litre hot water tank, a weather-based controller and an easy-to-operate control unit.

Statement by the jury
Thanks to a design that is compact and unobtrusive yet also high in quality, the Basic Line Ai1 Geo can be integrated well into any living quarters.

Die Basic Line Ai1 Geo ist ein Komplettsystem, das alle nötigen Heizfunktionen bietet. Die Erdwärmepumpe bezieht ihre Energie aus dem Erdreich und sorgt im Winter für Wärme, im Sommer für Kühlung und das ganze Jahr hindurch für warmes Wasser. Zur Grundausstattung gehören ein 170-Liter-Warmwasserspeicher, ein witterungsgeführter Regler sowie eine einfach zu bedienende Steuereinheit.

Begründung der Jury
Dank ihrer kompakten, unaufdringlichen und zugleich hochwertigen Gestaltung lässt sich die Basic Line Ai1 Geo gut in den Wohnbereich integrieren.

Sensor Comfort Compact
Heat Pump
Wärmepumpe

Manufacturer
Heliotherm Wärmepumpentechnik
Ges.m.b.H., Langkampfen, Austria
In-house design
Andreas Bangheri
Web
www.heliotherm.com

The Sensor Comfort Compact is a fully modulating air-water heat pump in compact design for outdoor installation in single- and multifamily homes. Using innovative modulation technology and optional active cooling, the unit creates and ensures a comfortable indoor climate. It is combinable with photovoltaic systems and various other storage and heat distribution systems. Sensor Comfort Compact works very efficiently and attains favourable seasonal efficiency (SCOP).

Statement by the jury
Thanks to a large number of combination options, this heat pump offers significant leeway in heating system planning.

Sensor Comfort Compact ist eine vollmodulierende Luft-Wasser-Wärmepumpe in kompakter Bauweise zur Außenaufstellung für Ein- und Mehrfamilienhäuser. Ein angenehmes Raumklima wird durch den Einsatz innovativer Modulationstechnik sowie optional durch aktive Kühlung sichergestellt. Das Gerät kann mit Photovoltaikanlagen sowie verschiedenen Speicher- und Wärmeabgabesystemen kombiniert werden. Sensor Comfort Compact arbeitet sehr effizient und erreicht einen sehr hohen saisonalen Wirkungsgrad (SCOP).

Begründung der Jury
Dank zahlreicher Kombinationsmöglichkeiten bietet diese Wärmepumpe viel Freiraum bei der Planung der Heizungsanlage.

Heat Pump Water Heater
Wärmepumpe

Manufacturer
Midea Group, Foshan, China
In-house design
Jiawei Chen, Hualong Li
Web
www.midea.com
Honourable Mention

An important aspect in the design of this heat pump water heater was to heighten acceptance in the Chinese market for an eco-friendly heat pump drawing energy from the air. The design of the corpus of the device follows a strict geometric language of form. The metallic reflecting surface is designed to ensure that the unit integrates optimally into its environment, while visually conveying the cleanliness of the underlying technology.

Statement by the jury
This heat pump water heater shows a consistent design that builds confidence in its energy-saving and eco-friendly functionality.

Ein wichtiger Aspekt bei der Gestaltung dieser Warmwasser-Wärmepumpe war, im chinesischen Markt die Akzeptanz einer umweltfreundlichen Wärmepumpe, die ihre Energie aus der Luft bezieht, zu erhöhen. Die Gestaltung des Korpus folgt einer streng geometrischen Formensprache. Die metallisch-spiegelnde Oberfläche wiederum soll sicherstellen, dass sich das Gerät bestmöglich in seine Umgebung integriert, während sie gleichzeitig visuell die Sauberkeit der zugrundeliegenden Technologie vermittelt.

Begründung der Jury
Diese Warmwasser-Wärmepumpe zeigt eine konsequente Gestaltung, die Vertrauen in ihre energiesparende und umweltfreundliche Funktionsweise schafft.

Buderus Logasol SKR10 CPC
Vacuum Tube Collector
Vakuumröhrenkollektor

Manufacturer
Bosch Thermotechnik GmbH, Buderus Deutschland, Wetzlar, Germany
Design
TEAMS Design, Esslingen, Germany
Web
www.buderus.de
www.teamsdesign.com

The Logasol SKR10 CPC vacuum tube collector is compatible with the most varied architectural concepts, whether pitched roof, flat roof or facade. With protective covers between the collectors and the edge of the array, a uniform appearance ensues. Thanks to compact dimensions and a weight of merely 18 kg, the ready-mounted modules can easily be transported and mounted. Depending on the heat demand, the modules may be flexibly combined to collector arrays of different sizes.

Der Vakuumröhrenkollektor Logasol SKR10 CPC ist mit den unterschiedlichsten architektonischen Konzepten kompatibel, vom Spitzdach übers Flachdach bis hin zur Fassade. Durch Abdeckkappen zwischen den Kollektoren und am Rand des Feldes entsteht ein einheitliches Erscheinungsbild. Dank kompakter Abmessungen und einem Gewicht von nur 18 kg können die fertig montierten einzelnen Module leicht transportiert und angebracht werden. Je nach Wärmebedarf lassen sich die Module flexibel zu Kollektorfeldern unterschiedlicher Größe kombinieren.

Statement by the jury
Thanks to the symmetrical design and high-grade workmanship of the Logasol SKR10 CPC, the collector array fosters a homogeneous overall impression.

Begründung der Jury
Durch die symmetrische Gestaltung und hochwertige Verarbeitung des Logasol SKR10 CPC lassen sich Kollektorenfelder mit homogenem Gesamteindruck erstellen.

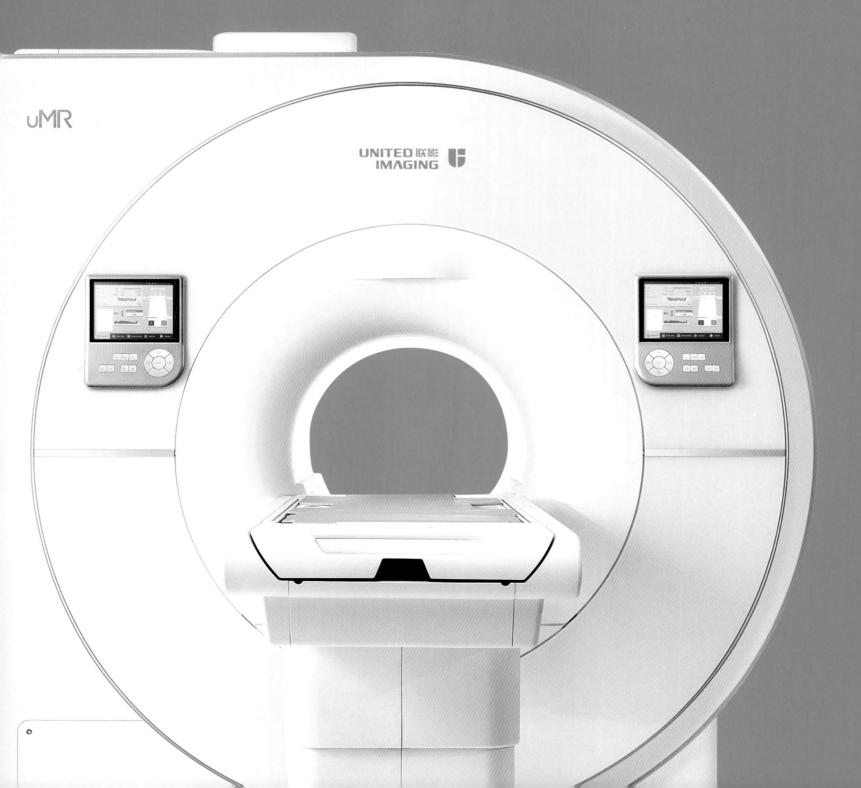

General practice and hospital
fittings
Healthcare
Laboratory technology and
furniture
Medical devices and equipment
Mobility, care and
communication aids
Orthopaedic aids
Orthoses and prostheses
Rehabilitation

Healthcare
Labortechnik und -mobiliar
Medizinische Geräte und
Ausrüstungen
Mobilitäts-, Pflege- und
Kommunikationshilfen
Orthesen und Prothesen
Orthopädische Hilfsmittel
Praxis- und
Krankenhausausstattung
Rehabilitation

uMR

UNITED 联影
IMAGING

Life science and medicine
Life Science und Medizin

Lumify
Ultrasound System
Ultraschallsystem

Manufacturer
Royal Philips,
Eindhoven, Netherlands

In-house design
Philips Design

Web
www.philips.com

reddot **award 2016**
best of the best

New transparency
Quick assessments and speedy access to patient data is of vital importance in today's medical treatment environment. Against this backdrop, Lumify presents a solution that convinces with designed simplicity. Complemented by an app, the innovative system offers the possibility to use ultrasound in a highly contemporary manner. As such, it presents a simple mobile solution for clinicians who need quick results in daily patient screening tasks. It can be controlled via any compatible smartphone or tablet that connects to the ultrasound transducer. Speedy assessments are thus enabled, needed for instance when testing in order to rule out acute diseases such as appendicitis. Furthermore, the app also allows clinicians and other staff to have quick access to detailed patient information and offers the possibility to share images, video and notes. The clear arrangement of the Lumify app is influenced by the simplicity of modern photo apps. The ultrasound transducer is pleasing to the touch and features easy-to-clean surfaces. It is quick and easy to familiarise with for getting quick diagnostic answers right from the start. The concept delivers a convincing system comprising an app and transducer, web portal and e-store. It facilitates uncomplicated collaboration and provides clinicians with all the tools needed for quick diagnostic answers. Lumify embodies an outstandingly practical solution for the daily work of clinicians.

Neue Transparenz
Eine möglichst zeitnahe Bereitstellung von Patientendaten ist in der Medizin von zentraler Bedeutung. Das Konzept von Lumify stellt hier eine in ihrer Einfachheit beeindruckende Lösung dar. Unterstützt von einer App, bietet dieses innovative System die Möglichkeit, ein Ultraschallgerät auf zeitgemäße Art zu nutzen. Als solches ist es eine einfache mobile Lösung für Ärzte, die für das tägliche Patientenscreening rasche Ergebnisse benötigen. Die Anwendung lässt sich über jedes kompatible Smartphone oder Tablet steuern, an welches der Ultraschallkopf angeschlossen wird. So werden schnelle Diagnosen ermöglicht, wenn es beispielsweise darum geht, eine akute Erkrankung wie eine Blinddarmentzündung auszuschließen. Mittels der App haben der Arzt oder das Personal zudem einen leichten Zugang zu weiteren Patienteninformationen. Möglich ist auch der Austausch von Bildern, Videos und Notizen. Beeinflusst von der Einfachheit heutiger Foto-Apps ist die Lumify-App klar gestaltet. Der Ultraschallkopf hat eine haptisch angenehme und leicht zu reinigende Oberfläche. Mit der Bedienung ist man rasch vertraut, um schnelle Diagnoseergebnisse zu erzielen. Das Konzept bietet ein stimmiges System aus App und Ultraschallkopf, Web-Portal und E-Store. Es begünstigt eine unkomplizierte Zusammenarbeit und gibt die für die prompte Diagnose nötigen Werkzeuge an die Hand. Lumify steht für eine bestechend praktikable Lösung im medizinischen Alltag.

Statement by the jury
The Lumify ultrasound system offers an uncomplicated solution for screening patients. It facilitates simple yes/no answers during patient screening as well as a useful management of patient information. Its innovative design concept offers just the right form for today's complexities in the medical field. With its clear arrangement and appealing design, it is portable, cost-effective and easily accessible.

Begründung der Jury
Das Ultraschallsystem Lumify ist eine unkompliziert nutzbare Lösung für das Patientenscreening. Es ermöglicht einfache Ja/Nein-Diagnosen und bietet eine sinnvolle Verwaltung der Patientendaten. Sein innovatives Gestaltungskonzept findet genau die richtige Form für die heutige Komplexität der Abläufe im Medizinbereich. Dieses klar und ansprechend gestaltete System ist dabei mobil, erschwinglich und leicht zugänglich.

Designer portrait
See page 48
Siehe Seite 48

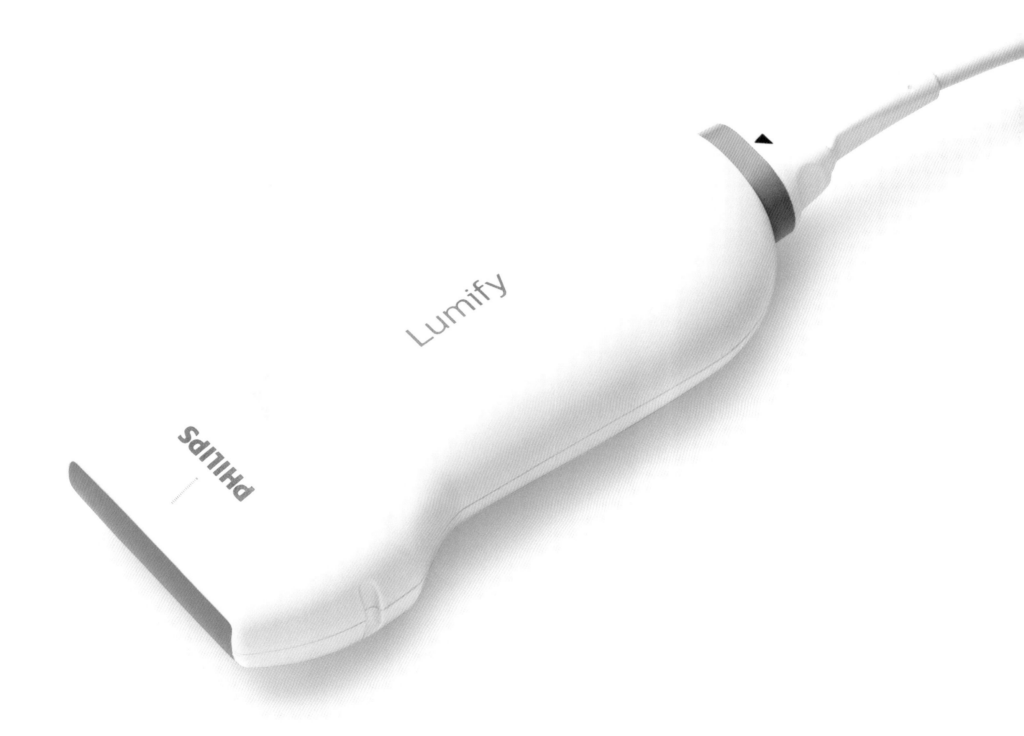

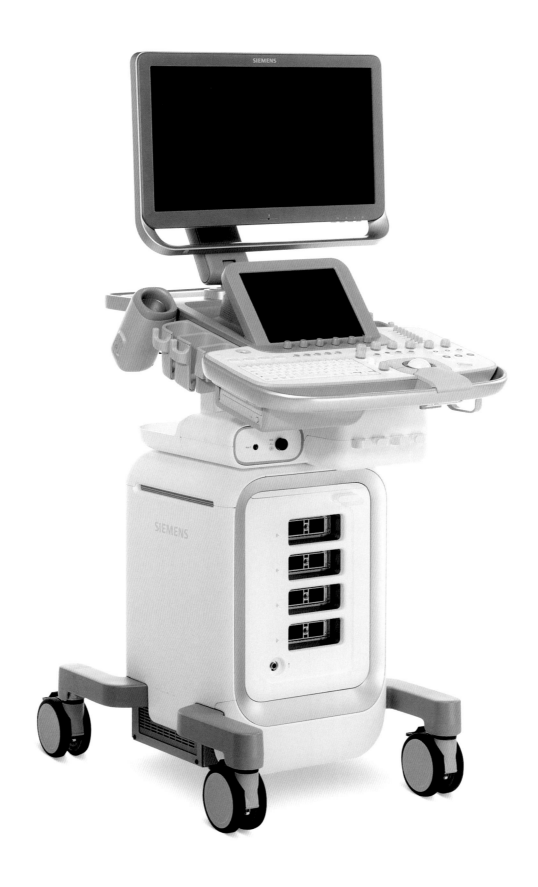

ACUSON NX3
Ultrasound System
Ultraschallsystem

Manufacturer
Siemens Healthcare, Seongnam, South Korea
In-house design
Design
RND+ (Jae Hwa Moon), Seoul, South Korea
Web
www.healthcare.siemens.com/ultrasound
www.rndplus.co.kr

The Acuson NX3 is an ultrasound system of the latest generation, with a design specifically geared towards an effective workflow. Thanks to its clearly structured operating console, up to 28 per cent fewer keystrokes are required as compared to similar devices. At the same time, users can specify numerous key settings according to their requirements, speeding up the scanning process even more. The 10.4" touch display enables quick selection of imaging parameters, while details are displayed particularly clearly on the 21.5" ultrasound monitor.

Statement by the jury
The Acuson NX3 captivates with its structured layout and generously dimensioned monitors. The other components display a markedly unobtrusive design.

Das Acuson NX3 ist ein Ultraschallsystem der neuesten Generation, dessen Design auf eine effiziente Arbeitsweise ausgelegt ist. Dank der übersichtlichen Bedienkonsole werden bis zu 28 Prozent weniger Tastenanschläge benötigt als bei vergleichbaren Geräten. Gleichzeitig kann der Anwender zahlreiche Tasteneinstellungen nach seinen Bedürfnissen festlegen, was das Scannen zusätzlich beschleunigt. Das 10,4"-Touchdisplay ermöglicht eine schnelle Auswahl der Bildgebungsparameter, während sich Details auf dem 21,5"-Ultraschallmonitor besonders gut erkennen lassen.

Begründung der Jury
Das Acuson NX3 begeistert durch seine strukturierte Ordnung und die großzügig dimensionierten Bildschirme. Die übrigen Komponenten sind betont zurückhaltend gestaltet.

Resona 7
Ultrasound System
Ultraschallsystem

Manufacturer
Shenzhen Mindray Bio-Medical Electronics Co., Ltd.,
Shenzhen, China
In-house design
Jinzhou Zhao, Jun Luo, Qi Zhang, Xiang Zhou
Web
www.mindray.com

The Resona 7 ultrasound system combines, in a single platform, several innovative technologies that critically enhance, for example, the examination of vascular blood flow and the imaging of the central nervous system in unborn children. It is operated via a tiltable touchscreen as well as a patented control panel, which provides a large work surface with clearly arranged keys and buttons.

Das diagnostische Ultraschallsystem Resona 7 stellt auf einer einzigen Plattform verschiedene innovative Technologien zur Verfügung, die beispielsweise die Untersuchung des Blutstroms in den Gefäßen oder die Darstellung des Zentralnervensystems bei Ungeborenen entscheidend verbessern. Es wird über den kippbaren Touchscreen bedient sowie über das patentierte Kontrollpanel, welches eine große Arbeitsoberfläche mit übersichtlich angeordneten Tasten und Knöpfen bietet.

Statement by the jury
The fact that the Resona 7 is a high-end device is reflected by its high-quality appearance. The design is characterised by expansive forms and rich colours.

Begründung der Jury
Dass es sich beim Resona 7 um ein High-End-Gerät handelt, spiegelt sich in der wertigen Optik wider. Diese ist durch ausladende Formen und eine satte Farbgebung geprägt.

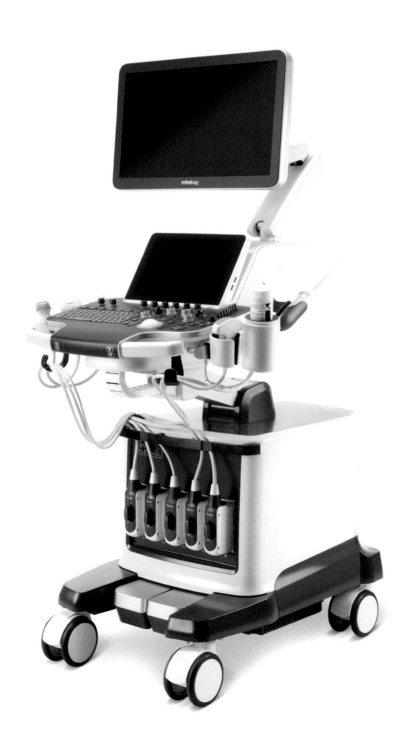

AX8
Laptop Ultrasound System
Laptop-Ultraschallsystem

Manufacturer
Edan Instruments, Inc., Shenzhen, China
In-house design
Richard Henderson
Web
www.edan.com.cn

The AX8 ultrasound system produces high-quality diagnostic images, serving the worldwide human and veterinary markets in a convenient laptop format. The sealed user interface, with two touch panels and elastomeric keys, allows users to focus on the patient and image. The display tilts and rotates for optimal off-angle viewing, and the broad palm rest provides ergonomic support while also serving as the handle. Within the handle, a proximity sensor displays the system's battery status automatically.

Das Ultraschallsystem AX8 im praktischen Laptop-Format erzeugt diagnostische Bilder in hoher Qualität für die human- und tiermedizinischen Weltmärkte. Die versiegelte Benutzeroberfläche mit zwei Touchpanels und Elastomer-Tasten erlaubt es dem Anwender, sich auf den Patienten und das Bild zu konzentrieren. Das dreh- und kippbare Display lässt sich auf den optimalen Winkel einstellen. Die breite, ergonomische Handauflage dient gleichzeitig als Griff. Ein Annäherungssensor im Griff zeigt automatisch den Akkustand an.

Statement by the jury
With its compact design, this ultrasound system makes an extremely robust impression. Thanks to its integrated handle, it is particularly easy to carry.

Begründung der Jury
Mit seiner kompakten Bauweise macht das Ultraschallsystem einen überaus stabilen Eindruck. Durch den integrierten Griff ist es besonders einfach zu transportieren.

uDR 370i
Mobile X-Ray System
Mobiles Röntgengerät

Manufacturer
Shanghai United Imaging Healthcare Co., Ltd.,
Shanghai, China
In-house design
Corporate Design Innovation Center
Web
www.united-imaging.com

The objective pursued in designing the uDR 370i was to create an X-ray unit for use in developing countries. The system is only 58 cm wide and therefore able to fit through narrow corridors. The batteries for the trolley and the X-ray unit are separate, which enables uninterrupted use for 21 days. The 19" LCD touchscreen presents all data clearly. With the help of a tablet PC, operators can do imaging remotely, which thus optimally protects them from radiation damage.

Das Ziel bei der Gestaltung des uDR 370i war es, ein Röntgengerät für den Einsatz in Entwicklungsländern zu konzipieren. Das System ist nur 58 cm breit und passt daher durch schmale Korridore. Die Batterien für den Trolley und das Röntgengerät sind getrennt verbaut, was einen unterbrechungsfreien Betrieb über 21 Tage ermöglicht. Auf dem 19"-LCD-Touchscreen werden alle Informationen anschaulich dargestellt. Mithilfe eines Tablet-PCs kann der Anwender das Röntgen aus der Entfernung koordinieren, sodass er optimal vor Strahlenschäden geschützt ist.

Statement by the jury
Although this X-ray system is impressively slim, it has a very generous appearance due to its balanced proportions and smooth surfaces.

Begründung der Jury
Obwohl das Röntgengerät beeindruckend schmal ist, mutet es aufgrund seiner ausgewogenen Proportionen und glatten Oberflächen überaus großzügig an.

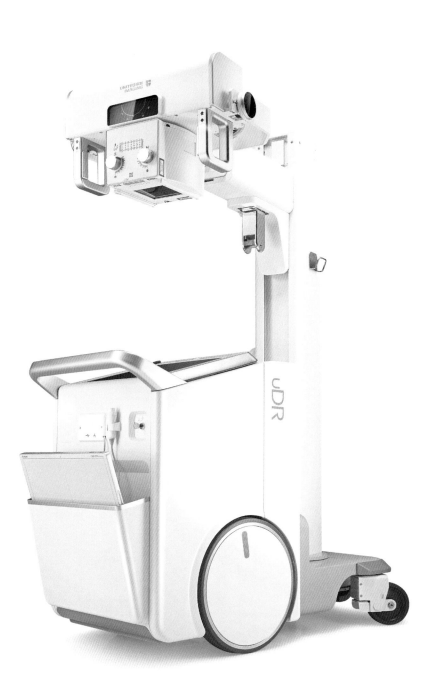

uDR 550i
X-Ray System
Röntgengerät

Manufacturer
Shanghai United Imaging Healthcare Co., Ltd.,
Shanghai, China
In-house design
Corporate Design Innovation Center
Web
www.united-imaging.com

The uDR 550i X-ray system was specifically tailored to meet requirements in developing countries, where high efficiency and low costs have the highest priority. The device's prominent features are thus a small footprint and high energy efficiency. The light on the column displays the unit's operational status. The high-quality metallic finish of the control unit makes it resistant to wear. Thanks to an antibacterial nano coating, the contact surfaces display especially favourable hygienic properties.

Das Röntgengerät uDR 550i wurde speziell auf die Anforderungen in Entwicklungsländern zugeschnitten, wo hohe Effizienz und niedrige Kosten oberste Priorität haben. Besondere Merkmale des Geräts sind deshalb sein geringer Platzbedarf und niedriger Stromverbrauch. Die Lampe an der Säule zeigt den Betriebszustand an. Die hochwertige Metallausführung der Steuereinheit ist verschleißbeständig. Durch die antibakterielle Nanobeschichtung haben die Kontaktflächen besonders gute hygienische Eigenschaften.

Statement by the jury
This X-ray system appeals with its minimalism, clear lines and slimness – design characteristics that excellently embody its functionality.

Begründung der Jury
Das Röntgengerät gefällt durch Minimalismus, Geradlinigkeit und Schlankheit – Gestaltungsmerkmale, die seine Leistungsfähigkeit hervorragend verkörpern.

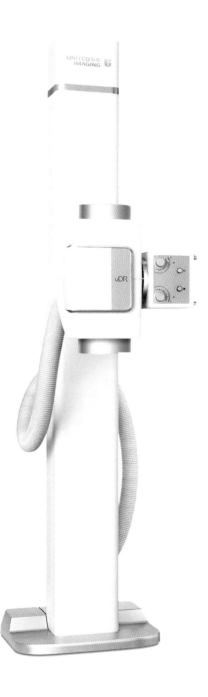
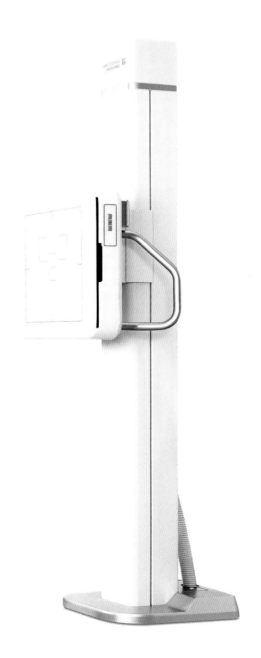

Planmed Clarity
Digital Mammography System
Digitales Mammographiegerät

Manufacturer
Planmed Oy, Helsinki, Finland
In-house design
Tapio Laukkanen
Web
www.planmed.com

In addition to conventional 2D imaging, the Planmed Clarity digital mammography system offers innovative 3D tomosynthesis imaging, which depicts the breast tissue without superposition of overlaying tissue. Its rounded contours and friendly colours help to remove any inhibitions that patients may have when it comes to touching or leaning against it. The concave face guard, which provides room to move, and the forward-curving support handles, which patients can hold onto in many ways, help them to relax during the examination.

Das digitale Mammographiegerät Planmed Clarity bietet neben einer konventionellen 2D-Mammographie auch eine innovative 3D-Tomosynthese-Bildgebung, bei der das Brustgewebe überlagerungsfrei dargestellt wird. Durch seine gerundeten Formen und sympathischen Dekorfarben hat die Patientin keine Scheu, das Gerät zu berühren und sich anzulehnen. Der gewölbte Gesichtsschutz, der Bewegungsfreiheit lässt, und die nach vorne gekrümmte Griffstange, die auf vielseitige Weise gehalten werden kann, helfen der Patientin, sich während der Untersuchung zu entspannen.

Statement by the jury
The soft lines of the Planmed Clarity harmoniously flow into one another. Its feminine appearance conveys a feeling of trust and well-being.

Begründung der Jury
Die sanften Linien des Planmed Clarity fließen harmonisch ineinander. Sein feminines Erscheinungsbild vermittelt ein Gefühl von Vertrauen und Wohlbefinden.

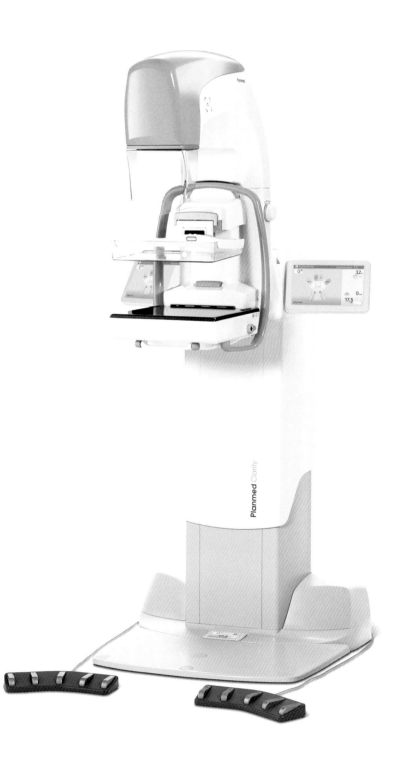

RIID
PET Dispensing System
PET-Infusionssystem

Manufacturer
Uniteko Co., Ltd., Gwangju, South Korea
Design
Fusion Design Co., Ltd., Seoul, South Korea
Web
www.uniteko.co.kr
www.fusiondesign.co.kr

During a PET examination, a computed tomography scan is carried out after the injection of a radioactively marked substance. The intelligent RIID PET dispensing system is used for the automated intravenous injection of such a radiopharmaceutical. The system is controlled via an easy-to-use touchscreen. The heavy construction weighs 550 kg and is supported by a strong enclosure made of stainless steel. The shielded chamber protects medical personnel from radiation exposure.

Statement by the jury
The RIID captivates with its compact structure, which is characterised by straight, clear lines. The large dimensioning of the handles facilitates easy access.

Für eine PET-Untersuchung wird nach Einspritzen einer radioaktiv markierten Substanz eine Computertomographie durchgeführt. Das intelligente PET-Infusionssystem RIID wird zur automatisierten intravenösen Injektion solch eines Radiopharmazeutikums eingesetzt. Die Steuerung erfolgt über einen einfach zu bedienenden LCD-Touchscreen. Die 550 kg schwere Konstruktion wird von einem stabilen Gehäuse aus Edelstahl getragen. Die abgeschirmte Kammer schützt das medizinische Personal vor radioaktiver Strahlung.

Begründung der Jury
Das RIID überzeugt durch seine Kompaktheit, die von geraden, klaren Linien geprägt ist. Die großzügige Dimensionierung der Griffe erlaubt einen einfachen Zugang.

MAGNETOM Amira
Magnetic Resonance Imaging System
Magnetresonanztomograph

Manufacturer
Siemens Healthcare, Imaging & Therapy Systems Magnetic Resonance, Erlangen, Germany
Design
designaffairs, Erlangen, Germany
Web
www.healthcare.siemens.com
www.designaffairs.com

The Magnetom Amira magnetic resonance imaging system increases patient comfort and optimises the examination process. Its noise level is extremely low and operations are streamlined with ten minute exams. With intelligent monitoring and control of the helium liquid, the Eco-Power technology reduces power consumption in standby mode. The new illumination concept, which includes the patient table, indicates the path of the patient during the examination.

Statement by the jury
The well-proportioned dimensions of the Magnetom Amira create an aesthetic balance. The silver edging skilfully highlights its soft contours.

Der Magnetresonanztomograph Magnetom Amira erhöht den Patientenkomfort und optimiert die Untersuchungsabläufe. Sein Geräuschpegel ist extrem niedrig und die Behandlungsdauer kann auf zehn Minuten reduziert werden. Die Eco-Power-Technologie verringert durch intelligente Überwachung und Steuerung der Heliumverflüssigung den Stromverbrauch während des Stand-by-Betriebs. Das neu entwickelte Beleuchtungskonzept, das den Patiententisch einbezieht, zeichnet den Weg des Patienten während der Untersuchung nach.

Begründung der Jury
Die wohlproportionierten Dimensionen des Magnetom Amira schaffen eine ästhetische Balance. Die silberfarbenen Einfassungen unterstreichen gekonnt seine weichen Konturen.

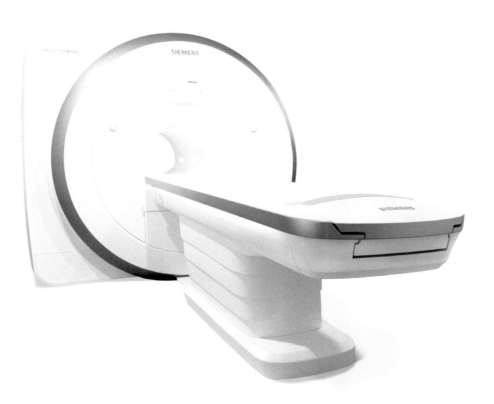

uMR 770
Magnetic Resonance Imaging System
Magnetresonanztomograph

Manufacturer
Shanghai United Imaging Healthcare Co., Ltd.,
Shanghai, China
In-house design
Corporate Design Innovation Center
Web
www.united-imaging.com

The 3-Tesla magnetic resonance imaging system uMR 770 delivers excellent image quality and a sophisticated operational design. The touchscreen and key panel are integrated into the device, allowing the operator to stay focused on the patient at all times throughout the examination process. Furthermore, the unibody control panels are arranged at an ergonomic 12-degree angle and feature slightly convex buttons for an enhanced feel. Operators can adjust music, ventilation and ambient light to provide patients with as pleasant of a scan experience as possible.

Der 3-Tesla-Magnetresonanztomograph uMR 770 bietet ausgezeichnete Bildqualität und ein durchdachtes Bedienkonzept. Der Touchscreen und die Tastenkonsole sind in das Gerät integriert, sodass der Anwender während der Untersuchung stets Kontakt zum Patienten halten kann. Zudem sind die aus einem Stück gefertigten Bedienkonsolen in einem ergonomischen 12-Grad-Winkel angeordnet und mit leicht gewölbten Tasten für eine verbesserte Haptik versehen. Der Anwender kann die Musik, die Belüftung und das Umgebungslicht anpassen, um die Untersuchung für den Patienten so angenehm wie möglich zu gestalten.

Statement by the jury
The high performance of the uMR 770 is highlighted by its uncompromising puristic design. The shining acrylic ring in the middle is an aesthetic eye-catcher.

Begründung der Jury
Die hohe Leistungsstärke des uMR 770 wird durch das kompromisslos puristische Design unterstrichen. Der glänzende Acrylring in der Mitte gerät zum ästhetischen Blickfang.

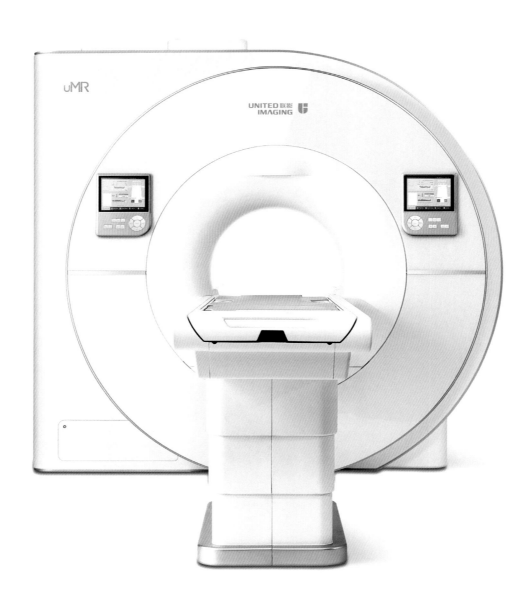

uMI 780
PET/CT System

Manufacturer
Shanghai United Imaging Healthcare Co., Ltd.,
Shanghai, China
In-house design
Corporate Design Innovation Center
Web
www.united-imaging.com

With the uMI 780 PET/CT system, a whole-body scan can be completed in just five minutes. Compared to conventional units, it reduces both the radioactive tracer and X-ray doses by 50 per cent. The warm ambient light intuitively acts as a breathing guide for patients. The special finishing on the buttons and the unibody aluminium frame make the control panel remarkably resistant to wear and tear. The integrated sensors prevent patients from unintentionally colliding with the device.

Mit dem PET/CT-System uMI 780 kann ein kompletter Ganzkörperscan in nur fünf Minuten durchgeführt werden. Im Vergleich zu herkömmlichen Geräten werden sowohl die Dosis der radioaktiven Tracer als auch die Röntgendosis um 50 Prozent reduziert. Das warme Umgebungslicht dient als intuitive Atmungshilfe für den Patienten. Die speziell beschichteten Tasten und der aus einem Stück gefertigte Aluminiumrahmen verleihen der Bedienkonsole außerordentliche Verschleißbeständigkeit. Die integrierten Sensoren verhindern unbeabsichtigte Kollisionen des Geräts mit dem Patienten.

Statement by the jury
The uMI 780 is a PET/CT system without visual interruptions. The smooth surfaces in monochrome white give rise to a coherent design.

Begründung der Jury
Das uMI 780 ist ein PET/CT-System ohne optische Brüche. Die glatten Oberflächen in monochromem Weiß stellen eine gestalterische Einheit her.

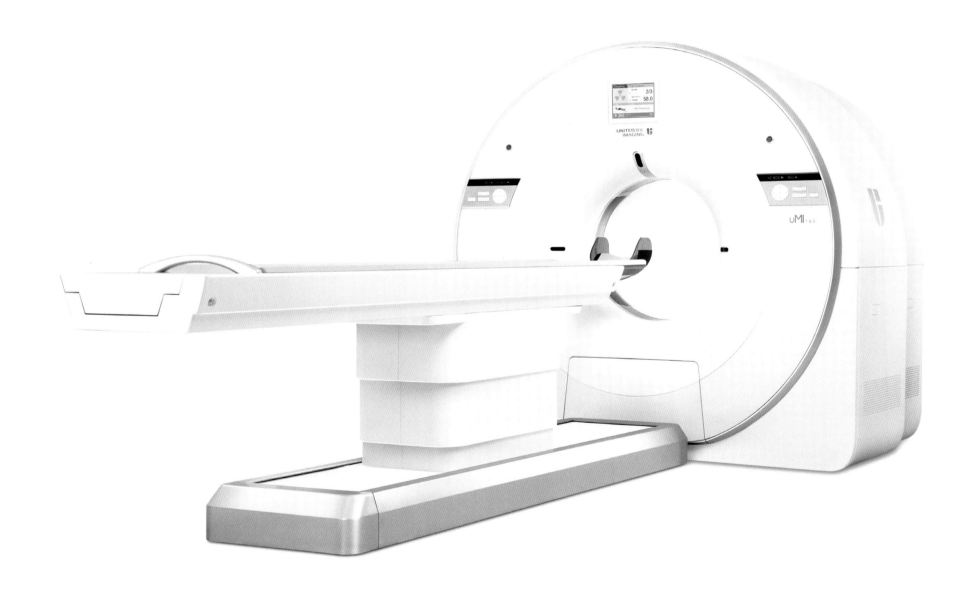

LiteTouch™
Dental Laser

Manufacturer
Light Instruments Ltd (Syneron Dental Lasers), Yokneam, Israel
In-house design
Design
Joel Rapoport – Industrial Design, Tel Aviv, Israel
Web
www.synerondental.com
www.joelr.co.il

The LiteTouch dental laser is based on an innovative technology that integrates the laser directly into the handpiece. The dentist thus enjoys unrestricted freedom of movement during the treatment process. The touchscreen display can be adjusted to provide a clear and unobstructed view from any position, while the headpiece, which rotates by 360 degrees, provides optimal access to the mouth cavity. Furthermore, the device is characterised by its compact size, leight weight and small footprint. It can easily be transported from room to room and requires very little space.

Der Dentallaser LiteTouch beruht auf einer innovativen Technologie, bei der sich der Laser direkt im Handstück befindet. Der Zahnarzt erlangt dadurch uneingeschränkte Bewegungsfreiheit während der Behandlung. Der Touchscreen-Monitor ist verstellbar, um eine klare und freie Sicht aus allen Arbeitspositionen zu ermöglichen, während das um 360 Grad schwenkbare Kopfstück einen idealen Zugang zur Mundhöhle bietet. Des Weiteren zeichnet sich das Gerät durch seine kompakte Größe, sein leichtes Gewicht und eine geringe Standfläche aus. Es kann einfach von Zimmer zu Zimmer transportiert werden und braucht kaum Platz.

Statement by the jury
With its rounded forms and soft edges, this dental laser not only looks robust but also makes a particularly friendly impression.

Begründung der Jury
Der Dentallaser wirkt durch seine gerundeten Formen und weichen Kanten nicht nur robust, sondern macht darüber hinaus einen besonders sympathischen Eindruck.

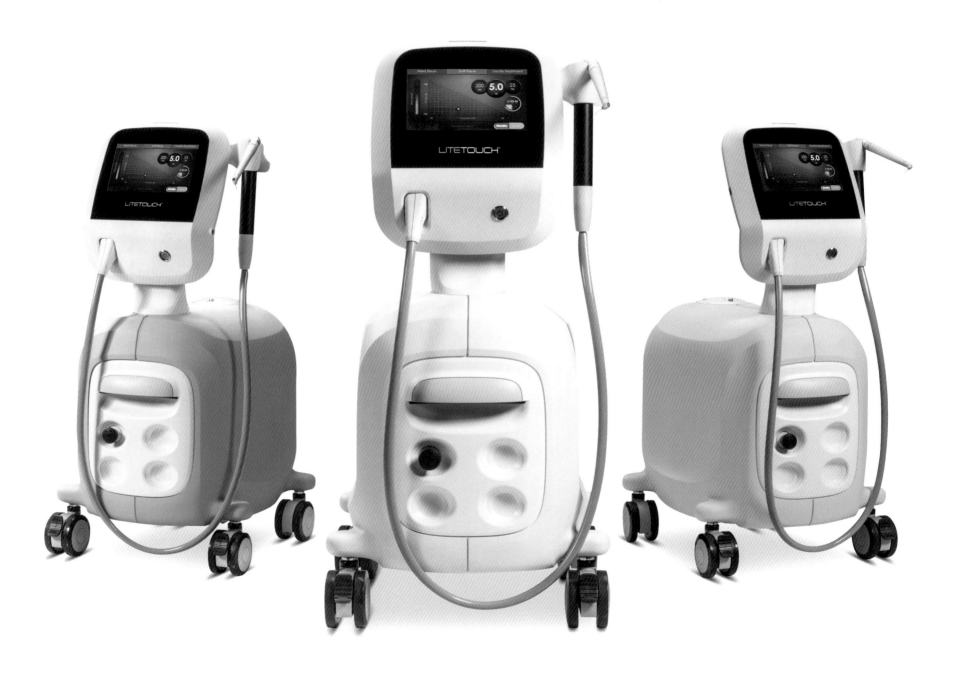

POC-W22A-H81
Medical Panel PC
Medizinischer Panel-PC

Manufacturer
IEI Integration Corp., New Taipei City, Taiwan
In-house design
Fu Tzu Wei, Chen Shih Chia
Web
www.ieiworld.com

The POC-W22A-H81 is a medical panel PC that can be used flexibly in hospitals thanks to its modular structure. It is characterised by a lightweight and slim design, which blends in with the surrounding environment. Due to a magnetic mechanism and its screwless chassis, the rear cover can be dismantled easily in order to replace the fan, the memory module, the HDD module and the PCIe Mini module. Furthermore, IT personnel may access the PC remotely via the IEI Remote Intelligent System for maintenance or repair tasks.

Der POC-W22A-H81 ist ein medizinischer Panel-PC, der durch seinen modularen Aufbau flexibel im Krankenhaus eingesetzt werden kann. Er zeichnet sich durch ein leichtes und schlankes Design aus, das sich harmonisch in die Umgebung einfügt. Durch einen Magnetmechanismus und das schraubenlose Gehäuse ist die Rückwand leicht auseinanderzubauen, um den Lüfter, das Speichermodul sowie das HDD- oder Mini-PCIe-Modul auszutauschen. Darüber hinaus können IT-Mitarbeiter über das IEI Remote Intelligent System von außen auf den PC zugreifen, um ihn zu warten und zu reparieren.

Statement by the jury
Besides its appealing puristic aesthetic, this panel PC captivates with an impressively rapid, easy assembly and disassembly of its main functional components.

Begründung der Jury
Neben seiner ansprechend puristischen Ästhetik besticht der Panel-PC durch eine beeindruckend schnelle und einfache Montage und Demontage der Hauptfunktionsteile.

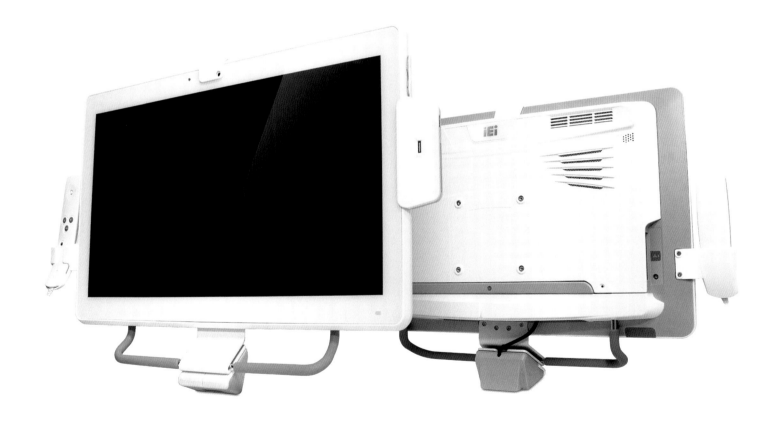

207

FS 5–33
Floor Stand for Operating Microscopes
Stativ für Operationsmikroskope

Manufacturer
Haag-Streit Surgical GmbH,
Wedel, Germany

Design
Held+Team, Hamburg, Germany

Web
www.haag-streit-surgical.com
www.heldundteam.de

reddot award 2016
best of the best

Perfectly positioned

Surgeries often require the need for many different tools, tools that can ideally be integrated smoothly into the entire process. The FS 5-33 floor stand is a slide unit for operating microscopes as used, for instance, during neurosurgery. It serves to easily move microscopes into place where needed and then position them stably. Its premium-quality design convinces with a concentration to the essential, complemented by a functionality that is perfectly honed to address the highest demands. Thanks to innovative dampening, there are no vibrations blurring the sight of the microscope attached to the holder. This ensures a safe and reliable working process. Based on auto-mated equilibration, weights within the holder arm are shifted to balance the microscope system in almost any position at any time. For the purpose of safe, effortless sliding and positioning, electro-magnetic brakes in the joints are first released by pushing the orange buttons on the stand or microscope, and then automatically fixed by releasing the buttons after exact positioning. In addition, the smooth surfaces of the stand comply ideally with the strict disinfection requirements in operating theatres. With its ergo-nomics and precise functionality, the stand delivers a high degree of safety and user convenience – its clear design idiom truly enriches the surroundings.

Perfekt positioniert

Während Operationen kommen oftmals mehrere Geräte zum Einsatz, die im Idealfall fließend in den Ablauf integriert werden können. Das Stativ FS 5-33 fungiert als Trägereinheit für Operationsmikroskope bei Opera-tionen zum Beispiel in der Neurochirurgie. Es wird ein-gesetzt, um die Mikroskope an den Ort der Anwendung zu bewegen und dort stabil zu positionieren. Seine hochwertige Gestaltung besticht mit ihrer Konzentra-tion auf das Wesentliche. Dies geht einher mit einer perfekt den Anforderungen entsprechenden Funktiona-lität. So verhindert eine innovative Dämpfung mögliche Vibrationen des am Ende des Stativs montierten Mikro-skops. Dies garantiert einen sicheren und zuverlässigen Ablauf. Dank eines automatisierten Gewichtsausgleichs werden Gewichte im Stativarm so verschoben, dass sich das Mikroskop stets im Gleichgewicht befindet. Um zudem ein sicheres, kraftloses Bewegen zu ermög-lichen, werden zunächst elektromagnetische Bremsen in den Gelenken durch Drücken der orangefarbenen Tasten am Stativ oder Mikroskop gelöst und nach der exakten Positionierung durch Loslassen wieder auto-matisch fixiert. Den strengen Anforderungen an die Desinfektion im Operationssaal wird dieses Stativ durch seine glatten Oberflächen bestens gerecht. Mit seiner Ergonomie und präzisen Funktionalität bietet es ein hohes Maß an Komfort und Sicherheit – seine klare Formensprache bereichert das Umfeld.

Statement by the jury

The FS 5-33 floor stand for operating microscopes embodies a highly technical and aesthetically advanced solution in the medical surgeon field. Thanks to its compact and clear design, it emerged as a well-structured and easy-to-clean system. Its well-arranged screen design ensures easy readability of data. This floor stand lends itself to excellent inte-gration into the most diverse operating theatres.

Begründung der Jury

Das Stativ für Operationsmikroskope FS 5-33 stellt eine ästhetische und technologisch sehr ausgereifte Ent-wicklung für den Operationsbereich dar. Mittels einer klaren und kompakten Gestaltung wurde hier ein gut strukturiertes und leicht zu reinigendes System reali-siert. Sein übersichtliches Screendesign erlaubt eine leichte Ablesbarkeit. Dieses Stativ lässt sich ausge-zeichnet in unterschiedlichste Operationsräume integ-rieren.

Designer portrait
See page 50
Siehe Seite 50

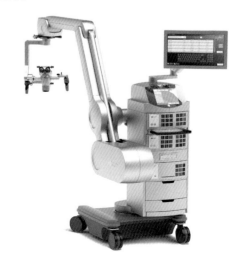

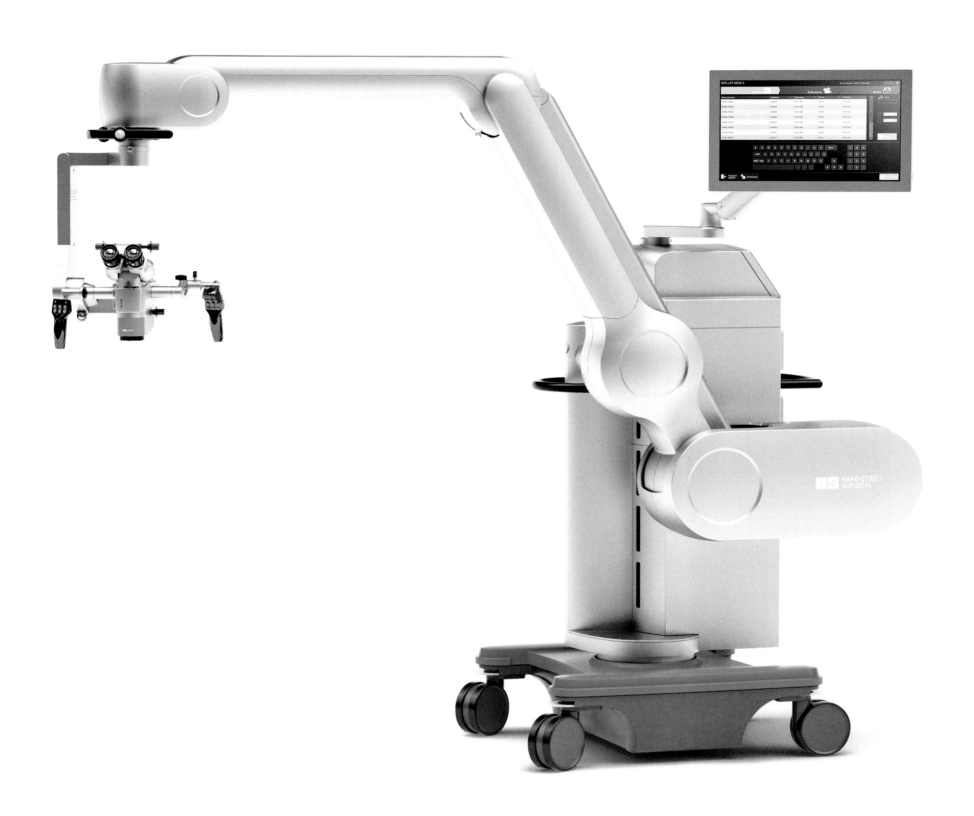

PolyAxNail Targeting Device
PolyAxNail Zielinstrumentarium
Implement for Emergency Surgery
Arbeitsgerät für die Unfallchirurgie

Manufacturer
Königsee Implantate, Allendorf, Germany
Design
OTM Orthopädie & Traumatologie Medizintechnik (Ulrich Schreiber), Munich, Germany
Web
www.koenigsee-implantate.de
www.otmedtec.de

With the PolyAxNail targeting device, an implant for the treatment of bone fractures can be safely inserted and optimally positioned. The patented joystick is used for easy individual adjustment of the implant to the anatomy and the fracture line. The use of a carbon-fibre-reinforced synthetic material in connection with glass-bead-blasted stainless steel enables the surgeon to see the bone fracture in the X-ray image; at the same time, the material is distinguished by high stability.

Statement by the jury
The PolyAxNail targeting device impresses with its innovative character and great ease of use, as well as with its high-quality materials.

Mit dem PolyAxNail Zielinstrumentarium wird ein Implantat zur Versorgung von Knochenbrüchen sicher im Körper eingebracht und optimal positioniert. Der patentierte Joystick dient zur einfachen, individuellen Anpassung des Implantats an die Anatomie und den Bruchverlauf. Die Verwendung von carbonfaserverstärktem Kunststoff in Verbindung mit glasperlengestrahltem Edelstahl ermöglicht dem Chirurgen, die Knochenfraktur im Röntgenbild zu sehen, und zeichnet sich zugleich durch eine hohe Beständigkeit aus.

Begründung der Jury
Das PolyAxNail Zielinstrumentarium überzeugt durch seinen innovativen Charakter und die einfache Bedienbarkeit sowie durch seine hochwertige Materialität.

corpuls cpr
Chest Compression Device
Thoraxkompressionsgerät

Manufacturer
GS Elektromedizinische Geräte
G. Stemple GmbH, Kaufering, Germany
Design
polyform industrie design
(Martin Nußberger), Munich, Germany
Web
www.corpuls.com
www.polyform-design.de

The corpuls cpr chest compression device enables uninterrupted mechanical reanimation. The system consists of a swivelling, rotatable arm with an integrated pressure stamp and different reanimation boards. They are made from a radiolucent material and have been developed especially for varied requirements in emergency medical services, air ambulances and hospitals. Due to the fact that it is only attached on one side, the device offers free access to the patient's upper body during use.

Statement by the jury
With its functional design language, the corpuls cpr supports intuitive use. The most important adjustment points are clearly identified in red.

Das Thoraxkompressionsgerät corpuls cpr ermöglicht eine maschinelle, unterbrechungsfreie Reanimation. Das System besteht aus einem schwenk- und drehbaren Arm mit eingesetztem Druckstempel und verschiedenen Reanimationsboards. Diese sind aus röntgendurchlässigem Material und wurden speziell für die unterschiedlichen Anforderungen in Rettungsdienst, Luftrettung und Klinik entwickelt. Durch die einseitige Anbringung bietet das Gerät während des laufenden Betriebs freien Zugang zum Thorax des Patienten.

Begründung der Jury
Das corpuls cpr unterstützt durch seine funktionale Formensprache eine intuitive Bedienung. Die wichtigsten Justierungspunkte sind in Rot klar gekennzeichnet.

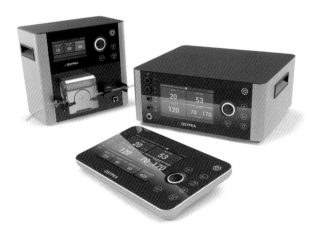

HAT500
Radio Frequency Ablation System
Hochfrequenz-Ablationssystem

Manufacturer
Osypka AG, Rheinfelden, Germany
Design
Imago Design GmbH (Stefan Thalhammer), Gilching, Germany
Web
www.osypka.de
www.imago-design.de

The HAT500 radio frequency ablation system is used for the treatment of cardiac arrhythmia. The ablation generator and the pump for irrigating the ablation catheter are centrally operated via a remote control featuring a touchscreen. All functions are neatly arranged, making the most important parameters visible at a glance. Moreover, clear colour coding prevents errors and saves time; for instance the connector jacks have the same shade as the cables that connect to them.

Statement by the jury
The design of the HAT500 has been developed specifically for this sophisticated interventional task. The components give rise to a cohesive overall appearance.

Das Hochfrequenz-Ablationssystem HAT500 kommt bei der Behandlung von Herzrhythmusstörungen zum Einsatz. Über eine Fernbedienung mit Touchscreen lassen sich sowohl der Ablationsgenerator als auch die Pumpe zum Spülen des Ablationskatheters zentral steuern. Die klar strukturierte Darstellung macht die wichtigsten Werte auf einen Blick ablesbar. Zusätzlich hilft die eindeutige Farbgebung, Fehler zu vermeiden und Zeit zu sparen. So entsprechen die Anschlussbuchsen z. B. der Farbe der anzuschließenden Kabel.

Begründung der Jury
Die Gestaltung des HAT500 ist ganz und gar auf die anspruchsvolle interventionelle Tätigkeit abgestimmt. Die Komponenten ergeben ein stimmiges Gesamtbild.

SE-301
ECG
EKG-Gerät

Manufacturer
Edan Instruments, Inc., Shenzhen, China
In-house design
Wuchao Mao, Kai Yang
Web
www.edan.cn.com

The SE-301 is a three-channel ECG for mobile use with a 5" colour touchscreen and an integrated lithium-ion battery. Furthermore, the device features an internal thermal printer and can take twelve measurements simultaneously. A variety of external devices like data carriers and a barcode scanner can be connected using its two USB ports and the micro SD card slot. Patient data may be transmitted via a cord or, optionally, using Wi-Fi.

Statement by the jury
The ECG captivates with its ultra-compact format. The touchscreen makes keys unnecessary and provides a seamless surface.

Das SE-301 ist ein mobil einsetzbares 3-Kanal-EKG-Gerät mit einem 5" großen Farbtouchscreen und eingebautem Lithium-Ionen-Akku. Darüber hinaus ist das Gerät mit einem internen Thermodrucker ausgestattet und kann zwölf Messungen simultan aufnehmen. Über zwei USB-Anschlüsse sowie einen Micro-SD-Karten-Slot lassen sich verschiedene externe Geräte wie Speichermedien oder ein Barcodescanner anschließen. Die Patientendaten können mit einem Kabel oder optional via Wi-Fi übermittelt werden.

Begründung der Jury
Das EKG-Gerät begeistert durch sein ultrakompaktes Format. Der Touchscreen macht Tasten überflüssig und bildet eine nahtlose Oberfläche.

maXium smart C
Electrosurgical Unit
Elektrochirurgiegerät

Manufacturer
Gebrüder Martin GmbH & Co. KG,
Tuttlingen, Germany
Design
Weinberg & Ruf, Filderstadt, Germany
Web
www.klsmartin.com
www.weinberg-ruf.com

With the maXium smart C electrosurgical unit, a range of applications in high-frequency surgery can be carried out. Three different socket modules are made available for this purpose, which can be connected to a wide variety of instruments. The clear horizontal assignment of the three outputs and the permanent display of all relevant parameters on the screen give the surgeon a clear overview at all times. The touchscreen technology makes the unit easy to use.

Statement by the jury
This surgical instrument evinces a distinctly tidy and clear appearance. Thanks to touchscreen operation, the interfaces are reduced to a minimum.

Mit dem Elektrochirurgiegerät maXium smart C können eine Vielzahl von Anwendungen in der Hochfrequenzchirurgie verwirklicht werden. Zu diesem Zweck stehen drei verschiedene Buchsenmodule zur Verfügung, an die sich die unterschiedlichsten Instrumente anschließen lassen. Durch die klare horizontale Zuordnung der drei Ausgänge und die permanente Darstellung aller relevanten Parameter auf dem Display behält der Chirurg stets den Überblick. Die Touchscreen-Technologie ermöglicht eine unkomplizierte Bedienung.

Begründung der Jury
Das Chirurgiegerät wirkt ausgesprochen aufgeräumt und übersichtlich. Durch die Touchscreen-Bedienung konnten die Schnittstellen auf ein Minimum reduziert werden.

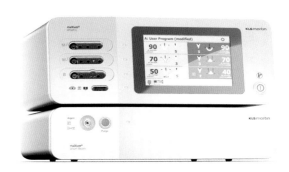

Jenny
Multifunctional Device for Critical Care
Multifunktionsgerät für die Intensivversorgung

Manufacturer
MS Westfalia GmbH, Troisdorf, Germany
In-house design
Design
Werk-m Design Agentur,
Neunkirchen-Seelscheid, Germany
Web
www.mswestfalia.com

Jenny is a patented modular critical care all-in-one solution. Compact plug-in modules with the functionality of a high-end ventilator, monitor and defibrillator provide continuous patient attendance throughout all critical care phases. The flat design in line with rubberised protection materials and the ergonomic handle allow both mobile and stationary application. One user interface for all critical care functions and a capacitive touchscreen support quick, intuitive interaction.

Statement by the jury
Due to the fact that the individual components can be extended and converted, Jenny provides remarkable versatility in a compact system.

Jenny ist ein patentiertes All-in-one-Gerät für die Intensivversorgung. Die Einsteckmodule mit den Funktionen eines High-End-Ventilators, Monitors und Defibrillators bieten eine kontinuierliche Patientenversorgung. Das flache Design im Einklang mit den stoßfesten gummierten Außenmaterialien und dem ergonomischen Griff ermöglichen den mobilen und stationären Einsatz. Ein einfaches User Interface für alle Pflegefunktionen und ein Touchscreen unterstützen eine schnelle, intuitive Bedienung.

Begründung der Jury
Dadurch, dass die einzelnen Bauteile aus- und umbaufähig sind, bietet Jenny eine bemerkenswerte Vielseitigkeit in einem kompakten System.

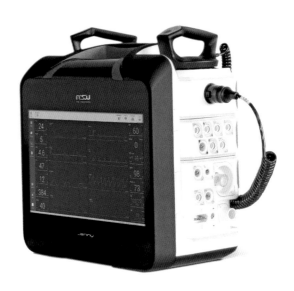

iMAC12
ECG
EKG-Gerät

Manufacturer
Wuhan Zoncare Bio-Medical Electronics Co.,
Ltd., Wuhan, China
In-house design
Web
www.zoncare.com

iMAC12 is an ultra-thin ECG unit with a 10.4" touchscreen and integrated printer, which is particularly suitable for hospital rounds and house calls. It features an infrared scanner for reading barcodes and supports both wireless and wired networking. The sliding paper tray and the automatic print adjustment function ensure a clearly legible ECG printout in any conditions. The most important commands are executed using the short-cut keys.

Statement by the jury
The ECG displays a particularly slim design. At the same time, it makes a very robust impression thanks to its alumini-um frame.

iMAC12 ist ein ultraflaches EKG-Gerät mit 10,4"-Touchscreen und eingebautem Drucker, das besonders für die Kranken-hausvisite und Hausbesuche geeignet ist. Es verfügt über einen Infrarotscanner zum Einlesen von Barcodes und kann kabellos oder kabelgebunden mit einem Netzwerk kommunizieren. Das ausziehbare Papier-schubfach und die automatische Druck-anpassungsfunktion sorgen für sauber lesbare EKG-Ausdrucke unter allen Bedin-gungen. Die wichtigsten Befehle werden über die Shortcut-Tasten eingegeben.

Begründung der Jury
Das EKG-Gerät präsentiert sich in einem äußerst schlanken Design. Gleichzeitig macht es durch den Aluminiumrahmen einen sehr robusten Eindruck.

iT20 & SE-2003 / SE-2012
Telemetry Transmitter and Holter System
Telemetrischer Sender und EKG-Langzeit-Rekorder

Manufacturer
Edan Instruments, Inc., Shenzhen, China
In-house design
Wuchao Mao, Kai Yang
Web
www.edan.com.cn

The iT20 is a telemetry transmitter that sends heart frequency and pulse data wirelessly to a central network at the hospital. Patients can thus move around freely in the ward during the real-time monitoring process. The SE-2003 recorder with three channels and the SE-2102 with twelve channels register the data. The devices are lightweight, compact and watertight, so that they may be carried in a pocket or worn around the neck, even while in the shower.

Statement by the jury
The convenient size and advanced tech-nology of this transmitter and the recorders are highly geared towards meeting the needs of the users.

Das iT20 ist ein telemetrischer Sender, der Herzfrequenz- und Pulsdaten über eine drahtlose Funkverbindung an ein zentrales Netzwerk im Krankenhaus weiterleitet. So können sich die Patienten während der Echtzeitüberwachung frei auf der Station bewegen. Die Rekorder SE-2003 mit drei Kanälen und SE-2012 mit zwölf Kanälen dienen der Aufzeichnung der Daten. Die Geräte sind leicht, kompakt und wasser-fest, sodass sie in der Hosentasche oder um den Hals getragen werden können, auch unter der Dusche.

Begründung der Jury
Das handliche Format und die fortschritt-liche Technologie des Senders und der Re-korder orientieren sich in besonders hohem Maße an den Bedürfnissen der Nutzer.

Four Series
Four-Serie
Cardiovascular Diagnostic Devices
Geräte für die Herz-Kreislauf-Diagnostik

Manufacturer
Zimmer MedizinSysteme, Neu-Ulm, Germany
Design
ID Design Agentur GbR, Krailling, Germany
Web
www.zimmer.de
www.id-design.de

Four Series provides comprehensive cardiovascular diagnostics from one source. It consists of the Spiro Four spirometer, the CardioPort Four ECG device and the PremoPort Four long-term blood pressure monitor, all of which are connected through a shared computer system. Patient results can thus be compiled easily, and process management in surgeries and hospitals optimised. The products' cohesiveness is reflected in their uniform, ergonomic design.

Statement by the jury
The simplicity of the Four Series devices communicates their uncomplicated use. The semi-transparent accents in blue foster a unique look.

Die Four-Serie bietet eine umfassende Herz-Kreislauf-Diagnostik aus einer Hand. Sie besteht aus dem Spirometer Spiro Four, dem EKG-Gerät CardioPort Four sowie dem Langzeit-Blutdruckmessgerät PremoPort Four, die alle über ein Computersystem miteinander verbunden sind. Dadurch lassen sich diagnostische Patientenergebnisse einfacher zusammenfassen und das Prozessmanagement in Praxen und Kliniken optimieren. Die Zusammengehörigkeit der Produktlösungen spiegelt sich visuell in dem einheitlichen ergonomischen Design wider.

Begründung der Jury
Die Schlichtheit der Four-Serie kommuniziert ihre unkomplizierte Bedienung. Die halbtransparenten Akzente in Blau verleihen den Geräten ein eigenständiges Profil.

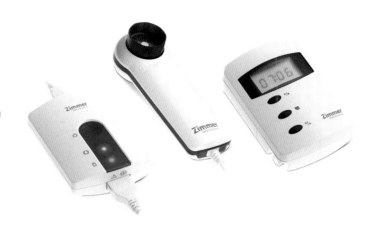

IPS
Integrated Pressure Sensor
Integrierter Drucksensor

Manufacturer
Xenios AG, Heilbronn, Germany
In-house design
Matthias Beurer, Sven Filipon
Web
www.xenios-ag.com

The IPS integrated pressure sensor is used in tube systems for blood circuits that are outside of the body, such as in heart-lung machines. Due to the fact that the sensor surface is integrated directly into the tubing wall, blood leakage and dead spaces are prevented. An innovative over-moulding process ensures reliable sealing. The casting material developed especially for this application is biocompatible and sterilisable. The gap at the back of the housing serves as an inspection window.

Statement by the jury
This pressure sensor convinces with its well-thought-out, functional design and with its use of innovative materials and manufacturing methods.

Der integrierte Drucksensor IPS wird in Schlauchsystemen für Blutkreisläufe eingesetzt, die außerhalb des Körpers liegen, z. B. in Herz-Lungen-Maschinen. Dadurch, dass die aktive Sensorfläche unmittelbar in die Schlauchwand integriert ist, werden Blutleckagen und Toträume verhindert. Ein innovatives Umspritzverfahren sorgt für eine zuverlässige Abdichtung. Das speziell für diese Anwendung entwickelte Vergussmaterial ist biokompatibel und sterilisierbar. Die Aussparung auf der Rückseite des Gehäuses dient als Sichtfenster.

Begründung der Jury
Der Drucksensor überzeugt durch seine durchdachte, funktionale Gestaltung sowie durch den Einsatz innovativer Materialien und Fertigungstechniken.

Air Smart Spirometer
Device for Measuring Lung Volume
Gerät zur Messung der Lungenkapazität

Manufacturer
Pond Healthcare Innovation AB, Stockholm, Sweden
Design
Pond Innovation & Design AB (Fredrik Aidehag, Nicolas Trudel), Stockholm, Sweden
Web
www.healthcareinnovation.se
www.pondsthlm.com

Spirometry devices are normally expensive and therefore not available in every medical practice. The Air Smart Spirometer was developed as a cost-efficient, mobile alternative in order to give every patient access to a pulmonary function test. It consists of the spirometer and a disposable turbine, which ensures perfect hygienic conditions. The spirometer is connected to an iOS device using a cable. It comes with a free app that guides users through the testing procedure.

Statement by the jury
The Air Smart Spirometer provides a state-of-the-art solution for a digital world. The minimalist aesthetic reflects the uncomplicated handling of the device.

Spirometrie-Geräte sind in der Regel teuer und stehen deshalb nicht in jeder Arztpraxis zur Verfügung. Der Air Smart Spirometer wurde als kostengünstige, mobile Alternative entwickelt, um jedem Patienten Zugang zu einem Lungenfunktionstest zu verschaffen. Er besteht aus dem Spirometer und einer Einwegturbine, die hygienisch einwandfreie Bedingungen sicherstellt. Über ein Kabel wird der Spirometer mit einem iOS-Gerät verbunden. Eine zugehörige, kostenlose App führt durch den Testvorgang.

Begründung der Jury
Der Air Smart Spirometer stellt eine zeitgemäße Lösung für eine digitale Welt dar. Die reduzierte Ästhetik spiegelt den unkomplizierten Umgang mit dem Gerät wider.

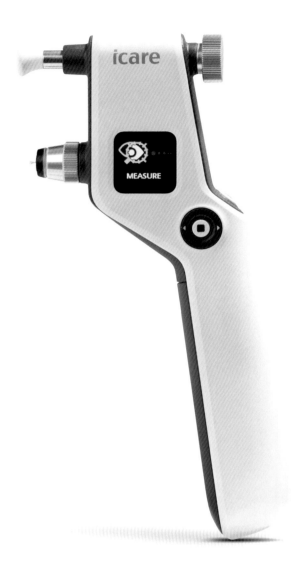

Icare ic100
Tonometer

Manufacturer
Icare Finland Oy, Vantaa, Finland
Design
Veryday (Madlene Lindström, Marcus Heneen),
Bromma, Sweden
Web
www.icarefinland.com
www.veryday.com

The Icare ic100 tonometer enables a quick and pain-free examination of intraocular pressure for the early detection of glaucoma. The instrument is based on a measuring procedure in which the cornea is briefly touched with a probe. Due to the ergonomic shape of the handle, ophthalmologists can freely choose their physical position in relation to the patient, be it standing up or sitting down. The LED screen and keys are positioned on the handpiece in such a way that the ophthalmologist can also keep an eye on the patient during the measurement process.

Der Tonometer Icare ic100 ermöglicht eine schnelle und schmerzlose Untersuchung des Augeninnendrucks zur Früherkennung des grünen Stars. Das Instrument basiert auf einem Messprinzip, bei dem mit einer Sonde kurz die Hornhaut berührt wird. Durch die ergonomische Griffgeometrie des Handstücks steht es dem Augenarzt frei, wie er sich während der Untersuchung zum Patienten positioniert, ob im Sitzen oder im Stehen. Der LED-Bildschirm und die Tasten sind so am Handstück angeordnet, dass der Arzt den Patienten auch während des Messvorgangs stets im Blick hat.

Statement by the jury
The design of the tonometer is characterised by its extremely flat shape and gentle contours, which make an important contribution to patients' acceptance of the device.

Begründung der Jury
Die Gestaltung des Tonometers ist geprägt von einer äußerst flachen Form und sanften Konturen. Diese leisten einen wichtigen Beitrag zur Akzeptanz bei den Patienten.

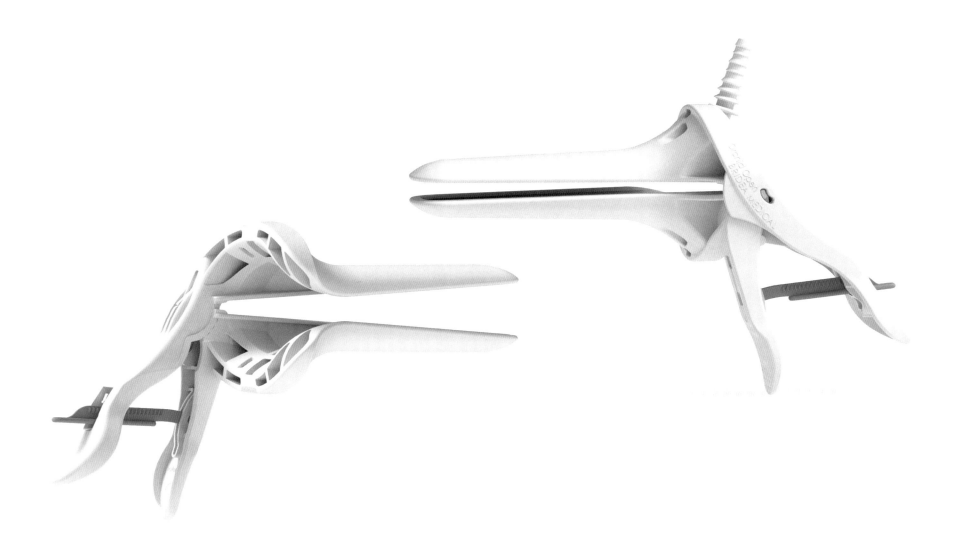

Orchid Open
Speculum
Spekulum

Manufacturer
Bridea Medical b.v., Amsterdam, Netherlands
In-house design
Bob Roeloffs
Web
www.brideamedical.com

The Orchid Open is a high-quality plastic speculum designed for single use. It is open on one side, giving the physician an unobstructed view and optimal access during the gynaecological examination. The patented hinge design is unique in providing high stability and rigidity, regardless of the opening angle, whilst retaining frictionless operation. Furthermore, the locking mechanism allows for superior single-handed use. Thanks to its rounded, smooth edges, the speculum inserts particularly well. It is available in white and transparent with and without smoke extraction nozzle.

Das Orchid Open ist ein hochqualitatives Kunststoffspekulum für den einmaligen Gebrauch. Es ist auf einer Seite offen, um während der gynäkologischen Untersuchung freie Sicht und optimalen Zugriff zu ermöglichen. Das patentierte Scharnierdesign gewährleistet eine hohe Stabilität und Steifigkeit sowie eine reibungsfreie Handhabung. Außerdem ermöglicht der Verriegelungsmechanismus die einhändige Nutzung. Dank der abgerundeten, weichen Kanten lässt sich das Spekulum sanft einführen. Es ist in Weiß und Transparent sowie mit oder ohne Rauchabzugssystem erhältlich.

Statement by the jury
The skin-friendly Orchid Open has a very high-quality finish for a disposable instrument. The innovative hinge technology enables simple and safe use.

Begründung der Jury
Das hautsympathische Orchid Open ist für ein Einweginstrument sehr hochwertig verarbeitet. Die innovative Scharniertechnik ermöglicht eine einfache, sichere Handhabung.

Stent System
System for the Treatment of Narrowed Blood Vessels
System zur Behandlung
verengter Blutgefäße

Manufacturer
Suzhou InnoMed Medical Device Co., Ltd.,
Suzhou, China
In-house design
Jian Wang, Pengchong Chiu
Web
www.innomed.com.cn

The Stent System consists of a frame-like prosthesis, which widens and supports a blocked blood vessel, and an applicator, with which the prosthesis is deployed into the vessel using a catheter. The elegant, curved shape of the applicator facilitates its use with only one hand. The system is compatible with various stent sizes. The stents are made of nitinol, a nickel and titanium alloy, which is particularly flexible and resistant to breakage.

Statement by the jury
Its distinct colour scheme and curved forms give this stent system a unique look and high recognition value.

Das Stent System besteht aus einer gerüstartigen Prothese, die ein verstopftes Blutgefäß aufdehnt und stützt, und einem Applikator, mit dem die Prothese über einen Katheter in das Gefäß eingesetzt wird. Die elegante Kurvenform des Applikators erleichtert die Bedienung mit nur einer Hand. Das System ist mit verschiedenen Stent-Größen kompatibel. Die Stents sind aus Nitinol gefertigt, einer Legierung aus Nickel und Titan, die besonders flexibel und bruchsicher ist.

Begründung der Jury
Durch seine markante Farbgebung und geschwungene Form erhält das Stent System ein eigenständiges Aussehen und hat einen hohen Wiedererkennungswert.

Khelix 10E Steerable EP Catheter
Steuerbarer Herzkatheter

Manufacturer
CathRx Ltd, Sydney, Australia
In-house design
Web
www.khelixmedical.com

The Khelix 10E Steerable EP Catheter was developed to decrease the risk of contamination and functional degradation resulting from multiple use. It features a detachable sheath, which is disposed of after the operation. The handle and the guidewire can be reused after sterilisation. This results in large savings with regard to materials and accordingly minimised costs. Thanks to a push-and-pull mechanism on the handle, the guidewire can be accurately steered towards the heart.

Statement by the jury
The design of this heart catheter shows a careful and responsible use of materials, which greatly enhances efficiency and hygiene.

Der Khelix 10E Steerable EP Katheter wurde entwickelt, um das Risiko von Verunreinigungen und der Funktionsbeeinträchtigung durch Mehrfachbenutzung zu verringern. Er verfügt deshalb über einen abnehmbaren Schaft, der nach der Operation entsorgt wird. Handgriff und Führungsdraht können nach der Sterilisation wiederverwendet werden. Dies sorgt für hohe Materialeinsparungen und entsprechend geringere Kosten. Der Führungsdraht lässt sich über einen Vor- und Zurückmechanismus am Handgriff präzise bis zum Herzen manövrieren.

Begründung der Jury
Die Gestaltung des Herzkatheters zeigt einen sorgfältigen, verantwortungsbewussten Umgang mit Materialien, der in hohem Maße die Effizienz und Hygiene fördert.

X-SMART IQ
Cordless Endodontic Motor
Kabelloser Endomotor

Manufacturer
Dentsply Maillefer, Ballaigues, Switzerland
In-house design
Web
www.dentsplymaillefer.com

The X-Smart IQ is an advanced endodontic motor for root canal treatments, which is controlled wirelessly via an iPad Mini. Not only does this enable graphically simplified operation of the device, but the planned treatment can be better explained to patients using imagery. The slim, well-balanced handpiece has a battery runtime long enough to carry out 16 treatments. The particularly small head and the angle piece, which rotates by 360 degrees, provide optimal access and unrestricted visibility.

Statement by the jury
This endodontic motor impresses with its technical and aesthetic qualities. Its compact and functional design language lends the unit a premium and professional appearance.

X-Smart IQ ist ein fortschrittlicher Endomotor für die Zahnwurzelbehandlung, der kabellos mit einem iPad Mini verbunden wird. Dies ermöglicht nicht nur eine grafisch vereinfachte Bedienung, sondern die geplante Behandlung kann dem Patienten anhand von Bildern besser erklärt werden. Das schlanke, ausbalancierte Handstück hat eine Akkulaufzeit für 16 Behandlungen. Der besonders kleine Kopf und das um 360 Grad drehbare Winkelstück sorgen für einen optimalen Zugang und uneingeschränkte Sicht.

Begründung der Jury
Der Endomotor beeindruckt in technischer wie ästhetischer Hinsicht. Seine kompakte, funktionale Formensprache mutet ebenso edel wie professionell an.

VistaCam iX HD
Intraoral Camera
Intraoralkamera

Manufacturer
Dürr Dental AG,
Bietigheim-Bissingen, Germany
Design
formstudio
(Christina Koch, Ulrich Merkle),
Stuttgart, Germany
Web
www.duerrdental.com
www.formstudio.com

The VistaCam iX HD intraoral camera consists of a handpiece with several interchangeable heads. Each head has a different camera function: exposure with autofocus, infrared or fluorescence. Furthermore, the camera is characterised by its slim, rounded form, which can be comfortably moved around in the patient's mouth. For ease of use, buttons for focusing and shutter release are installed on both sides of the handpiece.

Statement by the jury
The design of this intraoral camera has successfully translated sophisticated technology into a remarkably small form.

Die Intraoralkamera VistaCam iX HD besteht aus einem Handstück und verschiedenen austauschbaren Wechselköpfen. Jeder Kopf verfügt über eine andere Kamerafunktion: Aufnahmen mit Autofokus, Infrarot oder Fluoreszenz. Zudem zeichnet sich die Kamera durch eine schlanke, abgerundete Form aus, die sich komfortabel im Mund des Patienten bewegen lässt. Für eine vereinfachte Bedienung sind an beiden Seiten des Handstücks jeweils eine Fokustaste und eine Auslösetaste angebracht.

Begründung der Jury
Bei der Konstruktion der Intraoralkamera ist es gelungen, anspruchsvolle Technologie in eine bemerkenswert kleine Bauart zu überführen.

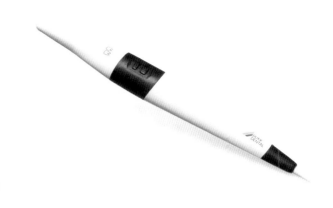

SIROLaser Blue Handpiece
SIROLaser-Blue-Handstück
Handpiece for Dental Laser
Handstück für Dentallaser

Manufacturer
Sirona Dental Systems GmbH,
Bensheim, Germany
Design
Puls Produktdesign
(Andreas Ries, Phillip Sorge),
Darmstadt, Germany
Web
www.sirona.com
www.puls-design.de

The compact and ergonomic design of the handpiece for the SiroLaser Blue dental laser facilitates easy use in areas of the oral cavity that are hard to access. The newly developed packaging and assembly concept of the sterile, single-use fibre tips and the stainless-steel sleeve, which can be removed easily for sterilisation, create immaculate hygienic conditions. An integrated finger switch allows fatigue-free working without the need for an additional foot switch.

Statement by the jury
With its flowing, elongated form and stainless-steel finish, the handpiece for the SiroLaser Blue possesses an elegant appearance.

Die kompakte und ergonomische Gestaltung des Handstücks für den Dentallaser SiroLaser Blue erleichtert die Behandlung in schwer zugänglichen Bereichen des Mundraums. Durch das neu entwickelte Verpackungs- und Montagekonzept der sterilen Einmalfaserspitzen und die zur Sterilisation leicht abnehmbare Edelstahlhülse ergeben sich tadellose hygienische Bedingungen. Ein integrierter Fingerschalter sorgt für ein ermüdungsfreies Arbeiten und macht einen zusätzlichen Fußschalter überflüssig.

Begründung der Jury
Das Handstück für den SiroLaser Blue besitzt durch seine fließende, lang gezogene Form und die Edelstahl-Optik eine elegante Anmutung.

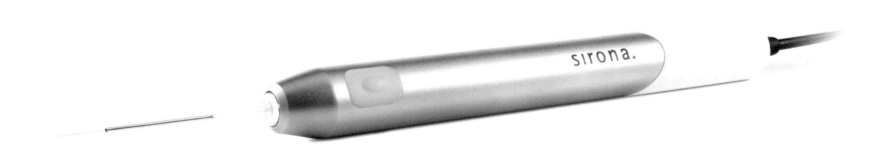

ONE
Loupe Glasses
Lupenbrille

Manufacturer
Univet, Rezzato (Brescia), Italy
In-house design
Fabio Borsani
Web
www.univet-optic.com

The frame of the One loupe glasses combines the stability of titanium with the lightness of aluminium. The high-definition optical system is made to measure based on individual requirements, such as pupillary distance and working distance of the user. The spectacles therefore provide an optimal fit and create ideal working conditions for surgeons and dentists. Furthermore, optional accessories such as side protectors, a headband and the connection with the illumination system are designed to offer a comfortable integrated ensemble.

Statement by the jury
These loupe glasses feature a convincingly clear and distinct design language, which expressively reflects the precision of this optical system.

Das Rahmengestell der Lupenbrille One vereint die Stabilität von Titan mit der Leichtigkeit von Aluminium. Das hochauflösende optische System wird nach individuellen Anforderungen wie Pupillendistanz und Arbeitsabstand des Benutzers angefertigt. Somit bietet die Brille eine optimale Anpassung und schafft ideale Arbeitsbedingungen für Chirurgen und Zahnärzte. Das weitere Zubehör wie der Seitenschutz, das Kopfhalteband und der Anschluss für das Beleuchtungssystem ist so designt, dass alles zusammen ein komfortabel zu tragendes, einheitliches Ganzes ergibt.

Begründung der Jury
Die Lupenbrille überzeugt durch ihre klare und markante Formensprache, die auf ausdrucksstarke Weise die Präzision dieses optischen Systems widerspiegelt.

DIPLOMAT
Pedicle Screw System
Pedikelschraubensystem

Manufacturer
SIGNUS Medizintechnik GmbH, Alzenau, Germany
In-house design
Web
www.signus.com

The Diplomat pedicle screw system includes two implants: the screw and the tulip. According to the surgical situation, the screw can be combined with different tulips, thus enabling different procedures for the stabilisation of the spine. The thread pitch of the screws has been designed for faster insertion and reduces the implantation time. The tulip profile is extremely low, thus guaranteeing optimum adjustment. The patented locking mechanism ensures a very high strength of the tulip-screw connection.

Das Pedikelschraubensystem Diplomat besteht aus zwei Implantaten: der Schraube und der Tulpe. Je nach klinischer Situation kann die Schraube mit verschiedenen Tulpen kombiniert werden, sodass sich ganz unterschiedliche Eingriffe zur Stabilisierung der Wirbelsäule realisieren lassen. Die Gewindesteigung der Schraube ist für ein schnelles Eindrehen ausgelegt und reduziert die Implantationszeit. Das Tulpenprofil ist extrem niedrig und garantiert eine optimale Anpassung. Der patentierte Verriegelungsmechanismus sorgt für höchste Festigkeit der Tulpen-Schrauben-Verbindung.

Statement by the jury
This modular pedicle screw system impresses with its enormous versatility. Featuring high-quality workmanship, the design has been thought out down to the smallest detail.

Begründung der Jury
Das Pedikelschraubensystem beeindruckt durch seine enorme Vielseitigkeit. Die hochwertig verarbeitete Konstruktion ist bis ins Detail durchdacht.

LINOS
Hand Fracture System
Handfraktursystem

Manufacturer
Gebrüder Martin GmbH & Co. KG,
Tuttlingen, Germany
In-house design
Klaus Kohler
Design
Inkutec® GmbH, Barsbüttel, Germany
Web
www.klsmartin.com
www.inkutec.de

The Linos hand fracture system provides a complete range of anatomically pre-shaped plates that can be combined with both standard and multidirectional-locking screws. The elements are freely interchangeable, which guarantees the best possible hand fracture treatment. The colour-coded, ergonomically designed instruments facilitate easy identification and intuitive application. Storage according to the sequence of use during surgery proves to be especially user-friendly.

Statement by the jury
The design of this hand fracture system has been thought out down to the smallest detail. It provides many options for combination and is thus flexible to use.

Das Handfraktursystem Linos bietet ein komplettes Sortiment an anatomisch vorgeformten Platten, die sowohl mit Standard- als auch mit multidirektional-winkelstabilen Schrauben besetzt werden können. Diese sind frei kombinierbar, um eine bestmögliche Versorgung bei jeder Handfraktur zu gewährleisten. Die farbcodierten, ergonomisch gestalteten Instrumente erlauben eine eindeutige Zuordnung und intuitive Verwendung. Die entsprechend dem OP-Ablauf angeordnete Lagerung ist besonders nutzerfreundlich.

Begründung der Jury
Die Gestaltung des Handfraktursystems ist bis ins Detail durchdacht. Es bietet vielseitige Kombinationsmöglichkeiten und ist dadurch flexibel einsetzbar.

CapFlex PIP
Prosthesis for the Second Knuckle
Prothese für das Fingermittelgelenk

Manufacturer
Gebrüder Martin GmbH & Co. KG,
Tuttlingen, Germany
In-house design
Frank Rebholz
Design
Inkutec® GmbH, Barsbüttel, Germany
Web
www.klsmartin.com
www.inkutec.de

The CapFlex PIP prosthesis is an innovative joint replacement for the second knuckle. In order to meet the anatomical requirements of individual patients, the modularly designed components are available in a range of sizes. The advantages for the patient resulting from the new design are a primary solid bone anchorage, the improved lateral joint stability and the optimised conditions for revision. For a safe step-by-step implantation intuitive, colour-coded instruments are available.

Statement by the jury
This prosthesis meets high standards with its combination of a modular design concept and anatomical aspects, thus enabling highly effective treatment.

Bei der Prothese CapFlex PIP handelt es sich um einen innovativen Gelenkersatz für das Fingermittelgelenk. Um der individuellen Anatomie des Patienten gerecht zu werden, sind die modular gestalteten Komponenten in unterschiedlichen Dimensionen verfügbar. Die aus dem Design resultierenden Vorteile sind eine hohe Primärstabilität, die verbesserte Seitwärtsstabilität sowie die optimierte Revisionsmöglichkeit. Für eine sichere Implantation stehen intuitive und farbcodierte Instrumente zur Verfügung.

Begründung der Jury
Auf hohem Niveau verbindet die Prothese ein modulares Gestaltungskonzept mit anatomischen Gesichtspunkten. Dies ermöglicht eine äußerst effektive Behandlung.

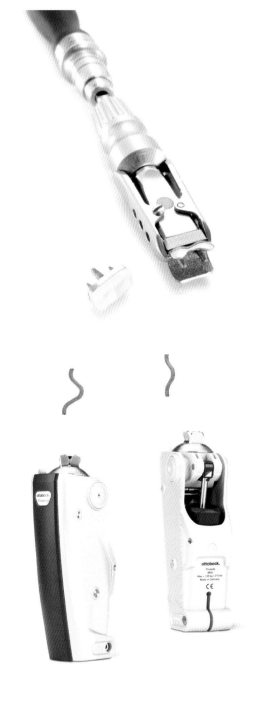

3R31 Prosedo
Prosthetic Knee Joint
Prothesenkniegelenk

Manufacturer
Otto Bock HealthCare GmbH,
Duderstadt, Germany
In-house design
Christian Noack
Web
www.ottobock.com

The 3R31 Prosedo prosthetic knee joint was developed for above-knee amputees, whose radius of mobility is limited to the domestic area. The knee joint features an individually adjustable hydraulic system, which gives the user improved balance during the process of sitting down. The intact side of the patient's body is relieved considerably in the process. The use of a glass-fibre-reinforced synthetic material for the joint chassis enables a lightweight, compact and simultaneously robust design.

Statement by the jury
This prosthetic knee joint is a mature construction, both technically and aesthetically. The compact design is emphasised by the strip of blue along the front.

Das Prothesenkniegelenk 3R31 Prosedo wurde für oberschenkelamputierte Menschen entwickelt, deren Bewegungsradius auf den häuslichen Bereich beschränkt ist. Das Kniegelenk verfügt über eine individuell einstellbare Hydraulik, die dem Anwender beim Hinsetzen eine bessere Balance ermöglicht. Die erhaltene Körperseite wird dabei deutlich entlastet. Für das Gelenkchassis wurde ein glasfaserverstärkter Kunststoff verwendet, was eine leichte, kompakte und zugleich robuste Konstruktion erlaubt.

Begründung der Jury
Bei dem Prothesenkniegelenk handelt es sich um eine technisch und ästhetisch ausgereifte Konstruktion. Die kompakte Bauart wird durch die blaue Frontlinie betont.

mylife™ YpsoPump®
Insulin Pump
Insulinpumpe

Manufacturer
Ypsomed AG, Burgdorf, Switzerland
In-house design
Web
www.ypsomed.com

The mylife YpsoPump is one of the smallest and lightest insulin pumps on the market. It only weighs 83 grams including battery and filled cartridge. Since the functions have been reduced to the essentials, the operation of the pump is particularly easy to learn. It is operated using a high-contrast OLED touchscreen. Icons that are language-neutral and thus immediately understandable guide the user through the menu. The pump is used with pre-filled cartridges, which simplifies the cartridge change considerably, as well as with self-filled cartridges for the insulin of choice. Therapy data can be transferred via Bluetooth.

Die mylife YpsoPump ist eine der kleinsten und leichtesten Insulinpumpen auf dem Markt. Sie wiegt nur 83 Gramm inklusive Batterie und gefüllter Ampulle. Da die Funktionen auf das Wesentlichste reduziert sind, ist der Umgang mit der Pumpe besonders leicht zu erlernen. Sie wird über einen kontraststarken OLED-Touchscreen bedient. Icons, die sprachunabhängig und daher unmittelbar verständlich sind, führen durch das Menü. Die Pumpe wird mit vor-gefüllten Ampullen angewendet, was einen schnellen und einfachen Ampullenwechsel gewährleistet, wie auch mit selbst befüllba-ren Ampullen für das Insulin nach Wahl. Die Therapiedaten können via Bluetooth übertragen werden.

Statement by the jury
This insulin pump captivates with its convenient handling. The simple black design directs the user's full attention to the display.

Begründung der Jury
Die Insulinpumpe besticht durch ihre Handlichkeit. Das schlichte Design in Schwarz lenkt die volle Aufmerksamkeit auf das Display.

Equashield
Closed System Transfer Device
Geschlossenes
Arzneimitteltransfersystem

Manufacturer
Equashield LLC, New York, USA
In-house design
Marino Kriheli
Web
www.equashield.com

Equashield is a medication transfer device developed for the safe handling of toxic drugs. It prevents outside contaminants from entering the system and dangerous liquids from escaping. Instead of applying the conventional approach of using an external balloon to give the container an airtight seal, the system uses an encapsulated syringe barrel in which pressure equalisation is achieved directly. The syringe barrel is made of metal, which is more hygienic and provides smoother motion than plastic.

Statement by the jury
The self-contained design of the transfer system is exemplary and meets the highest standards of hygiene and safety.

Equashield ist ein Arzneimitteltransfersystem für die sichere Handhabung toxischer Arzneimittel. Es verhindert das Eindringen von Verunreinigungen und das Austreten gefährlicher Flüssigkeiten. Um den Behälter luftdicht zu versiegeln, verwendet das System nicht wie üblich einen externen Ballon, sondern einen verkapselten Spritzenzylinder, in dem der Druckausgleich direkt erzeugt wird. Der Spritzenkolben besteht aus Metall, das im Vergleich zu Kunststoff hygienischer und leichtgängiger im Gebrauch ist.

Begründung der Jury
Die in sich geschlossene Konstruktion des Transfersystems ist vorbildlich und wird Ansprüchen an die Hygiene und Sicherheit in hohem Maße gerecht.

REVITIVE Medic
Circulation Booster
Durchblutungsstimulator

Manufacturer
Actegy Limited, Bracknell, Great Britain
Design
Team Consulting Ltd (Patrick Douloubakas, Paul Greenhalgh), Cambridge, Great Britain
Web
www.actegy.co.uk
www.team-consulting.com

Revitive Medic uses electrical muscle stimulation to enhance blood flow to the legs. The device's design is characterised by a combination of soft, organic forms and precise geometric detailing, which emphasises the technical dimension of the therapy without having an intimidating effect on elderly people. The unit may be operated using controls on the device, a remote control or a smartphone app. The integrated handle makes it highly portable.

Statement by the jury
The design language of this circulation booster looks sporty, modern and fresh. The strong colour contrasts skilfully direct attention to the controls.

Revitive Medic verwendet elektrische Muskelstimulation, um die Durchblutung in den Beinen zu verbessern. Das Gerätedesign zeichnet sich durch ein Zusammenspiel aus weichen, organischen Formen und präzisen geometrischen Details aus, welche die technische Dimension der Therapie unterstreichen, ohne auf ältere Menschen einschüchternd zu wirken. Die Bedienung erfolgt wahlweise direkt am Gerät, über eine Fernbedienung oder eine Smartphone-App. Der integrierte Griff ermöglicht den einfachen Transport.

Begründung der Jury
Die Formensprache des Durchblutungsstimulators wirkt sportlich, modern und frisch. Die hohen Farbkontraste lenken den Fokus geschickt auf die Bedienelemente.

Planmeca Lumo™
Work Chair for Dentistry
Zahnärztlicher Behandlerstuhl

Manufacturer
Planmeca Oy, Helsinki, Finland
In-house design
Juho Sutinen, Timo Silvonen
Web
www.planmeca.com

The Planmeca Lumo work chair for dentistry provides a variety of adjustment options and a generous range of movement. The height-adjustable backrest stabilises the practitioner's hip in an ergonomic position. The forward-tilting seat is flexible, which minimises strain and pressure on the thighs. Together, the seat and backrest ensure that the practitioner's back remains in a straight position while sitting. The horizontally sliding seat may be enlarged if required.

Statement by the jury
This work chair supports a healthier posture. The frame, chair and backrest, along with strong colour contrasts, engender an emotionally appealing appearance.

Der Behandlerstuhl Planmeca Lumo bietet eine Vielzahl von Einstellungen und einen großzügigen Bewegungsbereich. Die höhenverstellbare Rückenlehne stabilisiert die Hüfte des Behandlers in einer ergonomisch günstigen Haltung. Der sich nach vorne neigende Sitz ist flexibel, was die Beanspruchung und den Druck im Bereich der Oberschenkel minimiert. Im Zusammenspiel stellen Sitz und Rückenlehne sicher, dass der Rücken aufgerichtet ist. Die horizontal verschiebbare Sitzfläche lässt sich bei Bedarf vergrößern.

Begründung der Jury
Der Behandlerstuhl unterstützt eine gesündere Haltung. Gestell, Sitz und Lehne sowie kräftige Farbkontraste ergeben eine emotional ansprechende Erscheinung.

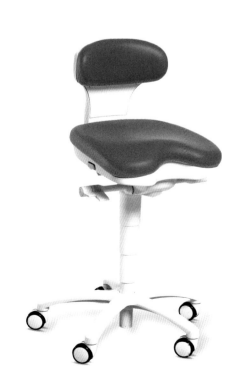

V-Compact
Rotational Viscometer
Rotationsviskosimeter

Manufacturer
Fungilab S.A., Sant Feliu de Llobregat
(Barcelona), Spain
In-house design
Ernest Buira
Web
www.fungilab.com

The V-Compact is a high-performance rotational viscometer that measures the flow resistance of fluids. In contrast to conventional models, the device has a digital interface and is controlled wirelessly via an app. This newly developed software provides full functionality and control over the entire instrument; all input settings, functions and parameters can be accessed on mobile devices like smartphones or tablet PCs that support the application. This allows authorised laboratory staff to remotely access the test data from anywhere.

Statement by the jury
Thanks to cordless functionality, it was possible to imbue the V-Compact with a fluent, minimalist design. The circumferential frame completes its unified appearance.

Das V-Compact ist ein Hochleistungs-Rotationsviskosimeter, das den Fließwiderstand von Flüssigkeiten misst. Im Unterschied zu herkömmlichen Modellen verfügt das Gerät über eine digitale Schnittstelle und wird kabellos über eine App bedient. Diese neu entwickelte Software bietet volle Funktionalität und Kontrolle über das gesamte Instrumentarium; alle mobilen Endgeräte wie Smartphone oder Tablet-PC, welche die App unterstützen, haben Zugriff auf sämtliche Eingabeeinstellungen, Funktionen und Parameter. So können befugte Labormitarbeiter die Testdaten von überallher abrufen.

Begründung der Jury
Durch die kabellose Bedienung war es möglich, bei dem V-Compact ein fließendes, reduziertes Design zu schaffen. Der umlaufende Rahmen vervollkommnet das einheitliche Bild.

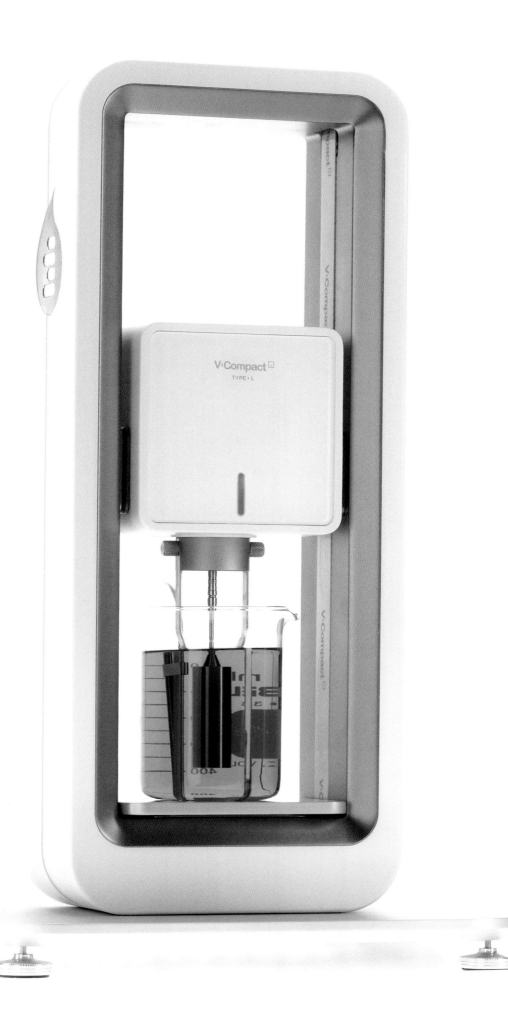

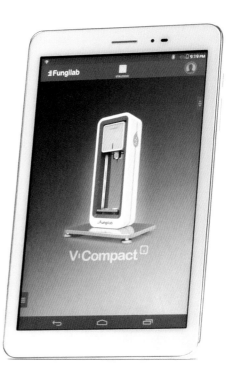

GeneReader NGS System
DNA Sequencer
DNA-Sequenziergerät

Manufacturer
QIAGEN GmbH, Hilden, Germany
Design
ID WEBER Industrial Design,
Altensteig, Germany
Web
www.qiagen.com

The GeneReader NGS System is a complete solution for decoding DNA. The unit combines the QIAcube, which prepares the sample, with two newly developed instruments, the GeneRead QIAcube and the GeneReader, creating a highly automated work process. Integrated software monitors the progress of the samples, while a bioinformatics platform takes over the otherwise time-consuming tasks of data analysis and interpretation. The rotary table concept of the GeneReader allows several samples to be sequenced independently, both in parallel and successively.

Das GeneReader NGS System ist eine Komplettlösung zur Entschlüsselung der DNA. Das System verbindet den QIAcube, der die Probe vorbereitet, mit zwei neu entwickelten Instrumenten, dem GeneRead QIAcube und dem GeneReader, zu einem hoch automatisierten Arbeitsprozess. Eine integrierte Software verfolgt den Verlauf der Proben, während eine Bioinformatik-Plattform die sonst zeitraubende Datenanalyse und Interpretation übernimmt. Durch das Drehtisch-Konzept des GeneReaders können mehrere Proben unabhängig voneinander sowohl in paralleler als auch in gestaffelter Weise sequenziert werden.

Statement by the jury
This DNA sequencer stands for simplification, which is impressively reflected in its plain aesthetics. The viewing window pleasantly disrupts the self-contained form.

Begründung der Jury
Das DNA-Sequenziergerät steht für Vereinfachung, was sich eindrucksvoll in seiner schlichten Ästhetik widerspiegelt. Die Sichtfenster lockern die geschlossene Form auf.

Sequel System
DNA Sequencer
DNA-Sequenziergerät

Manufacturer
Pacific Biosciences, Menlo Park, California, USA
Design
Whipsaw Inc, San Jose, USA
Web
www.pacb.com
www.whipsaw.com

The Sequel System is a human genome sequencing machine that is more powerful, cost-efficient and smaller than its predecessor. To prevent the door from obstructing the user, it glides down when opening, giving unrestricted access to the cells, which are arranged neatly on a stainless-steel platform. When the door glides back up again, an airtight chamber is created and the robotic arm dispenses chemicals onto the cells in order to start the analysis process.

Das Sequel System dient der Analyse des menschlichen Genoms und ist leistungsfähiger, kosteneffizienter und kleiner als das Vorgängermodell. Damit die Tür nicht den Arbeitsweg behindert, gleitet sie beim Öffnen nach unten. So hat der Anwender uneingeschränkten Zugang zu den Zellen, die übersichtlich auf einer Edelstahlplattform angeordnet sind. Wenn die Tür wieder nach oben gleitet, entsteht eine luftdichte Kammer und der Roboterarm dosiert Chemikalien auf den Zellen, um die Analyse zu starten.

Statement by the jury
The extraordinary compactness of the Sequel System is cleverly broken up by the forward-curving front. The device has an open and clearly structured look.

Begründung der Jury
Die außergewöhnliche Kompaktheit des Sequel Systems wird durch die nach vorne gewölbte Front geschickt aufgelockert. Das Gerät wirkt unverbaut und ist klar gegliedert.

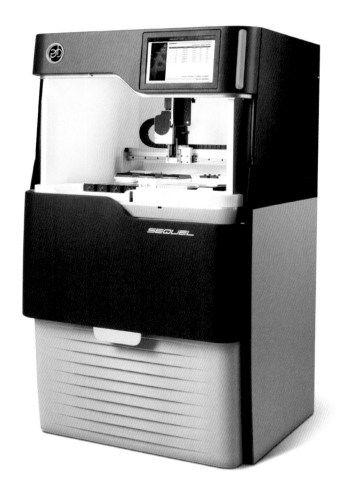

SA3800
Spectral Flow Cytometer
Spektral-Durchflusszytometer

Manufacturer
Sony Corporation, Tokyo, Japan
In-house design
Katsuhisa Hakoda
Web
www.sony.net/design

The fully automatic SA3800 spectral flow cytometer facilitates the fast and easy analysis of a large number of samples. The cells are illuminated with a broad spectrum of light and directed towards a prism, which separates them into the spectral colours. After a careful study of desk-based workflow procedures for research purposes, the controls, which are clearly distinguished by high-contrast materials, were arranged on the right side of the device. The surfaces have been designed as smooth and flush as possible in order to meet the high hygiene standards for laboratory equipment.

Der vollautomatische Spektral-Durchfluss-zytometer SA3800 ermöglicht eine schnelle und einfache Analyse zahlreicher Proben. Die Zellen werden mit Licht aus einem breiten Spektrum beleuchtet und auf ein Prisma gelenkt, das sie in die Spektralfarben zerlegt. Nach eingehender Untersuchung von tischbasierten Arbeitsabläufen wurden die Bedienelemente, die durch kontrast-reiche Materialien klar erkennbar sind, auf der rechten Seite des Geräts angeordnet. Die Oberflächen sind so glatt und bündig wie möglich gehalten, um die hohen Hygi-enestandards im Labor zu erfüllen.

Statement by the jury
This cytometer appears as if hewn from a single block. Only the functional area enjoys strong visual emphasis, thus becoming the clear point of focus.

Begründung der Jury
Der Zytometer wirkt wie aus einem Block gehauen. Einzig der Funktionsbereich ist optisch prägnant hervorgehoben und wird so klar in den Fokus gerückt.

Idylla
System for Molecular Diagnostics
System für die Molekulardiagnostik

Manufacturer
Biocartis, Mechelen, Belgium
In-house design
Web
www.biocartis.com

The fully automatic Idylla system was developed to offer fast access to clinical molecular diagnostic information. From patient sample to result, it only takes 40 to 150 minutes. The system consists of the analyser, the operating console with touchscreen interface and integrated barcode scanner and the separate cartridges. In order to avoid contamination by the sample in the laboratory, the sample is first put into the cartridge and then inserted into the analyser.

Das vollautomatische System Idylla wurde für einen schnellen Zugriff auf Informationen zur Molekulardiagnostik entwickelt. Von der Patientenprobe bis zum Ergebnis dauert es nur 40 bis 150 Minuten. Das System besteht aus dem Analysegerät, der Bedienkonsole mit Touchscreen-Oberfläche und integriertem Barcodescanner sowie separaten Kartuschen. Um im Labor eine Kontamination durch die Probe zu vermeiden, wird diese erst in die Kartusche gegeben und dann in das Analysegerät eingesetzt.

Statement by the jury
Idylla conveys smooth and clear workflows through its immaculate aesthetic, which is characterised by fluent transitions in pure white.

Begründung der Jury
Durch die makellose Ästhetik, die von fließenden Übergängen in reinem Weiß geprägt ist, kommuniziert Idylla reibungslose und klare Arbeitsabläufe.

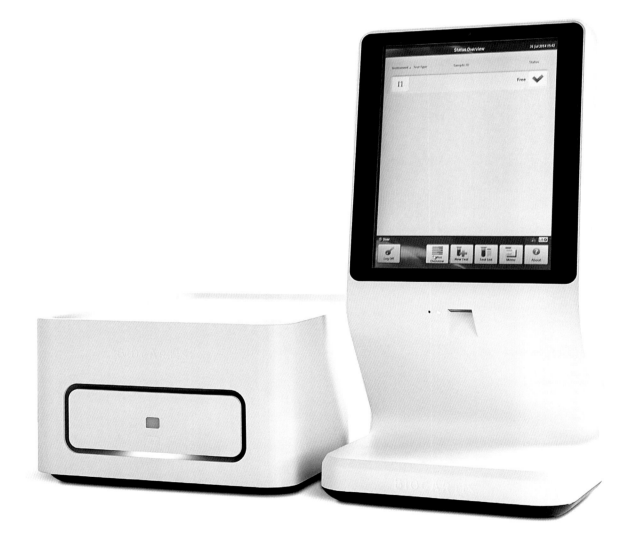

UV5Nano
Spectrophotometer
Spektralphotometer

Manufacturer
Mettler-Toledo GmbH,
Schwerzenbach, Switzerland
In-house design
Design
Produkt Design Zürich GmbH
(Marcel Delavy, Reto Berger, Livia Weder,
Martin Wilhelm), Zürich, Switzerland
Web
www.mt.com/uv-vis
www.produktdesign.ch

The UV5Nano spectrophotometer takes measurements in protein and nucleic acid samples in just two seconds. The terminal is separate from the device and can be positioned as required. The top of the housing with the sample arm and separate cuvette shaft has a clear design. The slightly curved, ergonomic form enables convenient and safe pipetting. The one-click user interface is quickly mastered and offers high ease of use.

Statement by the jury
The spectrophotometer captivates with its clear, cubist design language, which conveys the impression of a precise and high-performance laboratory device.

Das Spektralphotometer UV5Nano führt Messungen an Protein- oder Nukleinsäureproben in nur zwei Sekunden durch. Das vom Gerät separierte Terminal kann je nach Bedarf positioniert werden. Die Gehäuseoberseite mit dem Probenarm und dem separaten Küvettenschacht ist übersichtlich gestaltet; das leicht geschwungene, ergonomische Design ermöglicht ein bequemes und sicheres Pipettieren. Die One-Click-Benutzeroberfläche ist in ihrer Anwendung schnell zu erlernen und sehr einfach in der Bedienung.

Begründung der Jury
Das Spektralphotometer besticht durch seine klare, kubistische Formensprache, die den Eindruck eines präzisen und leistungsfähigen Laborgeräts vermittelt.

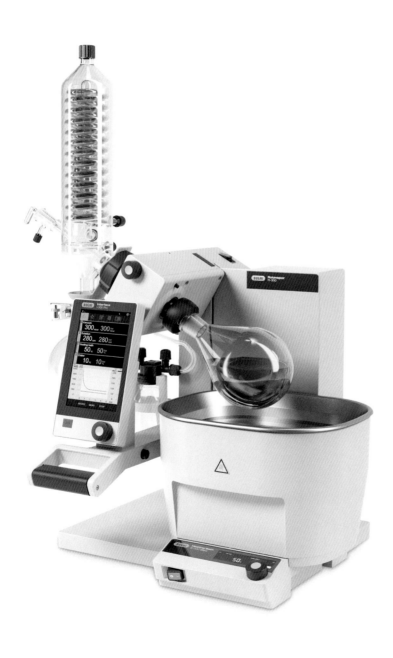

Rotavapor R-300
Rotary Evaporator
Rotationsverdampfer

Manufacturer
BÜCHI Labortechnik,
Flawil, Switzerland
Design
NOSE Design (Ruedi Müller),
Zürich, Switzerland
Web
www.buchi.com
www.nose.ch

The Rotavapor R-300 rotary evaporator, developed for the distillation of liquids, consists of various modules, allowing individual configurations. Different lift types, baths, process controllers and glass accessories are offered. The patented Combi-Clip with a snap-lock enables the user to connect the evaporator flask with one hand. All relevant data, such as bath and vapor temperature, rotational speed and vacuum pressure, can be monitored and managed via the prominently positioned display.

Statement by the jury
The open structure of this rotary evaporator fosters a sense of clarity. Thanks to its deliberately simple design, the components combine to form a cohesive unit.

Der Rotationsverdampfer Rotavapor R-300 zur Destillation von Flüssigkeiten besteht aus verschiedenen frei kombinierbaren Modulen. Je zwei Lifttypen, Bäder und Steuergeräte sowie diverse Glasaufbauten stehen zur Auswahl. Der patentierte Combi-Clip mit Schnappverschluss ermöglicht es, den Verdampferkolben einhändig anzuschließen. Alle wichtigen Werte wie Bad- und Dampftemperatur, Rotationsgeschwindigkeit und Vakuumdruck werden über ein zentrales Display übersichtlich angezeigt und eingestellt.

Begründung der Jury
Die offene Architektur des Rotationsverdampfers sorgt für klare Verhältnisse. Durch die betont schlichte Gestaltung ergeben die Bauteile ein stimmiges Ganzes.

PIPETMAN M
Electronic Pipette
Elektronische Pipette

Manufacturer
Gilson SAS, Villiers-le-Bel, France
In-house design
Web
www.gilson.com

The Pipetman M is a lightweight, electronic pipette that can aspirate liquid volumes of up to 1,200 microlitres. Thanks to the motor, the aspiration and dispensing of samples is almost effortless. All pipetting functions and menu options can be selected with just two buttons. The user may conveniently switch between five different operator modes, including a repetitive mode for repeated pipetting.

Statement by the jury
Due to its well-balanced weight, the Pipetman M is comfortable to grasp, thus facilitating effortless single-handed use.

Die Pipetman M ist eine leichte, elektronische Pipette, die Flüssigkeitsmengen von bis zu 1.200 Mikroliter aufnehmen kann. Dank des Motors erfordert die Probenaufnahme und -abgabe nahezu keinen Kraftaufwand. Mit nur zwei Tasten lassen sich alle Pipettierfunktionen und Menüoptionen sehr einfach ausführen. Der Anwender kann bequem zwischen fünf unterschiedlichen Anwendungsmodi wechseln, darunter auch ein Repetitivmodus für wiederholtes Pipettieren.

Begründung der Jury
Die Pipetman M liegt dank ihrer ausgewogenen Gewichtsverteilung gut in der Hand. Die einhändige Bedienung gelingt somit mühelos.

Tacta
Mechanical Pipette
Mechanische Pipette

Manufacturer
Sartorius Biohit Liquid Handling Oy, Helsinki, Finland
In-house design
Ville Hintikka
Web
www.sartorius.com

The ergonomic design of the Tacta mechanical pipette allows laboratory staff to pipette several thousand times a day without effort. Thanks to the finger brace, there is no need to grip the pipette tightly; instead, it rests lightly in the user's hand. The pipetting volume can be easily adjusted using just one hand. The large display is readable from any angle. Furthermore, with only three parts to disassemble, the pipette is easy to clean.

Statement by the jury
Due to its sophisticated ergonomics and pleasant volume, the pipette is easy on the hand. The individual functional areas are clearly structured.

Das ergonomische Design der mechanischen Pipette Tacta erlaubt es Mitarbeitern im Labor, ohne Anstrengung mehrere tausend Mal zu pipettieren. Dank des Fingerbügels muss die Pipette nicht mit Kraft festgehalten werden, sondern liegt locker in der Hand. Das Pipettiervolumen kann sehr einfach mit einer Hand angepasst werden. Das große Display lässt sich aus allen Blickwinkeln leicht ablesen. Zudem ist die Pipette mit nur drei abnehmbaren Teilen einfach zu reinigen.

Begründung der Jury
Die ausgeklügelte Ergonomie und das angenehme Volumen der Pipette schonen die Hand. Die einzelnen Funktionsbereiche sind klar strukturiert.

XPR Ultra-Microbalance
XPR Ultra-Mikrowaage

Manufacturer
Mettler-Toledo GmbH, Greifensee, Switzerland
In-house design
Daniel Mock, Stefan Bühler
Design
Held+Team (Fred Held, Thilo Hogrebe), Hamburg, Germany
Web
www.mt.com
www.heldundteam.de

The XPR Ultra-Microbalance features an active cooling mechanism that ensures accuracy down to one tenth of a microgram. It provides a user terminal at the weighing unit for carrying out weighing tasks and a touchscreen for the configuration of the device, which can be placed anywhere. This separation allows users to optimally focus on their tasks. Furthermore, the LED indicators display the status of the scale, while infrared sensors enable hands-free operation.

Statement by the jury
The XPR Ultra-Microbalance is inspired by the idea of a markedly clean design, the strength of which lies in its high functionality and simple operability.

Die XPR Ultra-Mikrowaage hat eine aktive Kühlung, die eine Genauigkeit bis auf ein Zehntel Mikrogramm zulässt. Es ist sowohl ein Bedienterminal an der Waageneinheit vorhanden, um die Wiegearbeiten durchzuführen, als auch ein frei platzierbarer Touchscreen, um das Gerät zu konfigurieren. Durch diese Unterteilung kann sich der Anwender optimal auf seine Tätigkeit konzentrieren. Des Weiteren zeigen LED-Indikatoren den Zustand der Waage an, während Infrarotsensoren eine berührungslose Steuerung ermöglichen.

Begründung der Jury
Die XPR Ultra-Mikrowaage ist inspiriert von der Idee einer betont sauberen Gestaltung, deren Stärke in der hohen Funktionalität und einfachen Bedienbarkeit liegt.

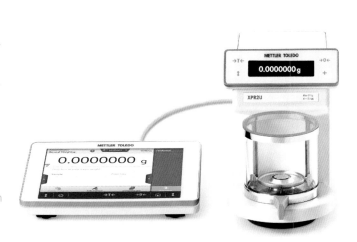

D2000
Dental Lab Scanner
Dentallaborscanner

Manufacturer
3Shape A/S, Copenhagen, Denmark
Design
Eskild Hansen Design Studios, Copenhagen, Denmark
Web
www.3shape.com
www.eskildhansen.com

The D2000 dental lab scanner increases scanning speed by capturing several lines in one scan. Four cameras with 5 MP each ensure high accuracy. Thanks to the two scan plates, models of the upper and lower jaws may be scanned at the same time. The tinted glass door can be opened with the tap of a finger; it gently glides upwards, ensuring easy access to the scanner's interior and guaranteeing improved ergonomics.

Der Dentallaborscanner D2000 steigert die Scangeschwindigkeit, indem er mehrere Scanzeilen in einer einzigen Aufnahme erfasst. Vier Kameras mit je 5 MP sorgen für eine hohe Genauigkeit. Durch die zwei Scanteller können Modelle des Ober- und Unterkiefers gleichzeitig gescannt werden. Die getönte Glasklappe lässt sich mit einem Fingertippen öffnen und gleitet leise nach oben. Dies gewährleistet einen einfachen Zugang zum Innenraum des Scanners und eine verbesserte Ergonomie.

Statement by the jury
This dental lab scanner impresses with its extravagant silhouette that tilts backwards, visually expressing the scanner's extraordinary speed.

Begründung der Jury
Der Dentallaborscanner besticht durch seine extravagante, nach hinten gekippte Silhouette, die seine außergewöhnliche Schnelligkeit visuell zum Ausdruck bringt.

CEREC SpeedFire
High-Temperature Dental Furnace
Dental-Hochtemperaturofen

Manufacturer
Sirona Dental Systems GmbH, Bensheim, Germany
Design
Puls Produktdesign (Andreas Ries, Torsten Richter),
Darmstadt, Germany
Web
www.sirona.com
www.puls-design.de

The Cerec SpeedFire is an all-in-one high-temperature furnace for use in dental practices. By applying innovative technologies, the sintering of zirconium oxide and the firing of dental ceramics can be combined in one furnace. The induction technology applied here allows the fastest heating rates, enabling the sintering of zirconium oxide restorations in less than 15 minutes. The dentist is thus able to provide patients with restorations from this material in a single treatment session. The device is operated via a separate control panel that features a touchscreen.

Der Cerec SpeedFire ist ein All-in-one-Hochtemperaturofen zur Verwendung in der Zahnarztpraxis. Durch den Einsatz innovativer Technologien werden das Sintern von Zirkonoxid und das Glasieren von Dentalkeramiken in einem Ofen vereint. Die angewandte Induktionstechnologie erlaubt höchste Aufheizraten, sodass Zirkonoxid-Restaurationen in weniger als 15 Minuten gesintert werden können. Der Zahnarzt ist somit in der Lage, Patienten in einer Behandlungssitzung mit Restaurationen aus diesem Werkstoff zu versorgen. Die Bedienung erfolgt über ein separates Control Panel mit Touchscreen.

Statement by the jury
The furnace presents a successful combination of an open and closed design, as well as rounded and austere lines, thus creating a fascinating tension of form.

Begründung der Jury
Der Ofen zeigt ein gekonntes Zusammenspiel aus offener und geschlossener Bauform, aus gerundeten und strengen Linien – so entsteht eine aufregende formale Grundspannung.

ASTORE
Medication Management System
Medikamentenmanagementsystem

Manufacturer
Acibadem Teknoloji, Istanbul, Turkey
Design
DesignUM, Istanbul, Turkey
Web
www.acibademtechnology.com
www.acibadem.com/en
www.design-um.com
Honourable Mention

The Astore management system enables safe, accurate and fast dispensing of medication in hospitals. It consists of three modules: the main station, the external cabinet and the wall station. Only authorised clinicians have access to the system, using a password, fingerprint identification or an ID card. Besides the dispensing of medication in specific doses for individual patients, the system also monitors stock to avoid shortages in patient care. The smooth, flat surfaces of the individual modules have antibacterial properties and are thus easy to keep hygienically clean.

Das Managementsystem Astore ermöglicht eine sichere, präzise und schnelle Medikamentenausgabe im Krankenhaus. Es besteht aus drei Modulen: der Haupteinheit, dem externen Schrank und der Wandeinheit. Ein autorisierter Zugang ist nur über ein Passwort, die Identifizierung des Fingerabdrucks oder mit einem Ausweis möglich. Neben der Medikamentenausgabe von patientenbezogenen Einzeldosen überwacht und kontrolliert das System auch die Lagerbestände, damit es bei der Versorgung der Patienten nicht zu Engpässen kommt. Die glatten, ebenen Flächen der einzelnen Module sind antibakteriell und dadurch einfach hygienisch sauber zu halten.

Statement by the jury
Astore is characterised by its precise, straight lines, which convey a feeling of efficiency and care.

Begründung der Jury
Astore zeichnet sich durch seine präzise Geradlinigkeit aus, die ein Gefühl von Effizienz und Sorgfalt vermittelt.

Rowa Dose
Blistering Machine
Blisterautomat

Manufacturer
CareFusion Germany 326 GmbH, Kelberg,
Germany
Design
Henssler und Schultheiss Fullservice
Productdesign GmbH,
Schwäbisch Gmünd, Germany
Web
www.carefusion.com/rowa
www.henssler-schultheiss.de

Rowa Dose is a blistering machine for pharmacies, hospitals and blister-pack centres. Pills are blister-packed for individual patients within seconds. A blister pack corresponds to the dose prescribed by a doctor for a specific time of intake, thus preventing medication errors. Furthermore, all medication intake instructions are printed in an easy-to-read manner on the filled blister packs. The canisters in which the pills are stored can be easily exchanged.

Statement by the jury
This blistering machine is characterised by a minimalist, geometric style, the strength of which lies in its clarity and functionality.

Rowa Dose ist ein Blisterautomat für Apotheken, Krankenhäuser und Blisterzentren. Die Tabletten werden innerhalb von Sekunden patientenindividuell verpackt. Ein Blisterbeutel entspricht dabei der vom Arzt verordneten Dosierung zu einem bestimmten Einnahmezeitpunkt. Fehlmedikationen werden so vermieden. Zudem sind sämtliche Einnahmehinweise gut lesbar auf den fertigen Schlauchblistern aufgedruckt. Die Kanister, in denen die Tabletten aufbewahrt werden, können schnell und einfach ausgetauscht werden.

Begründung der Jury
Der Blisterautomat zeichnet sich durch einen reduzierten, geometrischen Stil aus, dessen große Stärke in seiner Klarheit und Funktionalität liegt.

Rowa VMax 210
Storage and Dispensing System
Kommissioniersystem

Manufacturer
CareFusion Germany 326 GmbH,
Kelberg, Germany
Design
Henssler und Schultheiss Fullservice
Productdesign GmbH,
Schwäbisch Gmünd, Germany
Web
www.carefusion.com/rowa
www.henssler-schultheiss.de

The Rowa VMax 210 storage and dispensing system automatically sorts medications in the pharmacy and dispenses them at a sales counter within seconds. The system makes use of all available space for storage and situates packs next to each other with great precision. In spite of its high speed, the unit operates almost silently. The innovative HD multi-picking technology enables the safe handling of several packs simultaneously. The system can be individually adapted to any pharmacy layout.

Statement by the jury
The compact, cubist form of this storage and dispensing system is distinctly emphasised by its diverse rectangular surfaces. The operating functions are the focal element.

Das Kommissioniersystem Rowa VMax 210 sortiert in der Apotheke Arzneimittel automatisch ein und stellt sie bei Bedarf in Sekundenschnelle am Verkaufstresen bereit. Die Maschine nutzt jede Lücke zur Warenlagerung und sortiert präzise Packung an Packung. Trotz der hohen Geschwindigkeit arbeitet sie nahezu geräuschlos. Die innovative HD-Multi-Picking-Technologie ermöglicht das sichere Greifen von mehreren Packungen gleichzeitig. Das System kann individuell an jeden Apothekenraum angepasst werden.

Begründung der Jury
Die kompakte, kubische Form des Kommissioniersystems wird durch die unterschiedlichen rechteckigen Flächen deutlich betont. Die Bedienfunktionen stehen klar im Fokus.

DAYDOSE™
Packaging Concept for Dietary Supplement
Verpackungskonzept für
Nahrungsergänzungsmittel

Manufacturer
Abacus Medicine, Copenhagen, Denmark
Design
Medcomb, Copenhagen, Denmark
Web
www.daydose.com

DayDose is a dietary supplement that comes in highly practical packaging. It is convenient for users to carry along with them and helps to track intake easily. Each compartment is labelled with the respective day of the week and contains the recommended daily dose of micro-nutrients, antioxidants and omega-3 fatty acids. The four available product variants have different combinations of content. The daily doses are sealed and thus protected from external contaminants such as bacteria and viruses. The refillable packaging reduces waste.

DayDose ist ein Nahrungsergänzungsmittel in einer besonders praktischen Verpackung. Diese ist leicht zu transportieren und ermöglicht eine überschaubare Einnahme. Jedes Fach ist mit dem entsprechenden Wochentag gekennzeichnet und enthält die empfohlene Tagesdosis an Mikronähr-stoffen, Antioxidantien und Omega-3-Fett-säuren. Bei den vier erhältlichen Produktva-rianten sind die Inhaltsstoffe unterschiedlich zusammengesetzt. Die Tagesdosen sind versiegelt und so vor äußeren Einflüssen wie Bakterien und Viren geschützt. Durch die Nachfüllpackungen entsteht weniger Müll.

Statement by the jury
The design of the DayDose is as simple as it is self-explanatory. The design lan-guage is deliberately modelled after the pharmaceutical industry and exudes trustworthiness.

Begründung der Jury
Die Gestaltung von DayDose ist so simpel wie selbsterklärend. Die gezielt an der Pharmaindustrie orientierte Formensprache strahlt Vertrauenswürdigkeit aus.

AURA
Low Care Bed
Niedrigpflegebett

Manufacturer
Betten Malsch GmbH, Wildeck, Germany
In-house design
Web
www.bettenmalsch.com

The Aura low care bed, with its floor height of only 25 cm and vertical side rails in premium-quality aluminium, has been specially designed to prevent falls. The chassis with its concealed castors provides optimum mobility without compromising the bed's homelike character. The side rail is situated along the outside so that it blends in with the overall appearance and saves space. When lowered, it also makes for easy cleaning and provides additional space for accessories.

Statement by the jury
The side rails are mounted on the low care bed in an extremely discreet way. Thanks to the combination of wood and metal elements, it exudes warmth and elegance.

Das Niedrigpflegebett Aura ist mit 25 cm Bodenhöhe und einem vertikalen Seiten-gitter in edler Aluminiumausführung insbe-sondere für die Sturzprophylaxe gedacht. Das Fahrgestell mit verdeckten Laufrollen bietet optimale Mobilität, ohne den wohn-lichen Charakter zu beeinträchtigen. Das Seitengitter liegt außen, sodass es sich platzsparend und harmonisch in das Ge-samtbild einfügt. Im abgesenkten Zustand begünstigt es zudem die Reinigung und bietet zusätzliche Aufnahmemöglichkeiten für Zubehör.

Begründung der Jury
Die Seitengitter sind bei dem Pflegebett äußerst dezent angebracht. Durch die Kombination von Holz und metallenen Ele-menten strahlt es Wärme und Eleganz aus.

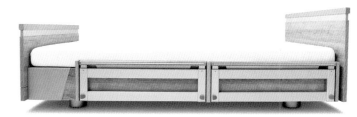

Arthritis Nurse Call Pendant
Pflegerufsystem

Manufacturer
Hills Limited, Sydney, Australia
Design
University of South Australia
(Robert White, Daniel Weiss, Sandy Walker, Peter Schumacher),
Adelaide, Australia
Web
www.hills.com.au
www.unisa.edu.au

The Arthritis Nurse Call Pendant has been developed especially for people with restricted finger strength and movement. The alarm is not activated at the touch of a button, but rather by pressing the transmitter with a hand, arm or any other body part. The silicone lamp is equipped with four bright col-our-changing LEDs that are lit when the alarm is activated, thus giving the user clear visual feedback. The system is wa-terproof and can be disassembled quick-ly, making it easy to clean.

Statement by the jury
This nurse call pendant gives people with limited motor skills more independence. Its design is particularly intuitive and elegant.

Das Pflegerufsystem wurde speziell für Personen mit Arthritis entwickelt, deren Fingerkraft und -beweglichkeit einge-schränkt ist. Der Alarm wird nicht per Knopfdruck, sondern durch Drücken des Senders mit der Hand, dem Arm oder ei-nem anderen Körperteil ausgelöst. Die Lampe aus Silikon ist mit vier hellen Farbwechsel-LEDs ausgestattet, die auf-leuchten, wenn der Alarm aktiv ist, und dem Anwender so eine eindeutige visuelle Rückmeldung geben. Das System ist wasserdicht und zum Reinigen einfach auseinanderzunehmen.

Begründung der Jury
Das Pflegenotrufsystem verhilft Personen mit eingeschränkter Motorik zu mehr Selb-ständigkeit. Sein Design ist ausgesprochen intuitiv und formschön.

Memo Box
Smart Pillbox
Intelligente Tablettenbox

Manufacturer
Tinylogics Ltd, Cambridge, Great Britain
In-house design
Web
www.tinylogics.com

The folding hinge of the Memo Box houses a microcomputer that continu-ously tracks medication intake. When a planned dose is missed, a notification is sent to a relative. The smooth and struc-tured surfaces, coupled with the robust aluminium trim, foster an elegant sen-sory impression. The smart pillbox can be filled with a medication dispenser or conventional blister packs.

Statement by the jury
With its high-quality appearance, the Memo Box is reminiscent of a notebook or diary, which makes an important con-tribution to arousing positive emotions in the user.

Im Klappscharnier der Memo Box befindet sich ein Mikrocomputer, der die Medika-menteneinnahme kontinuierlich überwacht. Sollte der Anwender eine vorgesehene Tablettendosis nicht eingenommen haben, wird eine Mitteilung an einen Angehörigen versendet. Die glatten und strukturierten Flächen verbunden mit der robusten Alu-miniumverkleidung machen einen optisch eleganten und sinnlichen Eindruck. Die Box kann mit einem Medikamentendispenser oder mit herkömmlichen Tablettenverpa-ckungen gefüllt werden.

Begründung der Jury
Mit ihrem wertigen Aussehen erinnert die Memo Box an ein Notiz- oder Tagebuch, was entscheidend dazu beiträgt, positive Emotionen beim Benutzer zu wecken.

Alcotest 3820
Alcohol Screening Device
Atemalkohol-Testgerät

Manufacturer
Dräger Safety AG & Co. KGaA, Lübeck, Germany
In-house design
Dräger Design Team
Web
www.draeger.com

The Alcotest 3820 alcohol screening device ensures exact and reliable measurements due to its electrochemical sensor technology. Furthermore, it meets the highest hygienic standards: the ergonomically designed mouthpiece can be replaced easily and is protected by a plug-on cap that keeps out dirt, regardless of where the device is stored. A backlit user interface with acoustic feedback facilitates use of the device in the dark and supports the test sequence with clear instructions.

Statement by the jury
Due to its minimalist design language, this screening device has a highly functional look. Its simplified controls make it intuitive to operate.

Das Atemalkohol-Testgerät Alcotest 3820 stellt durch seine elektrochemische Sensorik genaue und zuverlässige Messergebnisse sicher. Zudem erfüllt es höchste hygienische Ansprüche: Das ergonomisch gestaltete Mundstück ist einfach und schnell zu wechseln und wird von einer aufsteckbaren Kappe vor Schmutz geschützt, unabhängig vom Ort der Aufbewahrung. Ein hinterleuchtetes Bedieninterface mit akustischem Feedback erleichtert den Einsatz im Dunkeln und unterstützt den Testprozess durch klar verständliche Informationen.

Begründung der Jury
Das Testgerät mutet durch seine reduzierte Formensprache äußerst sachlich an. Dank seiner vereinfachten Bedienfunktionen ist es intuitiv zu verwenden.

Elvie
Pelvic Floor Exercise Tracker
Fitnesstracker für die Beckenbodenmuskulatur

Manufacturer
Chiaro, Makers of Elvie, London, Great Britain
In-house design
Jonathan O'Toole
Design
Goodwin Hartshorn, London, Great Britain
Web
www.elvie.com
www.goodwin-hartshorn.co.uk

Elvie is a patented exercise tracker designed to strengthen and tone pelvic-floor muscles. Made from the highest quality medical-grade silicone, the device links to an app via Bluetooth, giving biofeedback during exercises. This method is shown to help users improve control and endurance of this muscle group. Elvie has passed rigorous testing, resulting in a distinctly small kegel tracker with an optional cover for a custom fit and a discreet carry case that doubles up as an induction charger.

Statement by the jury
This pelvic floor exercise tracker has an appealing organic shape with a smooth, body-friendly surface. Thanks to an unobtrusive design, it is very discreet.

Elvie ist ein patentierter Fitnesstracker zur Stärkung und Straffung des Beckenbodens. Das Gerät aus hochwertigem medizinischen Silikon ist via Bluetooth mit einer App verbunden, die während der Übungen ein Biofeedback gibt. Die Methode hilft nachweislich, die Kontrolle und Belastbarkeit dieser Muskelgruppe zu verbessern. Nach ausgiebigen Tests ist ein besonders kleiner Tracker entstanden; die optionale Schutzhülle erlaubt eine individuelle Passform und das diskrete Etui dient gleichzeitig als Ladegerät.

Begründung der Jury
Der Fitnesstracker gefällt durch seine organische Form mit glatter, körperfreundlicher Oberfläche. Dank der zurückhaltenden Gestaltung ist er sehr diskret.

Provox® Coming Home™
Support after Laryngeal Surgery
Hilfsmittel nach Kehlkopfentfernung

Manufacturer
Atos Medical AB, Malmö, Sweden
Design
eye-d Innovation (Elin Persson, Pernille Sax),
Copenhagen, Denmark
Web
www.atosmedical.com
www.eye-d.com

The Provox Coming Home is an intuitive tool for patients whose larynx has been surgically removed. It makes discharging the patient easier for the health care professional and the return home from hospital smoother for the patient. The tool includes a durable carrying case with selected products and information in the local language. Simple icons give an overview of which products to use when, and the innovative and flexible pocket and folding system introduces the products and information in a step-by-step manner.

Das Provox Coming Home ist ein intuitives Hilfsmittel für Patienten, denen der Kehlkopf operativ entfernt wurde. Nach der Entlassung aus der Klinik erleichtert es dem Patienten die Rückkehr nach Hause. Es besteht aus einem strapazierfähigen Etui, das ausgewählte Produkte und Informationen in der jeweiligen Landessprache enthält. Einfache Symbole geben einen Überblick, wann welches Produkt zu benutzen ist. Das innovative und flexible Fächer- und Faltsystem führt Schritt für Schritt an die Produkte und Informationen heran.

Statement by the jury
The Provox Coming Home skilfully addresses patients' concerns in a sensitive way. The well-structured order provides the necessary support.

Begründung der Jury
Gekonnt und sensibel geht das Provox Coming Home auf die Belange der Patienten ein. Die gut strukturierte Ordnung gibt die notwendige Hilfestellung.

O² Rescue Bag
O²-Rettungsrucksack

Manufacturer
Top Bagage International,
Montauban-de-Bretagne, France
In-house design
Alexandre de Sousa
Web
www.topbagage.com

The O² rescue bag was developed especially for fire brigade operations. Its interior layout consists of removable pocket modules that can accommodate both a five-litre oxygen bottle and respiratory equipment. A colour-coded organisation system provides a quick overview of the contents: the pockets and openings are marked in blue and red, and the inside compartments are black. The four lateral reflector stripes enhance the visibility of the firefighters.

Statement by the jury
This rescue bag embodies excellent functionality. Its components are clearly visible from all sides and thus easy to access.

Der O²-Rettungsrucksack wurde speziell für Einsätze der Feuerwehr entwickelt. Die Innenausstattung besteht aus abnehmbaren Modultaschen, die eine Fünf-Liter-Sauerstoffflasche und Atemschutzgeräte aufnehmen können. Ein farbcodiertes Ordnungssystem schafft eine schnelle Übersicht über den Inhalt: Die Taschen und Öffnungen sind blau und rot gekennzeichnet, die innenliegenden Fächer sind in Schwarz gehalten. Die vier reflektierenden Streifen an den Seiten erhöhen die Sichtbarkeit der Feuerwehrleute.

Begründung der Jury
Der Rettungsrucksack zeichnet sich durch seine hervorragende Funktionalität aus. Die Komponenten sind von allen Seiten sehr gut einsehbar und schnell zu erreichen.

P5/11
Emergency Backpack
Notfallrucksack

Manufacturer
X-CEN-TEK GmbH & Co. KG,
Wardenburg, Germany
Design
Held+Team, Hamburg, Germany
Web
www.pax-bags.de
www.heldundteam.de

The P5/11 emergency backpack is a modular system that can be configured from a variety of different transparent and functional sets. The indestructible welding seams of the robust exterior materials create a smooth interior, which is easy to clean. At the same time, the backpack's weight is reduced considerably. The interior bags are held in place with extremely strong neodym magnets instead of with difficult-to-clean Velcro fasteners, which are commonly used in conventional models.

Statement by the jury
The emergency backpack captivates with its seamless, closed design, which is the result of the careful selection and processing of materials.

Der Notfallrucksack P5/11 ist ein Modulsystem, das sich aus verschiedenen Klarsicht- und Funktionssets konfigurieren lässt. Durch die unzerstörbaren Schweißverbindungen der robusten Außenmaterialien entsteht im Innenteil ein glattflächiges Volumen, das leicht zu reinigen ist. Gleichzeitig sinkt das Gesamtgewicht deutlich. Die Innentaschen werden mit extrem starken Neodym-Magneten an ihrem Platz gehalten und nicht wie bei herkömmlichen Modellen mit schwer zu reinigendem Klettband.

Begründung der Jury
Der Notfallrucksack beeindruckt mit seinem nahtlosen, geschlossenen Design, das durch die sorgfältige Auswahl und Fertigung der Materialien erzielt wird.

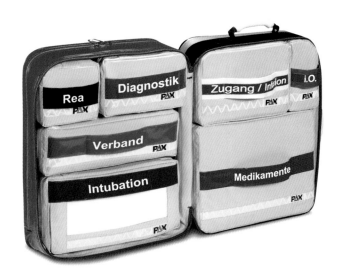

Cederroth First Aid Kit
Erste-Hilfe-Koffer

Manufacturer
Orkla Care AB (former Cederroth AB),
Upplands Väsby, Sweden
Design
Veryday (Anna Carell, Pelle Reinius),
Bromma, Sweden
Web
www.firstaid.cederroth.com
www.veryday.com

The Cederroth First Aid Kit enables users without previous training to provide first aid. In order to be able to act quickly in an emergency situation, the kit has a clear structure and contains directions which are easy to understand. The equipment is available in three sizes: M, L and XL. The double-walled, blow-moulded parts of the XL kit allow the integration of a plaster dispenser, which is accessible from the exterior. The inner cover made of Plexiglas is marked with a white cross as an emergency symbol, intuitively guiding users to the first aid products.

Mit dem Cederroth First Aid Kit ist es möglich, auch ohne Vorkenntnisse Erste Hilfe zu leisten. Um im Falle einer Notsituation schnell handeln zu können, ist der Koffer übersichtlich strukturiert und enthält leicht verständliche Anweisungen. Die Ausrüstung ist in drei Größen erhältlich: M, L und XL. In die zweischaligen Spritzgussteile des XL-Koffers lässt sich ein Pflasterspender integrieren, auf den man einfach von außen zugreifen kann. Der Innenkoffer aus Plexiglas mit dem weißen Kreuz als Notfallsymbol führt intuitiv zu den Erste-Hilfe-Produkten hin.

Statement by the jury
This first aid kit stands out due to its unusual colour scheme and purposeful arrangement, with each object having a designated place.

Begründung der Jury
Der Erste-Hilfe-Koffer fällt durch sein ungewöhnliches Farbschema ebenso auf wie durch seine sinnhafte Ordnung – jeder Gegenstand hat seinen festen Platz.

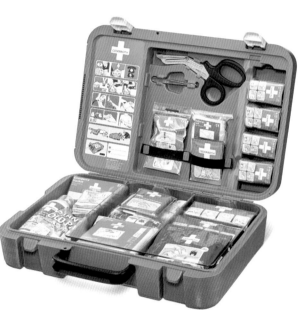

XY-211
Blood Pressure Meter
Blutdruckmessgerät

Manufacturer
Hangzhou Medzone Biotechnologies Co.,
Ltd., China, Shaoxing, China
Design
AUG Hangzhou Industrial Design Company
(Ying Gao, Xiaofeng Xu, Weihua Chai, Kai
Feng, Wei Zhang, Jinjin Zhang, Hualang
Zhong), Hangzhou, China
Web
www.mcloudlife.com
www.augid.com

The XY-211 blood pressure meter was developed especially for the Asian region. It is particularly geared towards families in which the care of the parents is traditionally carried out by their adult children, yet both generations live separately. With the help of an app, blood pressure information from the older family members is sent to the younger ones and depicted graphically. The look of the device is inspired by a jade gemstone symbolising health and harmony.

Statement by the jury
With its closed form, this blood pressure meter is particularly elegant and discreet. The smooth surfaces and organic lines engender a premium appearance.

Das Blutdruckmessgerät XY-211 wurde speziell für den asiatischen Raum entwickelt. Es richtet sich an Familien, in denen die Pflege der Eltern traditionell in der Hand der erwachsenen Kinder liegt, beide Generationen jedoch räumlich voneinander getrennt wohnen. Mithilfe einer App werden die Blutdruckwerte der älteren Familienmitglieder an die jüngeren verschickt und grafisch aufbereitet. Das Erscheinungsbild des Geräts ist von dem Edelstein Jade inspiriert, der für Gesundheit und Harmonie steht.

Begründung der Jury
Das Blutdruckmessgerät ist durch seine geschlossene Form besonders elegant und dezent. Die glatten Oberflächen und organischen Linien erzeugen eine wertige Optik.

Mobile Health Oximeter
Pulse Oximeter
Pulsoximeter

Manufacturer
Hangzhou Medzone Biotechnologies Co.,
Ltd., China, Shaoxing, China
Design
AUG Hangzhou Industrial Design Company
(Ying Gao, Xiaofeng Xu, Weihua Chai, Kai
Feng, Wei Zhang, Jinjin Zhang, Hualang
Zhong), Hangzhou, China
Web
www.mcloudlife.com
www.hzic.edu.cn

The Mobile Health Oximeter determines the pulse rate and the blood oxygen saturation. It is particularly small and lightweight and thus especially suitable for mobile monitoring. To make a measurement, a finger is placed in the bracket-like clip and illuminated by light from a sensor. Instead of featuring a built-in display, the measurement data are displayed on a smartphone. Bluetooth connectivity ensures ease of use and enables the storage of large amounts of data.

Statement by the jury
With its seamless, minimalist design and soft colours, the Mobile Health Oximeter fosters trust and a discreet sense of reserve.

Das Mobile Health Oximeter ermittelt die Pulsfrequenz und die Sauerstoffsättigung im Blut. Es ist besonders klein und leicht und daher insbesondere für die mobile Überwachung geeignet. Um die Messung vorzunehmen, wird ein Finger in den klammerartigen Clip hineingelegt und von einem Sensor durchleuchtet. Statt über ein eingebautes Display werden die Werte auf einem Smartphone dargestellt. Die Bluetooth-Konnektivität ermöglicht eine einfache Bedienung und die Speicherung großer Datenmengen.

Begründung der Jury
Das Pulsoximeter schafft durch seine nahtlose, reduzierte Gestaltung und die sanfte Farbgebung Vertrauen und strahlt diskrete Zurückhaltung aus.

Smart Health Ear
Thermometer
Smart Health
Ohrthermometer

Manufacturer
Hangzhou Medzone Biotechnologies Co.,
Ltd., China, Shaoxing, China
Design
AOZHI Hefei Industrial Design Company
(Weihua Chai, Wei Zhang, Fan Zhang, Kai
Feng, Jinjin Zhang, Hualang Zhong),
Hefei, China
Web
www.mcloudlife.com
www.augid.com

The Smart Health ear thermometer is characterised by reduced size and minimal weight, which make it highly portable. It can connect to a smartphone via the audio output jack to gain access to additional programme functions using the corresponding app. The measurement data may be forwarded to a physician in order to obtain medical advice. Furthermore, statistical analyses and history logs can be compiled.

Statement by the jury
This ear thermometer has an impressively small size. Its smooth surfaces and soft lines result in a flattering look and feel.

Das Smart Health Ohrthermometer zeichnet sich durch seine geringe Größe und sein leichtes Gewicht aus, wodurch es überallhin mitgenommen werden kann. Es lässt sich mit einem Smartphone über den Audioausgang verbinden, um die erweiterten Programmfunktionen über eine entsprechende App zu nutzen. Die Messdaten können außerdem an einen Arzt weitergeleitet werden, um sich medizinischen Ratschlag einzuholen. Des Weiteren lassen sich statistische Analysen und Verlaufsprotokolle erstellen.

Begründung der Jury
Das Ohrthermometer ist beeindruckend klein. Die glatten Oberflächen und weichen Linien ergeben eine schmeichelnde Optik und Haptik.

Mobile Fetal Monitor
Mobiler Fetaldoppler

Manufacturer
Zhejiang Medzone Medical Devices Co.,
Ltd., Shaoxing, China
Design
Institute of Zhejiang Medzone (Jian Yao),
Hangzhou, China
Web
www.medzone-biotech.com

This mobile fetal monitor makes the heartbeat of an unborn baby audible during pregnancy. The ultrasound device is connected to an app, which records the heartbeat, heart frequency and movements of the baby in the womb. The audio recordings can then be sent to friends and family. The device's design is inspired by the shape of a peanut, which is a symbol of happiness and long life in China.

Statement by the jury
With its app technology, this mobile fetal monitor is state of the art. Its playful design in pink or blue reflects the happy feelings of anticipation surrounding the new baby.

Der mobile Fetaldoppler macht den Herzton des ungeborenen Kindes während der Schwangerschaft hörbar. Das Ultraschallgerät ist mit einer App verbunden, die den Herzschlag, die Herzfrequenz und die Bewegungen des Babys im Mutterleib aufzeichnet und speichert. So kann das Audiodokument beispielsweise auch an Freunde und Verwandte verschickt werden. Das Gerätedesign ist an die Form einer Erdnuss angelehnt – in China steht die Erdnuss symbolisch für Glück und ein langes Leben.

Begründung der Jury
Mit seiner App-Technologie ist der Farbdoppler ganz auf der Höhe der Zeit. Sein verspieltes Design – in Rosa oder Blau – spiegelt die Vorfreude auf das Baby wider.

Lobob
Stethoscope
Stethoskop

Manufacturer
Chengdu Luobo Tech Co., Ltd., Chengdu,
China
Design
LKK Design Chengdu Co., Ltd., Chengdu,
China
Web
www.lkkdesign.com

The Lobob stethoscope was designed to take away children's fear of a medical examination. In order to make it look less like a medical device, this stethoscope only has a chestpiece that records sounds in the chest using a newly developed technology. Parents can access the results via an app or send them directly to a physician. The form, which has been inspired by a pebble, is designed to provide a pleasant look and feel for both parents and children.

Statement by the jury
This stethoscope breaks new ground with regard to technology and design. Its plain character strongly helps to increase acceptance by children.

Das Stethoskop Lobob wurde entworfen, um Kindern die Angst vor der Untersuchung zu nehmen. Damit es weniger wie ein medizinisches Gerät aussieht, besteht es nur aus dem Schalltrichter, der die Geräusche im Brustkorb über eine neu entwickelte Technologie aufzeichnet. Die Eltern können die Ergebnisse über eine App abrufen oder direkt an einen Arzt schicken. Die von einem Kieselstein inspirierte Form ist darauf ausgelegt, Kindern und Eltern gleichermaßen eine angenehme Optik und Haptik zu bieten.

Begründung der Jury
Das Stethoskop geht technisch wie gestalterisch neue Wege. Sein schlichter Charakter hilft, die Akzeptanz bei Kindern deutlich zu steigern.

Embrace
Smartwatch for Epilepsy Monitoring
Smartwatch für die Epilepsie-überwachung

Manufacturer
Empatica s.r.l., Milan, Italy
Design
Pearl Studios Inc., Montreal, Canada
Web
www.empatica.com
www.pearlstudios.com

The aim behind this product was to design a device for epilepsy monitoring that patients like to wear and that does not stigmatise them. Therefore, Embrace is designed like a fashionable smart-watch, which tells the time at a touch of a finger and activates an alarm in critical situations. Additional information about the health of the wearer can be accessed via a smartphone. The ultra-thin casing is fashioned from robust, polished metal, and the wristband is made of either elegant leather or an elastic fabric.

Statement by the jury
Embrace captivates with its cool, mini-malist look. The different wristbands can be adapted to the wearer's individual style.

Ziel bei der Produktentwicklung war es, ein Gerät für die Epilepsieüberwachung zu entwerfen, das die Betroffenen gerne tragen und sie nicht stigmatisiert. Deshalb ist Embrace als modische Smartwatch gestaltet, die auf Berührung die Uhrzeit anzeigt und in kritischen Situationen einen Alarm auslöst. Weitere Informationen über den gesundheitlichen Zustand des Trägers können über ein Smartphone abgerufen werden. Das ultradünne Gehäuse ist aus stabilem, poliertem Metall, das Armband entweder aus elegantem Leder oder elasti-schem Textil.

Begründung der Jury
Embrace begeistert durch seinen coolen, reduzierten Look. Die verschiedenen Arm-bänder lassen sich an den persönlichen Stil des Trägers anpassen.

DreamWear
Mask for Sleep Apnoea Therapy
Maske für die Schlafapnoe-Therapie

Manufacturer
Royal Philips, Eindhoven, Netherlands
In-house design
Philips Design
Web
www.philips.com

DreamWear is a barely noticeable mask that enables patients suffering from sleep apnoea to slumber comfortably without any restrictions. To achieve this, the nose pads and the frame form a unit, so that airflow is guided directly through the frame into the nose. Furthermore, the hose connector is attached not to the front of the mask, but to the top of the head. This results in fewer pressure marks on the face, and patients can sleep in any desired position without the hose getting in the way.

Statement by the jury
With its slim design, DreamWear pro-vides outstanding comfort. The mask's transparency emphasises its lightness.

DreamWear ist eine kaum spürbare Maske, die Patienten, die beim Schlafen unter Atemaussetzern leiden, eine angenehme, uneingeschränkte Nachtruhe ermöglicht. Dazu bilden Nasenpolster und Rahmen eine Einheit, sodass der Luftstrom direkt durch den Rahmen in die Nase geleitet wird. Zudem sitzt der Schlauchanschluss nicht vorne an der Maske, sondern oben am Kopf. Dadurch entstehen weniger Druck-stellen im Gesicht und der Patient kann jede gewünschte Schlafposition einneh-men, ohne dass der Schlauch im Weg ist.

Begründung der Jury
DreamWear erreicht durch sein schlankes Design einen herausragenden Komfort. Die Transparenz der Maske unterstreicht ihre Leichtigkeit.

Eargo
Hearing Aid
Hörgerät

Manufacturer
Eargo, Inc., Mountain View, USA
In-house design
Web
www.eargo.com

Eargo is a virtually invisible, recharge-able in-ear hearing aid that is inspired and modeled after the shape of a fishing fly. Made from medical-grade silicone, the patented Flexi Fibers allow air to flow naturally through the ear canal, while being strong enough to hold the device firmly in place. Furthermore, the design ensures for natural bass sounds to pass through into the ear canal, resulting in improved sound quality. When fully charged, the batteries last an entire day, eliminating the need for replacement batteries.

Eargo ist ein so gut wie unsichtbares, wie-deraufladbares Im-Ohr-Hörgerät. Die Ge-staltung wurde von der Form eines Fliegen-fischköders inspiriert. Die aus medizi-nischem Silikon gefertigten, patentierten Flexi Fibers erlauben, dass die Luft auf natürliche Weise durch den Gehörkanal strömen kann, gleichzeitig sind sie stabil genug, um das Gerät fest an seinem Platz zu halten. Darüber hinaus gewährleistet das Design, dass natürliche Basstöne in den Gehörgang gelangen, was die Klangqualität verbessert. Die aufgeladenen Batterien halten den ganzen Tag, ein Batteriewechsel ist nicht notwendig.

Statement by the jury
With its innovative form, Eargo clearly stands out from other in-ear hearing aids. It perfectly adjusts to individual differences in wearers' ear-canal anatomy.

Begründung der Jury
Eargo hebt sich durch seine innovative Form von anderen Im-Ohr-Hörgeräten deutlich ab. Es passt sich dem Gehörgang anatomisch hervorragend an.

Phonak Audéo™ V10
Hearing Aid
Hörgerät

Manufacturer
Sonova AG, Stäfa, Switzerland
In-house design
Martyn Beedham
Web
www.phonak.com

The Phonak Audéo V10 is a behind-the-ear hearing aid with a speaker that sits directly in the auditory canal. It features the new AutoSense OS, which automatically adjusts to any acoustic situation. Thanks to its reduced weight and slim design, the device is very comfortable and discreet to wear. The housing is made of robust high-tech materials. The models are available in various subtle hair and skin colours, as well as in fashionable shades. Furthermore, the device connects wirelessly to a variety of external audio sources.

Das Phonak Audéo V10 ist ein Hinter-dem-Ohr-Hörgerät, bei dem der Lautsprecher direkt im Gehörgang sitzt. Es verfügt über das neue AutoSense OS, das sich automatisch an die jeweilige Hörsituation anpasst. Durch sein geringes Gewicht und die schlanke Bauform ist das Gerät komfortabel und diskret zu tragen. Das Gehäuse besteht aus robusten Hightech-Materialien. Die Modelle sind in verschiedenen dezenten Haar- und Hauttönen sowie in modischen Farben erhältlich. Darüber hinaus kann das Gerät kabellos mit unterschiedlichen externen Audioquellen verbunden werden.

Statement by the jury
This hearing aid, which has a sculptural air, sits comfortably behind the ear. The softly gleaming finish emphasises its elegant form.

Begründung der Jury
Das skulptural anmutende Hörgerät schmiegt sich angenehm hinter dem Ohr an. Das matt schimmernde Finish unterstreicht die elegante Formgebung.

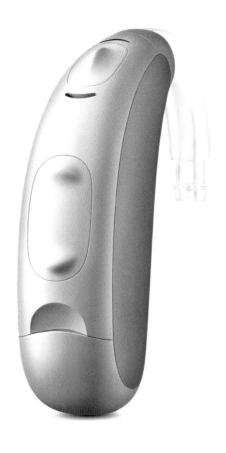

Stride P
Hearing Aid
Hörgerät

Manufacturer
Unitron, Kitchener, Canada
In-house design
Design
AWOL Company, Calabasas, USA
Web
www.unitron.com
www.awolcompany.com

The Stride P hearing aid successfully integrates a large battery – as is required for patients with more severe hearing loss – in an anatomical form, which sits discreetly behind the wearer's ear. The outer curvature of the housing results in a smooth, immaculate surface, while the darker accent on the inside creates the illusion of a smaller hearing aid. The user controls are characterised by an intuitive design featuring tactile differentiation of programme and volume buttons.

Das Hörgerät Stride P bringt eine große Batterie – wie sie für hochgradige Hörverluste erforderlich ist – mit einer anatomischen Form in Einklang, die sich diskret hinter dem Ohr anschmiegt. Die äußere Krümmung des Gehäuses ergibt eine glatte, makellose Oberfläche, während der innen liegende, dunklere Akzent die Illusion eines kleineren Hörgeräts vermittelt. Die Bedienelemente zeichnen sich durch ein intuitives Design mit einer fühlbaren Unterscheidung von Programm- und Lautstärkeregler aus.

Statement by the jury
This elegant hearing aid captivates with its balanced proportions. The tactile surface facilitates quick and safe operation.

Begründung der Jury
Das formschöne Hörgerät besticht durch seine ausgewogenen Proportionen. Die taktile Oberfläche erleichtert eine rasche und sichere Bedienung.

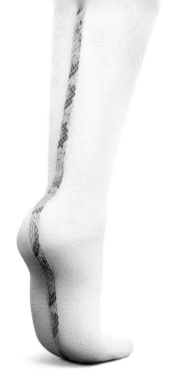

Lastofa Forte
Compression Stockings
Kompressionsstrumpf

Manufacturer
Ofa Bamberg GmbH, Bamberg, Germany
In-house design
Carola Essig
Web
www.ofa.de

The Lastofa Forte compression stockings innovatively combine the finest micro-fibre with refined merino wool. The internal air cushions allow the skin to breathe; they cool in summer and warm in winter. The six available colours navigate a natural, gentle spectrum. Instead of concealing the longitudinal seam of the flat-knitted material, it is embellished with an elegant decorative seam, which visually elongates the legs and turns the stockings into fashionable accessories.

Statement by the jury
This compression stocking is made from high-quality materials and is aesthetically appealing and fashionable thanks to the playful pattern of the decorative seam.

Der Kompressionsstrumpf Lastofa Forte kombiniert auf innovative Weise feinste Mikrofaser mit veredelter Merinowolle. Die innenliegenden Luftpolster lassen die Haut atmen; sie kühlen im Sommer und wärmen im Winter. Die sechs wählbaren Farben bewegen sich in einem natürlichen, sanften Spektrum. Statt die produktions-bedingte Längsnaht des Flachstrickmateri-als zu kaschieren, ist sie mit einer eleganten Schmucknaht veredelt. Diese streckt die Beine optisch und macht die Strümpfe zum modischen Accessoire.

Begründung der Jury
Der Kompressionsstrumpf aus hochwer-tigen Materialien ist dank des verspielten Musters seiner Schmucknaht ästhetisch ansprechend und modisch.

mediven elegance®
Catwalk Highlights
Compression Stocking
Kompressionsstrumpf

Manufacturer
medi GmbH & Co. KG, Bayreuth, Germany
In-house design
Web
www.medi.de

The design of the limited Catwalk High-lights edition of mediven elegance has managed to completely apply a motif print to this medical compression stock-ing. It is available either in black with a grey leopard pattern or in black with purple circles. The elastic knitting yarn ensures a lower sense of pressure, whilst the stocking hugs the leg like a second skin.

Statement by the jury
This compression stocking combines appealing aesthetics with premium quality. With an elegant, comfortable design, the stocking contributes to the wearer's well-being.

Bei der Gestaltung des mediven elegance in der limitierten Catwalk Highlights-Edition ist es gelungen, den medizinischen Kom-pressionsstrumpf rundum mit einem Motiv-druck zu versehen. Zur Auswahl stehen ein schwarzer Strumpf mit grauem Leoparden-muster und ein schwarzer Strumpf mit violetten Kreisen. Der elastische Strickfaden sorgt beim Tragen für weniger Druckem-pfinden und der Strumpf schmiegt sich wie eine zweite Haut an das Bein.

Begründung der Jury
Der Kompressionsstrumpf verbindet ansprechende Ästhetik mit hoher Qualität. Durch sein elegantes, komfortables Design trägt er zum Wohlbefinden der Trägerin bei.

Balance Seat
Seat Cushion
Sitzkissen

Manufacturer
Bullsone, Seoul, South Korea
In-house design
Daehee Kim, Jiseok Heo
Web
www.bullsone.com
www.balanceseat.co.kr

The inside of the Balance Seat is made of a highly elastic and durable gel material called Vetagel. It consists of several layers that have been shaped into a honeycomb structure, absorbing pressure and distributing it evenly. This increases blood circulation, which is particularly important when sitting for long periods. At the same time, any body movements create a pump effect in the honeycomb, which provides ongoing ventilation in the seat to prevent sweating. The outer fabric of the cover is breathable and non-slip. For cleaning purposes the seat may be simply rinsed with water.

Der Balance Seat besteht im Inneren aus einem hochelastischen, strapazierfähigen Gelmaterial, dem sogenannten Vetagel. Dies ist in mehreren Schichten zu einer Wabenstruktur verarbeitet, nimmt Druck auf und verteilt ihn gleichmäßig. Das fördert die Durchblutung, was insbesondere bei langem Sitzen wichtig ist. Gleichzeitig entsteht bei Körperbewegungen ein Pump-effekt in den Waben, der dafür sorgt, dass das Kissen permanent belüftet wird, was Schwitzen verhindert. Der äußere Stoffbezug ist atmungsaktiv und rutschfest. Zur Reinigung kann der Sitz einfach mit Wasser abgewaschen werden.

Statement by the jury
The Balance Seat provides excellent sitting comfort for any body weight. Moreover, its materials are very durable and easy to clean.

Begründung der Jury
Der Balance Seat bietet hervorragenden Sitzkomfort für jedes Körpergewicht. Seine Materialien sind zudem sehr langlebig und pflegeleicht.

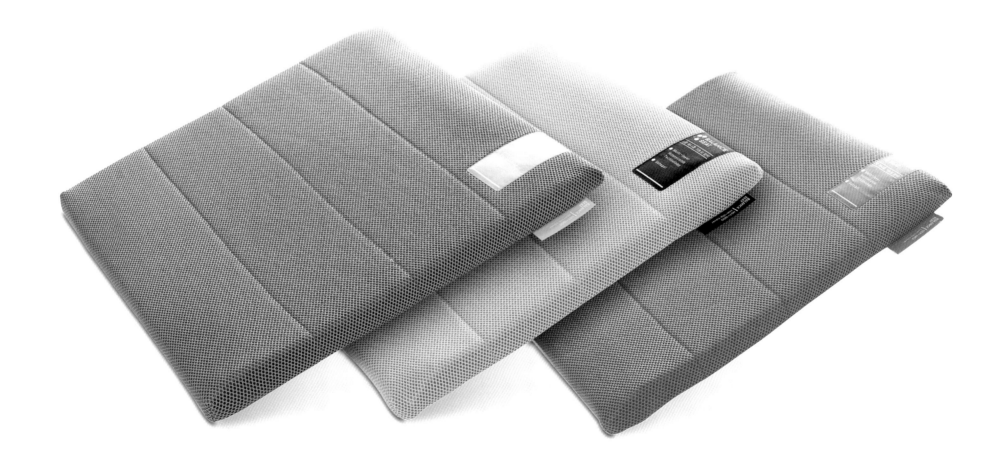

Genu PFS PROMASTER
Knee Orthosis
Knieorthese

Manufacturer
THUASNE Deutschland GmbH, Burgwedel,
Germany
In-house design
Web
www.thuasne.de

The Genu PFS Promaster knee orthosis
with joint splints and a patella traction
system provides an even distribution of
pressure. The direct skin contact with
the exposed pad ensures a comfortable
fit and improved body awareness.
Furthermore, the very shallow, laterally
integrated hinges with extension stop
stabilise the knee joint. Therefore, the
patella is centred during any movement,
which helps to reduce pain and to relieve
the knee joint of strain.

Statement by the jury
With its sophisticated functionality, this
knee orthosis sets standards of its own.
It not only stabilises but also corrects
malpositions.

Die Knieorthese Genu PFS Promaster mit
Gelenkschienen und Patella-Zugsystem
sorgt für eine gleichmäßige Druckvertei-
lung. Durch den direkten Hautkontakt der
freiliegenden Pelotte ergeben sich ein
komfortabler Sitz und eine verbesserte
Körperwahrnehmung. Darüber hinaus stabilisieren die sehr flachen, seitlich integrierten
Gelenke mit Extensionsanschlag das Kniegelenk. So wird die Kniescheibe bei jeder
Bewegung zentriert, das Kniegelenk wird
entlastet und Schmerzen werden reduziert.

Begründung der Jury
Die Knieorthese setzt durch ihre durchdachte Funktionalität eigene Maßstäbe.
Sie stabilisiert nicht nur, sondern korrigiert
auch Fehlstellungen.

JuzoPro® Lumbal
Orthoses Series
Orthesen-Serie

Manufacturer
Julius Zorn GmbH, Aichach, Germany
Design
supercreative (Marcus Wiedemann),
Munich, Germany
Web
www.juzo.com
www.supercreative.de

The orthoses of the JuzoPro Lumbal
series have a stabilising and pain-reliev-
ing effect in patients with issues in the
lumbar spine. Furthermore, a sacral pad
provides additional relief at the transition from the sacrum to the lumbar
spine. The pad features frictional nubs to
loosen the hardened muscle tissue. They
increase blood flow and provide a massaging effect. The particularly elastic and
breathable knitted fabric and the specifically developed fastening mechanism
ensure an optimal fit.

Statement by the jury
The orthoses fit particularly tightly
to the body and are hardly visible, thus
making them highly suitable for everyday use.

Die Orthesen der Serie JuzoPro Lumbal
zeigen eine entlastende und schmerzlin-
dernde Wirkung bei Beschwerden im
Lendenwirbelbereich. Zusätzlich schont
eine Kreuzbein-Pelotte den Übergang vom
Kreuzbein zur Lendenwirbelsäule. Um
Verspannungen der Muskeln aufzulockern,
ist die Pelotte mit Friktionsnoppen besetzt.
Sie fördern die Durchblutung und sorgen
für einen massageähnlichen Effekt. Das
besonders dehnfähige, atmungsaktive
Gestrick und ein speziell entwickelter Ver-
schluss garantieren eine optimale Passform.

Begründung der Jury
Die Orthesen liegen ausgesprochen nah am
Körper an und tragen kaum auf. Sie sind
dadurch absolut alltagstauglich.

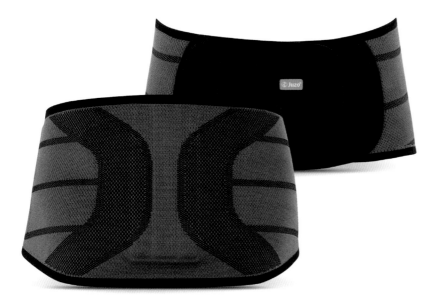

OPPO Mint Support Series
OPPO Mint-Support-Serie
Elastic Support
Elastische Bandagen

Manufacturer
OPPO Medical Corporation, Taipei, Taiwan
In-house design
Mei-Zhu Su, I-Ting Lin
Web
www.oppomedical.com

The 3D structure of the knitted fabric in the Mint Support Series forms a dynamic, reinforced protection system, which adjusts to body movements and provides stability in any situation. Moreover, it helps movements to be carried out in a controlled way. The incorporated rods at the joints and the torso provide additional support and stabilisation. The newly developed pads and reinforced straps exert an even pressure on the soft tissue and peripheral joints, thus facilitating blood circulation and alleviating pain and swelling.

Bei der Mint-Support-Serie bildet die 3D-Struktur des Gestricks ein dynamisches, verstärktes Schutzsystem, das sich der Körperbewegung anpasst und für konstanten Halt in jeder Situation sorgt. Zudem hilft es dabei, die Bewegungen kontrolliert auszuführen. Die eingearbeiteten Stäbe an Gelenken und Rumpf stützen und stabilisieren zusätzlich. Die neu entwickelten Pelotten und verstärkten Zuggurte üben einen gleichmäßigen Druck auf die Weichteile und peripheren Gelenke aus, wodurch das Blut besser zirkulieren kann und Schmerzen sowie Schwellungen gelindert werden.

Statement by the jury
The high-quality workmanship of the bandages is both visible and tangible. The pads and stabilisers provide an optimal anatomical fit.

Begründung der Jury
Die hochwertige Verarbeitung der Bandagen ist sowohl sichtbar als auch spürbar. Die Polster und Stabilisatoren sitzen anatomisch optimal.

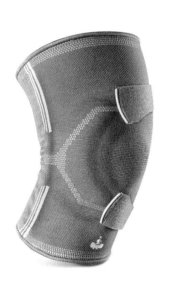
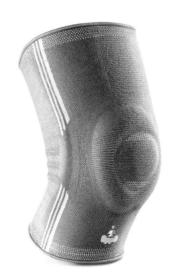

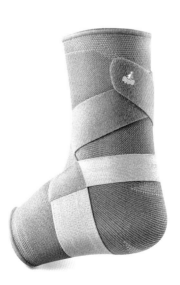

E⁺motion®
Support Series
Bandagen-Serie

Manufacturer
medi GmbH & Co. KG,
Bayreuth, Germany
In-house design
Web
www.medi.de
www.cepsports.com

The supports of the E⁺motion series stabilise and reduce stress on damaged joints. The elastic knitted fabric provides an optimal fit, while the silicone-quartz pads with 3D profile create a comfortable massaging effect when moving and thereby enhance the blood flow. Swelling and oedemata are thus reduced more quickly, which supports the healing process. The functional high-tech fibres, which have been partially combined with natural merino wool, are characterised by pleasant wearing comfort in varying temperatures.

Statement by the jury
Thanks to their sporty design in bright colours, the supports express an active lifestyle. Their supporting function is visualised through dynamic lines.

Die Bandagen der Serie E⁺motion stabilisieren und entlasten geschädigte Gelenke. Das elastische Gestrick sorgt für eine optimale Passform. Die Silikon-Quarz-Pelotte mit 3D-Profil entfaltet bei Bewegung einen wohltuenden Massageeffekt und regt die Durchblutung an. Dadurch werden Schwellungen und Ödeme effizienter abgebaut, was den Heilungsprozess unterstützt. Die funktionellen Hightech-Fasern, teilweise in Verbindung mit natürlicher Merinowolle, zeichnen sich durch ein angenehmes Trageklima aus.

Begründung der Jury
Durch ihr sportliches Design in leuchtenden Farben kommunizieren die Bandagen einen aktiven Lebensstil. Ihre Stützfunktion wird durch dynamische Linien visualisiert.

Xkelet
Custom-Made Orthosis
Individuell gefertigte Orthese

Manufacturer
Xkelet Easy Life S.L., Girona, Spain
In-house design
Andreu Carulla
Web
www.xkelet.com

Xkelet is an orthosis for the immobilisation of injured bones, which is custom-fitted using 3D printing. With the help of an iOS device, the affected limbs are scanned and measured. A 3D model is created from the data and can be configured further in an app. In the next step, the orthosis is ordered online, produced by the manufacturer and then sent to the customer. The individually manufactured orthosis provides more comfort and mobility than a cast and is also more hygienic.

Statement by the jury
The Xkelet translates cutting-edge technology into an unusual orthosis design that hardly restricts the user and looks fashionable.

Xkelet ist eine Orthese zur Ruhigstellung von verletzten Knochen, die mittels 3D-Druckverfahren maßgefertigt wird. Mithilfe eines iOS-Geräts wird die betroffene Gliedmaße abgetastet und vermessen. Aus den Daten entsteht ein 3D-Modell, das sich über eine App noch weiter konfigurieren lässt. Anschließend wird die Orthese online bestellt, vom Hersteller angefertigt und versendet. Die individuell gefertigte Orthese bietet mehr Komfort und Mobilität gegenüber Hartverbänden und ist zudem hygienischer.

Begründung der Jury
Bei Xkelet führt fortschrittliche Technologie zu einer gestalterisch ungewöhnlichen Orthese, die kaum einschränkt und modisch aussieht.

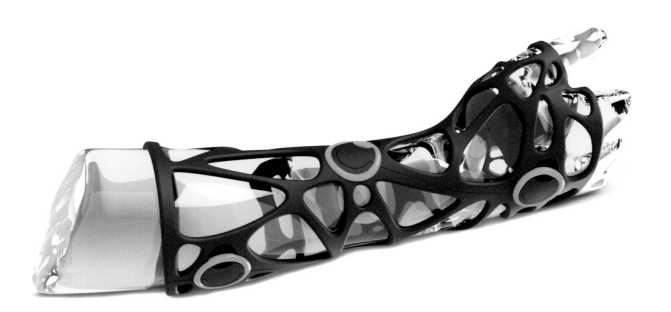

THERA-Trainer mobi
Therapeutic Exerciser
Therapeutischer
Bewegungstrainer

Manufacturer
medica Medizintechnik GmbH,
Hochdorf, Germany
Design
Slogdesign – Büro für Gestaltung
(Jürgen Hinderhofer), Biberach, Germany
Web
www.thera-trainer.de
www.slogdesign.de

The Thera-Trainer mobi is a lightweight and practical exerciser for the motor-supported training of arms and legs. It is designed for the mobilisation of the elderly and of people with slight physical limitations. The design focus is placed on high-quality ergonomics and intuitive use. Furthermore, the surfaces are easy to clean. The interlocking system enables a quick, tool-free exchange of footrests and therapy grips.

Der Thera-Trainer mobi ist ein leichter und handlicher Bewegungstrainer für das motorunterstützte Bein- und Armtraining. Er ist für die Mobilisation von älteren Menschen und von Menschen mit leichten körperlichen Beeinträchtigungen bestimmt. Die Gestaltung ist auf eine hohe Ergonomie und intuitive Bedienung ausgelegt. Zudem sind die Oberflächen einfach zu reinigen. Das Stecksystem ermöglicht einen schnellen werkzeuglosen Wechsel der Fußschalen und Therapiegriffe.

Statement by the jury
This compact exerciser requires very little space. Thanks to its rounded form and dynamic lines, it has a markedly friendly appearance.

Begründung der Jury
Der kompakte Trainer braucht nur sehr wenig Platz. Mit seiner rundlaufenden Form und dynamischen Linienführung erhält er einen betont freundlichen Charakter.

Adventurer HW6
Active Wheelchair
Aktivrollstuhl

Manufacturer
Heartway Medical Products Co., Ltd.,
Taichung, Taiwan
In-house design
Young Ho
Web
www.heartway.com.tw

The foldable Adventurer HW6 active
wheelchair is ultralight and easy to load,
but nevertheless very sturdy. The horizontal cross-brace under the seat is
designed like a bird with spread wings.
It thus achieves the same seating comfort as a model with a rigid frame. The
centre of gravity, the height of the drive
wheel and the backrest angle are continuously adjustable. In order to increase
safety, the wheelchair is equipped with
front bumper rolling guards, an anti-tilt
mechanism and a handbrake with anti-
pinch protection.

Statement by the jury
This wheelchair can be folded down to
an extremely flat size. Its design, without
any corners or edges, makes for simple
handling.

Der faltbare Aktivrollstuhl Adventurer HW6
ist ultraleicht und einfach zu verladen, aber
dennoch sehr stabil. Die horizontale Kreuz-
strebe unter dem Sitz ist wie ein Vogel mit
ausgebreiteten Flügeln gestaltet. Dadurch
erreicht der Rollstuhl denselben Sitzkomfort
wie ein Modell mit starrem Rahmen. Der
Schwerpunkt, die Antriebsradhöhe und der
Rückenwinkel sind stufenlos verstellbar. Zur
Sicherheit ist der Rollstuhl mit Frontschutz-
rollen, einem Kippschutz und einer Hand-
bremse mit Klemmschutz ausgestattet.

Begründung der Jury
Der Rollstuhl lässt sich extrem flach zusam-
menfalten. Seine Konstruktion ohne Ecken
und Kanten sorgt für ein ausgesprochen
einfaches Handling.

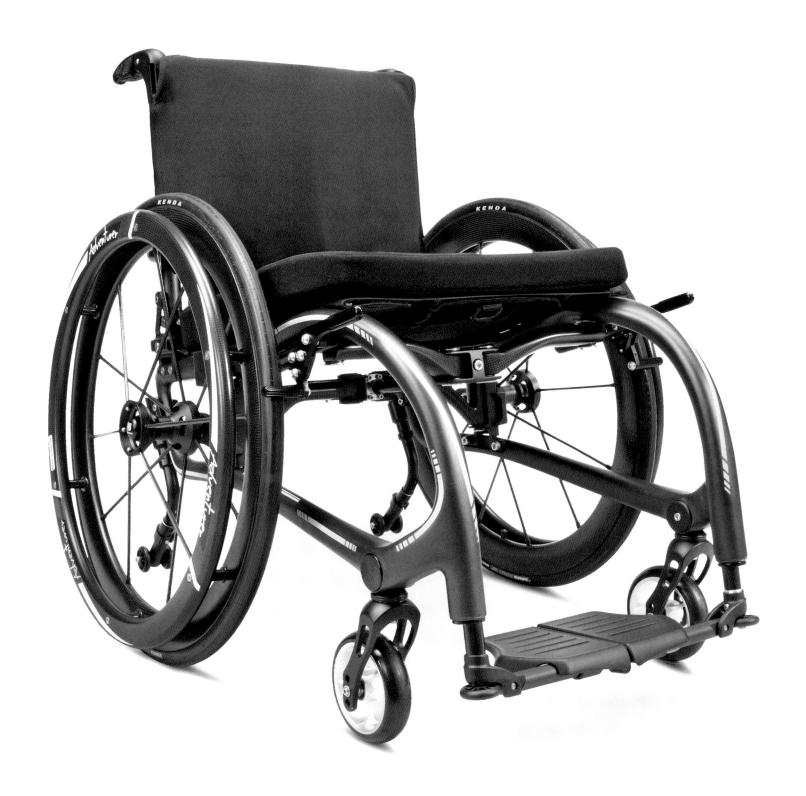

Computers and information technology
Computer und Informationstechnik

Dell Edge Gateway 5000 Series
Internet Gateway

Manufacturer
Dell Inc., Round Rock,
Texas, USA

In-house design
Experience Design Group

Web
www.dell.com

reddot award 2016
best of the best

Well-balanced transfer

Today's often highly complex network structures rely on gateways for trouble-free connection between computer networks and data centres. The Dell Edge Gateway 5000 Series is a system that collects, secures, analyses and acts on data from multiple disparate devices and sensors. It serves to communicate meaningful data to back-end systems in the cloud, control room or data centre. As one representative of the Dell Internet of Things (IoT) Gateways, the system is equipped with ample processing power and provides flexibility to perform analytics throughout an IoT ecosystem but especially at the edge of a distributed network, closer to the devices and sensors. It was designed for installation in distributed locations. Much like a PC, this gateway allows all peripherals and sensors to be attached easily. Like servers and routers, this gateway was designed to run continuously without interruption. It operates in headless fashion without regular human interaction such as via screens or keyboards. Coming in a solid enclosure primarily constructed from die-cast and extruded aluminium, it lends itself to being wall-mounted like a utility box or a typical electrical panel. Thanks to its overall consistent design concept, this gateway blends in perfectly into contemporary network scenarios – its distinctive design idiom conveys high competence.

Ausgewogener Transfer

In den heutigen oft sehr komplexen Netzwerkstrukturen dienen Gateways der problemlosen Verbindung von Daten- und Rechnernetzen. Das Dell Edge Gateway 5000 Series ist ein System, das Daten unterschiedlicher Einheiten und Sensoren sammelt, sichert, analysiert und entsprechend reagiert. Es ist in der Lage, relevante Daten an Backend-Systeme in der Cloud, eines Kontrollraums oder eines Rechenzentrums zu übermitteln. Als ein Vertreter von Dells Internet of Things (IoT) Gateways besitzt es die dafür notwendige, hohe Rechenleistung und die Flexibilität, um speziell an der Peripherie eines verteilten Netzes, in der Nähe der IoT-Geräte und Sensoren, ein gesamtes IoT-Ökosystem zu analysieren. Es wurde für die dezentrale Installation konzipiert. Ähnlich wie bei einem PC können alle Peripheriegeräte und Sensoren unkompliziert mit ihm verbunden werden. Dieses Gateway wurde zudem wie ein Server oder Router für den Dauerbetrieb ausgelegt. Es agiert autark und ohne regelmäßige menschliche Interaktion etwa mittels Bildschirm oder Tastatur. Mit seinem solide gestalteten Gehäuse aus vornehmlich Aluminiumdruckguss und stranggepressten Aluminiumprofilen kann es wie ein Verteilerkasten oder eine typische Schalttafel gut an die Wand montiert werden. Dank seines rundum durchdachten Gestaltungskonzepts passt dieses Gateway perfekt in zeitgemäße Szenarien der Vernetzung – seine markante Formensprache kommuniziert Kompetenz.

Statement by the jury

The design of the Dell Edge Gateway 5000 Series emerged with an outstandingly consistent form for the technology on the inside. The enclosure is compact and reduced to the essential elements, which makes the system easily accessible for users and impressively visualises the performance and processing power of this gateway. Functional and extremely solid, the unit is designed to be easily wall-mounted.

Begründung der Jury

Die Gestaltung des Dell Edge Gateway 5000 Series findet eine beeindruckend schlüssige Form für die innovative Technologie im Inneren. Das kompakte und auf die wesentlichen Elemente reduzierte Gehäuse bietet sich dem Nutzer leicht zugänglich dar. Es visualisiert eindringlich die Leistungsfähigkeit und Rechenleistung dieses Gateways. Funktional gestaltet und äußerst solide, lässt es sich einfach an die Wand montieren.

Designer portrait
See page 52
Siehe Seite 52

ASUS Sabertooth Z170 Mark1
Motherboard

Manufacturer
ASUSTeK Computer Inc., Taipei, Taiwan
In-house design
Web
www.asus.com

Inspired by futuristic military elements, the Asus Sabertooth Z170 Mark1 is a durable mainboard designed like exo armour. It has a flexible modular construction and sophisticated airflow channelling, while the component parts are protected for reliable performance. With its integrated M2 SSD slot and QLED lighting for identifying five important boot actions, the board also offers user-friendly equipment.

Statement by the jury
The futuristic design principle was consistently implemented in this motherboard, always taking into consideration both functionality and user.

Inspiriert von futuristisch-militärischen Elementen, ist das Asus Sabertooth Z170 Mark1 ein robustes Mainboard, das wie eine Exo-Panzerung anmutet. Es besitzt einen flexiblen, modularen Aufbau und eine ausgereifte Luftstromleitung, während die Bauteile für einen zuverlässigen Betrieb geschützt sind. Mit dem integrierten M2-SSD-Slot und dem QLED-Licht für die Anzeige von fünf wichtigen Boot-Aktionen bietet das Board zudem eine nutzerfreundliche Ausstattung.

Begründung der Jury
Das futuristische Gestaltungsprinzip wurde bei diesem Motherboard konsequent umgesetzt, wobei Funktion und Anwender stets berücksichtigt wurden.

ASUS ROG
Maximus VIII Formula
Motherboard

Manufacturer
ASUSTeK Computer Inc., Taipei, Taiwan
In-house design
Web
www.asus.com

The Asus ROG Maximus VIII Formula allows users the flexibility and freedom to compile a system that is both visually appealing and high-performance. Whereas conventional motherboards are limited to one dominating hue, this colour-neutral motherboard turns into the centrepiece upon which all systems are based. Carefully placed LEDs, in combination with clever laser-etching techniques, set striking accents.

Statement by the jury
This technically fully equipped motherboard conveys dynamics and durability, making it particularly attractive to demanding gamers.

Das Asus ROG Maximus VIII Formula gibt dem Benutzer die Flexibilität und Freiheit, ein System zusammenzustellen, das gleichermaßen leistungsfähig und visuell ansprechend ist. Wo herkömmliche Motherboards auf eine dominierende Farbe beschränkt sind, wird dieses farbneutrale Motherboard zum Herzstück, auf dem alle Systeme aufbauen. Akzente setzen sorgfältig platzierte LEDs in Kombination mit cleveren Lasergravur-Techniken.

Begründung der Jury
Dieses technisch voll ausgestattete Motherboard vermittelt Dynamik und Robustheit, was es insbesondere für anspruchsvolle Gamer attraktiv macht.

Raiden Series
Gaming Memory Modules
Gaming-Speicherbausteine

Manufacturer
AVEXIR Technologies Corp., Zhubei, Taiwan
In-house design
Web
www.avexir.com

The Raiden Series is conceived for gamers and modders who want to equip their PC with visually attractive, high-performance hardware. A particular highlight is the individual shaping of the modules with their three-coloured heat spreaders. An additional spectacular effect is created by pipes inserted at the top, in which blue lightning flashes streak when the modules are in operation. The technical equipment is likewise excellent with an eight-layer PCB and the hand-selected IC chips.

Die Raiden-Serie ist für Gamer und Modder konzipiert, die ihren PC mit leistungsfähiger und optisch attraktiver Hardware ausstatten wollen. Besonders hervorzuheben ist die eigenwillige Formgebung der Module mit ihrem dreifarbigen Hitzeleiter. Für einen spektakulären Effekt sorgen zusätzlich an der Oberseite eingelassene Röhren, in denen während des Betriebs blaue Blitze zucken. Die technische Ausstattung ist mit einem 8-Layer-PCB und handverlesenen IC-Chips ebenfalls vorzüglich.

Statement by the jury
The memory modules convince with their self-contained design and stunning lighting effects, which are especially impressive when used in gaming PCs.

Begründung der Jury
Diese Speicherbausteine überzeugen durch ihre eigenständige Gestaltung und den beeindruckenden Leuchteffekt, der besonders gut in Gaming-PCs zur Geltung kommt.

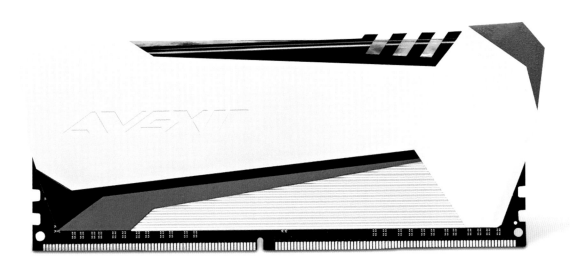

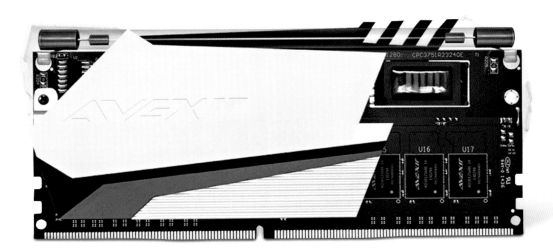

MasterWatt Maker
PC Power Supply
PC-Netzteil

Manufacturer
Cooler Master Technology Inc., New Taipei, Taiwan
In-house design
Eileen Chen
Web
www.coolermaster.com

The MasterWatt Maker is a high-performance PC power supply made of titanium with an efficiency factor of 94 per cent. This was achieved by reducing cabling and minimising heat loss. Settings for various parameters may be determined and implemented at any time using software or an app for iOS and Android. The integrated fan works silently, consumes minimal power and, in connection with the honeycomb mesh grille, ensures optimum ventilation of the power supply. The unit is made of brushed aluminium, underscoring its premium quality.

Der MasterWatt Maker ist ein leistungsstarkes PC-Netzteil aus Titan mit einem Wirkungsgrad von 94 Prozent. Dies wurde dadurch erreicht, dass Verkabelungen reduziert und Wärmeverluste minimiert wurden. Einstellungen verschiedener Parameter lassen sich über eine Software oder eine App für iOS und Android jederzeit ablesen und vornehmen. Der integrierte Lüfter arbeitet leise bei geringem Stromverbrauch und sorgt in Verbindung mit dem wabenförmigen Mesh-Gitter für die optimale Belüftung des Netzteils. Es ist aus gebürstetem Aluminium gefertigt, was seine Wertigkeit unterstreicht.

Statement by the jury
The MasterWatt Maker impresses with its well-conceived design, high efficiency and comprehensive control options.

Begründung der Jury
Der MasterWatt Maker beeindruckt durch seine durchdachte Gestaltung, seine hohe Effizienz und die umfangreichen Kontrollmöglichkeiten.

Suppressor F51
Midi-Tower Chassis
Midi-Tower-Gehäuse

Manufacturer
Thermaltake Technology Co., Ltd.,
Taipei, Taiwan
In-house design
Web
www.thermaltakecorp.com

The modularly constructed Suppressor F51 midi-tower chassis was designed exclusively for low-noise operation. The side parts and the front panel are acoustically insulated, and the high-grade insulation panels at the top can be removed to obtain space for additional cooling options. The chassis is suitable for all mainboards from Mini ITX to E-ATX solutions and offers much space for comprehensive liquid cooling loops and extra-long graphics cards.

Statement by the jury
The chassis impresses with its versatility and modular construction, offering a wide range of options for PC enthusiasts.

Das modular aufgebaute Midi-Tower-Gehäuse Suppressor F51 wurde gänzlich auf einen leisen Betrieb ausgelegt. Die Seitenteile und das Frontpanel sind gedämmt, die hochwertigen Dämmplatten an der Oberseite lassen sich entfernen, um Raum für weitere Kühlmöglichkeiten zu erhalten. Das Gehäuse ist für alle Mainboards vom Mini-ITX- bis zum E-ATX-Mainboard geeignet und bietet viel Platz für umfassende Wasserkühlungsloops und überlange High-End-Grafikkarten.

Begründung der Jury
Das Gehäuse besticht durch seine Vielseitigkeit und modulartige Bauweise, die zahlreiche Optionen für PC-Enthusiasten bietet.

Core P5
ATX Wall-Mount Chassis
ATX-Computergehäuse
für die Wandmontage

Manufacturer
Thermaltake Technology Co., Ltd.,
Taipei, Taiwan
In-house design
Web
www.thermaltakecorp.com

The Core P5 is a modularly constructed chassis that can be placed horizontally, vertically or mounted on the wall, according to personal preference. It has a large panoramic window made of acrylic glass, which permits a view of the interior while protecting the hardware components at the same time. The chassis is predestined for liquid cooling with radiators of a length of up to 480 mm and corresponding mounting points for pumps and compensation tanks.

Statement by the jury
The Core P5 offers gamers and modders a wide range of options for making their extraordinary hardware visible and for presenting it according to their aspirations.

Core P5 ist ein modular aufgebautes Gehäuse, das sich je nach persönlichem Geschmack horizontal oder vertikal platzieren oder an der Wand montieren lässt. Es besitzt ein großes Panoramafenster aus Acrylglas, das den Blick ins Innere ermöglicht und gleichzeitig die Hardware-Komponenten schützt. Das Gehäuse ist prädestiniert für Wasserkühlungen mit Radiatoren bis 480 mm Länge und entsprechenden Montagepunkten für Pumpen und Ausgleichsbehälter.

Begründung der Jury
Das Core P5 bietet Gamern und Moddern vielfältige Möglichkeiten, ihre außergewöhnliche Hardware sichtbar zu machen und nach Wunsch zu präsentieren.

Wiz Stick
Internet Security Dongle

Manufacturer
kt, korea telecom, Seoul, South Korea
In-house design
Design
Designmu, Seoul, South Korea
Web
www.kt.com
www.designmu.com

You can also find this product in
Dieses Produkt finden Sie auch in
Working
Page 127
Seite 127

The Wiz Stick is a dongle that connects via USB to a PC to heighten security when surfing the Internet. It detects unusual online activity and warns the user accordingly. Suspicious Internet websites are blocked, curbing online fraud. The stick has an ergonomic shape, is lightweight and, with its attached loop, can be comfortably worn around the neck. It is thus always handy and can be used with any computer.

Statement by the jury
With the stylish Wiz Stick, Internet usage risks are minimised, which is of particular advantage in the workplace.

Der Wiz Stick ist ein Dongle, der per USB an einen PC angeschlossen wird, um die Nutzung des Internets sicherer zu machen. Er erkennt ungewöhnliche Online-Aktivitäten und warnt den Benutzer. Verdächtige Internetseiten werden zudem gesperrt, sodass Internetbetrug erschwert wird. Der Stick besitzt eine ergonomische Form, ist leicht und kann dank einer Schlaufe auch bequem um den Hals getragen werden. So ist er immer zur Hand und kann an jedem Rechner eingesetzt werden.

Begründung der Jury
Mit dem formschönen Wiz Stick werden Risiken der Internetnutzung auf eine clevere Weise minimiert, was besonders am Arbeitsplatz von Vorteil ist.

MasterCase 5 Series
PC Chassis
Computergehäuse

Manufacturer
Cooler Master Technology Inc., New Taipei, Taiwan
In-house design
Mason Gi
Web
www.coolermaster.com

With the MasterCase 5 Series, users have the opportunity to design their PC chassis optically and functionally according to their own ideas. A range of replacement panels and doors are available, which can be compiled as desired. The chassis can also be easily adapted should any hardware require replacement. Users enjoy a high degree of freedom in the placement of hardware components, as the hard drive can be situated in any vertical position. Even three extra-long graphics cards can be accommodated in the chassis when the optical drive is removed.

Mit dem MasterCase 5 Series erhalten Anwender die Möglichkeit, ihre Computergehäuse nach eigenen Vorstellungen optisch und funktional zu gestalten. Eine Reihe von Ersatzpanels und Klappen stehen zur Verfügung, die sich nach Wunsch zusammenstellen lassen. Wird Hardware ausgetauscht, kann das Gehäuse leicht angepasst werden. Bei der Platzierung von Hardwarekomponenten hat der Nutzer viel Freiheit, denn die Festplatte lässt sich vertikal in jeder Position platzieren. Selbst drei überlange Grafikkarten finden in dem Gehäuse Platz, wenn das optische Laufwerk entfernt wird.

Statement by the jury
The modular construction of this computer chassis considerably simplifies the assembly of components in creating an individual PC, as well as the later exchange of hardware.

Begründung der Jury
Der modulare Aufbau dieses Computergehäuses vereinfacht die Zusammenstellung eines individuellen PCs und den späteren Austausch von Hardware erheblich.

Acer Veriton N Series
Computer

Manufacturer
Acer Incorporated, New Taipei, Taiwan
In-house design
Web
www.acer.com

Computers of the Veriton N series can be extended from a volume of one litre all the way to a three litre version, allowing for individual adjustment. With a rectangular profile and black colouring, it renders a solid impression. Moreover, up to three PCs can easily be coupled, due to the reserved linear shape. Thanks to its small dimensions, the computer can also be attached to the back of a screen.

Statement by the jury
This very compact computer series offers flexible working units that, due to their modular concept, can be configured and set up as desired.

Computer der Veriton-N-Serie können von einem Basis-Desktop mit einem Volumen von einem Liter bis zu einer Drei-Liter-Version ausgebaut und damit individuell angepasst werden. Mit ihrem rechteckigen Profil und der schwarzen Farbgebung vermitteln sie einen soliden Eindruck. Zudem können durch die gerade, schlichte Form bis zu drei PCs gekoppelt werden. Aufgrund seiner geringen Größe lässt sich der Computer auch an der Rückseite eines Bildschirms befestigen.

Begründung der Jury
Diese sehr kompakte Computerserie bietet flexible Arbeitsgeräte, die aufgrund ihrer Modularität nach Belieben konfiguriert und aufgestellt werden können.

ASUS VivoMini PC VC Series
Mini Computer
Minicomputer

Manufacturer
ASUSTeK Computer Inc., Taipei, Taiwan
In-house design
Web
www.asus.com

Computers of the Asus VivoMini PC VC series are high-performance devices with a compact format and an unobtrusively elegant design. They feature a modular construction and are available with three different top covers. The upper modules can be assembled to build a PC precisely catering to the user's demands. The CPU, motherboard, storage drives, thermal module and adapter are cleverly arranged to minimise the size of the chassis.

Statement by the jury
This compact PC fits well on any desk and enhances the surrounding environment with its stylish presence.

Computer der Serie Asus VivoMini PC VC sind leistungsstarke Geräte mit einem kompakten Format und unaufdringlich elegantem Design. Sie sind modular aufgebaut und mit drei verschiedenen Deckeln verfügbar. Die oberen Module können zu einem PC zusammengesetzt werden, der genau den Ansprüchen des Benutzers entspricht. Dabei sind CPU, Motherboard, Speicherlaufwerke, Kühlmodul und Adapter geschickt angeordnet, damit das Gehäuse so klein wie möglich bleibt.

Begründung der Jury
Dieser kompakte PC findet auf jedem Schreibtisch Platz und wertet die Umgebung mit seiner stilvollen Präsenz auf.

HP Envy Desktop
Computer

Manufacturer
HP Inc., Palo Alto, USA
In-house design
HP Industrial Design Team
Web
www.hp.com

The HP Envy Desktop premium computer combines elegant design with outstanding performance. Accommodated in its solid, brushed-aluminium chassis is hardware that is laid out for high demands when it comes to entertainment and work contexts. The minimalist design of the computer is disrupted only by a vertical slot behind which the optical hard drive is situated. The interfaces along the top are easily accessible.

Statement by the jury
The nearly seamless aluminium chassis renders a very high-grade impression, turning the computer into a gem in the office and at home.

Der Premium-Computer HP Envy Desktop vereint eine elegante Gestaltung mit einer ausgezeichneten Leistung. In seinem massiven Gehäuse aus gebürstetem Aluminium ist Hardware verbaut, die für hohe Ansprüche hinsichtlich Unterhaltung und Arbeit ausgelegt ist. Die minimalistische Form des Computers wird lediglich durch eine vertikale Klappe durchbrochen, hinter der sich das optische Laufwerk befindet. Die Schnittstellen an der Oberseite sind leicht zugänglich.

Begründung der Jury
Das nahezu nahtlose Aluminiumgehäuse besitzt eine überaus wertige Ausstrahlung. Damit wird der Computer zum Schmuckstück im Büro und zu Hause.

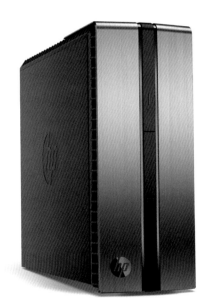

HP Envy Phoenix
Computer

Manufacturer
HP Inc., Palo Alto, USA
In-house design
HP Industrial Design Team
Web
www.hp.com

The HP Envy Phoenix can be equipped with high-end hardware to configure a PC for gaming, entertainment or other demanding tasks. The sturdy chassis made of anodised aluminium underscores the high-level performance of these components. The tapered bezel reflects the dynamics of the system, while the reduced vertical element with the light strip attests to a sophisticated sense of style.

Statement by the jury
Thanks to an unobtrusive yet dynamic design, this high-end computer is suited for both gamers and professional users.

Der HP Envy Phoenix lässt sich mit High-End-Hardware bestücken, um einen PC für Gaming, Unterhaltung oder andere anspruchsvolle Anwendungen zu konfigurieren. Das robuste Gehäuse aus eloxiertem Aluminium unterstreicht die hohe Leistungsfähigkeit dieser Komponenten. Die sich verjüngende Einfassung betont die Dynamik des Systems, während das reduzierte vertikale Element mit dem Lichtstreifen von einem ausgereiften Stilempfinden zeugt.

Begründung der Jury
Dank seiner unaufdringlichen, gleichwohl dynamischen Gestaltung ist dieser High-End-Computer für Gamer ebenso geeignet wie für professionelle Anwender.

HP Pavilion Mini
Mini Computer
Minicomputer

Manufacturer
HP Inc., Palo Alto, USA
In-house design
HP Industrial Design Team
Web
www.hp.com

The HP Pavilion Mini is a complete Windows PC with small dimensions that can be used anywhere. Equipped with Intel i3 or i7 processors, it is suitable for both demanding office tasks and home entertainment. Dual display ports enable the connection of multiple monitors for effective working. Its design is characterised by soft, friendly curves, making it a modern alternative to conventional desktop computers.

Statement by the jury
This very compact, high-performance PC, with its reserved design, integrates well into any work or living environment.

Der HP Pavilion Mini ist ein vollständiger Windows-PC mit geringen Abmessungen, der überall eingesetzt werden kann. Ausgestattet mit Intel-i3- oder -i7-Prozessoren, eignet er sich für anspruchsvolle Aufgaben im Büro ebenso wie für Home-Entertainment. Dual-Display-Ports erlauben den Anschluss von mehreren Bildschirmen für das effektive Arbeiten. Seine durch weiche Kurven geprägte freundliche Anmutung macht ihn zu einer modernen Alternative zu den traditionellen Desktop-Computern.

Begründung der Jury
Dieser sehr kompakte und leistungsfähige PC lässt sich mit seiner zurückhaltenden Gestaltung in jedes Arbeits- und Wohnzimmer integrieren.

ideacentre Y 900
Gaming Computer

Manufacturer
Lenovo (Beijing) Ltd., Beijing, China
In-house design
Web
www.lenovo.com

An outstanding characteristic of the ideacentre Y 900 is its generous space of 34 litres, offering users a wide range of options for installing state-of-the-art hardware. Installation and modification of components can be done without tools and is accordingly simple. A removable dust filter at the front side can be cleaned easily. The internal and external LEDs are a visual highlight, emitting a soft glow as computer power increases.

Bezeichnend für den ideacentre Y 900 ist sein großzügiges Platzangebot von 34 Litern, das Anwendern weitreichende Möglichkeiten bietet, zeitgemäße Hardware einzubauen. Der Einbau und Umbau von Komponenten geschieht ohne Werkzeug und ist entsprechend einfach. Ein entnehmbarer Staubfilter an der Vorderseite kann leicht gereinigt werden. Ein optisches Highlight sind die internen und externen LEDs, die sanft leuchten, sobald die Rechenleistung steigt.

Statement by the jury
With its angular front side, discreet ribbed finish and prominently placed LED elements, the ideacentre Y 900 is a gaming PC that embodies consistent design.

Begründung der Jury
Mit seiner kantigen Vorderseite, einem dezenten Streifendekor und den prominent platzierten LED-Elementen ist der ideacentre Y 900 ein konsequent gestalteter Gaming-PC.

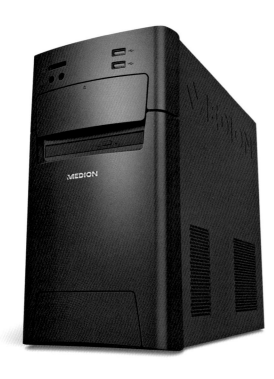

MEDION® Akoya M70
Computer

Manufacturer
Medion AG, Essen, Germany
In-house design
Medion Design Team
Design
INDX Design, Mülheim an der Ruhr
Web
www.medion.com

The Medion Akoya M70 is a computer with an excellent price-performance ratio. It is equipped with a wide range of functions like Media Bay and a hot-swap drive, thus offering extensive capacity for multimedia applications. The characteristic Edge Design conveys its performance, as does the all-black colour scheme. The textured surface does without spray painting, resulting in an especially eco-friendly product.

Statement by the jury
With its plain design and economical use of decorative elements, this computer places value on the bare essentials.

Der Medion Akoya M70 ist ein Computer mit einem ausgezeichneten Preis-Leistungs-Verhältnis. Er ist mit vielfältigen Funktionen wie Media Bay und Hot-Swap-Laufwerk ausgestattet und bietet damit eine umfassende Leistung für Multimedia-Anwendungen. Das charakteristische Edge Design vermittelt seine Leistungsfähigkeit ebenso wie die komplett schwarze Farbgestaltung. Die strukturierte Oberfläche kommt ohne Spraylackierung aus und ist damit besonders umweltfreundlich.

Begründung der Jury
Mit seiner schlichten Gestaltung und den sparsam eingesetzten dekorativen Elementen vermittelt dieser Computer die Konzentration auf das Wesentliche.

MEDION® ERAZER® X77
Gaming Computer

Manufacturer
Medion AG, Essen, Germany
In-house design
Medion Design Team
Design
INDX Design, Mülheim an der Ruhr
Web
www.medion.com

Equipped with high-performance, premium components like an Intel Core i7 processor and an Nvidia Geforce GTX 980 graphics card, the Medion Erazer X77 is a gaming computer for demanding users. It shows the Edge Design of the Erazer product line and thus positions itself unmistakably as a representative of the gaming field. This is emphasised by a circumferential, multicolour edge of light and a striking geometric design.

Statement by the jury
This gaming computer impresses with an angular, multifaceted design that conveys independence and underscores its high performance.

Ausgestattet mit leistungsfähigen High-End-Komponenten wie einem Intel-Core-i7-Prozessor und einer Nvidia-Geforce-GTX-980-Grafikkarte, ist der Medion Erazer X77 ein Gaming-Computer für hohe Ansprüche. Er zeigt das Edge Design der Erazer-Linie und positioniert sich dadurch unmissverständlich als Vertreter im Gaming-Bereich. Betont wird dies durch eine umlaufende vielfarbige Lichtkante und eine markante geometrische Linienführung.

Begründung der Jury
Der Gaming-Computer beeindruckt durch ein kantige, facettenreiche Gestaltung. Sie verleiht ihm Eigenständigkeit und betont seine hohe Leistungsfähigkeit.

Revo Build
Mini Computer
Minicomputer

Manufacturer
Acer Incorporated, New Taipei, Taiwan
In-house design
Web
www.acer.com

The Revo Build is a mini computer with a reduced design based on the concept of simplicity. It may be assembled without having to open the chassis or equip the motherboard. The individual components in the shape of blocks, such as a rechargeable battery, portable hard drive, or audio and graphics blocks, are assembled using magnetic connectors and can be arranged as desired.

Statement by the jury
With the Revo Build, it is possible even for non-technophile users to assemble a computer according to their own preferences.

Der Revo Build ist ein reduziert gestalteter Minicomputer, der auf dem Konzept der Einfachheit basiert. Er lässt sich zusammenbauen, ohne dass das Gehäuse geöffnet und das Motherboard bestückt werden muss. Die einzelnen Komponenten, wie kabelloser Akku, tragbare Festplatte, Audio- und Grafik-Blöcke, haben die Form von Blöcken und werden über magnetische Verbindungen zusammengefügt. So können sie nach Belieben angeordnet werden.

Begründung der Jury
Mit dem Revo Build haben auch wenig technikaffine Anwender die Möglichkeit, einen Computer nach Maß zusammenzustellen.

HP Pavilion Desktop
Computer

Manufacturer
HP Inc., Palo Alto, USA
In-house design
HP Industrial Design Team
Web
www.hp.com

The HP Pavilion Desktop meets the basic demands of a computer, while simultaneously featuring a sophisticated design at an affordable price. With its minimalist appearance, it blends into any environment; moreover, it shows surprising details like a fine conical pattern giving the chassis spatial depth. The vertical ribbon at the front with ports and an optical disk drive fosters an appealing contrast.

Statement by the jury
The HP Pavilion Desktop is a computer with a state-of-the-art design offering all functions for everyday work.

Der HP Pavilion Desktop erfüllt grundsätzliche Ansprüche an einen Computer und besitzt zugleich ein ausgefeiltes Design zu einem erschwinglichen Preis. Mit seiner minimalistischen Anmutung passt er in jede Umgebung; zusätzlich zeigt er überraschende Details, beispielsweise ein feines kegelförmiges Muster, das dem Gehäuse eine räumliche Tiefe verleiht. Das vertikale Band an der Vorderseite mit Anschlüssen und Laufwerk bildet dazu einen ansprechenden Kontrast.

Begründung der Jury
Der HP Pavilion Desktop ist ein modern gestalteter Computer, der sämtliche Funktionen für das tägliche Arbeiten bietet.

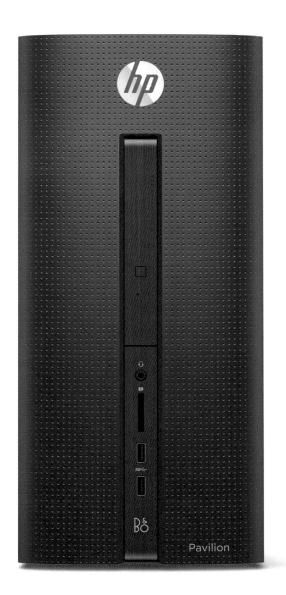

ideacentre AIO 510s
All-in-One PC

Manufacturer
Lenovo (Beijing) Ltd., Beijing, China
In-house design
Web
www.lenovo.com

The ideacentre AIO 510s all-in-one PC is a slim, fully fledged computer. It is merely 7.5 mm thick, with a narrow bezel of only 3.5 mm, thus making the screen appear virtually frameless. With its slim design, the PC has an unobtrusive appeal and takes up but little space on a desk. On the bottom side, it has a concealed panel with interfaces that can be flipped out as needed. The PC is supported by an elegantly designed stand featuring a filigree appearance.

Statement by the jury
The objective to create a slim and high-performance all-in-one PC was implemented here in an exemplary way.

Der All-in-one-PC ideacentre AIO 510s ist ein schlanker vollwertiger Computer. Er ist nur 7,5 mm dick und der Bildschirm erscheint mit seiner Einfassung von lediglich 3,5 mm fast rahmenlos. Durch seine schlanke Gestalt wirkt der PC unaufdringlich und nimmt nur wenig Platz auf dem Schreibtisch ein. An seiner Unterseite besitzt er ein verdecktes Panel mit Schnittstellen, das bei Bedarf ausgeklappt werden kann. Getragen wird der PC von einem elegant geformten, filigran wirkenden Standfuß.

Begründung der Jury
Das Ziel, einen leistungsstarken, schlanken All-in-one-PC mit einer stilvollen Anmutung zu kreieren, wurde hier vorbildlich umgesetzt.

HP Pavilion AIO
All-in-One PC

Manufacturer
HP Inc., Palo Alto, USA
In-house design
HP Industrial Design Team
Web
www.hp.com

The HP Pavilion AIO is a stylish all-in-one computer with touchscreen offering an intuitive user experience. Its familiar shape is complemented by a slim stand in a sculptural design. A contributing factor to the purist appearance of the computer is the clever concealment of elements that might make it look bulky or clunky. The easily accessible interface ports also blend smoothly into the design so that the discreet appearance is retained.

Statement by the jury
The design of this computer is characterised by elegant minimalism, with its appearance upgrading any interior.

Die HP Pavilion AIO ist ein stilvoll gestalteter All-in-one-Computer mit Touchscreen, der eine intuitive Nutzererfahrung bietet. Seine vertraute Form wird durch einen schlanken, skulpturalen Standfuß ergänzt. Zur puristischen Erscheinung des Computers trägt bei, dass Elemente, die ihn klobig wirken lassen könnten, geschickt verborgen werden. Auch die leicht zugänglichen Schnittstellen und Anschlüsse fügen sich so ein, dass die zurückhaltende Anmutung gewahrt bleibt.

Begründung der Jury
Dieser Computer besitzt eine elegante, von Minimalismus geprägte Formgebung. Dadurch wertet er jedes Interieur auf.

HP Envy AIO
All-in-One PC

Manufacturer
HP Inc., Palo Alto, USA
In-house design
HP Industrial Design Team
Web
www.hp.com

A remarkable feature of the HP Envy AIO is its curved 34" panel offering a completely immersive experience for the user. It also provides generous space and allows for simultaneous work with two applications, which can be comfortably displayed side by side. The two lateral speakers round off the comprehensive user experience. Completing the design are two appealingly curved supporting feet.

Statement by the jury
With its large screen and integrated speakers, this computer is superbly equipped for entertainment, yet using the device for work is also an enjoyable experience.

Bemerkenswert am HP Envy AIO ist vor allem sein gekrümmter 34"-Bildschirm, der den Benutzer ganz in das Geschehen eintauchen lässt. Zusätzlich bietet er reichlich Platz und gestattet es, mit zwei Anwendungen gleichzeitig zu arbeiten, die in einer komfortablen Fenstergröße dargestellt werden können. Die Lautsprecher an den Außenseiten runden das umfassende Nutzererlebnis ab. Komplettiert wird das Design durch zwei ansprechend geschwungene Standfüße.

Begründung der Jury
Mit seinem großen Bildschirm und den Lautsprechern ist dieser Computer hervorragend für die Unterhaltung ausgestattet, macht aber auch das Arbeiten zum Vergnügen.

ThinkCentre M900z AIO
Computer

Manufacturer
Lenovo, Morrisville, North Carolina, USA
In-house design
Web
www.lenovo.com

The ThinkCentre M900z AIO combines functional design, advanced performance features and well-conceived options. This includes three screen sizes and three different stand solutions, such as an elegantly curved chrome stand and a transformer stand allowing the screen to be positioned in a nearly flat position for comfortable touch input. The anti-glare screen has a rear service access cover, which can be removed without tools.

Statement by the jury
This slim and versatile all-in-one PC convinces with its sophisticated design and proves to be a device with high usage value.

Der ThinkCentre M900z AIO kombiniert eine funktionale Gestaltung, fortschrittliche Leistungsmerkmale und durchdachte Optionen. Dazu zählen drei Bildschirmgrößen und drei verschiedene Standlösungen, wie ein elegant gebogener Ständer aus Chrom und ein Standfuß, der es gestattet, den Bildschirm für die bequeme Touch-Eingabe nahezu flach zu positionieren. Der Bildschirm ist entspiegelt und besitzt an seiner Rückseite eine Wartungsklappe, die ohne Werkzeug abgenommen werden kann.

Begründung der Jury
Dieser schlanke und vielseitige All-in-one-PC punktet mit seiner überlegten Gestaltung, dank derer er sich als Gerät mit hohem Gebrauchswert erweist.

ThinkCentre X1 AIO
Computer

Manufacturer
Lenovo, Morrisville, North Carolina, USA
In-house design
Web
www.lenovo.com

The ThinkCentre X1 AIO features a 23.8" IPS display housed between Infinity glass and a durable and elegant aluminium enclosure measuring only 11 mm thick. Fine ribbing on the back of the system provides visual interest and cleanly integrates venting where it is needed. Thanks to the stand's small-diameter steel arm and polished chrome finish that reflects its surroundings, the X1 AIO appears to float weightlessly above the desk.

Statement by the jury
An airy and reduced design ensures that this all-in-one PC can be superbly placed on virtually any desktop.

Der ThinkCentre X1 AIO besitzt ein 23,8"-IPS-Display, das zwischen Infinity-Glas und einer stabilen wie eleganten Einfassung aus Aluminium untergebracht ist, die lediglich 11 mm dick ist. Eine feine Rippenstruktur an der Rückseite des Systems zieht die Blicke auf sich und integriert die Belüftung dort, wo sie benötigt wird. Dank des Stahlarms mit seinem kleinen Durchmesser und dank des polierten Chroms, das die Umgebung reflektiert, scheint der X1 AIO schwerelos über dem Schreibtisch zu schweben.

Begründung der Jury
Die luftige Formgebung und die reduzierte Gestaltung sorgen dafür, dass sich der All-in-one-PC auf jedem Schreibtisch hervorragend aufstellen lässt.

ThinkCentre Tiny-in-One
Computer

Manufacturer
Lenovo, Morrisville, North Carolina, USA
In-house design
Web
www.lenovo.com

The ThinkCentre Tiny-in-One consists of a monitor with a dock at the rear for a Tiny PC. Once a Tiny PC is installed, the system transforms into a fully fledged all-in-one PC. In order to upgrade the system, the old PC can be effortlessly taken out and replaced by a new one. The front chin provides speakers and easy-access USB and audio ports, while the rear housing channels cables for a clean appearance.

Statement by the jury
The system convinces with its modular construction, which is not only user-friendly but, due to the simple interchangeability of components, sustainable as well.

Der ThinkCentre Tiny-in-One besteht aus einem Monitor mit einem Dock für einen Tiny-PC an seiner Rückseite. Wird ein Tiny-PC installiert, verwandelt sich das System in einen vollwertigen All-in-one-PC. Um das System upzugraden, kann der alte PC mühelos entnommen und durch einen neuen ersetzt werden. Die Vorderseite beherbergt Lautsprecher und leicht zugängliche USB- und Audio-Ports, während die hintere Abdeckung zugunsten einer sauberen Erscheinung Kabel aufnimmt.

Begründung der Jury
Das System überzeugt mit seinem modularen Aufbau, der nicht nur nutzerfreundlich, sondern aufgrund der einfachen Austauschbarkeit der Komponenten auch nachhaltig ist.

31.5 inch AIO
All-in-One PC

Manufacturer
Shenzhen Inno&Cn Co., Ltd., Shenzhen, China
Design
Xivo Design (Chao Jing, Jiuzhou Zhang), Shenzhen, China
Web
www.ondamnt.com
www.xivodesign.com

This all-in-one computer with a 35″ display cleverly accommodates the processor in a self-contained base, underscoring the reduced weight of the device. The T-Con board is positioned upside down so that the back design of the computer is as slim and lightweight as possible. The speaker occupies the entire length of the stand, so in connection with the large screen a comprehensive audio and video experience is achieved. The speaker can also be used for music playback independently of the computer.

Dieser All-in-one-PC mit 35″-Display bringt den Prozessor geschickt in der eigenständig gestalteten Basis unter, wodurch die Leichtigkeit des Geräts betont wird. Das T-Con-Board steht auf dem Kopf, damit die Rückseite des Computers so schlank und leicht wie möglich gestaltet werden konnte. Der Lautsprecher nimmt die gesamte Länge des Standfußes ein; in Verbindung mit dem großen Bildsch rm wird eine umfassende Audio- und Video-Erfahrung erreicht. Der Lautsprecher lässt sich auch unabhängig für die Wiedergabe von Musik verwenden.

Statement by the jury
With its geometrically shaped base, the 31.5 inch AIO renders an autonomous, sculptural impression.

Begründung der Jury
Der 31,5 inch AIO zeigt mit seiner geometrisch geformten Basis und dem abgewinkelten Bildschirm eine eigenständige skulpturale Anmutung.

T9plus
Keyboard
Tastatur

Manufacturer
Delux Technology Company Limited, Shenzhen, China
In-house design
Mengyao Yu, Tao Xiao
Web
www.deluxworld.com

The T9plus is a mechanical single-hand keyboard providing the essential keys needed for the control of games. Its 29 keys are arranged according to frequency of use. With its special design, the keyboard can be placed on a desk in a position optimally suiting the gamer. Each key has a special switch providing a comfortable feel when operated, while also extending the life cycle of the keys. The RGB backlighting is configurable in ten different modes, fostering a special gaming atmosphere that is especially helpful in the dark.

Die mechanische Einhand-Tastatur T9plus bietet die wesentlichen Tasten, d'e für die Steuerung von Spielen benötigt werden. Ihre 29 Tasten sind nach der Häufigkeit ihrer Verwendung angeordnet. Durch die besondere Form kann die Tastatur in einer für den Spieler optimalen Position auf dem Schreibtisch abgelegt werden. Jede Taste besitzt einen gesonderten Schalter, was ein angenehmes Gefühl beim Betätigen liefert und die Lebensdauer der Tasten erhöht. Die in zehn Modi konfigurierbare RGB-Hintergrundbeleuchtung erzeugt eine besondere Atmosphäre beim Spielen und ist im Dunkeln hilfreich.

Statement by the jury
The T9plus keyboard is perfectly aligned to the demands of computer gamers. It is space-saving, functional and durable.

Begründung der Jury
Die Tastatur T9plus ist perfekt an die Bedürfnisse von Computerspielern angepasst. Sie ist platzsparend, funktional und langlebig.

273

Quick Fire XTi
Mechanical Gaming Keyboard
Mechanische Gaming-Tastatur

Manufacturer
Cooler Master Technology Inc., New Taipei, Taiwan
In-house design
Shaujiun Huang
Web
www.coolermaster.com

The Quick Fire XTi mechanical gaming keyboard is distinguished by a plain and minimalist design. It has UV-coated Cherry MX keys that can be backlit individually in a broad range of colours. The keyboard is automatically detected per plug and play and is immediately operational. Profiles and keys can also be programmed without complex software to optimise individual input. The USB cable is removable so that the keyboard can be stowed away easily when not in use, also preventing cable breakage.

Die mechanische Gaming-Tastatur Quick Fire XTi zeichnet sich durch eine schlichte und minimalistische Gestaltung aus. Sie besitzt UV-beschichtete Cherry-MX-Tasten und eine Hintergrundbeleuchtung, die für jede Taste in den verschiedensten Farben konfiguriert werden kann. Die Tastatur wird einfach per Plug-and-Play erkannt und kann sofort eingesetzt werden. Profile und Tasten können auch ohne komplexe Software programmiert werden, um die individuelle Eingabe zu optimieren. Das USB-Kabel ist abnehmbar, damit die Tastatur bei Nichtgebrauch leicht verstaut werden kann und Kabelbruch verhindert wird.

Statement by the jury
With its straightforward design and slim shape, this gaming keyboard sets a visual contrast in an environment characterised by dynamics and sportiness.

Begründung der Jury
Mit ihrer schlichten Anmutung und schlanken Gestalt setzt diese Gaming-Tastatur einen visuellen Kontrast in einem Umfeld, das von Dynamik und Sportlichkeit geprägt ist.

Poseidon Z RGB
Gaming Keyboard
Gaming-Tastatur

Manufacturer
Thermaltake Technology Co., Ltd., Taipei, Taiwan
In-house design
Web
www.thermaltakecorp.com

The Poseidon Z RGB mechanical gaming keyboard features keys with RGB backlighting that can be individually adjusted, thus lending an individual sense of dynamics to the game. The user may choose between 16.8 million colours with which each single light-emitting diode can be lit up as desired. The keyboard switches have been optimised with regard to durability, precision and speed for an optimum gaming experience.

Die mechanische Gaming-Tastatur Poseidon Z RGB besitzt Tasten m t RGB-Hintergrundbeleuchtung, die sich individuell anpassen lässt und dem Spiel eine eigene Dynamik verleiht. Der Nutzer kann aus 16,8 Millionen Farben wählen und damit jede einzelne Diode in der Farbe leuchten lassen, die er wünscht. Die Schalter der Tastatur wurden auf Haltbarkeit, Präzision und Geschwindigkeit hin optimiert, um dem Spieler das bestmögliche Nutzererlebnis zu ermöglichen.

Statement by the jury
With its solid design, this keyboard conveys longevity and durability, which is of particular advantage to intensive gamers.

Begründung der Jury
Mit ihrer soliden Bauweise vermittelt die Tastatur Langlebigkeit und Robustheit, was besonders für Intensivspieler von Vorteil ist.

K380
Bluetooth Keyboard
Bluetooth-Tastatur

Manufacturer
Logitech, Newark, California, USA
In-house design
Logitech Design
Design
Feiz Design, Amsterdam, Netherlands
Web
www.logitech.com
www.feizdesign.com

With its compact design, the K380 Bluetooth keyboard provides a comfortable, flexible typing experience in connection with smartphones and tablets, similar to a desktop PC. The Easy-Switch buttons enable seamless movement between up to three devices: the adaptive technology automatically recognises the respective operating system and selects the corresponding key arrangement. With a two-year battery life, the keyboard is always ready for use.

Die kompakt gestaltete Bluetooth-Tastatur K380 bietet auf Smartphones und Tablets ein komfortables, flexibles Tipperlebnis wie auf einem Desktop-PC. Mit den Easy-Switch-Tasten kann problemlos zwischen bis zu drei Geräten umgeschaltet werden: Die anpassungsfähige Technologie erkennt automatisch das jeweilige Betriebssystem und wählt die zugehörige Tastenanordnung. Mit einer Batterielebensdauer von zwei Jahren ist die Tastatur immer einsatzbereit.

Statement by the jury
With its friendly contours, intelligent device identification and long battery runtime, this keyboard is a perfect accessory for mobile use.

Begründung der Jury
Mit ihren freundlichen Kurven, der intelligenten Geräteerkennung und der langen Akkulaufzeit ist diese Tastatur ein perfektes Zubehör für unterwegs.

ASUS ROG Claymore / Spatha
Keyboard and Mouse
Tastatur und Maus

Manufacturer
ASUSTeK Computer Inc., Taipei, Taiwan
In-house design
Web
www.asus.com

The ROG Claymore keyboard and ROG Spatha mouse consist primarily of metal, rendering them especially robust and durable. Both devices offer options for individual adjustment: the numeric keypad may be separated from the keyboard, and the mouse can be used with or without a cable. Moreover, the mouse includes 12 function keys that can be programmed using macros, as well as six thumb keys for shortcuts.

Die Tastatur ROG Claymore und die Maus ROG Spatha bestehen beide überwiegend aus Metall, was sie besonders robust und haltbar macht. Möglichkeiten zur individuellen Anpassung bieten beide Geräte: Der Nummernblock kann von der Tastatur getrennt werden, die Maus lässt sich sowohl mit als auch ohne Kabel verwenden. Zudem besitzt die Maus zwölf Tasten, die mit Makros programmiert werden können, sowie sechs Daumentasten für Shortcuts.

Statement by the jury
Both mouse and keyboard offer a wide range of configuration options and impress with a powerful design that renders a solid impression.

Begründung der Jury
Maus und Tastatur lassen sich umfangreich konfigurieren und beeindrucken durch ihre kraftvolle Gestaltung, die ihnen eine massive Anmutung verleiht.

M335
Wireless Mouse
Kabellose Maus

Manufacturer
Logitech, Newark, California, USA
In-house design
Logitech Design
Design
Design Partners, Bray, Ireland
Web
www.logitech.com
www.designpartners.com

The M335 wireless mouse allows for the connection and operation of virtually any Bluetooth-capable device, regardless of whether the device uses MacOS, Windows, Chrome or Android. With its compact, curved shape and rubber grip, it rests comfortably in the hand even after hours of use and can be stowed away easily in a bag. With a battery runtime of ten months, the mouse is ready for use anytime and anywhere.

Die kabellose Maus M335 ermöglicht den Anschluss und Betrieb über nahezu jedes Bluetooth-fähige Gerät, sei es ein MacOS-, Windows-, Chrome- oder Android-Gerät. Mit ihrer kompakten, geschwungenen Form und den gummierten Griffflächen liegt sie selbst nach stundenlanger Nutzung noch bequem in der Hand und sie lässt sich problemlos in einer Tasche verstauen. Bei einer Batterielebensdauer von zehn Monaten ist die Maus zudem immer und überall einsatzbereit.

Statement by the jury
This mouse convinces with its plain shape, which is appealingly complemented by a striking colour scheme and offset grip surfaces.

Begründung der Jury
Die Maus besticht durch ihre schlichte Form, die durch die auffällige Farbgebung und die abgesetzten Griffflächen ansprechend ergänzt wird.

ThinkPad X1
Wireless Touch Mouse
Kabellose Maus
für das ThinkPad X1

Manufacturer
Lenovo, Morrisville, North Carolina, USA
In-house design
Web
www.lenovo.com

This wireless mouse evokes the slim profile of the ThinkPad X1 Carbon notebook and proves useful for travellers, easily slipping into a shirt pocket or small travel case. It connects via Bluetooth or a wireless dongle. The bottom of the mouse features a touchpad, allowing presenters to navigate screens and advance slides during a presentation.

Die kabellose Maus erinnert an das schlanke Profil des Notebooks ThinkPad X1 Carbon und erweist sich damit für Reisende als nützliches Gerät, das leicht in eine Hemd- oder Reisetasche gleitet. Sie kann sowohl per Bluetooth als auch über einen Dongle verbunden werden. An der Unterseite der Maus befindet sich ein Touchpad, das es den Vortragenden ermöglicht, durch Bildschirme zu navigieren und Folien weiterzuschalten.

Statement by the jury
This mouse impresses with its dual function as mouse and presenter, but also with its slim shape, allowing it to be stowed away in any bag.

Begründung der Jury
Diese Maus beeindruckt mit ihrer Doppelfunktion als Maus und Presenter sowie mit ihrer schlanken Form, dank derer sie sich in jeder Tasche verstauen lässt.

MX Master
Wireless Mouse
Kabellose Maus

Manufacturer
Logitech, Newark, California, USA
In-house design
Logitech Design
Design
Design Partners, Bray, Ireland
Web
www.logitech.com
www.designpartners.com

The MX Master wireless mouse is a precision instrument offering an optimal experience for users who place value on productivity and efficiency. Its advanced functionality and powerful design have been optimised for Windows PCs and Macs. The hand-sculpted, comfortable shape of the mouse is defined by curved sides that function as health-promoting support for hand and wrist. In addition, intelligently positioned buttons and wheels enable precise motion control and a smooth working experience.

Die kabellose Maus MX Master ist ein Präzisionsgerät, das Anwendern, die auf Produktivität und Effizienz setzen, ein optimales Steuerungserlebnis bietet. Ihre fortschrittlichen Funktionen und die kraftvolle Gestaltung wurden für Windows-PCs und Macs optimiert. Die handgerechte, komfortable Form der Maus ist durch geschwungene Seiten definiert, die als gesundheitsfördernde Stütze für Hand und Handgelenk fungieren. Daneben sorgen intelligent platzierte Tasten und Rädchen für eine präzise Bewegungssteuerung und flüssiges Arbeiten.

Statement by the jury
This mouse presents a convincing ergonomic design that guarantees fatigue-free and precise work over extended periods of time.

Begründung der Jury
Die Maus punktet mit ihrer ergonomischen Gestaltung, wodurch sie ermüdungsfreies und präzises Arbeiten über längere Zeiträume gewährleistet.

Play Collection
Wireless Mouse
Kabellose Maus

Manufacturer
Logitech, Newark, California, USA
In-house design
Logitech Design
Web
www.logitech.com

The Logitech Play Collection mice are available in eight versions, each showing an independent, colourful design. They connect wirelessly to a notebook or PC with a USB receiver plugged into the corresponding device so that no irritating cables disturb the workflow. Each mouse is powered by a single AA battery with a runtime of up to 12 months. With a slim, symmetrical shape, each mouse can be stowed away easily and is suitable for both right- and left-handers.

Die Mäuse der Logitech Play Collection gibt es in acht Varianten, von denen jede ein eigenwilliges, farbenfrohes Muster zeigt. Sie werden kabellos mit einem USB-Empfänger, der in Notebook oder PC gesteckt wird, verbunden, sodass kein Kabel beim Arbeiten stört. Energie beziehen die Geräte über eine AA-Batterie, die bis zu zwölf Monate lang hält. Da die Mäuse eine schlanke, symmetrische Form haben, sind sie leicht zu verstauen und für Rechts- wie für Linkshänder geeignet.

Statement by the jury
These colourful mice bring a high degree of zest for life and individuality into a technically dominated environment.

Begründung der Jury
Diese farbenfrohen Mäuse bringen ein hohes Maß an Lebensfreude und Individualität in eine von Technik bestimmte Umgebung.

Yoga Mouse
Yoga Maus

Manufacturer
Lenovo (Beijing) Ltd., Beijing, China
In-house design
Web
www.lenovo.com

The Yoga Mouse is a multifunctional input device that can be adapted to different usage scenarios. This is brought about by a rotation hinge dividing the mouse into two halves of nearly the same size. It can be moved in such a way that the device is angled, resulting in the hand position typical for a mouse. In flat mode, it takes on the function of a remote control for presentation software or other applications. The travel mode is suitable for energy-saving transport.

Statement by the jury
A clever rotation mechanism adds sensible functionality to the mouse. This is particularly helpful during presentations when both mouse and remote are required.

Die Yoga Maus ist ein multifunktionales Eingabegerät, das sich an unterschiedliche Anwendungsszenarien anpassen lässt. Möglich wird dies über ein Drehscharnier, das die Maus in etwa gleich große Hälften teilt. Es kann so bewegt werden, dass das Gerät abgewinkelt ist und die maustypische Handhaltung ermöglicht. Im flachen Zustand übernimmt das Gerät die Funktion einer Fernbedienung für Präsentationen oder andere Anwendungen. Der Reise-Modus schließlich dient zum energiesparenden Transport.

Begründung der Jury
Der clevere Drehmechanismus erweitert die Maus um sinnvolle Funktionen. Dies ist vor allem bei Präsentationen, bei denen Maus und Fernbedienung benötigt werden, hilfreich.

Ventus X
Gaming Mouse
Gaming-Maus

Manufacturer
Thermaltake Technology Co., Ltd.,
Taipei, Taiwan
In-house design
Web
www.thermaltakecorp.com

The Ventus X gaming mouse combines a classic design with state-of-the-art technology. The matt coating and rubber pads on the sides offer comfort and a secure grip, while the honeycomb grille design allows fresh air to reach the palms, which reduces sweating. The mouse is ergonomically shaped for right-handers and features a precise 5,700 DPI laser sensor. It addresses those gamers who place value on state-of-the-art technology yet prefer classic designs.

Statement by the jury
With the Ventus X, computer gamers have a discreetly designed gaming mouse at their fingertips, which also impresses with its up-to-date technical features.

Die Gaming-Maus Ventus X verbindet eine klassische Gestaltung mit zeitgemäßer Technik. Die matte Beschichtung und Gummi-Pads an den Seiten bieten Komfort und Griffsicherheit, während das Honigwaben-Gitter Frischluft an die Handfläche lässt und die Schweißbildung verhindert. Die ergonomisch für Rechtshänder geformte Maus besitzt einen präzisen 5.700-DPI-Laser-Sensor und wendet sich an Gamer, die Wert auf neueste Technologie legen, aber klassische Formen bevorzugen.

Begründung der Jury
Mit der Ventus X erhalten Computerspieler eine zurückhaltend gestaltete Gaming-Maus, die gleichzeitig mit aktuellen technischen Merkmalen überzeugt.

007 Gaming Mouse
007 Gaming-Maus

Manufacturer
Shenzhen Lofree Culture Co., Ltd.,
Shenzhen, China
In-house design
Web
www.lofree.com.cn

With its sleek design, the 007 Gaming Mouse specifically appeals to technophiles. The mouse comes with eleven replaceable accessories, which can be conveniently attached using magnets. This makes it possible to configure the high-performance mouse according to one's own requirements in a total of 54 different ways. This is particularly important for gamers since the mouse plays a crucial role in gaming.

Statement by the jury
With its range of accessories, this gaming mouse turns into a customised input device for the involved players, adapting to various situations.

Die schnittig gestaltete 007 Gaming-Maus spricht Menschen an, die sich für Technik begeistern können. Sie wird mit elf austauschbaren Zubehörteilen geliefert, die sich bequem mit Magneten auf dem Mauskörper anbringen lassen. Dadurch gibt es insgesamt 54 verschiedene Möglichkeiten, die leistungsfähige Maus nach eigenen Bedürfnissen zu konfigurieren. Dies ist besonders für Gamer wichtig, da die Maus beim Spielen entscheidend ist.

Begründung der Jury
Mit ihren verschiedenen Zubehörteilen wird die Gaming-Maus für die jeweiligen Spieler in unterschiedlichen Situationen zum maßgeschneiderten Eingabegerät.

Mouse with Emergent Power Bank
Maus mit integriertem Ladegerät

Manufacturer
kt, korea telecom, Seoul, South Korea
In-house design
Design
seymourpowell, London, Great Britain
Web
www.kt.com
www.seymourpowell.com

This mouse with a sleek sports-car design can be used both with and without a cable. It is moreover equipped with power bank functionality for charging other mobile devices via USB. The mouse itself is charged when it is connected to the computer with the mouse cable. Due to its compact dimensions, it can be used anywhere, such as in tight spaces like cafe tables.

Diese Maus im schnittigen Sportwagendesign kann mit und ohne Kabel verwendet werden. Sie fungiert zudem als Ladegerät für andere Mobilgeräte, die per USB angeschlossen werden. Die Maus selbst wird aufgeladen, während sie an einem Computer im Kabelbetrieb verwendet wird. Durch ihre kompakte Größe lässt sie sich bequem mitnehmen und ist überall einsetzbar, auch wenn, wie z. B. auf Cafétischen, nicht viel Platz ist.

Statement by the jury
With its well-conceived design, this mouse with emergent power bank conveys a dynamic feel and is predestined for use in small spaces.

Begründung der Jury
Mit ihrer durchdachten Gestaltung vermittelt die Maus with Emergent Power Bank Dynamik und ist prädestiniert für die Nutzung auf kleinstem Raum.

HP ZBook Dock
Docking Station
Dockingstation

Manufacturer
HP Inc., Palo Alto, USA
In-house design
HP Industrial Design Team
Web
www.hp.com

This docking station is equipped with the Thunderbolt 3.1 universal interface, thus offering comprehensive connectivity. It is designed to be linked with mobile workstations, adding various connection ports and also providing an external power supply. Two 4K displays can be hooked up to the station while simultaneously charging a notebook. With a discreet and reserved design, it blends into any environment.

Die Dockingstation ist mit der Universalschnittstelle Thunderbolt 3.1 ausgestattet und bietet damit umfassende Konnektivität. Sie ist für den Anschluss an mobile Workstations konzipiert, erweitert diese um diverse Anschlüsse und gewährleistet zusätzlich eine externe Stromversorgung. So lassen sich beispielsweise zwei 4K-Displays anschließen, während gleichzeitig ein Notebook aufgeladen wird. Da das Design so zurückhaltend ist, fügt sie sich in jede Umgebung ein.

Statement by the jury
With its minimalist design, the ZBook Dock not only complements state-of-the-art IT devices but also asserts a visually reduced presence in the workplace.

Begründung der Jury
Mit seiner minimalistischen Gestaltung passt das ZBook Dock nicht nur zu aktuellen IT-Geräten, sondern ordnet sich auch am Arbeitsplatz optisch unter.

HP USB-C/USB Travel Dock
Reise-Dockingstation

Manufacturer
HP Inc., Palo Alto, USA
In-house design
HP Industrial Design Team
Web
www.hp.com

This handy travel dock, which is very lightweight at 95 grams, accommodates connector ports for VGA, HDMI, USB 2.0 and 3.0, as well as RJ-45. This for instance enables a larger screen to be connected. The dock itself is linked via USB C to a notebook; the USB cable can be placed flat in a recess at the bottom of the dock for easy transport. This not only ensures that the USB plug is protected but also achieves a closed dock form so that it may be conveniently stowed away.

In dieser handlichen, mit einem Gewicht von nur 95 Gramm sehr leichten Reise-Dockingstation sind die Anschlüsse VGA, HDMI, USB 2.0 und 3.0 sowie RJ-45 integriert. Dadurch lässt sich zum Beispiel ein größerer Bildschirm anschließen. Verbunden wird sie selbst per USB-C-Anschluss am Notebook, wobei das USB-Kabel für den Transport flach in eine Aussparung an der Unterseite der Dockingstation gelegt werden kann. So wird nicht nur der USB-Stecker geschützt, sondern eine geschlossene Form der Dockingstation erzielt, sodass sie leicht verstaut werden kann.

Statement by the jury
With its slim design and clever cable management, this compact dock is particularly suitable for mobile use.

Begründung der Jury
Diese kompakte Dockingstation eignet sich mit ihrer schlanken Form und dem cleveren Kabelmanagement besonders gut für die Mitnahme.

ES3000 V3
Enterprise-Class SSD
Enterprise-Klasse-SSD

Manufacturer
Huawei Technologies Co., Ltd.,
Shenzhen, China
In-house design
Yu Ni, Ganwei Li
Web
www.huawei.com

Thanks to an innovative LDPC algorithm, this SSD has a life cycle that is more than five times as long as conventional solid-state drives. At the same time, it was possible to reduce costs for core applications in this way. With its aluminium alloy case, the SSD is robust and reliable. The innovative heat dissipation mechanism not only reduces power consumption but also allows the memory to be used under demanding climatic conditions.

Statement by the jury
Heat dissipation via a deep groove structure at the bottom of the case is an outstanding technical solution offered by this SSD.

Dank eines innovativen LDPC-Algorithmus besitzt diese SSD eine mehr als fünfmal so hohe Lebensdauer im Vergleich zu herkömmlichen Solid-State-Drives. Gleichzeitig werden dadurch die Kosten für Kernanwendungen reduziert. Mit ihrem Gehäuse aus einer Aluminiumlegierung ist die SSD robust und zuverlässig. Die innovative Wärmeableitung verringert nicht nur den Stromverbrauch, sondern erlaubt auch den Einsatz des Speichers bei anspruchsvollen klimatischen Bedingungen.

Begründung der Jury
Intelligent gelöst ist bei dieser SSD vor allem die Ableitung der Wärme über die tiefe Rillenstruktur an der Unterseite des Gehäuses.

Visual Compute Accelerator
Add-In Card
Add-in-Karte

Manufacturer
Intel Corporation, Santa Clara, USA
In-house design
Design
Huge Design, San Francisco, USA
Web
www.intel.com
www.huge-design.com

The Visual Compute Accelerator is a computing add-in card for the commercial computer field that accelerates media and graphics performance on Xeon processor E5 platforms. It is characterised by a high-grade design highlighted in particular by its sophisticated aluminium finish with polished graphics and blacked-out PCB components. This conveys a subtle sense of refinement, while also underscoring the high performance and technology of its interior.

Statement by the jury
The Visual Compute Accelerator impresses with its elegant design, which is rather the exception when it comes to high-end solutions for the commercial field.

Der Visual Compute Accelerator ist eine Add-in-Karte für den kommerziellen Computerbereich, mit der Media- und Grafikleistungen von E5-Plattformen mit Xeon-Prozessor beschleunigt werden. Er zeichnet sich durch eine wertige Gestaltung aus, die vor allem durch sein edel anmutendes Aluminium-Finish mit polierten Schriftzügen und geschwärzten Leiterplatten geprägt ist. Dies vermittelt eine subtile Raffinesse und betont gleichzeitig die hohe Leistung und Technologie im Inneren.

Begründung der Jury
Der Visual Compute Accelerator beeindruckt mit seiner eleganten Formgebung, die bei High-End-Lösungen für den kommerziellen Bereich eher die Ausnahme ist.

KunLun 9032
Server

Manufacturer
Huawei Technologies Co., Ltd.,
Shenzhen, China
In-house design
Jules Parmentier, Changye Jia
Web
www.huawei.com

The KunLun 9032 is a 32-socket high-end server with a modular design. It can be flexibly configured and expanded to meet all demands. The server design maximises space utilisation. Moreover, the airflow is streamlined in an intelligent, low-noise way, thus increasing the cooling area and improving energy efficiency. Diagnosis and maintenance is controlled via a 7" touchscreen.

Statement by the jury
All equipment features of this server enable secure, efficient and maintenance-friendly operation.

KunLun 9032 ist ein 32-Sockel-High-End-Server mit einem modularen Aufbau. Er lässt sich flexibel konfigurieren und erweitern, um allen Anforderungen gerecht zu werden. Der Server ist so gestaltet, dass er den Platz bestmöglich ausnutzt. Zudem wird der Luftstrom intelligent und geräuscharm geführt, um den gekühlten Bereich zu vergrößern und die Energieeffizienz zu erhöhen. Diagnose und Wartung erfolgen über einen 7"-Touchscreen.

Begründung der Jury
Sämtliche Ausstattungsmerkmale dieses Servers ermöglichen einen sicheren, effizienten und wartungsfreundlichen Betrieb.

Chromé
Hard-Drive System
Festplattensystem

Manufacturer
Seagate Technology, Cupertino, USA
Design
Neil Poulton Industrial & Product Design
(Neil Poulton), Paris, France
Web
www.seagate.com
www.neilpoulton.com

Similar to a concept vehicle, the Chromé RAID system defines the future of its class. It combines innovative technology with an astonishing visionary design. The RAID 0 system is equipped with two SATA SSDs with 500 GB and m2 interface ports. This ensures high transmission rates of up to 940 MB/s. The hard-drive system connects to other devices with a USB C cable appropriate for the newest generation of computers.

Statement by the jury
This hard-drive system, with its purist design and optimally selected technology, is an eye-catcher on any desktop.

Ähnlich wie ein Konzeptfahrzeug definiert das RAID-System Chromé die Zukunft seiner Klasse. Es vereint eine innovative Technologie mit einer verblüffenden, visionären Gestaltung. Bestückt ist das RAID-0-System mit zwei SATA-SSDs mit 500 GB und m2-Schnittstellen. Dies gewährleistet hohe Übertragungsraten von bis zu 940 MB/s. Angeschlossen wird das Festplattensystem mit einem USB-C-Kabel, das für die neueste Generation von Computern geeignet ist.

Begründung der Jury
Mit seiner puristischen Gestaltung wird dieses technisch bestens ausgestattete Festplattensystem zum Blickfang auf jedem Schreibtisch.

Intenso 2,5" Memory Board
2,5" External Hard Drive
Externe 2,5"-Festplatte

Manufacturer
Intenso GmbH, Vechta, Germany
In-house design
Web
www.intenso.de

The external hard drive Intenso 2.5" Memory Board is a state-of-the-art memory solution for transferring and securing photos, videos, music and other data. Its housing features a contemporary design, is made of premium aluminium in an anthracite hue and is easily stowed away thanks to its small dimensions. The modest logo engraving, in combination with the blue LED display, is another optical highlight. Due to its compact design, the hard drive uses very little space on a desk.

Statement by the jury
With its aluminium enclosure, this hard drive renders a durable and classy impression. It is a modern memory solution and attractive accessory in one.

Die externe Festplatte Intenso 2,5" Memory Board ist eine moderne Speicherlösung zum Übertragen und Sichern von Fotos, Videos, Musik und anderen Daten. Sie besitzt ein zeitgemäß gestaltetes Gehäuse aus hochwertigem Aluminium in Anthrazit und lässt sich durch ihr kleines Format leicht verstauen. Die schlichte Logogravur in Verbindung mit der blauen LED-Anzeige ist ein weiteres optisches Highlight. Durch ihre kompakte Gestalt beansprucht die Festplatte auf dem Schreibtisch nur wenig Platz.

Begründung der Jury
Mit ihrem Gehäuse aus Aluminium wirkt diese Festplatte wertig und edel. Sie ist moderne Speicherlösung und attraktives Accessoire in einem.

Intenso 2,5" Memory Safe
2,5" External Hard Drive
Externe 2,5"-Festplatte

Manufacturer
Intenso GmbH, Vechta, Germany
In-house design
Web
www.intenso.de

This external hard drive, which comes in a handy format, protects all stored data with certified AES 256-bit hardware encryption. An individually selected PIN code of four to 12 digits ensures that all personal content on the hard drive is protected from unauthorised access, even when the drive gets lost. The PIN code may be entered, deleted and changed exclusively using the keypad integrated into the hard drive.

Statement by the jury
With its discreet design, this hard drive conveys durability, pointing to high security standards with regard to encryption.

Die externe Festplatte im handlichen Format schützt dank zertifizierter AES-256-Bit-Hardware-Verschlüsselung alle auf der Festplatte abgespeicherten Daten. Ein individuell wählbarer Zahlencode aus vier bis zwölf Ziffern stellt sicher, dass alle persönlichen Inhalte selbst bei Verlust der Festplatte vor fremdem Zugriff geschützt sind. Die Eingabe, Löschung und Änderung des Zahlencodes erfolgt ausschließlich über das in der Festplatte integrierte Tastenfeld.

Begründung der Jury
Die Festplatte strahlt mit ihrem reduziert gestalteten Gehäuse eine Robustheit aus, die auf die hohen Sicherheitsstandards in puncto Verschlüsselung verweist.

Innov8
External Hard Drive
Externe Festplatte

Manufacturer
Seagate Technology, Cupertino, USA
Design
Huge Design, San Francisco, USA
Web
www.seagate.com
www.huge-design.com

The Innov8 is an external hard drive with a large memory capacity of 8 TB. It connects to a PC and is sufficiently supplied with power via a single USB C cable. Its case is fashioned from high-grade aluminium, making the hard drive particularly durable. Its design features overlapping layers, which gives the hard drive a technical, industrial appearance.

Statement by the jury
The Innov8 hard drive impresses with its one-cable solution and is also a successful homage to industrial design.

Innov8 ist eine externe Festplatte mit einem großen Speichervolumen von 8 TB. Angeschlossen an den PC und ausreichend mit Strom versorgt wird sie über ein einziges USB-C-Kabel. Das Gehäuse besteht aus hochwertigem Aluminium, wodurch die Festplatte besonders widerstandsfähig ist. Es ist in übereinanderliegenden Schichten gestaltet und verleiht der Festplatte dadurch eine technische, industrielle Anmutung.

Begründung der Jury
Die Festplatte Innov8 punktet mit ihrer Ein-Kabel-Lösung und ist zudem eine gelungene Hommage an das Industrial Design.

LaCie Porsche Design Desktop Drive
External Hard Drive
Externe Festplatte

Manufacturer
Seagate Technology, Cupertino, USA
Design
Studio F. A. Porsche (Nadine Cornehl), Zell am See, Austria
Web
www.seagate.com
www.studiofaporsche.com

This external hard drive was developed in collaboration with Porsche and displays a functional, precious appearance thanks to its aluminium enclosure. Aside from serving as memory-storage device, it is also capable of charging the battery of a laptop when connected via a USB-C cable. During the charging process, the user still can access the data stored on the hard drive.

Statement by the jury
This stylishly designed hard drive convinces in its dual function as memory-storage and charging device for which just one cable is required.

Diese externe Festplatte wurde in Zusammenarbeit mit Porsche entwickelt und besitzt dank ihres Aluminiumgehäuses eine funktionale, edle Anmutung. Neben ihrer Eigenschaft als Datenspeicher bietet sie die Möglichkeit, zugleich den Akku eines Laptops aufzuladen, wenn sie mit einem USB-C-Kabel angeschlossen wird. Während des Ladevorgangs kann der Anwender noch auf Daten zugreifen, die auf der Festplatte abgelegt sind.

Begründung der Jury
Die stilvoll gestaltete Festplatte überzeugt mit ihrer Doppelfunktion als Datenspeicher und Ladegerät, für die lediglich ein Kabel benötigt wird.

LaCie Porsche Design Mobile Drive
External Hard Drive
Externe Festplatte

Manufacturer
Seagate Technology, Cupertino, USA
Design
Studio F. A. Porsche (Nadine Cornehl), Zell am See, Austria
Web
www.seagate.com
www.studiofaporsche.com

This external hard drive combines pioneering technology by LaCie with the distinctive Porsche design style. Its minimalist shaping is characterised by timeless elegance, impressively underscoring its functionality. The all-aluminium enclosure is at once lightweight and robust. Rounded corners, highly polished bevelled edges and a sandblast finish harmonically combine to create a stylish state-of-the-art design.

Statement by the jury
This external hard drive with its purist design renders a precious impression. The aluminium enclosure adds stability and elegance to the device.

Diese externe Festplatte verbindet die zukunftsweisende Technologie von LaCie mit dem unverwechselbaren Stil von Porsche. Ihre minimalistische Formgebung ist von einer zeitlosen Eleganz geprägt, was ihre Funktionalität eindrucksvoll unterstreicht. Das vollständig aus Aluminium gefertigte Gehäuse ist leicht und robust zugleich. Abgerundete Ecken, polierte, abgeschrägte Kanten und eine sandgestrahlte Oberfläche fügen sich harmonisch zu einem zeitgemäßen Stil zusammen.

Begründung der Jury
Mit ihrer puristischen Gestaltung wirkt diese Festplatte überaus edel. Das Aluminiumgehäuse verleiht ihr Stabilität und Eleganz.

SSD2GO PKT
Portable SSD
Tragbare SSD

Manufacturer
Angelbird Technologies GmbH, Lustenau, Austria
In-house design
Web
www.angelbird.com

The SSD2GO PKT is an external SSD with a casing precisely machined from one solid block of aluminium. This not only ensures excellent protection of the sophisticated electronic components but also gives the SSD a noble and timeless appearance. With its very compact shape, the drive weighs merely 50 grams; it is smaller than a credit card and only 9.5 mm thick. As it is equipped with USB 3.1 Type-C, it offers a high data transmission rate of 10 GB/s and is also optimally equipped for future standards.

Die SSD2GO PKT ist eine externe SSD mit einem Gehäuse, das aus einem massiven Block Aluminium präzise gefertigt wurde. Dies gewährleistet nicht nur einen hervorragenden Schutz der ausgefeilten Elektronik, sondern verleiht der SSD eine edle und zeitlose Anmutung. Mit seiner sehr kompakten Form wiegt das Laufwerk lediglich 50 Gramm, ist kleiner als eine Kreditkarte und nur 9,5 mm dick. Da es mit USB 3.1 Typ C ausgestattet ist, bietet es eine hohe Datenübertragungsrate von 10 GB/s und ist zudem für zukünftige Standards bestens ausgerüstet.

Statement by the jury
With this ultra-compact, innovative memory solution, mobile users can also benefit from the advantages of an SSD.

Begründung der Jury
Mit dieser ultrakompakten innovativen Speicherlösung können Anwender von den Vorteilen einer SSD auch unterwegs profitieren.

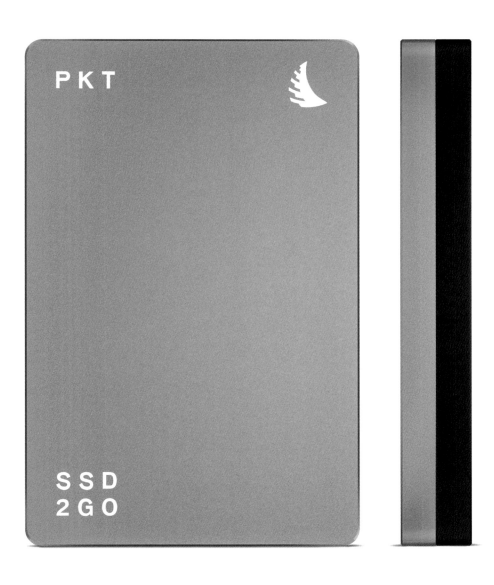

ThinkVision T2364t
Monitor

Manufacturer
Lenovo, Morrisville, North Carolina, USA
In-house design
Web
www.lenovo.com

The 23" ThinkVision T2364t monitor is equipped with an HD touchscreen with a nearly borderless viewing area. The slim geometric shape of the monitor is favourably highlighted by the tilt stand. Moreover, the stand ensures stable positioning and facilitates operation. The monitor features a practical integrated cable support and serves as an eye-catcher with its strong colouring. The anti-glare screen enables the user to optimally view content in all stand positions from 15–70 degrees.

Statement by the jury
The monitor is characterised by a well-conceived, state-of-the-art design, particularly benefiting from the very functional tilt stand.

Der 23"-Monitor ThinkVision T2364t ist mit einem HD-Touchscreen ausgestattet, der einen sehr schmalen Rand besitzt. Die schlanke, geometrische Form des Monitors kommt durch den Kippständer gut zur Geltung, zudem sorgt der Ständer für einen stabilen Stand und erleichtert die Bedienung. Integriert ist ein praktischer Kabelhalter, der mit seiner kräftigen Farbe die Blicke auf sich zieht. Der Bildschirm ist blendfrei, sodass die Inhalte in den möglichen Ständerpositionen von 15–70 Grad optimal betrachtet werden können.

Begründung der Jury
Der Monitor zeichnet sich durch eine durchdachte, zeitgemäße Gestaltung aus, die besonders von dem überaus funktionalen Kippständer profitiert.

ThinkVision X1
Monitor

Manufacturer
Lenovo, Morrisville, North Carolina, USA
In-house design
Web
www.lenovo.com

The ThinkVision X1 monitor has a nearly frameless 4K panel thanks to which the visible screen area could be laid out as generously as possible. A large number of video connections are included, as well as a USB C port, a sound system and a USB 3.0 hub. The tiltable stand has an almost delicate appearance, yet provides enough stability to safely support the 27" screen. The camera at the top can be swivelled and rotated by nearly 360 degrees to simplify the sharing of content.

Statement by the jury
This monitor impresses with its nearly frameless, high-resolution screen. Another highlight is the swivelling and rotating camera, giving rise to many possibilities.

Der Monitor ThinkVision X1 besitzt ein nahezu rahmenloses 4K-Panel, wodurch der sichtbare Bildschirmbereich so groß wie möglich angelegt werden konnte. Zahlreiche Videoanschlüsse sowie USB C sind ebenso vorhanden wie ein Soundsystem und ein USB-3.0-Hub. Der neigbare Standfuß wirkt nahezu grazil, bietet aber genügend Stabilität, um den 27"-Bildschirm sicher zu stützen. Seine an der Oberseite angebrachte Kamera lässt sich schwenken und fast um 360 Grad drehen, was das Teilen von Inhalten vereinfacht.

Begründung der Jury
Der Monitor überzeugt mit seinem fast randlosen, hochauflösenden Bildschirm. Weiteres Highlight ist die schwenk- und drehbare Kamera, die viele Möglichkeiten bietet.

ThinkVision X24 Pro
Monitor

Manufacturer
Lenovo, Morrisville, North Carolina, USA
In-house design
Web
www.lenovo.com

This 24" HD monitor combines a large number of equipment features in a device with a seamless design. It includes built-in speakers, an adjustable 3D camera with LED lighting, a USB 3.0 hub and a charging stand for mobile phones. These elements are all integrated through a consistent design, so that a desktop may remain as tidy as possible. Interface ports are thus accommodated in the stand, while speakers and a WiGig module are housed in the same bar.

Statement by the jury
Technical details are cleverly concealed in the monitor and stand, giving the ThinkVision X24 Pro an impeccable look.

Dieser 24"-HD-Monitor vereint zahlreiche Ausstattungsmerkmale in einem nahtlos wirkenden Gerät. Er verfügt beispielsweise über eingebaute Lautsprecher, eine verstellbare 3D-Kamera mit LED-Beleuchtung, einen USB-3.0-Hub und eine Ladestation für Mobiltelefone. Diese Elemente sind im Sinne einer konsistenten Gestaltung integriert, damit der Schreibtisch möglichst frei bleiben kann. So sind Schnittstellen im Standfuß untergebracht, Lautsprecher und WiGig-Modul befinden sich in einer gemeinsamen Leiste.

Begründung der Jury
Technische Details sind geschickt in Monitor und Standfuß verborgen und verleihen dem ThinkVision X24 Pro ein makelloses Aussehen.

Dell Medical Review 24
Monitor

Manufacturer
Dell Inc., Round Rock, Texas, USA
In-house design
Experience Design Group
Web
www.dell.com

The Medical Review 24 monitor was designed specifically to meet day-to-day demands in the health-care field. It features an anti-reflective, frameless glass front and a smooth, fully sealed enclosure capable of withstanding cleaning agents with a strong alcohol concentration. The device includes laterally movable power and OSD switches, which can also be operated with medical gloves. The screen can be easily tilted, swivelled and adjusted in height.

Statement by the jury
With its well-conceived design, the Medical Review 24 monitor is ideal for spaces with strict hygienic demands.

Der Monitor Medical Review 24 wurde speziell für die alltäglichen Bedürfnisse im Gesundheitsbereich entwickelt. Er verfügt über eine entspiegelte, rahmenlose Glasfront und ein fugenloses, vollständig abgedichtetes Gehäuse, das auch stark alkoholhaltige Reinigungsmittel verträgt. Das Gerät besitzt an der Seite herausfahrbare Netz- und OSD-Schalter, die mit Handschuhen bedient werden können. Der Bildschirm lässt sich neigen, schwenken und in der Höhe verstellen.

Begründung der Jury
Mit seiner durchdachten Gestaltung ist der Monitor Medical Review 24 ideal für Bereiche mit hohen hygienischen Anforderungen geeignet.

Dell UltraSharp 30
Ultra-HD 4K OLED Monitor

Manufacturer
Dell Inc., Round Rock, Texas, USA
In-house design
Experience Design Group
Web
www.dell.com

The UltraSharp 30 Ultra-HD 4K OLED monitor shows a clear aesthetic design focusing on screen content and allowing the monitor enclosure to integrate into the background. It was developed for professional users who require realistic screen displays, a wide colour gamut and high-end performance. The monitor is available either with a height-adjustable stand or a swivel arm. Both are designed in such a way that nothing distracts from the screen content.

Statement by the jury
The striking stand highlights the technical aspects of this product and, at the same time, provides a solid, secure standing position for the monitor.

Der Ultra-HD-4K-OLED-Monitor UltraSharp 30 zeigt eine ästhetisch klare Gestaltung, die das Gehäuse zugunsten des Bildschirminhalts in den Hintergrund treten lässt. Er wurde für professionelle Anwender entwickelt, die eine wirklichkeitsgetreue Darstellung, eine hochwertige Farbwiedergabe und High-End-Performance benötigen. Der Monitor ist entweder mit einem höhenverstellbaren Fuß oder mit einem Schwenkarm erhältlich. Beides ist so gestaltet, dass nichts vom Bildschirminhalt ablenkt.

Begründung der Jury
Der markante Fuß betont die technische Seite des Produkts und sorgt gleichzeitig für einen soliden, sicheren Stand des Monitors.

Dell UltraSharp
InfinityEdge Displays
Monitors

Manufacturer
Dell Inc., Round Rock, Texas, USA
In-house design
Experience Design Group
Web
www.dell.com

With a thin circumferential bezel, the new UltraSharp InfinityEdge displays are ideal for multi-monitor setups. They are mounted on an adjustable arm so that they can be – depending on the working situation – optimally adjusted as an individual device or in group settings. The monitors are available in 24" und 27" displays. Their appearance is characterised by high-grade surfaces, which also include the injection-moulded enclosure parts and elegant back cover with anti-scratch metallic look.

Statement by the jury
These monitors have a clear and tidy appearance from all sides, always creating a good impression independent from the swivelling position.

Mit einem dünnen umlaufenden Rahmen eignen sich die neuen UltraSharp-InfinityEdge-Monitore ideal für Multi-Monitor-Anordnungen. Sie sind an einem verstellbaren Arm montiert, sodass sich mehrere Monitore – je nach Arbeitssituation – optimal einzeln oder in Gruppen ausrichten lassen. Die Monitore sind in 24" und 27" erhältlich. Ihr Erscheinungsbild ist geprägt von hochwertigen Oberflächen, die auch die Spritzguss-Gehäuseteile und die elegante Rückenabdeckung im kratzfesten Metallic-Look umfassen.

Begründung der Jury
Diese Monitore bieten von allen Seiten ein aufgeräumtes Erscheinungsbild. Damit machen sie stets eine gute Figur, ganz gleich, in welche Position sie geschwenkt werden.

U Surfing
Curved Display
Gekrümmter Bildschirm

Manufacturer
TPV Technology Group,
Top Victory Electronics Co., Ltd., New Taipei, Taiwan
In-house design
Yao-Hsing Tsai, Li-Shwu Fu, Yi-Ting Chung, Doc Ho
Web
www.tpvholdings.com

With its 21:9 aspect ratio and curvature of 1800R, the U Surfing curved display provides high viewing comfort. Instead of a conventional interface, it features a magnetic platform in which a smartphone can be placed for wireless charging. This also enables the user to transmit audio and video files or to access smartphone functions. The control for bass and treble is accommodated in the unconventionally shaped stand. The display can also be connected to a keyboard and mouse.

Mit seinem Seitenverhältnis von 21:9 und der Krümmung von 1800R liefert der gekrümmte Bildschirm U Surfing einen hohen Sehkomfort. Statt einer traditionellen Schnittstelle besitzt er eine magnetische Plattform, in die ein Smartphone gelegt wird, um es kabellos aufzuladen. Zusätzlich kann der Nutzer so Audio- und Videodateien übertragen oder auf die Smartphone-Funktionen zugreifen. Im eigenwillig geformten Standfuß befindet sich die Einstellung für Bässe und Höhen, zudem kann der Bildschirm mit Tastatur und Maus verbunden werden.

Statement by the jury
The U Surfing display convinces with its distinct stand, which conveys high quality and renders an impression that is both precious and solid.

Begründung der Jury
U Surfing besticht mit seinem eigenständigen Standfuß. Er vermittelt eine hohe Wertigkeit und wirkt edel und solide zugleich.

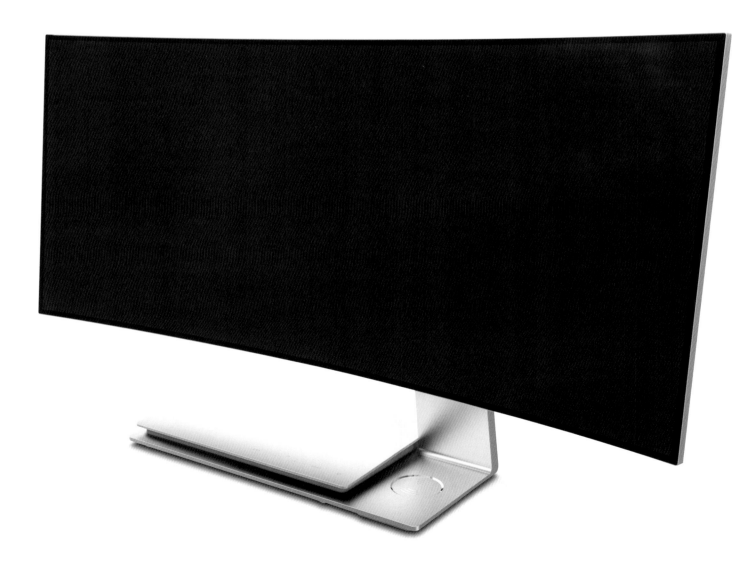

34UC98
Curved Monitor
Gekrümmter Monitor

Manufacturer
LG Electronics Inc., Seoul, South Korea
In-house design
Sooyoung Park, Sunghoon Oh,
Jaeneung Jung
Web
www.lg.com

This 34" ultra-wide curved monitor possesses an ideal curve ratio of 1900R. Despite the very large screen, it provides the user with an optimum viewing angle and level of focus on the screen while preventing screen distortion along the edges. To avoid distraction, all unnecessary decorative elements were eliminated. The stand is equipped with a height-tilt mechanism, enabling easy adjustment to the desired position.

Statement by the jury
The 34UC98 curved monitor rests on a solid stand with appealing rounded contours, offering a large number of adjustment options.

Dieser 34"-Ultra-Wide-Curved-Monitor besitzt einen idealen Krümmungsradius von 1900R. Dadurch bietet sich dem Benutzer trotz des sehr großen Bildschirms ein Optimum bei Betrachtungswinkel und Fokussierung des Bildes, ohne Verzerrung an den Bildschirmrändern. Um Ablenkung zu vermeiden, wurde auf unnötige Verzierungen verzichtet. Der Standfuß ist mit einem Höhen- und Schwenkmechanismus ausgestattet, wodurch der Bildschirm leicht in die gewünschte Position ausgerichtet werden kann.

Begründung der Jury
Der Bildschirm 34UC98 ruht auf einem soliden Standfuß mit ansprechender Rundung, der vielfältige Einstellmöglichkeiten bietet.

Acer XR342CK
Monitor

Manufacturer
Acer Incorporated, New Taipei, Taiwan
In-house design
Web
www.acer.com

An unmistakably shaped aluminium stand gives the XR342CK UltraWide monitor a striking presence, paired with unobtrusive lightness. The stand is both solid and slim and thus has an attractive appeal from all sides. A cable management slot helps the user to discreetly stow away additional cables. The monitor can be tilted from –5 to 35 degrees and shifted up and down by 13 cm to achieve the most comfortable viewing position.

Statement by the jury
The stand of the monitor unites supposed opposites in an ingenious way. It appears airy, rigid, noble and sporty, all at the same time.

Der unverwechselbar geformte Standfuß aus Aluminium verleiht dem UltraWide-Monitor XR342CK eine hohe Präsenz, gepaart mit einer unaufdringlichen Leichtigkeit. Der Standfuß ist ebenso solide wie schlank und erscheint damit von allen Seiten attraktiv. Eine Aussparung hilft dem Anwender, zusätzliche Kabel diskret zu verstauen. Der Monitor kann von –5 bis 35 Grad geneigt und um 13 cm nach oben und unten geschoben werden, um die für den Betrachter angenehmste Position einzunehmen.

Begründung der Jury
Der Standfuß des Monitors führt geschickt vermeintliche Gegensätze zusammen. Er wirkt gleichzeitig luftig und robust, edel und sportlich.

Philips Brilliance Curved UltraWide LCD Display

Manufacturer
MMD Philips Displays TPV Technology,
New Taipei City, Taiwan
Design
Philips Design, Eindhoven, Netherlands
Web
www.philips.com

The Philips Brilliance Curved UltraWide LCD Display features DTS-certified speakers which are integrated into the centre of the stand. Viewers can immerse themselves fully in the visual and acoustic experience. The self-contained arc design of the stand and the innovative surfaces underscore the elegant appearance of this monitor, which enables high productivity both at home and at work.

Statement by the jury
The speaker is integrated into the stand in such a way that both parts form a harmonious whole in terms of design and function.

Der Philips Brilliance Curved UltraWide LCD-Monitor besitzt DTS-zertifizierte Lautsprecher, die im Zentrum des Standfußes eingebettet sind. Dadurch kann der Betrachter visuell und klanglich vollständig in das Geschehen eintauchen. Die eigenständige Bogenform des Standfußes und die innovativen Oberflächen unterstreichen die elegante Anmutung des Monitors, der zu Hause und am Arbeitsplatz für eine hohe Produktivität sorgt.

Begründung der Jury
Der Lautsprecher ist harmonisch in den Standfuß integriert, wodurch eine gestalterische wie funktionale Einheit entsteht.

MacBook
Notebook

Manufacturer
Apple, Cupertino, USA
In-house design
Web
www.apple.com

Every component of the new MacBook has been meticulously redesigned to create a product that only weighs 900 grams, with a thickness of merely 13.1 mm. It features an impressive, very slim 12" Retina display for razor-sharp reproduction of content. The full-size keyboard is also extremely thin; thanks to innovative key mechanics, it has a fast response time and offers better typing control. The Force Touch trackpad recognises pressure and delivers tactile feedback, comparable to a mouse click. This simplifies interaction with the notebook.

Jede Komponente des neuen MacBooks wurde sorgfältig überarbeitet, um ein Produkt zu schaffen, das lediglich 900 Gramm wiegt und nur 13,1 mm dick ist. Es besitzt ein beeindruckendes, sehr schlankes 12"-Retina-Display, auf dem Inhalte gestochen scharf dargestellt werden. Auch die vollwertige Tastatur ist extrem dünn und bietet dank der innovativen Tastenmechanik eine schnelle Reaktionszeit und bessere Kontrolle beim Tippen. Das Force Touch Trackpad erkennt Druck und liefert ein haptisches Feedback, das vergleichbar mit einem Mausklick ist. Dies erleichtert die Interaktion mit dem Notebook.

Statement by the jury
The MacBook combines a design consistently geared to minimal weight and slimness with high-grade functionality attuned to the individual user.

Begründung der Jury
Das MacBook vereint eine konsequent auf geringes Gewicht und Schlankheit ausgerichtete Gestaltung mit einer hochwertigen, ganz auf den Nutzer abgestimmten Funktionalität.

Surface Book
Three-in-One Notebook
3-in-1-Notebook

Manufacturer
Microsoft Corporation, Redmond, USA
In-house design
Web
www.microsoft.com/surface

The Surface Book is a very thin notebook with a special hinge that allows it to be transformed into a clipboard or tablet. The touch display is optimally aligned for input with the included stylus and offers space for creative tasks. The design of the notebook is functional, with the characteristic hinge as a striking feature. It is equipped with four rotational points to allow the notebook screen to bend easily and steadily all the way around to become a clipboard folio. As an additional option, the keyboard may be detached to operate the device in tablet mode. Detaching and reattaching the keyboard is achieved at the simple push of a button.

Das Surface Book ist ein sehr dünnes Notebook mit einem besonderen Scharnier, das die Verwandlung in ein Notizbuch oder Tablet erlaubt. Das Touchdisplay ist bestens auf die Eingabe mit dem mitgelieferten Stift abgestimmt und gibt Raum für kreative Aufgaben. Die Gestaltung des Notebooks ist funktional. Einen Großteil davon nimmt das charakteristische Scharnier ein, das mit vier Rotationspunkten ausgestattet ist, um den Bildschirm leicht und stetig umzuklappen und das Notebook wie ein Notizbuch zu verwenden. Als weitere Option kann die Tastatur abgenommen werden, um in den Tablet-Modus zu gelangen. Um die Tastatur abzunehmen und wieder anzufügen, genügt ein Knopfdruck.

Statement by the jury
The Surface Book benefits from its hinge, presenting itself as a self-contained solution. The hinge is a striking design feature and eminently functional.

Begründung der Jury
Das Surface Book profitiert von seinem Scharnier, das sich als eigenständige Lösung präsentiert. Es ist ein hervorstechendes gestalterisches Merkmal und überaus funktional.

HP Elitebook 1040 G3
Notebook

Manufacturer
HP Inc., Palo Alto, USA
In-house design
HP Industrial Design Team
Web
www.hp.com

With a thickness of merely 16 mm, the HP Elitebook 1040 G3 is a very thin 14" notebook for business users. The elegant form, tapering from front to back, is a design feature underscoring its high performance and mobility. Despite its slimness, the notebook is exceedingly durable thanks to the materials selected: aluminium is combined with a thin, lightweight magnesium bottom cover, thus enabling the unit to withstand impact and critical environmental conditions. Additional features are the high-grade audio components, a clickpad with gesture recognition and a brilliant HD display.

Das HP Elitebook 1040 G3 ist mit seinen 16 mm ein sehr dünnes 14"-Notebook für Business-Anwender. Die sich nach vorne verjüngende Gestalt lässt es elegant wirken und verdeutlicht seine hohe Leistungs-fähigkeit und Mobilität. Dank der verwen-deten Materialien ist das Notebook trotz seiner geringen Dicke äußerst widerstands-fähig: Aluminium wird mit einer dünnen, leichten Magnesium-Abdeckung an der Unterseite kombiniert, damit es Stöße und widrige Umwelteinflüsse aushält. Weitere Merkmale sind hochwertige Audiokompo-nenten, ein Clickpad mit Gestenerkennung aus Glas und ein brillantes HD-Display.

Statement by the jury
This notebook shows that elegance and robustness can go hand in hand in an impressive way, making it an ideal work-ing device for business users.

Begründung der Jury
Dieses Notebook zeigt eindrucksvoll, dass Eleganz und Robustheit Hand in Hand gehen können. Für Business-Anwender ist es damit ein ideales Arbeitsgerät.

HP EliteBook 840 G3
Notebook

Manufacturer
HP Inc., Palo Alto, USA
In-house design
HP Industrial Design Team
Web
www.hp.com

The EliteBook 840 G3 is a very light-weight notebook in its class, geared towards performance and mobility. With its all-magnesium body, it weighs only 1.5 kg yet offers all connections required so that no additional dongles are necessary. A precision-stamped aluminium keyboard deck conveys high quality, while the splashproof keyboard provides the durability required. Two premium speakers facilitate an outstanding audio experience, which is of particular advantage at conferences. These speakers are just as strategically positioned as the microphone and the fingerprint sensor.

Das EliteBook 840 G3 ist ein für seine Klasse sehr leichtes Notebook, das auf Leistung und Mobilität ausgelegt ist. Mit seinem Gehäuse aus Magnesium wiegt es lediglich 1,5 kg, verfügt aber über alle notwendigen Anschlüsse, sodass keine zusätzlichen Dongles nötig sind. Ein präzise gestanztes Tastatur-Deck vermittelt eine hohe Wertigkeit, während die spritzwassergeschützte Tastatur für die notwendige Widerstandsfähigkeit sorgt. Zwei Premium-Lautsprecher ermöglichen ein hervorragendes Audio-Erlebnis, was besonders bei Konferenzen von Vorteil ist. Sie sind ebenso überlegt platziert wie das Mikrofon und der Fingerabdruck-Sensor.

Statement by the jury
With its comprehensive equipment oriented to the business workday, the HP EliteBook 840 G3 leaves nothing to be desired.

Begründung der Jury
Mit seiner umfangreichen, am Business-Alltag orientierten Ausstattung lässt das HP EliteBook 840 G3 keine Wünsche offen.

HP Elitebook Folio G1
Notebook

Manufacturer
HP Inc., Palo Alto, USA
In-house design
HP Industrial Design Team
Web
www.hp.com

This notebook is particularly suitable for mobile business professionals who frequently use their device in conference settings. Its display can be rotated by 180 degrees, simplifying presentations and the sharing of content. In addition, it is equipped with embedded Skype conference keys, high-grade speakers and specially tuned microphones. All this is accommodated in a very slim, robust aluminium enclosure with a thickness of only 12 mm and a weight of less than 1 kg. The tasteful, diamond-cut edges of the input area provide a touch of elegance.

Insbesondere für Geschäftsreisende, die ihr Gerät häufig in Konferenzen einsetzen, ist dieses Notebook sehr gut geeignet. Sein Display lässt sich um 180 Grad aufklappen, was das Teilen von Inhalten und das Präsentieren vereinfacht. Zusätzlich ist es mit gesonderten Skype-Tasten, hochwertigen Lautsprechern und besonders abgestimmten Mikrofonen ausgestattet. All dies findet Platz in einem sehr schlanken, lediglich 12 mm dicken Gehäuse aus robustem Aluminium, das insgesamt weniger als 1 kg wiegt. Für einen Hauch von Eleganz sorgen die geschmackvollen diamantgeschliffenen Kanten des Eingabebereichs.

Statement by the jury
The HP Elitebook Folio G1 is so thin and lightweight that it can be conveniently used while working outside the office. At the same time, it is both stylish and durable.

Begründung der Jury
Das HP Elitebook Folio G1 ist so dünn und leicht, dass es hervorragend auch außerhalb des Büros genutzt werden kann. Dabei zeigt es gleichermaßen Stil wie Haltbarkeit.

HP Envy 13
Notebook

Manufacturer
HP Inc., Palo Alto, USA
In-house design
HP Industrial Design Team
Web
www.hp.com

With a thickness of merely 12.9 mm, the HP Envy 13 is currently one of the thinnest notebooks. It is fashioned from aluminium, renders an elegant and noble impression, yet is very durable at the same time. One of its specific features is the hinge slightly lifting the notebook at the back when it is opened, positioning the keyboard for comfortable input. At the same time, this ensures more efficient heat dissipation. The HP Envy 13 includes a sixth-generation Intel processor, a full HD display, an SSD with up to 512 GB and a large number of ports for external devices.

Mit seiner Dicke von nur 12,9 mm ist das HP Envy 13 derzeit eines der flachsten Notebooks. Es besteht aus Aluminium, wirkt dadurch elegant und edel, ist aber gleichzeitig überaus widerstandsfähig. Eines seiner besonderen Merkmale ist das Scharnier, das das Notebook beim Öffnen hinten leicht anhebt und die Tastatur für eine bequeme Eingabe positioniert. Gleichzeitig kann dadurch die Wärme effizienter abgeführt werden. Das HP Envy 13 besitzt einen Intel-Prozessor der sechsten Generation, ein Full-HD-Display, eine SSD mit bis zu 512 GB und zahlreiche Anschlüsse für externe Geräte.

Statement by the jury
This very slim notebook combines excellent performance characteristics with a classy design. The hinge is both shapely and functional.

Begründung der Jury
Dieses sehr schlanke Notebook vereint eine ausgezeichnete Leistung mit einer edlen Anmutung. Das Scharnier ist formschön wie funktional.

HP Pavilion x360
Convertible Notebook

Manufacturer
HP Inc., Palo Alto, USA
In-house design
HP Industrial Design Team
Web
www.hp.com

The hinge of the HP Pavilion x360 convertible notebook holds the display in such a way that it can be steplessly angled from a closed to a completely opened position. This gives the user a large number of possibilities for operating the device in stand, tent, tablet or notebook mode, enjoying multimedia content or communicating with friends. The hard drive has a memory capacity of up to 1 TB, providing enough storage space for image and video files. Moreover, the notebook is equipped with a large number of ports for connecting external devices like printers or monitors.

Beim Convertible Notebook HP Pavilion x360 hält ein Scharnier das Display so, dass es stufenlos von einer geschlossenen bis zu einer komplett geöffneten Position angewinkelt werden kann. Dies eröffnet vielfältige Möglichkeiten, um z. B. im Stand-, Zelt-, Tablet- oder Notebook-Modus zu arbeiten, Multimedia-Inhalte zu genießen oder mit Freunden zu kommunizieren. Die bis zu 1 TB große Festplatte bietet genügend Platz auch für Bild- und Videodateien, zudem ist das Notebook mit zahlreichen Ports ausgestattet, um externe Geräte wie Drucker oder Bildschirme anzuschließen.

Statement by the jury
Whether used for work or entertainment, this notebook is so versatile and powerful that it is suitable for any kind of application area.

Begründung der Jury
Ob für die Arbeit oder die Unterhaltung, dieses Notebook ist so vielseitig und leistungsstark, dass es für jede Anwendung geeignet ist.

HP Pavilion x2
Convertible Notebook

Manufacturer
HP Inc., Palo Alto, USA
In-house design
HP Industrial Design Team
Web
www.hp.com

With its detachable keyboard, the HP Pavilion x2 offers the functionality of a notebook and tablet in one unit. Display and keyboard are connected by a durable magnetic hinge. The magnetic forces are so strong that the two elements stay together even if the user lifts the device at the display. The four variants – notebook, tablet, stand and tent mode – can be easily set up by separating or connecting and angling both the display and keyboard in the arrangement desired. In notebook mode, the fully fledged keyboard fosters a comfortable writing experience.

Mit seiner abnehmbaren Tastatur bietet das HP Pavilion x2 die Funktionalität eines Notebooks und Tablets in einem. Display und Tastatur sind mit einem robusten magnetischen Scharnier verbunden. Sein Magnet ist so stark, dass er beide Elemente zusammenhält, selbst wenn das Gerät nur am Display hochgehoben wird. Die vier Varianten – Notebook-, Tablet-, Stand- und Zelt-Modus – lassen sich einfach einrichten, indem Display und Tastatur getrennt und nach Wunsch zusammengesteckt und angewinkelt werden. Im Notebook-Modus gewährleistet die vollwertige Tastatur eine angenehme Schreiberfahrung.

Statement by the jury
The HP Pavilion x2 is a versatile device that can be individually adjusted in a simple and reliable way thanks to the clever magnet hinge mechanism.

Begründung der Jury
Das HP Pavilion x2 ist ein vielseitiges Gerät, das dank des cleveren Magnetmechanismus einfach und zuverlässig individuell angepasst werden kann.

HP Probook 11 G2 Education Edition
Notebook

Manufacturer
HP Inc., Palo Alto, USA
In-house design
HP Industrial Design Team
Web
www.hp.com

This notebook was conceived for students whose environment poses specific challenges to working devices. The edges of the 20-mm-thin HP Probook 11 G2 Educational Edition are wrapped in green or black rubber to absorb impact. The clean control panel features spill-resistant keys to withstand any mishap without difficulty. The screen can be folded out by 180 degrees, making collaborative work a pleasurable experience. With its rounded edges and slim shape, the notebook is easy to stow away in a bag.

Dieses Notebook wurde für Lernende konzipiert, deren Umfeld oftmals besondere Bedingungen an Arbeitsgeräte stellt. Die Kanten des 20 mm dünnen HP Probook 11 G2 Education Edition sind mit grünem oder schwarzem Gummi eingefasst, wodurch Stöße abgefangen werden. Das aufgeräumte Bedienfeld besitzt spritzgeschützte Tasten, sodass auch das eine oder andere Missgeschick problemlos verkraftet wird. Der Bildschirm lässt sich um 180 Grad aufklappen, was das Arbeiten mit anderen zum Vergnügen macht. Mit seinen gerundeten Kanten und der schlanken Form lässt sich das Notebook leicht in einer Tasche verstauen.

Statement by the jury
This robust, stylish notebook meets the special demands of a notebook for students in an exemplary way.

Begründung der Jury
Dieses robuste und formschöne Notebook wird den speziellen Anforderungen an ein Notebook für Schüler oder Studenten in vorbildlicher Weise gerecht.

HP Spectre x360
Convertible Notebook

Manufacturer
HP Inc., Palo Alto, USA
In-house design
HP Industrial Design Team
Web
www.hp.com

With its 360-degree hinge the Spectre x360 is particularly suitable for people who need a notebook that can be used seamlessly at home as well as in the workplace. As such, it may be used, for example, as a tablet on the go or for viewing movies in an upright position. Other options are provided by the tent mode for games and the notebook mode for work. With its powerful processor and tremendous versatility in switching between notebook and tablet modes, the Spectre x360 embodies a true convergence of culture, technology and design.

Mit seinem 360-Grad-Scharnier ist das Spectre x360 besonders gut für Menschen geeignet, die ein Notebook benötigen, das sich nahtlos sowohl zu Hause als auch am Arbeitsplatz verwenden lässt. So kann es beispielsweise als Tablet für unterwegs oder im Stand-Modus zum Betrachten von Filmen eingesetzt werden. Weitere Möglichkeiten bieten der Zelt-Modus für Spiele und der Notebook-Modus für die Arbeit. Mit seinem leistungsstarken Prozessor und seiner enormen Vielseitigkeit, mit der es zwischen Notebook- und Tablet-Modi wechselt, verkörpert das Spectre x360 eine echte Konvergenz von Kultur, Technologie und Design.

Statement by the jury
Its special hinge turns the Spectre x360 into an elegant multitalent capable of displaying content in any desired form.

Begründung der Jury
Sein besonderes Scharnier macht das Spectre x360 zu einem eleganten Multitalent, mit dem sich Inhalte in jeder gewünschten Weise darstellen lassen.

HP ZBook 15 G3
Mobile Workstation

Manufacturer
HP Inc., Palo Alto, USA
In-house design
HP Industrial Design Team
Web
www.hp.com

The HP ZBook 15 G3 mobile workstation offers state-of-the-art technology in an elegant design. A very powerful mobile computer with a full range of functions was developed for demanding users. With a weight of 2 kg, the 18-mm-thin device is optimally laid out for mobile professional use. Thanks to an aluminium-magnesium die-cast chassis, it is so robust that it easily masters everyday work challenges. Depending on the intended purpose, different configurations are available with regard to processor, memory storage or screen.

Die mobile Workstation HP ZBook 15 G3 bietet zeitgemäße Technologien und eine elegante Formgebung. Der sehr leistungsfähige mobile Computer mit vollem Funktionsumfang wurde für anspruchsvolle Anwender entwickelt. Mit einem Gewicht ab 2 kg ist das 18 mm flache Gerät ideal für den mobilen professionellen Einsatz geeignet. Dank des Aluminium-Magnesium-Druckguss-Gehäuses ist es darüber hinaus so robust, dass es Belastungen im Arbeitsalltag problemlos standhält. Je nach Einsatzzweck sind unterschiedliche Konfigurationen hinsichtlich Prozessor, Speicher oder Bildschirm möglich.

Statement by the jury
With its numerous intelligent functions and slim design, this workstation is a stylish, high-grade and very mobile working device.

Begründung der Jury
Mit seinen zahlreichen intelligenten Funktionen und dem schlanken Design ist das ZBook 15 G3 ein hochwertiges wie auch stilvolles und sehr mobiles Arbeitsgerät.

HP ZBook Studio G3
Mobile Workstation

Manufacturer
HP Inc., Palo Alto, USA
In-house design
HP Industrial Design Team
Web
www.hp.com

The ZBook Studio G3 is a workstation equipped with high-performance components laid out for computing-intensive applications as required, for instance, in the creative industry or in construction. Machined from one solid aluminium block, the chassis is only 18 mm thick yet particularly durable. The premium technical equipment is underscored by a sophisticated etch pattern on the display cover and the diamond-cut edge around the perimeter of the enclosure. The 4K-resolution display presents content with high brilliance. The large ventilation grille at the base provides sufficient cooling for the workstation.

Das ZBook Studio G3 ist ein mit leistungsfähigen Komponenten ausgestatteter Computer, der für rechenintensive Anwendungen ausgelegt ist, wie sie beispielsweise in der Kreativwirtschaft oder in der Konstruktion benötigt werden. Das aus einem Aluminiumblock gefräste Gehäuse ist nur 18 mm dick, aber dennoch besonders haltbar. Verdeutlicht wird die vorzügliche technische Ausstattung durch das raffinierte Muster auf der Display-Abdeckung und die Kante mit Diamantschliff, die sich um das Gehäuse zieht. Das Display mit 4K-Auflösung stellt Inhalte mit einer hohen Brillanz dar. Das große Lüftungsgitter an der Unterseite sorgt für die ausreichende Kühlung des Geräts.

Statement by the jury
This mobile workstation features outstanding technical equipment, ensuring that demanding tasks may be accomplished anywhere.

Begründung der Jury
Diese mobile Workstation besitzt eine ausgezeichnete technische Ausstattung, damit anspruchsvolle Aufgaben überall bewältigt werden können.

ASUS Chromebook C202SA
Notebook

Manufacturer
ASUSTeK Computer Inc., Taipei, Taiwan
In-house design
Mary Hsi
Web
www.asus.com

The Asus Chromebook C202SA with the Chrome OS operating system is a notebook that has been designed for the educational field. It is equipped with scratch-resistant, rounded edges and absorbs shock and impact comparable to a drop height of 90 cm. The keyboard markings have a comfortably large size, and the tactile feedback of the keys provides a secure typing feel. The matt screen of the notebook prevents irritating reflections, which is of particular advantage when experiencing unfavourable lighting conditions.

Statement by the jury
The Asus Chromebook C202SA has a congenial appearance and is so robust that it is particularly suitable for educational purposes.

Das Asus Chromebook C202SA mit dem Betriebssystem Chrome OS ist ein für den Bildungsbereich entwickeltes Notebook. Es ist mit kratzfesten, gerundeten Kanten ausgestattet und verkraftet Stöße vergleichbar einer Fallhöhe von 90 cm. Die Schrift auf der Tastatur ist angenehm groß und das taktile Feedback der Tasten sorgt für ein sicheres Tippgefühl. Das matte Display macht das Notebook unempfindlich gegen Spiegelungen, was besonders bei ungünstigen Lichtverhältnissen von Vorteil ist.

Begründung der Jury
Das Asus Chromebook C202SA zeigt eine sympathische Anmutung und ist gleichzeitig so robust, dass es besonders gut für schulische Zwecke geeignet ist.

ASUS X556/X456/X756 Series
Notebooks

Manufacturer
ASUSTeK Computer Inc., Taipei, Taiwan
In-house design
Web
www.asus.com

User-friendliness, sustainability and cost reduction were the most important factors during the development of this notebook series. In order to enhance the working experience, a streamlined look was conceived for the housing. The surfaces are made in such a way that they show an elegant gloss or premium brushed metallic finish, while simultaneously reducing the visibility of fingerprints and enabling easy cleaning. The unibody housing is recyclable and does without toxic paint.

Statement by the jury
Design and equipment are optimally harmonised in the X Series notebooks. Another plus point is the consideration of environmental concerns.

Bei der Entwicklung dieser Notebooks standen Benutzerfreundlichkeit, Nachhaltigkeit und Kostenreduzierung im Vordergrund. Um das Arbeiten angenehmer zu gestalten, wurden die Gehäuse stromlinienförmig gehalten. Die Oberflächen sind so beschaffen, dass sie einerseits elegant glänzen oder eine edel gebürstete Metalllackierung zeigen, andererseits können sie leicht gereinigt werden und Fingerabdrücke sind kaum sichtbar. Das Unibody-Gehäuse lässt sich recyceln und kommt ohne giftige Lackierung aus.

Begründung der Jury
Gestaltung und Ausstattung sind bei den Notebooks der X-Serie bestens aufeinander abgestimmt. Ein Pluspunkt ist zudem die Beachtung des Umweltgedankens.

ASUS Zenbook UX330
Notebook

Manufacturer
ASUSTeK Computer Inc., Taipei, Taiwan
In-house design
Web
www.asus.com

The innovative Asus Zenbook UX330 offers the performance and versatility of a Core I processor and the high mobility of the Zenbook series. With ten hours of battery life, the all-aluminium notebook measures barely 13.6 mm at its thickest point. The unibody construction consists of an anodised, sandblasted finish with an attractive brushed coating. Polished gold edges create an elegant contrast to the deep-blue exterior.

Statement by the jury
The carefully selected surface textures and decorative gold edges convey the high quality of this notebook in an unobtrusive way.

Das innovative Asus Zenbook UX330 bietet die Leistung und Vielseitigkeit eines Core-I-Prozessors und die hohe Mobilität der Zenbook-Serie. Mit zehn Stunden Akkulaufzeit misst das vollständig aus Aluminium bestehende Notebook an der dicksten Stelle nur 13,6 mm. Die Unibody-Konstruktion besteht aus einer eloxierten, sandgestrahlten Oberfläche mit einer attraktiven gebürsteten Beschichtung. Polierte Goldkanten bilden zudem einen eleganten Kontrast zum dunkelblauen Gehäuse.

Begründung der Jury
Die sorgfältig ausgewählten Oberflächentexturen und dekorativen Goldkanten vermitteln unaufdringlich die hohe Wertigkeit dieses Notebooks.

ASUS GL502 Series
Gaming Notebooks

Manufacturer
ASUSTeK Computer Inc., Taipei, Taiwan
In-house design
Web
www.asus.com

The GL502 series disproves the inherent notion that high-performance gaming notebooks must be heavy. It was conceived for powerful gaming situations yet is mobile enough for transport. The chassis is furnished with fluorescent orange elements to emphasise a vibrant attitude towards life. The cooling system ensures maximal cooling efficiency to provide the stability required for intense gaming marathons.

Statement by the jury
This notebook impresses with attractive contrasts ranging from deep black to fluorescent orange, conveying dynamics and gaming enjoyment.

Die GL502-Serie widerlegt den Eindruck, dass leistungsstarke Gaming-Notebooks schwer sein müssen. Es wurde so konzipiert, dass es einerseits über eine auf das Gaming ausgelegte Leistung verfügt und andererseits mobil genug für den Transport ist. Das Gehäuse ist mit fluoreszierenden Elementen in Orange versehen, um eine positive Haltung zum Leben zu betonen. Das Kühlsystem gewährleistet maximale Kühleffizienz und bietet damit die notwendige Beständigkeit für intensive Spielemarathons.

Begründung der Jury
Das Notebook beeindruckt mit attraktiv gesetzten Kontrasten zwischen tiefem Schwarz und leuchtendem Orange, die Dynamik und Freude am Spiel vermitteln.

ASUS GX700VO
Gaming Notebook

Manufacturer
ASUSTeK Computer Inc., Taipei, Taiwan
In-house design
Web
www.asus.com

The GX700VO is a lightweight notebook with a sophisticated cooling system: during mobile operation, it is cooled by an internal dual fan arrangement; during stationary use, it can be docked to a high-performance water-cooling system. This solves the problem of elevated temperatures during intensive gaming using powerful hardware. It also enables overclocking without hardware damage.

Statement by the jury
The external cooling system is an intelligent solution to overheating problems that may arise while using gaming notebooks.

Das GX700VO ist ein leichtes Notebook mit einem ausgefeilten Kühlsystem: Beim mobilen Betrieb wird es mit einer internen Kühlung aus Doppellüftern versorgt, im stationären Betrieb kann es an eine leistungsfähige Flüssigkühlung angedockt werden. Diese Kühlung löst das Problem der hohen Temperaturen, die bei intensivem Gaming mit Hochleistungshardware auftreten. Das bietet auch Möglichkeiten zum Übertakten, ohne dass die Hardware Schaden nimmt.

Begründung der Jury
Die externe Kühlung ist eine intelligente Lösung für Hitzeprobleme, die bei Gaming-Notebooks auftreten können. Damit kann das Notebook zum Spielen und Arbeiten verwendet werden.

ASUS ROG G752 Series
Gaming Notebooks

Manufacturer
ASUSTeK Computer Inc., Taipei, Taiwan
In-house design
Mary Hsi
Web
www.asus.com

With its unorthodox contours, the ROG G752 series gaming notebook deviates from the look of classic representatives of this genre. Its titanium-like body with decorative copper detailing highlights reliability and heat resistance during overclocking periods. Moreover, the keyboard arrangement has been optimised to help gamers intuitively find the best ergonomic hand position. The high-performance notebook is equipped with a Nvidia GTX graphics card and a 4K/2K ultra-HD display.

Statement by the jury
The striking design gives this gaming notebook an unmistakable character and underscores its high-performance capabilities.

Mit seiner unorthodoxen Linienführung bricht das Gaming-Notebook ROG G752 Series mit den klassischen Vertretern seines Genres. Sein titanähnliches Gehäuse mit Kupferdekoration veranschaulicht die Zuverlässigkeit und Hitzebeständigkeit beim Übertakten. Zudem wurde die Tastatur optimiert, damit Gamer intuitiv die beste ergonomische Handposition finden können. Das leistungsfähige Notebook ist mit einer Nvidia-GTX-Grafikkarte und einem 4K/2K-Ultra-HD-Display ausgestattet.

Begründung der Jury
Die markante Formgebung verleiht diesem Gaming-Notebook einen unverwechselbaren Charakter und unterstreicht seine hohe Leistungsfähigkeit.

Aspire S 13
Notebook

Manufacturer
Acer Incorporated, New Taipei, Taiwan
In-house design
Lihsuan Chou, Paul Huang
Web
www.acer.com

The Aspire S 13 notebook is characterised by a contemporary design with defined angles. The aptly placed metal elements also render a high-grade impression. A particular eye-catcher is the silver-grey hinge, as it creates an appealing contrast with the groove pattern of the display cover. The backlit keys of the notebook are generously arranged for comfortable typing, especially under dark conditions.

Statement by the jury
The striking hinge and the groove pattern on the cover are two style elements lending the notebook an unmistakable, noble appearance.

Das Notebook Aspire S 13 ist von einer zeitgemäßen Formgebung mit definierten Winkeln gekennzeichnet. Überlegt platzierte Metallelemente verleihen ihm darüber hinaus eine wertige Anmutung. Besonders das silbergraue Scharnier ist ein Blickfang, denn es bildet mit der gerillten Struktur des Displaydeckels einen ansprechenden Kontrast. Auf der Tastatur mit Hintergrundbeleuchtung sind die Tasten großzügig angeordnet, was das Tippen besonders im Dunkeln komfortabel macht.

Begründung der Jury
Das auffällige Scharnier und die Rillenstruktur des Deckels sind zwei Stilelemente, die dem Notebook ein unverwechselbares, edles Äußeres verleihen.

Aspire R 15
Convertible Notebook

Manufacturer
Acer Incorporated, New Taipei, Taiwan
In-house design
Zoey Huang
Web
www.acer.com

The hairline-brush metallic top cover and input area give this notebook an elegant look and special feel. With the 360-degree tiltable screen, it can be easily used in different operational modes. The 15.6" display is accommodated in a relatively small enclosure, which is particularly helpful in limited spaces. With its aluminium cover and base made of both plastic and 40 per cent glass fibre, the notebook is also extremely durable.

Statement by the jury
The Aspire R 15 features a comparatively large display and thus offers a wide range of options for entertainment and work contexts.

Die Haarlinienstruktur der Metallabdeckung und des Eingabebereichs verleiht diesem Notebook ein elegantes Aussehen und eine besondere Haptik. Dank des um 360 Grad neigbaren Bildschirms lässt es sich leicht in verschiedenen Modi verwenden. Das 15,6"-Display ist in einem relativ kleinen Gehäuse untergebracht, was besonders bei beengten Verhältnissen hilfreich ist. Mit seiner Abdeckung aus Aluminium und dem Boden aus Kunststoff mit Glasfaseranteil ist das Gerät zudem widerstandsfähig.

Begründung der Jury
Das Aspire R 15 besitzt ein vergleichsweise großes Display und bietet dadurch vielfältige Möglichkeiten für Unterhaltung und Arbeit.

TravelMate P6
Notebook

Manufacturer
Acer Incorporated, New Taipei, Taiwan
In-house design
George Huang
Web
www.acer.com

The TravelMate P6 is a notebook designed for high performance and security. Its top cover is made of durable carbon- and glass-fibre materials, while the casing itself is fashioned from aluminium alloy, making the notebook durable and longlasting. These features are underscored by the matt-black colour of the casing and its striking profile. A fingerprint sensor, dust-protected ventilation system and shock-resistant hard drive are additional features of the notebook.

Statement by the jury
The TravelMate P6 impresses with various design details, making it a reliable working device for professional users.

Das TravelMate P6 ist ein ganz auf Leistung und Sicherheit ausgelegtes Notebook. Seine Abdeckung besteht aus strapazierfähigem Carbon und Glasverbundmaterialien, das Gehäuse aus einer Aluminiumlegierung. Dadurch ist das Gerät robust und langlebig. Unterstrichen werden diese Eigenschaften durch die mattschwarze Farbe des Gehäuses und das prägnante Profil. Ein Fingerabdrucksensor, ein staubgeschütztes Lüftersystem sowie eine stoßgeschützte Festplatte sind weitere Merkmale des Notebooks.

Begründung der Jury
Das TravelMate P6 punktet mit zahlreichen Ausstattungsdetails, die es zu einem zuverlässigen Arbeitsgerät für professionelle Anwender machen.

Dell XPS 15
Notebook

Manufacturer
Dell Inc., Round Rock, Texas, USA
In-house design
Experience Design Group
Web
www.dell.com

The Dell XPS 15 notebook has a nearly frameless 15" display in a comparatively small enclosure. The chassis is precision cut from a single block of solid aluminium and is thus very robust and durable. The Gorilla Glass of the display is extremely scratch-resistant. The wedge-shaped enclosure is no thicker than 17 mm and weighs only 2 kg. It accommodates an SSD, quad core processors and 2 GB of video memory.

Statement by the jury
This notebook convinces with its compact format and special features making it particularly robust and suitable for daily use.

Das Notebook Dell XPS 15 besitzt ein nahezu rahmenloses 15"-Display in einem vergleichsweise kleinen Gehäuse. Dies wird im Präzisionsschnittverfahren aus einem massiven Aluminiumblock hergestellt und ist dadurch robust und widerstandsfähig. Auch das Gorilla-Glas des Displays ist äußerst kratzfest. Das keilförmige Gehäuse misst im geschlossenen Zustand maximal 17 mm und wiegt nur 2 kg. Es beherbergt eine SSD, 4-Kern-Prozessoren und 2 GB Videospeicher.

Begründung der Jury
Das Notebook punktet mit seinem kompakten Format sowie mit Merkmalen, die es besonders robust und geeignet für die tägliche Verwendung machen.

15Z960
Ultrabook

Manufacturer
LG Electronics Inc., Seoul, South Korea
In-house design
Sooyoung Park, Heechang Lee, Taejin Lee
Web
www.lg.com

The 15Z960 weighs less than 1 kg and is one of the most lightweight 15.6" ultrabooks. It is thus a very portable device optimally suited for work thanks to its ample screen size. The enclosure consists of a magnesium alloy, providing the required ruggedness for mobile use. A particular feature of the ultrabook is the webcam located around the hinge and not at the upper edge of the screen. The frame as a seamless circumferential style element is therefore retained.

Statement by the jury
With its very slim form and reduced weight, this ultrabook is a stylish companion for both leisure and business users.

Das 15Z960 wiegt weniger als 1 kg und ist eines der leichtesten 15,6"-Ultrabooks. Es ist damit ein sehr mobiles Gerät, das dank seiner großzügigen Bildschirmgröße hervorragend zum Arbeiten geeignet ist. Da sein Gehäuse aus einer Magnesiumlegierung besteht, bietet es auch die benötigte Robustheit für den Einsatz unterwegs. Eine Besonderheit des Ultrabooks ist die Webcam, die nicht wie üblich am oberen Bildschirmrand, sondern im Scharnier untergebracht ist. Dadurch bleibt der Rahmen als nahtlos umlaufendes Stilelement erhalten.

Begründung der Jury
Mit seiner sehr schlanken Form und dem geringen Gewicht ist dieses Ultrabook ein stilvoller Begleiter für Freizeit- wie auch für Business-Anwender.

ThinkPad Yoga 260
Convertible Notebook

Manufacturer
Lenovo (Japan) Ltd., Yokohama, Japan
In-house design
Web
www.lenovo.com

The new ThinkPad Yoga 260 is a portable ultrabook which can be transformed into a tablet in an instant, thanks to its 360-degree hinge. Additional applications are the tent or stand mode such as for presentations or watching videos. With this broad range of options, the lightweight and slim device can be easily adjusted to the challenges of day-to-day work. An integrated stylus for creative input is automatically charged in the notebook.

Statement by the jury
This versatile notebook is a useful aid for people who are frequently on the go and require a fitting device for divergent situations.

Das neue ThinkPad Yoga 260 ist ein tragbares Ultrabook, das sich dank seines 360-Grad-Scharniers blitzschnell in ein Tablet verwandeln lässt. Weitere Anwendungen sind der Zelt- oder Stand-Modus beispielsweise für Präsentationen oder das Betrachten von Videos. Durch diese vielfältigen Möglichkeiten kann das leichte und schlanke Gerät einfach an die Herausforderungen im Arbeitsalltag angepasst werden. Ein integrierter Stift für die kreative Eingabe wird im Notebook automatisch aufgeladen.

Begründung der Jury
Das vielseitige Notebook ist ein nützlicher Helfer für Menschen, die viel unterwegs sind und für die unterschiedlichsten Situationen das passende Gerät benötigen.

Yoga 900
Ultrabook

Manufacturer
Lenovo (Beijing) Ltd., Beijing, China
In-house design
Web
www.lenovo.com

The Yoga 900 is a stylish, elegant hybrid ultrabook. It is very slim and, with its Core i7 processor, delivers high performance. The innovative watchband hinge allows the user to position the display quickly and naturally in the angle desired, for instance switching from tablet to tent mode. As the frame around the display is rubberised, the device stands securely upright in tent mode, and the edges are protected as well.

Statement by the jury
State-of-the-art technology is accommodated in an extremely slim format in the Yoga 900. The hinge, in the style of a watchband, is an appealing eyecatcher.

Das Yoga 900 ist ein stilvolles, elegantes Hybrid-Ultrabook. Es ist sehr dünn und bietet mit einem Core-i7-Prozessor eine hohe Leistung. Das innovative Gliederscharnier erlaubt dem Anwender, das Display schnell und natürlich in einem anderen Winkel zu positionieren, um z. B. in den Tablet- oder Zelt-Modus zu wechseln. Da der Rahmen um das Display gummiert ist, steht das Gerät im Zelt-Modus sicher und auch die Kanten sind geschützt.

Begründung der Jury
Im Yoga 900 ist zeitgemäße Technik in einem äußerst schlanken Format untergebracht. Das Scharnier im Stil eines Uhrenarmbands ist ein ansprechender Blickfang.

ThinkPad X1 Yoga
Convertible Notebook

Manufacturer
Lenovo (Japan) Ltd., Yokohama, Japan
In-house design
Web
www.lenovo.com

The new ThinkPad X1 Yoga is a business notebook made of durable carbon fibre with a slim design. Its OLED display convinces with detailed imaging, which is significant both for a work setting and for enjoying entertainment. In tablet mode, the keys are automatically retracted for protection, preventing inadvertent activation. A digitiser stylus provided with the notebook and stowed away in the device is thus always on hand.

Statement by the jury
With well-conceived functions and practical accessories, the ThinkPad X1 Yoga offers central elements crucial for today's mobile professional world.

Das neue ThinkPad X1 Yoga ist ein Business-Notebook aus widerstandsfähiger Kohlefaser mit einer schlanken Formgebung. Sein OLED-Display überzeugt mit einer detailreichen Darstellung, was für das Arbeiten ebenso wichtig ist wie für den Genuss von Unterhaltung. Im Tablet-Modus werden die Tasten automatisch zurückgezogen, um sie zu schützen und zu verhindern, dass sie unabsichtlich betätigt werden. Ein mitgelieferter Digitalisierstift wird im Notebook verstaut und ist immer zur Hand.

Begründung der Jury
Mit durchdachten Funktionen und praktischem Zubehör bietet das ThinkPad X1 Yoga zentrale Elemente, die in der mobilen Arbeitswelt von heute entscheidend sind.

ideapad 710s
Notebook

Manufacturer
Lenovo (Beijing) Ltd., Beijing, China
In-house design
Web
www.lenovo.com

The design of this notebook is focused on the idea of developing a high-performance device at an affordable price. The 13" notebook offers a high degree of mobility as it is merely 13.9 mm thick and weighs only 1.16 kg. With a very narrow bezel, the screen appears to be virtually frameless so that pictures and videos may be viewed comfortably. Moreover, the screen can be flipped open by 180 degrees, offering more usage possibilities.

Statement by the jury
The very slim and lightweight ideapad 710s can be easily taken along and is thus always ready for use anywhere.

Bei der Gestaltung dieses Notebooks stand der Gedanke im Vordergrund, ein leistungsfähiges, erschwingliches Gerät zu entwickeln. Das 13"-Notebook bietet eine hohe Mobilität, da es lediglich 13,9 mm dick ist und nur 1,16 kg wiegt. Mit seiner sehr schmalen Einfassung erscheint der Bildschirm nahezu rahmenlos, sodass sich Filme und Videos angenehm betrachten lassen. Der Bildschirm kann zudem um 180 Grad aufgeklappt werden, was mehr Möglichkeiten bei der Nutzung bietet.

Begründung der Jury
Das sehr schlanke und leichte ideapad 710s kann einfach mitgenommen werden und ist damit immer und überall einsatzbereit.

ThinkPad X1 Carbon
Notebook

Manufacturer
Lenovo (Japan) Ltd., Yokohama, Japan
In-house design
Web
www.lenovo.com

The new ThinkPad X1 Carbon is a robust notebook in state-of-the-art design for professional users. The carbon-fibre casing is very durable so that the notebook is capable of withstanding extreme conditions. The slim and lightweight device is equipped with high-performance components such as an Intel i7 processor and a fast SSD, thus meeting the high demands of a business notebook.

Statement by the jury
This notebook impresses with its slim design, first-class technical equipment and a ruggedness that masters extreme conditions.

Das neue ThinkPad X1 Carbon ist ein robustes Notebook mit zeitgemäßer Formgebung für professionelle Anwender. Das Gehäuse aus Kohlefaser ist sehr widerstandsfähig, sodass das Notebook auch extremen Bedingungen standhält. Das schlanke und leichte Gerät ist mit leistungsfähigen Komponenten wie beispielsweise einem Intel-i7-Prozessor und einer schnellen SSD bestückt und erfüllt damit problemlos die hohen Anforderungen an ein Business-Notebook.

Begründung der Jury
Dieses Notebook beeindruckt mit seiner schlanken Bauform, der erstklassigen technischen Ausstattung und seiner Unempfindlichkeit gegenüber widrigen Bedingungen.

MEDION® ERAZER® X7841
Gaming Notebook

Manufacturer
Medion AG, Essen, Germany
In-house design
Medion Design Team
Web
www.medion.com

The Medion Erazer X7841 is a high-performance 17.3" gaming notebook. Equipped with high-end hardware, particularly with regard to the processor, graphics card and memory, it provides an outstanding gaming experience. With its rubberised surface, the notebook is rugged and has a pleasant feel. The technical equipment is underscored by the characteristic Edge Design, which highlights the self-contained character of the notebook.

Statement by the jury
The luminescent blue lines are brought out particularly well on the brushed surface, giving this gaming notebook a sporty appearance.

Das Medion Erazer X7841 ist ein leistungsfähiges 17,3"-Gaming-Notebook. Ausgestattet mit High-End-Hardware, insbesondere hinsichtlich Prozessor, Grafikkarte und Speicher, bietet es ein ausgezeichnetes Spielerlebnis. Dank seiner gummierten Oberfläche ist es unempfindlich und fasst sich angenehm an. Unterstrichen wird die technische Ausstattung durch das charakteristische Edge Design, das den eigenständigen Charakter des Notebooks hervorhebt.

Begründung der Jury
Die blau leuchtenden Linien kommen auf der gebürsteten Oberfläche gut zur Geltung und verleihen diesem Gaming-Notebook eine sportliche Anmutung.

iPad Pro

Manufacturer
Apple, Cupertino, USA
In-house design
Web
www.apple.com

With its 12.9" Retina display, this iPad – the largest so far – is merely 6.9 mm thick and weighs only 713 grams. The iPad Pro is equipped with a high-performance A9X chip with 64-bit architecture, four speakers, front and back camera, Wi-Fi and LTE. It also includes a fingerprint sensor to protect it from unauthorised access. The battery powers the iPad Pro for up to ten hours. With its already installed apps, the device provides many options for creative and productive users. Additional apps are available in the App Store.

Mit seinem 12,9"-Retina-Display ist dieses bisher größte iPad lediglich 6,9 mm dick und wiegt nur 713 Gramm. Das iPad Pro ist mit einem leistungsstarken A9X-Chip mit 64-Bit-Architektur, vier Lautsprechern, Front- und Rückkamera, Wi-Fi und LTE ausgestattet. Zudem besitzt es einen Fingerabdrucksensor, um es vor unbefugtem Zugriff zu schützen. Der Akku erlaubt bis zu zehn Stunden Betrieb. Das iPad Pro bietet dank seiner bereits installierten Apps viele Möglichkeiten für kreative und produktive Anwender, weitere Apps lassen sich aus dem App Store beziehen.

Statement by the jury
The extremely light and slim iPad Pro convinces with its elegant design, comprehensive range of functions and powerful performance.

Begründung der Jury
Das überaus leichte und schlanke iPad Pro überzeugt durch seine elegante Gestaltung ebenso wie durch seine umfangreichen Funktionen und die hohe Leistungsfähigkeit.

ASUS ZenPad Series + Clutch Cover
Tablets and Accessories
Tablets und Zubehör

Manufacturer
ASUSTeK Computer Inc., Taipei, Taiwan
In-house design
Web
www.asus.com

The Asus ZenPad is a slim tablet with a design inspired by the style of a fashionable clutch. It is available in a large number of trendy colours, textures and patterns, thus appealing to different user groups. Specifically designed for the ZenPad was the Clutch Cover – a stylish leather case protecting the device and usable as stand with different positioning angles. The colour spectrum is diverse and ranges from discrete to striking.

Statement by the jury
With its elegant Clutch Cover, the Asus ZenPad turns into an attractive accessory for a fashion-conscious target group.

Das Asus ZenPad ist ein schlankes Tablet, dessen Gestaltung vom Stil einer modischen Clutch inspiriert wurde. Es ist in zahlreichen schicken Farben, Texturen und Mustern erhältlich und spricht damit verschiedene Nutzergruppen an. Speziell hierfür entwickelt wurde das Clutch Cover – eine stilvolle Lederhülle, die das Gerät schützt und als Ständer mit unterschiedlichen Stellwinkeln verwendet werden kann. Ihr Farbspektrum ist vielfältig und reicht von dezent bis auffällig.

Begründung der Jury
Mit dem geschmackvollen Clutch Cover wird das Asus ZenPad zum attraktiven Accessoire für eine modebewusste Zielgruppe.

Pixel C
Tablet

Manufacturer
Google, Mountain View, USA
In-house design
Web
www.google.com

The Pixel C consists of two elements, a tablet and keyboard, optimally harmonising with each other thanks to their uniform design. Docking and detaching is exceptionally simple due to the magnetic connection. With its rounded edges, the tablet rests comfortably in the hand. Equipped with a durable aluminium body, the combination is sturdy enough to be used on one's lap. The keyboard is inductively charged by the tablet and thus does not require a battery of its own.

Statement by the jury
Tablet and keyboard enter into a stylish symbiotic relationship and appear as a unit, both functionally and visually.

Pixel C besteht aus zwei Elementen, Tablet und Tastatur, die aufgrund ihrer einheitlichen Gestaltung bestens miteinander harmonieren. Das Andocken und Trennen ist dank der magnetischen Verbindung kinderleicht, zudem liegt das Tablet mit seinen runden Kanten gut in der Hand. Ausgestattet mit einem stabilen Aluminiumgehäuse, ist die Kombination robust genug, um auch auf dem Schoß verwendet zu werden. Den Strom bezieht die Tastatur per Induktion vom Tablet, sodass sie keinen eigenen Akku benötigt.

Begründung der Jury
Tablet und Tastatur gehen eine formschöne Symbiose ein und erscheinen dadurch funktional wie auch optisch als Einheit.

ThinkPad X1
Tablet

Manufacturer
Lenovo (Japan) Ltd., Yokohama, Japan
In-house design
Web
www.lenovo.com

The concept of the ThinkPad X1 is characterised by the maxim of offering the fitting device for any utilisation purpose. Additional modules like different interface ports, a stylus or a projector can be conveniently added or interchanged. The detachable keyboard with trackpoint and trackpad serves as a protective cover and is attached to the tablet magnetically. It is available in the attractive colours silver, red and black.

Das Konzept des ThinkPad X1 ist von der Maxime geprägt, für jeden Anwendungszweck das passende Gerät bereitstellen zu können. Zusatzmodule wie verschiedene Schnittstellen, ein Eingabestift oder auch ein Beamer können einfach hinzugefügt oder ausgetauscht werden. Die abnehmbare Tastatur mit Trackpoint und Trackpad dient als Schutz und wird magnetisch an das Tablet angeschlossen. Sie ist in den attraktiven Farben Silber, Rot und Schwarz erhältlich.

Statement by the jury
With its modular design, the ThinkPad X1 offers a wide range of options, making it the perfect companion for any application area.

Begründung der Jury
Mit seinem modularen Design bietet das ThinkPad X1 eine Fülle an Möglichkeiten, die es perfekt für jede Art von Anwendung machen.

HP Elite x2 1012
Tablet

Manufacturer
HP Inc., Palo Alto, USA
In-house design
HP Industrial Design Team
Web
www.hp.com

The HP Elite x2 1012 is an 8-mm-thick tablet for business users. Its chassis consists of precision-cut aluminium, with a cover made of Gorilla Glass. This gives the slim device the durability required for everyday use. The elegant stand allows for infinitely variable positioning as desired. Just like the tablet, the keyboard is extremely durable, thanks to the stiffened aluminium deck.

Statement by the jury
This stylish tablet convinces with a timeless aesthetics and solidity that makes it particularly suitable for professional users.

Das HP Elite x2 1012 ist ein 8 mm dickes Tablet für Business-Anwender. Sein Gehäuse besteht aus präzisionsgeschnittenem Aluminium und die Abdeckung aus Gorilla-Glas. Dies gibt dem schlanken Gerät die nötige Robustheit für den täglichen Einsatz. Der elegante Ständer lässt sich stufenlos in die gewünschte Position bringen. Wie das Tablet, so ist auch die Tastatur dank ihrer Oberseite aus versteiftem Aluminium äußerst haltbar.

Begründung der Jury
Dieses stilvolle Tablet überzeugt mit seiner zeitlosen Ästhetik und Robustheit, womit es sich besonders gut für professionelle Anwender eignet.

Dell Latitude 12
7000 Series
Two-in-One Tablet PC
2-in-1-Tablet-PC

Manufacturer
Dell Inc., Round Rock, Texas, USA
In-house design
Experience Design Group
Web
www.dell.com

The Dell Latitude 12 of the 7000 series is a very thin and lightweight two-in-one system in the business class. The four edges of the aluminium alloy casing are designed to include impact zones in order to ensure optimum drop protection. The textile-coated, magnetic cover with keyboard turns the tablet into a notebook in an instant. This cover provides scratch protection and complements the system with an adjustable stand.

Statement by the jury
The functional keyboard cover turns this discreetly designed tablet into a notebook for professional users who require a reliable mobile system.

Das Dell Latitude 12 der 7000er-Serie ist ein sehr dünnes und leichtes 2-in-1-System der Business-Klasse. Die vier Kanten des Gehäuses aus einer Aluminiumlegierung besitzen Aufprallzonen, um ein Optimum an Fallschutz zu gewährleisten. Die textilbeschichtete, magnetische Hülle mit Tastatur macht aus dem Tablet im Handumdrehen ein Notebook. Sie schützt als Abdeckung vor Kratzern und ergänzt das System um einen verstellbaren Ständer.

Begründung der Jury
Die funktionale Tastaturhülle verwandelt das schlicht gestaltete Tablet in ein Notebook für professionelle Anwender, die ein zuverlässiges mobiles System benötigen.

Envy 8 Note
Detachable Tablet and Keyboard
Abnehmbares Tablet und Tastatur

Manufacturer
HP Inc., Palo Alto, USA
In-house design
HP Industrial Design Team
Web
www.hp.com

The approach pursued in developing the Envy 8 Note was to turn an 8" tablet into a work tool for maximum productivity. One primary challenge with such a reduced display size relates to input via keyboard – be it directly on the screen or using a small, integrated keypad. The solution is a keyboard dock into which the tablet is easily inserted. The tablet is held upright and is ready for input. A stylus serves as additional input device that can be attached to the keyboard for safekeeping.

Beim Envy 8 Note wurde der Ansatz verfolgt, ein 8"-Tablet in ein möglichst produktives Arbeitsgerät zu verwandeln. Eine Herausforderung bei dieser geringen Display-Größe ist vor allem die Eingabe mittels Tastatur – sei es auf dem Display oder über eine kleine integrierte Tastatur. Gelöst wird dies mit einem Tastatur-Dock, in das das Tablet einfach hineingesteckt wird. Es wird dadurch aufrecht gehalten und ist bereit für die Eingabe. Als weiteres Eingabegerät dient ein Stylus, der in einer an der Tastatur befestigten Schlaufe verwahrt werden kann.

Statement by the jury
The Envy 8 Note is a handy electronic notepad for use on the go. With a touchscreen, keyboard and stylus, it offers a wide range of input options.

Begründung der Jury
Das Envy 8 Note ist ein handliches elektronisches Notizbuch für unterwegs. Dank Touchscreen, Tastatur und Stylus bietet es vielfältige Eingabemöglichkeiten.

HP Spectre X2
Convertible Notebook

Manufacturer
HP Inc., Palo Alto, USA
In-house design
HP Industrial Design Team
Web
www.hp.com

The HP Spectre X2 is a fully fledged notebook with the mobility of a tablet thanks to its detachable keyboard. The chassis of the tablet was designed to be as slim as possible without impairing stability and performance. At nearly 5 mm, the keyboard is very flat, yet it features all keys in standard size and also includes a trackpad. The base consists of aluminium, making the keyboard extremely lightweight. A robust stainless-steel stand holds the tablet in any position for comfortable viewing.

Das HP Spectre X2 ist ein vollwertiges Notebook, das dank seiner abnehmbaren Tastatur die Mobilität eines Tablets besitzt. Das Gehäuse des Tablets wurde so schlank wie möglich gehalten, ohne dabei seine Stabilität und Leistung zu beeinträchtigen. Die Tastatur ist mit 5 mm sehr flach, besitzt aber alle Tasten in Standardgröße sowie ein Trackpad. Die Bodenabdeckung besteht aus Aluminium, wodurch die Tastatur extrem leicht ist. Ein robuster Edelstahlständer hält das Tablet in jeder Position, damit das Display bequem betrachtet werden kann.

Statement by the jury
The slim, lightweight keyboard turns this tablet into an elegant notebook in an instant, allowing the user to enjoy the full functional range of a computer, even on the go.

Begründung der Jury
Die leichte und flache Tastatur verwandelt das Tablet im Handumdrehen in ein elegantes Notebook, sodass man auch unterwegs alle Funktionen eines Computers genießen kann.

Smart Keyboard
Smart-Tastatur

Manufacturer
Apple, Cupertino, USA
In-house design
Web
www.apple.com

The new Smart Keyboard for the iPad Pro offers the functionality of a full-size keyboard, implementing unconventional technology in the process. The entire keyboard is draped with a special fabric that has been laser-ablated to precisely define each key and to offer a natural feel. Below the woven surface is a 0.1-mm-thin conductive material transmitting finger pressure to the keys of the iPad. For this reason, the Smart Keyboard does not need an external power supply like batteries or a cable connection.

Das neue Smart Keyboard für das iPad Pro bietet die Funktionalität einer Tastatur in voller Größe und setzt hierfür eine unkonventionelle Technologie ein. Die gesamte Tastatur ist aus einem besonderen Gewebe gefertigt, das mit dem Laser geformt wurde, um jede Taste präzise zu definieren und eine natürliche Haptik zu bieten. Unter der gewebten Oberfläche befindet sich ein 0,1 mm dünnes leitendes Material, das den beim Tippen eingesetzten Druck der Finger auf die Tastenfelder des iPads überträgt. Deshalb benötigt das Smart Keyboard auch keine eigene Energieversorgung wie Akkus oder Kabel.

Statement by the jury
The Smart Keyboard's innovative approach to transmitting energy directly to the keys of the iPad display through pressure is implemented in an exemplary way.

Begründung der Jury
Der innovative Ansatz, Druckenergie unmittelbar auf die Tasten des iPad-Displays zu übertragen, wird bei dem Smart Keyboard in vorbildlicher Weise umgesetzt.

Blok Family for iPad Air 2
Keyboard with Case for the iPad Air 2
Tastatur mit Hülle für das iPad Air 2

Manufacturer
Logitech, Newark, California, USA
In-house design
Logitech Design
Design
Notion, Dublin, Ireland
Web
www.logitech.com
www.designbynotion.com

The Blok protective cases for the iPad Air 2 are made of a shock-absorbing polymer structure that protects the iPad from impact. Drops from a height of up to 1.8 metres onto concrete can be effectively absorbed. The delicate corners of the iPad are protected particularly well since the protective case contains extra polymers in sensitive areas. The range includes three products designed to meet different customer demands: the protective shell, the protective case for use at practically any angle and the protective case with integrated keyboard for users who intend to work more productively with the iPad.

Die Blok-Schutzhüllen für das iPad Air 2 bestehen aus einer stoßabsorbierenden Polymerstruktur, die das iPad bei Krafteinwirkung schützt. Stürze auf Beton aus einer Höhe von bis zu 1,8 Metern können dadurch abgefangen werden. Die empfindlichen Kanten des iPads sind besonders gut geschützt, da die Schutzhülle in den entsprechenden Bereichen zusätzliche Polymere besitzt. Die Familie umfasst drei Produkte für unterschiedliche Kundenanforderungen: die Schutzhülle, das Schutzcase mit nahezu frei verstellbarem Neigungswinkel und das Schutzcase mit integrierter Tastatur für Anwender, die mit dem iPad produktiver arbeiten wollen.

Statement by the jury
With its well-conceived design, these slim cases are proof that effective protection can be achieved in a stylish, functional way.

Begründung der Jury
Mit ihrer durchdachten Gestaltung beweisen diese schlanken Hüllen, dass ein effektiver Schutz auf eine formschöne, funktionale Weise möglich ist.

Rolly Keyboard 2
Bluetooth Keyboard
Bluetooth-Tastatur

Manufacturer
LG Electronics Inc., Seoul, South Korea
In-house design
Hyunwoo Yoo, Sera Park
Web
www.lg.com

This Bluetooth keyboard may be simply rolled up and is so compact that it can be stowed away anywhere. With two hinges on the backside, it holds a mobile phone or tablet vertically or horizontally in an upright position so that the user has a good view of the screen when typing. The opening tab made of fabric indicates the spot where the keyboard can be opened and is a visual highlight as well.

Diese Bluetooth-Tastatur lässt sich einfach zusammenrollen und ist dann so kompakt, dass sie überall verstaut werden kann. Mit zwei Scharnieren auf der Rückseite hält sie ein Mobiltelefon oder Tablet vertikal oder horizontal in aufrechter Position, damit der Anwender beim Tippen das jeweilige Display gut im Blick hat. Die aus Stoff gefertigte Öffnungslasche zeigt an, wo die Tastatur geöffnet werden kann, und ist zudem ein visuelles Highlight.

Statement by the jury
When the Rolly Keyboard 2 is rolled up, it requires but little storage space and conveys a look that is both solid and original.

Begründung der Jury
Wenn das Rolly Keyboard 2 zusammengerollt ist, beansprucht es nur wenig Stauraum und wirkt gleichermaßen solide wie originell.

BrydgeAir
Bluetooth Keyboard for the iPad
Bluetooth-Tastatur für das iPad

Manufacturer
Brydge Global Pte Ltd, Singapore
In-house design
Web
www.brydgekeyboards.com

With its minimalist design, the BrydgeAir mirrors the contours of the iPad Air all the way to the placement of switches and buttons. This enables a seamless transition between keyboard and iPad. The housing is fashioned from high-grade aluminium and is anodised to reflect the iPad colours. The iPad is inserted into the U-shaped hinge mechanism, allowing viewing angles from 0 to 180 degrees.

Mit ihrer minimalistischen Formgebung folgt BrydgeAir den Linien und Winkeln des iPad Air bis hin zur Platzierung der Schalter und Knöpfe. Dadurch ermöglicht sie den nahtlosen Wechsel zwischen Tastatur und iPad. Das Gehäuse besteht aus hochwertigem Aluminium und ist in den Farben eloxiert, in denen auch das iPad erhältlich ist. Eingesetzt wird das iPad in das U-Scharnier, das einen Blickwinkel von 0 bis 180 Grad ermöglicht.

Statement by the jury
This keyboard is perfectly adapted to the iPad Air and considerably simplifies use, providing many new options for prolific writers.

Begründung der Jury
Mit dieser perfekt auf das iPad Air abgestimmten Tastatur wird die Bedienung des iPads noch einfacher, was auch Vielschreibern neue Möglichkeiten eröffnet.

Typo Keyboard for iPad Mini
Typo-Tastatur für das iPad Mini

Manufacturer
Typo Innovations, Las Vegas, USA
Design
Bluemap Design, New York, USA
Web
www.gettypo.com
www.bluemapdesign.com

The Typo keyboard for iPad Mini combines a protective case with an adjustable stand and a slim Bluetooth keyboard. It was designed with the objective of expanding input options for the iPad Mini so as to close the gap between tablet and notebook. The integrated stand positions the iPad Mini at any desired viewing angle. Since the keyboard is detachable, the stand can also be used by itself, for instance to watch videos.

Statement by the jury
Perfectly aligned to the iPad Mini, Typo is a well-conceived, multifunctional solution that facilitates text input considerably.

Die Typo-Tastatur für das iPad Mini kombiniert eine Schutzhülle mit einem verstellbaren Ständer und einer flachen Bluetooth-Tastatur. Sie wurde mit dem Ziel entwickelt, die Eingabemöglichkeiten des iPad Mini zu erweitern, um die Lücke zwischen Tablet und Notebook zu schließen. Der integrierte Ständer nimmt das iPad Mini in jedem gewünschten Betrachtungswinkel auf. Da sich die Tastatur abnehmen lässt, kann der Ständer auch alleine verwendet werden, um beispielsweise Videos zu betrachten.

Begründung der Jury
Perfekt auf das iPad Mini abgestimmt, ist Typo eine durchdachte multifunktionale Lösung, die die Texteingabe erheblich erleichtert.

Typo Keyboard for iPad Air
Typo-Tastatur für das iPad Air

Manufacturer
Typo Innovations, Las Vegas, USA
Design
Bluemap Design, New York, USA
Web
www.gettypo.com
www.bluemapdesign.com

The Typo keyboard for iPad Air combines a protective case with an adjustable stand and an extraordinarily thin Bluetooth keyboard. It was designed with the objective of facilitating an enhanced input experience on the iPad. The very small hinge deserves special consideration. It holds the iPad securely in any desired viewing angle so that the user can type on the keyboard in the most comfortable position. Matching the iPad Air, the keyboard also features a very slim design.

Statement by the jury
This multifunctional keyboard sensibly complements the iPad Air. It offers more operational comfort and protects the device when not in use.

Die Typo-Tastatur für das iPad Air kombiniert eine Schutzhülle mit einem verstellbaren Ständer und einer außergewöhnlich flachen Bluetooth-Tastatur. Sie wurde mit dem Ziel entwickelt, das Tippen auf einem iPad komfortabler zu machen. Besondere Beachtung verdient das sehr kleine Scharnier. Es hält das iPad in jedem beliebigen Betrachtungswinkel sicher, sodass der Anwender es in der für ihn angenehmsten Position bedienen kann. Passend zum iPad Air ist die Tastatur sehr schlank gestaltet.

Begründung der Jury
Diese multifunktionale Tastatur ist eine sinnvolle Ergänzung für das iPad Air. Sie sorgt für mehr Komfort bei der Bedienung und schützt das Gerät bei Nichtgebrauch.

HP Neoprene Sleeve
Notebook Sleeve
Notebook-Hülle

Manufacturer
HP Inc., Palo Alto, USA
In-house design
HP Industrial Design Team
Web
www.hp.com

This sleeve made of neoprene fits all notebooks ranging from 12" to 17". Available in four sizes and colours, it is also reversible, offering two colour options at once. Handling the sleeve is very simple: it is pulled over the notebook and protects it from scratching and impact. Since the sleeve is thin and lightweight, the notebook can be readily stowed away in a backpack or schoolbag.

Statement by the jury
This sleeve impresses with its very easy handling. It appeals to a younger target group, in particular due to the selection of modern colours.

Diese Hülle aus Neopren ist für Notebooks von 12" bis 17" geeignet. Sie ist in vier Größen und Farben erhältlich, außerdem lässt sie sich umstülpen, sodass jede Hülle zwei Farbvarianten bietet. Die Hülle ist denkbar einfach zu handhaben: Sie wird über das Notebook gezogen und schützt es so vor Kratzern und Stößen. Da sie kaum aufträgt, findet das Notebook auch im Rucksack oder in einer Schultasche problemlos Platz.

Begründung der Jury
Diese Hülle punktet mit ihrer kinderleichten Handhabung und ist aufgrund der modernen Farben besonders für eine jüngere Zielgruppe attraktiv.

ASUS ZenPad Audio Cover
Tablet Audio Cover
Audio-Abdeckung für Tablets

Manufacturer
ASUSTeK Computer Inc., Taipei, Taiwan
In-house design
Web
www.asus.com

The Asus ZenPad Audio Cover is a protective cover and speaker at the same time. Equipped with six speakers, it delivers powerful DTS-HD sound for spatial music reproduction. Additionally, it serves as a stand to hold the tablet in an upright position for comfortable viewing. As the audio cover consists of durable materials, the tablet is well protected against damage in everyday life.

Statement by the jury
The dual function of high-grade speaker and robust protective cover has been adeptly applied to the Asus ZenPad Audio Cover.

Das Asus ZenPad Audio Cover ist Schutzhülle und Lautsprecher zugleich. Ausgestattet mit sechs Lautsprechern liefert es einen kraftvollen DTS-HD-Sound für die räumliche Musikwiedergabe. Zusätzlich dient es als Ständer, um das Tablet in einer aufrechten Position zu halten, damit es bequem betrachtet werden kann. Da das Audio Cover aus robusten Materialien besteht, ist das Tablet im Alltag gut gegen Beschädigungen geschützt.

Begründung der Jury
Die Doppelfunktion als hochwertiger Lautsprecher und widerstandsfähige Schutzhülle ist im Asus ZenPad Audio Cover überlegt umgesetzt.

World to Europe USB
Travel Adapter
Reiseadapter

Manufacturer
Q2Power AG, Ruggell, Liechtenstein
Design
i Design (Michael Koch), Biberist, Switzerland
Web
www.q2-power.com
www.i-design.ch

The World to Europe USB is an earthed travel adapter and USB charger in one. In all countries that follow the Schuko standard, travellers from all over the world can safely connect and charge their devices using two- and three-pole connectors or a USB plug. An innovative feature is the patented safety mechanism which guarantees that the user does not accidentally plug in two connectors at the same time. The contemporary design is complemented by functional recessed grips and rounded edges.

Statement by the jury
This travel adapter offers an exemplary safety concept that virtually excludes incorrect connections to electrical sockets.

Der World to Europe USB ist ein geerdeter Reiseadapter und USB-Ladegerät zugleich. Reisende aus aller Welt können damit in allen Ländern mit Schuko-Standard Geräte mit zwei- und dreipoligen Steckern sowie USB-Stecker sicher einstecken und die entsprechenden Geräte laden. Innovativ ist der patentierte Sicherheitsmechanismus, der garantiert, dass nicht versehentlich zwei Stecker gleichzeitig eingesteckt werden. Die moderne Formensprache wird durch funktionale Griffmulden und abgerundete Kanten ergänzt.

Begründung der Jury
Dieser Reiseadapter bietet ein vorbildliches Sicherheitskonzept, das eine Fehlbelegung von Steckdosen nahezu ausschließt.

ISD-55
Double-Sided Information Column
Doppelseitige Informationsstele

Manufacturer
MOStron Elektronik GmbH, Viersen, Germany
In-house design
Web
www.mostron.de

The slim, double-sided ISD-55 information column shows a purist and straightforward design. Its plain black anodised aluminium housing is robust and thus optimally suited for public space. With its nearly seamless shape, the column is also easy to clean. It features two 55" full HD displays that can be operated separately or in parallel. The displays are protected by anti-glare, single-pane safety glass.

Statement by the jury
As an unobtrusive, functionally designed product, this information column is a successful solution for public space.

Die schlanke, doppelseitige Informationsstele ISD-55 zeigt sich puristisch und geradlinig. Ihr schlichtes Gehäuse aus schwarz eloxiertem Aluminium ist robust und damit für öffentliche Bereiche bestens geeignet. Zudem ist die Stele dank ihrer nahezu nahtlosen Form einfach zu reinigen. Sie besitzt zwei Full-HD-55"-Displays, die einzeln oder parallel angesteuert werden können. Die Displays werden durch entspiegeltes, unempfindliches Einscheibensicherheitsglas geschützt.

Begründung der Jury
Als unaufdringliches, funktional gestaltetes Produkt ist diese Informationsstele eine gelungene Lösung für den öffentlichen Raum.

Apple Pencil
Stylus
Eingabestift

Manufacturer
Apple, Cupertino, USA
In-house design
Web
www.apple.com

The Apple Pencil is a stylus that shows its strength on an iPad Pro with a multi-touch system. It delivers results in pixel-perfect precision, offering a wide range of creative possibilities. With its very sensitive pressure and tilt sensors, the stylus instantly recognises when the user is pressing harder or changes the writing angle. Just as with a classic pencil, the user can vary line weight, create subtle shading and produce a wide range of artistic effects. The design of the stylus is reminiscent of a pencil and illustrates its functionality at first glance.

Statement by the jury
The Apple Pencil renders a very familiar impression as it can be handled just as easily as a pencil. Moreover, its reduced design facilitates access to the product.

Der Apple Pencil ist ein Eingabestift, der seine Stärken auf einem iPad Pro mit Multitouch-System ausspielt. Er liefert Ergebnisse in pixelgenauer Präzision, was vielfältige kreative Möglichkeiten bietet. Dank seiner sehr empfindlichen Druck- und Neigesensoren erkennt der Stift direkt, wenn stärker gedrückt wird oder sich der Aufsetzwinkel verändert. Dadurch können wie mit einem klassischen Bleistift Strich-breiten variiert, feine Schattierungen er-zeugt und zahlreiche künstlerische Effekte umgesetzt werden. Die an einen Bleistift angelehnte Gestaltung des Stiftes lädt zur intuitiven Benutzung ein und verdeutlicht seine Funktionsweise auf den ersten Blick.

Begründung der Jury
Der Apple Pencil wirkt sehr vertraut, da er sich genauso einfach wie ein Bleistift handhaben lässt. Seine reduzierte Gestal-tung erleichtert zudem die Annäherung an das Produkt.

Bamboo Smart
Stylus
Eingabestift

Manufacturer
Wacom Co. Ltd., Tokyo, Japan
In-house design
Naoya Nishizawa
Web
www.wacom.com

The Bamboo Smart is a stylus which can be used with a large number of Samsung devices. It rests very comfortably in the hand and thus allows for natural writing positioning. Its thin tip is designed for long-term use and enables precise strokes. This facilitates the input of handwritten notes or the smooth sketching of drawings. The stylus is compatible with apps like Autodesk SketchBook, ArtRage, S Note and Bamboo Paper.

Statement by the jury
This slim stylus can be held in a very natural way, allowing the user to write or scribble intuitively on a tablet.

Der Bamboo Smart ist ein Eingabestift, der mit zahlreichen Samsung-Geräten verwendet werden kann. Er liegt sehr gut in der Hand und ermöglicht dadurch eine natürliche Schreibhaltung. Seine dünne Spitze ist für einen langen Gebrauch ausgelegt und gestattet eine präzise Strichführung. Dies erleichtert die Eingabe von handschriftlichen Notizen sowie das flüssige Zeichnen von Skizzen. Der Stift ist kompatibel mit Apps wie Autodesk SketchBook, ArtRage, S Note oder Bamboo Paper.

Begründung der Jury
Dieser schlanke Stift kann ganz natürlich gehalten werden, sodass der Benutzer auf einem Tablet intuitiv schreiben oder skribbeln kann.

DTU-1141
Pen Display
Stift-Display

Manufacturer
Wacom Co. Ltd., Tokyo, Japan
In-house design
Giles Mitchell
Web
www.wacom.com

With a thickness of merely 11 mm, the DTU-1141 pen display is very slim and compact. Its 10.6" full HD colour LCD panel is particularly suited for viewing and signing electronic documents. The hardened anti-reflection surface of the display is durable, provides a natural pen-on-paper feel and enables a wide viewing angle. Only a single USB cable is required to connect the screen to a monitor and supply it with power.

Statement by the jury
This pen display with its durable construction and full HD panel is optimally equipped for the sensitive field of electronic document signing.

Das Stift-Display DTU-1141 ist mit einer Dicke von nur 11 cm schlank und kompakt. Sein 10,6"-Full-HD-LCD-Farbdisplay eignet sich besonders für das Anzeigen und Unterzeichnen von elektronischen Dokumenten. Die gehärtete, entspiegelte Oberfläche des Displays ist langlebig und bietet ein natürliches Stift-auf-Papier-Gefühl sowie einen großen Blickwinkel. Für den Anschluss an einen Bildschirm und die Stromversorgung ist nur ein einziges USB-Kabel nötig.

Begründung der Jury
Für den sensiblen Bereich der elektronischen Dokumentensignatur ist dieses Stift-Display mit seiner robusten Ausführung und dem Full-HD-Panel bestens ausgestattet.

Intuos
Creative Pen Tablet
Kreatives Stifttablett

Manufacturer
Wacom Co. Ltd., Tokyo, Japan
In-house design
Giles Mitchell
Web
www.wacom.com

The Intuos pen tablet is very lightweight and has a slim shape. The polycarbonate shell seamlessly transitions across the front and back surfaces of the tablet, giving it a comfortable feel. With its 1,024 pressure sensitivity levels, the pen facilitates natural brushstrokes and precise lines. Thanks to multi-touch, other functions like zooming and rotating are controlled using finger gestures. The pen tablet also features four ExpressKeys, which can be customised as desired.

Statement by the jury
This creative pen tablet is especially easy and convenient to use thanks to its reduced weight and intuitive functionality.

Das Intuos Stifttablett ist sehr leicht und besitzt eine schlanke Gestalt. Das Gehäuse aus Polycarbonat geht nahtlos über die vordere und hintere Tablett-Oberfläche, was dem gesamten Tablett eine angenehme Haptik verleiht. Mit seinen 1.024 Druckstufen erlaubt der Stift natürliche Pinselstriche und eine präzise Linienführung. Dank Multitouch werden weitere Funktionen wie Zoomen oder Rotieren über Fingergesten gesteuert. Zudem sind vier ExpressKeys vorhanden, die sich nach Wunsch anpassen lassen.

Begründung der Jury
Dieses kreative Stifttablett lässt sich dank seines geringen Gewichts und der intuitiv nutzbaren Funktionen besonders einfach und bequem handhaben.

HP PageWide XL
Large-Format Printer
Großformatdrucker

Manufacturer
HP Inc., Sant Cugat del Vallès
(Barcelona), Spain

In-house design
Javier A. Cesar, Andreu Oliver,
Andreina Saranz, Pascual Bilotta,
Roel Geerts

Design
Nacar Design, Barcelona, Spain

Web
www.hp.com
www.nacardesign.com

reddot award 2016
best of the best

Perfect format

Large-format prints are part of everyday work, for instance in the architecture and engineering professions. Explicitly designed for such tasks, the HP PageWide XL fascinates with a consistent concept. Its well-balanced design merges the output performance of two printers into one unit. The innovative PageWide printing technology offers large-format production printing in both colour and black and white at excellent breakthrough speeds. Providing up to 30 D/A1-size prints per minute, this printer is thus 60 per cent faster than other LED printers today. This helps users achieve outstandingly high productivity, a streamlined workflow and a significant reduction of overall costs. The innovative performance power of this printer is also seen in the user-friendly and appealingly structured user interface. Accessible from all sides around the printer, the interface provides constant remote printer status updates and is easy to understand even for users without long experience. Boasting such qualities, the HP PageWide XL large-format printer sets new standards. The unit works fast and impresses with an outstandingly convenient lightness in use – it enriches the working environment with both extraordinary ergonomics and a solid, self-reliant appearance.

Perfektes Format

In Bereichen wie etwa der Architektur oder den Ingenieurberufen werden häufig großformatige Ausdrucke benötigt. Der explizit für solche Formate entworfene HP PageWide XL begeistert hier mit einem schlüssigen Konzept. Seine ausgewogene Gestaltung vereint in einem Gerät die Kapazität von zwei Druckern. Die innovative PageWide-Drucktechnologie erlaubt den Großformatdruck in Schwarz-Weiß oder in Farbe mit einer exzellenten Druckgeschwindigkeit. Bis zu 30 Ausdrucke im Format D/A1 pro Minute kann dieses Gerät bereitstellen und ist damit 60 Prozent schneller als herkömmliche LED-Drucker. Dies bedingt eine ausgesprochen hohe Produktivität, die auch einen zügigen Workflow und stark reduzierte Kosten impliziert. Die innovative Leistungsfähigkeit dieses Druckers zeigt sich ebenso in einer ansprechenden und nutzerfreundlich strukturierten Bedienoberfläche. Sie ist von allen Seiten zugänglich, gibt eine stetige Rückmeldung über den Status des Gerätes und ist auch ohne aufwendige Eingewöhnung gut verständlich. Mit diesen Qualitäten setzt der Großformatdrucker HP PageWide XL neue Standards. Er arbeitet rasch, mit einer verblüffend komfortablen Leichtigkeit – und bereichert das Arbeitsumfeld mit seiner gediegenen, selbstbewussten Ausstrahlung und ausgezeichneten Ergonomie.

Statement by the jury

This large-format printer convinces with a careful design. Elegant in appearance, its form is complemented by easy accessibility and perfectly thought out functionality. The HP PageWide XL delivers intuitive operation, quickly making its use self-evident and integration meaningful. This printer impresses with a technical and aesthetic quality that immediately casts a spell on users.

Begründung der Jury

Dieser Großformatdrucker überzeugt durch die Sorgfalt seiner Gestaltung. Die elegant anmutende Form geht einher mit leichter Zugänglichkeit und einer perfekt durchdachten Funktionalität. Der HP PageWide XL erlaubt eine sehr einfache Art der Bedienung, wobei schnell deutlich wird, wie man ihn nutzt und sinnvoll mit ihm interagiert. Er beeindruckt mit einer ästhetischen und technischen Qualität, die den Nutzer unmittelbar in ihren Bann zieht.

Designer portrait
See page 54
Siehe Seite 54

Color LaserJet Enterprise MFP M577
Laser Printer
Laserdrucker

Manufacturer
HP Inc., Boise, USA
In-house design
HP Imaging and Printing Design
Web
www.hp.com

The Color LaserJet Enterprise MFP M577 is a compact printer with a timeless design. It is characterised by smooth surfaces with very few lines and fosters a calm overall impression so that the printer blends unobtrusively into the surrounding environment. Thanks to innovative toner technology, the printing speed has increased while energy consumption has been reduced considerably. Moreover, the printer features multilevel security functions providing protection from unauthorised network access.

Statement by the jury
With its small footprint and reserved design, this printer is optimally suited for modern workplaces.

Der Color LaserJet Enterprise MFP M577 ist ein kompakter Drucker mit einer zeitlosen Gestaltung. Diese ist geprägt von glatten Flächen mit nur wenigen Linien und erzeugt ein ruhiges Gesamtbild, sodass sich der Drucker unauffällig in die Umgebung einfügt. Dank innovativer Tonertechnologie ist die Druckgeschwindigkeit erhöht, und dies bei einem deutlich reduzierten Energieverbrauch. Weiterhin verfügt der Drucker über mehrstufige Sicherheitsfunktionen, die im Netzwerk Schutz vor unerlaubtem Zugriff bieten.

Begründung der Jury
Mit seinem geringen Platzbedarf und der zurückhaltenden Gestaltung ist dieser Drucker hervorragend für moderne Arbeitsplätze geeignet.

HP DeskJet 3630
All-in-One Printer
All-in-one-Drucker

Manufacturer
HP Inc., San Diego, USA
In-house design
HP Imaging and Printing Design
Web
www.hp.com

The design of the HP DeskJet 3630 is focused on the development of a compact, cost-effective wireless printer with a complete functional spectrum and modern exterior. The shape, surface and workmanship of this printer, no longer reminiscent of the conventional plastic enclosures of electronic devices, stand out with their elegant design. With well-conceived details and easy operation, this DeskJet model is suitable for the entire family.

Statement by the jury
With its white housing and friendly colour accents, this printer has a very amicable appearance and thus enriches the home environment.

Bei der Gestaltung des HP DeskJet 3630 lag der Schwerpunkt darauf, einen kompakten, kostengünstigen kabellosen Drucker mit vollständigem Funktionsspektrum und einem modernen Äußeren zu entwickeln. Form, Oberfläche und Ausführung des Druckers erinnern nicht mehr an herkömmliche Kunststoffgehäuse von elektronischen Geräten, sondern bestechen durch ihre Eleganz. Mit durchdachten Details und einfacher Bedienung ist dieser DeskJet für die ganze Familie geeignet.

Begründung der Jury
Mit seinem hellen Gehäuse und den freundlichen Farbakzenten wirkt dieser Drucker überaus sympathisch und wird zur Bereicherung für die häusliche Umgebung.

HP OfficeJet 3830
All-in-One Printer
All-in-one-Drucker

Manufacturer
HP Inc., San Diego, USA
In-house design
HP Imaging and Printing Design
Web
www.hp.com

The HP OfficeJet 3830 is a multifunctional device for printing, copying, scanning and faxing. Due to its user-friendly concept, it fits well into small home offices. Additionally contributing to this is its discreet design, which is characterised by soft, friendly shapes. The printer is operated via the touchscreen or else wirelessly using a smartphone or tablet when connected to the home network.

Statement by the jury
With its plain elegance, this compact device can be used in both private domains and home office settings.

Der HP OfficeJet 3830 ist ein multifunktionales Gerät, mit dem sich drucken, kopieren, scannen und faxen lässt. Aufgrund seines nutzerfreundlichen Konzepts kann er problemlos in kleinen Homeoffices eingesetzt werden. Dazu trägt auch seine zurückhaltende Gestaltung bei, die von weichen, freundlichen Formen geprägt ist. Bedient wird der Drucker über einen Touchscreen oder kabellos per Smartphone oder Tablet, wenn er in das Heimnetzwerk eingebunden ist.

Begründung der Jury
Mit seiner schlichten Eleganz kann dieses kompakte Gerät im privaten Bereich ebenso eingesetzt werden wie im Homeoffice.

HP Envy 4520
All-in-One Printer
All-in-one-Drucker

Manufacturer
HP Inc., San Diego, USA
In-house design
HP Imaging and Printing Design
Web
www.hp.com

The HP Envy 4520 is a stylish and compact all-in-one printer for the home office. The graphical touch control panel is conveniently angled towards the user and thus easily accessible. A subtle glossy ribbon across the front, sides and back creates an elegant contrast to the matt finish of the dark housing. The semi-automated paper feed enables mobile printing at any time using a smartphone or tablet.

Statement by the jury
With its smooth surfaces and fine contours, the HP Envy 4520 has a very likeable appearance, making it an ideal device for private settings.

Der HP Envy 4520 ist ein schicker und kompakter All-in-one-Drucker für das Homeoffice. Das grafische Bedienfeld mit Touch-Funktion ist zum Benutzer hin angewinkelt und daher bequem erreichbar. Ein dezent glänzendes Band an der Vorder- und Rückseite und an den Seiten sorgt für einen eleganten Kontrast zur matten Oberfläche des dunklen Gehäuses. Die halbautomatisierte Papieraufnahme ermöglicht, dass über ein Smartphone oder Tablet jederzeit mobil gedruckt werden kann.

Begründung der Jury
Mit seinen glatten Flächen und den feinen Rundungen wirkt der HP Envy 4520 überaus sympathisch. Somit ist er ein ideales Gerät für private Räume.

HP OfficeJet 4650
All-in-One Printer
All-in-one-Drucker

Manufacturer
HP Inc., San Diego, USA
In-house design
HP Imaging and Printing Design
Web
www.hp.com

The HP OfficeJet 4650 is a compact all-in-one printer enabling comfortable mobile printing. It is equipped with an automatic document feeder, which can easily be closed when not in use. This contributes to a more elegant appearance and guarantees that no dust or dirt can make its way into the printer. The control panel is conveniently angled in the direction of the user, allowing for easy input of commands or reading of the printer status.

Statement by the jury
The HP OfficeJet 4650 shows a self-contained design with which it blends into home office surroundings in an especially harmonious way.

Der kompakte All-in-one-Drucker HP OfficeJet 4650 ermöglicht ein komfortables, mobiles Drucken. Er ist mit einer automatischen Dokumentenzuführung ausgestattet, die sich leicht zuklappen lässt, wenn sie nicht benötigt wird. Dies trägt zu einem eleganten Erscheinungsbild bei und sorgt dafür, dass kein Staub und Schmutz in das Gerät gelangen. Das Bedienfeld ist zum Benutzer hin angewinkelt und erlaubt die bequeme Eingabe von Befehlen oder das Ablesen des Status.

Begründung der Jury
Der HP OfficeJet 4650 zeigt eine in sich geschlossene Gestaltung, dank derer er sich besonders harmonisch in ein Homeoffice einfügt.

HP OfficeJet 200
Mobile Printer
Mobiler Drucker

Manufacturer
HP Inc., Singapore
In-house design
HP Imaging and Printing Design
Web
www.hp.com

The very compact HP OfficeJet 200 mobile printer is designed for professionals frequently on the move. Its long battery runtime and high-capacity toner cartridges guarantee smooth and trouble-free operation throughout the workday. The printer is convenient and intuitive to operate so that mobile users enjoy productive freedom. Equipped with Wi-Fi, the printer is set up easily using a smartphone or tablet app.

Statement by the jury
This printer is optimally suitable for mobile use. It is compact, enables wireless printing and has a long service life.

Der sehr kompakte mobile Drucker HP OfficeJet 200 wurde für Nutzer entwickelt, die beruflich viel unterwegs sind. Seine lange Akkulaufzeit und Tintenpatronen mit hoher Kapazität garantieren einen reibungslosen Betrieb während eines ganzen Arbeitstages. Der Drucker lässt sich einfach und intuitiv bedienen, damit mobile Anwender ihn produktiv einsetzen können. Er ist mit Wi-Fi ausgestattet und wird einfach per App über Smartphones oder Tablets eingerichtet.

Begründung der Jury
Der Drucker ist bestens für den mobilen Einsatz ausgestattet. Er ist kompakt, erlaubt das kabellose Drucken und hat eine lange Betriebsdauer.

DesignJet T830
Large-Format Multifunction Printer
Großformat-Multifunktionsdrucker

Manufacturer
HP Inc., Sant Cugat del Vallès, Spain
In-house design
Javier A. Cesar, Iñigo Oraa
Design
Nacar Design, Barcelona, Spain
Web
www.hp.com
www.nacardesign.com

The DesignJet T830 is a robust 36"
multifunction printer for offices and the
construction sector. On a very small
footprint it offers printing, scanning and
copying, which makes it suitable for
tight spaces. It is equipped with Wi-Fi
and prints documents in colour as well
as in a small format. As it is very compact for a device of its category, the
printer is ideally suitable for mobile use,
such as in construction site offices.
Thanks to durable workmanship, it can
be utilised in a safe and reliable way,
even in demanding environments.

Der DesignJet T830 ist ein widerstandsfähiger 36"-Multifunktionsdrucker für
Büros und die Bauwirtschaft. Drucken,
Scannen und Kopieren bietet er auf einer
sehr kleinen Standfläche, sodass er auch
für beengte Platzverhältnisse geeignet ist.
Er ist mit Wi-Fi ausgestattet und druckt
Dokumente sowohl in Farbe als auch in
einem kleinen Format aus. Da er für ein
Gerät seiner Klasse sehr kompakt ist, kann
er auch mobil, beispielsweise in Büros
direkt auf der Baustelle, seinen Dienst tun.
Dank seiner robusten Ausführung lässt
er sich auch in schwierigen Umgebungen
zuverlässig einsetzen.

Statement by the jury
This space-saving multifunction printer
enables large-format prints, scans and
copies to be easily created on site in any
place where they are required.

Begründung der Jury
Mit diesem platzsparenden Multifunktions-
drucker werden großformatige Drucke,
Scans und Kopien überall dort möglich, wo
sie benötigt werden.

Sindoh 3DWOX
3D Printer
3D-Drucker

Manufacturer
Sindoh Co., Ltd., Seoul, South Korea
Design
tangerine
(Martin Darbyshire, Young Choo, Gavin Flowers),
London, Great Britain
Web
www.sindoh.com
www.tangerine.net

The Sindoh 3DWOX combines innovative technology, wide-ranging functionality and a stylish, user-oriented design. All control elements are arranged ergonomically, while the 5" touchscreen enables intuitive navigation. The filament is auto-loading and is conveniently accessed through the front door panel to allow effortless refilling. All moving parts are safely enclosed, which reduces noise and ensures secure printer operation.

Der Sindoh 3DWOX vereint innovative Technologien, umfangreiche Funktionen und eine stilvolle, am Nutzer ausgerichtete Gestaltung. So sind die Bedienelemente ergonomisch angeordnet, während der 5"-Touchscreen die intuitive Navigation erlaubt. Das Filament wird automatisch geladen und ist bequem über eine Klappe an der Vorderseite zugänglich, damit es mühelos nachgefüllt werden kann. Alle beweglichen Teile befinden sich in einem geschlossenen Bauraum, was die Betriebsgeräusche reduziert und die sichere Bedienung des Druckers gewährleistet.

Statement by the jury
With its well-thought-out design, the Sindoh 3DWOX makes innovative 3D printing technology accessible to everyone.

Begründung der Jury
Mit seiner durchdachten Gestaltung macht der Sindoh 3DWOX die innovative Technologie des 3D-Druckens für jedermann zugänglich.

The jury 2016
International orientation and objectivity
Internationalität und Objektivität

The jurors of the Red Dot Award: Product Design
All members of the Red Dot Award: Product Design jury are appointed on the basis of independence and impartiality. They are independently working designers, academics in design faculties, representatives of international design institutions, and design journalists.

The jury is international in its composition, which changes every year. These conditions assure a maximum of objectivity. The members of this year's jury are presented in alphabetical order on the following pages.

Die Juroren des Red Dot Award: Product Design
In die Jury des Red Dot Award: Product Design wird als Mitglied nur berufen, wer völlig unabhängig und unparteiisch ist. Dies sind selbstständig arbeitende Designer, Hochschullehrer der Designfakultäten, Repräsentanten internationaler Designinstitutionen und Designfachjournalisten.

Die Jury ist international besetzt und wechselt in jedem Jahr ihre Zusammensetzung. Unter diesen Voraussetzungen ist ein Höchstmaß an Objektivität gewährleistet. Auf den folgenden Seiten werden die Jurymitglieder des diesjährigen Wettbewerbs in alphabetischer Reihenfolge vorgestellt.

01

Prof.
Werner Aisslinger
Germany
Deutschland

While still a student at the Berlin University of the Arts, Werner Aisslinger already worked for Ron Arad and Jasper Morrison in London and Michele de Lucci in Milan. In 1993 he founded the "studio aisslinger" in Berlin with a focus on experimental design, product design, material innovation and architectural concepts. Aisslinger's special interest is the use of cutting-edge technologies and unusual materials. For instance, with the "Juli Chair" for Cappellini he designed the first piece of furniture ever made from integral polyurethane foam, which was the first German chair for the permanent collection of the Museum of Modern Art in New York since 1964. Furthermore, with nomadic architectural modules such as the Loftcube he was the groundbreaker of a new urban lifestyle. Werner Aisslinger received several awards; his products are part of many museum collections around the world and were presented at a comprehensive exhibition of his works entitled "Home of the Future" in 2013 at the Berlin museum Haus am Waldsee. In 2014 Werner Aisslinger was awarded the renowned title "A&W Designer of the Year" in Cologne combined with an exhibition at the Kölnischer Kunstverein art museum.

Werner Aisslinger arbeitete bereits als Student der Universität der Künste Berlin für Ron Arad und Jasper Morrison in London sowie für Michele de Lucci in Mailand. 1993 gründete er das „studio aisslinger" in Berlin mit den Schwerpunkten Experimentelles Design, Produktdesign, Materialinnovationen und Architekturkonzepte. Das besondere Interesse Aisslingers gilt dem Einsatz neuester Technologien und ungewöhnlicher Materialien. So entwarf er mit dem „Juli Chair" für Cappellini das erste Möbelstück aus Polyuretan-Integralschaum – seit 1964 der erste deutsche Stuhl für die permanente Kollektion des Museum of Modern Art in New York – und mit nomadischen Architekturmodulen wie dem „Loftcube" Wegbereiter eines neuen urbanen Lebensgefühls. Werner Aisslinger wurde vielfach ausgezeichnet; seine Produkte sind in Museumssammlungen weltweit vertreten und wurden 2013 in einer umfassenden Werkschau unter dem Titel „Home of the Future" im Museum Haus am Waldsee in Berlin gezeigt. 2014 erhielt Werner Aisslinger in Köln den renommierten Titel „A&W-Designer des Jahres" mit einer Ausstellung im Kölnischen Kunstverein.

01 **The sea and the shore**
A hybrid between a well and a
storage space, hand-made in clay,
on the occasion of the Axor
WaterDream 2016, for Hansgrohe SE
Ein Hybrid aus Brunnen und Ablage-
fläche, handgefertigt aus Ton, im
Rahmen des Axor WaterDream 2016,
für Hansgrohe SE

02 **Luminaire**
Osram OLED, concept study, 2014
Osram OLED, Konzeptstudie, 2014

02

"An up and coming designer must,
above all, be interested in economic
and social topics as well as in those
that focus on sustainability and
that have a promising future."
„Ein Nachwuchsdesigner muss vor
allem an ökonomischen und sozialen
sowie an nachhaltigkeitsorientier-
ten und zukunftsträchtigen Themen
interessiert sein."

Which everyday product could you not live without?
My Bose SoundLink Mini speaker – which has now also become my constant travel companion. Nothing is more beautiful than being able to listen to one's playlists wherever one is.

How would you describe your work as a designer?
Designers are generalists. They therefore have to travel the world with a keen eye in order to be aware of the upheavals or problems of civilisation so that they can use them as future sources for ideas. In other words, designers need to be creative and productive input-output organisms.

What does winning the Red Dot say about the product?
It is the most important international design "seal of quality".

Welches Alltagsprodukt möchten Sie nicht mehr missen?
Meine Bose-Box SoundLink Mini – mittlerweile auch mein Reisebegleiter. Nichts ist schöner, als seine eigenen Playlists in guter Qualität überall hören zu können.

Wie würden Sie Ihre Tätigkeit als Designer beschreiben?
Designer sind Generalisten und müssen deshalb interessiert durch die Welt reisen, um zivilisatorische Umwälzungen oder Probleme zu erkennen und daraus zukünftige Ideen zu schöpfen – es geht also darum, als Designer ein kreativer und produktiver Input-Output-Organismus zu sein.

Was sagt die Auszeichnung mit dem Red Dot über ein Produkt aus?
Sie ist das international wichtigste „Qualitätssiegel" im Design.

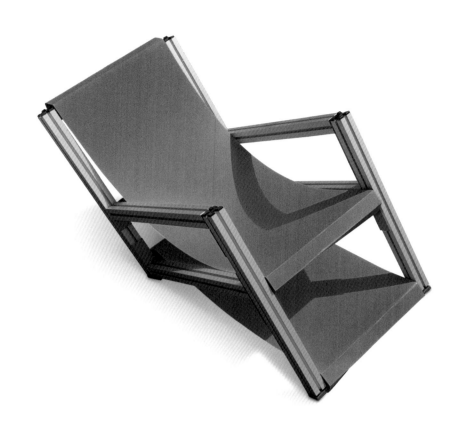

01

Manuel
Alvarez Fuentes
Mexico
Mexiko

Manuel Alvarez Fuentes studied industrial design at the Universidad Iberoamericana, Mexico City, where he later served as Director of the Design Department. In 1975, he also received a Master of Design from the Royal College of Art, London. He has over 40 years of experience in the fields of product design, furniture and interior design, packaging design, signage and visual communications. From 1992 to 2012, he was Director of Diseño Corporativo, a product design consultancy. Currently, he is head of innovation at Alfher Porcewol in Mexico City. He has acted as consultant for numerous companies and also as a board member of various designers' associations, including as a member of the Icsid Board of Directors, as Vice President of the National Chamber of Industry of Mexico, Querétaro, and as Director of the Innovation and Design Award, Querétaro. Furthermore, Alvarez Fuentes has been senior tutor in Industrial Design at Tecnológico de Monterrey Campus Querétaro since 2009. In 2012 and 2013, he was president of the jury of Premio Quorum, the most prestigious design competition in Mexico.

Manuel Alvarez Fuentes studierte Industriedesign an der Universidad Iberoamericana, Mexiko-Stadt, wo er später die Leitung des Fachbereichs Design übernahm. 1975 erhielt er zudem einen Master of Design vom Royal College of Art, London. Er hat über 40 Jahre Erfahrung in Produkt- und Möbelgestaltung, Interior Design, Verpackungsdesign, Leitsystemen und visueller Kommunikation. Von 1992 bis 2012 war er Direktor von Diseño Corporativo, einem Beratungsunternehmen für Produktgestaltung. Heute ist Alvarez Fuentes Head of Innovation bei Alfher Porcewol in Mexiko-Stadt. Er war als Berater für zahlreiche Unternehmen sowie als Vorstandsmitglied in verschiedenen Designverbänden tätig, z. B. im Icsid-Vorstand, als Vizepräsident der mexikanischen Industrie- und Handelskammer im Bundesstaat Querétaro und als Direktor des Innovation and Design Award, Querétaro. Seit 2009 ist Alvarez Fuentes Senior-Dozent für Industriedesign am Tecnológico de Monterrey Campus Querétaro. 2012 und 2013 war er Präsident der Jury des Premio Quorum, des angesehensten Designwettbewerbs in Mexiko.

01 **SolForm**
Beach chair, anodised
aluminium structure
and canvas, 2016
Strandstuhl, Rahmen aus
eloxiertem Aluminium
und Segeltuch, 2016

"It is fascinating to evaluate
the constant progress made in
technologies and manufacturing
capabilities that is reflected in
the various products coming from
so many different places in the
world."

„Ich finde es überaus faszinierend,
den konstanten Fortschritt in
Technik und Herstellungsverfahren
zu bewerten, der sich in den unterschiedlichen Produkten aus so
vielen Teilen der Welt widerspiegelt."

**What is the difference between good and bad
product design?**
Good product design is always pertinent to users and
understandable, sustainable and beautiful. And it is
durable and in many ways timeless.

Which skills does a successful designer have?
He is a keen observer, strategist and ecologist;
a generous person who thoroughly looks after other
people. He is well prepared to meet users' needs
with a technical and systematic approach and create
a suitable design language and aesthetic.

**Which developments would you like to see in
product design in the future?**
In the future I would like to see more reliable and
durable products; products that deliver an improved
quality of life, while interacting safely with users,
and are easy to maintain. I hope to see an increase in
more meaningful designs which provide real and
honest solutions to people's needs and expectations.

**Was unterscheidet gutes von schlechtem
Produktdesign?**
Gutes Produktdesign ist stets zweckdienlich für die
Nutzer. Es ist verständlich, nachhaltig und schön,
außerdem langlebig und in vielfältiger Weise zeitlos.

Welche Fähigkeiten hat ein erfolgreicher Designer?
Er ist ein guter Beobachter, Stratege und Ökologe;
ein großzügiger Mensch, der sich eingehend um andere
Menschen kümmert. Er ist gut darauf vorbereitet, die
Nutzerbedürfnisse mit einem technischen und systema-
tischen Ansatz zu lösen und eine passende Designsprache und -ästhetik zu schaffen.

**Welche Entwicklungen im Produktdesign
würden Sie sich für die Zukunft wünschen?**
Ich würde mir mehr zuverlässige und langlebige Pro-
dukte für die Zukunft wünschen. Produkte, die die
Lebensqualität verbessern und gleichzeitig sicher mit
Benutzern interagieren und einfach zu warten sind.
Ich hoffe auf einen Zuwachs an bedeutsamen Gestal-
tungen, die wahre und ehrliche Lösungen für die
Bedürfnisse und Erwartungen von Menschen bieten.

01

David Andersen
Denmark
Dänemark

David Andersen, born in 1978, graduated from the Glasgow School of Art in 2003 and the Copenhagen Academy of Fashion and Design. In 2004, he was awarded "Best Costume Designer" and received the award "Wedding Gown of the Year" from the Royal Court Theatre in Denmark. He has developed designs for ready-to-wear clothes, shoes, perfume, underwear and home wear and emerged as a fashion designer working as chief designer at Dreams by Isabell Kristensen as well as designing couture for artists and dance competitions under his own name. He debuted his collection "David Andersen" in 2007 and apart from Europe it also conquered markets in Japan and the US. In 2010 and 2011, the Danish Fashion Award nominated him in the category "Design Talent of the Year", and in 2010 as well as 2012, David Andersen received a grant from the National Art Foundation. He regularly shows his sustainable designs, which are worn by members of the Royal Family, politicians and celebrities, at couture exhibitions around the world. David Andersen is now Vice President Design at Rosendahl Design Group which represents a portfolio of design classics.

David Andersen, 1978 geboren, ist ein Absolvent der Glasgow School of Art des Jahrgangs 2003 und der Copenhagen Academy of Fashion and Design. 2004 wurde er als „Best Costume Designer" sowie für das „Hochzeitskleid des Jahres" vom Royal Court Theatre in Dänemark prämiert. Er entwirft Konfektionskleidung, Schuhe, Parfüm, Unterwäsche und Heimtextilien und wurde als Modedesigner bekannt, als er als Chefdesigner bei Dreams von Isabell Kristensen sowie unter seinem eigenen Namen für Künstler und Tanzwettbewerbe arbeitete. Seine im Jahr 2007 eingeführte Kollektion „David Andersen" eroberte neben Europa Märkte in Japan und den USA. 2010 und 2011 nominierte ihn der Danish Fashion Award in der Kategorie „Design Talent of the Year" und 2010 sowie 2012 erhielt er ein Stipendium der National Art Foundation. David Andersen präsentiert seine nachhaltigen Entwürfe, die von Mitgliedern der Königsfamilie, Politikern und Prominenten getragen werden, regelmäßig in Couture-Ausstellungen weltweit. David Andersen ist zurzeit Vice President Design der Rosendahl Design Group, die eine Reihe von Design-Klassikern vertritt.

02

"A young design talent should follow his dreams even if it can be tough! The opposite can be even tougher."

„Ein junges Designtalent sollte seinen Träumen folgen, selbst wenn das schwer ist! Das Gegenteil kann noch schwerer sein."

Which everyday product could you not live without?
I could not live without my shoes – especially my Rick Owens shoes that suit my personality and are so comfortable to wear.

Which skills does a successful designer have?
You need to be able to express yourself and not be afraid of doing so. Be able to take in impressions and signals from the daily life around you and then convert them into great ideas.

How would you describe your work as a designer?
Keywords in my design are personality, humour, sensibility and a great eye for graphic lines. Designing for me is a creative process, where the product finds its form along the way.

What does winning the Red Dot say about the product?
That it's an interesting product that stands out. It often has a good story and hits the zeitgeist.

Welches Alltagsprodukt möchten Sie nicht mehr missen?
Meine Schuhe möchte ich nicht missen – insbesondere nicht meine Rick-Owens-Schuhe, die zu meiner Persönlichkeit passen und so bequem sind.

Welche Fähigkeiten hat ein erfolgreicher Designer?
Man muss fähig sein und keine Angst davor haben, sich auszudrücken. Fähig sein, Eindrücke und Signale aus dem täglichen Leben um sich herum aufzunehmen und dann in große Ideen umzuwandeln.

Wie würden Sie Ihre Tätigkeit als Designer beschreiben?
Schlüsselworte in meiner Tätigkeit als Designer sind Persönlichkeit, Sensibilität und ein ausgezeichnetes Auge für grafische Linien. Für mich ist Gestalten ein kreativer Prozess, währenddessen das Produkt seine Form findet.

Was sagt die Auszeichnung mit dem Red Dot über ein Produkt aus?
Dass es ein interessantes Produkt ist, das sich von anderen abhebt. Oft steckt hinter dem Produkt eine gute Geschichte und es entspricht dem Zeitgeist.

01

Prof. Masayo Ave
Japan/Germany
Japan/Deutschland

The architect and designer Masayo Ave founded her own design studio "Ave design corporation" in 1992. Since 2001 she has been a leader in advanced sensory design research and conducted numerous multidisciplinary design workshops. During her guest professorship from 2004 to 2007, Masayo Ave founded the Experimental Design Institute of Haptic Interface Design at the Berlin University of the Arts. During the following two years she was professor and head of the product design department at the Estonian Academy of Arts. From 2012 to 2013 she was a guest professor at the textile and surface design department at Berlin Weissensee School of Art. Furthermore, she has held a teaching position at the architecture department of Hosei University, at the Kanazawa College of Arts in Japan, since 2009. Since 2006 her design studio "MasayoAve creation" and the Haptic Interface Design Institute have been based in Berlin. In addition, Masayo Ave is actively involved in the development of new educational design programmes for children and youth in cooperation with design institutes such as the DesignSingapore Council and the Red Dot Design Museum Essen, Germany.

Die Architektin und Designerin Masayo Ave eröffnete 1992 ihr Designstudio „Ave design corporation". Seit 2001 hat sie eine Führungsposition in der sensorischen Designforschung inne und gibt zahlreiche multidisziplinäre Design-Workshops. Während ihrer Gastprofessur zwischen 2004 und 2007 gründete sie das experimentelle Designinstitut „Haptic Interface Design" an der Universität der Künste Berlin. In den folgenden zwei Jahren war sie als Professorin und Leiterin des Produktdesign-Instituts der Estonian Academy of Arts tätig. Von 2012 bis 2013 erhielt sie eine Gastprofessur im Fachbereich „Textildesign und Oberflächengestaltung" an der Kunsthochschule Berlin Weißensee. Außerdem unterrichtet sie seit 2009 an der Architektur-Fakultät der Hosei University am Kanazawa College of Arts in Japan. Seit 2006 sind ihr Designstudio „MasayoAve creation" und das Haptic Interface Design Institute in Berlin ansässig. Masayo Ave beschäftigt sich außerdem mit Programmen für die Designlehre von Kindern und Jugendlichen in Kooperation mit Designinstituten wie dem DesignSingapore Council und dem Red Dot Design Museum Essen.

02

01 BLOCK

Modular sofa and cool cushions made from an open-cell foam based on polyester, launched in her own collection "MasayoAve creation", 1999/2000

Modulares Sofa und coole Kissen, hergestellt aus einem offenporigen Schaum, basierend auf Polyester; erschienen in ihrer eigenen Kollektion „MasayoAve creation", 1999/2000

02 GENESI

Table light designed with a cover made from a washable open-cell polyester and a body in chromed steel, launched in her own collection "MasayoAve creation", 1998

Tischleuchte, die mit einem Lampenschirm aus waschbarem, offenporigem Polyester und einem Körper aus verchromtem Stahl entworfen wurde; erschienen in ihrer eigenen Kollektion „MasayoAve creation", 1998

"I would like to design good educational tools and spaces to cultivate children's sensitivity, imagination and perceptive powers."

„Ich würde gerne pädagogisch wertvolle Instrumente und Räume kreieren, die die Sensibilität, die Fantasie und das Wahrnehmungsvermögen von Kindern kultivieren."

How would you describe your work as a designer?
In my design work I explore the intrinsic quality of industrial materials with the aim of enriching the sensory experience of industrial products and living spaces.

Which developments in the category "Babies and children" did you perceive as particularly positive?
Products for babies and children have the most complex requirements because they are the most sensitive and perceptive human beings and their body dimensions and abilities change day by day. Thus, haptic comfort, scents of materials or the enrichment of sensory experience are becoming key criteria for this category.

Which type of product has undergone the greatest development in the last five years?
Products which support and enhance the physical ability of human beings, such as wheelchairs and prosthetic legs. They are not merely designed as technical and functional tools, but increasingly as natural extensions of the human body.

Wie würden Sie Ihre Tätigkeit als Designerin beschreiben?
In meiner Tätigkeit als Designerin erforsche ich die intrinsische Qualität industrieller Materialien mit dem Ziel, die sinnliche Erfahrung industrieller Produkte und Lebensräume zu bereichern.

Welche Entwicklungen im Bereich „Baby und Kind" fanden Sie besonders positiv?
Produkte für Babys und Kinder haben die komplexesten Anforderungen, da sie die sensibelsten und aufnahmefähigsten Menschen sind und sich ihre Körpermaße und Fähigkeiten jeden Tag verändern. Daher entwickeln sich haptisches Wohlbefinden, Gerüche von Materialien oder die Bereicherung der sinnlichen Erfahrung zu den Schlüsselkriterien dieser Kategorie.

Welche Produktart hat sich im Laufe der letzten fünf Jahre am meisten verändert?
Produkte, die die physischen Fähigkeiten des Menschen unterstützen und verbessern, wie zum Beispiel Rollstühle und Beinprothesen. Sie werden nicht bloß als technische und funktionale Werkzeuge gestaltet, sondern mehr und mehr als natürliche Erweiterungen des menschlichen Körpers.

01

Chris Bangle
USA / Italy
USA / Italien

Chris Bangle studied at the University of Wisconsin, graduated from the Art Center College of Design in Pasadena, California and began his career at Opel in 1981. In 1985 he moved on to Fiat, before becoming the first American Chief of Design at BMW in 1992, where he was in charge of the designs for BMW, Mini Cooper and Rolls-Royce. In 2007 he was awarded, together with the Design Team BMW Group, the honorary title "Red Dot: Design Team of the Year" for his outstanding overall design achievements. Since leaving the automotive industry in 2009 Chris Bangle has continued his own design projects and innovations in his design studio Chris Bangle Associates s.r.l. (CBA) near Clavesana in Piemonte, Italy. As Managing Director of CBA he currently heads a team of designers and engineers, who use the studio as a design residence and creative think tank together with the staff of its clients. His 25 years of experience and competence make Chris Bangle a sought-after speaker. He frequently travels around the world to give lectures, teach design and consult clients.

Chris Bangle studierte an der University of Wisconsin, machte seinen Abschluss am Art Center College of Design in Pasadena, Kalifornien, und begann seine Karriere 1981 bei Opel. 1985 wechselte er zu Fiat, bevor er 1992 der erste „American Chief of Design" bei BMW wurde und für die Entwürfe von BMW, Mini Cooper und Rolls-Royce verantwortlich zeichnete. 2007 wurde ihm für seine herausragende gestalterische Gesamtleistung zusammen mit dem Design Team BMW Group der Ehrentitel „Red Dot: Design Team of the Year" verliehen. Seit seinem Ausstieg aus der Automobilbranche 2009 führt Chris Bangle eigene Gestaltungsvorhaben und Innovationen in seinem Studio Chris Bangle Associates s.r.l. (CBA) bei Clavesana im Piemont, Italien, fort und leitet derzeit als Managing Director von CBA ein Team von Designern und Ingenieuren, die das Studio gemeinsam mit den Mitarbeitern der Auftraggeber als Designresidenz und kreative Ideenfabrik nutzen. Seine 25-jährige Erfahrung und Kompetenz machen Chris Bangle zu einem gefragten Referenten. Er reist regelmäßig um die Welt, um Vorträge zu halten, Design zu lehren und seine Kunden zu beraten.

01

"It's an honour to be asked for your opinion in matters of good design and the challenge to live up to the standards of such a premium award."

„Es ist eine Ehre, nach seiner Meinung über gutes Design gefragt zu werden, und eine Herausforderung, den Maßstäben eines so erstklassigen Wettbewerbs gerecht zu werden."

Which skills does a successful designer have?
Almost all design depends on communication skills of some sort such as drawing or speaking; both contain the power of persuasion and the skills of logic and rhetoric. I encourage young people to buttress their technical skills with experiences in art of any nature.

How would you describe your work as a designer?
I follow a three-phase process that I learned at BMW – Understanding, Believing, Seeing. To understand means to listen and question in depth what the clients' true needs are. After that, one must try to discover solutions that don't need immediate proof of plausibility but must be compelling enough to inspire the belief in their eventual reality. What people believe in is more powerful than what they know, which is the source of all innovation. After that the fine-tune work we call seeing begins.

Welche Fähigkeiten hat ein erfolgreicher Designer?
Nahezu jegliche Gestaltung hängt von irgendwelchen Kommunikationsfähigkeiten ab, zum Beispiel Zeichnen oder Sprechen. Beide beinhalten Überzeugungskraft und logische wie rhetorische Fähigkeiten. Ich ermuntere junge Leute dazu, ihre technischen Fähigkeiten mit Erfahrungen in Künsten jeglicher Art zu untermauern.

Wie würden Sie Ihre Tätigkeit als Designer beschreiben?
Ich folge einem dreiphasigen Prozess, den ich bei BMW gelernt habe – Understanding, Believing, Seeing (Verstehen, Glauben, Sehen). Etwas zu verstehen bedeutet, zuzuhören und eingehend zu fragen, was die wahren Bedürfnisse der Kunden sind. Danach muss man versuchen, Lösungen zu entdecken, die keinen unmittelbaren Plausibilitätsbeweis benötigen, aber dennoch schlüssig genug sind, um den Glauben an ihre spätere Verwirklichung anzuregen. Woran Menschen glauben, ist viel einflussreicher als das, was sie wissen – der Ursprung jeglicher Innovation. Danach beginnt die Feinanpassungsarbeit, die wir „Seeing" nennen.

01

Martin Beeh
Germany
Deutschland

Martin Beeh is a graduate in Industrial Design from the Darmstadt University of Applied Sciences in Germany and the ENSCI-Les Ateliers, Paris, and completed a postgraduate course in business administration. In 1995, he became design coordinator at Décathlon in Lille/France, in 1997 senior designer at Electrolux Industrial Design Center Nuremberg and Stockholm and furthermore became design manager at Electrolux Industrial Design Center Pordenone/Italy, in 2001. He is a laureate of several design awards as well as founder and director of the renowned student design competition "Electrolux Design Lab". In the year 2006 he became general manager of the German office of the material library Material ConneXion in Cologne. Three years later, he founded the design office beeh_innovation. Martin Beeh lectured at the Folkwang University of the Arts in Essen, the University of Applied Sciences Schwäbisch Gmünd and the University of Applied Sciences Hamm-Lippstadt and was professor for design management at the University of Applied Sciences Ostwestfalen-Lippe in Lemgo from 2012 to 2015. He is currently teaching management and planning methods at the department of design of the University of Applied Sciences Aachen.

Martin Beeh absolvierte ein Studium in Industriedesign an der Fachhochschule Darmstadt und an der ENSCI-Les Ateliers, Paris, sowie ein Aufbaustudium der Betriebswirtschaft. 1995 wurde er Designkoordinator bei Décathlon in Lille/Frankreich, 1997 Senior Designer im Electrolux Industrial Design Center Nürnberg und Stockholm sowie 2001 Design Manager im Electrolux Industrial Design Center Pordenone/Italien. Er ist Gewinner diverser Designpreise und gründete und leitete den renommierten Designwettbewerb für Studierende, das „Electrolux Design Lab". Im Jahr 2006 wurde er General Manager der deutschen Niederlassung der Materialbibliothek „Material ConneXion" in Köln. Drei Jahre später gründete Martin Beeh das Designbüro beeh_innovation. Martin Beeh hatte Lehraufträge an der Folkwang Universität der Künste in Essen, an der Hochschule für Gestaltung Schwäbisch Gmünd und an der Hochschule Hamm-Lippstadt und war von 2012 bis 2015 Professor für Designmanagement an der Hochschule Ostwestfalen-Lippe in Lemgo. Aktuell lehrt er Management und Planungsmethoden am Fachbereich Gestaltung der Fachhochschule Aachen.

02

"A young design talent is a master of his craft, is happy to engage in conversations and willing to learn, questions conventional solutions and can tell an industrial loft apartment from a working factory."

„Ein Nachwuchsdesigner beherrscht sein Handwerk, ist dialogfreudig und lernfähig, hinterfragt eingefahrene Lösungswege und kennt Fabriken nicht nur als Loft."

Which product would you like to design one day?
An electric coffee grinder – a device that makes everyday life easier, brings joy and has remained almost unchanged for a long time. Since the legendary 1976 Braun KMM 10 very little has changed here.

What does winning the Red Dot say about the product?
It has high design quality, stands out from the masses of competitors and is meaningful. Often award-winning products are pioneers for the company itself or even for the respective market. It is this courage which we support as jurors.

Which developments would you like to see in product design in the future?
Fewer, but better products. We only have to make those in charge of marketing see this as an opportunity.

What attracts you to the work as a Red Dot juror?
It is great fun for me to thoroughly test and scrutinise the products together with my dedicated colleagues.

Welches Produkt würden Sie gerne einmal gestalten?
Eine elektrische Kaffeemühle: ein Freude bereitender, seit Langem konstruktiv nahezu unveränderter Alltagshelfer. Seit der legendären Braun KMM 10 von 1976 hat sich hier wenig getan.

Was sagt eine Auszeichnung mit dem Red Dot über das Produkt aus?
Hohe Gestaltungsqualität, Herausragen aus dem Meer der Wettbewerber, Sinnhaftigkeit des Produktes. Oft sind ausgezeichnete Produkte Pioniere für das Unternehmen selbst oder gar für den jeweiligen Markt. Diesen Mut unterstützen wir als Juroren.

Welche Entwicklungen im Produktdesign würden Sie sich für die Zukunft wünschen?
Weniger, aber bessere Produkte. Das muss man nur noch den Verantwortlichen im Marketing als Chance vermitteln.

Was reizt Sie an der Arbeit als Red Dot-Juror?
Es macht mir unglaubliche Freude, die Produkte mit den engagierten Kollegen auf Herz und Nieren zu prüfen und kritisch zu hinterfragen.

01

Dr
Luisa Bocchietto
Italy
Italien

Luisa Bocchietto, architect and designer, graduated from the Milan Polytechnic. She has worked as a freelancer undertaking projects for local development, building renovations and urban planning. As a visiting professor she teaches at universities and design schools, she takes part in design conferences and international juries, publishes articles and organises exhibitions on architecture and design. Over the years, her numerous projects aimed at supporting the spread of design quality. From 2008 until 2014 she was National President of the ADI, the Italian Association for Industrial Design. Currently, she is a member of the Icsid Board and is President Elect for the period from 2017 to 2019. From September 2014 to February 2015 she was Editorial Director of PLATFORM, a new magazine about Architecture and Design.

Luisa Bocchietto, Architektin und Designerin, graduierte am Polytechnikum Mailand. Sie arbeitet freiberuflich und führt Projekte für die lokale Entwicklung, Gebäudeumbauten und Stadtplanung durch. Als Gastprofessorin lehrt sie an Universitäten und Designschulen, sie nimmt an Designkonferenzen und internationalen Jurys teil, veröffentlicht Artikel und betreut Ausstellungen über Architektur und Design. Ihre zahlreichen Projekte über die Jahre hinweg verfolgten das Ziel, die Verbreitung von Designqualität zu unterstützen. Von 2008 bis 2014 war sie Nationale Präsidentin der ADI, des italienischen Verbandes für Industriedesign. Aktuell ist sie Gremiumsmitglied des Icsid und President Elect für den Zeitraum 2017–2019. Von September 2014 bis Februar 2015 war sie Chefredakteurin von PLATFORM, einem neuen Magazin über Architektur und Design.

01 LAMIAITALIA
Design of ceramic contain-
ers, made with the pottery
factory Bottega Gatti
(Faenza, Italy) as part of the
Milano Makers project
"Ceramics, Food and Design:
when designers encounter
the master potters", 2015
Gestaltung von Keramikbe-
hältnissen, hergestellt mit der
Keramikwerkstatt Bottega
Gatti (Faenza, Italien) als Be-
standteil des „Milano Makers"-
Projekts „Keramik, Essen und
Design: Wenn Designer Töp-
fermeistern begegnen", 2015

02 PLATFORM
Six covers of the magazine
"PLATFORM Architecture
and Design", 2014/2015
Sechs Cover des Magazins
„PLATFORM Architecture and
Design", 2014/2015

02

"My work as a designer is to try
to improve the world around us
with passion, skill and humour."
„Meine Tätigkeit als Designerin
besteht darin, die Welt um uns
herum mit Leidenschaft, Kompetenz und Humor zu verbessern."

**Which everyday product could you not live
without?**
My car, because it's my mobile office, my home, my
thinking place and my personal retreat, as I move
from place to place.

**What is the difference between good and bad
product design?**
Innovation; any innovation, be it a little or a lot,
because it allows to build a richer world.

Which skills does a successful designer have?
Curiosity, attention and multidisciplinary expertise.

What attracts you to the work as a Red Dot juror?
Working with other people from around the world
who are competent in design is always an exciting
experience.

**Which type of product has undergone the greatest
development in the last five years?**
Apps and everything to do with the digital world as
well as design services.

**Welches Alltagsprodukt möchten Sie nicht
mehr missen?**
Mein Auto, da es mein mobiles Büro, mein Zuhause,
mein Raum zum Denken, mein persönlicher Zufluchts-
ort ist, während ich mich von einem Ort zum nächsten
bewege.

**Was unterscheidet gutes von schlechtem
Produktdesign?**
Innovation. Jegliche Innovation, sei sie groß oder klein,
da sie es ermöglicht, eine reichere Welt zu schaffen.

Welche Fähigkeiten hat ein erfolgreicher Designer?
Neugierde, Aufmerksamkeit und multidisziplinäre
Fachkenntnis.

Was reizt Sie an der Arbeit als Red Dot-Juror?
Mit anderen Menschen aus aller Welt, die Design-
kompetenz besitzen, zusammenzuarbeiten, ist immer
eine aufregende Erfahrung.

**Welche Produktart hat sich im Laufe der letzten
fünf Jahre am meisten entwickelt?**
Apps und alles, was mit der digitalen Welt zu tun hat,
sowie Designdienstleistungen.

01

Gordon Bruce
USA

Gordon Bruce is the owner of Gordon Bruce Design LLC and has been a design consultant for 40 years working with many multinational corporations in Europe, Asia and the USA. He has worked on a very wide range of products, interiors and vehicles – from aeroplanes to computers to medical equipment to furniture. From 1991 to 1994, Gordon Bruce was a consulting vice president for the Art Center College of Design's Kyoto programme and, from 1995 to 1999, chairman of Product Design for the Innovative Design Lab of Samsung (IDS) in Seoul, Korea. In 2003, he played a crucial role in helping to establish Porsche Design's North American office. For many years, he served as head design consultant for Lenovo's Innovative Design Center (IDC) in Beijing and he is presently working with Bühler in Switzerland and Huawei Technologies Co., Ltd. in China. Gordon Bruce is a visiting professor at several universities in the USA and in China and also acts as an author and design publicist. He recently received Art Center College of Design's "Lifetime Achievement Award".

Gordon Bruce ist Inhaber der Gordon Bruce Design LLC und seit mittlerweile 40 Jahren als Designberater für zahlreiche multinationale Unternehmen in Europa, Asien und den USA tätig. Er arbeitete bereits an einer Reihe von Produkten, Inneneinrichtungen und Fahrzeugen – von Flugzeugen über Computer bis hin zu medizinischem Equipment und Möbeln. Von 1991 bis 1994 war Gordon Bruce beratender Vizepräsident des Kioto-Programms am Art Center College of Design sowie von 1995 bis 1999 Vorsitzender für Produktdesign beim Innovative Design Lab of Samsung (IDS) in Seoul, Korea. Im Jahr 2003 war er wesentlich daran beteiligt, das Büro von Porsche Design in Nordamerika zu errichten. Über viele Jahre war er leitender Designberater für Lenovos Innovative Design Center (IDC) in Beijing. Aktuell arbeitet er für Bühler in der Schweiz und Huawei Technologies Co., Ltd. in China. Gordon Bruce ist Gastprofessor an zahlreichen Universitäten in den USA und in China und als Buchautor sowie Publizist tätig. Kürzlich erhielt er vom Art Center College of Design den Lifetime Achievement Award.

01 **CM1 and CM 2**
Connection Machine,
Massively Parallel Processor
for Thinking Machines, 1984
Consulting Industrial
Designers: Gordon Bruce,
Allen Hawthorne
Thinking Machines designers:
Danny Hillis (inventor) and
Tamiko Thiel
Maschinenanschluss,
Massenparallelrechner für
Thinking Machines, 1984
Consulting Industrial
Designers: Gordon Bruce,
Allen Hawthorne
Designer der Thinking Machines:
Danny Hillis (Erfinder) und
Tamiko Thiel

02 **Putter Golf Clubs**
Weighted customisable putters
for EnterBrands, a Porsche
Design subsidiary, 2003
Beschwerte, einstellbare Putter
für EnterBrands, ein Tochterun-
ternehmen von Porsche Design,
2003

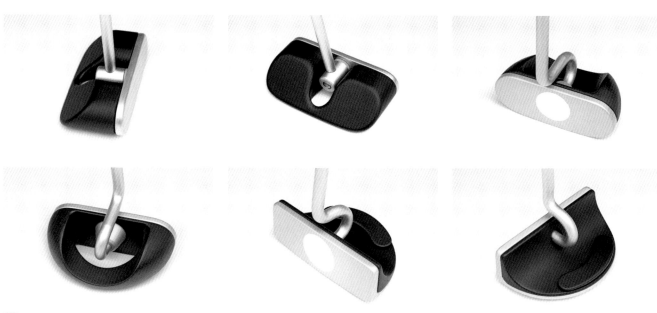

02

"More and more companies are learning that a well thought-out design is not only achievable but necessary in order to be competitive."

„Mehr und mehr Unternehmen beginnen zu verstehen, dass eine gut durchdachte Gestaltung nicht nur realisierbar, sondern notwendig ist, um wettbewerbsfähig zu sein."

What is the difference between good and bad product design?
Well-designed products result from the inside out. That is, well-designed products result from solving all the important issues that enable a product to accommodate its users in the most comfortable and natural way possible while performing tasks and achieving goals with good results in the most effective and efficient way possible.

How would you describe your work as a designer?
I always begin by asking myself, what are the key design performance issues that are at the heart of the concept and how do I fit the task to the user and prevent them from having to compensate for possible shortcomings of the concept.

Which developments would you like to see in product design in the future?
I would like to see design education rethought, redesigned and improved. In some areas necessary skills for attaining good judgement have been discarded in favour of technological expediencies.

Was unterscheidet gutes von schlechtem Produktdesign?
Gut gestaltete Produkte entstehen, wenn alle wichtigen Probleme gelöst sind, die das Produkt befähigen, dem Benutzer auf die komfortabelste und natürlichste Weise entgegenzukommen und gleichzeitig Aufgaben und Ziele mit guten Ergebnissen so effektiv und effizient wie möglich zu erreichen.

Wie würden Sie Ihre Tätigkeit als Designer beschreiben?
Ich beginne immer damit, mich zu fragen: Was sind die zentralen Leistungen, die das Designkonzept erzielen muss, und wie bewerkstellige ich es, die Aufgabe auf den Nutzer zuzuschneiden und zu verhindern, dass der Nutzer eventuelle Mängel am Konzept ausgleichen muss?

Welche Entwicklungen im Produktdesign würden Sie sich für die Zukunft wünschen?
Dass die Designlehre überdacht, umgestaltet und verbessert wird. In manchen Bereichen sind Fähig-keiten, die für ein gutes Urteilsvermögen notwendig sind, zugunsten technologischer Zweckdienlichkeiten ausgemustert worden.

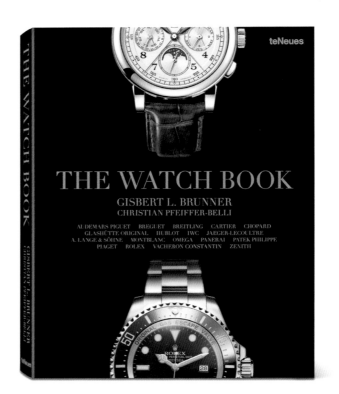

01

Gisbert L. Brunner
Germany
Deutschland

Since 1964 Gisbert Brunner has been involved with wristwatches, pendulum clocks and other precision chronometers. During the quartz watch crisis in the 1970s his affection for the timekeepers that appeared to be dying out grew even stronger. And from the early 1980s onwards his collector's passion led him to write his first articles for magazines and more than 20 books. In addition, Gisbert Brunner writes for publications such as ZEIT Magazin, Chronos, Handelszeitung, Prestige, Red Bulletin, Flair, #ich and Terra Mater. Furthermore, he blogs at redbulletin.com and gives lectures around the world on mechanical watches and renowned watch manufacturers.

Gisbert Brunner beschäftigt sich seit 1964 mit Armbanduhren, Pendeluhren und anderen Präzisionszeitmessern. Während der Quarzuhren-Krise in den 1970er Jahren wuchs seine Liebe zu den scheinbar aussterbenden mechanischen Zeitmessern. Und ab den frühen 1980er Jahren veranlasste ihn sein leidenschaftliches Sammelhobby dazu, die ersten Zeitschriftenartikel und bis heute mehr als 20 Bücher über dieses Metier zu verfassen. Gisbert Brunner schreibt außerdem für Publikationen wie ZEIT Magazin, Chronos, Handelszeitung, Prestige, Red Bulletin, Flair, #ich und Terra Mater. Zudem bloggt der Uhrenexperte auf redbulletin.com und hält weltweit Vorträge über mechanische Uhren und renommierte Uhrenmanufakturen.

01 **The Watch Book**
Published by teNeues in three
languages in September 2015
In drei Sprachen erschienen bei
teNeues im September 2015

"What distinguishes good from
bad watch design is the level of
haphazardness with which design
aspects occur."

„Gutes von schlechtem Uhrendesign
unterscheidet die Zufälligkeit,
mit der gestalterische Aspekte
geschehen."

**Which developments would you like to see in
product design in the future?**
Design innovations without neglecting functionality
and traditional values.

**Which emotions does a day spent in a jury session
arouse in you?**
Extremely pleasant ones. And that is due to the
relaxed atmosphere, in which the highly focused
assessment of the submitted products takes place.

**Which developments in the watches category have
you perceived as particularly positive?**
That tried and tested timeless design, paired with
some progressive design elements, utterly survives
in the market.

**To what extent are materials currently influencing
watch design?**
Especially when it comes to casings, the choice of
materials becomes increasingly important because
of their weight and scratch-resistance or simply in
order to achieve a different look.

**Welche Entwicklungen im Produktdesign
würden Sie sich für die Zukunft wünschen?**
Gestalterische Innovation ohne Vernachlässigung
der Funktionalität und der tradierten Werte.

**Welche Emotionen weckt ein Jurierungstag
in Ihnen?**
Ausgesprochen angenehme. Und zwar wegen der
entspannten Atmosphäre, in der die hoch konzen-
trierte Beurteilung der eingereichten Produkte
abläuft.

**Welche Entwicklung in der Uhren-Kategorie
haben Sie als besonders positiv wahrgenommen?**
Dass sich bewährtes, zeitloses Design, gepaart
mit einigen gestalterisch progressiven Elementen,
schlichtweg nicht überlebt.

**Inwieweit sind Materialien Thema im
Uhrendesign?**
Speziell bei den Gehäusen werden die verwendeten
Materialien wegen des Gewichts, der Kratzfestigkeit
oder einfach einer andersartigen Optik immer
wichtiger.

01

Rüdiger Bucher
Germany
Deutschland

Rüdiger Bucher, born in 1967, graduated in political science from the Philipps-Universität Marburg and completed the postgraduate study course "Interdisciplinary studies on France" in Freiburg, Germany. Since 1995 for five years, he was in charge of "Scriptum. Die Zeitschrift für Schreibkultur" (Scriptum. The magazine for writing culture) at the publishing house Verlagsgruppe Ebner Ulm where in 1999 he became Editorial Manager of Chronos, the leading German-language special interest magazine for wrist watches. As Chief Editor since 2005 Chronos has positioned itself internationally with subsidiary magazines and licensed editions in China, Korea, Japan and Poland. At the same time, Rüdiger Bucher established a successful corporate publishing department for Chronos. Since 2014, he has been Editorial Director and besides Chronos he has also been in charge of the sister magazines "Uhren-Magazin" (Watch Magazine), "Klassik Uhren" (Classic Watches) and the New York-based "WatchTime". Rüdiger Bucher lectures as an expert for mechanical wrist watches and is a sought-after interview partner for various media.

Rüdiger Bucher, geboren 1967, absolvierte ein Studium in Politikwissenschaft an der Philipps-Universität Marburg und das Aufbaustudium „Interdisziplinäre Frankreich-Studien" in Freiburg. Ab 1995 betreute er beim Ebner Verlag Ulm fünf Jahre lang „Scriptum. Die Zeitschrift für Schreibkultur", bevor er im selben Verlag 1999 Redaktionsleiter von „Chronos", dem führenden deutschsprachigen Special-Interest-Magazin für Armbanduhren, wurde. Ab 2005 Chefredakteur, hat sich Chronos seitdem mit Tochtermagazinen und Lizenzausgaben in China, Korea, Japan und Polen international aufgestellt. Gleichzeitig baute Rüdiger Bucher für Chronos einen erfolgreichen Corporate-Publishing-Bereich auf. Seit 2014 verantwortet er als Redaktionsdirektor neben Chronos auch die Schwestermagazine „Uhren-Magazin", „Klassik Uhren" sowie die in New York beheimatete „WatchTime". Als Experte für mechanische Armbanduhren hält Rüdiger Bucher Vorträge und ist ein gefragter Interviewpartner für verschiedene Medien.

01 Chronos Special Uhrendesign
Published once a year each
September since 2013
Erscheint seit 2013 einmal
jährlich im September

02 Chronos is present around the
globe with issues of differing
themes plus special issues
Mit verschiedenen Ausgaben
und Sonderheften ist Chronos
rund um den Globus vertreten

02

"Emotion and colour are the topics in watch design in the coming years. And high-quality mechanical wristwatches are increasingly supplemented with extravagant ideas and forms."

„Emotion und Farbe sind die Themen im Uhrendesign der nächsten Jahre. Auch hochwertige mechanische Armbanduhren werden zunehmend durch extravagante Ideen und veränderte Formen ergänzt."

What is the difference between good and bad watch design?
The crucial point is that the proportions are right. The watch mustn't be too bulky, the wristband not too narrow and the dial should neither be cluttered nor have any empty space for no apparent reason.

If you could design your personal watch, which characteristics would it have?
It should cleverly combine classical with modern aspects and arouse positive emotions. I would prefer a sporty-robust tool watch, which has extraordinary functions and its elements such as wristband, dial and/or housing would be in one of my favourite colours of either blue or green.

What does winning the Red Dot say about the product?
Receiving a Red Dot is as if the product is being knighted. The Red Dot confirms that the product has a good and high-quality design, that it is innovative and arouses positive emotions.

Was unterscheidet gutes von schlechtem Uhrendesign?
Entscheidend ist, dass die Proportionen stimmen. Die Uhr darf nicht zu klobig sein, das Band nicht zu schmal und das Zifferblatt sollte weder überladen sein noch irgendwo unmotiviert freien Platz lassen.

Wenn Sie Ihre persönliche Uhr gestalten dürften, welche Charakteristika hätte diese?
Sie sollte klassische Elemente geschickt mit modernen verbinden und positive Emotionen freisetzen. Ich würde eine sportlich-robuste Toolwatch bevorzugen, die etwas Außergewöhnliches kann und bei der Elemente wie Armband, Zifferblatt und/oder Gehäuse in einer meiner Lieblingsfarben Blau oder Grün gehalten sind.

Was sagt eine Auszeichnung mit dem Red Dot über das Produkt aus?
Die Verleihung des Red Dot ist ein Adelsschlag für jedes Produkt. Der Red Dot bezeugt, dass das Produkt gut und hochwertig gestaltet ist, dass es einen gewissen Innovationsgrad besitzt und positive Emotionen weckt.

01

Tony K. M. Chang
Taiwan

Tony K. M. Chang studied architecture at Chung Yuan Christian University in Chung Li, Taiwan. Today, he is Chief Advisor of the Taiwan Design Center, of which he has been chief executive officer since 2004. Until 2013, he has been the editor-in-chief of DESIGN magazine. Chang has made tremendous contributions to industrial design, both in his home country and across the entire Asia-Pacific region. As an expert in design management and design promotion, he has served as a consultant for governments and in the corporate sector for decades. Between 2005 and 2007, then 2009 and 2011 and again since 2013, he is an executive board member of the Icsid and also master-minded the 2011 IDA Congress in Taipei. In 2008, he was elected founding chairman of the Taiwan Design Alliance, a consortium of government-supported and private design entities aimed at promoting Taiwanese design. Tony K. M. Chang has lectured in Europe, the United States and Asia, and he frequently serves as a juror in prestigious international design competitions.

Tony K. M. Chang studierte Architektur an der Chung Yuan Christian University in Chung Li, Taiwan. Heute ist er Chefberater des Taiwan Design Centers, dessen Chief Executive Officer er seit 2004 war. Bis 2013 war er zudem Chefredakteur des Magazins DESIGN. Chang hat im Bereich Industriedesign Erhebliches geleistet, sowohl in seinem Heimatland als auch im gesamten Asien-Pazifik-Raum. Als Experte in Designmanagement und Designförderung ist er seit Jahrzehnten als Berater in Regierungs- und Unternehmenskreisen tätig. Von 2005 bis 2007, von 2009 bis 2011 und erneut seit 2013 ist er Vorstandsmitglied des Icsid und leitete 2011 den IDA Congress in Taipeh. Im Jahr 2008 wurde er zum Founding Chairman der Taiwan Design Alliance gewählt, einer Vereinigung staatlich geförderter und privater Designorgane zur Förderung taiwanesischen Designs. Tony K. M. Chang hält Vorträge in Europa, den USA und Asien und fungiert häufig als Juror hochrangiger internationaler Designwettbewerbe.

02

"A young design talent should have multiple solutions to a problem and be capable of integrating various ideas and resources."

„Ein junges Designtalent sollte für jedes Problem mehrere Lösungen haben und in der Lage sein, verschiedene Ideen und Ressourcen integrieren zu können."

Which everyday product could you not live without?
Of course my smartphone. It is your 24 hour convenience store for all the information you need for everyday life.

Which skills does a successful designer have?
He or she should have good taste and know how to make use of various colours and materials for a practical project or product that could sell on the market.

How would you describe your professional work?
I regard myself as a professional design consultant and manager for the industrial, academic and governmental field persisting in promoting the value of design to the wider public.

What attracts you to the work as a Red Dot juror?
I am really glad to be here as a Red Dot juror, seeing excellent pieces of work from all around the world and, at the same time, having the opportunity to exchange professional opinions with other jury members.

Welches Alltagsprodukt möchten Sie nicht mehr missen?
Natürlich mein Smartphone. Es ist der 24-Stunden-Verbrauchermarkt für sämtliche Informationen, die man zum täglichen Leben braucht.

Welche Fähigkeiten hat ein erfolgreicher Designer?
Sie oder er sollte einen guten Geschmack haben und wissen, wie man verschiedene Farben und Materialien für ein praktisches Projekt oder Produkt einsetzen kann, damit es sich im Markt verkaufen lässt.

Wie würden Sie Ihre berufliche Tätigkeit beschreiben?
Ich halte mich für einen professionellen Designberater und -manager für den Industrie-, Bildungs- und Regierungsbereich, der in der Öffentlichkeit beharrlich für den Wert von Design wirbt.

Was reizt Sie an der Arbeit als Red Dot-Juror?
Ich freue mich sehr, als Red Dot-Juror dabei zu sein. Man sieht hervorragende Arbeiten aus der ganzen Welt und hat gleichzeitig die Gelegenheit, sich mit anderen Mitgliedern der Jury auf professioneller Ebene auszutauschen.

01

Vivian Wai-kwan Cheng
Hong Kong
Hongkong

On leaving Hong Kong Design Institute after 19 years of educational service, Vivian Cheng founded "Vivian Design" in 2014 to provide consultancy services and promote her own art in jewellery and glass. She graduated with a BA in industrial design from the Hong Kong Polytechnic University and was awarded a special prize in the Young Designers of the Year Award hosted by the Federation of Hong Kong Industries in 1987, and the Governor's Award for Industry: Consumer Product Design in 1989, after joining Lambda Industrial Limited as the head of the Product Design team. In 1995 she finished her Master degree and joined the Vocational Training Council teaching product design and later became responsible for, among others, establishing an international network with design-related organisations and schools. Vivian Cheng was the International Liaison Manager at the Hong Kong Design Institute (HKDI) and member of the Chartered Society of Designers Hong Kong, member of the Board of Directors of the Hong Kong Design Centre (HKDC), and is board member of the Icsid from 2013 to 2017. Furthermore, she has been a panel member for the government and various NGOs.

Nach 19 Jahren im Lehrbetrieb verließ Vivian Cheng 2014 das Hong Kong Design Institute und gründete „Vivian Design", um Beratungsdienste anzubieten und ihre eigene Schmuck- und Glaskunst weiterzuentwickeln. 1987 machte sie ihren BA in Industriedesign an der Hong Kong Polytechnic University. Im selben Jahr erhielt sie einen Sonderpreis im Wettbewerb „Young Designers of the Year", veranstaltet von der Federation of Hong Kong Industries, sowie 1989 den Governor's Award for Industry: Consumer Product Design, nachdem sie bei Lambda Industrial Limited als Leiterin des Produktdesign-Teams angefangen hatte. 1995 beendete sie ihren Master-Studiengang und wechselte zum Vocational Training Council, wo sie Produktdesign unterrichtete und später u. a. für den Aufbau eines internationalen Netzwerks mit Organisationen und Schulen im Designbereich verantwortlich war. Vivian Cheng war International Liaison Manager am Hong Kong Design Institute (HKDI), Mitglied der Chartered Society of Designers Hong Kong, Vorstandsmitglied des Hong Kong Design Centre (HKDC) und ist Gremiumsmitglied des Icsid von 2013 bis 2017. Außerdem war sie Mitglied verschiedener Bewertungsgremien der Regierung und vieler Nichtregierungsorganisationen.

01 AIR
    Casting in silver
    Silberguss

02 FIRE
    Casting in Shibuichi
    (metal alloy)
    Shibuichi-Guss
    (Metalllegierung)

02

"If your product wins a
Red Dot you have great
potential of achieving
success."
„Wenn ein Produkt einen
Red Dot gewinnt, hat es
großes Erfolgspotenzial."

Which everyday product could you not live without?
I cannot live without my spectacles. Not only because they improve my vision, but also because they have become part of my identity. My spectacles are now a part of me.

How would you describe your work as a designer?
Design is an extremely challenging discipline. As designers, we are ambassadors aiming to introduce a better alternative of living to people.

Which topics will influence the field of jewellery the most in the coming years?
I think the way jewellery will be designed and manufactured using the latest technology such as laser cutting, rapid prototyping and 3D modelling is going to become increasingly influential in the coming years.

Welches Alltagsprodukt möchten Sie nicht mehr missen?
Ich kann nicht ohne meine Brille leben. Nicht nur, weil sie meine Sehleistung verbessert, sondern weil sie ein Teil meiner Identität ist. Meine Brille ist jetzt ein Teil von mir.

Wie würden Sie Ihre Tätigkeit als Designerin beschreiben?
Design ist eine extrem anspruchsvolle Disziplin. Als Designer sind wir Botschafter, die versuchen, Menschen eine bessere Lebensalternative nahe-zubringen.

Welche Themen werden den Schmuckbereich in den nächsten Jahren am meisten beeinflussen?
Ich glaube, dass die Art und Weise, wie Schmuck mithilfe der neuesten Technologien, zum Beispiel Laserschneiden, schnelle Prototypenerstellung und 3D-Modellierung, gestaltet und hergestellt wird, in den kommenden Jahren mehr und mehr Einfluss gewinnen wird.

01

Datuk Prof.
Jimmy Choo OBE
Malaysia/
Great Britain
Malaysia/
Großbritannien

Datuk Professor Jimmy Choo is descended from a family of Malaysian shoemakers and learned the craft from his father. He studied at Cordwainers College, which is today part of the London College of Fashion. After graduating in 1983, he founded his own couture label and opened a shoe shop in London's East End whose regular customers included the late Diana, Princess of Wales. In 1996, Choo launched his ready-to-wear line with Tom Yeardye and sold his share in the business in November 2001 to Equinox Luxury Holdings Ltd. He is a Malaysia Tourism advisor and promotes design education through a variety of roles; he is an ambassador for footwear education at the London College of Fashion, a spokesperson for the British Council in their promotion of British Education to foreign students as well as the Honorary President at the International School of Creative Arts (ISCA), and he also spends time working with the non-profit programme, Teach For Malaysia. In 2003, Jimmy Choo was honoured for his contribution to fashion by Queen Elizabeth II who appointed him "Officer of the Order of the British Empire".

Datuk Professor Jimmy Choo, der einer malaysischen Schuhmacher-Familie entstammt und das Handwerk von seinem Vater lernte, studierte am Cordwainers College, heute Teil des London College of Fashion. Nach seinem Abschluss 1983 gründete er sein eigenes Couture-Label und eröffnete ein Schuhgeschäft im Londoner East End, zu dessen Stammkundschaft auch Lady Diana, die verstorbene Prinzessin von Wales, gehörte. 1996 führte Choo gemeinsam mit Tom Yeardye seine Konfektionslinie ein und verkaufte seine Anteile an dem Unternehmen im November 2001 an die Equinox Luxury Holdings Ltd. Er ist zurzeit als Berater für Tourism Malaysia tätig und fördert die Designlehre in verschiedenen Rollen: Er ist Botschafter für Footwear Education am London College of Fashion, Sprecher des British Council für die Förderung der Ausbildung ausländischer Studenten in Großbritannien sowie Ehrenpräsident der International School of Creative Arts (ISCA) und arbeitet darüber hinaus für das gemeinnützige Programm „Teach for Malaysia". Für seine Verdienste in der Mode verlieh ihm Königin Elisabeth II. 2003 den Titel „Officer of the Order of the British Empire".

02

"I would like to see improvements in design to make travelling more comfortable for passengers such as being able to charge mobile phones on the go."
„Ich würde mir Designinnovationen wünschen, die das Reisen für Passagiere komfortabler gestalten, zum Beispiel die Möglichkeit, Mobiltelefone unterwegs aufzuladen."

Which skills does a successful designer have?
He has been trained by experts to continue to practise and learn throughout his career to achieve a fine level of quality. And he has an eye for detail.

Do you have a design role model?
My late father and all of my teachers at Cordwainers, who taught me the design process and the craft of shoemaking.

What attracts you to the work as a Red Dot juror?
It is a privilege to see so many unique and cutting edge designs from design professionals from across the globe. And it is a privilege to be in the company of my fellow jurors – all of them exceptionally talented designers with unique skills.

What emotions does a day spent in a jury session arouse in you?
Excitement and awe. My eyes are opened to what is possible in the world of design, and it is incredibly exciting to see things that have never been talked about before.

Welche Fähigkeiten hat ein erfolgreicher Designer?
Er ist von Experten dazu trainiert worden, während seiner gesamten Karriere ständig zu üben und zu lernen, um einen hohen Grad an Qualität zu erlangen. Und er hat einen Blick für Details.

Haben Sie ein Vorbild in Sachen Gestaltung?
Meinen verstorbenen Vater und alle meine Lehrer bei Cordwainers, die mir den Gestaltungsprozess und das Handwerk der Schuhmacherei beigebracht haben.

Was reizt Sie an der Arbeit als Red Dot-Juror?
Es ist ein Privileg, so viele einzigartige und innovative Gestaltungen von professionellen Designern aus aller Welt zu sehen. Und es ist ein Privileg, Zeit mit meinen Jurykollegen zu verbringen, die alle bemerkenswert talentierte Gestalter mit einzigartigen Fähigkeiten sind.

Welche Emotionen weckt ein Jurierungstag in Ihnen?
Begeisterung und Ehrfurcht. Mir wird vor Augen geführt, was in der Designwelt möglich ist, und es ist unglaublich aufregend, Dinge zu sehen, über die noch nie vorher geredet wurde.

01

Vincent Créance
France
Frankreich

After graduating from the Ecole Supérieure de Design Industriel, Vincent Créance began his career in 1985 at the Plan Créatif Agency where he became design director in 1990 and developed, among other things, numerous products for high-tech and consumer markets, for France Télécom and RATP (Paris metro). In 1996 he joined Alcatel as Design Director for all phone activities on an international level. In 1999, he became Vice President Brand in charge of product design and user experience as well as all communications for the Mobile Phones BU. During the launch of the Franco-Chinese TCL and Alcatel Mobile Phones joint venture in 2004, Vincent Créance advanced to the position of Design and Corporate Communications Director. In 2006, he became President and CEO of MBD Design, one of the major design agencies in France, providing design solutions in transport design and product design. Créance is a member of the APCI (Agency for the Promotion of Industrial Creation), on the board of directors of ENSCI (National College of Industrial Creation), and a member of the Strategic Advisory Board for Strate College.

Vincent Créance begann seine Laufbahn nach seinem Abschluss an der Ecole Supérieure de Design Industriel 1985 bei Plan Créatif Agency. Hier stieg er 1990 zum Design Director auf und entwickelte u. a. zahlreiche Produkte für den Hightech- und Verbrauchermarkt, für die France Télécom oder die RATP (Pariser Metro). 1996 ging er als Design Director für sämtliche Telefon-aktivitäten auf internationaler Ebene zu Alcatel und wurde 1999 Vice President Brand, zuständig für Produktdesign und User Experience sowie die gesamte Kommunikation für den Geschäftsbereich „Mobile Phones". Während des Zusammenschlusses des französisch-chinesischen TCL und Alcatel Mobile Phones 2004 avancierte Vincent Créance zum Design and Corporate Communications Director. 2006 wurde er Präsident und CEO von MBD Design, einer der wichtigsten Designagenturen in Frankreich, und entwickelte Designlösungen für Transport- und Produktdesign. Créance ist Mitglied von APCI (Agency for the Promotion of Industrial Creation), Vorstand des ENSCI (National College of Industrial Design) und Mitglied im wissenschaftlichen Beirat des Strate College.

02

"A successful designer is skilful at synthesising information and ideas, has broad general knowledge resulting from permanent curiosity."

„Ein erfolgreicher Designer hat die Fähigkeit, Informationen und Ideen zu synthetisieren, und besitzt ein breites Allgemeinwissen dank beständiger Neugierde."

What attracts you to the work as a Red Dot juror?
As a juror, you immerse yourself in a maelstrom of creation, innovation and aesthetics for several days. The Red Dot is like a fantastic exhibition of contemporary objects: seeing so many pretty things is very refreshing and rejuvenating. It is like stepping into a fountain of youth. It also requires stepping back from your daily life, asking yourself key questions on what makes a good design, especially in a world that is changing so rapidly.

Which emotions does a day spent in a jury session arouse in you?
A blend of excitement and pleasure in the face of such high creative quality, but also a lot of stress related to the responsibility you feel, when you have to judge the work of your peers, and even more when the general quality of the entries increases every year. And frankly, sometimes it is also a lot of fun!

Was reizt Sie an der Arbeit als Red Dot-Juror?
Als Juror vertiefen Sie sich mehrere Tage lang in einen Sog aus Kreation, Innovation und Ästhetik. Der Red Dot ist wie eine fantastische Ausstellung zeitgenössischer Objekte: So viele schöne Dinge zu sehen, ist sehr erfrischend und belebend. Es ist, als ob man in einen Jungbrunnen steigt. Darüber hinaus macht es die Arbeit als Juror notwendig, vom täglichen Leben Abstand zu gewinnen und sich selbst Schlüsselfragen zu stellen, was gutes Design gerade in einer sich so schnell verändernden Welt ausmacht.

Welche Emotionen weckt ein Jurierungstag in Ihnen?
Eine Mischung aus Aufgeregtheit und Genuss angesichts derartig hochgradiger, kreativer Qualität. Aber auch eine Menge Stress bezüglich der Verantwortung, die ich empfinde, wenn ich Arbeiten meiner Kollegen bewerten muss. Und das wird noch dadurch verstärkt, dass jedes Jahr die allgemeine Qualität der Einreichungen steigt. Ehrlich gesagt macht es manchmal auch sehr viel Spaß!

01

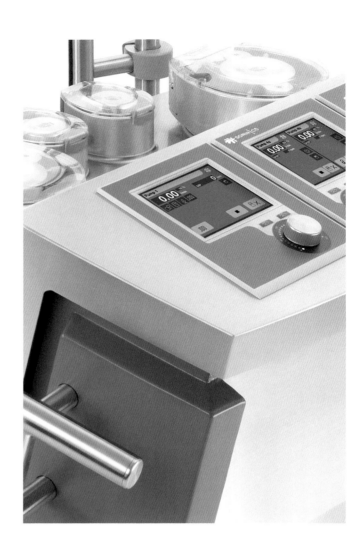

Stefan Eckstein
Germany
Deutschland

Stefan Eckstein studied industrial design at the Muthesius Academy of Fine Arts and Design and ergonomics at the Anthropological Institute of the Christian Albrecht University of Kiel. In 1989 he founded ECKSTEIN DESIGN, a studio for industrial design, interaction design and corporate industrial design in Munich, of which he is managing director. Following his philosophy which states that "reduction to the essentials leads to a better result" he combines streamlined concept and development phases in a structured iteration process thus creating "Agile Design Development", a user-oriented innovation method. For more than 25 years Stefan Eckstein has been a member of the Association of German Industrial Designers (VDID) and in 2012 he became its president. The VDID Codex, which today represents a guideline for the ethical values of the profession of industrial designers, was developed under his direction. Stefan Eckstein has received many design awards in national and international award competitions and has been a juror several times, incorporating the guiding values of responsible design into the process.

Stefan Eckstein studierte Industrial Design an der Muthesius-Hochschule und Ergonomie am Anthropologischen Institut der Christian-Albrechts-Universität zu Kiel. 1989 gründete er ECKSTEIN DESIGN, ein Studio für Industriedesign, Interaction Design und Corporate Industrial Design in München, dessen Geschäftsführer er ist. Gemäß seiner Philosophie „Reduzierung auf das Wesentliche führt zu einem besseren Ergebnis" verbindet er in einem strukturierten Iterationsprozess schlanke Konzept- und Entwicklungsphasen und erarbeitet so die „Agile Designentwicklung", eine nutzerorientierte Innovationsmethode. Seit über 25 Jahren ist Stefan Eckstein Mitglied im Verband Deutscher Industrie Designer (VDID) und seit 2012 Präsident des Verbandes. Der VDID Codex wurde unter seiner Leitung entwickelt und steht heute als Leitbild für die ethischen Werte des Berufsstandes. Stefan Eckstein wurde vielfach national und international ausgezeichnet, war mehrfach als Juror tätig und bezog dabei die Leitwerte für verantwortungsvolles Gestalten in den Prozess mit ein.

01 **SORIN C5**
The heart-lung machine
based on a modular principle
was created for the Sorin
group
Die Herz-Lungen-Maschine
mit modularem Aufbau
entstand für die Sorin group

02 **VDW.CONNECT Drive®**
A cordless endo motor that
may be operated both
directly or via tablet app
Ein kabelloser Endomotor, der
sowohl singulär als auch über
eine App mit einem Tablet
eingesetzt werden kann

02

"A young design talent should have the courage to experiment with alternatives which may initially appear unsuitable in order to create truly innovative solutions."

„Ein Nachwuchsdesigner sollte sich trauen, das Denken in zunächst abwegig erscheinenden Alternativen zu experimentieren, damit wirklich innovative Lösungen entstehen."

How would you describe your work as a designer?
Industrial designers fulfil users' needs with fascinating solutions. They influence the supply of goods, help companies achieve great success and channel enormous streams of capital indirectly. They influence everyday culture and anticipate the future.

Which developments in the field of tool design would you like to see in the future?
An increased consistency of form down to the smallest detail, so that the repertoire of the creative means that has been chosen will be applied to all details of the tool with the same precision and care.

What attracts you to the work as a Red Dot juror?
I like analysing the practical application of the submitted products and to put myself into the user's shoes for that purpose. Furthermore, I appreciate having exciting discussions with my colleagues and identifying the best design solution together with them.

Wie würden Sie Ihre Tätigkeit als Designer beschreiben?
Industriedesigner erfüllen Anwenderbedürfnisse mit faszinierenden Lösungen. Sie beeinflussen das Warenangebot, verhelfen Unternehmen zu großen Erfolgen und lenken indirekt enorme Kapitalströme. Sie wirken prägend an der Alltagskultur mit und greifen der Zukunft voraus.

Welche Entwicklungen im Werkzeug-Design würden Sie sich für die Zukunft wünschen?
Eine noch höhere formale Konsequenz bis ins Detail, sodass das Repertoire der einmal gewählten bildnerischen Mittel mit gleicher Präzision und Sorgfalt auf alle Einzelheiten des Werkzeuges angewendet wird.

Was reizt Sie an der Arbeit als Red Dot-Juror?
Mich reizt es, mich mit der Anwendungspraxis der angemeldeten Produkte zu befassen und mich dazu in die Anwender zu versetzen. Außerdem schätze ich es, mich in spannenden Diskussionen mit den Kollegen auseinanderzusetzen und gemeinsam mit ihnen die besten Designlösungen zu ermitteln.

01

Prof. Lutz Fügener
Germany
Deutschland

Professor Lutz Fügener began his studies at the Technical University Dresden, where he completed a foundation course in mechanical engineering. He then transferred to the Burg Giebichenstein University of Art and Design in Halle/Saale, Germany, where he obtained a degree in industrial design in 1995. In the same year, he became junior partner of Fisch & Vogel Design in Berlin. Since then, the firm (today called "studioFT") has increasingly specialised in transportation design. Two years after joining the firm, Lutz Fügener became senior partner and co-owner. In 2000, he was appointed as Professor of Transportation Design/3D Design by Pforzheim University and there chairs the prestigious BA degree course in transportation design. Lutz Fügener is also active as an author and journalist for a number of different daily newspapers, weekly magazines and periodicals, as well as blogs in which he writes on mobility-related design topics.

Professor Lutz Fügener absolvierte ein Grundstudium in Maschinenbau an der Technischen Universität Dresden und nahm daraufhin ein Studium für Industrial Design an der Hochschule für Kunst und Design, Burg Giebichenstein, in Halle an der Saale auf. Sein Diplom machte er im Jahr 1995. Im selben Jahr wurde er Juniorpartner des Büros Fisch & Vogel Design in Berlin. Seit dieser Zeit spezialisierte sich das Büro (heute „studioFT") mehr und mehr auf den Bereich „Transportation Design". Zwei Jahre nach seinem Einstieg wurde Lutz Fügener Seniorpartner und gleichberechtigter Mitinhaber des Büros. Im Jahr 2000 wurde er von der Hochschule Pforzheim auf eine Professur für Transportation Design/3D-Gestaltung berufen und ist Leiter des renommierten BA-Studiengangs für Fahrzeugdesign. Lutz Fügener ist als Autor und Journalist für verschiedene Tageszeitungen, Wochenmagazine, Periodika und Blogs tätig und schreibt über Themen des Designs im Zusammenhang mit Mobilität.

01 **SpeedE project**
Redesign of an experimental
car of the Institute for Automotive Engineering of RWTH
Aachen University in the
course of a research project
Redesign eines Experimental-
fahrzeugs des Instituts
für Kraftfahrzeuge (ika) an
der RWTH Aachen im Rahmen
eines Forschungsprojektes

01

"A successful designer can grasp the task at hand in its entirety, take previously unimagined, innovative paths and implement them with high quality."

„Ein erfolgreicher Designer kann die ihm vorliegende Aufgabe in ihrer Gesamtheit begreifen, bisher nicht gedachte, innovative Wege gehen und diese in hoher Qualität umsetzen."

How would you describe your work as a designer?
I deeply enjoy the challenges of projects in which you have to work within narrow boundaries, trying to shift them bit by bit, converting what appear to be disadvantages into advantages and having to exploit the potential of new technologies in order to achieve something that was previously impossible. I like questioning well-trodden paths.

What does winning the Red Dot say about the product?
The Red Dot is a quality seal. It indicates that a solution with high aesthetic quality has been created, which was implemented well to meet its purpose.

Which innovations did you see during the jury session?
The innovations ranged from successful attempts to give fully electric vehicles a new appearance to the creation of a system for the interior fittings of aircraft, which provides advantages to both manufacturers and customers at previously unattained functional and aesthetic levels.

Wie würden Sie Ihre Tätigkeit als Designer beschreiben?
Ich habe große Freude an den Herausforderungen von Projekten, bei denen man sich in engen Grenzen bewegen muss, versucht, diese Stück für Stück zu verschieben, scheinbare Nachteile in Vorteile verwandelt, Potenziale von neuen Technologien ausnutzen muss, um bisher nicht Mögliches zu ermöglichen. Gerne stelle ich ausgetretene Wege infrage.

Was sagt die Auszeichnung mit dem Red Dot über ein Produkt aus?
Ein Red Dot ist ein Qualitätssiegel. Es signalisiert, dass hier eine überdurchschnittlich gute, dem Zweck des Gegenstandes entsprechend umgesetzte Lösung in hoher ästhetischer Qualität entstanden ist.

Welche Innovationen haben Sie während der Jurierung gesehen?
Sie reichten von dem gelungenen Versuch, vollelektrischen Fahrzeugen ein neues Erscheinungsbild zu geben, bis zur Gestaltung eines Systems für den Innenausbau von Flugzeugen, das auf unerreicht hohem funktionalen und ästhetischen Niveau Hersteller und Kunden gleichermaßen Vorteile bringt.

01

Hideshi Hamaguchi
USA / Japan

Hideshi Hamaguchi graduated with a Bachelor of Science in chemical engineering from Kyoto University. Starting his career with Panasonic in Japan, Hamaguchi later became director of the New Business Planning Group at Panasonic Electric Works, Ltd. and then executive vice president of Panasonic Electric Works Laboratory of America, Inc. In 1993, he developed Japan's first corporate Intranet and also led the concept development for the first USB flash drive. Hideshi Hamaguchi has over 15 years of experience in defining strategies and decision-making, as well as in concept development for various industries and businesses. As Executive Fellow at Ziba Design and CEO at monogoto, he is today considered a leading mind in creative concept and strategy development on both sides of the Pacific and is involved in almost every project this renowned business consultancy takes on. For clients such as FedEx, Polycom and M-System he has led the development of several award-winning products.

Hideshi Hamaguchi graduierte als Bachelor of Science in Chemical Engineering an der Kyoto University. Seine Karriere begann er bei Panasonic in Japan, wo er später zum Direktor der New Business Planning Group von Panasonic Electric Works, Ltd. und zum Executive Vice President von Panasonic Electric Works Laboratory of America, Inc. aufstieg. 1993 entwickelte er Japans erstes Firmen-Intranet und übernahm zudem die Leitung der Konzeptentwicklung des ersten USB-Laufwerks. Hideshi Hamaguchi verfügt über mehr als 15 Jahre Erfahrung in der Konzeptentwicklung sowie Strategie- und Entscheidungsfindung in unterschiedlichen Industrien und Unternehmen. Als Executive Fellow bei Ziba Design und CEO bei monogoto wird er heute als führender Kopf in der kreativen Konzept- und Strategieentwicklung auf beiden Seiten des Pazifiks angesehen und ist in nahezu jedes Projekt der renommierten Unternehmensberatung involviert. Für Kunden wie FedEx, Polycom und M-System leitete er etliche ausgezeichnete Projekte.

01 Cintiq 24HD
for Wacom, 2012
für Wacom, 2012

02 Toy blocks for everyone
A collection of 202 building blocks crafted from beech-wood, coming in beautifully arranged units. Infused with the stories of twelve elements, each unique piece embodies a small fragment of nature. For Felissimo, Japan, in collaboration with Marie Uno.
Bauklötze für alle
Eine Kollektion von 202 Bauklötzen, die aus Buchen-holz gefertigt und in attraktiv arrangierten Sets erhältlich sind. Durchtränkt mit den Geschichten von zwölf Elementen, verkörpert jedes einzigartige Stück ein kleines Fragment der Natur. Für Felissimo, Japan, in Zusam-menarbeit mit Marie Uno.

02

"A young design talent should enjoy uncertainty."
„Ein Nachwuchsdesigner sollte die Ungewissheit genießen."

Which everyday product could you not live without?
My Moleskine large plain reporter notebook and my Lamy white medium Safari fountain pen. This set is the sandbox for my thoughts.

What is the difference between good and bad product design?
It's all about the degree of beauty in the intention.

What does winning the Red Dot say about the product?
That the product is at the pinnacle of design. People regard it as being at the top and the designer knows that he has reached the peak.

Which emotions does a day spent in a jury session arouse in you?
Fun, playing with the mixture of quality and quantity at hand.

Which innovations did you see during the jury session?
Many innovations regarding the communication between products and users.

Welches Alltagsprodukt möchten Sie nicht mehr missen?
Mein großes Blanko-Reporternotizbuch von Moleskine und meinen weißen Lamy-Safari-Füllfederhalter mit mittlerer Federspitze. Dieses Set ist der Sandkasten für meine Gedanken.

Was unterscheidet gutes von schlechtem Produktdesign?
Es geht immer um den Schönheitsgrad der Absicht.

Was sagt die Auszeichnung mit dem Red Dot über ein Produkt aus?
Dass das Produkt den Gipfel der Gestaltung erreicht hat. Die Menschen sehen, dass es auf dem Höhepunkt ist, und der Designer weiß, dass er den Gipfel erreicht hat.

Welche Emotionen weckt ein Jurierungstag in Ihnen?
Freude – und zwar dabei, mit der vorliegenden Mischung aus Qualität und Quantität zu spielen.

Welche Innovationen haben Sie während der Jurierung gesehen?
Viele Innovationen im Bereich der Kommunikation zwischen Produkten und Benutzern.

01

Prof. Renke He
China

Professor Renke He, born in 1958, studied civil engineering and architecture at Hunan University in China. From 1987 to 1988, he was a visiting scholar at the Industrial Design Department of the Royal Danish Academy of Fine Arts in Copenhagen and, from 1998 to 1999, at North Carolina State University's School of Design. Renke He is dean and professor of the School of Design at Hunan University and is also director of the Chinese Industrial Design Education Committee. Currently, he holds the position of vice chair of the China Industrial Design Association.

Professor Renke He wurde 1958 geboren und studierte an der Hunan University in China Bauingenieurwesen und Architektur. Von 1987 bis 1988 war er als Gastprofessor für Industrial Design an der Royal Danish Academy of Fine Arts in Kopenhagen tätig, und von 1998 bis 1999 hatte er eine Gastprofessur an der School of Design der North Carolina State University inne. Renke He ist Dekan und Professor an der Hunan University, School of Design, sowie Direktor des Chinese Industrial Design Education Committee. Er ist derzeit zudem stellvertretender Vorsitzender der China Industrial Design Association.

02

"A young design talent should
have roots in his local culture and
at the same time have a global
perspective."
„Ein Nachwuchsdesigner sollte
Wurzeln in seiner lokalen Kultur
und zugleich eine globale Perspek-
tive haben."

Which skills does a successful designer have?
He understands and identifies the real needs of the
users and transforms them into products or services.

How would you describe your work as a designer?
Creating valuable products and services for both
consumers and clients.

Which product would you like to design some day?
My dream is to design a truly wearable camera some
day.

**What does winning the Red Dot say about the
product?**
It is the best confirmation that the product has a
world class design.

What attracts you to the work as a Red Dot juror?
The great opportunity to see the latest trends in
global design and meet good friends from all over
the world.

Welche Fähigkeiten hat ein erfolgreicher Designer?
Er versteht und identifiziert die wahren Bedürfnisse
der Benutzer und verwandelt sie in Produkte oder
Dienstleistungen.

Wie würden Sie Ihre Tätigkeit als Designer
beschreiben?
Als das Schaffen von wertigen Produkten und Dienstleistungen für Konsumenten und Auftraggeber.

Welches Produkt würden Sie gerne einmal
gestalten?
Mein Traum ist es, eines Tages eine wirklich tragbare
Kamera zu gestalten.

Was sagt die Auszeichnung mit dem Red Dot
über ein Produkt aus?
Sie ist die beste Bestätigung, dass das Produkt ein
Weltklassedesign hat.

Was reizt Sie an der Arbeit als Red Dot-Juror?
Die großartige Gelegenheit, die neuesten Trends im
internationalen Design zu sehen und gute Freunde
aus aller Welt zu treffen.

01

Prof.
Herman Hermsen
Netherlands
Niederlande

Professor Herman Hermsen, born in 1953 in Nijmegen, Netherlands, studied at the ArtEZ Institute of the Arts in Arnhem from 1974 to 1979. Following an assistant professorship, he began his career in teaching in 1985. Since 1979, he is an independent jewellery and product designer. Until 1990, he taught product design at the Utrecht School of the Arts (HKU), after which time he returned to Arnhem as lecturer at the Academy. Hermsen has been professor of product and jewellery design at the University of Applied Sciences in Düsseldorf since 1992. He gives guest lectures at universities and colleges throughout Europe, the United States and Japan, and began regularly organising specialist symposia in 1998. He has also served as juror for various competitions. Herman Hermsen has received different international awards for his work in product and jewellery design, which is shown worldwide in solo and group exhibitions and held in the collections of renowned museums, such as the Cooper-Hewitt Museum, New York; the Pinakothek der Moderne, Munich; and the Museum of Arts and Crafts, Kyoto.

Professor Herman Hermsen, 1953 in Nijmegen in den Niederlanden geboren, studierte von 1974 bis 1979 am ArtEZ Institute of the Arts in Arnheim und ging nach einer Assistenzzeit ab 1985 in die Lehre. Seit 1979 ist er unabhängiger Schmuck- und Produktdesigner. Bis 1990 unterrichtete er Produktdesign an der Utrecht School of the Arts (HKU) und kehrte anschließend nach Arnheim zurück, um an der dortigen Hochschule als Dozent zu arbeiten. Seit 1992 ist Hermsen Professor für Produkt- und Schmuckdesign an der Fachhochschule Düsseldorf; er hält Gastvorlesungen an Hochschulen in ganz Europa, den USA und Japan, organisiert seit 1998 regelmäßig Fachsymposien und ist Juror in verschiedenen Wettbewerbsgremien. Für seine Arbeiten im Produkt- und Schmuckdesign, die weltweit in Einzel- und Gruppenausstellungen präsentiert werden und sich in den Sammlungen großer renommierter Museen befinden – z. B. Cooper-Hewitt Museum, New York, Pinakothek der Moderne, München, und Museum of Arts and Crafts, Kyoto –, erhielt Herman Hermsen verschiedene internationale Auszeichnungen.

01 Brooch "Men in rain", 2015,
aluminium print with rock
crystal drops
Brosche „Men in rain", 2015,
Aluminiumdruck mit Berg-
kristalltropfen

02 Pendant "Monalisa chained",
2015, aluminium print with
silver and zirconias
Anhänger „Monalisa chained",
2015, Aluminiumdruck mit
Silber und Zirkonien

03 Pendant "Woman and stone",
2015, aluminium print with
synthetic spinel
Anhänger „Woman and stone",
2015, Aluminiumdruck mit
synthetischem Spinell

02

03

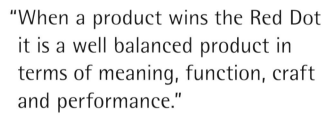

"When a product wins the Red Dot
it is a well balanced product in
terms of meaning, function, craft
and performance."
„Wenn ein Produkt den Red Dot
gewinnt, dann ist es ausgewogen
in Bezug auf seine Bedeutung,
Funktion, Verarbeitung und
Leistung."

Which skills does a successful designer have?
A wide spectrum of creativity and a talent for
improvisation.

How would you describe your work as a designer?
Next to my work as a professor for jewellery and
product design, I concentrate more and more on
concepts of jewellery and small products. My collection can be based on different approaches ranging
from purely material based and formal to conceptual
or associative and humoristic.

What attracts you to the work as a Red Dot juror?
In a very compact time frame you are confronted
with a wide product range with interesting differences
or shared approaches regarding their functionality,
aesthetics and implementation. Every year it is a
challenge to pick out the best and most complete
designs.

Welche Fähigkeiten hat ein erfolgreicher Designer?
Ein breites Spektrum an Kreativität und ein Talent
fürs Improvisieren.

**Wie würden Sie Ihre Tätigkeit als Designer
beschreiben?**
Neben meiner Tätigkeit als Professor für Schmuck- und
Produktgestaltung konzentriere ich mich mehr und
mehr auf Konzepte für Schmuck oder kleine Produkte.
Meine Kollektion kann auf unterschiedlichen Ansätzen
basieren, deren Spektrum von ausschließlich material-
basiert über formal und konzeptionell hin bis zu asso-
ziativ-humoristisch reicht.

Was reizt Sie an der Arbeit als Red Dot-Juror?
In einem sehr knappen Zeitrahmen werden Sie mit
einer großen Auswahl an Produkten konfrontiert, die
interessante Unterschiede oder gemeinsame Ansätze in
Bezug auf ihre Funktionalität, Ästhetik und Umsetzung
aufweisen. Es ist jedes Jahr eine Herausforderung, die
besten und vollständigsten Entwürfe auszuwählen.

01

Prof.
Carlos Hinrichsen
Chile

Professor Carlos Hinrichsen graduated as an industrial designer in Chile in 1982 and earned his master's degree in engineering in Japan in 1991. Currently, he is dean of the Faculty of Engineering and Business at the Gabriela Mistral University in Santiago and director of its Institute of Economy, Innovation and Entrepreneurship. Chile is in transition from an efficiency-based towards an innovation-based economy where the Institute contributes with actions and initiatives to get this important aim for the country mixing business, design, innovation, applied research and engineering spheres. From 2007 to 2009 Carlos Hinrichsen was president of Icsid and currently serves as senator within the organisation. In 2010 he was honoured with the distinction "Commander of the Order of the Lion of Finland". From 1992 to 2010 he was director of the School of Design DuocUC, Chile and from 2011 to 2014 director of the DuocUC International Affairs. He has led initiatives that integrate business, engineering, design, innovation, management and technology in Asia, Africa and Europe.

Professor Carlos Hinrichsen erlangte 1982 seinen Abschluss in Industriedesign in Chile und erhielt 1991 seinen Master der Ingenieurwissenschaft in Japan. Aktuell ist er Dekan der Fakultät „Engineering and Business" an der Universität Gabriela Mistral in Santiago und Direktor ihres Institute of Economy, Innovation and Entrepreneurship. Chile ist im Übergang von einer effizienzbasierten zu einer innovationsbasierten Wirtschaft, in der das Institut mit Maßnahmen und Initiativen dazu beiträgt, dieses wichtige Landesziel durch die Integration der Bereiche Handel, Design, Innovation, angewandte Forschung und Ingenieurwesen zu erreichen. Von 2007 bis 2009 war Carlos Hinrichsen Icsid-Präsident und heute ist er Senator innerhalb der Organisation. 2010 wurde er mit der Auszeichnung „Commander of the Order of the Lion of Finland" geehrt. Von 1992 bis 2010 war er Direktor der School of Design DuocUC in Chile und von 2011 bis 2014 Direktor der DuocUC International Affairs. In Asien, Afrika und Europa leitete er Initiativen, die Handel, Ingenieurwesen, Design, Innovation, Management und Technologie integrieren.

01 **Foguita**
Kerosene heater, designed for
Compañía Tecno Industrial CTI in
1993: It is still in production in
Chile and sold in local and regional
markets – currently the company
is part of Electrolux Chile
Ölheizgerät, entworfen 1993 für
Compañía Tecno Industrial CTI:
Das Gerät wird immer noch in Chile
hergestellt und lokal und regional
vertrieben – derzeit gehört die Firma
zu Electrolux Chile

02 **Gabriela Mistral University
campus gate – the place where
the Institute of Economy,
Innovation and Entrepreneurship
is located**
Das Campustor der Universität
Gabriela Mistral – hier befindet sich
das Institute of Economy, Innovation
and Entrepreneurship

02

"The Red Dot Award is like a
mirror, always current and
reflective of what is going on
in the design industry and the
international market."

„Der Red Dot Award ist wie ein
Spiegel, der immer aktuell ist und
reflektiert, was in der Designbranche und auf dem internationalen Markt vorgeht."

Which skills does a successful designer have?
One important ability is to decode the present and
future needs of specific users and to shape products and services that respond to their needs and
expectations.

What attracts you to the work as a Red Dot juror?
Being part of a jury that has a wide range of experience and comes from different backgrounds and, of
course, also provides an independent professional
assessment. I enjoy seeing how innovation is incorporated in all areas of design.

**Which developments in the category "Heating
and air conditioning technology" did you perceive
as particularly positive?**
Product design and quality are getting better and
better. The products have a high degree of simplicity
while a sophisticated design language and usability
are cleverly combined with technology with users
or customers in mind.

Welche Fähigkeiten hat ein erfolgreicher Designer?
Eine wichtige Fähigkeit besteht darin, die aktuellen
und zukünftigen Bedürfnisse bestimmter Nutzer zu
entschlüsseln und die Produkte und Dienstleistungen
so zu gestalten, dass sie auf deren Bedürfnisse und
Erwartungen reagieren.

Was reizt Sie an der Arbeit als Red Dot-Juror?
Teil einer Jury zu sein, die über ein sehr breites Wissen
und über unterschiedliche Erfahrungen verfügt, und
natürlich auch Teil einer unabhängigen, professionellen Jurierung zu sein. Ich genieße es zu sehen, wie
Innovationen in allen Gestaltungsbereichen Einzug
halten.

**Welche Entwicklungen in der Kategorie
„Heiz- und Klimatechnik" erachten Sie als
besonders positiv?**
Die Produktgestaltung und -qualität verbessert sich
ständig. Die Produkte haben einen hohen Grad an
Einfachheit, wobei eine hoch entwickelte Designsprache und Gebrauchsfreundlichkeit geschickt mit
einer auf den Nutzer und Kunden ausgerichteten
Technik kombiniert werden.

01

Prof. Song Kee Hong
Singapore
Singapur

Prof. Song Kee Hong is a deputy head at the Industrial Design Division, National University of Singapore. He is also the design director at cross-disciplinary consultancy Design Exchange and has more than two decades of design experience, including work at global innovation consultancy Ziba in the US and at HP. He has worked with notable brands across diverse industries including Apple, Dell, Epson, HP, Intel, Lenovo, P&G, Philips, Sanyo, Sennheiser, and WelchAllyn. His portfolio lists over twenty international design awards. He currently serves as an executive committee member in the Design Business Chamber Singapore and has previously served on the advisory committees of National University of Singapore's School of Design and Environment, Singapore government's Ministry of Education's Design and Technology programme, Singapore Polytechnic's School of Mechanical and Manufacturing Engineering and the Singapore Design Council.

Prof. Song Kee Hong ist ein stellvertretender Leiter der Industrial Design Division an der National University of Singapore. Er ist ebenfalls Designdirektor der interdisziplinären Unternehmensberatung Design Exchange und verfügt über mehr als zwei Jahrzehnte Designerfahrung, u. a. durch Tätigkeiten bei der globalen Innovations-Unternehmensberatung Ziba in den USA und bei HP. Er arbeitete bereits mit namhaften Marken unterschiedlicher Branchen zusammen, u. a. Apple, Dell, Epson, HP, Intel, Lenovo, P&G, Philips, Sanyo, Sennheiser und WelchAllyn. Sein Portfolio verzeichnet mehr als 20 internationale Designauszeichnungen. Aktuell ist er Vorstandsmitglied der Design Business Chamber Singapore. Zuvor war er in den Fachbeiräten der Fakultät „Design und Umwelt" an der Nationaluniversität Singapur sowie des Design- und Technologieprogramms des Bildungsministeriums aktiv. Zudem saß er im Beirat der Fachhochschule für Maschinenbau und Fertigungstechnik in Singapur sowie des landeseigenen Singapore Design Councils.

02

"A young design talent is someone who has not made enough mistakes yet."

„Ein Nachwuchsdesigner ist jemand, der noch nicht genug Fehler gemacht hat."

Do you have a design role model?
When I was a design student, Tadao Ando was my role model. There are no redundant details in his designs created at that time and that really inspired me. I still follow that principle but have extended it beyond styling to include usability and sustainability, striving to achieve more with less in my design.

What does winning the Red Dot say about the product?
It means the product design has survived thorough scrutiny by a pool of international design experts. Entering this award also demonstrates the manufacturer's confidence in the quality of their product.

Which developments would you like to see in product design in the future?
I would like to see more products that are designed for a longer lifespan.

Haben Sie ein Designvorbild?
Als ich ein Designstudent war, war Tadao Ando mein Vorbild. Es gibt keine überflüssigen Details in seinen Entwürfen aus dieser Zeit und das war sehr inspirierend für mich. Ich folge diesem Prinzip noch heute, aber ich habe es über das Styling hinaus auf Benutzerfreundlichkeit und Nachhaltigkeit ausgedehnt. Das Ziel meiner Gestaltung ist, mit weniger mehr zu erreichen.

Was sagt die Auszeichnung mit dem Red Dot über ein Produkt aus?
Es bedeutet, dass das Produktdesign die umfassende Prüfung einer Gruppe internationaler Designexperten bestanden hat. Darüber hinaus besagt die Tatsache, dass dieses Produkt am Wettbewerb teilnimmt, dass der Hersteller Vertrauen in die Qualität seines Produktes hat.

Welche Entwicklungen im Produktdesign würden Sie sich für die Zukunft wünschen?
Ich würde gerne mehr Produkte sehen, die für eine längere Lebensdauer gestaltet sind.

01

Tapani Hyvönen
Finland
Finnland

Tapani Hyvönen graduated as an industrial designer from the present Aalto University School of Arts, Design and Architecture. In 1976, he founded the design agency "Destem Ltd." and was co-founder of ED-Design Ltd. in 1990. He has served as CEO and president of both agencies until 2013. He has been a visiting professor at Guangdong University of Technology in Guangzhou and Donghua University in Shanghai, China. His many award-winning designs for which e.g. he was honoured with the Industrial Designer of the Year Award of the Finnish Association of Industrial Designers TKO in 1991 or the Pro Finnish Design Award by the Design Forum Finland, are part of the collections of the Design Museum Helsinki and the Cooper-Hewitt Museum, New York.
Tapani Hyvönen was an advisory board member of the Design Leadership Programme at the University of Art and Design Helsinki 1989–2000, and a board member of the Icsid 1999–2003 and 2009–2013. He was president of the Finnish Association of Designers Ornamo 2009–2012 and has been a board member of the Finnish Design Museum since 2011.

Tapani Hyvönen graduierte an der heutigen Aalto University School of Arts, Design and Architecture zum Industriedesigner. 1976 gründete er die Design-agentur „Destem Ltd." und war 1990 Mitbegründer der ED-Design Ltd., die er beide bis 2013 als CEO und Präsident leitete. Er lehrt als Gastprofessor u. a. an der Guangdong University of Technology in Guangzhou und der Donghua University in Shanghai, China. Seine vielfach ausgezeichneten Arbeiten, für die er u. a. mit der Auszeichnung Industriedesigner des Jahres der Finnish Association of Industrial Designers TKO 1991 oder dem Pro Finnish Design Award des Design Forum Finland geehrt wurde, sind in den Sammlungen des Design Museum Helsinki und des Cooper-Hewitt Museum, New York, vertreten. Tapani Hyvönen war 1989–2000 in der Beratungskommission des Design Leadership Programme der University of Art and Design Helsinki und 1999–2003 sowie 2009–2013 Vorstandsmitglied des Icsid. Er war Präsident der Finnish Association of Designers Ornamo 2009–2012 und ist seit 2011 Vorstandsmitglied des Finnish Design Museum.

"A talented young designer finds connections between things that have not been connected before, which leads to new designs and innovation."

„Ein Nachwuchsdesigner findet Beziehungen zwischen Dingen, die vorher nicht miteinander verbunden waren, was zu neuen Gestaltungen und Innovationen führt."

Which skills does a successful designer have?
Curiosity in all areas of life.

What attracts you to the work as a Red Dot juror?
Two things: meeting the greatly talented jury members and sharing the experience of reviewing the most attractive and best quality products from all over the world year after year.

Which types of products in the category "Bathrooms, spas and personal care" have undergone the greatest development in the last five years?
The strongest development has taken place in the details. Shower room floor and drain solutions are becoming more sophisticated. Drains are now integrated and hidden in floor elements. Taps and other water fittings have become simpler and their function understandable. Automatic water fittings have become more common.

Welche Fähigkeiten hat ein erfolgreicher Designer?
Neugierde in allen Lebensbereichen.

Was reizt Sie an der Arbeit als Red Dot-Juror?
Zwei Dinge: jedes Jahr die hochgradig talentierten Jurymitglieder zu treffen und die Erfahrung mit ihnen zu teilen, die attraktivsten und hochwertigsten Produkte aus aller Welt zu begutachten.

Welche Produkttypen der Kategorie „Bad, Wellness und Personal Care" haben sich in den letzten fünf Jahren am meisten verändert?
Die stärkste Entwicklung hat bei den Details stattgefunden. Boden- und Abflusslösungen für Duschräume werden immer komplexer. Abflüsse werden jetzt in das Bodenelement integriert und damit verborgen. Wasserhähne und andere Armaturen sind einfacher geworden und ihre Funktionen sind leichter verständlich. Automatische Armaturen haben eine stärkere Verbreitung gefunden.

01

Guto Indio da Costa
Brazil
Brasilien

Guto Indio da Costa, born in 1969 in Rio de Janeiro, studied product design and graduated from the Art Center College of Design in Switzerland in 1993. He is design director of Indio da Costa A.U.D.T, a consultancy based in Rio de Janeiro, which develops architectural, urban planning, design and transportation projects. It works with a multidisciplinary strategic-creative group of designers, architects and urban planners, supported by a variety of other specialists. Guto Indio da Costa is a member of the Design Council of the State of Rio de Janeiro, former Vice President of the Brazilian Design Association (Abedesign) and founder of CBDI (Brazilian Industrial Design Council). He has been active as a lecturer and contributing writer to different design magazines and has been a jury member of many design competitions in Brazil and abroad.

Guto Indio da Costa, geboren 1969 in Rio de Janeiro, studierte Produktdesign und machte 1993 seinen Abschluss am Art Center College of Design in der Schweiz. Er ist Gestaltungsdirektor von Indio da Costa A.U.D.T, einem in Rio de Janeiro ansässigen Beratungsunternehmen, das Projekte in Architektur, Stadtplanung, Design- und Transportwesen entwickelt und mit einem multidisziplinären, strategisch-kreativen Team aus Designern, Architekten und Stadtplanern sowie mit der Unterstützung weiterer Spezialisten operiert. Guto Indio da Costa ist Mitglied des Design Councils des Bundesstaates Rio de Janeiro, ehemaliger Vize-Präsident der brasilianischen Designvereinigung (Abedesign) und Gründer des CBDI (Industrial Design Council Brasilien). Er ist als Lehrbeauftragter aktiv, schreibt für verschiedene Designmagazine und ist als Jurymitglied zahlreicher Designwettbewerbe in und außerhalb Brasiliens tätig.

01 VLT
Design: Indio da Costa
A.U.D.T and Yellow Window

02 Planos
Line of modular sofas,
made of leather-covered steel
Kollektion modularer Sofas aus
mit Leder bezogenem Stahl

02

"As a Red Dot juror I particularly enjoy the analysis of the wide variety of products and the rich exchange with other jury members from all around the world."

„Als Red Dot-Juror gefällt mir besonders die Analyse der breit gefächerten Produkte sowie der interessante Austausch mit den anderen Jurymitgliedern aus aller Welt."

Which everyday product could you not live without?
The smartphone. It has become the "remote control of our lives", the channel through which we connect worldwide and ask and pay for different services.

Which developments would you like to see in product design in the future?
The future is full of challenges, especially ecological challenges. I would like to see design as the leading driving force and designers as the leading voice towards a sustainable society.

Which developments in the category "Lighting and lamps" did you perceive as particularly positive?
This category is going through a major change due to improvements in LED technology, which have already taken lamp design to the next stage. However, despite the technology, lighting is much more than its source, so we must judge both the object itself and its lighting effect.

Welches Alltagsprodukt möchten Sie nicht mehr missen?
Das Smartphone. Es ist zur „Fernsteuerung" unseres Lebens geworden. Es ist der Kanal, über den wir weltweit mit anderen Menschen in Verbindung treten, nach verschiedenen Dienstleistungen suchen und für diese bezahlen.

Welche Entwicklungen im Produktdesign würden Sie sich für die Zukunft wünschen?
Die Zukunft ist voller Herausforderungen, besonders ökologischer. Ich würde mir wünschen, dass Design die führende Triebfeder und Designer die führende Stimme hin zu einer nachhaltigen Gesellschaft sind.

Welche Entwicklungen in der Kategorie „Licht und Leuchten" erachten Sie als besonders positiv?
Diese Kategorie durchlebt zurzeit eine große Veränderung aufgrund der Fortschritte in der LED-Technologie, die das nächste Stadium in der Gestaltung von Leuchten eingeleitet haben. Ungeachtet der Technologie ist eine Lampe jedoch viel mehr als ihre Lichtquelle, daher müssen wir sowohl das Objekt als auch seinen Beleuchtungseffekt bewerten.

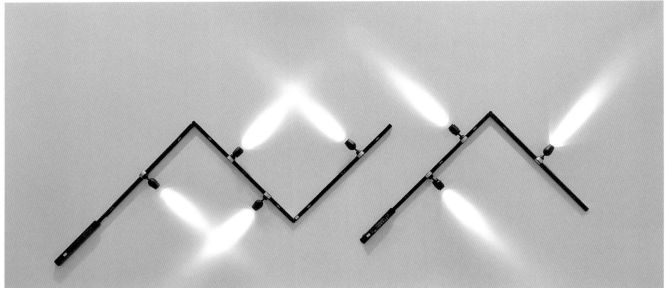

01

Prof.
Cheng-Neng Kuan
Taiwan

In 1980, Professor Cheng-Neng Kuan earned a Master's degree in Industrial Design (MID) from the Pratt Institute in New York. He is currently a full professor and the vice president of Shih-Chien University, Taipei, Taiwan. With the aim of developing a more advanced design curriculum in Taiwan, he founded the Department of Industrial Design, in 1992. He served as department chair until 1999. Moreover, Professor Kuan founded the School of Design in 1997 and had served as the dean from 1997 to 2004 and as the founding director of the Graduate Institute of Industrial Design from 1998 to 2007. Professor Kuan had also held the position of the 16th chairman of the Board of China Industrial Designers Association (CIDA), Taiwan. His fields of expertise include design strategy and management as well as design theory and creation. Having published various books on design and over 180 research papers and articles, he is an active member of design juries in his home country and internationally. He is a consultant to major enterprises on product development and design strategy.

1980 erwarb Professor Cheng-Neng Kuan einen Master-Abschluss in Industriedesign (MID) am Pratt Institute in New York. Derzeit ist er ordentlicher Professor und Vizepräsident der Shih-Chien University in Taipeh, Taiwan. 1992 gründete er mit dem Ziel, einen erweiterten Designlehrplan zu entwickeln, das Department of Industrial Design in Taiwan. Bis 1999 war Professor Kuan Vorsitzender des Instituts. Darüber hinaus gründete er 1997 die School of Design, deren Dekan er von 1997 bis 2004 war. Von 1998 bis 2007 war er Gründungsdirektor des Graduate Institute of Industrial Design. Zudem war er der 16. Vorstandsvorsitzende der China Industrial Designers Association (CIDA) in Taiwan. Seine Fachgebiete umfassen Designstrategie, -management, -theorie und -kreation. Neben der Veröffentlichung verschiedener Bücher über Design und mehr als 180 Forschungsarbeiten und Artikel ist er aktives Mitglied von Designjurys in seiner Heimat sowie auf internationaler Ebene. Zudem ist er als Berater für Großunternehmen im Bereich Produktentwicklung und Designstrategie tätig.

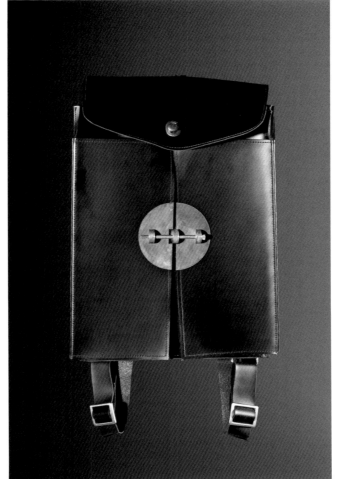

02

"A young design talent should be humble and learn as much as he can, be bold when venturing into the unknown and develop his design regardless of success or failure."

„Ein Nachwuchsdesigner sollte bescheiden sein, so viel wie möglich lernen, mutig sein, wenn er sich an Unbekanntes wagt, und seine Gestaltung ohne Rücksicht auf Erfolg oder Misserfolg entwickeln."

What is the difference between good and bad product design?
Good design will usually come with some risks, it is stimulating and yet not out of control; it appears to be somewhat adventurous. In contrast, bad design leans more towards the conservative, mediocre and even tasteless.

Which skills does a successful designer have?
All the skills related to prototyping: thinking the unthinkable, making the impossible possible and creating visuals.

Which emotions does a day spent in a jury session arouse in you?
It is a journey of curiosity and discovery, combined with analytical thinking and excitement. Also, I feel an appreciation of beauty and satisfaction when encountering the winning works.

Was unterscheidet gutes von schlechtem Produktdesign?
Für gewöhnlich birgt gutes Design einige Risiken: Es ist anregend und doch nicht gänzlich unkontrollierbar; es erscheint ein bisschen abenteuerlich. Im Gegensatz dazu tendiert schlechtes Design dazu, konservativ, mittelmäßig und sogar geschmacklos zu sein.

Welche Fähigkeiten hat ein erfolgreicher Designer?
Alle Fähigkeiten, die zur Prototypenentwicklung gehören: das Undenkbare zu denken, das Unmögliche möglich zu machen und die Kreation visueller Darstellungen.

Welche Emotionen weckt ein Jurierungstag in Ihnen?
Er ist eine Reise voller Neugier und Entdeckungen, gepaart mit analytischem Denken und Begeisterung. Darüber hinaus empfinde ich eine Wertschätzung für die Schönheit und Befriedigung, wenn ich auf die Gewinnerarbeiten stoße.

01

Kristiina Lassus
Finland/Italy
Finnland/Italien

Kristiina Lassus, born in Helsinki in 1966, graduated from the University of Industrial Arts of Helsinki with a Master of Arts in Design Leadership in 1992. This was followed by postgraduate studies in product development at the Helsinki Polytechnic in 1993, and her second MA in Interior Architecture and Furniture Design from the University of Industrial Arts in Helsinki in 1995. After working in renowned architectural practices in Finland and Australia, she developed her first products for Alessi, Poltronova and Zanotta. Her specialisation in design management and product development led to managerial positions in international design companies. She worked as Design Coordinator for Artek Oy Ab in Finland from 1994 to 1997 and as Design Manager for Alessi SpA in Italy from 1998 to 2004. In 2003, she founded Kristiina Lassus Studio which provides consultancy services in creative direction, project management, product design, brand development and design promotion. In 2007, she registered her own trademark, "Kristiina Lassus", as a symbol of independent and personal production.

Kristiina Lassus, 1966 in Helsinki geboren, graduierte 1992 an der University of Industrial Arts in Helsinki mit einem Master of Arts in Design Leadership. Ab 1993 studierte sie Product Development an der Helsinki Polytechnic und legte 1995 ihren zweiten Master of Arts in Interior Architecture und Furniture Design an der University of Industrial Arts in Helsinki ab. Sie arbeitete in renommierten Architekturbüros in Finnland und Australien, bevor sie ihre ersten Produkte für Alessi, Poltronova und Zanotta entwarf. Dank ihrer Spezialisierung auf Design Management und Product Development hatte sie geschäftsführende Positionen in internationalen Designfirmen inne. Von 1994 bis 1997 arbeitete sie als Design Coordinator für Artek Oy Ab in Finnland und von 1998 bis 2004 als Design Manager für Alessi SpA in Italien. 2003 gründete sie das Kristiina Lassus Studio, dessen Beratungstätigkeit die Bereiche Creative Direction, Projektmanagement, Produktdesign, Markenentwicklung und Designförderung umfasst. 2007 ließ sie ihre eigene Schutzmarke „Kristiina Lassus" eintragen, als Symbol einer unabhängigen und persönlichen Produktion.

01 Iota + Tibidabo
    Salad bowl and salad set –
    stainless steel; for Alessi
    Salatschüssel und Salat-Set –
    Edelstahl; für Alessi

02 Akana
    Rug, handknotted in Nepal –
    wool, bamboo silk, linen;
    for Rugs Kristiina Lassus
    Teppich, handgeknotet in Nepal –
    Wolle, Bambusseide, Leinen;
    für Rugs Kristiina Lassus

02

"Young design talents will hopefully have a chance to devote at least part of their time and skills to resolving some important social and ecological problems."

„Ein Nachwuchsdesigner wird hoffentlich die Gelegenheit haben, zumindest einen Teil seiner Zeit und Fähigkeiten der Lösung wichtiger sozialer und ökologischer Probleme zu widmen."

How would you describe your work as a designer?
In my work I find the triangle of design-marketing-production fascinating. My approach is analytical and practical and I aim for uniqueness and durability.

Which product would you like to design one day?
Something truly necessary.

What does winning the Red Dot say about the product?
It means excellence in various forms: well made, appropriate, functional, practical, problem solving, innovative, aesthetically pleasing, long lasting and environmentally responsible.

Which developments would you like to see in product design in the future?
The waste problem of used products is huge and I hope we will find solutions both to minimise waste and to improve recycling.

Wie würden Sie Ihre Tätigkeit als Designerin beschreiben?
In meiner Arbeit fasziniert mich das Dreieck aus Design, Marketing und Herstellung. Mein Ansatz ist analytisch und praktisch und mein Ziel Einzigartigkeit und Langlebigkeit.

Welches Produkt würden Sie gerne einmal gestalten?
Etwas, das wirklich notwendig ist.

Was sagt die Auszeichnung mit dem Red Dot über ein Produkt aus?
Sie bedeutet Exzellenz in vielen Bereichen: Das Produkt ist gut verarbeitet, zweckmäßig, funktional, praktisch, problemlösend, innovativ, ästhetisch ansprechend, dauerhaft und umweltverträglich.

Welche Entwicklungen im Produktdesign würden Sie sich für die Zukunft wünschen?
Das Abfallproblem benutzter Produkte ist riesig und ich hoffe, dass wir Lösungen finden werden, die zur Minimierung von Abfällen und zur Verbesserung des Recyclings führen.

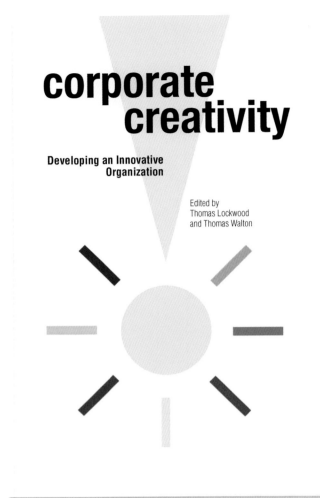

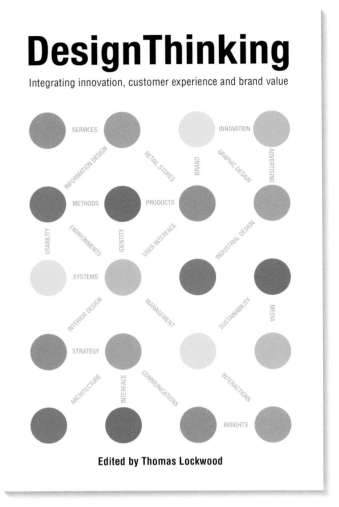

01/02

Dr Thomas Lockwood
USA

Thomas Lockwood is the author of books on design thinking, design management, corporate creativity and design strategy. He has a PhD in design management, and is regarded as a pioneer in the integration of design, innovation and design thinking practices within business, as well as for founding international design and user-experience organisations. He was a visiting professor at Pratt Institute in New York City, is a Fellow at the Royal Society of the Arts in London, and a frequent design award judge. Lockwood is a founding partner of Lockwood Resource, an international recruiting firm specialising in design leadership recruiting. From 2005 to 2011, he was president of DMI, the Design Management Institute, a non-profit research association in Boston. From 1995 to 2005, he was design director at Sun Microsystems and StorageTek, and creative director at several design and advertising firms for a number of years. In addition, he manages a blog about design leadership at lockwoodresource.com.

Thomas Lockwood ist Autor von Büchern zu den Themen Design Thinking, Designmanagement, Corporate Creativity und Designstrategie. Mit einem Doktor in Designmanagement gilt er als Vordenker für die Integration von Design, Innovation und Design Thinking-Praxis ins Geschäftsleben sowie für die Gründung internationaler Design- und User-Experience-Organisationen. Er war Gastprofessor am Pratt Institute in New York City, ist Mitglied der Royal Society of the Arts in London und regelmäßig Juror bei Designwettbewerben. Lockwood ist Gründerpartner von Lockwood Resource, einer internationalen Rekrutierungsfirma, die sich auf die Anwerbung von Führungspersonal für den Designbereich spezialisiert hat. Von 2005 bis 2011 war er Präsident des DMI (Design Management Institute), einer gemeinnützigen Forschungsorganisation in Boston. Von 1995 bis 2005 war er Designdirektor bei Sun Microsystems und StorageTek und über mehrere Jahre hinweg Kreativdirektor in verschiedenen Design- und Werbefirmen. Darüber hinaus führt er den Blog lockwoodresource.com über Mitarbeiterführung im Designsektor.

"Winning a Red Dot for a product is the most important seal of recognition with regards to its design, innovation, usability, style and ecological quality."

„Gewinnt ein Produkt einen Red Dot, erhält es das wichtigste Siegel der Anerkennung in Sachen Gestaltung, Innovation, Nutzerfreundlichkeit, Stil und ökologischer Qualität."

What is the difference between good and bad product design?
The difference is the degree of pleasure for the user. After all, design is about people, it's as simple as that.

Do you have a design role model?
Yes, Robert Blaich. He was the first head of design at Philips, and led the company from being a house of brands to a branded house. He got design a seat at the table, literally, and was an early thought leader on design leadership.

Which emotions does a day spent in a jury session arouse in you?
Almost all of my emotions! I experience happiness, sadness and curiosity; I feel challenged, have to use my intellect, require stamina, have to push myself to explain my thoughts and opinions, and I feel personal satisfaction.

Was unterscheidet gutes von schlechtem Produktdesign?
Der Unterschied liegt in dem Grad der Freude, die das Produkt dem Nutzer bereitet. Letztlich geht es bei Design um Menschen – so einfach ist das.

Haben Sie ein Vorbild in Sachen Gestaltung?
Ja, und zwar Robert Blaich. Er war der erste Leiter der Designabteilung bei Philips und entwickelte die Firma von einem Unternehmen, das Markenprodukte anbietet, zu einem, das eine eigene Marke ist. Er verschaffte Design ein Mitspracherecht und war ein früher Vordenker in Design Leadership.

Welche Emotionen weckt ein Jurierungstag in Ihnen?
Fast alle! Ich erfahre Glück, Traurigkeit und Neugierde, fühle mich herausgefordert, nutze meinen Intellekt, benötige Ausdauer, versuche alles zu geben, um meine Gedanken und Meinung gut darzulegen, und empfinde persönliche Zufriedenheit.

01

Lam Leslie Lu
Hong Kong
Hongkong

Lam Leslie Lu received a Master of Architecture from Yale University in Connecticut, USA in 1977, and was the recipient of the Monbusho Scholarship of the Japanese Ministry of Culture in 1983, where he conducted research in design and urban theory in Tokyo. He is currently the principal of the Hong Kong Design Institute and academic director of the Hong Kong Institute of Vocational Education. Prior to this, he was head of the Department of Architecture at the University of Hong Kong. Lam Leslie Lu has worked with, among others, Cesar Pelli and Associates, Hardy Holzman Pfeiffer Associates, Kohn Pedersen Fox Associates and Shinohara Kazuo on the design of the Centennial Hall of the Tokyo Institute of Technology. Moreover, he was visiting professor at Yale University and the Delft University of Technology as well as assistant lecturer for the Eero Saarinen Chair at Yale University. He also lectured and served as design critic at major international universities such as Columbia, Cambridge, Delft, Princeton, Yale, Shenzhen, Tongji, Tsinghua and the Chinese University Hong Kong.

Lam Leslie Lu erwarb 1977 einen Master of Architecture an der Yale University in Connecticut, USA, und war 1983 Monbusho-Stipendiat des japanischen Kulturministeriums, an dem er die Forschung in Design und Stadttheorie in Tokio leitete. Derzeit ist er Direktor des Hong Kong Design Institute und akademischer Direktor des Hong Kong Institute of Vocational Education. Zuvor war er Leiter des Architektur-Instituts an der Universität Hongkong. Lam Leslie Lu hat u. a. mit Cesar Pelli and Associates, Hardy Holzman Pfeiffer Associates, Kohn Pedersen Fox Associates und Shinohara Kazuo am Design der Centennial Hall des Tokyo Institute of Technology zusammengearbeitet, war Gastprofessor an der Yale University und der Technischen Universität Delft sowie Assistenz-Dozent für den Saarinen-Lehrstuhl in Yale. Er hielt zudem Vorträge und war Designkritiker an großen internationalen Universitäten wie Columbia, Cambridge, Delft, Princeton, Yale, Shenzhen, Tongji, Tsinghua und der chinesischen Universität Hongkong.

"A young design talent is in need of a broad understanding of global culture and civility, but also possesses the considered resolve to ignore all of it."

„Ein Nachwuchsdesigner benötigt ein umfassendes Verständnis globaler Kultur und globalen Anstands, aber er besitzt ebenso die wohlüberlegte Entschlossenheit, dieses Wissen zu ignorieren."

Which everyday product could you not live without?
A fountain pen, as I still write and sketch a lot.

Which developments would you like to see in product design in the future?
An even closer relationship between thinking, conceptualisation, mechanisation and craft.

What attracts you to the work as a Red Dot juror?
The opportunity to observe social and cultural changes in very naked form and the competitiveness of thoughts inherent in the proposals.

Which emotions does a day spent in a jury session arouse in you?
I feel humbled every time, because I realise that I need to think more, then unthink even more, in order to work harder to overcome my ignorance. It's a real learning experience, just like at school.

Welches Alltagsprodukt möchten Sie nicht mehr missen?
Einen Füllfederhalter, da ich noch viel schreibe und zeichne.

Welche Entwicklungen im Produktdesign würden Sie sich für die Zukunft wünschen?
Eine noch engere Beziehung zwischen Denken, Konzeption, Mechanisierung und Handwerk.

Was reizt Sie an der Arbeit als Red Dot-Juror?
Die Gelegenheit, soziale und kulturelle Veränderungen in sehr unverhüllter Form zu beobachten, und die Konkurrenzfähigkeit der Gedanken, die den Vorschlägen innewohnen.

Welche Emotionen weckt ein Jurierungstag in Ihnen?
Ich fühle jedes Mal Demut, da ich feststelle, dass ich mehr denken und dann noch mehr umdenken muss, um meine Unwissenheit noch stärker zu überwinden. Es ist eine echte Lernerfahrung, genau wie in der Schule.

01

Wolfgang K. Meyer-Hayoz
Switzerland
Schweiz

Wolfgang K. Meyer-Hayoz studied mechanical engineering, visual communication and industrial design and graduated from the Stuttgart State Academy of Art and Design. The professors Klaus Lehmann, Kurt Weidemann and Max Bense have had formative influence on his design philosophy. In 1985, he founded the Meyer-Hayoz Design Engineering Group with offices in Winterthur, Switzerland and Constance, Germany. The design studio offers consultancy services for national as well as international companies in the five areas of design competence: design strategy, industrial design, user interface design, temporary architecture and communication design, and has received numerous international awards. From 1987 to 1993, Wolfgang K. Meyer-Hayoz was president of the Swiss Design Association (SDA). He is a member of the Association of German Industrial Designers (VDID), Swiss Marketing and the Swiss Management Society (SMG). Wolfgang K. Meyer-Hayoz also serves as juror on international design panels and supervises Change Management and Turnaround projects in the field of design strategy.

Wolfgang K. Meyer-Hayoz absolvierte Studien in Maschinenbau, Visueller Kommunikation sowie Industrial Design mit Abschluss an der Staatlichen Akademie der Bildenden Künste in Stuttgart. Seine Gestaltungsphilosophie prägten die Professoren Klaus Lehmann, Kurt Weidemann und Max Bense. 1985 gründete er die Meyer-Hayoz Design Engineering Group mit Büros in Winterthur/Schweiz und Konstanz/ Deutschland. Das Designstudio bietet Beratungsdienste für nationale wie internationale Unternehmen in den fünf Designkompetenzen Designstrategie, Industrial Design, User Interface Design, Temporäre Architektur und Kommunikationsdesign und wurde bereits vielfach ausgezeichnet. Von 1987 bis 1993 war Wolfgang K. Meyer-Hayoz Präsident der Swiss Design Association (SDA); er ist Mitglied im Verband Deutscher Industrie Designer (VDID), von Swiss Marketing und der Schweizerischen Management Gesellschaft (SMG). Wolfgang K. Meyer-Hayoz engagiert sich auch als Juror internationaler Designgremien und moderiert Change-Management- und Turnaround-Projekte im designstrategischen Bereich.

01 Robotic systems for the
micro- and nano-scale.
Corporate design for the
ETH spin-off FemtoTools AG,
Switzerland
Robotersysteme für den
Mikro- und Nanobereich.
Corporate Design für die
ETH-Spin-off FemtoTools AG,
Schweiz

02 Venezuela
Product design, usability
optimisation and design of
an independent icon-based
language for the fully-
automatic coffee machine
by Aequator AG, Switzerland
Produktdesign, Usability-
Optimierung sowie Entwurf
einer eigenständigen Icon-
Sprache für den Kaffeevoll-
automaten der Aequator AG,
Schweiz

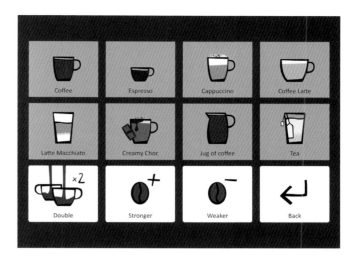

02

"Young design talents have fantastic opportunities for professional development today, provided they are exceptional, can communicate well and have management expertise."

„Ein Nachwuchsdesigner hat heute fantastische professionelle Entwicklungsmöglichkeiten – vorausgesetzt, er ist eine Ausnahmeerscheinung, kann gut kommunizieren und besitzt Management-Know-how."

Which skills does a successful designer have?
He is curious and interested in current developments, has a sense of aesthetics, can think in a structured and anticipatory way, can express himself verbally and graphically and is a team player.

What does winning the Red Dot say about the product?
Receiving the Red Dot virtually puts the product on a winner's podium. It confirms that it fully meets the high standards of the defined assessment criteria and therefore has high customer value.

Which developments would you like to see in product design in the future?
I would like to see more networked thinking and development in companies.

What attracts you to the work as a Red Dot juror?
Again and again I'm attracted and inspired by the dialogue, the exchange of opinions, meeting the jury colleagues from around the world and the most diverse industries in person and the unique team spirit of the Red Dot staff members.

Welche Fähigkeiten hat ein erfolgreicher Designer?
Er ist neugierig und interessiert an aktuellen Entwicklungen, er hat ein Gefühl für Ästhetik, kann strukturiert und antizipatorisch denken, sich verbal und zeichnerisch ausdrücken und ist teamfähig.

Was sagt eine Auszeichnung mit dem Red Dot über das Produkt aus?
Die Auszeichnung mit dem Red Dot stellt das Produkt quasi auf ein Siegerpodest. Sie bestätigt, dass es den hohen Anforderungen der definierten Bewertungs-kriterien voll entspricht und hiermit einen hohen Kundennutzen darstellt.

Welche Entwicklungen im Produktdesign würden Sie sich für die Zukunft wünschen?
Gerne würde ich mir mehr vernetztes Denken und Entwickeln in den Unternehmen wünschen.

Was reizt Sie an der Arbeit als Red Dot-Juror?
Mich reizt und begeistert immer wieder aufs Neue der Dialog, der Austausch, das persönliche Zusammen-treffen mit den Jury-Kolleginnen und -Kollegen aus aller Welt und aus den verschiedensten Branchen sowie der einzigartige Team-Spirit der Red Dot-Mitarbeiter.

01

Prof. Jure Miklavc
Slovenia
Slowenien

Professor Jure Miklavc graduated in industrial design from the Academy of Fine Arts in Ljubljana, Slovenia, and has nearly 20 years of experience in the field of design. Miklavc started his career working as a freelance designer, before founding his own design consultancy, Studio Miklavc. Studio Miklavc works in the fields of product design, visual communications and brand development and is a consultancy for a variety of clients from the industries of light design, electronic goods, user interfaces, transport design and medical equipment. Sports equipment designed by the studio has gained worldwide recognition. From 2013 onwards, the team has been working for the prestigious Italian motorbike manufacturer Bimota. Designs by Studio Miklavc have received many international awards and have been displayed in numerous exhibitions. Jure Miklavc has been involved in design education since 2005 and is currently a lecturer and head of industrial design at the Academy of Fine Arts and Design in Ljubljana.

Professor Jure Miklavc machte seinen Abschluss in Industrial Design an der Academy of Fine Arts and Design in Ljubljana, Slowenien, und verfügt über nahezu 20 Jahre Erfahrung im Designbereich. Er arbeitete zunächst als freiberuflicher Designer, bevor er sein eigenes Design-Beratungsunternehmen „Studio Miklavc" gründete. Studio Miklavc ist in den Bereichen Produktdesign, Visuelle Kommunikation und Markenentwicklung sowie in der Beratung zahlreicher Kunden der Branchen Lichtdesign, Elektronische Güter, Benutzeroberflächen, Transport-Design und Medizinisches Equipment tätig. Die von dem Studio gestalteten Sportausrüstungen erfahren weltweit Anerkennung. Seit 2013 arbeitet das Team für den angesehenen italienischen Motorradhersteller Bimota. Studio Miklavc erhielt bereits zahlreiche Auszeichnungen sowie Präsentationen in Ausstellungen. Seit 2005 ist Jure Miklavc in der Designlehre tätig und aktuell Dozent und Head of Industrial Design an der Academy of Fine Arts and Design in Ljubljana.

01 AchillX Relaxroll
An integral project which comprises the building of a brand and corporate identity as well as developing products and packaging for a new sports company
Ein integrales Projekt, das den Aufbau einer Marke und Firmenidentität sowie die Entwicklung von Produkten und Verpackungen für ein neues Sportunternehmen umfasst

02 Helmet
for Bimota SA as part of the redesign of the corporate identity and strategy, new communication materials, fair stand design and merchandise products
für Bimota SA als Teil der Neugestaltung der Firmenidentität und -strategie, der Kommunikationsmaterialien, des Messestanddesigns und der Handelswaren

02

"A young design talent could be the person who changes the way we live in the future."
„Ein Nachwuchsdesigner könnte die Person sein, die unser zukünftiges Leben verändert."

What is the difference between good and bad product design?
Good design serves many key purposes very well, whereas bad design usually only pretends to do so. Beyond that, good design influences us deeply and can change us.

How would you describe your work as a designer?
I have a fairly methodical approach, but I'm never tired of experimenting with things that can produce truly innovative solutions.

What does winning the Red Dot say about the product?
That it stands for absolute quality in the broadest sense of the word. Besides the usual "hard" values there is also an emphasise on "soft" values. It means that some serious thought went into creating the solution.

Was unterscheidet gutes von schlechtem Produktdesign?
Gutes Design erfüllt viele zentrale Aufgaben mit großem Erfolg, wohingegen schlechtes Design normalerweise nur vorgibt, das zu tun. Darüber hinaus beeinflusst uns gutes Design zutiefst und kann uns verändern.

Wie würden Sie Ihre Tätigkeit als Designer beschreiben?
Ich habe einen recht methodischen Ansatz, aber ich werde niemals müde, mit Dingen zu experimentieren, die wahrhaft innovative Lösungen hervorbringen können.

Was sagt die Auszeichnung mit dem Red Dot über ein Produkt aus?
Dass das Produkt für absolute Qualität steht – im weitesten Sinne des Wortes. Neben den üblichen „harten" Werten liegt hier auch ein Augenmerk auf „weichen" Werten. Das bedeutet, dass wir es hier mit einer wohldurchdachten Lösung zu tun haben.

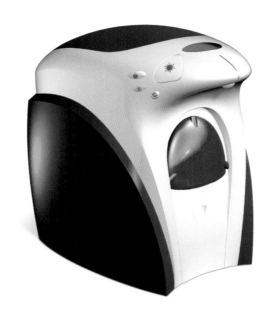

01

Prof. Ron A. Nabarro
Israel

Professor Ron A. Nabarro is an industrial designer, strategist, entrepreneur, researcher and educator. He has been a professional designer since 1970 and has designed more than 750 products to date in a wide range of industries. He has played a leading role in the emergence of age-friendly design and age-friendly design education. From 1992 to 2009, he was a professor of industrial design at the Technion Israel Institute of Technology, where he founded and was the head of the graduate programme in advanced design studies and design management. Currently, Nabarro teaches design management and design thinking at DeTao Masters Academy in Shanghai, China. From 1999 to 2003, he was an executive board member of Icsid and now acts as a regional advisor. He is a frequent keynote speaker at conferences, has presented TEDx events, has lectured and led design workshops in over 20 countries and consulted to a wide variety of organisations. Furthermore, he is co-founder and CEO of Senior-touch Ltd. and design4all. The principle areas of his research and interest are design thinking, age-friendly design and design management.

Professor Ron A. Nabarro ist Industriedesigner, Stratege, Unternehmer, Forscher und Lehrender. Seit 1970 ist er praktizierender Designer, gestaltete bisher mehr als 750 Produkte für ein breites Branchenspektrum und spielt eine führende Rolle im Bereich des altersfreundlichen Designs und dessen Lehre. Von 1992 bis 2009 war er Professor für Industriedesign am Technologie-Institut Technion Israel, an dem er das Graduiertenprogramm für fortgeschrittene Designstudien und Designmanagement einführte und leitete. Aktuell unterrichtet Nabarro Designmanagement und Design Thinking an der DeTao Masters Academy in Shanghai, China. Von 1999 bis 2003 war er Vorstandsmitglied des Icsid, für den er aktuell als regionaler Berater tätig ist. Er ist ein gefragter Redner auf Konferenzen, hat bei TEDx-Veranstaltungen präsentiert, hielt Vorträge und Workshops in mehr als 20 Ländern und beriet eine Vielzahl von Organisationen. Zudem ist er Mitbegründer und Geschäftsführer von Senior-touch Ltd. und design4all. Die Hauptbereiche seiner Forschung und seines Interesses sind Design Thinking, altersfreundliches Design und Designmanagement.

02

"Good product design is 'user-
centred' and 'non-excluding'
design, bad product design is
'designer-centred' design."
„Gutes Produktdesign ist auf den
Nutzer ausgerichtet und nicht aus-
grenzend, während sich schlechtes
Design um den Designer dreht."

Which skills does a successful designer have?
Apart from the traditional skills of creativity and
the ability to visualise new solutions, a successful
designer should have the ability to look at systems
from a meta-position and understand social and
environmental responsibility.

**Which developments would you like to see in
product design in the future?**
I would like to see a more humanistic approach and
designers contributing not only to the "look & feel"
of products, but also to the user's experience.

**Which emotions does a day spent in a jury session
arouse in you?**
The most dramatic emotion that I feel again and
again, even after so many years of adjudications,
happens when a design is excellent and all jury
members immediately agree. I'm always amazed that
excellent design is so easy to spot and gets such a
unanimous response from the jury.

Welche Fähigkeiten hat ein erfolgreicher Designer?
Neben traditionellen Fähigkeiten wie Kreativität und
der Imagination neuer Lösungen muss ein erfolgreicher Designer Systeme von einer Meta-Position aus
betrachten können und soziale und ökologische
Verantwortung verstehen.

**Welche Entwicklungen im Produktdesign
würden Sie sich für die Zukunft wünschen?**
Ich würde mir einen humanistischeren Ansatz wünschen und dass Designer nicht nur zu den optischen
und haptischen Qualitäten eines Produktes beitragen,
sondern auch zum Nutzererlebnis.

**Welche Emotionen weckt ein Jurierungstag
in Ihnen?**
Die dramatischste Emotion, die ich immer wieder –
selbst nach so vielen Jahren in der Jury – fühle,
passiert, wenn eine Gestaltung hervorragend ist und
alle Jurymitglieder sofort zustimmen. Ich bin immer
wieder verblüfft, dass ausgezeichnetes Design so klar
zu erkennen ist und eine so einstimmige Reaktion
von der Jury bekommt.

01

Prof. Dr. Ken Nah
Korea

Professor Dr Ken Nah graduated with a Bachelor of Science in industrial engineering from Hanyang University, South Korea, in 1983. He deepened his interest in human factors/ergonomics by earning a master's degree from Korea Advanced Institute for Science and Technology (KAIST) in 1985 and he gained a PhD from Tufts University in 1996. In addition, Ken Nah is also a USA Certified Professional Ergonomist (CPE). He is currently the dean of the International Design School for Advanced Studies (IDAS) and a professor of design management as well as director of the Human Experience and Emotion Research (HE.ER) Lab at IDAS, Hongik University, Seoul. Since 2002 he has been the director of the International Design Trend Center (IDTC). Ken Nah was the director general of "World Design Capital Seoul 2010". Alongside his work as a professor, he is also the president of the Korea Institute of Design Management (KIDM), vice president of the Korea Association of Industrial Designers (KAID) as well as the chairman of the Design and Brand Committee of the Korea Consulting Association (KCA).

Professor Dr. Ken Nah graduierte 1983 an der Hanyang University in Südkorea als Bachelor of Science in Industrial Engineering. Sein Interesse an Human Factors/Ergonomie vertiefte er 1985 mit einem Master-Abschluss am Korea Advanced Institute for Science and Technology (KAIST) und promovierte 1996 an der Tufts University. Darüber hinaus ist Ken Nah ein in den USA zertifizierter Ergonom (CPE). Derzeit ist er Dekan der International Design School for Advanced Studies (IDAS) und Professor für Design Management sowie Direktor des „Human Experience and Emotion Research (HE.ER)"-Labors an der IDAS, Hongik University, Seoul. Seit 2002 ist er zudem Leiter des International Design Trend Center (IDTC). Ken Nah war Generaldirektor der „World Design Capital Seoul 2010". Neben seiner Lehrtätigkeit ist er Präsident des Korea Institute of Design Management (KIDM), Vizepräsident der Korea Association of Industrial Designers (KAID) sowie Vorsitzender des „Design and Brand"-Komitees der Korea Consulting Association (KCA).

01 Workbook for Design Ideas
Korean, Chinese, and Taiwanese
editions co-authored by
Prof. Dr. Ken Nah and Prof. Sunah Kim
Arbeitsbuch für Designideen
Koreanische, chinesische und taiwa-
nesische Ausgabe, von den Autoren
Prof. Dr. Ken Nah und Prof. Sunah Kim
gemeinsam verfasst

01

"A young design talent needs to know how to listen."

„Ein Nachwuchsdesigner muss gut zuhören können."

What attracts you to the work as a Red Dot juror?
The great community spirit among the Red Dot jurors and the opportunity to experience great products from all around the world in the judging hall.

Which type of product in the category "Consumer electronics and cameras" has undergone the greatest development in the last five years?
Television. Technological advancements such as flexible displays and OLED technology have allowed designers to completely rethink TVs and even their shapes.

To what extent are materials a topic in the design of consumer electronics and cameras?
Materials are one of the most, if not the most, crucial and difficult factor to consider when designing consumer electronics and cameras. The material of a product is the medium through which the user makes both a physical and emotional connection with the product. Only when a product's material has been appropriately selected and engineered a product can be truly captivating.

Was reizt Sie an der Arbeit als Red Dot-Juror?
Der großartige Gemeinschaftsgeist der Red Dot-Juroren und die Gelegenheit, ausgezeichnete Produkte aus aller Welt in der Jurierungshalle zu erleben.

Welche Produkte im Bereich „Unterhaltungselektronik und Kameras" haben sich in den letzten fünf Jahren am meisten entwickelt?
Fernseher. Technologische Neuerungen, wie zum Beispiel flexible Displays und die OLED-Technologie, haben es Designern ermöglicht, Fernseher und sogar deren Form komplett neu zu denken.

Inwieweit sind Materialien ein Thema bei der Gestaltung von Unterhaltungselektronik und Kameras?
Materialien sind einer der wichtigsten und schwierigsten – wenn nicht sogar der wichtigste und schwierigste – Aspekt bei der Gestaltung von Unterhaltungselektronik und Kameras. Das Material eines Produktes ist das Medium, durch das der Benutzer sowohl physikalisch als auch emotional in Kontakt mit dem Produkt tritt. Nur wenn das Material eines Produktes passend ausgewählt und verarbeitet worden ist, kann ein Produkt wirklich faszinierend sein.

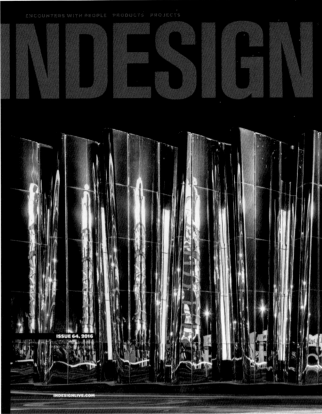

01

Raj Nandan
Australia
Australien

In 1998, Raj Nandan completed a Bachelor of Commerce/Marketing at Charles Sturt University in Sydney. At the age of 22, he purchased his first magazine, Architectural Review Australia, and launched publications in the design and architecture sector. In 2000, Nandan started his own boutique-publishing house. Indesign Media Asia Pacific (IMAP) found instant success with the magazine Indesign, which now circulates in 41 countries. Today, IMAP produces a range of well-respected design and architecture titles that include, among others, Indesign, Habitus, DQ (Design Quarterly) and The Collection. In 2003, Nandan founded the emerging design programme Launch Pad, a prototype-to-production mentoring programme. He has since been invited onto several boards, including the Strategic Advisory Board of the International Federation of Interior Architects/Designers and the Advisory Board for Emergency Architects Australia. He is also an ambassador for Unlimited: Designing for the Asia Pacific. Now with a significant digital audience, IMAP continues to champion design in the region.

Raj Nandan erlangte 1998 einen Bachelor in Commerce/Marketing an der Charles Sturt University in Sydney. Mit 22 Jahren erwarb er seine erste Zeitschrift, die Architectural Review Australia, und brachte Publikationen im Bereich Design und Architektur heraus. Im Jahr 2000 startete Nandan seinen eigenen Boutique-Verlag. Indesign Media Asia Pacific (IMAP) hatte sofort Erfolg mit dem Magazin Indesign, das mittlerweile in 41 Ländern vertrieben wird. Heute produziert IMAP angesehene design- und architekturbasierte Titel, unter anderem Indesign, Habitus, DQ (Design Quarterly) und The Collection. 2003 gründete Raj Nandan das aufstrebende Designprogramm Launch Pad, ein Prototyp-zu-Produktion-Programm mit Beratung. Er ist Mitglied verschiedener Gremien, einschließlich des Strategic Advisory Board der International Federation of Interior Architects/Designers und des Beratungsgremiums für Emergency Architects Australia. Außerdem ist er Repräsentant für Unlimited: Designing for the Asia Pacific. Mit einem heute bedeutenden digitalen Publikum engagiert sich IMAP weiterhin für Design in der Region.

02

"Ironically this small Red Dot says very big things: It says that the design has excelled in a manner that deserves recognition on a global level."

„Ironischerweise macht dieser kleine Red Dot eine sehr große Aussage: Er besagt, dass das Design so her-ausragend ist, dass es internationale Anerkennung verdient."

Do you have a role model?
Muhammad Ali.

Which everyday product could you not live without?
Ear plugs – they keep the noise out of my world so I can think.

What is the difference between good and bad product design?
Good design solves a simple problem in a simple way with a great aesthetic. Bad design complicates a simple problem and provides a complicated solution.

What characterises a product you would immediately like to write about?
It's so unique and simple that it verges on genius.

Which emotions does a day spent in a jury session arouse in you?
Excitement in the morning, exhaustion in the evening.

Haben Sie ein Vorbild in Sachen Design?
Muhammad Ali.

Welches Alltagsprodukt möchten Sie nicht mehr missen?
Ohrstöpsel. Sie halten Lärm fern von meiner Welt, sodass ich denken kann.

Was unterscheidet gutes von schlechtem Produktdesign?
Gutes Design löst einfache Probleme auf einfache Weise mit großartiger Ästhetik. Schlechtes Design verkompliziert ein einfaches Problem und bietet eine komplizierte Lösung.

Was macht ein Produkt aus, über das Sie sofort schreiben möchten?
Es ist so einzigartig und einfach, dass es an Genialität grenzt.

Welche Emotionen weckt ein Jurierungstag in Ihnen?
Begeisterung am Morgen, Erschöpfung am Abend.

01

Prof. Dr. Yuri Nazarov
Russia
Russland

Professor Dr Yuri Nazarov, born in 1948 in Moscow, teaches at the National Design Institute in Moscow where he is also provost. As an actively involved design expert, he serves on numerous boards, for example as president of the Association of Designers of Russia, as a corresponding member of Russian Academy of Arts, and as a member of the Russian Design Academy. Yuri Nazarov has received a wide range of accolades for his achievements: he is a laureate of the State Award of the Russian Federation in Literature and Art as well as of the Moscow Administration's Award, and he also has received a badge of honour for "Merits in Development of Design".

Professor Dr. Yuri Nazarov, 1948 in Moskau geboren, lehrt am National Design Institute in Moskau, dessen Rektor er auch ist. Als engagierter Designexperte ist er in zahlreichen Gremien des Landes tätig, zum Beispiel als Präsident der Russischen Designervereinigung, als korrespondierendes Mitglied der Russischen Kunstakademie sowie als Mitglied der Russischen Designakademie. Für seine Verdienste wurde Yuri Nazarov mit einer Vielzahl an Auszeichnungen geehrt. So ist er Preisträger des Staatspreises der Russischen Föderation in Literatur und Kunst sowie des Moskauer Regierungspreises und besitzt zudem das Ehrenabzeichen für „Verdienste in der Designentwicklung".

02

"A young design talent must work hard and be knowledgeable in all areas."

„Ein Nachwuchsdesigner muss hart arbeiten und ein fundiertes Wissen in allen Bereichen haben."

Which skills does a successful designer have?
A professional designer must have two important skills. He must be able to listen to his clients and explain to them how to solve their problems.

Which product would you like to design some day?
I currently try to only work on important social projects or projects representing our culture and country, such as recently the city design of the post-Olympic Sochi and the mascot for the Russian pavilion at the 2015 Milan Expo.

Which developments would you like to see in product design in the future?
I would like to see fewer commercial products and more items meeting social needs.

Welche Fähigkeiten hat ein erfolgreicher Designer?
Ein professioneller Designer muss zwei wichtige Fähigkeiten haben. Er muss seinen Klienten zuhören und ihnen erklären können, wie sie ihre Probleme lösen können.

Welches Produkt würden Sie gerne einmal gestalten?
Zurzeit versuche ich, ausschließlich an wichtigen sozialen Projekten oder Projekten, die unsere Kultur und unser Land repräsentieren, zu arbeiten, wie zuletzt die Stadtgestaltung des post-olympischen Sochi und das Maskottchen für den russischen Pavillon auf der Expo 2015 in Mailand.

Welche Entwicklungen im Produktdesign wünschen Sie sich für die Zukunft?
Ich wünsche mir weniger kommerzielle Produkte und mehr Produkte für soziale Bedürfnisse.

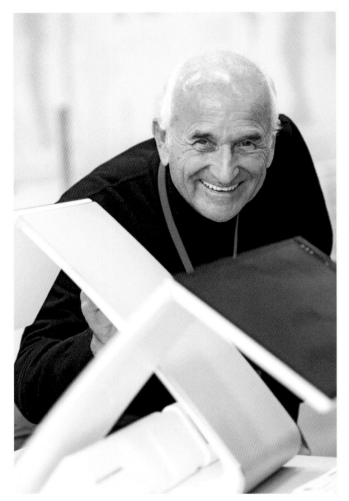

01

Alexander Neumeister
Germany/Brazil
Deutschland/Brasilien

Alexander Neumeister is a high-tech industrial designer, who lives both in Germany and Brazil. A graduate of the Ulm School of Design and a one-year scholarship student at the Tokyo University of Arts, he specialised in the fields of medicine, professional electronics and transportation. Among some of his best-known works are the "Transrapid" Maglev trains, the German ICE trains, the Japanese Shinkansen "Nozomi 500", as well as numerous regional trains and subways for Japan, China and Brazil, and the C1 and C2 trains for the Munich Metro. His last Transrapid was chosen as the motif for a special postage stamp about design in Germany. Besides working for German companies like MBB, Deutsche Bahn, BMW, Thyssen Henschel or Siemens, for 21 years he was design consultant for Hitachi/Japan. From 1983 to 1987 he was board member and later vice-president of the Icsid. In 1992, Alexander Neumeister & Neumeister Design received the honorary title "Red Dot: Design Team of the Year" for outstanding design achievements.

Alexander Neumeister arbeitet als Hightech-Industriedesigner und ist in Deutschland wie in Brasilien zu Hause. Absolvent der Hochschule für Gestaltung in Ulm und ein Jahr lang Stipendiat der Tokyo University of Arts, spezialisierte er sich auf die Bereiche Medizin, Professionelle Elektronik und Verkehr. Die Magnetschwebebahn „Transrapid", die deutschen ICE-Züge, der japanische Shinkansen „Nozomi 500", aber auch zahlreiche Regionalzüge und U-Bahnen in Japan, China und Brasilien sowie die U-Bahnen C1 und C2 für München zählen zu seinen bekanntesten Entwürfen. Sein letzter Transrapid war Motiv einer Sonderbriefmarke über Design in Deutschland. Neben Projekten für deutsche Großunternehmen wie MBB, Deutsche Bahn, BMW, Thyssen Henschel oder Siemens war er 21 Jahre lang Designberater für Hitachi/Japan. Von 1983 bis 1987 war er Vorstandsmitglied und später Vizepräsident des Icsid. 1992 wurde Alexander Neumeister & Neumeister Design mit dem Ehrentitel „Red Dot: Design Team of the Year" für herausragende Designleistungen ausgezeichnet.

01 JR-West Shinkansen
"Nozomi 500" at the train
station Tokyo
JR-West Shinkansen
„Nozomi 500" am Bahnhof
Tokio

02 ICE-3 at the long-distance
train station,
Frankfurt Airport
ICE-3 am Fernbahnhof,
Flughafen Frankfurt

02

"I am fascinated by the potential inherent in 3D printing technology, which turns all my know-how as a designer upside down."

„Ich bin fasziniert von dem Potenzial, das in der 3D-Drucker-Technologie steckt, die mein ganzes Know-how als Designer auf den Kopf stellt."

What skills should a successful designer have?
Each designer should follow his own path. And if he expertly manages to combine his specific skills with his special interests, he will be successful. Successful in many different ways, because success is not just a financial criteria!

Is there an object which you admire as designer?
Yes, it is a small tea brush, more than 300 years old, used in Japanese tea ceremonies. When I saw it for the first time, during my scholarship in Japan, I was fascinated by the ingenious combination of material and function that formed a coherent whole, as well as by its design – perfect for the purpose. Over this long period of time, it has not lost any of its quality.

What fascinated you most during the jury session?
I was fascinated by the speed with which Asian countries implement new ideas and concepts and do so while maintaining high quality design, often in a very unconventional and innovative way.

Welche Fähigkeiten hat ein erfolgreicher Designer?
Ich glaube, jeder Designer sollte seinen eigenen Weg gehen. Und wenn es ihm gelingt, seine ganz speziellen Fähigkeiten optimal mit seinen Interessen zu verbinden, wird er erfolgreich sein. Erfolgreich auf vielen Ebenen, denn Erfolg ist nicht nur ein wirtschaftliches Kriterium!

Haben Sie ein Vorbild in Sachen Gestaltung?
Ja, und zwar den kleinen Teebesen für die japanische Teezeremonie – mehr als 300 Jahre alt. Als ich ihn während meines Stipendiums in Japan zum ersten Mal sah, war ich fasziniert von der Genialität, mit der Material und Funktion eine Einheit bilden, und von der Gestaltung – perfekt für den Zweck –, die über diese lange Zeit nichts von ihrer Qualität eingebüßt hat.

Welche Innovationen haben Sie während der Jurierung am meisten fasziniert?
Mich hat die Geschwindigkeit fasziniert, mit der asiatische Länder mit hoher Designqualität neue Ideen und Konzepte umsetzen – und dies oft sehr innovativ und unkonventionell.

01

Ken Okuyama
Japan

Ken Kiyoyuki Okuyama, industrial designer and CEO of KEN OKUYAMA DESIGN, was born in 1959 in Yamagata, Japan, and studied automobile design at the Art Center College of Design in Pasadena, California. He has worked as a chief designer for General Motors, as a senior designer for Porsche AG, and as design director for Pininfarina S.p.A., being responsible for the design of Ferrari Enzo, Maserati Quattroporte and many other automobiles. He is also known for many different product designs such as motorcycles, furniture, robots and architecture. KEN OKUYAMA DESIGN was founded in 2007 and provides business consultancy services to numerous corporations. Ken Okuyama also produces cars, eyewear and interior products under his original brand. He is currently a visiting professor at several universities and also frequently publishes books.

Ken Kiyoyuki Okuyama, Industriedesigner und CEO von KEN OKUYAMA DESIGN, wurde 1959 in Yamagata, Japan, geboren und studierte Automobildesign am Art Center College of Design in Pasadena, Kalifornien. Er war als Chief Designer bei General Motors, als Senior Designer bei der Porsche AG und als Design Director bei Pininfarina S.p.A. tätig und zeichnete verantwortlich für den Ferrari Enzo, den Maserati Quattroporte und viele weitere Automobile. Zudem ist er für viele unterschiedliche Produktgestaltungen wie Motorräder, Möbel, Roboter und Architektur bekannt. KEN OKUYAMA DESIGN wurde 2007 als Beratungsunternehmen gegründet und arbeitet für zahlreiche Unternehmen. Ken Okuyama produziert unter seiner originären Marke auch Autos, Brillen und Inneneinrichtungsgegenstände. Derzeit lehrt er als Gastprofessor an verschiedenen Universitäten und publiziert zudem Bücher.

02/03

"A young design talent should go abroad and develop his talent."
„Ein Nachwuchsdesigner sollte ins Ausland gehen und sein Talent entwickeln."

What is the difference between good and bad product design?
Good design always provides a value beyond what customers expect.

How would you describe your work as a designer?
I don't merely design the styling of products, but the industry's system and the structure itself.

Which developments would you like to see in car design in the future?
By shifting to electric vehicles or some other energy source, the proportions of a car can become entirely different from those of cars with internal combustion engines.

What attracts you to the work as a Red Dot juror?
Coming in contact with unexpected ideas and products.

Was unterscheidet gutes von schlechtem Produktdesign?
Gute Gestaltung bietet immer einen Wert, der über das, was Kunden erwarten, hinausgeht.

Wie würden Sie Ihre Tätigkeit als Designer beschreiben?
Ich gestalte nicht nur das Design von Produkten, sondern das industrielle System und die Struktur an sich.

Welche Entwicklungen im Fahrzeug-Design würden Sie sich für die Zukunft wünschen?
Durch einen Wechsel hin zu Elektromotoren oder einer anderen Energiequelle können die Proportionen eines Fahrzeugs komplett anders gestaltet werden als bei Autos mit Verbrennungsmotor.

Was reizt Sie an der Arbeit als Red Dot-Juror?
Auf unerwartete Ideen und Produkte zu treffen.

01

Simon Ong
Singapore
Singapur

Simon Ong, born in Singapore in 1953, graduated with a master's degree in design from the University of New South Wales and an MBA from the University of South Australia. He is the group managing director and co-founder of Kingsmen Creatives Ltd., a leading communication design and production group with 19 offices across the Asia-Pacific region and the Middle East. Kingsmen has won several awards, such as the President's Design Award, Singapore Good Design Mark, SRA Best Retail Concept Award, SFIA Hall of Fame, Promising Brand Award, A.R.E. Retail Design Award and RDI International Store Design Award USA. Simon Ong is actively involved in the creative industry as chairman of the design group of Manpower, the Skills & Training Council of Singapore Workforce Development Agency. Moreover, he is a member of the advisory board of the Singapore Furniture Industries Council, Design Business Chamber Singapore and Interior Design Confederation of Singapore. An ardent advocate of education, Simon Ong currently serves as a board director of Nanyang Academy of Fine Arts and a member of the advisory board to the School of Design & Environment at the National University of Singapore.

Simon Ong, geboren 1953 in Singapur, erhielt einen Master in Design der University of New South Wales und einen Master of Business Administration der University of South Australia. Er ist Vorstandsvorsitzender und Mitbegründer von Kingsmen Creatives Ltd., eines führenden Unternehmens für Kommunikationsdesign und Produktion mit 19 Geschäftsstellen im asiatisch-pazifischen Raum sowie im Mittleren Osten. Kingsmen wurde vielfach ausgezeichnet, u. a. mit dem President's Design Award, Singapore Good Design Mark, SRA Best Retail Concept Award, SFIA Hall of Fame, Promising Brand Award, A.R.E. Retail Design Award und RDI International Store Design Award USA. Simon Ong ist als Vorsitzender der Designgruppe von Manpower, der „Skills & Training Council of Singapore Workforce Development Agency", aktiv in die Kreativindustrie involviert, ist unter anderem Mitglied des Beirats des Singapore Furniture Industries Council, der Design Business Chamber Singapore und der Interior Design Confederation of Singapore. Als leidenschaftlicher Befürworter von Bildung ist Simon Ong zurzeit als Vorstandsvorsitzender der Nanyang Academy of Fine Arts und als Mitglied des Beirats der School of Design & Environment an der National University of Singapore tätig.

02

"A young design talent must possess vast knowledge of the environment and industry that he or she is operating in, besides having creativity."

„Neben Kreativität muss ein Nachwuchsdesigner eine enorme Kenntnis der Umwelt und der Branche haben, in der er oder sie tätig ist."

Which skills does a successful designer have?
A good designer must have empathy for others and the environment. He or she should always keep the user's needs, convenience and limitations in mind, because good design enhances our everyday lives.

What does winning the Red Dot say about the product?
The Red Dot Design Award is the most recognised award in the design industry, much like the Grammy awards for music. Winning the Red Dot is testament to the designer's capabilities on an international playing field.

Which developments would you like to see in product design in the future?
I would like to see product design venture further afield into robotics, artificial intelligence and the Internet of Things. Design and technology have the immense potential to come together in the form of a unique product that respects the environment and enhances our lifestyle.

Welche Fähigkeiten hat ein erfolgreicher Designer?
Ein guter Designer muss Einfühlungsvermögen haben, für andere und die Umwelt. Er oder sie sollte sich immer der Bedürfnisse, des Komforts und der Einschränkungen der Nutzer bewusst sein, da gute Gestaltung unser tägliches Leben verbessert.

Was sagt die Auszeichnung mit dem Red Dot über ein Produkt aus?
Der Red Dot Design Award ist der renommierteste Wettbewerb in der Designbranche, ähnlich den Grammy Awards in der Musikindustrie. Den Red Dot zu gewinnen, ist ein Beweis für die hervorragenden Fähigkeiten des Designers im internationalen Vergleich.

Welche Entwicklungen im Produktdesign würden Sie sich für die Zukunft wünschen?
Ich würde mir wünschen, dass Produktdesign sich weiter vorwagt in Bereiche wie Robotik, künstliche Intelligenz und das Internet der Dinge. Design und Technologie haben das enorme Potenzial, gemeinsam ein einzigartiges Produkt hervorzubringen, das die Umwelt respektiert und unser Leben verbessert.

01

Prof. Martin Pärn
Estonia
Estland

Professor Martin Pärn, born in Tallinn in 1971, studied industrial design at the University of Industrial Arts Helsinki (UIAH). After working in the Finnish furniture industry he moved back to Estonia and undertook the role of the ambassadorial leader of design promotion and development in his native country. He was actively involved in the establishment of the Estonian Design Centre that he directed as chair of the board. Martin Pärn founded the multidisciplinary design office "iseasi", which creates designs ranging from office furniture to larger instruments and from interior designs for the public sector to design services. Having received many awards, Pärn began in 1995 with the development of design training in Estonia and is currently head of the Design and Engineering's master's programme, he established in 2010. The joint initiative of the Tallinn University of Technology and the Estonian Academy of Arts aims, among other things, to create synergies between engineers and designers.

Professor Martin Pärn, geboren 1971 in Tallinn, studierte Industriedesign an der University of Industrial Arts Helsinki (UIAH). Nachdem er in der finnischen Möbelindustrie gearbeitet hatte, ging er zurück nach Estland und übernahm die Funktion des leitenden Botschafters für die Designförderung und -entwicklung des Landes. Er war aktiv am Aufbau des Estonian Design Centres beteiligt, das er als Vorstandsvorsitzender leitete. Martin Pärn gründete das multidisziplinäre Designbüro „iseasi", das Büromöbel, größere Instrumente oder Interior Designs für den öffentlichen Sektor gestaltet und Designservices anbietet. Vielfach ausgezeichnet, startete Pärn 1995 mit der Entwicklung der Designlehre in Estland und ist heute Leiter des Masterprogramms „Design und Engineering", das er 2010 aufgebaut hat. Es ist eine gemeinsame Initiative der Tallinn University of Technology und der Estonian Academy of Arts und verfolgt u. a. das Ziel, durch den Zusammenschluss Synergien von Ingenieuren und Designern zu erreichen.

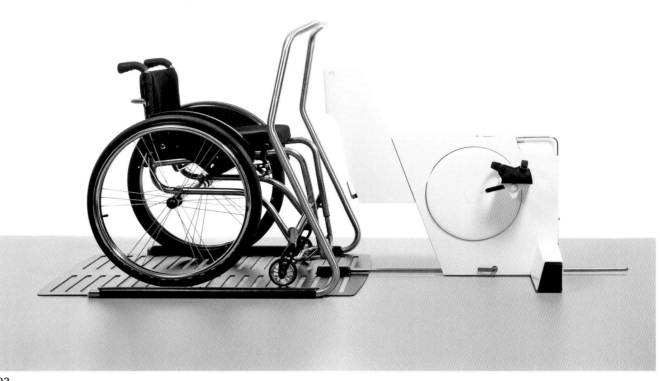

02

"A young design talent is a promise for a better future; a future that is more exciting, more engaging and more responsible."
„Ein Nachwuchsdesigner ist das Versprechen für eine bessere Zukunft. Eine Zukunft, die aufregender, fesselnder und verantwortungsvoller ist."

What is the difference between good and bad product design?
Design can change the way we behave and feel about the world: good design for better attitudes and towards more responsibility, bad design towards the opposite direction.

Which skills does a successful designer have?
The ability to read and understand the world around us and to notice invisible nuances that hide possibilities, the ability to turn these possibilities into tangible solutions that tell stories in the form of things and systems and the skill to create something new in an elegant and functional manner.

How would you describe your work as a designer?
Creating sense in a man-made world.

Was unterscheidet gutes von schlechtem Produktdesign?
Design kann unser Verhalten und die Art, wie wir die Welt sehen, verändern: gutes Design hin zu besseren Einstellungen und mehr Verantwortung, schlechtes Design in die entgegengesetzte Richtung.

Welche Fähigkeiten hat ein erfolgreicher Designer?
Die Fähigkeit, die Welt um uns herum zu lesen und zu verstehen sowie unsichtbare Nuancen zu bemerken, die Möglichkeiten verbergen; die Fähigkeit, diese Möglichkeiten in greifbare Lösungen zu verwandeln, die Geschichten in Form von Dingen und Systemen erzählen, und die Fähigkeit, auf elegante und sachliche Art und Weise etwas Neues zu schaffen.

Wie würden Sie Ihre Tätigkeit als Designer beschreiben?
Ich schaffe Sinn in einer von Menschenhand gestalteten Welt.

01

Dr Sascha Peters
Germany
Deutschland

Dr Sascha Peters is founder and owner of the agency for material and technology HAUTE INNOVATION in Berlin. He studied mechanical engineering at the RWTH Aachen, Germany, and product design at the ABK Maastricht, Netherlands. He wrote his doctoral thesis at the University of Duisburg-Essen, Germany, on the complex of problems in communication between engineering and design. From 1997 to 2003, he led research projects and product developments at the Fraunhofer Institute for Production Technology IPT in Aachen and subsequently became deputy head of the Design Zentrum Bremen until 2008. Sascha Peters is author of various specialised books on sustainable raw materials, smart materials, innovative production techniques and energetic technologies. He is a leading material expert and trend scout for new technologies. Since 2014, he has been an advisory board member of the funding initiative "Zwanzig20 – Partnerschaft für Innovation" (2020 – Partnership for innovation) by order of the German Federal Ministry of Education and Research.

Dr. Sascha Peters ist Gründer und Inhaber der Material- und Technologieagentur HAUTE INNOVATION in Berlin. Er studierte Maschinenbau an der RWTH Aachen und Produktdesign an der ABK Maastricht. Seine Doktorarbeit schrieb er an der Universität Duisburg-Essen über die Kommunikationsproblematik zwischen Engineering und Design. Von 1997 bis 2003 leitete er Forschungsprojekte und Produktentwick-lungen am Fraunhofer-Institut für Produktions-technologie IPT in Aachen und war anschließend bis 2008 stellvertre-tender Leiter des Design Zentrums Bremen. Sascha Peters ist Autor zahlreicher Fachbücher zu nach-haltigen Werkstoffen, smarten Materialien, innovativen Fertigungsverfahren und energetischen Technologien und zählt zu den führenden Material-experten und Trendscouts für neue Technologien. Seit 2014 ist er Mitglied im Beirat der Förderinitiative „Zwanzig20 – Partnerschaft für Innovation" im Auftrag des Bundesministeriums für Bildung und Forschung.

02

"One special innovation in the jury session was tiles, which exude a range of smells after being touched, sometimes smelling of myriads of flowers, other times of milk or chocolate."

„Eine besondere Innovation während der Jurierung waren Kacheln, denen nach Berührung verschiedene Gerüche entströmten – mal nach einem Blumenmeer, mal nach Milch oder Schokolade."

What attracts you to the work as a Red Dot juror?
The exchange of ideas with experts from other continents, who assess products according to different standards. Time and again, I find it highly interesting to see which differences but also commonalities exist between Asia and America, Europe, Africa and Australia.

What do you pay particular attention to when assessing a product?
To the innovative quality of the materials used in a product. And this is definitely meant in a technological sense. Which resources are used in the production? Does the company use regenerative energy sources? Does a new material have an essential function or does it merely serve to convey superficial values?

Which topics in particular will influence the materials sector in the coming years?
Climate change and the turnaround in energy policy. It is already becoming apparent now that companies are abandoning manufacturing processes which are based on oil and are returning to regenerative sources with regards to resources as well as use of energy.

Was reizt Sie an der Arbeit als Red Dot-Juror?
Der Austausch mit Experten unterschiedlicher Kontinente, die nach anderen Maßstäben bewerten. Ich finde es immer wieder interessant zu sehen, welche Unterschiede, aber auch Gemeinsamkeiten zwischen Asien und Amerika, Europa, Afrika und Australien herrschen.

Worauf achten Sie besonders, wenn Sie ein Produkt bewerten?
Auf den Innovationsgrad der für ein Produkt verwendeten Materialien. Und das ist durchaus technologisch gemeint. Welche Ressourcen werden bei der Herstellung verwendet? Greift das Unternehmen auf regenerative Energiequellen zurück? Wird ein neuer Werkstoff strukturell verwendet oder dient er lediglich dem Transport oberflächlicher Werte?

Welche Themen werden die Material-Branche in den kommenden Jahren besonders beeinflussen?
Der Klimawandel und die Energiewende. Man sieht bereits jetzt, dass sich Unternehmen von Herstellungsprozessen abwenden, die auf Erdöl basieren, und sowohl bei den verwendeten Ressourcen als auch bei der benutzten Energie auf regenerative Quellen zurückgreifen.

01

Nils Toft
Denmark
Dänemark

Nils Toft, born in Copenhagen in 1957, graduated as an architect and designer from the Royal Danish Academy of Fine Arts in Copenhagen in 1985. He also holds a Master's degree in Industrial Design and Business Development. Starting his career as an industrial designer, Nils Toft joined the former Christian Bjørn Design in 1987, an internationally active design studio in Copenhagen with branches in Beijing and Ho Chi Minh City. Within a few years, he became a partner of CBD and, as managing director, ran the business. Today, Nils Toft is the founder and managing director of Designidea. With offices in Copenhagen and Beijing, Designidea works in the following key fields: communication, consumer electronics, computing, agriculture, medicine, and graphic arts, as well as projects in design strategy, graphic and exhibition design.

Nils Toft, geboren 1957 in Kopenhagen, machte seinen Abschluss als Architekt und Designer 1985 an der Royal Danish Academy of Fine Arts in Kopenhagen. Er verfügt zudem über einen Master im Bereich Industrial Design und Business Development. Zu Beginn seiner Karriere als Industriedesigner trat Nils Toft 1987 bei dem damaligen Christian Bjørn Design ein, einem international operierenden Designstudio in Kopenhagen, das mit Niederlassungen in Beijing und Ho-Chi-Minh-Stadt vertreten ist. Innerhalb weniger Jahre wurde er Partner bei CBD und leitete das Unternehmen als Managing Director. Heute ist Nils Toft Gründer und Managing Director von Designidea. Mit Büros in Kopenhagen und Beijing operiert Designidea in verschiedenen Hauptbereichen: Kommunikation, Unterhaltungselektronik, Computer, Landwirtschaft, Medizin und Grafikdesign sowie Projekte in den Bereichen Designstrategie, Grafik- und Ausstellungsdesign.

01

"Good design is able to make promises about a great product experience and keep them."

„Gutes Design verspricht eine hervorragende Produkterfahrung und hält sein Versprechen."

Which everyday product could you not live without?

One of the many things I would not like to be without is my Fiat 124 Spider by Pininfarina. For me it captures the essence and beauty of what a classic Italian sports car is. Living in Scandinavia with long dark winters you need an open-top car to take in as much of the summer as you can when the summer is there.

What is the difference between good and bad product design?

Good design is a visual language that without words tells the story about the idea behind the product and the positive experience it will offer the user. Bad design is often a lot of styling that tries to hide the fact that there is no real idea behind the product.

What attracts you to the work as a Red Dot juror?

I take so much inspiration and knowledge back with me after each jury session. The Red Dot also gives a fantastic insight into the latest trends from around the world.

Welches Alltagsprodukt möchten Sie nicht mehr missen?

Eines der vielen Dinge, die ich nicht missen möchte, ist mein Fiat 124 Spider von Pininfarina. In meinen Augen verkörpert er das Wesen und die Schönheit eines klassischen italienischen Sportwagens. Wenn man in Skandinavien lebt, wo die Winter lang und dunkel sind, braucht man ein Cabriolet, um so viel Sonne wie möglich zu bekommen, wenn der Sommer da ist.

Was unterscheidet gutes von schlechtem Produktdesign?

Gutes Design ist eine visuelle Sprache, die ohne Worte die Geschichte von der Idee, die hinter dem Produkt steckt, erzählt und davon, welche positive Nutzererfahrung es bietet. Schlechtes Design ist oft eine Menge Styling, das versucht, die Tatsache zu verbergen, dass hinter dem Produkt keine echte Idee steckt.

Was reizt Sie an der Arbeit als Red Dot-Juror?

Jede Jurierung ist so inspirierend und ich lerne so viel. Darüber hinaus gibt mir der Red Dot einen fantastischen Einblick in die neuesten Trends aus aller Welt.

01

Prof. Danny Venlet
Belgium
Belgien

Professor Danny Venlet was born in 1958 in Victoria, Australia and studied interior design at Sint-Lukas, the Institute for Architecture and Arts in Brussels. Back in Australia in 1991, Venlet started to attract international attention with large-scale interior projects such as the Burdekin hotel in Sydney and Q-bar, an Australian chain of nightclubs. His design projects range from private mansions, lofts, bars and restaurants all the way to showrooms and offices of large companies. The interior projects and the furniture designs of Danny Venlet are characterised by their contemporary international style. He says that the objects arise from an interaction between art, sculpture and function. These objects give a new description to the space in which they are placed – with respect, but also with relative humour. Today, Danny Venlet teaches his knowledge to students at the Royal College of the Arts in Ghent.

Professor Danny Venlet wurde 1958 in Victoria, Australien, geboren und studierte Interior Design am Sint-Lukas Institut für Architektur und Kunst in Brüssel. Nachdem er 1991 wieder nach Australien zurückgekehrt war, begann er, mit der Innenausstattung großer Projekte wie dem Burdekin Hotel in Sydney und der Q-Bar, einer australischen Nachtclub-Kette, internationale Aufmerksamkeit zu erregen. Seine Designprojekte reichen von privaten Wohnhäusern über Lofts, Bars und Restaurants bis hin zu Ausstellungsräumen und Büros großer Unternehmen. Die Innenausstattungen und Möbeldesigns von Danny Venlet sind durch einen zeitgenössischen, internationalen Stil ausgezeichnet und entspringen, wie er sagt, der Interaktion zwischen Kunst, Skulptur und Funktion. Seine Objekte geben den Räumen, in denen sie sich befinden, eine neue Identität – mit Respekt, aber auch mit einer Portion Humor. Heute vermittelt Danny Venlet sein Wissen als Professor an Studenten des Royal College of the Arts in Gent.

01 View into the exhibition "Power of Objects" in Brussels – with Easy Rider (chair for Bulo), D2V2 (light for DARK) and Viteo garden shower
Blick in die Ausstellung „Power of Objects" (Kraft der Objekte) in Brüssel – mit Easy Rider (Stuhl für Bulo), D2V2 (Leuchte für DARK) und der Viteo-Gartendusche

"I would like to design products with an interior such as a boat, car or aeroplane. This would allow me to combine my skills as an interior and product designer."
„Ich würde gerne Produkte gestalten, die einen Innenraum haben, zum Beispiel ein Boot, Auto oder Flugzeug. Das würde mir ermöglichen, meine Fähigkeiten als Innenarchitekt und Produktdesigner zu kombinieren."

What is the difference between good and bad product design?
I believe there are obvious visual and emotional indicators of good and bad design. Of course there are even more indicators, but I would like to highlight the emotional ones. Good design reflects good virtues such as honesty, clarity, courage, substance and detailing. As Marty Neumeier describes bad design: "A wealth of information leads to a poverty of attention."

How would you describe your work as a designer?
As behaviouristic, intuitive, constructive, collaborative, sensory, three dimensional poetry.

Which developments would you like to see in product design in the future?
I would like to see more products that the world really needs instead of the one-hundredth version of an already existing product.

Was unterscheidet gutes von schlechtem Produktdesign?
Ich glaube, dass es offensichtliche visuelle und emotionale Kennzeichen für gutes und schlechtes Design gibt. Natürlich gibt es noch mehr, aber ich möchte die emotionalen hervorheben. Gute Gestaltung spiegelt gute Eigenschaften wider, zum Beispiel Ehrlichkeit, Klarheit, Mut, Substanz und Detailtreue. Und schlechte Gestaltung ist, wie Marty Neumeier sie beschreibt: „Ein Überfluss an Informationen führt zu einem Mangel an Aufmerksamkeit."

Wie würden Sie Ihre Tätigkeit als Designer beschreiben?
Als behavioristische, intuitive, konstruktive, kollaborative, sinnliche, dreidimensionale Poesie.

Welche Entwicklungen im Produktdesign würden Sie sich für die Zukunft wünschen?
Ich würde mir mehr Produkte wünschen, die die Welt wirklich braucht, und nicht die einhundertste Version eines bereits existierenden Produktes.

01

Günter Wermekes
Germany
Deutschland

Günter Wermekes, born in Kierspe, Germany in 1955, is a goldsmith and designer. After many years of practice as an assistant and head of the studio of Prof. F. Becker in Düsseldorf, he founded his own studio in 1990. He attracted great attention with his jewellery collection "Stainless Steel and Diamond", which he has been presenting at national and international fairs since 1990. His designs are also appreciated by renowned manufacturers such as BMW, Rodenstock, Niessing or Tecnolumen, for which he designed, among other things, accessories, glasses, watches and door openers. In exhibitions and lectures around the world he has illustrated his personal design philosophy, which is: "Minimalism means reducing things more and more to their actual essence, and thus making it visible." He has also implemented this motto in his design of the Red Dot Trophy. In 2014, Günter Wermekes was one of ten finalists in the design competition for the medal of the Tang Prize, the "Asian Nobel Prize". His works have won numerous prizes and are part of renowned collections.

Günter Wermekes, 1955 geboren in Kierspe, ist Goldschmied und Designer. Nach langjähriger Tätigkeit als Assistent und Werkstattleiter von Prof. F. Becker in Düsseldorf gründete er 1990 sein eigenes Studio. Große Aufmerksamkeit erregte er mit seiner Schmuckkollektion „Edelstahl und Brillant", die er ab 1990 auf nationalen und internationalen Messen präsentierte. Sein Design schätzen auch namhafte Hersteller wie BMW, Rodenstock, Niessing oder Tecnolumen, für die er u. a. Accessoires, Brillen, Uhren und Türdrücker entwarf. In Ausstellungen und Vorträgen weltweit verdeutlicht er seine persönliche Gestaltungsphilosophie, dass „Minimalismus bedeutet, Dinge so auf ihr Wesen zu reduzieren, dass es dadurch sichtbar wird". Diesen Leitspruch hat er auch in seinem Entwurf der Red Dot Trophy umgesetzt. 2014 war Günter Wermekes einer von zehn Finalisten des Gestaltungswettbewerbs für die Preismedaille des „Tang Prize", des „Asiatischen Nobelpreises". Seine Arbeiten wurden mehrfach prämiert und befinden sich in bedeutenden Sammlungen.

01 The gold set
Ring models R0042 to
46 made of stainless steel
and 999 gold for the
collection "Stainless Steel
and Diamond"
Ringmodelle R0042 bis 46
aus Edelstahl und 999er
Gold für die Kollektion
„Edelstahl und Brillant"

"The most important skill of a successful designer is definitely the ability to persistently pursue his/her goal. Everything else is talent and craftsmanship."

„Die wichtigste Fähigkeit eines erfolgreichen Designers ist ganz sicher, beharrlich sein Ziel zu verfolgen. Alles andere ist Talent und Handwerk."

Which everyday product could you not live without?
The Faber Castell Finepen 1511 drawing pen, which has been the perfect "extension" of my brain for many years.

What is the difference between good and bad jewellery design?
Good jewellery design convinces with its form while at the same time appealing to people's emotions.

How would you describe your work as a designer?
I try to give form to things, which is based on the materials and which will last a long time.

What attracts you to the work as a Red Dot juror?
The complexity of the task of coming to a fair assessment of the products is definitely a great challenge and incentive at the same time.

Welches Alltagsprodukt möchten Sie nicht mehr missen?
Den Zeichenstift „Faber Castell Finepen 1511", seit vielen Jahren die perfekte „Verlängerung" meines Gehirns.

Was unterscheidet gutes von schlechtem Schmuckdesign?
Gutes Schmuckdesign überzeugt formal und spricht die Menschen gleichzeitig emotional an.

Wie würden Sie Ihre Tätigkeit als Designer beschreiben?
Ich versuche, Dingen eine Gestalt zu geben, die sich an den Materialien orientiert und über einen langen Zeitraum Bestand hat.

Was reizt Sie an der Arbeit als Red Dot-Juror?
Die Komplexität der Aufgabe, eine gerechte Bewertung der Produkte zu erreichen, ist sicher die große Herausforderung und Ansporn zugleich.

Alphabetical index manufacturers and distributors
Alphabetisches Hersteller- und Vertriebs-Register

Alphabetical index manufacturers and distributors
Alphabetisches Hersteller- und Vertriebs-Register

Alphabetical index manufacturers and distributors
Alphabetisches Hersteller- und Vertriebs-Register

Alphabetical index designers
Alphabetisches Designer-Register

Alphabetical index designers
Alphabetisches Designer-Register

Alphabetical index designers
Alphabetisches Designer-Register

Alphabetical index designers
Alphabetisches Designer-Register

Alphabetical index designers
Alphabetisches Designer-Register

reddot edition

Editor | Herausgeber
Peter Zec

Project management | Projektleitung
Jennifer Bürling

Project assistance | Projektassistenz
Sophie Angerer
Maren Boots
Stefan Dierkes
Marie Eigner
Kirsten Frink
Caroline König
Judith Lindner
Saskia Verhees
Mareike Britta Winciers

Editorial work | Redaktion
Bettina Derksen, Simmern, Germany
Eva Hembach, Vienna, Austria
Karin Kirch, Essen, Germany
Karoline Laarmann, Dortmund, Germany
Bettina Laustroer, Wuppertal, Germany
Kirsten Müller, Mülheim an der Ruhr, Germany
Astrid Ruta (Red Dot: Design Team of the Year), Essen, Germany
Martina Stein, Otterberg, Germany

Proofreading | Lektorat
Klaus Dimmler (supervision), Essen, Germany
Mareike Ahlborn, Essen, Germany
Jörg Arnke, Essen, Germany
Wolfgang Astelbauer, Vienna, Austria
Sabine Beeres, Leverkusen, Germany
Dawn Michelle d'Atri, Kirchhundem, Germany
Annette Gillich-Beltz, Essen, Germany
Karin Kirch, Essen, Germany
Norbert Knyhala, Castrop-Rauxel, Germany
Laura Lothian, Vienna, Austria
Regina Schier, Essen, Germany
Anja Schrade, Stuttgart, Germany

Translation | Übersetzung
Heike Bors-Eberlein, Tokyo, Japan
Patrick Conroy, Lanarca, Cyprus
Stanislaw Eberlein, Tokyo, Japan
William Kings, Wuppertal, Germany
Cathleen Poehler, Montreal, Canada
Tara Russell, Dublin, Ireland
Jan Stachel-Williamson, Christchurch, New Zealand
Philippa Watts, Exeter, Great Britain
Andreas Zantop, Berlin, Germany
Christiane Zschunke, Frankfurt am Main, Germany

Layout | Gestaltung
Lockstoff Design GmbH, Grevenbroich, Germany
Susanne Coenen
Katja Kleefeld
Judith Maasmann
Stephanie Marniok
Iris Mecklenburg
Lena Overkamp
Nicole Slink

Cover | Umschlag
Idea | Idee
Burkhard Jacob, Red Dot Institute, Essen, Germany
Implementation | Umsetzung
Lockstoff Design, Grevenbroich, Germany

Photographs | Fotos
Stefano Campo Antico (BLOCK, juror Masayo Ave)
Dragan Arrigler (AchillX, juror Jure Miklavc)
Design Exchange (Alexis Eyewear retail shops,
juror Song Kee Hong)
East Japan Railway Company (E7/W7 Hokuriku Shinkansen,
juror Ken Okuyama)
ELMTL (view into the exhibition, juror Danny Venlet)
IKA Institut für Kraftfahrzeuge Aachen
(SpeedE, juror Lutz Fügener)
Piero Martinello (PLATFORM Architecture and Design,
juror Luisa Bocchietto)
Perphoto Professional (VLT, juror Guto Indio da Costa)
Christophe Recoura (French TGV 3G and Paris Tramway
T7-T8, juror Vincent Créance)
Alltin Sezer (GENESI, juror Masayo Ave)
Giovanni Tagini (Invisible Swimming Pool,
juror Chris Bangle)
Roberto Turci (Helmet, juror Jure Miklavc)
Hisanori Watanabe (JR-West Shinkansen "Nozomi 500",
juror Alexander Neumeister)

Page | Seite
388
Name | Name
Tokyo_Institute_of_Technology_Centennial_Hall_2009
Copyright | Urheber
Wiiii
Source | Quelle
http://commons.wikimedia.org/wiki/File:Tokyo_
Institute_of_Technology_Centennial_Hall_2009.jpg

Distribution of this photograph is protected by copyright
law. A license is required for distribution. More information
is available at
Diese Fotografie unterliegt hinsichtlich der Verbreitung
dem Urheberrechtsschutz. Die Verbreitung bedarf einer
Lizenz. Nähere Angaben dazu finden Sie unter
http://creativecommons.org/licenses/by-sa/3.0/deed.en

Jury photographs | Jurorenfotos
Simon Bierwald, Dortmund, Germany

In-company photos | Werkfotos der Firmen

Production and lithography |
Produktion und Lithografie
tarcom GmbH, Gelsenkirchen, Germany
Gregor Baals
Jonas Mühlenweg
Bernd Reinkens
Gundula Seraphin

Printing | Druck
Dr. Cantz'sche Druckerei Medien GmbH,
Ostfildern, Germany

Bookbinding | Buchbinderei
BELTZ Bad Langensalza GmbH
Bad Langensalza, Germany

Red Dot Design Yearbook 2016/2017
Living: 978-3-89939-185-5
Doing: 978-3-89939-186-2
Working: 978-3-89939-187-9
Enjoying: 978-3-89939-189-3
Set (Living, Doing, Working & Enjoying): 978-3-89939-184-8

Publisher + worldwide distribution |
Verlag + Vertrieb weltweit
Red Dot Edition
Design Publisher | Fachverlag für Design
Contact | Kontakt
Sabine Wöll
Gelsenkirchener Str. 181
45309 Essen, Germany
Phone +49 201 81418-22
Fax +49 201 81418-10
E-mail edition@red-dot.de
www.red-dot-edition.com
www.red-dot-shop.com
Book publisher ID no. | Verkehrsnummer
13674 (Börsenverein Frankfurt)

**Bibliographic information published
by the Deutsche Nationalbibliothek**
The Deutsche Nationalbibliothek
lists this publication in the Deutsche
Nationalbibliografie; detailed bibliographic
data are available on the Internet at
http://dnb.ddb.de
Bibliografische Information
der Deutschen Nationalbibliothek
Die Deutsche Nationalbibliothek verzeichnet
diese Publikation in der Deutschen
Nationalbibliografie; detaillierte
bibliografische Daten sind im Internet über
http://dnb.ddb.de abrufbar